The Texas Landscape Project

Kathie and Ed Cox Jr. Books on Conservation Leadership

SPONSORED BY

THE MEADOWS CENTER
FOR WATER AND THE ENVIRONMENT
TEXAS STATE UNIVERSITY

Andrew Sansom, General Editor

The Texas Landscape Project

•

Nature and People

David Todd and Jonathan Ogren

with assistance from Clare Crosby, Matt Fougerat, Johanna Arendt, and Brad Peter

Foreword by Andrew Sansom

TEXAS A&M UNIVERSITY PRESS   COLLEGE STATION

This paper meets the requirements of ANSI/NISO Z39.48-1992
(Permanence of Paper).
Binding materials have been chosen for durability.
Manufactured in China by Everbest Printing Co.
through FCI Print Group

Library of Congress Cataloging-in-Publication Data

Todd, David, 1959– author.

 The Texas Landscape Project: nature and people / text by David Todd; exhibits by Jonathan Ogren; with assistance from Clare Crosby, Matt Fougerat, Johanna Arendt, and Brad Peter; foreword by Andrew Sansom. — First edition.

   pages cm. — (Kathie and Ed Cox Jr. books on conservation leadership)

 Includes bibliographical references and index.

 ISBN 978-1-62349-372-1 (flex: alk. paper) — ISBN 978-1-62349-373-8 (ebook) 1. Texas Landscape Project. 2. Conservation projects (Natural resources)—Texas. 3. Natural resources management areas—Texas. 4. Natural resources management areas—Texas—Maps. 5. Nature—Effect of human beings on—Texas. 6. Nature—Effect of human beings on—Texas—Maps. 7. Human ecology—Texas. 8. Human ecology—Texas—Maps. 9. Biodiversity conservation—Texas—Sources. 10. Ecology—Texas—Sources. I. Ogren, Jonathan, cartographer. II. Crosby, Clare. III. Title. IV. Series: Kathie and Ed Cox Jr. books on conservation leadership.

 GE155.T4T537 2016

 333.709764—dc23

                    2015029205

Maps in this book use base data layers obtained from ESRI, USGS, NRCS, TPWD, TCEQ, TWDB, and other sources identified for individual figures. The maps have been produced using several projections to convert three-dimensional locations into two-dimensional representations. State maps used the NAD 1983, Texas Centric Mapping System Albers projection, in meters. National maps relied on the NAD 1983, USGS version of the USA Contiguous Albers Equal-Area Conic projections, in meters. Global maps were drawn from the WGS 84, World Robinson projection, in meters. Local maps were developed from an appropriate state plane system or UTM projection. Some maps have been altered to give an oblique view that allows a focus on Texas or a particular locale. Finished maps were created with a combination of software applications, including ESRI ArcGIS, Google Earth Pro, Corel DRAW, Photoshop, and Indiemapper.

A list of other titles in this series may be found at the back of the book.

To Hannah and Margaret,
with hopes that you and your generation
will always enjoy exploring and sharing this wonderful place.

David Todd

———————————

To Crescent and Simon,
with thanks for helping me to see the world and Texas
through new eyes and with new purpose.

Jonathan Ogren

Contents

Foreword

As I sit down on a gorgeous winter day in the Texas Hill Country to write the foreword to the latest edition of the Kathie and Ed Cox Jr. Books on Conservation Leadership, I am, quite frankly, humbled.

The absolutely monumental *Texas Landscape Project* is the latest contribution to the conservation movement by one of its true unsung heroes, David Todd. An unsung hero, it seems to me, is a person who has a profound and positive impact on our lives and times but goes mostly unrecognized, a person who demonstrates extraordinary compassion, dedication, and determination without seeking credit for his or her contribution.

Such a person is David Todd.

David is the founder, interviewer, and executive director for the Conservation History Association of Texas. Part of a family whose conservation efforts span three generations, he has worked as an environmental attorney, a conservation donor, and a cattle rancher. He has served on the boards of Audubon Texas, the Texas League of Conservation Voters, the Texas Conservation Alliance, and the Lone Star Chapter of the Sierra Club. David Todd is a cofounder of the Texas Environmental Grantmakers Group—which brings together philanthropists from across the state to better inform them about conservation issues, institutions, and challenges—and the creator of the *Texas Legacy Project*, which chronicles the profiles and experiences of twentieth-century leaders of the conservation movement in Texas.

Now, David has teamed up with another extraordinary behind-the-scenes-operator, Jonathan Ogren. Jonathan is founder, principal, and environmental planner of Siglo Group, which exists to integrate natural systems into land planning and design. He has worked at NASA, Sequoia National Park, and the Lady Bird Johnson Wildflower Center and specializes in environmental assessment, regional analysis, conservation planning, mapping, and land use feasibility studies. Ogren's remarkable ability to interpret landscape conditions, trends, and challenges through geographic information science has had a profound impact on our understanding of the enormous environmental difficulties facing Texas today.

Together, these two exceptional professionals have created a breathtaking compendium of insights into the natural history, the environmental richness, and the manifold conservation dilemmas confronting the Lone Star State today. On these pages, the incredible diversity of Texas is portrayed in meticulous yet stunning illustrative detail, providing us not only with the most comprehensive picture of the Texas environment ever assembled but an intimate rendering of both its treasures and its challenges.

Publication of this great work by the unique partnership of Texas A&M University Press and The Meadows Center for Water and the Environment at Texas State University would not have been possible without the support of Mr. and Mrs. Cox and the Cynthia and George Mitchell Foundation, which is currently launching its own landscape conservation project.

The pages that follow are sure not only to inspire and inform a higher level of conservation leadership but also to profoundly demonstrate for us how unsung heroes can contribute to our understanding and respect of the world around us, our place in it, and our power and responsibility to protect it for future generations.

—Andrew Sansom
General Editor, Kathie and
Ed Cox Jr. Books on
Conservation Leadership

Preface

When we try to pick out anything by itself, we find it hitched to everything else in the Universe.

—John Muir, *My First Summer in the Sierra*, 1911

"Hitches": The Texas Landscape Project is sponsored by the Conservation History Association of Texas, a nonprofit focused on research and education about efforts to protect the Texas environment and public health. The Landscape Project is tied in with an earlier association work, the Texas Legacy Project, which compiled, archived, and distributed oral histories of leading conservationists in the state. Both the Landscape Project and the Legacy Project look at the intertwined connections among people, places, and the broader environment. They are both efforts to explore that "hitch" or link that Muir saw. The Legacy Project focused on the personal stories that could be sewn together from Texan environmentalists' memories, perspectives, and audio records. On the other hand, the Landscape Project is an account of Texas places, stitched together from databases, maps, aerial photos, charts, and visual images.

Views: The Landscape Project is an exercise in visual storytelling. Its goal is to create an atlas that gives a clear, graphic look into the sometimes confusing and opaque environmental history of the state. While there are many kinds of exhibits in the book, the focus is on maps. At a level of color and line, these maps in the atlas are just pictures, abstractions of the real world. However, the maps offer the visual clues that can give a direct way to explain and understand the behavior of that world, better sometimes than what pages of convoluted text might provide. And, in the special case of environmental issues, maps have a distinct power, beyond plots, photographs, drawings, and other graphic tools that are not so place-based. Many green issues are closely tied to their location in a given watershed, ecoregion, town, or neighborhood; mapping those issues shows their context and consequences. Understanding the origin and impact of an ecological or public health problem often requires seeing what is upwind or downwind, upstream or downriver, nearby or far away. A map helps a great deal in seeing these aspects of our natural world more clearly.

Places: Using maps and supporting text and images, the atlas focuses on environmental issues that affect the entire state of Texas, sometimes reach outside the state, and even stretch beyond the country. The Landscape Project also covers regional topics that are tied to the Panhandle, Pineywoods, Trans-Pecos, Gulf Coast, or Hill Country, as well as controversies that are unique to a single city. A caveat may be in order here. We hope you find these country, state, regional, and local frames useful, but it is good to remember that they can also be artificial and limiting. The first causes and last effects of many environmental problems can sometimes extend well beyond the neat political boundaries shown in the maps.

Topics: With this geographic lens, the Project looks at a variety of subjects. The topics include surface and ground water, land and structures, livestock and wildlife, air quality and climate, fossil and renewable energy. Interwoven throughout, the Project touches on many questions of public health, environmental justice, politics, and economics. In terms of time, the Project focuses mostly on events that occurred after the mid-twentieth century, when the growth and impact of the state's population and economy accelerated. However, the atlas also looks at older issues, such as the effects of grazing, farming, hunting, mining, and timbering.

Explorations: The maps here may seem to be small, flat, and static, but a second look should reveal a more complete picture of the data locked inside. We hope that readers will open the maps up and dig into them. For instance, while the maps measure just inches on a side, they represent very big places—deep canyons, tall forests, long rivers, and broad prairies. Please use the scale, and stretch the maps in your mind to reach across and into these big pieces of the Texas landscape. Also, please remember that many of the two-dimensional maps hold stacks of disparate information. A map's single point or polygon may contain a hodgepodge of data, including population counts, resource use, financial cost, waste load, and other information, mixed and matched and combined. It may take time to unpack all these related but different layers, but we hope that you will gain a better sense of their many connections and cumulative effects. Finally, a single-frame map may span a number of years, collapsing a filmstrip of images that flicker through time with early causes segueing into later effects. While the paper maps shown here freeze the frame, please imagine how the map might move through history.

Readers: As you can see, we have many plans, ambitions, and instructions for the Texas Landscape Project. Basically, though, we hope that readers find the Project useful in some way. For us, it would be wonderful if readers enjoyed learning about the array of data collection and research efforts conducted by so many agencies, academics, and nonprofits. We would also be grateful if users felt that they got a stronger understanding and love for the many distinct and wonderful places in Texas. And last, we would be thrilled if readers of *The Texas Landscape Project* found some renewed value and purpose in conserving Texas for the future. Please contact us at www.texaslandscape. org, and tell us what, if anything, the Project might have meant for you. Thank you very much for taking part in this look at Texas.

The Texas
Landscape Project

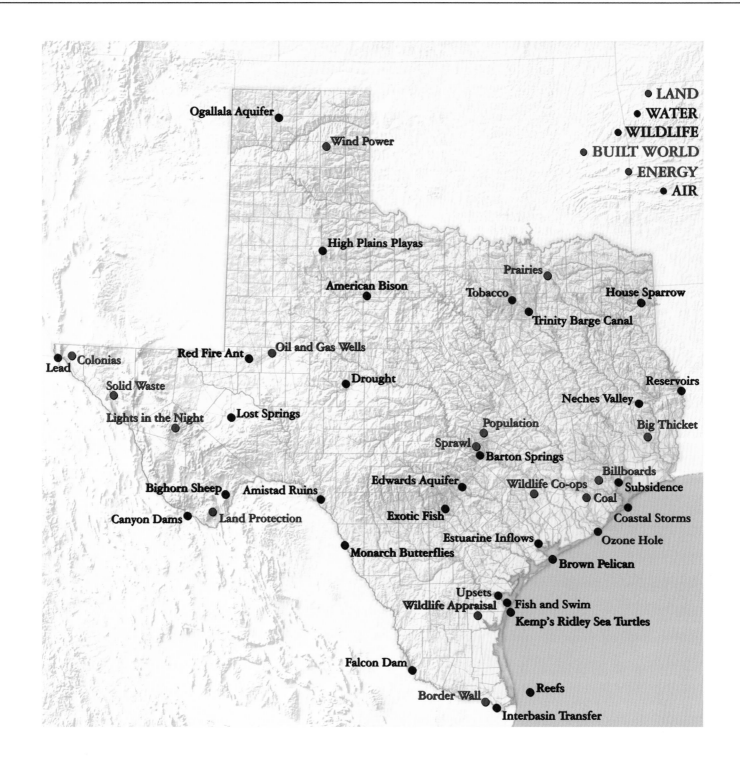

LAND
WATER
WILDLIFE
BUILT WORLD
ENERGY
AIR

Ogallala Aquifer
Wind Power
High Plains Playas
Prairies
Tobacco
House Sparrow
Trinity Barge Canal
American Bison
Oil and Gas Wells
Red Fire Ant
Colonias
Lead
Reservoirs
Drought
Neches Valley
Solid Waste
Big Thicket
Lights in the Night
Lost Springs
Population
Sprawl
Barton Springs
Bighorn Sheep
Amistad Ruins
Edwards Aquifer
Billboards
Subsidence
Wildlife Co-ops
Coal
Exotic Fish
Canyon Dams
Land Protection
Coastal Storms
Estuarine Inflows
Ozone Hole
Monarch Butterflies
Brown Pelican
Upsets
Wildlife Appraisal
Fish and Swim
Kemp's Ridley Sea Turtles
Falcon Dam
Reefs
Border Wall
Interbasin Transfer

Overview Map

American Bison [Wildlife]: The American buffalo nearly went extinct in the late 1800s, but has been restored with several generations' work throughout the nation. **Rath City** was a major Panhandle trading post during the great bison slaughter of the 1870s, seeing more than 1.5 million hides pass through in just three years.

Amistad Ruins [Water]: Inundation of cultural resources is a problem for many dams. The **Doss** site, dating to perhaps 9000 BC, is one of the older prehistoric Native American settlements that were flooded by the waters of Lake Amistad.

Barton Springs [Water]: Groundwater protection strategies have required combinations of watershed acquisition and nonpoint source controls, as illustrated by the efforts to protect **Barton Springs**.

Big Thicket [Land]: Creating parks is an expensive and politically charged, but ecologically valuable, effort. The cost, tension, and value are shown by work to protect the **Big Thicket National Preserve**, a highly diverse set of ecoregions that provides an early example of stream and wildlife corridor protection.

Bighorn Sheep [Wildlife]: The native bighorn mountain sheep, eliminated in Texas by 1960, began its recovery with transplanting of sheep from Nevada, followed by captive breeding at the **Black Gap Wildlife Management Area**.

Billboards [Built World]: Once known as the billboard capital of the world, Houston has become a leader in removing and restricting outdoor signs with strong advocacy from its municipal government.

Border Wall [Built World]: The US-Mexico fence helps reduce illegal immigration, but also cuts through key wildlife preserves and blocks some migrations. One hundred ten miles of fencing exist along the Texas-Mexico border, with the majority found in the **Lower Rio Grande Valley**.

Brown Pelican [Wildlife]: The brown pelican almost went extinct due to market hunting for the millinery trade, and because of pesticide use and habitat loss. Texas' **Chester Island** is home to a rookery of the birds, helping the birds with their dramatic recovery.

Canyon Dams [Water]: Dams on the Rio Grande, which would have inundated many of the famous segments of the Big Bend, were proposed during the first half of the 1900s. The **Santa Elena Canyon** was one site considered by Caracristi (1915) and Henderson (1942) for such a dam.

Coal [Energy]: The nation is enmeshed in a conversation about the future of coal, a cheap source of energy that has offsetting public health and climate change costs. The **Parish** coal power plant is the largest in Texas, and among the largest nationally, and provides an example of these controversies.

Coastal Storms [Water]: The Texas coast has been a magnet for development but has also been a target for high winds and severe flooding from tropical storms. For example, **Galveston** lost over six thousand citizens to the terrible hurricane of 1900 and has continued to bear the brunt of later storms, including Carla (1961), Alicia (1983), Allison (2001), and Ike (2008).

Colonias [Built World]: Texas has many colonias, settlements without adequate water, wastewater, flood control, roads, or other infrastructure. **El Paso**, as well as the Lower Rio Grande Valley, is home to many of these communities, which fortunately have been improved by tighter regulations and more generous subsidies.

Drought [Water]: In many parts of the state, Texas has recently struggled with historic drought, triggering resourceful water conservation efforts. In August 2011, **Lake O. C. Fisher** stood essentially empty, a victim of these dry times.

Edwards Aquifer [Water]: Texas is fortunate to have enormous groundwater resources. However, they need to be protected from overpumping and pollution. **Comal Springs** provides the major outflow from the Edwards aquifer, and is thus affected by contamination and drawdown in the aquifer.

Estuarine Inflows [Water]: Texas' growing population and economy is colliding with limited surface waters, as exemplified by **Matagorda Bay**, which is threatened by reductions in freshwater and nutrient inflows due to the high percentage of permitted diversions.

Exotic Fish [Wildlife]: Exotic fish have been brought to Texas for food, amusement, and water quality protection, but sometimes have proved to be invasive and troublesome for native wildlife. Numerous nonnative fish have been surviving in streams and lakes near **San Antonio**, due to the high human population and the warm local climate.

Falcon Dam [Water]: Dams have flooded important historic structures in the state, including those affected by the Falcon Reservoir at **Old Falcon**, where buildings date to as early as 1749.

Fish and Swim [Water]: Since the passage of the Clean Water Act, Americans have invested billions in making the country's streams and lakes "fishable and swimmable," but the challenge has been great, and **Corpus Christi** has still had to close many of its beaches to visitors due to contaminated water.

High Plains Playas [Water]: Playas form a key link in the migration of birds through the Panhandle, but many of these wetlands, such as those in **McAdoo**, Texas, have been pitted, cultivated, diked, or cut by roads, and have become the subject of a variety of efforts for their restoration.

House Sparrow [Wildlife]: Conservationists often say that the impact of invasive species is one of the gravest ecological challenges facing our society. In 1882, **Jefferson** was the first location for a sighting of a house sparrow in Texas, later followed by many other sparrows and nonnative starlings and the Eurasian collared dove.

Interbasin Transfer [Water]: In order to accommodate Texas populations, farms, and industries, many of the state's rivers have been considered for diversions and canals, including Burleigh's Ditch, an ambitious proposal to shift water from Louisiana and East Texas to the **Rio Grande Valley**.

Kemp's Ridley Sea Turtles [Wildlife]: Through a pioneering international effort to protect and transplant highly endangered Kemp's ridley sea turtles, **North Padre Island** now sees many ridleys returning to nest on its shores.

Land Protection [Land]: Texas has a wonderful array of habitat protected by federal, state, and private efforts. Comprising more than 800,000 acres, **Big Bend National Park** is the largest park in the state.

Lead [Air]: Lead is a very useful, but also very toxic metal. **El Paso**, home to the ASARCO lead smelter, one of the leading sources of lead pollution during its operation, became the scene of crucial public health research that alerted the United States to the need to control lead exposure.

Lights in the Night [Built World]: Dark skies support nocturnal wildlife, and also allow people to connect with the heritage and natural beauty of the stars, planets, and other heavenly bodies. **McDonald Observatory** is a leader in the effort to protect astronomical research by limiting light pollution.

Lost Springs [Water]: In the vast and arid reaches of Texas, springs often formed essential early stops for trails, water supplies for agriculture, and hosts for community events. Many were later drained by overpumping, including **Government Springs** in Fort Stockton.

Monarch Butterflies [Wildlife]: Millions of monarch butterflies funnel through a narrow section of South Texas, centered near **Eagle Pass**, on their way through during the fall and spring migrations.

Neches Valley [Water]: Federal and state agencies work both to develop water supplies and protect habitat. Sometimes these efforts collide, as they did at the proposed **Fastrill Reservoir**, which was blocked by designation of the Neches National Wildlife Refuge at the same site.

Ogallala Aquifer [Water]: The Panhandle is home to some of the nation's great grain and fiber farms, but many of those irrigated operations are very vulnerable to overpumping and decline in the Ogallala aquifer. The area near **Cactus**, Texas, has experienced water level drops in the Ogallala aquifer of over 150 feet, some of the steepest declines seen throughout the aquifer.

Oil and Gas Wells [Energy]: From more than a century of drilling for oil and gas, the state has thousands of orphan wells needing plugging, many in the Permian Basin near **Midland**.

Ozone Hole [Air]: Declines in stratospheric ozone have been seen in Antarctica, and around the world, with many chemicals, producers, and users playing a part. Over the past two decades, numerous facilities, including one in **Freeport**, have made drastic reductions in chemical releases to protect the ozone layer.

Prairies [Land]: Texas is a grassland state, yet many of its native prairies have been lost over the years to cultivation, overgrazing, fire suppression, and development. The Nature Conservancy's Clymer Meadow, near **Celeste**, is one of the few tallgrass prairies that remain.

Population [Built World]: Texas' vibrant economy and warm climate have resulted in rapid population growth and consequent environmental strains. For instance, **Georgetown** is the seat of Williamson County, one of the fastest growing areas in the United States, and also a region struggling with sprawl, traffic, and water shortages.

Red Fire Ant [Wildlife]: The red imported fire ant is a good example of the complicated, and often unpredictable, impact of exotic species. **Ward County** represents Texas' current western edge of the fast-moving spread of the red imported fire ant.

Reefs [Water]: While the Gulf is home to natural reefs at the Flower Gardens, their rarity has led government and private entities to use abandoned rigs, ships (such as the **Texas Clipper**), and other structures as artificial reefs, to serve as aquatic sanctuaries and nurseries.

Reservoirs [Water]: Following the great drought of the 1950s, Texas embarked on a twenty-year dam-building effort, including work to construct the **Toledo Bend** reservoir, the largest in Texas. While these dams have helped manage water for people, they have reduced bottomland hardwoods, wetlands, and estuarine inflows.

Solid Waste [Built World]: Modern solid waste management has made great strides in protecting people from nuisance and disease, but there remain environmental justice concerns about the ultimate home of these wastes. These justice issues were raised by the way in which the poor Hispanic town of **Sierra Blanca** became the host for sludge transported all the way from New York City.

Sprawl [Built World]: Despite its green reputation, Austin struggles with the collateral damage of its growth, including sprawl into the **Balcones Canyonlands** habitat protection areas.

Subsidence [Water]: Brownwood was a subdivision that was flooded and abandoned by 1984. The neighborhood became a victim of land surface subsidence related to overpumpage of groundwater, as well as withdrawals of oil, gas, and sulfur.

Tobacco [Air]: Second-hand smoke has become both a serious public health concern and a successful regulatory program. Some of the first objections and control efforts came from American Airlines flight attendants based at the **Dallas/Fort Worth International Airport**.

Trinity Barge Canal [Water]: Dallas sought to become a port for ocean-going traffic through dredging and lock construction on the Trinity River. One example of the work, **Lock 1**, was built in the 1910s at river mile 488.1, just southeast of Dallas, as the first of a series of more than two dozen planned structures.

Upsets [Air]: Texas industry uses a variety of complex and volatile chemical processes, which sometimes suffer upsets that lead to accidents, and major releases. Refinery Row, in **Corpus Christi**, has seen a high density of these upsets at refineries sited quite close to residential areas.

Wildlife Appraisals [Land]: Reduced tax appraisals through use of wildlife exemptions have helped protect thousands of acres of privately held habitat in Texas. Over 410,000 acres in **Kleberg County** are appraised for wildlife use, the largest expanse of any county in Texas.

Wildlife Co-ops [Land]: As bigger ranches are subdivided, cooperative efforts through wildlife management associations can be a key tool in improving habitat and animal populations. The **Oakridge Ranch** is an example of one effective co-op that has coordinated management among contiguous tracts as small as 20 acres.

Wind Power [Energy]: Texas has become home to the largest wind farm complex in the United States, and **Pampa** is believed to be the location of the first wind turbines erected in Texas and connected to its grid.

Land

Texas is a vast land of wide plains, tall forests, and big skies. But it is also a place that is being rapidly settled, subdivided, and developed. In this section of the atlas, we track the efforts to protect the state's lands, focusing on the conservation of prairies, Neches river bottoms, Big Thicket sloughs and forests, and working farms and ranches.

Often the data on these land trends are incomplete or indirect, and we have had to use other indicators to understand the history and causes of these changes, especially those of long ago, before there were thorough and accurate records.

For instance, the atlas describes changes in Texas native grasslands through reports on branding registries, cotton gins, grain mills, and sod farms. The routes of short-haul railroads and the rise and fall of old ghost town post offices are used to trace the areas of long-past timber cuts in the Big Thicket. The fate of the Neches bottomlands is laid out by dam site proposals and flood contour lines, while the future of private farms and ranches is outlined by landowner association boundaries and tax appraisal numbers.

By using these other, indirect ways of gauging change, we hope we can point out how multifaceted and complex this evolution in Texas lands has been.

Source

Omernik, J. M. 2009. *Level III and IV Ecoregions of Texas, Polygon Coverage*. US Environmental Protection Agency. http://www.tpwd.state.tx.us/landwater/land/maps/gis/data_downloads/shp/ecoregpy.zip, accessed January 1, 2013.

Texas Ecoregions

OKLAHOMA

NEW MEXICO

ARKANSAS

Amarillo

High Plains

Southwestern
Tablelands

Lubbock

Central Great
Plains

Fort Worth   Dallas

LOUISIANA

Arizona/New Mexico
Mountains

Midland

Texas
Blackland
Prairies

South
Central
Plains

El Paso

Cross
Timbers

East Central
Texas Plains

Chihuahuan Desert

Edwards Plateau

Austin

San Antonio

Houston

Western Gulf
Coastal Plain

MEXICO

Southern
Texas
Plains

Gulf of Mexico

Brownsville

0   50 miles

This map outlines the eleven distinct ecoregions found in Texas. From the High Plains of the Panhandle, the state stretches 860 miles south to the Southern Texas Plains and Rio Grande Valley. From the high Chihuahuan Desert of the Trans-Pecos, Texas reaches 770 miles to the tall pines of the South Central Plains. Within these boundaries, there is a wide range of elevation, longitude, rainfall, and soil that contributes to the state's ecological diversity. Adding to this original variety, some ecoregions have been more affected by cultivation and development, while others are more intact, and are targets for protection and restoration (Omernik 2009).

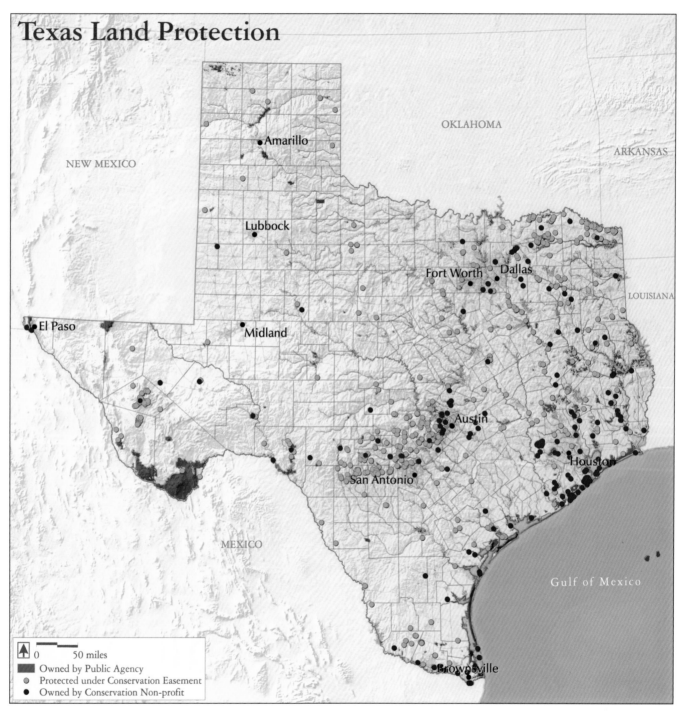

Texas Land Protection

NEW MEXICO

OKLAHOMA

ARKANSAS

Amarillo

Lubbock

Fort Worth • Dallas

LOUISIANA

El Paso

Midland

Austin

San Antonio

Houston

MEXICO

Gulf of Mexico

0   50 miles

■ Owned by Public Agency
● Protected under Conservation Easement
● Owned by Conservation Non-profit

Brownsville

This figure shows where protected lands are found across the state, within both public parks and private preserves (Texas Land Trust Council 2015; Texas Parks and Wildlife 2012).

Land Protection

Texas shall retain all the vacant and unappropriated lands lying within its limits, to be applied to the payment of the debts and liabilities of said republic of Texas, and the residue of said lands, after discharging said debts and liabilities, to be disposed of as said state may direct.

—Annexation of Texas, Joint Resolution of the Congress of the United States, 1845

Texas came into the union in 1845 with a huge expanse of public lands spread across 225 million acres (Texas General Land Office 1942). However, by the current day, Texas has lost all but roughly 3 percent of its public property. The reasons for the loss of its public lands go back over a century and a half. For many years, Texas was rich in land but poor in cash. So the state used some 87–95 million acres to lure in settlers, reward veterans, and to encourage the construction of railroads, irrigation canals, shipyards, and factories. Texas ceded other acreage to the US government under the Compromise of 1850. The compromise allowed the state to trade its title to 67 million acres in exchange for $10 million in US bonds and $2.75 million in cash. The swap reduced debt that the Republic of Texas had run up and settled persistent boundary questions (Miller 1972).

In the years since, Texas has gained a rapidly growing urban population with little access to rural family land to visit and enjoy. The state has also seen its trove of ecological resources fragmented and converted into great cities. As a result, Texas has sought to reverse its historic loss of public lands and safeguard property for future tourism, outdoor recreation, and habitat protection.

State History

Land protection efforts in the state began with campaigns to protect

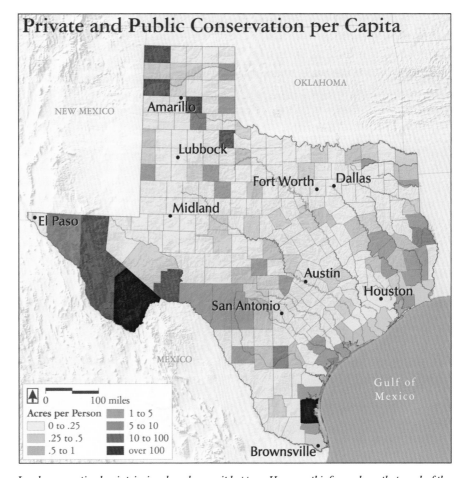

Land conservation has intrinsic value wherever it happens. However, this figure shows that much of the protected acreage in Texas is located quite far from the major population centers in the eastern half of the state. Future conservationists will face the challenge of finding and acquiring open space that is more easily and quickly accessible to most Texans (Olson 2015; Steinbach 2011 and 2012; Texas Department of State Health Services 2015; Texas Land Trust Council 2015; Texas Parks and Wildlife 2015).

important historical sites, including the Alamo mission (1883), San Jacinto battleground (1897), and the spot at Washington-on-the-Brazos where Texas declared its independence from Mexico (1916). Much of the pressure for these early parks came from private citizens. The Alamo was saved in large part due to generous giving and strenuous political arm twisting by the Daughters of the Republic of Texas, especially one of its leaders, Clara Driscoll (Ables 1967). The San Jacinto monument grew out of more than forty years of lobbying from the Texas Veterans Association for a

memorial to those lost in the Texas Revolution, with support, again, from the Daughters of the Republic of Texas (Bell 1999).

Nothing is more conducive to the health and contentment and happiness of a people than for them to commune with nature, loitering on blue-bonneted hills or daisy decked meadows, with bees and birds for companions, in an atmosphere sweet with the perfume from flowers of a thousand hues.

**—"The Battles of Peace,"
Governor Pat Neff, 1925**

Governor Neff

During his 1921–25 tenure, Governor Pat Neff was perhaps the first state leader to push for land protection efforts in Texas. The Progressive-era governor and his mother, Isabella Eleanor Neff, donated land for the vast majority of the first official state park, Mother Neff, established in 1921. Two years later, Governor Neff persuaded the legislature to create the Texas State Parks Board (Senate Bill 73, 38th Legislature, 1st sess.). Members of the board toured the state widely, soliciting gifts of land for parks, and

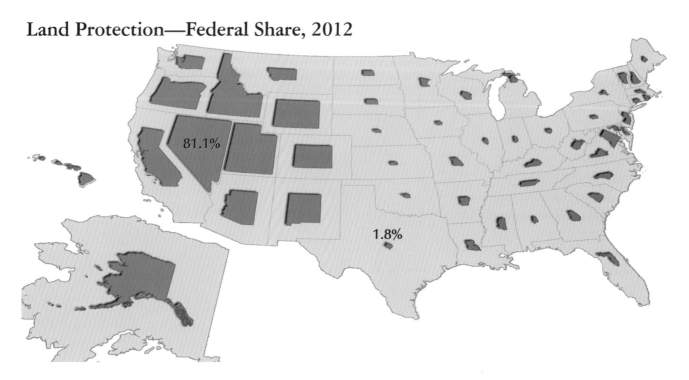

Land Protection—Federal Share, 2012

81.1%

1.8%

The federal government owns and manages roughly 28 percent of US acreage, but its presence varies a great deal from state to state. Some states, such as Alaska and Nevada, have very high percentages of their land held by the US government. On the other hand, the federal government controls only 1.8 percent of lands in Texas (Gorte et al. 2012; US Census Bureau 2010).

later managed to get state appropriations and federal support. The board's
efforts were focused on acquiring
campgrounds and travel destinations,
and eventually led to the protection of
lands at Caddo Lake (1933), Goose
Island (1931), Palo Duro Canyon
(1933), Big Spring (1934), and Big
Bend (née Texas Canyons) State Park
(1933) (Anderson 2010; Liles and
Seidel 2010; Long 2010a and 2010b;
Tyler 2007).

Federal Efforts

Federal agencies were early and active
proponents of safeguarding lands in
Texas. Nationwide, the US government has long been a major force for
land conservation, controlling close
to 28 percent of the national landscape, and as much as 81 percent in
one state—Nevada (Gorte et al. 2012).
While the federal government owns
only 1.8 percent of the Lone Star
State, it is still a significant landlord,
with close to 3 million acres to its
name.

The US Forest Service undertook
the first major federal venture in Texas
with its 1935 purchase of more than
600,000 acres of overcut and drought-
struck forest lands for the Davy
Crockett, Sam Houston, and Angelina
National Forests. Later, the National
Park Service set aside spectacular
landscapes and rich habitats in the Big
Bend (1955), Padre Island (1962),
Guadalupe Mountains (1966), and
Big Thicket (1972) (49 Stat. 393, June
20, 1935; 76 Stat. 650, September 28,

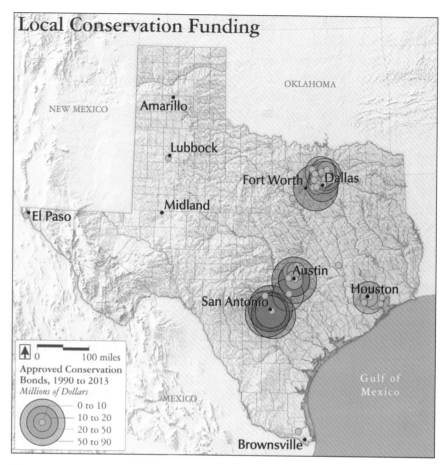

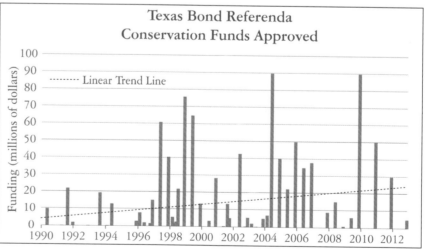

*Support for land conservation in Texas is often underwritten by bonds issued by counties, cities, and
utility districts. It is fortunate that more bond dollars are being approved each year. However, it is
worrisome that much of the spending is concentrated in just a few, if highly populated, parts of the
state (Trust for Public Land 2014).*

1962; 80 Stat. 920, October 15, 1966; 88 Stat. 1256, October 11, 1974). The US Fish and Wildlife Service has been active in Texas as well. The service acquired bird and waterfowl habitat at Muleshoe (1935), Aransas (1937), Santa Ana (1943), Hagerman (1946), Anahuac (1963), Brazoria (1966), and San Bernard National Wildlife Refuges (1968) (US Fish and Wildlife Service 1975, A-11). Unlike the national parks and forests, these refuges were not bought with general revenues. Instead, Fish and Wildlife bought the refuges using Duck Stamp and Pittman-Robertson Act revenues, drawing on hunting and fishing taxes (Federal Aid in Wildlife Restoration Act, 16 U.S.C. 669, September 2, 1937; Migratory Bird Hunting and Conservation Stamp Act, 16 U.S.C. 718, July 1, 1934).

Local Referenda

One of the most vibrant arenas for Texas land conservation is local. County, city, and regional utility districts have taken the bull by the horns and regularly raised millions of dollars for land protection in the state. In this way, thousands of acres have been acquired and developed for ball fields, hike-and-bike trails, nature sanctuaries, and other kinds of parks. Interestingly, some 1.3 billion in conservation dollars have come over the last twenty-four years from bonds and sales taxes endorsed by public referenda. That is certainly a massive sum, but it is even more impressive that the money was raised in a bottom-up way, with genuine grassroots support. The bond and tax funds are surely impor-

tant sources of revenue, but the referenda themselves are also a key validation of the kind of broad and deep public support that exists for parkland. Citizens will voluntarily tax themselves to have access to public land. In fact, ninety out of one hundred votes on Texas conservation initiatives, held from 1990 to 2015, were approved. And the margin was not narrow: the average "yes" vote was 65 percent, very close to a supermajority (Trust for Public Land 2015)!

Private Lands

While these bonds have enabled local governments to get involved in land protection, the big state and federal land protection campaigns of past years have scaled back. Land prices have run up and discretionary government funds have fallen, leaving the state and US governments with few opportunities. Fortunately, though, private efforts have picked up some of the slack.

In fact, a number of the private land protection sites date back many years. Some include early hunting and fishing grounds. The Little Sandy Hunting and Fishing Club of 1902 and the Eagle Lake Rod and Gun Club of the 1920s are examples of some old private hunting properties (Sawyer 2012). Also, from its early days the National Audubon Society has invested heavily in protecting Texas' coastal rookery sanctuaries. Since 1923, Audubon has managed 13,000 acres of tidal mudflats and bay islands for the General Land Office. Local

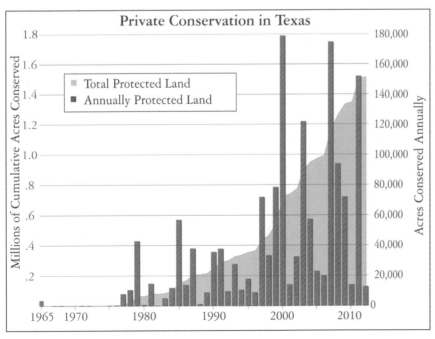

Land protected by no-profit organizations under fee simple title or by easement has soared in recent years and now approaches half of all real estate set aside in the state.

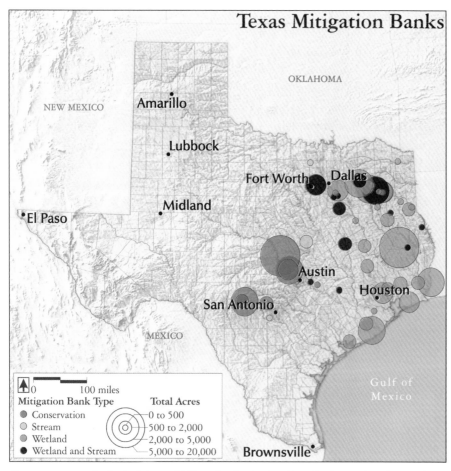

Fees to compensate for the dredging and filling of wetlands, the taking of endangered species, or other damage to habitat, have helped fund conservation and restoration of land in Texas (Neumann 2014 and 2015; US Army Corps of Engineers 2014).

donors in less than four weeks to acquire a prairie jewel near Deer Park (Lorenz and Buckingham 2014).

Mitigation Banks

Another new form of land conservation has grown out of efforts to mitigate dredging and filling of wetlands and offset construction activities affecting endangered species. First begun in 1983 with guidance from the US Fish and Wildlife Service, a basic strategy for these "mitigation banks" has gradually evolved with input from the US Army Corps of Engineers, the EPA, the USDA, NOAA, and the Department of the Interior (Federal Guidance for the Establishment, Use, and Operation of Mitigation Banks 1995; US Fish and Wildlife Service 1983).

Typically, a protected piece of "bank" land is first licensed through the US Army Corps of Engineers, but sometimes through other agencies. Once the bank is licensed, the cost of protecting it, and even restoring it, can be underwritten by selling mitigation credits to agencies and developers who need to offset estimated impacts on their own separate tracts. This is an exciting source of new land conservation funds. In fact, the Army Corps of Engineers has approved fifty Texas mitigation banks, covering over 58,000 acres in total. Two of the Texas banks have been so successful they have already sold out (US Army Corps of Engineers 2014; Neumann 2014; Williams 2014).

However, some critics believe these banks present some drawbacks. The

organizations were active too (Barcott 2010). In the 1950s, Houston's Outdoor Nature Club gathered money and members to acquire the Little Thicket Nature Sanctuary, a nature preserve and study site in San Jacinto County (Peterson and Brown 1983).

The first broad-membership, statewide, private land protection efforts got underway with the 1959 arrival of the Nature Conservancy in Texas, and the 1983 creation of its state-based analogue, the Texas Land Conservancy (Bartlett 1995). In the years since, over forty private land trusts have been established in the state. Together, they have succeeded in protecting over 1.52 million acres, often using conservation easements and other strategies (Texas Land Trust Council 2014). One of the most extraordinary outpourings of support for land conservation occurred in 2013. In September of that year, the Bayou Land Conservancy raised over $4 million from more than 1,500

concerns revolve around two main problems. One is that each piece of land is unique in its distinctive mix of wildlife, vegetation, soils, hydrology, and other features. In that view, it is unclear whether impacts to one tract can truly be balanced by protecting another parcel since, in a strict sense, it will never be an identical match. The impacts, and the conservation benefits, do not translate that directly. Another concern is almost philosophical: is it right to conserve a tract of land if it enables the harm or destruction of another piece of land? This ethical concern rises for the 88 percent of Texas mitigation banks that are run for profit (US Army Corps of Engineers 2014; Williams 2014).

Both concerns may be allayed somewhat by requiring more than a 1:1 match of protected to harmed land, but these criticisms will likely persist. On the other hand, maybe we all need to be more pragmatic, given the enormous cost of land conservation and the rapid pace of habitat destruction. And, we might all try not to shy away from this idea of mitigation. Perhaps mitigation is behind all land conservation. Maybe offsetting the growth of the built world has been the motor driving land protection for many years, just without the direct licenses, fees, and other financial ties.

Family Lands

While mitigation banks empower the market to drive conservation, sometimes love can be just as powerful a land protection tool. The Texas Department of Agriculture has developed a project that offers a sign of the strong tie that many Texans have to land. Through the Family Land Heritage program, the agency recognizes families who have owned and operated a farm or ranch for one hundred years or more. As of 2014, the department had identified over 4,700 tracts that had been in the same family for more than a century, including more than 1,070 parcels that had been held for 150 years or more (Texas Department of Agriculture 2015a and 2015b).

Sources

Ables, Robert. 1967. "The Second Battle for the Alamo." *Southwestern Historical Quarterly* 70 (3): 372–413.

Anderson, H. Allen. 2010. "Palo Duro Canyon State Scenic Park." Handbook of Texas Online. Texas State Historical Association. http://www.tshaonline.org/handbook/online/articles/gkp03, accessed August 9, 2014.

Barcott, Bruce. 2010. "Coast Guard." *Audubon* (July–August).

Bartlett, Richard. 1995. *Saving the Best of Texas: A Partnership Approach to Conservation.* Austin: University of Texas Press.

Bell, Paul G., Jr. 1999. "Monumental Myths." *Southwestern Historical Quarterly* 103 (1): 1–16.

Bezanson, David. 2015. Land Protection and Easements Manager, Texas Chapter, The Nature Conservancy. Personal communication.

Commission for Environmental Cooperation. 2015. Terrestrial Protected Areas, 2010. North American Environmental Atlas. http://www.cec.org/atlas/files/Terrestrial_Protected_areas_2010/TerrProtectedAreas_2010_Shapefile.zip, accessed May 1, 2015.

Federal Guidance for the Establishment, Use, and Operation of Mitigation Banks. 1995. *Federal Register* 60 (228): 58605–15.

Gorte, Ross, Carol Vincent, Laura Hanson, and Marc Rosenblum. 2012. "Federal Land Ownership: Overview and Data." Report 7–5700, R42432. Congressional Research Service. February 8.

Liles, Vernen, and Marjorie Seidel. 2010. "Caddo Lake State Park." Handbook of Texas Online. Texas State Historical Association. http://www.tshaonline.org/handbook/online/articles/gkc02, accessed August 9, 2014.

Long, Christopher. 2010a. "Big Spring State Recreation Area." Handbook of Texas Online. Texas State Historical Association. http://www.tshaonline.org/handbook/online/articles/gkb06, accessed August 9, 2014.

———. 2010b. "Goose Island State Park." Handbook of Texas Online. Texas State Historical Association. http://www.tshaonline.org/handbook/online/articles/gkg07, accessed August 9, 2014.

Lorenz, Jennifer, and Matt Buckingham. 2014. "Fundraising Wisdom." *Saving Land* (Winter). Land Trust Alliance.

Miller, Thomas Lloyd. 1972. *Public Lands of Texas, 1519–1970.* Norman: University of Oklahoma Press.

National Park Service. 2015. Administrative Boundaries of National Park System Units, National Geospatial Data Asset. National Park Service,

US Department of the Interior. http://gstore.unm.edu/apps/rgis/datasets/7bbe8af5–029b-4adf-b06c-134f0dd57226/nps_boundary.original.zip, accessed May 1, 2015.

Neff, Pat. 1925. The Battles of Peace. Administrative Files, Texas State Park Board Records, Archives and Information Services Division, Texas State Library and Archives Commission.

Neumann, Matt. 2014 and 2015. GIS Specialist, Advanced Ecology. Personal communications, August 2014 and March 2015.

Olson, Lori. 2015. Executive Director, Texas Land Trust Council. Personal communication, March.

Peterson, Charles, and Larry Brown. 1983. "Vascular Flora of the Little Thicket Nature Sanctuary, San Jacinto County, Texas: A Sanctuary of the Outdoor Nature Club." Outdoor Nature Club.

Sawyer, R. K. 2012. *A Hundred Years of Texas Waterfowl Hunting: The Decoys, Guides, Clubs, and Places, 1870s to 1970s.* College Station: Texas A&M University Press.

Steinbach, Mark. 2011 and 2012. Executive Director, Texas Land Conservancy. Personal communications, April 2011 and July 2012.

Texas Department of Agriculture. 2015a. All Family Land Heritage Honorees from 1974–2013. http://www.texasagriculture.gov/LinkClick.aspx?fileticket=Dsi8TYq4i6I%3d&tabid=666&portalid=0&mid=2271, accessed May 27, 2015.

———. 2015b. Family Land Heritage Honorees. http://www.texasagriculture.gov/Portals/0/forms/COMMFLH/2014%20Honoree%20List.pdf, accessed May 27, 2015.

Texas Department of State Health Services. 2015. Projected Texas Population by County, 2015. Center for Health Statistics, Texas Department of State Health Services. https://www.dshs.state.tx.us/chs/popdat/ST2015.shtm, accessed April 1, 2015.

Texas General Land Office. 1942. History and Disposition of the Texas Public Domain.

Texas Land Trust Council. 2014. Texas Land Trust Council Conservation Lands Inventory. http://www.texaslandtrustcouncil.org/images/TLTC_General_2013_03_29_forweb.jpg, accessed August 9, 2014.

———. 2015. Conservation Lands Inventory. Shapefile. http://www.texaslandtrustcouncil.org/index.php/what-we-do/cli, accessed March 2, 2015.

Texas Natural Resources Information System. 2015. StratMap Park Boundaries, Boundaries, Texas Statewide Datasets, Data Search and Download. Geographic Information Office, Texas Natural Resources Information System, Texas Water Development Board. https://tg-twdb-gemss.s3.amazonaws.com/d/stratmap_bnd/stratmap_park.zip, accessed May 1, 2015.

Texas Parks and Wildlife. 2012. Land and Water Resources Conservation and Recreation Plan Statewide Inventory 2012, Geodatabase. http://tpwd.texas.gov/gis/apps/lwrcrp/, accessed May 1, 2013.

———. 2015. Counties, Boundaries, GIS Data Downloads. Shapefile. http://tpwd.texas.gov/gis/data/baselayers/counties-zip, accessed April 1, 2015.

Thompson, Michelle. 2014. Software analyst. Applied Research Associates.

Personal communication, August.

Trust for Public Land. 2015. LandVote Database. https://tpl.quickbase.com/db/bbqna2qct?a=dbpage&pageID=10, accessed May 28, 2015.

Tyler, Ron. 2007. *The Big Bend: A History of the Last Texas Frontier.* College Station: Texas A&M University Press.

US Army Corps of Engineers. 2015. Regulatory In-Lieu Fee and Bank Information Tracking System (RIBITS). https://ribits.usace.army.mil, accessed March 27, 2015.

US Fish and Wildlife Service. 1975. Operation of the National Wildlife Refuge System, DES 75–57. Draft Environmental Statement. Department of the Interior.

———. 1983. US Fish and Wildlife Service Interim Guidance on Mitigation Banking. ES Instruction Memorandum No. 80, June 23.

———. 2015. USFWS Interest Shapefile. Boundaries showing USFWS acquired lands (March 1, 2015). http://ecos.fws.gov/ServCatFiles/Reference/Holding/45000, accessed May 1, 2015.

US Forest Service. 2015. Administrative Forest Boundaries, Shapefile. FSGeoData Clearinghouse. US Forest Service, US Department of Agriculture. http://data.fs.usda.gov/geodata/edw/edw_resources/shp/S_USA.AdministrativeForest.zip, accessed May 1, 2015.

US Geological Survey. 2014. Protected Areas Database of the United States (PAD-US). http://gapanalysis.usgs.gov/padus/data/download/, accessed August 8, 2014.

Williams, Beattie. 2014. Director, Computer Sciences and Consulting Services, Applied Research Associates. Personal communication, August.

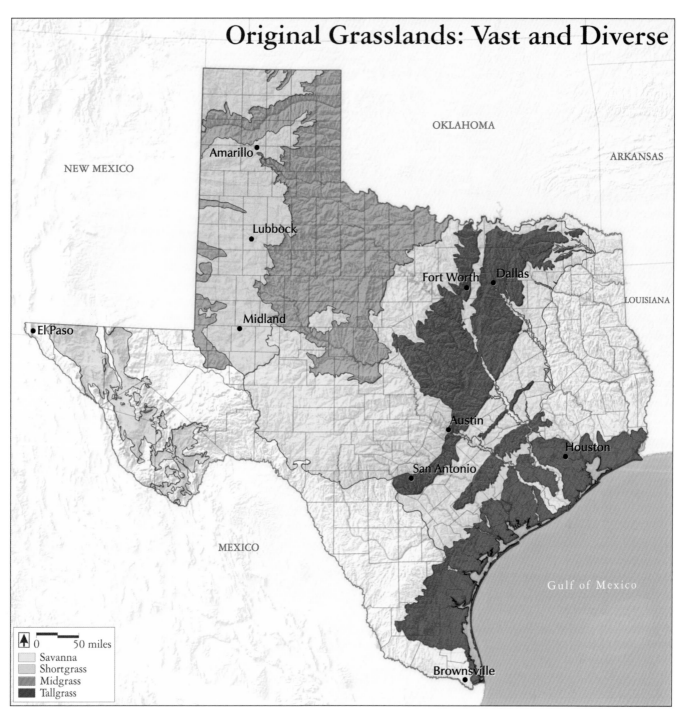

Original Grasslands: Vast and Diverse

NEW MEXICO

OKLAHOMA

ARKANSAS

Amarillo

Lubbock

Fort Worth · Dallas

LOUISIANA

El Paso

Midland

Austin

Houston

San Antonio

MEXICO

Gulf of Mexico

0   50 miles

Savanna
Shortgrass
Midgrass
Tallgrass

Brownsville

This Texas map highlights the state's original immense grasslands (Omernik 2009; Bezanson 2015).

Prairies, Pastures, Cropfields, and Lawns

I reached some plains so vast, that I did not find their limit anywhere I went, although I traveled over them for more than 300 leagues . . . with no more land marks than if we had been swallowed up by the sea . . . there was not a stone, nor bit of rising ground, nor a tree, nor a shrub, nor anything to go by.

—Francisco Vázquez de Coronado, 1541

The prairie in which I now found myself presented the appearance of a perfect flower garden, with scarcely a square foot of green to be seen. The most variegated carpet of flowers I ever beheld lay unrolled before me; red, yellow, violet, blue, every color was there; millions of the most magnificent prairie roses, tuberoses, asters, dahlias, and fifty other kinds of flowers.

—Charles Webber, 1852

Crossing this stream [the Trinity River in 1835], we entered, on rising the western bank, the first large prairie we ever saw, stretching further to the west than the eye could reach. It is hard to describe the emotions of the soul on looking for the first time across a vast prairie. The feeling is somewhat akin to that experienced on the first visit to the beach. Land and water there bore some resemblance.

—Z. N. Morrell, 1872

The plain gives man new and novel sensations of elation, of vastness, of romance, of awe, and often nauseating loneliness.

—Walter Prescott Webb, 1931

Texas has high mountains, deep canyons, thick woodlands, and long coastlines. However, grassland is the state's defining landscape, and one that, for hundreds of years, has brought visitors wonder, delight, and some fear. Nearly every part of the state can claim a distinctive grassland as its own. Texas stretches from the coastal prairie along the Gulf, to the Blackland and Crosstimbers of Central Texas, to the shortgrass prairies of the Chihuahuan Desert and High Plains. Little and big bluestem, eastern gamagrass, brownseed paspalum, yellow Indiangrass, and hundreds of other grasses, forbs, and legumes are found throughout the state. And, beyond their ecological value, these plants support the huge herds of cattle, sheep, and goats, and the pioneering farmers and ranchers that have long been a vital part of Texan culture.

"Gone"

However, in the years since western settlement, the extent, diversity, and integrity of those grasslands have declined markedly. Just a small fraction of the native prairies once found in Texas remains today. For example, Bill Neiman, a grower of native grasses and forbs, estimates that only 4/1,000 of 1 percent of the Blackland's tallgrass prairie still exists in Texas (Neiman 2002). And the remnants continue to become even scarcer. As Bob Burleson, an early Texas prairie advocate and restorer, said, "my wife and I took a tour of prairies that we had plotted and studied thirty years ago. And out of all the ones that we went back to, something over twenty, they were all gone, except parts of a couple of them. And even the one that was remaining had been sprayed and so all the broad-leafed forbs and legumes were gone from it. Others had just disappeared" (Burleson 1999).

Creatures, Great and Small

With the loss of prairies, there has also been a drop-off in the wildlife that depends on these grasslands. Many grassland birds have seen declines in the 1966–2010 period, including such well-known birds as the eastern meadowlark (-2.8 percent/year) and the painted bunting (-0.8 percent/year) (Sauer et al. 2012). The highly endangered Attwater's prairie chicken has gone from populations of a million in the coastal prairie of Texas and Louisiana to fewer than fifty in the wild today (Turner 2012). Game birds, such as the northern bobwhite quail, have suffered a great deal as well. The quail's numbers have fallen by 2.9 percent annually, on average, as native bunch grasses have declined (Telfair 2012; Sauer et al. 2012). It is important to remember that prairies' value extends far beyond birds, and also affects a wide array of reptiles (the threatened Texas horned lizard), many key pollinating insects (including bees, moths, and butterflies), and numerous mammals (from the magnificent bison that once roamed the land to the less famous eastern spotted skunk) (Texas Parks and Wildlife 2005).

Continuous Grazing

The loss of prairies has been due to many causes, gradually played out over many years. Grazing is one practice that has had an early and ongo-ing impact. Grazing alone, as millions of buffalo (as well as deer, antelope, and elk) did for eons, helped the prairies. The forbs and grasses benefited from these animals eating the older grass, churning the soil, and fertilizing the land with their dung and urine. However, grazing by domestic livestock has been a different matter. For one thing, some of the new grazers, such as the sheep and horses that were brought to this country in the 1500s, had a mouth structure that allowed them to graze very close to the ground and permanently damage plants. But another problem ran across all species: because these animals were privately owned, it was important to keep the herds separate, whether through herding or fencing. As a result, the ranchers' cattle, sheep, goats, and horses tended to remain on a given piece of land, grazing continuously. There was no respite, as there had been with the migratory herds of wild animals. Grasses and forbs had no recovery time to rebuild their root systems after intense grazing.

With time and continuous grazing, the Texas grasslands' plant diversity fell. The famous Texas naturalist Roy Bedichek reported the result

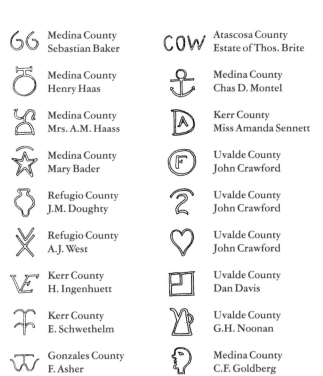

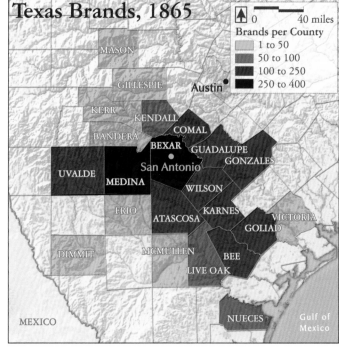

This map plots the ownership of livestock brands, based on an 1865 county-by-county registry. Coming so shortly after the Civil War and its cutoff of national markets, it is impressive that the inventory turned up so many brands and cattle operations in Texas. Further, this map likely fails to include the many ranching operations that were too distant from the San Antonio–based publisher to be included. In any case, the map's basic point is that the large number of brands required extensive herding and fencing to keep the branded livestock apart. By concentrating livestock in a single area, continuous grazing increased, with fewer opportunities for plants' rest and regrowth. Over time, the native grasses and forbs inevitably suffered (Jackson and Long 1865).

in the 1940s, when he walked along fence lines that paralleled Texas roads. In one cow pasture, he saw twenty-four species of forbs, while on the road's swale only a few feet away, he found sixty-eight; in a goat pasture, he counted just eight types of forbs, and in the nearby roadside, he noted forty-six; in a sheep pasture, he found only a single rain lily, while fifty-four species of wildflowers grew close by along the road (Bedichek 1947). The endless grazing in the fenced pastures doomed much of the native vegetation. Sometimes, where overstocking and drought conspired, the impact extended beyond a slide in diversity and resulted in almost an entire loss of the prairie. The drought of 1885–86 was so serious in West Texas that 25 to 40 percent of the cattle in the Big Bend died, and much of the black, blue, and white grama grasses found in the high desert prairie were lost as well (Utley 1962).

This long-standing problem of confined, continuous grazing was accelerated by the advent of wire fencing in the last quarter of the 1800s. Wire turned out to be cheaper to buy and easier and quicker to install than its predecessors—the fences of rails and planks, the walls of rocks, and the hedgerows of bois d'arc, thorn locust, mesquite, and pyracantha. Some of the earliest wire fencing in Texas was made of slick wire imported from Belgium. Early deliveries of wire arrived as ballast on immigrant ships and were installed at the King Ranch in 1871. The popularity of wire fenc-

ing grew with the addition of barbs, and because of old-fashioned salesmanship by a young man named John Gates. Gates arrived in San Antonio in 1876 with the pitch, "this fence is the finest in the world: light as air, stronger than whiskey, cheaper than dirt, and all steel and miles long. The cattle ain't born that can get through it." Litigation over patent rights and legislative battles over the end of the open range slowed the adoption of wire fencing during the early years. However, cattlemen were soon convinced of the newfangled fence's value. National barbed wire production soared, from 5 tons in 1874, to 40,000 in 1880, and then 200,000 in 1890. Huge fencing projects were undertaken in the state, including 800 miles of fence installed in 1881 at the XIT Ranch, and many thousands of miles strung along the new Texas railroad tracks of the 1880s and '90s (McCallum 1957; Hayter 1939).

The Prairie Dog

While the American grasslands are often associated with the one-ton bison, the three-pound prairie dog may well have had an equally important role in the prairie. Enormous prairie dog towns were once found in the Panhandle and western portions of the state. J. Frank Dobie estimated that in 1852 a single town of about fifty million prairie dogs covered a million acres of the Llano Estacado (Dobie 1961, 90). In 1905, a federal biologist calculated that 800 million prairie

dogs occupied some 90,000 square miles in Texas (Bailey 1905). These prairie dogs were not only numerous, they were also a keystone species of the prairie. Their grass clipping helped open areas for recycling soil nutrients and provided space for plants and animals that relied on bare soil, such as the mountain plover. Their burrowing helped churn the soil, and their networks of tunnels provided shelter for burrowing owls, rabbits, hares, Texas horned lizards, black-footed ferrets, and snakes. The prairie dogs served as prey for badgers, black-footed ferrets, coyotes, wolves, and raptors, such as the ferruginous hawk and Swainson's hawk. Unfortunately, their role has fallen dramatically. Ninety-six to ninety-nine percent of prairie dogs have been poisoned, gassed, or had their colonies bulldozed. Some have been shot for sport. Others have been killed to control sylvatic plague and limit forage competition with cattle (Texas Parks and Wildlife 2012; Singhurst et al. 2010).

The Plow

Another and perhaps more abrupt change in the prairie was caused by its plowing and seeding for crops. The extent of cultivation can be suggested by these maps of grain mills and cotton gins, showing how food and textile crops spread quickly and widely across the state, usurping most of the grasslands in the eastern half of Texas. The early yet intense effect of cultivation, and other changes in land use, can

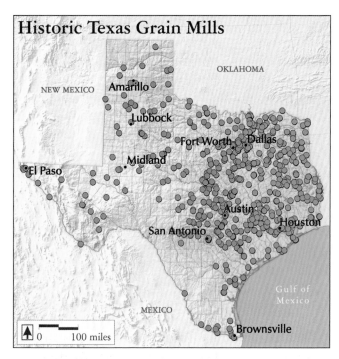

Grain mills and cotton gins are indicators of cultivation and prairie loss in Texas. This map marks where more than 680 early grain mills are reported to have existed (Firsching 2012; Julien 2012; Shelton 2012; Texas Historical Commission 2012).

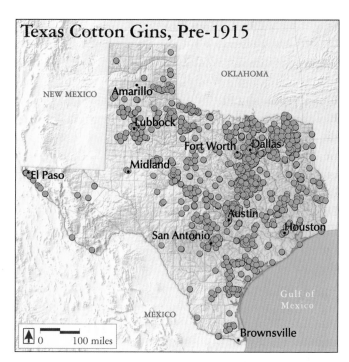

This map shows over 3,900 locations of cotton gins in the state. Roughly 45 percent of the gins represented here are estimated to have been built before 1915, indicating that grassland loss began quite early in Texas (Moore 2012).

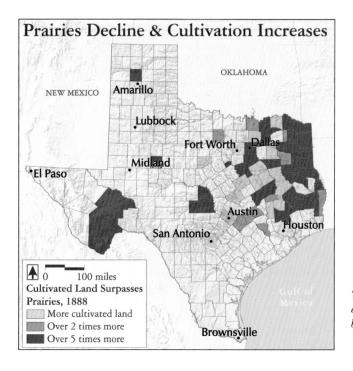

This map is based on a Texas agricultural census published in 1888. The census reported those counties where prairie acreage had already dropped below the extent of cultivated areas (Rozek 2001).

be seen in the following map based on an 1888 state census of Texas. Even before our modern age of powerful tractors, and multirow plows and disks, many counties, particularly in the Blackland Prairie, had already seen the disappearance of large stretches of prairie. For example, prairie acreage, seen as a portion of cultivated lands, had sunk below 20 percent in Henderson, Dallas, Red River, Fannin, Rockwall, Ellis, Hill, Delta, and Hunt Counties as early as 1888 (Rozek 2001).

Fire Suppression

Prairies have evolved with periodic fires that controlled the woody species that competed with grasses, forbs, and sedges. Also, fires traditionally removed litter and dead vegetation, put down a layer of rich minerals, and promoted the right soil temperature for seeds to germinate. However, as the prairie was settled, fire grew into a much-feared threat, both for the risk to the people who had come to live there and for the danger to their structures and possessions. Disastrous wildfires, such as the Peshtigo fire of 1871 in Wisconsin and the Big Burn of 1910 in Washington State, brought national attention to the peril. Fire control became a high priority throughout the country.

Texans continue to take this risk of grassland and forest fire very seriously, and they work hard to control it. In September 2011, during the height of a severe drought, all but four of the state's 254 counties implemented burn bans to reduce the chance that a spark might get away. In the case that a fire does get started, the state can react with impressive resources. There are over 60,000 paid and volunteer firefighters on call in the state. Additionally, the Texas Forest Service has a powerful fleet of wildfire-fighting equipment, including sixty-six bulldozers, nine engines, and two maintainers and tenders, all staged for quick deployment (Texas Forest Service 2012).

Exotic Plants

Introduced species also caused trouble for Texas' native grasslands. With the Dust Bowl of the 1930s and the

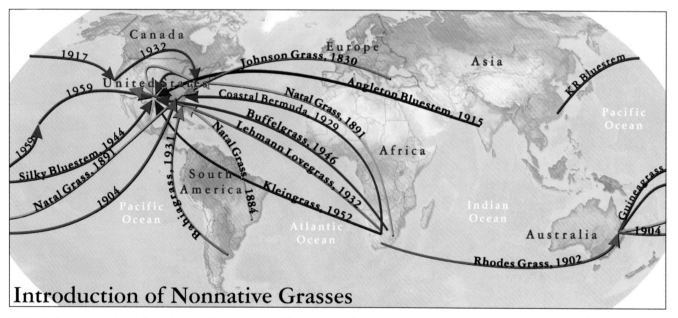

Introduction of Nonnative Grasses

This global map shows the origins and routes of some introduced forage grasses that are now common, and in some cases, invasive, in Texas. They include Angleton bluestem, bahiagrass, buffelgrass, coastal Bermuda, guineagrass, Johnsongrass, kleingrass, KR bluestem, Lehmann lovegrass, Rhodes grass, and silky bluestem (Agricultural Journal 1904; Ball 1902; Bisset and Sillar 1984; Burr 1955; Chomley and Hunter 1907; Bogdan 1977; Cox et al. 1988; Hanson 1959; Harlan 1952; Piper 1925; Redmon 2001; Smith 2012; Tracy 1916; Tracy 1919).

great Texas drought of the 1950s, and under continued grazing pressure, the state's pastures had suffered greatly. Post–World War II years had also seen the rise of the automobile and the expansion of a 300,000-mile network of streets and roads in the state. The new cars and pavement created a vast right-of-way needing sodding and stabilizing (Alvarez 2006). Worry grew about how native vegetation would be able to hold on to Texas soil and feed its livestock.

So, land grant colleges, the Soil Conservation Service, and private landowners and nurseries turned to grasses from Africa, China, the Middle East, Australia, and South America to cover and tie down the soil. Introductions, both intentional and inadvertent, began in the early 1800s if not before. Trials of introducing new plants became more common in the 1930s and ran well into the 1950s. Such grasses as Angleton bluestem, Australian bluestem, bahiagrass, Bermudagrass, buffelgrass, guineagrass, Johnsongrass, KR and Kleberg bluestems, kleingrass, Lehmann lovegrass, natal grass, silky bluestem, Rhodes grass, and yellow bluestem eventually found their way into Texas roadways and pastures. Without local competitors, insects, and diseases, and with selection for high germination and rapid growth rates, these exotics were often robust, and even invasive. In some cases, the new plants grew into monocultures that replaced diverse native prairies (Agricultural Journal of the Cape of Good Hope

These aerial photos show the gradual disappearance of a coastal tallgrass prairie near League City, Texas. Once home to mottled ducks and the very rare Attwater's prairie chicken, the prairie was lost through construction of a subdivision from 1996 to 2010 (Rosen 2012; US Geological Survey 2012).

1904; Bisset and Sillar 1984; Ball 1902; Bogdan 1977; Burr 1955; Chomley and Hunter 1907; Cox et al. 1988; Hanson 1959; Harlan 1952; Piper 1925; Redmon 2001; Smith 2012; Tracy 1916; Tracy 1919).

Grading and Building

Many former prairies have provided ideal building sites in Texas. As open, reasonably level spots, prairies have often been scraped, regraded, paved, built on, and replanted. Even before building begins, leveling grasslands can do irreparable harm, since the subtle topographic relief of prairie's characteristic mima mounds and gilgai—its bumps and divots—can be quickly erased. As a consequence, many Texas prairies have been buried under residential subdivisions, shopping centers, and office complexes over the past generation.

Our Love of Lawns

In the United States, more land is devoted to growing turf grass than any other plant. Many reasons are offered for its popularity. Some saw and admired an egalitarian value in shared lawns connecting and wrapping suburban American homes. Others claimed that there were aristocratic roots in the manicured swards that might be associated with the European estates of Capability Brown or André Le Nôtre. And no doubt, many found a practical value in how residential turf could be simply maintained with the new and handy sprinklers, edgers, and lawn mowers (Steinberg 2006).

In any case, the great height (as much as 6 feet or more!), bunchy form, and the seasonal flowers and seed heads of prairie grasses and forbs have traditionally had little place in American gardens (Falck 2002). Our lawn-loving culture is illustrated by the network of sod farms supplying turf to houses, office complexes, and institutional grounds, as well as by the pervasive ordinances outlawing tall grasses in many Texas cities and towns.

The map of municipal weed ordinances shows where cities and towns require that lots be cut to at most 12 inches in height, and in some cases, as low as 6 inches. With the rising interest in native grasses, and concerns about drought tolerance, there has been some erosion in these local laws. In one famous case, the noted Texas environmental attorney Ned Fritz was repeatedly charged by the city of Dallas under its weed ordinances. On the third charge, Mr. Fritz took the case to a jury and won (City of Abilene 2014; City of Atlanta 2014; City of Dallas 2014; City of Fort Worth 2014; City of Houston 2014; City of La

Here we chart our love of lawns, and our preference for sod grass, kept short and tidy, over bunch grass, high and wild. This map shows the locations of major sod farms selling turf grasses in Texas. The farms provide more than sixty-five different varieties of carpet grass, including types of bentgrass, Bermuda, bluegrass, fescue, St. Augustine, and zoysia (Turfgrass Producers of Texas 2012).

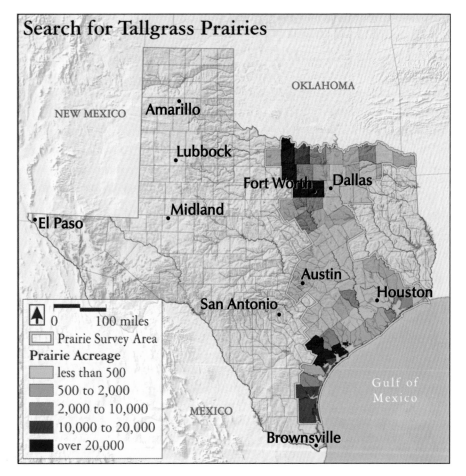

Search for Tallgrass Prairies

0   100 miles

☐ Prairie Survey Area

Prairie Acreage

less than 500

500 to 2,000

2,000 to 10,000

10,000 to 20,000

over 20,000

This map is a compilation of more than ninety county surveys searching for tallgrass prairie remnants in the eastern half of the state. The Native Prairies Association of Texas and Texas Parks and Wildlife collaborated on the research from the year 2000 through 2010. They found remnants ranging from less than an acre to over 40,000 acres, with a wide variance in their diversity of grasses and forbs, and their encroachment by exotic plants and woody cover. Some are held as parks and private preserves, but most are not protected (Alderson and JSA Company 2010 and 2011; Alderson 2011, 2010a, 2010b; Anderson 2009 and 2010, Anderson 2003, 2007, 2009; Bahm 2009a, 2009b, 2009c, 2009d, 2009e, 2009f, 2009g, 2009h; Bezanson 2015; Green 2009a, 2009b, 2009c, 2009d; Hammons 2010, 2009a, 2009b; Kane 2007a, 2007b; Kiphart 2001 and 2002; Merkord 2009a, 2009b, 2009c, 2009d, 2009e; Merkord and Merkord 2009a, 2009b, 2009c, 2009d; Moss and Hammons 2007; Native Prairies Association of Texas 2010; Naylor 2010, 2009; Quayle 2000; Rhodes 2010a, 2010b, 2009; Rosen 2008, 2007a, 2007b; Rowe 2010, 2009, 2008, 2007; Singhurst 2012, 2015; Sommerville 2010, 2009a, 2009b, 2009c, 2009d, 2009e; Spangler 2005a; Spangler 2004a and 2005a; Spangler 2004b and 2005b; Toledo 2010, 2009a, 2009b, 2009c, 2009d, 2009e, 2009f, 2009g; White 2010, 2009a, 2009b, 2009c, 2008 and 2009, 2007a, 2007b; Wolverton 2010).

Porte 2014; City of Lubbock 2014; City of Madisonville 2014; City of San Antonio 2014; City of Waco 2014; City of Yoakum 2014; Fritz 1999).

The Traces

As prairies have grown more rare, there has been a simultaneous recognition of the beauty, complexity, and value of the prairie, in Texas and beyond. Efforts have budded to locate and protect the intact prairies that remain.

It is interesting to speculate about why some prairies have survived and why others have disappeared. There are surely many reasons. Some factors are probably environmental. For instance, relatively large grassland tracts have persisted in the ranchlands west of Fort Worth. This is likely because annual rainfall is under 35 inches, limiting dryland farming and the sod-busting, seeding, and herbicide use that cultivation involves. Other factors may be cultural. For example, many five- to ten-acre prairie remnants survive in the country west of Houston. Czech farmers there—in Fayette, Washington, and Austin Counties—had a long tradition of setting aside native hay meadows for feeding farm livestock through drought and winter (Singhurst 2012; Mauro 1986).

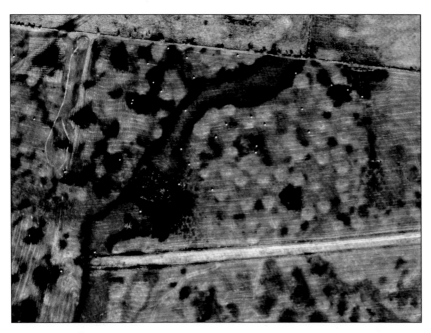

Prairies have very distinctive topography, as shown in this 2010 aerial photograph of Nash Prairie, a coastal prairie southwest of Houston in Fort Bend County. Nash has a clay-soil prairie's characteristic microrelief, with low areas known as hogwallows, and higher areas, typically fifteen to eighteen feet across, called mima or pimple mounds. The mounds appear here as the round, light-colored regions. The relief may be as little as eighteen inches, but Nash Prairie's varied topography underpins the great diversity of its plant life by offering a range of areas that are slightly wetter or a bit drier than the norm. When a grassland is plowed or bulldozed, these slightly low and high areas are typically lost (Gustavson 1975; US Geological Survey 2012).

A Revival

Prairies are being rebuilt in many parts of Texas. Grassland enthusiasts harvest seed from intact preserves, ranchlands, hay meadows, cemeteries, and railroad rights-of-way where these native grasses persevere. Restorers then use jury-rigged seed harvesters, cleaners, drills, and broadcasters to spread seed to new refuges. Sometimes they work alone, but they often band together. Statewide organizations, such as the Native Prairies Association of Texas, Nature Conservancy of Texas, Texas Land Conservancy, and Texas R.I.C.E., promote prairie recovery. Regional grassland groups, such as the Coastal Prairie Partnership, Katy Prairie Conservancy, and Wildlife Habitat Federation also exist. Many of these private groups work in partnership with government agencies, such as Texas Parks and Wildlife and the US Fish and Wildlife Service.

Seed

As interest has grown in prairie recovery, a small market for native seed has blossomed. Seed farmers, such as Native American Seed in Junction, and prairie harvesters, such as the Pierce Ranch, near El Campo, have become active. South Texas Natives, in cooperation with the Garza Plant Materials Center and Texas AgriLife Research, has helped supply native seed to commercial growers to expand supply and lower prices for replanting prairies.

Prairie remnants are held in both public and private hands. The US government has extensive acreage at the Anahuac, Brazoria, and Attwater Prairie Chicken National Wildlife Refuges. The nonprofit Texas Nature Conservancy maintains Clymer Meadow (1,068 acres in Hunt County), Nash Prairie (400 acres in Brazoria County), and the Texas City Prairie (2,303 acres in Galveston County). Meanwhile, the Native Prairies Association of Texas protects Maddin Prairie Preserve (1,114 acres in Mitchell County), Russell Grasslands and Forest Preserve (831 acres in San Jacinto County), Simpson Prairie (50 acres in McLennan County), and other smaller remnants. The Texas Land Conservancy also looks after a number of prairies: Kachina Prairie (30 acres in Ellis County), Malone Preserve (146 acres in Johnson County), Marysee Prairie (10 acres in Liberty County), and Tanglewood Prairie (31 acres in Lee County) (Bezanson 2012; Singhurst 2012).

Substantial reseedings have been done at federal sites, such as the Anahuac National Wildlife Refuge (NWR), Attwater Prairie Chicken NWR, and Brazoria NWR (Halls Bayou Unit). Plantings have also happened at state parks, such as Stringfellow WMA, at nonprofit sanctuaries, such as the Texas Nature Conservancy's Mad Island Preserve, and on private ranches, including tracts near Celeste, Columbus, Crawford, Edna, Midfield, Temple, and Weimar (Stransky 2012).

Caution

Another encouraging sign for prairie protection is that there are increasing safeguards used against introducing more nonnatives into the Texas landscape. Many private landowners now require contractors such as well drillers and pipeline operators to use native grass mixes when reseeding new rights-of-way and other disturbed areas. Farmers who participate in restoring cropfields to grasslands through the federal Conservation Reserve Program are often choosing now to use more native grasses. Also, research is underway to develop native grasses, such as hooded and shortspike windmill grass, to include in roadside seeding mixes, while the Texas Department of Transportation is allowing more of such native species to be used in stabilizing rights-of-way (Lund 2009).

COMMON NAME	EFFECTS OF GRAZING		
	Coefficient	*Net Effect*	*Net Effect Key*
Eastern gamagrass	7	↓	*increases* ↑ *neutral* *decreases* ↓
Roemer's mimosa	3	↑	
Little bluestem	4	↑	
Big bluestem	7	↓	
Maximilian sunflower	4	↑	
Prairie acacia	5	●	
White prairie clover	5	●	
Canada goldenrod	2	↑	
Texas wintergrass	2	↑	
Canda wild rye	4	↑	
Tall fescue	-3	*nonative*	
Fringeleaf wild petunia	3	↑	
Downy phlox	7	↓	
White aster	3	↑	
Groovestem Indian plantain	5	●	
Ground cherry	2	↑	
Branched noseburn	3	↑	
Milkweed	2	↑	
Prairie bishop	3	↑	
Littletooth sedge	5	●	

Prairies have extraordinarily diverse vegetation. Here is the result of Daubenmire plant surveys made in June 2006 of Clymer Meadow, a 1,068-acre blackland prairie, northeast of Dallas, near Celeste, Texas. Each transect was 60 meters long, with samples taken from half-meter by half-meter quadrats, spaced out on 2-meter centers. Over 250 vascular plants have been recorded at Clymer, many of them "decreasers," the special grasses and forbs that decrease, or become rarer, as grazing and other disturbances proceed. In this particular set of summer transects, the surveys showed the prairie to be dominated by eastern gamagrass, Roemer's mimosa, little bluestem, Maximilian sunflower, and big bluestem, all natives, and two considered "decreasers" (Eidson 2013; Reemt 2013).

Paddocks, Buffalos, and Prairie Dogs

Sometimes native grasses persist in the seedbed, but need a boost to thrive. Livestock and wildlife can help. One way is through "intensive rotation," where ranchers move cattle, sheep, and goats among fifteen to more than one hundred paddocks. The frequent moves and long rests allow grasses to recover before being grazed again.

Bison are being reintroduced as well. The buffalo tend to graze most on grasses, leaving the forbs to lend more diversity to the prairie. Buffalo hoof action can remove the litter that shelters invasive nonnative plants. Bison also roll and wallow, creating open areas that allow new prairie plants to germinate.

Prairie dogs are also being restored to their old haunts, sometimes using premade burrows of PVC pipe. Colonies are being reestablished on private property (such as Jesse Wood's ranch in Callahan County), nonprofit lands (including the Texas Land Conservancy's Maddin Prairie Preserve), and on public parcels (such as Caprock Canyon State Park) (Merkord 2007; Sheehan 2006).

Herbicides and Burns

In other situations, prairies are intact but have gotten overgrown with invasive woody or exotic species, such as Chinese tallow, deep-rooted sedge, McCartney rose, huisache, and mesquite. In those cases, grasslands at Armand Bayou Nature Center, Brazoria NWR, and Justin Hurst WMA have been brought back with herbicide treatments (Grazon X, Tordon, Sendero, and other chemicals) (Stransky 2012).

There has also been interest in using fire to promote prairies and control nonnative grasses. The Lady Bird Johnson National Wildflower Center has had success curbing KR bluestem using prescribed burns during the summer months (Simmons 2005, 4). In fact, some landowners in West Texas have banded together to do cooperative burns. The Edwards Plateau Prescribed Burning Association is one such group, and it has the catchy motto, "Happiness is smoke on the horizon!" (Pyne 2012).

Healing

Despite the many efforts to restore prairies in Texas, it remains undeniably difficult. Too many pieces have been lost, and too little is known about how the pieces once fit together. Resown prairie plants often fail to sprout or survive. Even those that persist sometimes become reinvaded by nonnative plants.

However, just the effort to rebuild a prairie may have its own value. A nonprofit known as the Great Plains Restoration Council has organized troubled youth to help in reassembling prairies along the Gulf Coast and in the Crosstimbers. The council has found that this work can help the young people find meaning and purpose in their lives. In this way, perhaps, this ecological work can be more than just about restoring lands; it can also be about healing people (Manos 2009).

Sources

Agricultural Journal of the Cape of Good Hope. 1904. *Agricultural Journal of the Cape of Good Hope* 24 (January–June): 293.

Alderson, James. 2010a. Survey of Milam County, Texas. Native Prairies Association of Texas. August and December.

———. 2010b. Survey of Native Prairie in Johnson County, Texas. Native Prairies Association of Texas. June and July.

———. 2011. Survey of Waller County, Texas. Native Prairies Association of Texas. May.

Alderson, James, and JSA Company. 2010 and 2011. Survey of McLennan County, Texas. Native Prairies Association of Texas. May 2010 and January 2011.

Alvarez, Elizabeth Cruce, ed. 2006. *Texas Almanac, 2006–7.* College Station: Texas A&M University Press.

Anderson, Charles. 2003, 2007, 2009. Survey of Native Prairie in Navarro County, Texas. Native Prairies Association of Texas. February 2003, January 2007, March and September 2009.

———. 2009. Survey of Native Prairie in Comal County, Texas. Native Prairies Association of Texas. October.

———. 2009 and 2010. Survey of Native Prairie in Hays County, Texas. Native Prairies Association of Texas. April 2009 and May 2010.

Bahm, Matt. 2009a. Survey of Native Prairie in Collin County, Texas. Native Prairies Association of Texas. February.

——. 2009b. Survey of Native Prairie in Dallas County, Texas. Native Prairies Association of Texas. March.

——. 2009c. Survey of Native Prairie in Denton County, Texas. Native Prairies Association of Texas. October.

——. 2009d. Survey of Native Prairie in Fannin County, Texas. Native Prairies Association of Texas. February and May.

——. 2009e. Survey of Native Prairie in Hill County, Texas. Native Prairies Association of Texas. October.

——. 2009f. Survey of Native Prairie in Kaufman County, Texas. Native Prairies Association of Texas. July.

——. 2009g. Survey of Native Prairie in Rockwall County, Texas. Native Prairies Association of Texas. March.

——. 2009h. Survey of Native Prairie in Van Zandt County, Texas. Native Prairies Association of Texas. August and September.

Bailey, Vernon. 1905. *Biological Survey of Texas: Life Zones, with Characteristic Species of Mammals, Birds, Reptiles, and Plants.* Washington, DC: Government Printing Office.

Ball, Carleton R. 1902. "Johnson Grass: Report of Investigations Made during the Season of 1901." Bulletin No. 11. Bureau of Plant Industry, US Department of Agriculture. Washington, DC: Government Printing Office.

Bedichek, Roy. 1947. *Adventures with a Texas Naturalist.* Austin: University of Texas Press.

Bezanson, David. 2012, 2014, and 2015. Protection and Easements Manager, Texas Chapter, The Nature Conservancy. Personal communications, December 2012, December 2014 through May 2015.

Bisset, W. J., and D. I. Sillar. 1984. "Angleton Grass (*Dichanthium aristatum*) in Queensland." *Tropical Grasslands* 18 (4).

Bogdan, A. V. 1977. *Tropical Pasture and Fodder Plants.* New York: Longman, 77–86.

Burleson, Bob. 1999. Oral history interview conducted June 19, in Temple, Texas. Texas Legacy Project. Conservation History Association of Texas.

Burr, Richard. 1955. "An Australian Grass in Texas." *Journal of Range Management* 8: 8–10.

Chomley, F. G., and Percy Hunter. 1907. *Agricultural Gazette of New South Wales* 17 (December 3): 1210, 1211.

City of Abilene. 2014. Grass, Weeds, or Brush. Section 19, Article II, Chapter 19. Code of Ordinances of the City of Abilene.

City of Atlanta. 2014. Litter and Weed Ordinance. City Ordinance 460, Adopted 11/20/95, Section 1. Code of Ordinances of the City of Atlanta.

City of Dallas. 2014. High Grass/Weeds. Ordinance Section 18-13(a). Code of Ordinances of the City of Dallas.

City of Fort Worth. 2014. High Weeds and Grass. Appendix B, Article II, Division 2, Section 11A-8. Code of Ordinances of the City of Fort Worth.

City of Houston. 2014. Neighborhood Nuisances. Article XI, Section 10-451(a)(10). Code of Ordinances of the City of Houston.

City of La Porte. 2014. Chapter 34. Code of Ordinances of the City of La Porte.

City of Lubbock. 2014. Weeds, Rubbish, and Unwholesome Situations. Part 1, Division 2, Section 34.02. Code of Ordinances of the City of Lubbock.

City of Madisonville. 2014. Amended Ordinance No. 165A, Section 4. Code of Ordinances of the City of Madisonville.

City of Plano. 2014. Weeds, Rubbish, or Unsanitary Matter. Article I, Chapter 14. Code of Ordinances of the City of Plano.

City of San Antonio. 2014. Areas Required to Be Kept Clear. Section 14–61(a)(4). Code of Ordinances of the City of San Antonio.

City of Waco. 2014. Unsanitary or Unsightly Matter, Weeds, and Rubbish. Article II, Chapter 16. Code of Ordinances of the City of Waco.

City of Yoakum. 2014. Prohibited Nuisances. Section 26-2(b), Part II. Code of Ordinances of the City of Yoakum.

Coronado, Francisco Vázquez de. 1541. A letter to the King of Spain, October 20.

Cox, Jerry, G. B. Ruyle, Jan H. Fourie, and Charlie Donaldson. 1988. "Lehmann Lovegrass—Central South Africa and Arizona, USA." *Rangelands* 10 (2).

Dobie, J. Frank. 1961. *The Voice of the Coyote.* Bison Book edition, published by arrangement with Little, Brown.

Eidson, Jim. 2012. Range Ecologist, Nature Conservancy of Texas. Personal communications, December 2012 through January 2013.

Falck, Zachary. 2002. "Controlling the Weed Nuisance in Turn-of-the-Century American Cities." *Environmental History* 7 (4): 611–31.

Firsching, Donald. 2012. Database Programmer, Texas Historical Commission. Personal communication, December.

Frisvold, George, et al. 2007. Decision

Model for Controlling Buffelgrass Invasion in an Urban-Wildland Interface. Program of Research on the Economics of Invasive Species Management Workshop. Economic Research Service, USDA. Washington, DC, October 18–19.

Fritz, Ned. 1999. Oral history interview conducted June 17, in Dallas, Texas. Texas Legacy Project. Conservation History Association of Texas.

Green, Carrol. 2009a. Survey of Native Prairie in Brown County, Texas. Native Prairies Association of Texas. April.

———. 2009b. Survey of Native Prairie in Lampasas County, Texas. Native Prairies Association of Texas. August.

———. 2009c. Survey of Native Prairie in Mills County, Texas. Native Prairies Association of Texas. June.

Gustavson, Thomas C. 1975. Microrelief (Gilgai) Structures on Expansive Clays of the Texas Coastal Plain. Geological Circular 75-7. Bureau of Economic Geology, University of Texas at Austin.

Hammons, Ryan. 2009a. Survey of Native Prairie in Freestone, Grayson, and Victoria Counties, Texas. Native Prairies Association of Texas. March.

———. 2009b. Survey of Native Prairie in Lee County, Texas. Native Prairies Association of Texas. June.

———. 2010. Survey of Native Prairie in Walker County, Texas. Native Prairies Association of Texas. March.

Hanson, B. A. 1959. Grass Varieties of the United States. Agriculture Handbook No. 170. US Department of Agriculture, Agricultural Research Service. Washington, DC.

Harlan, Jack. 1952. "Origin of King Ranch bluestem in America." Oklahoma Forage Leaflet No. 11.

Hayter, Earl. W. 1939. "Barbed Wire Fencing—A Prairie Invention: Its Rise and Influence in the Western States." *Agricultural History* 13 (4): 189–207.

Jackson, W. H., and S. A. Long. 1865. *The Texas Stock Directory; or, Book of Marks and Brands*. Herald Office. San Antonio, Texas.

Julien, Dan. 2012. Information Technology Coordinator, Texas Historical Commission. Personal communication, December.

Kane, Jay. 2006. Survey of Native Prairie in Limestone County, Texas. Native Prairies Association of Texas. January through July 2006.

———. 2007a. Survey of Native Prairie in Austin County, Texas. Native Prairies Association of Texas. August.

———. 2007b. Survey of Native Prairie in Fayette County, Texas. Native Prairies Association of Texas. August.

Kiphart, Tim. 2001 and 2002. Survey of Native Prairie in Washington County, Texas. Native Prairies Association of Texas. November 2001; September, November, and December 2002.

Lund, Anna Shae. 2009. "Evaluation of Texas Native Grasses for Texas Department of Transportation's Right of Ways." Thesis submitted in partial fulfillment of the master of science degree, Texas A&M University–Kingsville.

Manos, Jared. 2009. Prairie and Spiritual Restoration. Texas Environmental Grantmakers Group. Houston, Texas (September 18). http://www.texasegg.org/discussions/prairierestoration.php, accessed December 7, 2012.

Mauro, Garry. 1986. "The Texas Prairie." In "The Prairie, Roots of Our Culture, Foundation of Our Economy." Proceedings of the Tenth North American Prairie Conference, June

22–26. Texas Women's University, Denton.

McCallum, Henry D. 1957. "Barbed Wire in Texas." *Southwestern Historical Quarterly* 61 (2): 207–19.

Merkord, Glenn. 2009a. Survey of Native Prairie in Brazoria County, Texas. Native Prairies Association of Texas. April and May.

———. 2009b. Survey of Native Prairie in Galveston County, Texas. Native Prairies Association of Texas. June.

———. 2009c. Survey of Native Prairie in Hardin County, Texas. Native Prairies Association of Texas. September and November.

———. 2009d. Survey of Native Prairie in Jefferson County, Texas. Native Prairies Association of Texas. September, October, and November.

———. 2009e. Survey of Native Prairie in Orange County, Texas. Native Prairies Association of Texas. October.

Merkord, Glenn, and Pat Merkord. 2009a. Survey of Native Prairie in Chambers County, Texas. Native Prairies Association of Texas. June.

———. 2009b. Survey of Native Prairie in Fort Bend County, Texas. Native Prairies Association of Texas. April.

———. 2009c. Survey of Native Prairie in Harris County, Texas. Native Prairies Association of Texas. March.

———. 2009d. Survey of Native Prairie in Montgomery County, Texas. Native Prairies Association of Texas. January and February.

Merkord, Pat. 2007. "Prairie Dogs Reintroduced to Maddin Prairie Preserve." *Texas Nature Tracker*. Texas Parks and Wildlife.

Moore, Jerry. 2012. Curator, Texas Cotton Gin Museum. Personal communication, December.

Morrell, Zenos. 1872. *Flowers and Fruits from the Wilderness; or, Thirty-Six Years in Texas and Two Winters in Honduras.* Boston: Gould and Lincoln.

Moss, Randy, and Ryan Hammons. 2007. Survey of Native Prairie in Colorado County, Texas. Native Prairies Association of Texas. August.

Native Prairies Association of Texas. 2010. Survey of Tallgrass Prairies of Texas.

Naylor, Loren. 2009. Survey of Native Prairie in Liberty County, Texas. Native Prairies Association of Texas. January and March.

———. 2010. Survey of Native Prairie in Aransas County, Texas. Native Prairies Association of Texas. August.

Neiman, Bill. 2002. Oral history interview conducted April 20, in Junction, Texas. Texas Legacy Project. Conservation History Association of Texas. http://www.texaslegacy.org/bb/transcripts/neimanbilltxt.html, accessed December 4, 2012.

Omernik, James. 2009. Level III and IV Ecoregions of Texas, 2009 polygon coverage data, at 1:250,000 scale. US Environmental Protection Agency. http://www.tpwd.state.tx.us/land water/land/maps/gis/data_downloads/, accessed December 4, 2012.

Piper, Charles, 1925. "Cultivated Grasses of Secondary Importance." Farmers' Bulletin 1433, p. 31. Washington, DC. UNT Digital Library. http://digital.library.unt.edu/ark:/67531/metadc 1769/, accessed December 7, 2012.

Pyne, Stephen. 2012. "Texas Takes on Fire." In *To the Last Smoke.* Arizona State University.

Quast, Phillip. 2015. Outreach Coordinator and Program Director, Native Prairies Association of Texas. Personal communication, April.

Quayle, Jeff. 2000. Survey of Native Prairie in Grayson County, Texas. Native Prairies Association of Texas. May, September, December.

Redmon, Larry. 2001. Bahiagrass Utilization in East Texas, SCS-2001-12. http://forages.tamu.edu/PDF/scs2001-12.pdf, accessed December 3, 2012.

Reemt, Charlotte. 2013. Research and Monitoring Ecologist, Nature Conservancy of Texas. Personal communications, December 2012 through January 2013.

Rhodes, Ed. 2009. Survey of Native Prairie in Jack County, Texas. Native Prairies Association of Texas. June–September, and November.

———. 2010a. Survey of Native Prairie in Aransas County, Texas. Native Prairies Association of Texas. August.

———. 2010b. Survey of Native Prairie in Hamilton County, Texas. Native Prairies Association of Texas. April, May, and June.

Rosen, David. 2007a. Survey of Native Prairie in Jackson County, Texas. Native Prairies Association of Texas. July.

———. 2007b. Survey of Native Prairie in Matagorda County, Texas. Native Prairies Association of Texas. June and July.

———. 2008. Survey of Native Prairie in Wharton County, Texas. Native Prairies Association of Texas. July.

———. 2012. Biology Professor, Lee College. Personal communication, December.

Rowe, Brian. 2007. Survey of Native Prairie in Cook County, Texas. Native Prairies Association of Texas. July and August.

———. 2008. Survey of Native Prairie in Parker County, Texas. Native Prairies

Association of Texas. February, April, and May.

———. 2009. Survey of Native Prairie in Montague County, Texas. Native Prairies Association of Texas. August and September.

———. 2010. Survey of Native Prairie in Tarrant County, Texas. Native Prairies Association of Texas. August.

Rozek, Barbara J., ed. 2001. *The Forgotten Texas Census: The First Annual Report of the Agricultural Bureau of the Department of Agriculture, Insurance, Statistics, and History, 1887–1888.* College Station: Texas A&M University Press.

Sauer, J. R., J. E. Hines, J. E. Fallon, K. L. Pardieck, D. J. Ziolkowski Jr., and W. A. Link. 2011. The North American Breeding Bird Survey, Results and Analysis 1966–2010. Version 12.07.2011, USGS Patuxent Wildlife Research Center. Laurel, MD.

Sheehan, Jason. 2006. "Prairie Dogs to Get New Home." *Abilene Reporter-News*, April 3.

Shelton, Anne. 2012. Texas Historical Commission. Personal communication, December.

Simmons, Mark. 2005. Prairie Restoration Management Plan: Lyndon B. Johnson National Historical Park, Johnson City, Texas. Lady Bird Johnson Wildflower Center.

Singhurst, Jason. 2012 and 2015. Botanist, Texas Parks and Wildlife. Personal communications, December 2012 and April 2015.

Singhurst, Jason, John Young, Greg Kerouac, and Heather Whitlaw. 2010. "Estimating Black-Tailed Prairie Dog Distribution in Texas." *Texas Journal of Science* 62 (4): 243–62.

Smith, Forrest. 2012. The Invasive Grass Phenomenon. South Texas Natives. Caesar Kleberg Wildlife Research Institute, Texas A&M University at Kingsville. http://ckwri.tamuk .edu/fileadmin/user_upload/docs/ STN/Presentations/Invasive_Grass_ Phenomenon.pdf, accessed November 19, 2012.

Sommerville, Austin. 2009a. Survey of Native Prairie in Bosque County, Texas. Native Prairies Association of Texas. April.

———. 2009b. Survey of Native Prairie in Clay County, Texas. Native Prairies Association of Texas. October.

———. 2009c. Survey of Native Prairie in Erath County, Texas. Native Prairies Association of Texas. May.

———. 2009d. Survey of Native Prairie in Hood County, Texas. Native Prairies Association of Texas. May.

———. 2009e. Survey of Native Prairie in Wise County, Texas. Native Prairies Association of Texas. October.

———. 2010. Survey of Native Prairie in Sommervell County, Texas. Native Prairies Association of Texas. August.

Spangler, Jason. 2004a and 2005a. Survey of Native Prairie in Travis County, Texas. Native Prairies Association of Texas. November 2004; March, June, November, and December 2005.

———. 2004b and 2005b. Survey of Native Prairie in Williamson County, Texas. Native Prairies Association of Texas. November 2004; May and November 2005.

———. 2005. Survey of Native Prairie in Falls County, Texas. Native Prairies Association of Texas. October.

Steinberg, Ted. 2006. *American Green: The Obsessive Quest for the Perfect Lawn.* New York: W. W. Norton.

Stransky, Bill. 2012. Executive Director, Texas Rice Industry Coalition for the Environment. Personal communication, December.

Telfair, Raymond. 2012. Northern Bobwhite, Texas Breeding Bird Atlas. Texas A&M AgriLife Extension. http:// txtbba.tamu.edu/species-accounts/ northern-bobwhite/, accessed December 8, 2012.

Texas Forest Service. 2012. Outdoor Burn Bans, as of September 30, 2011.

Texas Historical Commission. 2012. Texas Historic Sites Atlas. http:// atlas.thc.state.tx.us/shell-county.htm, accessed November 26, 2012.

Texas Parks and Wildlife. 2005. Texas Wildlife Action Plan, 2005–2010, Section 2. http://www.tpwd.state.tx.us/ publications/pwdpubs/pwd_pl_w7000 _1187a/, accessed December 8, 2012.

———. 2012. Black-Tailed Prairie Dog (*Cynomys ludovicianus*). Texas Parks and Wildlife. http://www.tpwd.state .tx.us/huntwild/wild/species/prairie/, accessed December 9, 2012.

Toledo, David. 2009a. Survey of Native Prairie in Bee County, Texas. Native Prairies Association of Texas. April.

———. 2009b. Survey of Native Prairie in DeWitt County, Texas. Native Prairies Association of Texas. June.

———. 2009c. Survey of Native Prairie in Goliad County, Texas. Native Prairies Association of Texas. April and May.

———. 2009d. Survey of Native Prairie in Lavaca County, Texas. Native Prairies Association of Texas. June.

———. 2009e. Survey of Native Prairie in Kleberg County, Texas. Native Prairies Association of Texas. April and May.

———. 2009f. Survey of Native Prairie in Refugio County, Texas. Native Prairies Association of Texas. April and May.

———. 2009g. Survey of Native Prairie in San Patricio County, Texas. Native Prairies Association of Texas. April.

———. 2010. Survey of Native Prairie in Nueces County, Texas. Native Prairies Association of Texas. June.

Tracy, S. M. 1919. "Rhodes Grass." Farmers' Bulletin 1048. US Department of Agriculture. Washington, DC. UNT Digital Library. http://digital.library.unt.edu/ ark:/67531/metadc96645/, accessed December 5, 2012.

Tracy, Samuel. 1916. "Natal Grass: A Southern Perennial Hay Crop." Farmers' Bulletin 726. US Department of Agriculture. Washington, DC. UNT Digital Library. http://digital.library .unt.edu/ark:/67531/metadc96391/, accessed December 7, 2012.

Turfgrass Producers of Texas. 2012. Membership Directory—Producers. http://www.txsod.com/members.asp, accessed December 5, 2012.

Turner, Allan. 2012. "Drought Deals Setback to Prairie Chicken Recovery Efforts." *Houston Chronicle*, September 5.

US Geological Survey. 2012. Earth Explorer. Aerial photographs, digital format. http://earthexplorer.usgs.gov/, accessed December 15, 2012.

Utley, Robert M. 1962. "Longhorns of the Big Bend: A Special Report on the Early Cattle Industry of the Big Bend Country of Texas." National Park Service, US Department of the Interior. Santa Fe, New Mexico. April. http://www.nps.gov/history/history/ online_books/bibe/longhorns_bibe .pdf, accessed December 6, 2012.

Webb, Walter Prescott. 1931. *The Great Plains*. Lincoln: University of Nebraska Press.

Webber, Charles. 1852. *The Prairie Scout; or, Agatone the Renegade: A Romance of Border Life*. New York: Dewitt and Davenport.

White, Matt. 2007a. Survey of Native Prairie in Franklin County, Texas. Native Prairies Association of Texas. June–August.

———. 2007b. Survey of Native Prairie in Lamar County, Texas. Native Prairies Association of Texas. May and August.

———. 2008 and 2009. Survey of Native Prairie in Hopkins County, Texas. Native Prairies Association of Texas. January 2008, June 2008, and March 2009.

———. 2009a. Survey of Native Prairie in Delta County, Texas. Native Prairies Association of Texas. April.

———. 2009b. Survey of Native Prairie in Franklin County, Texas. Native Prairies Association of Texas. June.

———. 2009c. Survey of Native Prairie in Rains County, Texas. Native Prairies Association of Texas. June.

———. 2010. Survey of Native Prairie in Red River County, Texas. Native Prairies Association of Texas. May, June, and July.

Wolverton, Darrell. 2010. Survey of Native Prairie in Gonzales County, Texas. Native Prairies Association of Texas. August.

Desert Bighorn Sheep

Ancient Native American pictographs of desert bighorn sheep have been found on rock walls in West Texas' Culberson, El Paso, and Hudspeth Counties (Jackson 1938, 403).

Origins

For hundreds, perhaps thousands of years, people have coexisted with desert bighorn sheep (*Ovis canadensis nelsoni*) in Texas. Pictographs from the Trans-Pecos illustrate views of desert bighorn sheep recorded in times well before western settlement. Even as late as 1880, Texas was home to a herd of desert bighorn sheep numbering roughly 1,500, possibly running as high as 2,500 (Borderlands Research Institute 2014). The sheep ranged widely, finding their way through sixteen mountain ranges of the Trans-Pecos (Brewer 2001, 7).

While sweeping the slopes with the glass one evening near our camp in one of the big canyons opening into the Guadalupe Mountains, I located three sheep halfway up the face of the rocky slope, 1000 feet above me. . . . They jumped from rock to rock, pausing to look and listen. . . . I was amazed at the strength of the old ram, as, slowly lifting his massive horns, he flung himself with apparent ease to the rock above."

—Vernon Bailey, 1905

However, from 1850 to 1960, bighorn populations plummeted in Texas and throughout the West. Fortunately, the past fifty years have seen a successful effort to rebuild bighorn herds.

Conservationists have relied on a combination of patience, research, and partnership, with a great deal of support coming from the hunting community. This is the story of the sheep's decline and revival in the desert mountains of the Trans-Pecos and beyond.

Salt

Strain on the bighorn herds in Texas grew with early European settlements. In the seventeenth century, Spaniards found silver, gold, lead, and other minerals in northern Mexico (Orris et al. 1993, 4). By 1692, Diego de Vargas had located salt flats west of

Guadalupe Peak that could be used for processing the metal ores, as well as tanning leather and salting meats (Wade 2003, 147). For the next two hundred years, wagon trains came up out of Mexico to mine these salt beds. While they dug up and dried the salt, rested their oxen, and loaded the wagons for the return trip, the miners and teamsters killed many of the bighorn sheep for food (Carson 1941, V).

Mines and Rails

In the last two decades of the nineteenth century, new factors arose that cut into the bighorn herd in West Texas. The biggest impact came from market hunting. Contract hunters killed many animals to feed workers who were building the Texas & Pacific and the Southern Pacific railways in the Trans-Pecos during the late 1870s and early 1880s. As well, the hunters supplied bighorn meat to laborers at metal mines that opened near Shafter and Van Horn in the 1880s (McKinney 2001). Also, as bison herds were shot out in the Panhandle, former buffalo hunters drifted into West Texas. There, they found bighorns that could be killed and shipped out by rail to Kansas City and St. Louis meat markets (Carson 1941, 7; Doughty 1983, 199).

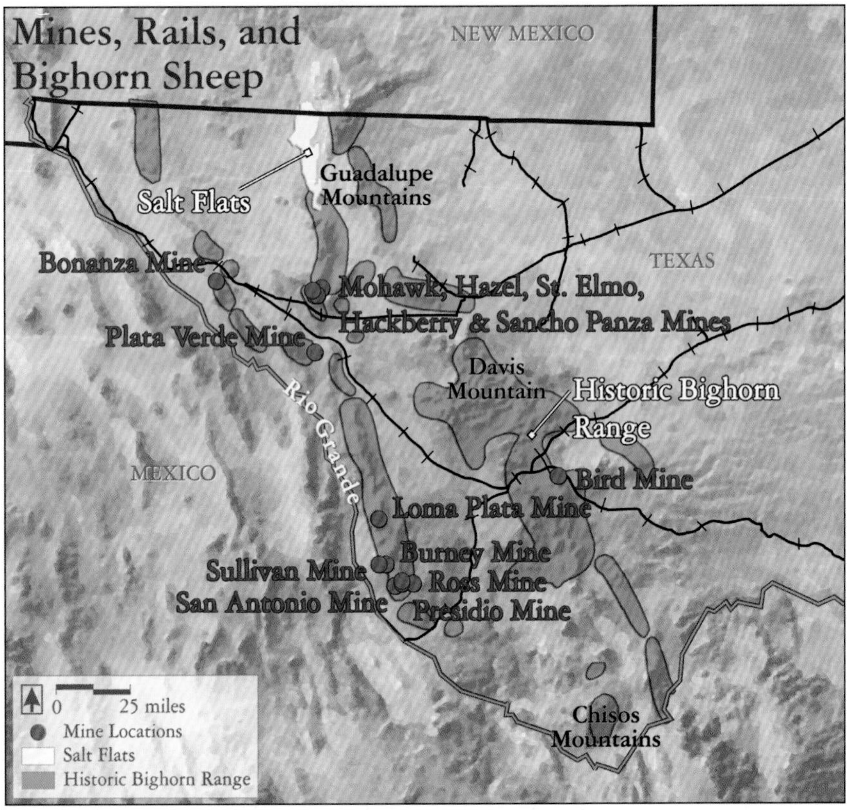

Trophies

Meat was not always the main draw for hunters. Sport hunters took their toll. As an early state biologist, Butch Carson, put it, "the large massive horns carried by the old rams, their many wrinkles and beautiful curling design, [were] enough to make any early pioneer want to kill a ram just to possess such a pair of horns" (Monson and Sumner 2003, 289). In fact, one Carlsbad deer hunter reportedly came across a bighorn band in 1908, killed nine rams in a single day, and left them to rot (Carson 1941, 11).

Early Conservation

Nevertheless, in the first decades of the 1900s, the bighorn population began to slowly rebuild in West Texas. The sheep benefited from several changes. For instance, in 1903, the state banned all bighorn hunting (Schmidly 2002, 402). While these new game laws were admittedly hard to enforce, mining

Providing meat for laborers in the salt, silver, lead, zinc, and gold mines of West Texas brought pressure on bighorns from the late seventeenth century into the early twentieth century. Feeding the cross-country railroad builders during the 1880s put yet more stress on the sheep numbers. The overlap of these mines and railroads with the traditional bighorn range can be seen here (Carson 1941, V; Evans 1975; Janke 2014).

tapered off in the 1920s and lowered the demand for bighorn meat in the area (Evans 1975, 7).

Predator control may have also helped rebuild bighorn numbers in the early twentieth century. To support the bighorn (and other wildlife and domestic livestock herds), state and federal trappers and hunters took more than seventy mountain lions from the Eagle Mountain area in the 1934–41 period (Carson 1941, 14). In addition, one West Texas game warden organized an antipredator campaign that reportedly killed 1,100 golden eagles (Davis and Taylor 1939, 452).

Sheep and Goats

However, these efforts to protect the bighorn were overwhelmed by other changes in the Trans-Pecos, particularly the rise of cattle, sheep, and goat ranching. By 1930, there were already 230,000 cattle, 88,000 sheep, and 91,000 goats in the five counties that made up the home range of the Texas bighorns (Brewster, Presidio, Jeff Davis, Culberson, and Hudspeth Counties) (Davis and Taylor 1939, 442). In a dry, harsh, mountainous country, this left little forage for the original wildlife there, including the bighorn.

The most direct competition seems to have come from the introduction of sheep to the high desert country. An additional 20,000 domestic sheep were brought into the heart of the Texas bighorn range from 1938

Western portions of Canada, the United States, and Mexico have long been home to American bighorn sheep, including three subspecies, the Rocky Mountain bighorn sheep (Ovis canadensis canadensis), the Sierra Nevada bighorn sheep (O. c. sierrae), and the desert bighorn sheep native to Texas and the Southwest (O. c. nelsoni). Their populations, and the extent of their range, fell dramatically from 1850 through 1960. By 1960, the desert bighorn was considered extirpated from Texas (Brewer 2014; Wild Sheep Working Group 2014b).

through 1941 (Carson 1941, 14). The livestock herds vied for forage and brought dangerous diseases (Carson 1941, 9, 16; Monson and Sumner 2003, 174; Davis and Taylor 1939, 453). Contagious respiratory infections, leading often to pneumonia, were (and continue to be) a particular problem (Brewer 2014). Competition with aoudads that had been introduced to West Texas was especially tough. The aoudads (also known as Barbary sheep) reproduced faster and dealt better with predation than the bighorns. Humans played a more direct role too, as they blocked off traditional watering sites and range with net wire fencing (Brewer 2001, 7, 9; Flores 1999, 161).

Decline

With these new pressures, the bighorn's fall was rapid. The Texas herd's count slid from about 500 in 1905 to 300 in 1940, 150 in 1941, and then to just 35 in 1945 (Bailey 1905; Carson 1941, 3; Hernandez et al. undated). Similar decreases were happening elsewhere: by the 1920s, the bighorn was largely eliminated from Washington, Oregon, North Dakota, South Dakota, and parts of Mexico (Defenders of Wildlife 2014).

Sanctuaries

The bighorn's decline did not go unnoticed. In 1939, lobbying from the Arizona Boy Scouts and Major Frederick Russell Burnham (known as the "Father of Scouting"), along with prodding from the National Wildlife Federation, Izaak Walton League, and Audubon Society, persuaded FDR to create the Cabeza Prieta and Kofa National Wildlife Refuges in Arizona (Friends of Kofa 2014). The federal government followed up with another preserve in 1941—the San Andres National Wildlife Refuge of New Mexico. Four years later, Texas established the Sierra Diablo Wildlife Management Area as a sanctuary for the last of the state's herd (Zarrella 2012).

The Last of the Herd

The help arrived too late in Texas. The last documented sighting of a wild sheep occurred in October 1958. By the early 1960s, the sheep had largely disappeared from the state (Blaney 2010; Cox 2011).

Early Restoration

Yet even before the native bighorn disappeared from Texas, there were fledgling efforts to return the sheep to the mountain ranges of the western part of the state. In 1954, representatives met from Texas, Arizona, the US Fish and Wildlife Service, the Wildlife Management Institute, and the Boone and Crockett Club to forge a cooperative agreement on sheep restoration (Chappell 2003).

Capture

Restocking work started with efforts to capture bighorn from areas in the southwestern United States and Mexico where the populations were still robust. Catching such agile, elusive animals from remote, tough terrain was not simple, especially in the early days. As one Texas Parks and Wildlife biologist put it, "they tried a lot of different things. They tried building traps around water holes. They tried driving these animals into various traps. They tried drive nets. They used steel leg hold traps. They built box traps. They did a lot of different things. None of them worked very well, but they were able to capture a few sheep and we were able to get some of them down here." In later years, biologists used net guns, shot from a hovering helicopter, to temporarily hold a sheep until handlers could drop to the ground to blindfold and load it (McKinney 2001).

At one time I saw four rams fighting over one ewe. These fights are very spectacular. . . . When they both get their temper worked up enough, they back off quite a distance from each other, and with a snort, they charge. Just before reaching each other, they rear up and then crash together. The report is about like the crack of a .410 shotgun.

—Butch Carson, 1941

Breeding

From 1957 through 1959, thirty sheep were successfully captured in the desert mountains of western Arizona. The sheep were then brought to Black Gap Wildlife Management Area to adjust to their new Texas home and begin breeding (Borderlands Research Institute 2014). A decade and more later, the Black Gap operation was followed by similar breeding efforts at Sierra Diablo Wildlife Management Area (1970) and Chilicote Ranch (1977) (Hernandez et al. undated). During 1983, the breeding program was expanded with four new 10-acre pens at the Sierra Diablo WMA, built with over $200,000 raised by the non-profit Texas Bighorn Society (Texas Bighorn Society 2014a). In 1985, C. G. Johnson gave his 23,000-acre Elephant Mountain Ranch in Brewster County to the state. Over the years, the Johnson ranch has become a major brood facility for bighorn restoration (Chappell 2003; Texas Bighorn Society 2014a).

Meanwhile, south of the Big Bend, in the Sierra del Carmen, the CEMEX concrete and aggregate firm was undertaking its own private breeding program for the desert bighorn. From 2001 through 2004, CEMEX sponsored the capture of eighty bighorn in the Mexican state of Sonora. Those sheep were then moved east and released to an 11,000-acre high-fenced area in the heart of over 257,000 acres owned and managed by CEMEX (McKinney 2010).

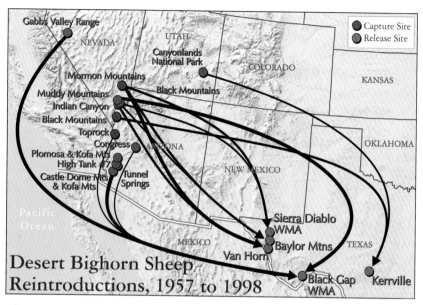

Desert Bighorn Sheep Reintroductions, 1957 to 1998

This map shows the many interstate bighorn reintroductions that were made from 1957 through 1998. Captures occurred in Arizona, Nevada, and Utah, as well as an undocumented effort in Mexico. Sheep were largely released in the Black Gap Wildlife Management Area (WMA), but were also brought to the Sierra Diablo WMA, the Baylor Mountains, and near Van Horn and Kerrville, Texas. Each transfer involved one to twenty-five sheep (Brewer 2014; Wild Sheep Working Group 2014a).

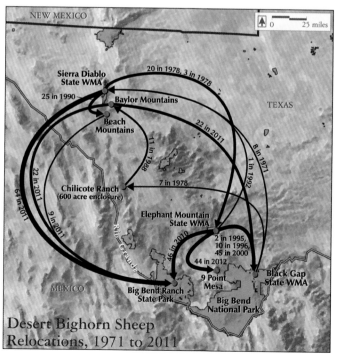

Desert Bighorn Sheep Relocations, 1971 to 2011

This map traces the transfers of bighorns that occurred within Texas from 1971 through 2011. Over those forty years, relocations were made from brood herds at Black Gap, Elephant Mountain, and Sierra Diablo Wildlife Management Areas, as well as other smaller facilities, to release sites throughout West Texas (Brewer 2014; Wild Sheep Working Group 2014a).

Releases

As populations built up through these breeding programs, it became possible to start transplants among Texas herds. In 1971, eight sheep were brought from Black Gap Wildlife Management Area to Sierra Diablo. Another seven animals were moved from Black Gap to the Chilicote Ranch site in 1978. In time, Sierra Diablo WMA began releasing its own sheep to other sites, with twenty-three going to Elephant Mountain WMA in 1987–88, twenty-five to the Beach Mountains in 1990, and sixty-four to Big Bend Ranch State Park in 2011. In turn, some of these release sites were also able to send extra sheep on to other locations. For instance, sheep from Elephant Mountain were sent to Sierra Diablo (one in 1992), Black Gap (fifty-eight from 1995 through 2000), Big Bend Ranch State Park (forty-six in 2010), and 9-Point Mesa (forty-four in 2012) (Brewer 2014; Hernandez et al. undated; Texas Parks and Wildlife 2009; Wild Sheep Working Group 2014a; Zarrella 2012).

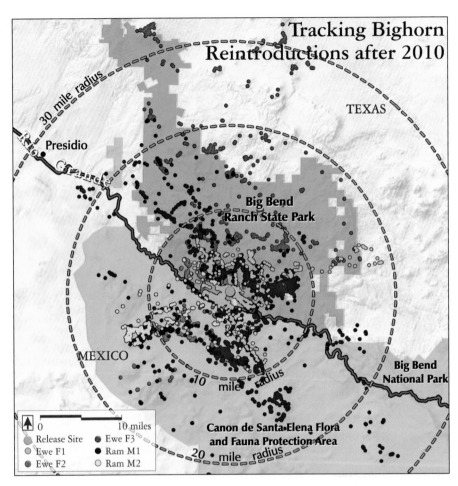

Very large releases of bighorn sheep were made in December 2010 and 2011 to Big Bend Ranch State Park, with 141 sheep coming in from the Beach Mountains, Baylor Mountains, Sierra Diablo WMA, and Elephant Mountain WMA. The introduced bighorn have done well. Sheep have reproduced and spread into the surrounding habitat, without regard to park or international boundaries. This map draws on reports from radio collars installed on five introduced sheep (Janke 2014).

Management

Since 1957, an impressive number of desert bighorn sheep have been relocated to Texas lands. Nearly 690 desert bighorn sheep have been reintroduced to the mountains of West Texas, with more than 370 of these animals coming from outside of Texas (Brewer 2014; Schmidly 2002, 402; Wild Sheep Working Group 2014a; Zarrella 2012). Yet transplanting the sheep has not been enough to ensure their survival. The sheep's full recovery has required control of forage competition (especially aoudads); management of brush; aerial surveys of herds (beginning in 1990); and research on animal health, diet, habitat preference, and predation (Hernandez et al. undated; Texas Parks and Wildlife 2009). Since the bighorn's home range is extremely dry, getting only eight to fifteen inches of rain a year, one key restocking step has involved helicopter-aided construction of "water guzzlers" in remote mountain areas. These "guzzlers" capture rainfall from slick rock slopes or inverted roofs to store in reservoirs for the sheep and other wildlife (McKinney 2001).

Progress

The goal of all this work has been to eventually return the sheep to sixteen mountain ranges of West Texas, with a total herd of 3,000 (Cox 2011). So far, the trends look good. Sheep numbers have increased more than eightfold over just the last twenty-five years, rising from less than 150 in 1990, to 352 in 2002, 822 in 2006, 1,115 in 2010, and 1,300 in 2012. This growing Texas herd now roams over eight mountain ranges in the state. (Borderlands Research Institute 2014; Texas Bighorn Society 2014b; Texas Parks and Wildlife 2009; Wild Sheep Working Group 2014b).

Hunting and Restoration

In 1988, state biologists determined that the Texas herd population was large and stable enough to support a limited hunting season after an eighty-five-year hiatus. Permits to kill older rams have been issued to private land-owners, nonprofit supporters (chiefly the Foundation for North American Wild Sheep), and to a public lottery (McKinney 2001). These permits can bring huge prices. The first Texas license sold for $61,000, and its successors generated $645,500 in income from 1989 through 2005 (Brewer 2005). The proceeds have been reinvested in restoration efforts (Library Index 2014).

A desert bighorn sheep, sporting a radio collar, is seen here just after a December 2011 release in the 300,000-acre Big Bend Ranch State Park. This ram was one of seventy-six ewes and nineteen rams captured and relocated by helicopter from several private West Texas ranches as well as the state's Sierra Diablo Wildlife Management Area (Fountain 2011).

Predators

While the relatively small population of bighorn gradually rebuilds in Texas, it remains very vulnerable. To protect the sheep, there has been a controversial effort to remove mountain lions that were preying on the bighorns. Some of the lions have been taken in live captures with dogs, leg-hold snares, traps, ropes, and tranquilizers. The Texas cats are then transported to Florida to improve the genetics of the inbred panthers there. However, many of the lions are not welcome either for wild release or for zoo use, and so they have been destroyed (McKinney 2001).

Partnerships

This effort to restore the bighorn to Texas has been a long-term and broad-based partnership among public agencies, nonprofits, and private individuals. Some of the key partners have included Texas Parks and Wildlife; state agencies in Arizona, Utah, and Nevada; regional alliances (the Wild Sheep Working Group); and not-for-profit groups (including the Texas Bighorn Society, Foundation for North American Wild Sheep, Wild Sheep Foundation, and the Dallas Safari Club). The joint effort now affects over 2.3 million acres of wilderness. The program has even reached across international borders, with significant contributions from CEMEX Corporation's restoration work to the south of the Big Bend (Brewer 2005).

Throughout the efforts to bring the bighorn back to Texas, hunters have played a key role. Some might think it is ironic, or at least counterintuitive, that the same people who will clamber for hours over dry washes and rocky slopes to shoot a bighorn, will also work equally hard to restore those animals. Maybe that hunt, that chase, is something that brings hunters closer to an understanding and appreciation for the animal. Whatever their private reasons, there is no doubt that hunter support has been vital to bighorn recovery. The taxes on weapons and ammunition, the fees for the Texas Parks and Wildlife Grand Slam hunt, and the volunteer time and gifts from the Texas Bighorn Society, the Foundation for North American Wild Sheep, and many individual sportsmen, have all been crucial to the partnership that has returned the bighorn to the Texas landscape (Pittman-Robertson Act, 16 U.S.C. 669).

Sources

Bailey, Vernon. 1905. North American Fauna, No. 25: Biological Survey of Texas. US Department of Agriculture. Washington, DC: Government Printing Office.

Blaney, Betsy. 2010. "Bighorn Sheep Move to a New Texas Home." Associated Press. December 26. http://www.nbcnews.com/id/40812213/ns/us_news-environment/t/bighorn-sheep-move-new-texas-home/#.U2Px4fldV8E, accessed May 2, 2014.

Borderlands Research Institute. 2014. "A Brief History of Texas Bighorns."

http://ww2.sulross.edu/brinrm/bg_bhs_history.html, accessed May 2, 2014.

Brewer, Clay. 2001. "Project No. WBB04: Diets and Seasonal Forage Utilization of Desert Bighorn Sheep at Elephant Mountain Wildlife Management Area." *Texas Parks and Wildlife* (December).

———. 2005. Briefing Item on Desert Bighorn Sheep, Agenda Item 3, May 25, 2005, Public Hearing, Texas Parks and Wildlife Commission, Austin.

———. 2014. Chair, Western Alliance of Fish and Wildlife Agency Wild Sheep Working Group. Biologist, Texas Parks and Wildlife. Personal communication, May.

Carson, Butch. 1941. Man, the Greatest Enemy of the Desert Bighorn Mountain Sheep: Bulletin 21. Texas Game, Fish, and Oyster Commission, Austin.

Chappell, Henry. 2003. "Counting Sheep." *Texas Parks and Wildlife* (June).

Cox, Mike. 2011. "State's Largest-Ever Desert Bighorn Sheep Release Completed in Big Bend." News Release. Texas Parks and Wildlife. http://www.tpwd.state.tx.us/news-media/releases/?req=20111221b, accessed May 2, 2014.

Davis, William, and Walter Taylor. 1939. "The Bighorn Sheep of Texas." *Journal of Mammalogy* 20 (4): 440–55.

Defenders of Wildlife. 2014. Basic Facts about the Bighorn Sheep. http://www.defenders.org/bighorn-sheep/basic-facts, accessed May 2, 2014.

Doughty, Robin. 1983. *Wildlife and Man in Texas: Environmental Change and Conservation*. College Station: Texas A&M University Press.

Evans, Thomas. 1975. Gold and Silver

in Texas: Mineral Resource Circular No. 56. Bureau of Economic Geology, University of Texas, Austin.

Flores, Daniel. 1999. *Horizontal Yellow: Nature and History in the Near Southwest*. Albuquerque: University of New Mexico Press.

Fountain, Chase. 2011. Photograph: Bighorn Mountain Sheep. Texas Parks and Wildlife.

Friends of Kofa. 2014. Refuge History. http://friendsofkofa.org/Refuge_History.html, accessed May 2, 2014.

Hernandez, Froylan, Louis Harveson, Thomas Janke, Reagan Gage, Clay Brewer, Justin Foster, and Shawn Locke. Undated. Restoration and Management of Desert Bighorn Sheep in Texas. http://www.scielpaso.org/membership/Desert%20Big%20Horn%20Sheep%20Restoration.pdf.

Holtcamp, Wendee. 2011. "Regal Return: Desert Bighorn Sheep Are being Restored to the Mountains of West Texas." *Texas Parks and Wildlife* (April).

Jackson, A. T. 1938. Picture-Writing of Texas Indians. Anthropological Papers, Vol. II. Bureau of Research in the Social Sciences, Study No. 27. University of Texas Publication, No. 3809. March 1. Austin.

Janke, Thomas. 2014. Desert Bighorn Sheep radio-collar data, 2011–14. Graduate Research Assistant, Borderlands Research Institute, Sul Ross State University. Personal communication, May.

Library Index. 2014. Endangered Mammals: Bighorn Sheep. http://www.libraryindex.com/pages/669/Endangered-Mammals-BIGHORN-SHEEP.html, accessed May 2, 2014.

McKinney, Billy Pat. 2001. Oral history interview conducted April 5, in Marathon, Texas. Texas Legacy Project, Conservation History Association of Texas.

McKinney, Bonnie. 2010. Desert Bighorn Sheep Restoration Program: CEMEX-El Carmen, Maderas del Carmen, Coahuila, Mexico. News Roundup. Texas Parks and Wildlife. http://www.tpwd.state.tx.us/news media/releases/news_roundup/bighorn_sheep_release_at_big_bend_ranch/cemex-el_carmen.phtml, accessed June 5, 2014.

Monson, Gale, and Lowell Sumner, eds. 2003. *The Desert Bighorn: Its Life History, Ecology, and Management*. Tucson: University of Arizona Press.

Orris, Greta, Norman Page, John-Mark Staude, Karen Bolm, Marguerite Carbonaro, Floyd Gray, and Keith Long. 1993. "Nonfuel Mineral Resources in the United States—Mexico Border Region." US Geological Survey Circular 1098.

Schmidly, David. 2002. *Texas Natural History: A Century of Change*. Lubbock: Texas Tech University Press.

Texas Bighorn Society. 2014a. History of Texas Bighorn Sheep—Bighorn Sheep Society. http://www.texasbighorn society.org/index.php/about-tbs/history, accessed May 18, 2014.

———. 2014b. Observed Population. http://www.texasbighornsociety.org/index.php/about-bighorns/from-tpwd, accessed May 14, 2014.

Texas Parks and Wildlife. 2009. Desert Bighorn Sheep. http://www.tpwd.state.tx.us/landwater/land/habitats/trans_pecos/big_game/desertbighornsheep/, accessed May 2, 2014.

US Environmental Protection Agency. 2013. Level III and IV Ecoregions of the Continental United States: Corvallis, Oregon, US EPA, National Health and Environmental Effects Research Laboratory. http://www.tpwd.state.tx.us/gis/data/baselayers/omernikregions-zip, accessed May 18, 2014.

Wade, Maria. 2003. *The Native Americans of the Texas Edwards Plateau*. Austin: University of Texas Press.

Wild Sheep Working Group. 2014a. Desert Bighorn Sheep Reintroduction Worksheet, 1957–2011.

———. 2014b. Wild Sheep Population Estimate, License Numbers, Ram Harvest (Winter 2012–2013). http://www.wildsheepworkinggroup.com/app/download/7132367804/Wild+Sheep+Population+Estimate%2C+License+Numbers%2C+Ram+Harvest+%28Winter+2012–2013%29.xls, accessed May 21, 2014.

Zarrella, Christina. 2012. Wildlife and Sport Fish Restoration Success Stories, updated February 6, 2012. US Fish and Wildlife Service. http://wsfr75.com/sites/default/files/Success_Stories-Region_2.pdf, accessed May 2, 2014.

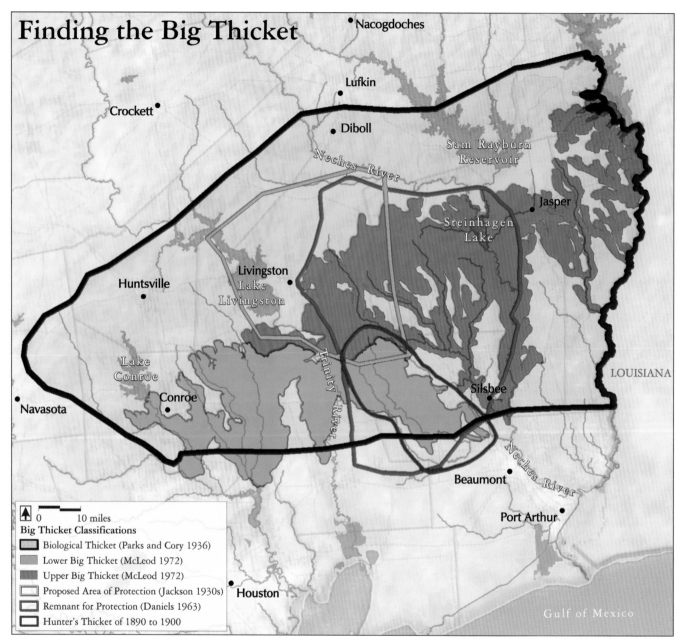

Finding the Big Thicket

Big Thicket Classifications

- Biological Thicket (Parks and Cory 1936)
- Lower Big Thicket (McLeod 1972)
- Upper Big Thicket (McLeod 1972)
- Proposed Area of Protection (Jackson 1930s)
- Remnant for Protection (Daniels 1963)
- Hunter's Thicket of 1890 to 1900

0   10 miles

What is the "Big Thicket"? It depends! The largest zone, shaded in a very light green, covers the 3.35-million-acre "biological" thicket described by Hal Parks and Victor Cory in 1938. Orange outlines the area proposed for protection by Jackson beginning in the 1930s. The dark blue boundary encircles a 450,000-acre remnant of the Thicket that governor Price Daniels believed was still available for protection in 1963. The region outlined in green is the "Lower Thicket," while the area marked in a darker green is the "Upper Thicket," both delineated by the ecologist Claude McLeod in 1972, and together amounting to over 2 million acres. The 400,000-acre traditional hunter's Thicket of 1890 through 1900, as drawn by the geologist Saul Aronow, is circumscribed in brown (Cozine 2004, 5; Gunter 1971, 47; Gunter 1993, 15; McLeod 1972).

The Big Thicket

"There . . . wild orchids (twenty-two varieties in all) and moss-bearded cypress flourish cheek by jowl with western mesquite, yucca and cactus, while plant growth patterns identical with those found in the temperate Appalachian highlands persist alongside subtropical forests of wild jasmine and jungle-like growth so thick that it can be penetrated only by hacking a trail with a knife."

—Pete Gunter, 1970

This is a story about a ninety-year effort to protect this place, the Big Thicket, a land of creeks, woodlands, bogs, and prairies in the southeastern corner of the state. As you will see, it is a long story, a complex one full of many economic and political hurdles. Perhaps it gives an example of how hard it is to set aside and protect a piece of this heavily used, largely privately owned state.

Those general trials for protecting land in Texas are joined by confusion over what the "Thicket" actually is, and where it starts and stops. The Thicket is a diverse and somewhat nebulous place. A pair of early biologists technically described the Thicket as a temperate mesophytic jungle, but added that the area reminded them of a "Lost Atlantis" (Parks, Cory, et al. 1936, 9).

Despite the confusion over the Thicket's exact boundaries, there is agreement that the Thicket has shrunk

a great deal over the past 150 years. Originally, the Thicket contained 3.35 million acres of wilderness. Less than one-tenth survives today. We are fortunate that a number of people among the public, the government, and industry worked for decades to preserve some valuable remnants of this extraordinary place (Peacock 1990, 25).

Isolation

While close to the large cities of Houston and Beaumont and to the

pine plantations of East Texas, the Big Thicket long remained less cutover and developed than many of its neighbors. Its semivirgin qualities were rooted in the dense, impenetrable nature of much of that area of the state. Large parts of the Thicket, with no surprise given its name, were heavily forested and crisscrossed by creeks, sloughs, and swamps. Given the tough terrain, the main roads into Texas had long skirted the Thicket. Also, the eastern edge of the Thicket abutted the Neutral Territory, a no

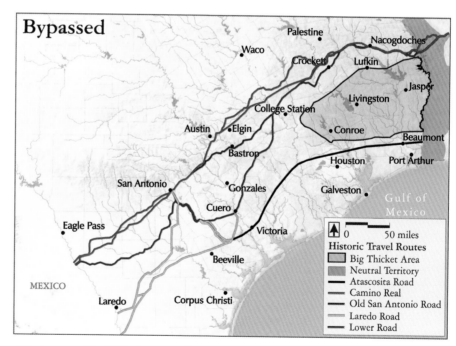

This is a map of the Thicket's heritage of solitude and freedom. For many years, the Big Thicket (shown in green) was isolated, bypassed to the north and south by the Camino Real (red), the Old San Antonio Road (blue), Laredo Road (orange), Lower Road (purple), and the Atascocita Road (black). On the east, the Thicket ran up against the Neutral Territory, a lawless, disputed area shown here in tan (National Park Service 2013; Pool 1975, 34).

man's land contested by the United States and Spain from 1806 to 1821, and through much of the eighteenth century by France and Spain. Without clear jurisdiction and control, a culture of independence and lawlessness grew up, some of which spilled over into the Thicket.

A Land Rush

Early residents of the Thicket included members of the Atakapan, Caddo, Alabama, and Coushatta tribes (Peacock 1984, 17–25). By the 1820s and 1830s, the Thicket began to change with the arrival of Anglo settlers and industry. Many of the new immigrants came from Tennessee and Georgia, drawn by a pledge of 4,000 acres of free land from the Mexican government (Douglas 1967, 4). Others fled debt, prison, slavery, or conscription (Callicot et al. 2006, 29; Keith 2007, 251; McLeod 1972, 5).

Timber!

Much of the early East Texas economy grew up around timber products. Many lumbermen came to Texas with hopes of harvesting the area's rich virgin forests as woodlands to the north and east became exhausted. Old-growth forests along the Atlantic seaboard had been largely cut from the south of Maine to the eastern section of Georgia in the early part of the nineteenth century. Yellow pine in the southeastern United States, and stands of northern white pine and hardwoods in Wisconsin, Michigan, and Pennsylvania were being rapidly logged by 1870 (Block 1994, 10; Liknes, Nelson, and Kaisershot 2013, 9; Turner et al. 1998, 40–41).

During the late 1860s through the early 1890s, the Texas forest attracted retail lumber firms such as Long-Bell; tie and timber contractors such as William Cameron; and wood-

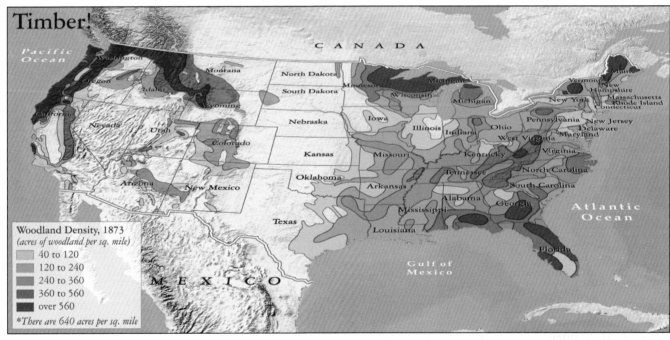

Woodland Density, 1873
(acres of woodland per sq. mile)
- 40 to 120
- 120 to 240
- 240 to 360
- 360 to 560
- over 560

*There are 640 acres per sq. mile

This map shows the density of woodlands in the United States in 1873. This was a time when primary woodlands in the northern Midwest and Atlantic seaboard were being rapidly cut and lumbermen had first come to survey and harvest the virgin longleaf pine, cypress, and other trees of East Texas. Density is shown in terms of acres of woodland per square mile, ranging from 0–40 (lightest green), 40–120, 120–240, 240–360, 360–560, and over 560 (darkest green) (Brewer 1874; Liknes, Nelson, and Kaisershot 2013).

land buyers such as Henry Lutcher, G. Bedell Moore, and Thomas L. L. Temple. Land sold for little ($1.25–$3.00/acre for virgin pine and cypress in the late 1870s). Sometimes the land could be had for nothing, under Texas' loose "use and possession" laws (Gunter 1971, 10; Bonney 2011, 52). Yet the property could yield fabulous returns ($200 for an acre with 20,000 board-feet of lumber!) (Sitton and Conrad 1998, 11). These kinds of profits pulled in big funds and major investors. By 1893, the timber industry had started to consolidate with the rise of some very large landowners, such as the East Texas Land and Improvement Company (260,000 acres), Kirby Lumber Corporation (140,000 acres), Texas Pine Land Association (140,000 acres), Texas Tram and Lumber Company (110,000 acres), and many others (Block 1994, 15–16; Maxwell and Baker 1983, 31).

"Sawmilling is logging, logging is railroading"

—Sitton and Conrad,
Nameless Towns

Sawmills

Following Texas independence, early settlers found many trees that were simply too large for the handsaws or mule- and oxen-powered machinery of the day. About three-quarters of the old growth trees were two to three feet

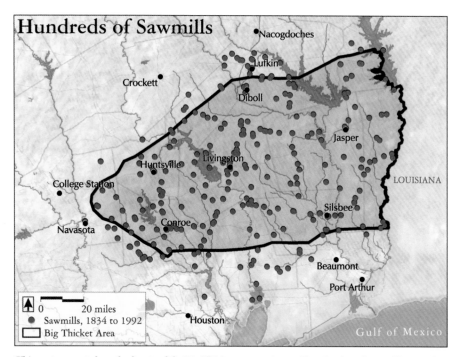

This map suggests how the forests of the Big Thicket were cut by tracking the sites of sawmills in and around the Big Thicket. The locations of close to 1,200 sawmills, built from 1834 through 1992, are shown here in red. They include mills that handled both pine and hardwoods, making dimensional lumber, stakes, shingles, ties, derrick timbers, and other products (Firsching 2014; Texas Forestry Museum 2014; Texas General Land Office 2014; Texas Historical Commission 2014).

in diameter, and at least one-quarter of the hardwoods, long leaf pines, and short leaf pines had trunks over three feet across! However, this soon began to change. In 1833, M. B. Menard and Thomas McKinney built one of the first sawmills in Texas. Located on Menard Creek, in northern Liberty County, the steam-powered mill could run about 3,000 board-feet of lumber daily through its upright sash saw.

The last two decades of the century saw much more powerful equipment come to East Texas. In the late 1870s,

circular saws were introduced, and by the 1890s, band saws were seen. The power to drive these saws grew immensely. By 1900, large mills in East Texas with 350–400 horsepower steam engines and 20-foot diameter, 50-ton flywheels were running over 50,000 board-feet per day (Firsching 2014; Texas Forestry Museum 2014). And these big sawmills multiplied across East Texas, growing from at least 166 in 1893, to over 320 in 1906, to more than 425 by 1927 (Block 1994, 11–18).

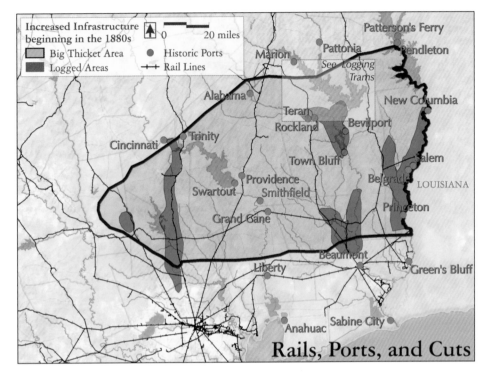

Rails, Ports, and Cuts

The development of sawmills would have been of little use without ways to get the raw timber to the mills, and the cut lumber then from the mills to market. This map shows the extensive network of larger railroads, often chartered common-carrier lines, that was built throughout the Thicket. Also, we can see how, from as early as 1881, logging (in brown) occurred in those areas near ports (marked in blue), river courses, and early rail lines that could be used to carry the wood for processing and sale (Block 1994; Gerland 2014; Maxwell and Baker 1983, 7, 8; Sargent 1884; Walker 2001; Williams 1988, 48).

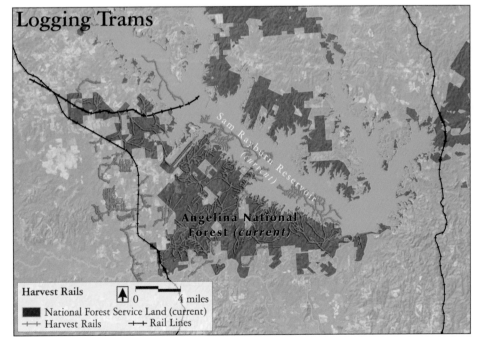

Logging Trams

The Logging Trams map gives a partial picture of the very dense network of railways (some now submerged) that was laid to pull timber out of the Big Thicket. This map shows the many spurs that ran throughout the forest (in this case, the southwestern part of today's Angelina National Forest). Oxen and mules would drag logs to these tracks to be loaded and carried on to a mill. After only about a half year, the rails would be pulled up, shifted, and put down again to harvest a new section of woodland (Dean, Neiman, and O'Neill 1948).

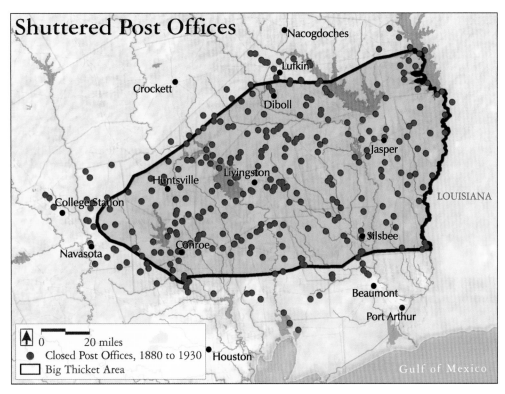

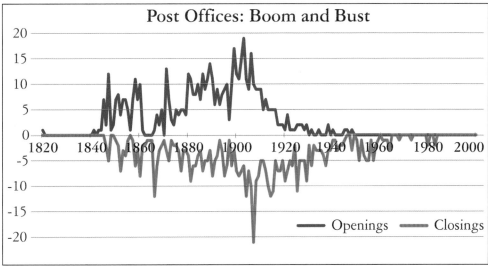

The logging of East Texas brought a boom that lasted from the 1880s through roughly 1930. Then came the bust. After the forests were cut, sawmills were closed and towns shuttered. This Big Thicket map of over 560 abandoned post offices shows how the bust closed down many logging towns. As the logging raced through the East Texas forests, the towns often had a very short lifetime. Of these abandoned post offices, the average opening date was 1886, at the onset of the great Texas logging campaign, and their typical life span was just seventeen years (Forte 2014; US Postal Service 1971).

Ports and Railroads

Timber is big, heavy, and hard to get to mills and markets. Many of the Big Thicket forests could not be harvested until there were ways to move the giant logs. Early logging occurred near rivers, where timber could be floated downstream. However, hundreds of thousands of acres of woodland lacked access to deep, easily traveled rivers. Construction of railroads (leveraged by generous state land grants of 10,240 acres per mile of tract) made it possible to get the wood out faster and in greater volume (Constitution of 1876, Article XIV, Section 3). Further, railways were themselves a major user of the lumber. With the exception of the steel engine and rails, the railroads ran on wood—ties, bridges, trestles, depots, cars, and even, in the early days, fuel. In this way, the Texas railroad and lumber industries fed each other and grew in partnership (Railroad Commission 1907, 20).

The last quarter of the nineteenth century saw rapid railroad construction throughout East Texas, in large part to serve the timber industry. In 1876, Paul Bremond began construction of one of the earliest railroads in East Texas— the Houston, East and West Texas. Bremond brought tracks from Houston to New Caney in 1877, to Livingston by 1879, to Moscow by 1880, and on to the Sabine River by 1885 (Cozine 2004, 47–50). Other railroad firms followed suit. The Sabine and East Texas Railroad was laid from Beaumont and on to Kountze in 1881, eventu-ally reaching Woodville and Rockland (McLeod 1972, 6). The Texas and New Orleans Railroad bought out the Sabine and East Texas rail line and extended service from Rockland on to Dallas. The Gulf, Beaumont and Kansas City Railroad first built tracks from Beaumont to Silsbee, and then ran rails on to Kirbyville (1895) and Roganville (1896). After purchase by Santa Fe, the Gulf, Beaumont and Kansas City lines stretched north to San Augustine, while a new line, called the Texas, Louisiana and Eastern Railroad, was completed from Cleveland to Silsbee by 1902 (Maxwell and Baker 1983, 35–43).

Boom and Bust

In the early days, particularly from 1880 through 1930, the philosophy of many timber operators was to "cut and run," to remove all the merchant-able timber, and then move on to a virgin parcel to repeat the process. In this way, much of the East Texas forest was razed. According to a Texas state forester count, of the 14 million acres of virgin pine forest standing in 1870, 90 percent had been cut by 1927 (Cruikshank and Eldredge 1939, 1; Texas Almanac 1927, 190).

At the same time that the Texas forests were shrinking to their last remnants, the national economy was entering the Depression. Wood supplies fell at the same time that demand plummeted. In 1932, the annual cut in Texas dropped to less than a fifth of 1913's peak-year harvest (Pierson and Reynolds 1936). With the woodlands depleted and the economy in freefall, the sawmills could not be fed and the equipment loans, logging crews, and mill employees could not be paid. The death knell rang for many Thicket logging communities. Scores of company towns—Old Fuqua, Votaw, Camden, Greyberg, Village Mills, Pineland— became ghost towns (Douglas 1967, 4). For many, the boom had been glorious, but all too brief.

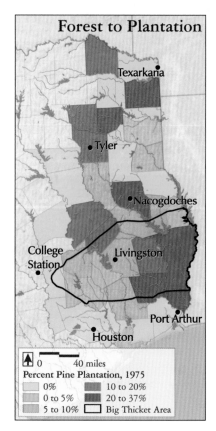

This map shows the extent of pine plantations in East Texas in 1975. At that time, 37 percent of Newton County's forests (darkest orange) were made up of plantations, while the figures for Jasper (31 percent), Hardin (27 percent), and Trinity (20 percent) were also quite high (Carraway 2014; Miles 2014).

Pine Plantations

As many of the primary forests in East Texas were cut out, there were endeavors to replant these lands as tree farms. In 1926, the first slash pine plantation was put in at the state forest near Kirbyville. Its success, tied with the construction in 1940 of the Southland Paper Mill in Lufkin, led to the rise of the pine, pulp, and paper industry in East Texas (Cozine 2004, 123). Beginning in the 1950s, and rising through the time the Big Thicket National Preserve was being created, many native forests in East Texas were replaced by plantations of loblolly and slash pine, with bulldozing and herbicides used to control hardwoods and other competing natives. While these plantations helped meet market demand for pulp and saw timber, there was concern that the Big Thicket's integrity and diversity were being eroded by these monoculture plantings (McLeod 1972, addendum). The conversion of native forests to pine plantations was a particular concern for the preserve because timber firms held over 60 percent of the land within its declared borders (Cozine 2004, 67).

Oil, Gas, Rice, and Suburbia

The timber industry likely had the greatest impact on the landscape of the Thicket, but there were other factors as well. As early as 1863, rice farming began in southeast Texas, centered near Beaumont, and led to flooding of local forests (Dethloff 1988). Local

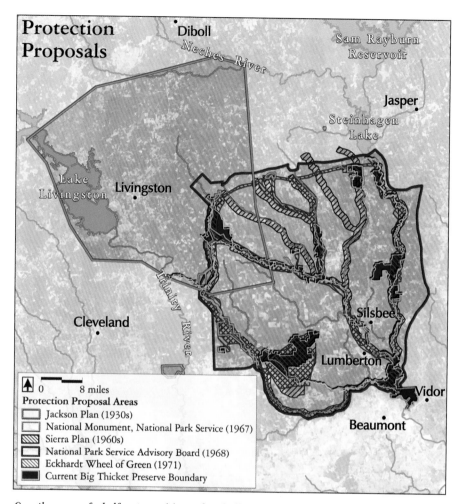

Over the course of a half century, citizens, elected officials, and government agencies proposed numerous plans for a park to protect elements of the Big Thicket. This map shows just a few. The area in light green shows the candidate area for a 430,000-acre park proposed by R. E. Jackson and the East Texas Big Thicket Association during the 1930s. In blue, we see a 270,000-acre vision of the late 1960s supported by the Sierra Club and the Big Thicket Coordinating Committee. In 1968, the Advisory Board on National Parks, Historical Sites, Buildings and Monuments suggested a 1.4-million acre "Environmental Conservation Zone" (marked in purple), where logging and oil and gas exploration would have been limited. The 1971 proposal from one leading political representative, congressman Bob Eckhardt, is shown in red. In orange, we see a 35,500-acre National Monument recommended by the Park Service in 1967, and within the yellow boundaries, we can pick out the area of the current 106,000-acre Preserve (Cozine 2004, 119–20; Johnston 2014; Jones 2013; National Park Service 1967; National Park Service 2011; Ogren 2014; Thompson-Buchanan 2014).

oil strikes came in the early 1900s: Spindletop and Saratoga in 1901, Sour Lake in 1903, Batson in 1904. And by the 1950s, land in the Thicket began to be subdivided on a larger scale and cleared for housing (National Park Service 2013).

Conservation Beginnings

For many years, there have been those who have watched the Thicket develop and change, and who have worked to save a portion of the area. The first preservation proposals for the Thicket came from R. E. Jackson, a railroad employee and business-man. He argued for protection of a 430,000-acre tract along and to the east of the Trinity River. To organize and press for this view, he worked with the Hardin County Cooperative Pasture and Game Preserve as early as the 1920s, and later via the East Texas Big Thicket Association, which first met in 1936 (Bonney 2011, 163). As well, he managed to secure a lease-hold of 22,000 acres of biologically rich land in the "Tight-Eye" country of Polk County, where he welcomed scientists and politicians interested in studying and safeguarding the area (Gunter 1993, 67).

Scientific study of the Thicket advanced during the 1930s. Associates of the Texas Agricultural Experiment Station, Hal Parks and Victor Cory (hosted by Jackson), published the *Biological Survey of the East Texas Big Thicket Area* in 1936. The *Survey* described the Thicket's characteristics, boundaries, and extent (estimated at over 3.35 million acres) (Parks, Cory, et al. 1936). A diverse array of scientists recognized the importance and value of the Thicket, and in 1937, the Texas Academy of Science closed its annual convention with a resolution calling for "scien-tific protection" of the Big Thicket (Gunter 1993, 67).

Protection of the Thicket garnered important political support in the 1930s. Governor Allred; lumberman John Henry Kirby; and W. M. Tucker, head of the Texas Game, Fish and Oyster Commission, all backed the idea of a park to protect the Thicket. US senator Morris Sheppard was also persuaded. In November 1938, Sheppard asked the National Park Service to investigate the Big Thicket as a possible addition to the National Park system (Anderson et al. 2005, 8). In early 1939, acting regional NPS director Herbert Maier and wildlife technician W. B. McDougal completed their study and recom-mended creation of a 400,000-acre Big Thicket National Park (Gunter 1993, 69).

Oil and War

During the late 1930s, however, other forces arose that cut momentum for a park in the Thicket. Oil was discovered in Polk County in 1936, sapping inter-est there in creating a sanctuary. Then, in September 1939, Germany invaded Poland, and World War II began in ear-nest. With the onset of the war, funding prospects for a park fell, and the new military activity raised rival demand for local timber. In 1936, the US gov-ernment had spent $3 million to buy 600,000 acres of national forest fifty miles north of the Thicket, and there was little enthusiasm in Washington for spending yet more money on acquiring public land in East Texas (Cozine 2004, 90). Also, with Senator Sheppard's death in 1943, the park lost its chief advocate in Washington, DC (Bonney 2011, 168–69).

The 1960s

Advocacy for a park in the Thicket finally resumed in the early 1960s with efforts on the state and private levels. Governor Price Daniel took up the banner in 1961 with a proposal for a 20,000-acre park, followed in 1962 with creation of a Big Thicket Study Commission to build political support for the idea (Cozine 2004, 93–95; Gunter 1971, 72). Then, in 1964, Lance Rosier, a local natural-ist known as the "St. Francis of the Forest"; Dempsie Henley, mayor of Liberty; and others formed the Big Thicket Association (Douglas 1967, xi). Rosier knew the flora and fauna of the Thicket well, and Henley was well connected in political circles, having served earlier as chair for Daniel's Big Thicket Study Commission.

The Big Thicket Association was dedicated to "expanding, enhancing and protecting the Big Thicket," and its work began to bear fruit within the year. The association held trail rides, beauty contests, and square dances, and also reached out to political and scientific leaders, including senator Ralph Yarborough; Clarence Cottam, director of the Welder Wildlife Foundation; Dr. Don Correll of the Texas Research Foundation; Jim Bowmer, president of the Texas Explorers Club; and Bill Bowen, superintendent of the Padre Island National Seashore (Bonney 2011, 143; Gunter 1993, 73; Henley 1970, 126). The state and federal governments began to respond. In March 1965, the state of Texas' Big Thicket Study Commission recommended a 52,200-acre park. During 1965 and 1966, the National Park Service held a series of studies of the Thicket that resulted in their endorsement of park protection as well.

However, Governor Connally failed to endorse the state commission's park recommendation, and timber owners resisted land purchase and lease offers from Texas Parks and Wildlife (Cozine 2004, 98, 108, 116). And meanwhile, the federal agency proposal of a relatively small, 35,000-acre park, scattered in an array of isolated tracts, disappointed proponents. Progress in Congress stalled as well. Senator Yarborough introduced Senate Bill 3929 in October 1966, only to see it and its successor bills languish in committee for almost five years.

While the political wheels turned painfully slowly, concern grew that the Thicket was disappearing rapidly—at the rate of fifty acres a day—and that soon there might be little left to protect (Douglas 1967, 37). Clearcutting of

pines became more common, followed by bulldozing, burning, and monoculture planting. Diverse hardwood stands of magnolia, beech, ash, gum, hickory, and oak were girdled to open lands for the more profitable pine, or cut to directly feed the market for pulp (McLeod 1972, addendum). During 1966 and 1967, virgin woodlands were sawed down in the Thicket, leaving large gaps in the proposed Beech Creek and Cypress Creek Units (Gunter 1972, 81). Some of the cuts, including roadside magnolias with 30-inch trunks, of little value on the lumber market, seemed to be designed simply as a way to make the land less appealing for park protection. Other damage to the Thicket, including the poisoning of a thousand-year-old magnolia, and of a rookery of herons, egrets, spoonbills, and anhingas, appeared to be calculated purely for spite (Cong. Record—Senate, January 19, 1970, 104; Douglas 1967, 19, 20). And conservationists feared that whatever pieces of the Thicket survived would cost more and more to purchase with each passing year; land prices had already jumped from $50/acre in 1960 to $300 in 1966 (Douglas 1967, 25).

The 1970s

Despite setbacks, public support for a park persisted. With time, a general consensus grew that protecting a set of river corridors would save the Thicket's more distinctive, diverse, and quickly restored plant communi-

ties. Fortunately, some of these river-bottom areas had been missed by the more devastating skidder operations and prescribed burns (McLeod 1972, 18). At the same time, set-asides of these riparian areas might avoid infringing on some of the upland areas that timber companies favored for commercial pine.

Still, disputes arose over the size (ranging from 35,500 to 191,000 acres) and shape (the contiguous "Wheel of Green" or the dispersed "String of Pearls") of the proposed parklands (Gunter 1993, 86–96). In fact, there were fully two dozen rival bills filed in Congress to protect "the Thicket" in the first half of the 1970s by a variety of politicians (including Senators Bentsen, Fannin, Jackson, Tower, and Yarborough and Representatives Brooks, Bush, Cabell, Dowdy, Eckhardt, Milford, Patman, Pickle, Roe, Steelman, and Wilson). The controversies over the preserve's outline also divided timber companies that might have to sell more or less of their lands. As well, disagreements divided many advocates for protection. However, the Big Thicket Coordinating Committee, led by Dempsie Henley, Lance Rosier, Maxine Johnston, Ned Fritz, and Pete Gunter, maintained a general consensus among some forty supportive citizens groups (Caldwell, Hayes, and MacWhirter 1976, 280–82; US Senate 1974, 139).

The Final Deal

Perhaps the key turning point in the Thicket's long-running legislative battle was the November 1972 election of Charlie Wilson to replace congressman John Dowdy. Dowdy had been a stalwart opponent to any sizable park, while Representative Wilson was more willing to accept a Big Thicket sanctuary. However, Wilson joined with the timber interests' opposition to large contiguous park parcels and defied the idea of a park in the Big Sandy–Village Creek corridor, with its scattering of private home sites. On June 13, 1973, Wilson introduced a bill for a 75,000-acre park, later expanded to 84,550 acres in a partnership with Congressman Eckhardt (H.R. 11546, 93rd Congress). With support from the powerful lumberman Arthur Temple, and sponsorship from the entire Texas House delegation, H.R. 11546 passed the House on December 4, 1973 (Cozine 2004, 156). The next day, senator Lloyd Bentsen (D-TX) introduced a bill for a yet larger park, including over 16,000 acres in the Big Sandy–Village Creek corridor. However, the conference committee deferred to Wilson, since the preserve fell within his district. In the end, it was the House bill, with Wilson's language, that President Ford signed into law on October 11, 1974 (Cozine 2004, 157–58; Public Law 93-439).

In creating the preserve, the nation had taken a huge step forward in protecting the "American Ark," the "Biological Crossroads of North America" (Parent 1993, 3). Aside from its great biological value, the new park also represented a landmark in the general philosophy behind land protection. For one thing, the National Park Service now had its first "preserve," an area protected for its biological richness, not for its beauty, or its standing timber, or its recreational opportunities, or its watershed. Secondly, according to William Lienesch of the National Parks

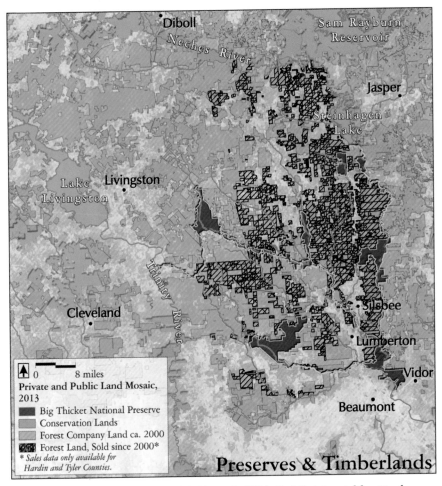

Preserves & Timberlands

Private and Public Land Mosaic, 2013

- ⬛ Big Thicket National Preserve
- Conservation Lands
- Forest Company Land ca. 2000
- ▨ Forest Land, Sold since 2000*

* Sales data only available for Hardin and Tyler Counties.

0 — 8 miles

This map shows, in yellow, the vast lands held near the Thicket by fully integrated forest products firms (typically, Temple-Inland, Champion, International Paper, and Louisiana Pacific) in roughly the year 2000 (Carraway 2014). As suggested by the cross-hatching in Hardin and Tyler Counties, most of these lands were sold during the first decade of the twenty-first century. Buyers included insurance companies, pension funds, universities, and REITs (including John Hancock Life Insurance, Crown Pine Timber, and others). While these new owners are bound by ongoing supply contracts that they have with mills, there is concern that the operators have less of a long-term commitment to keeping these private buffer forests intact (Adams 2014; Crocker 2014; Stevens 2014).

Conservation Association, the Big Thicket's layout pioneered the idea of securing corridors, especially riparian areas, to connect wildlife populations and maintain their diversity (Dixon 2009, 11). Lastly, the painful throes of the preserve's creation presaged future tensions between private property interests and public lands proponents. Some of the later struggles over property rights included the Sagebrush Rebellion in the 1970s, the James Watt era at the Department of the Interior in the 1980s, and the Take Back Texas movement of the 1990s.

Outside the Preserve

In the years since its creation, the preserve has grown in size to over 106,000 acres, thanks in good part to dedicated efforts by the Conservation Fund and the Texas Nature Conservancy (Conservation Fund 2013a, 2013b, 2013c). However, in that same time, the area outside the park boundaries has changed in worrisome ways. Pressure from activist investors, new tax strategies, high debt levels, and fierce global competition pushed timber companies near the preserve to sell vast acreage. From 2000 through 2005, Champion Paper, International Paper (IP), Louisiana-Pacific, and Georgia-Pacific sold 1.7 million acres in the state. In 2006, IP transferred 535,000 acres to new hands; and in 2007, Temple Inland let go of 1.1 million acres (Texas Environmental Grantmakers Group

2007). While the ultimate outcome is still unclear, critics fear that these sales will fragment ownership as title shifts to Real Estate Investment Trusts (REITs) held by university endowments, foundations, pension funds, and other institutional investors.

There are concerns that the REITs have shorter and broader investment goals than the old integrated timber firms that were anchored by sawmills, truck fleets, company towns, and long family connections to the East Texas woods.

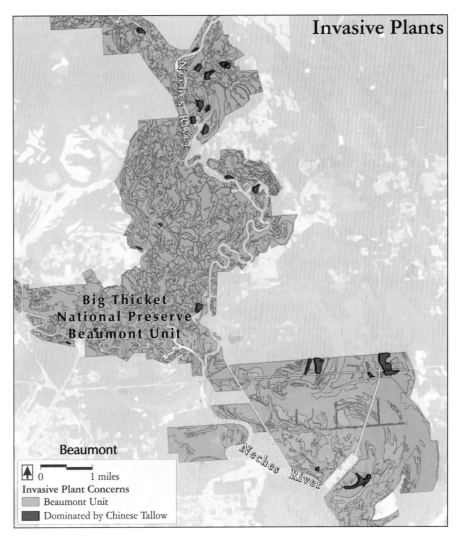

The Preserve is not pristine. This map shows areas in red where the nonnative invasive plant, Chinese tallow, has become dominant in parts of the Big Thicket's Beaumont Unit. The map draws on surveys conducted from 2011 through 2013 (DESCO 2013; Perkins 2014; Rowland 2014).

Inside the Preserve

Just as change occurs outside the preserve, so is there change within its boundaries. The encroachment of invasive exotic plants that can shunt aside the Thicket's natives is one change that has become a serious concern. Chinese tallow (*Triadica sebifera*) is one aggressive pioneer; other invasives in the Big Thicket include alligatorweed (*Alternanthera philoxeroides*), giant salvinia (*Salvinia molesta*), Japanese climbing fern (*Lygodium japonicum*), Japanese honeysuckle (*Lonicera japonica*), Japanese privet (*Ligustrum japonicum*), and water hyacinth (*Eichhornia crassipes*) (DESCO Environmental Consultants 2013, appendix E).

Nevertheless, the Thicket's biological riches still remain. The landscape contains an amazing catalog of eighty-five types of trees and sixty species of shrubs, more than 350 species of birds, and over one thousand types of flowering plants (including cacti, twenty-six ferns, twenty orchids, camellias, and even carnivorous plants) (Keith 2007, 251; National Park Service 2013; Peacock 1990, 25, 26, 83). Its diversity is even recognized globally; in 1981, UNESCO added the Big Thicket National Preserve to its international Biosphere Reserve network (Gunter 1993, 105).

And yet even these startlingly high counts probably fall below the real numbers. In recent years, many new species have been discovered in the preserve, thanks to inventory

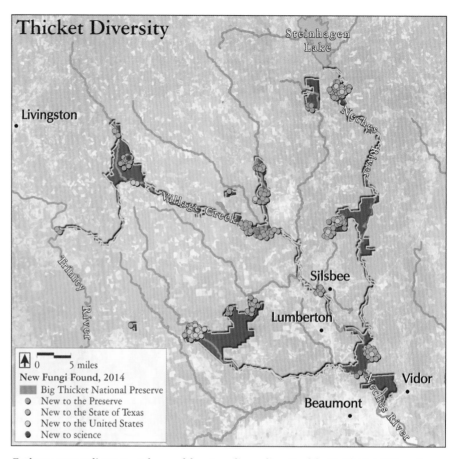

Explorers are revealing more and more of the extraordinary diversity of the Big Thicket. This map shows over 450 new species of fungi, of which 195 are new to the preserve (blue), 238 to the state (yellow), three to the United States (orange), and twenty-one that are entirely new to science (red)! (Halvorsen 2014; Lewis 2014).

work coordinated by the Big Thicket Association (BTA) and involving a number of individual scientists and research universities, including Rice University and Sam Houston State (Walker 2013). The BTA inventory, dubbed "Thicket of Diversity," has confirmed many species that are new to the preserve. The list of new finds includes nine freshwater fish, seven moths, fifty-eight slime molds, sixteen aquatic true bugs, and one whirligig

beetle (Big Thicket Association 2013a and 2013b). With many years of help from its friends, the Thicket continues to surprise and amaze!

Sources

Adams, Greg. 2014. GIS Analyst, Tyler County Appraisal District. Personal communication. July.

Anderson, Luke, Chris Allen, Leah Elrod, Melissa Forbes, Hannah

Harbin, and Diann Strom. 2005. "Big Thicket National Preserve: Trails to the Future, Capstone Project, Bush School of Government and Public Service." College Station: Texas A&M University.

Big Thicket Association. 2013a. Thicket of Diversity New Species Discovered: April 2, 2013. http://www.btatx.org/thicket-of-diversity/new-species, accessed December 11, 2013.

———. 2013b. TOD New Species Count: 413. http://www.btatx.org/thicket-of-diversity/new-species, accessed July 9, 2014.

Block, William T. 1994. *East Texas Mill Towns and Ghost Towns*. Vol. 1. Lufkin: Best of East Texas Publishers.

Bonney, Lorraine. 2011. *The Big Thicket Guidebook: Exploring the Backroads and History of Southeast Texas*. Denton: University of North Texas Press.

Brewer, William. 1874. "Map Showing in Five Degrees of Density the Distribution of Woodland within the Territory of the United States, 1873." In *Statistical Atlas of the United States Based on the Results of the Ninth Census, 1870*, compiled by Francis Walker. New York: Julius Bien.

Caldwell, Lynton, Lynton R. Hayes, and Isabel M. MacWhirter. 1976. *Citizens and the Environment: Case Studies in Popular Action*. Bloomington: Indiana University Press.

Callicot, J. Baird, Miguel Acevedo, Pete Gunter, Paul Harcombe, Christopher Lindquist, and Michael Monticino. 2006. "Biocomplexity in the Big Thicket." *Ethics, Place, and Environment* 9 (1): 21–45.

Carraway, Burl. 2014. Sustainable Forestry Department Head, Texas A&M Forest Service. Personal communication, April.

Conservation Fund. 2013a. Places We Work: Big Thicket National Preserve. www.conservationfund.org/projects/big-thicket-national-preserve, accessed December 10, 2013.

———. 2013b. Places We Work: Neches River. www.conservationfund.org/projects/neches-river, accessed December 10, 2013.

———. 2013c. Places We Work: Village Creek State Park. www.conservationfund.org/projects/village-creek-state-park/, accessed December 10, 2013.

Cozine, James. 2004. *Saving the Big Thicket: From Exploration to Preservation, 1685–2003*. Denton: University of North Texas Press.

Crocker, Theresa. 2014. Hardin County Appraisal District. Personal communication, July.

Cruikshank, J. W., and I. F. Eldredge. 1939. Forest Resources of Southeastern Texas. Miscellaneous Publication No. 326. US Department of Agriculture, Southern Forest Experiment Station, US Forest Service. Washington, DC: US Government Printing Office.

Daniels, Price. 1962. Proposal for a 435,000-acre Big Thicket Park. Map. Office of the Governor.

Dean, Anthony, L. I. Neiman, and Helen O'Neill. 1948. Angelina National Forest, Texas, 1948. Forest Service, US Department of Agriculture.

DESCO Environmental Consultants. 2013. Post-Operation Assessment of Vegetation in the Beaumont Unit and Other Adjacent Lands of the Big Thicket National Preserve, Hardin, Jasper, Jefferson, and Orange Counties, Texas.

Dethloff, Henry. 1988. *A History of the American Rice Industry, 1685–1985*. College Station: Texas A&M University Press.

Dixon, Suzanne. 2009. *Texas Pride: Celebrating and Protecting our National Parks in the Lone Star State*. Dallas: National Parks Conservation Association.

Douglas, William O. 1967. *Farewell to Texas*. New York: McGraw-Hill.

Firsching, Donald. 2014. Database Programmer, Texas Historical Commission. Personal communication, March.

Forte, Jim. 2014. Postal History, Post Offices: Texas. www.postalhistory.com/postoffices.asp?task=display&state=TX, accessed March 24, 2014.

Gerland, Jonathan. 2014. Director, The History Center, Diboll, Texas. Personal communication, March.

Gunter, Pete. 1970. The Big Thicket—Wilderness on a Death Bed. Congressional Record—Senate, January 19, p. 103.

———. 1971. *The Big Thicket: A Challenge for Conservation*. Austin: Jenkins Publishing.

———. 1993. *The Big Thicket: An Ecological Evaluation*. Denton: University of North Texas Press.

Halvorsen, Mona. 2014. Director, Thicket of Diversity, Big Thicket Association. Personal communications, February–July.

Henley, Dempsie. 1970. *The Murder of Silence: The Big Thicket Story*. Waco: Texian Press.

Johnston, Maxine. 2014. Advisory Board Member, Big Thicket Association. Personal communication, April.

Jones, Andy. 2013. Texas State Director, Conservation Fund. Personal communication, January.

Keith, Gary. 2007. *Eckhardt: There Once Was a Congressman from Texas*. Austin: University of Texas Press.

Lewis, David. 2014. Member, Fungal TWIG, Big Thicket National Preserve. Personal communication, March.

Liknes, Greg, Mark Nelson, and Daniel Kaisershot. 2013. Historical Woodland Density of the Coterminous United States, 1873. US Forest Service, US Department of Agriculture. Newtown Square, Pennsylvania. http://dx.doi.org/10.2737/RDS-2013-0006.

Maxwell, Robert, and Robert Baker. 1983. *Sawdust Empire: The Texas Lumber Industry, 1830–1940*. College Station: Texas A&M University Press.

McLeod, Claude. 1972. "The Big Thicket Forest of Eastern Texas: A Brief Historical, Botanical and Ecological Report." Sam Houston State University, Huntsville, Texas.

Miles, P. D. 2014. Forest Inventory EVALIDator web application version 1.5.1.06. US Department of Agriculture, Forest Service, Northern Research Station, St. Paul, Minnesota. http://apps.fs.fed.us/Evalidator/tmattribute.jsp.

Morin, G. A., K. Kuusela, D. B. Henderson-Howat, N. S. Efstathiadis, S. Oroszi, H. Sipkens, E. v. Hofsten, and D. W. MacCleery. 1996. "Long-Term Historical Changes in the Forest Resource." Geneva Timber and Forest Study Papers, No. 10. United Nations Economic Commission for Europe, Food and Agriculture Organization of the United Nations, Timber Section, Geneva, Switzerland.

National Park Service. 1967. Proposed Big Thicket National Monument, Texas: A Study of Alternatives. National Park Service, US Department of Interior.

———. 2011. Land Resources Division, Listing of Acreage, 12/31/2011. National Park Service. https://irma.nps.gov/Stats/DownloadFile/107.

———. 2013. Big Thicket Biological Crossroads. http://www.nps.gov/bith/bigthicketbiologicalcrossroads.htm, accessed December 11, 2013.

———. 2014. El Camino Real de los Tejas National Historic Trail. National Historic Trails and Routes. http://imgis.nps.gov/Trails, accessed March 6, 2014.

Ogren, Jonathan. 2014. Principal, Siglo Group. Personal communication, February.

Parent, Laurence. 1993. Big Thicket National Preserve. Southwest Parks and Monuments Association, Tucson.

Parks, Hal, Victor Cory, et al. 1936. *The Fauna and Flora of the Big Thicket Area*. Texas Agricultural Experiment Station.

Peacock, Howard. 1984. *The Big Thicket of Texas: America's Ecological Wonder*. Boston: Little, Brown.

———. 1990. *The Nature of Texas*. College Station: Texas A&M University Press.

Perkins, Arthur. 2014. Senior Biologist/Ecologist IV. DESCO Environmental Consultants. Personal communication, June.

Pierson, Albert, and R. V. Reynolds. 1936. Lumber Production, 1869–1934. US Department of Agriculture, Forest Service, Division of Forest Economics. Washington, DC.

Pool, William C. 1975. *A Historical Atlas of Texas*. Austin: Encino Press.

Railroad Commission of Texas. 1907. *Sixteenth Annual Report of the Railroad Commission of the State of Texas*. Austin: Von Boeckmann-Jones.

Rowland, Justin. 2014. Regulatory Permit Coordinator and Senior Biologist. DESCO Environmental Consultants. Personal communication, June.

Sargent, Charles S. 1884. Report on the Forest of North America (Exclusive of Mexico). Tenth Census of the United States. Department of the Interior, Office of the Census. Washington, DC: Government Printing Office.

Sitton, Thad, and James Conrad. 1998. *Nameless Towns: Texas Sawmill Communities, 1880–1942*. Austin: University of Texas Press.

Stevens, Alex. 2014. Hardin County Appraisal District. Personal communications, April–June.

Texas Almanac and Industrial Guide. 1927. Texas Forest and Woodland Resources. *Dallas Morning News*. http://texashistory.unt.edu/ark:/67531/metapth123785/m1/194/?q=lumber, accessed March 28, 2014.

Texas Environmental Grantmakers Group. 2007. Piney Woods Protection. http://www.texasegg.org/discussions/pineywoods.php, accessed April 23, 2014.

Texas Forestry Museum. 2014. Sawmill Database. http://www.treetexas.com/research/sawmill/, accessed March 27, 2014.

Texas General Land Office. 2014. Texas Railroads. https://koordinates.com/layer/686-texas-railroads/data/, accessed March 5, 2014.

Texas Historical Commission. 2014. Texas Historic Sites Atlas: Sawmills. http://atlas.thc.state.tx.us/shell-county.htm, accessed March 6, 2014.

Thompson-Buchanan, Scott. 2014. Cartographer, Intermountain Region, National Park Service. Personal communication, April.

Turner, Monica, Stephen Carpenter, Eric Gustafson, Robert Naiman, and Scott Pearson. 1998. "Land Use." In *Status and Trends of the Nation's Biological Resources*, vol. 1, edited by M. J. Mac, P. A. Opler, P. Doran, and C. Haecker. Washington, DC: National Biological Service.

US Senate. 1974. Big Thicket National Park: Hearings. Subcommittee on Parks and Recreation, Committee on Interior and Insular Affairs, US Senate. Ninety-Third Congress, Second Session. February 5 and 6.

US Postal Service. 1971. Record of Appointment of Postmasters, 1832–September 30, 1971. National Archive M841, Rolls, 121–27.

Walker, Bruce. 2013. Executive Director, Big Thicket Association. Personal communication, December.

Walker, Mike. 2001. *SPV's Comprehensive Railroad Atlas of North America*. Faversham, Kent, England: Ian Andrews.

Williams, Howard. 1988. *Gateway to Texas*. Orange, TX: Heritage House Museum of Orange.

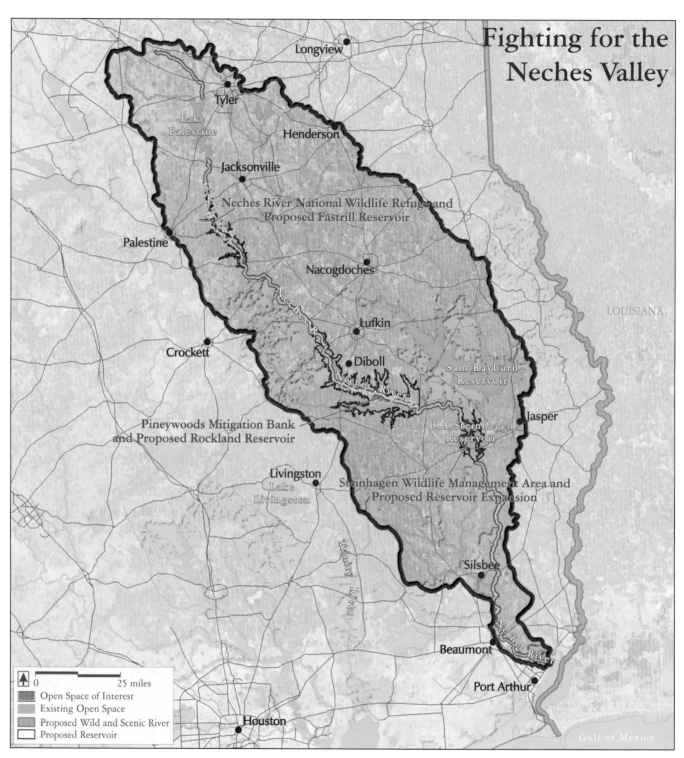

Here is the Neches River watershed, showing major parks, lakes, roads, and cities (Steinbach 2011 and 2012; Texas Natural Resources Information System 2012).

The Neches Valley

This is the story of a kind of Rorschach test, where some saw a landscape for its rich bottomland and diverse wildlife, while others saw this same country for its plentiful rain, strong runoff, and robust water supplies. Played out in the upper Neches basin, these two visions competed for the same site. Some pressed for a National Wildlife Refuge and a Wild and Scenic River designation. Others lobbied for dam construction at Fastrill, Weches, Rockland, and Town Bluff.

The Neches Bottomlands

In deep East Texas, from Lake Palestine downstream to the B. A. Steinhagen Reservoir, the Neches River flows wild for over 220 miles, without dams or diversions, through a valley of old history, long-lived customs, huge hardwood trees, and abundant wildlife.

In 1985, the US Fish and Wildlife Service recognized this stretch of the Neches River valley as a Priority 1 Conservation Area, largely due to its increasingly rare stands of overcup and swamp chestnut oaks, water elms, black willows, pecans, hickories, and other bottomland hardwoods (US Fish and Wildlife Service 2005, 6, 16). The valley's biological value comes from this rarity. It is a survivor of Texas' busy history. Over the years,

the state has lost more than 75 percent of this kind of ecosystem to logging, dam construction, and conversion of diverse stands to pine plantations (Texas Parks and Wildlife 2012). These changes have contributed to the disappearance of the ivory-billed woodpecker and red wolf, and the scarcity of the red-cockaded woodpecker, paddlefish, and black bear.

Protection for the bottomlands along the Neches has come slowly. Gradually, however, conservation groups and private individuals have

Richard Donovan paddles the Neches River, 3 miles north of Beaumont, in 2001 (Sloan 2012).

raised attention for the need to secure some remnants of this land. A number of nonprofit groups have been involved in the generation-long campaign, including the Big Thicket Association, Clean Air and Water, the Conservation Fund, Friends of the Neches, the National Wildlife Federation, Sierra Club, Texas Conservation Alliance, and others.

"In 1998, I picked up the Lufkin Daily News and there was this huge picture on the front page of the paper, full color, showing the Neches with Fastrill Reservoir up on the northern Neches . . . then Rockland Reservoir, 125,000 acres of that, and then Dam B on down below that. And it just was such a shock to me because I had grown up on the Neches. I have hunted and fished the Neches all of my life, since I was fourteen or fifteen years old. I grew up on the Neches and its tributaries, walking the creek banks and letting mosquitoes suck the blood out of my veins, and camping, and fishing, and hunting squirrel and deer and coons and possums, and just every matter of thing that you could think of, I hunted as a young man. And I saw that layout of those dams, and it just stunned me. It was just like I'd lost a family friend."

—Richard Donovan, 2008

Paddling the River

Richard Donovan, an East Texas native and veteran of the real estate and timber industries, undertook major canoe trips down the Neches in 1998 and 2001. These trips helped bring a great deal of attention to the need to appreciate and defend these bottomlands and the wildlife, history, and culture they support. Covered by camera crews (Beaumont's KTRM and KBMT, Lufkin's KTRE, and Texas Parks and Wildlife's team), and interviewed by reporters from papers in Houston, Beaumont, Tyler, Jasper, and Lufkin, Donovan became a natural spokesperson for the river. His concern for the river's life and culture found its way into his popular book, *Paddling the Wild Neches*, helping spread the word about the Neches yet further (Donovan 2006).

The Upper Neches is a rare thing in Texas—a free-flowing stream. These photographs of the Neches River show the effects of flood and drought, of high and low water levels (please note the marks A and B for comparison). The pair of images suggests the importance of natural pulses of water, silt, and nutrients in an undammed river segment. The photos were taken on the Neches at the Hobson Crossing bridge, five miles downstream from US Highway 84 (Van Dellen 2012).

Land Sales

Concern about the fate of the Upper Neches and its bottomlands was also raised by the large-scale breakup and sale of private timberlands. In 2000 through 2007, Champion Paper, Georgia-Pacific, International Paper, Louisiana Pacific, and Temple-Inland liquidated over 3.3 million acres of timberlands in East Texas (Texas Environmental Grantmakers Group 2007). With that pace and extent of land sales, conservationists realized that large, high-quality bottomland tracts might soon become prohibitively expensive, or after lumbering or subdivision, simply unavailable.

A Refuge Is Born

In June 2006, a 38-mile reach of the Neches gained approval by the US Fish and Wildlife Service as an area worthy of protection, pinned down by the receipt of the first acre for the Neches River National Wildlife Refuge. A gift from the great-granddaughter of a freed slave, this acre fell within a 25,231-acre boundary first identified in the 1980s (Holdcamp 2011). In 2009, the Conservation Fund brought the refuge another early gift of land, some 30 acres (Gooch 2009).

Fastrill Support

However, opposition to the refuge arose quickly due to its overlap with a proposed 35,000- to 45,000-acre water supply reservoir called Fastrill. In April 2005, Dallas added Fastrill to its Long-Range Water Supply Plan as a potential source of water for 2050 and beyond. The Texas legislature declared its support for Fastrill with an August 2005 resolution declaring the reservoir as a "critical resource." Later, in 2007, the legislature went further, designating Fastrill as a "unique reservoir site," a title with a good deal more legal force (Texas Senate Resolution 6 2005; Texas Water Development Board 2012b, 238–40; Texas Water Code, Section 16.051(g); Texas Water Development Board 2012b, 239). Numerous talks about shifting either the refuge or the

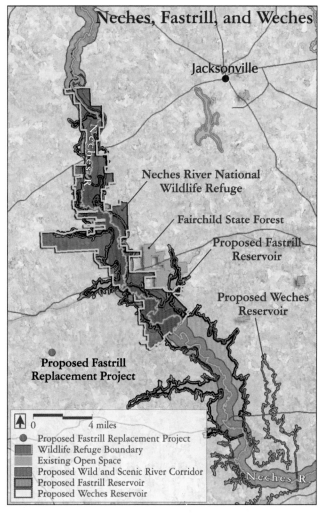

This map shows how the Neches River National Wildlife Refuge would overlap with the proposed Fastrill Reservoir. The map also suggests the wide effect that the Weches Reservoir would have had just downstream of Fastrill (Jones 2012; Texas Water Development Board 2006).

lake site to avoid the conflict ultimately failed. In January 2007, the city of Dallas and the Texas Water Development Board sued in federal court to block the refuge (Bush 2010). Their basic claim against the refuge was (rather ironically) filed under the National Environmental Policy Act, arguing that the environmental assessment for the park was inadequate.

Fastrill Critique

At the same time, there was criticism against the reservoir and strong support for the park. Some focused on the cheaper and less damaging water supply options that Dallas had available. For example, opponents of the $292 million Fastrill proposal, such as the Texas Conservation Alliance, argued that the city of Dallas could turn to other, already-existing reservoirs, such as Lake Texoma, Wright-Patman, or Toledo Bend, for any truly necessary water supplies (Quarles 2010; HDR Engineering et al. 2007, 3–80). In their March 2010 report, "Drop by Drop," the Sierra Club and National Wildlife Federation also pointed out that Dallas could satisfy much of its water need through conservation and efficiency measures, without building any new costly dams, canals, pipelines, or treatment plants. At 240 gallons/capita/day (gpcd), Dallas water use has been the highest in the state, and almost twice the 124 gpcd used by Brownsville, for instance (McCormick et al. 2010).

The Refuge and the Natural World

Other park advocates focused on the ecological merits of the refuge, stressing the free-flowing waters, diverse vegetation, and rich wildlife that would be protected within its lands. In addition, they argued that the environmental benefits of the refuge would reach well beyond its borders, by securing downstream flows and enabling movement of wildlife up and down the riparian corridor. These proponents saw the Neches Refuge as a key link within the extensive acreage that was already protected in the river's bottomlands, including Davy Crockett and Angelina National Forests, Martin Dies, Jr. State Park, Sandy Creek Park, and the Big Thicket National Preserve (Donovan, Lange, and van Dellen 2009).

The Refuge and Ecotourism

Refuge backers also touted the economic value of the park as a tourist draw, bringing in customers for hotels, restaurants, filling stations, outfitters, and other local businesses. Nature-based tourism, including birdwatching, hunting, and fishing, has been growing rapidly in Texas, and is already estimated to annually bring in $10.9 billion to the state (Staples 2007). National wildlife refuges evidently are a significant part of this economic benefit, attracting 4.9 million visitors and generating more than $125 million in Texas' four-

state region (including the Lone Star State as well as Arizona, New Mexico, and Oklahoma) during a recent year (Carver and Caudill 2007). As a consequence, there was a feeling that the refuge would help build a stronger, more sustainable, less cyclical economy in East Texas, one that would be less affected by the booms and busts of the timber industry.

The Refuge and Landowners

Those who preferred the refuge to the reservoir also felt that the park would be fairer to private landowners. They pointed out that the projected purchases of 25,000 acres of land for the refuge would be from willing sellers only, and far less than the 150,000 to 185,000 acres that would be condemned for the reservoir (35,000–45,000 acres for the lake itself, plus more taken for habitat mitigation). As well, critics of Fastrill Reservoir argued that various dam plans had been pending for this stretch of the Neches for too long, since as early as 1936. These dam proposals had cast a cloud over title, lowered land prices, and undermined landowners' abilities to make long-term plans (Kagan, Moreno, and Katselas 2010).

Fastrill Exports

Finally, there was resistance to the out-of-basin use of Fastrill's waters, when there were local needs for supplying downstream communities and ecosystems, diluting effluent from petrochemical industries in the Beaumont–Port Arthur area, and providing fresh water for the fishing and shrimping industries in Sabine Lake. As Richard Harrell of the Beaumont-based non-profit group Clean Air and Water put it, "we want to go down on the record that we are opposed to taking water from our upper basins and moving it to Houston, Dallas or the Fort Worth area. We need the water. There are shortages in this region; and we will need the water, especially in those times" (Texas Water Development Board 2011, 10–18, 10–19).

A Court Ruling

Nineteen months after Dallas's filing, a federal district judge rejected the city's arguments against the refuge (Bush 2008). The court basically deferred to the US Fish and Wildlife Service's expertise and accepted the agency's fact finding and reasoning in its environmental assessment for the refuge. The lower court's ruling was confirmed in March 2009 by the Fifth Circuit, and once again in February 2010, when the US Supreme Court denied a hearing to the city's appeal (*City of Dallas* v. *Hall* 2010). This series of rulings meant that the refuge could proceed, despite the plans for Fastrill (Bush 2010).

Refuge Growth

In little more than a year following the litigation, the refuge began to take shape with a 2,500-acre gift to the Fish and Wildlife Service from the Conservation Fund and the home-building firm PulteGroup, Inc. (RefugeWatch 2011). The Conservation Fund later bought an additional 6,715 acres for possible inclusion in the refuge. Despite these private contributions, getting federal or state government support has been difficult for the new refuge. In 2012, a congressional contribution of up to $11 million was denied (O'Toole-Pitts 2011). Further, Texas governor Rick Perry refused to sign off on a Migratory Bird Certificate for the state, effectively blocking use of $1 million in Duck Stamp funding for the refuge (Jones 2012).

Wild and Scenic River Proposal

Aside from the work to create the refuge, a separate effort has sought to create a 225-mile Wild and Scenic River segment in the area. In 1982, the National Park Service had described this reach of the river as having "outstandingly remarkable scenic, recreational, fish and wildlife values" (Donovan 2006, 7, 8). In 1996, the US Forest Service echoed this view, saying outright that "potential exists for designation of the Neches River as a segment of the Wild and Scenic River System of Waterways" (US Forest Service 1996, 116). Following up in 2012, Senator Hutchison (R-TX) introduced a bill to study its establishment (Upper Neches River Wild and Scenic Study Act, S. 2324). While Wild and Scenic designation would not necessarily involve any land acquisition, it would effectively block dams on the river itself, from Lake Palestine downstream, through the Davy Crockett and Angelina National Forests, and on to the B. A. Steinhagen Reservoir (Hodge 2011). If approved, the Neches would have only the second such protected segment in the state since the federal law's passage in 1968, a sole companion to the 196-mile reach of the Rio Grande that flows through the Lower Canyons of the Big Bend.

Fastrill's Offspring

With the creation of the Neches National Wildlife Refuge, the defeat of Fastrill Reservoir, and the progress on Wild and Scenic designation, it would seem that the waters and lowlands of the Neches valley would be well protected. However, dams are a slippery thing! They are frequently proposed, and when sometimes defeated, they often return. Conditions in Texas have been especially favorable to dams. The Lone Star State has over 7,100 dams, roughly a tenth of those in the entire United States, and far more than any other state (US Army Corps of Engineers 2012).

For instance, although it appears that Fastrill Reservoir has been trumped by the Neches National Wildlife Refuge, Fastrill's demise has led to a new water supply proposal: the paired Neches "Run-of-the-River Project" and "Fastrill Replacement Project" (Texas Water Development

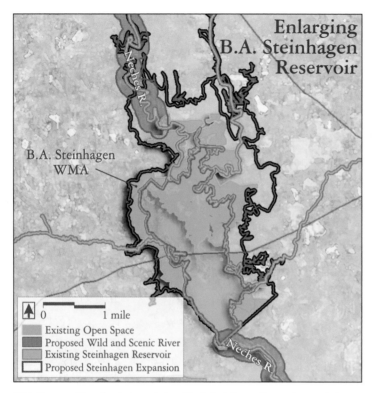

This figure outlines the shape and size of B. A. Steinhagen Reservoir, at existing 83-foot MSL and the proposed, raised 95-foot MSL elevations. The reservoir is shown with various nearby federal, state, and local parks, including Angelina-Neches Dam WMA, Magnolia Ridge Park, Martin Dies Jr. State Park, and Sandy Creek Park (Hallman 2012; Texas Water Development Board 2012a).

Board 2012a, plate 1). While this coupled project would evidently not include an impoundment on the main stem of the Neches, it would require a major diversion of scalped flows. Estimates by the proponents indicate that it could siphon off 112,100 acre-feet of water each year, and cost over $1.98 billion (Gooch 2010, 2, 4, 5).

In addition to Fastrill, there have been other water supply projects proposed for this same area. While not garnering the same level of support among utilities, agencies, and contrac- tors, they are certainly not to be dis- counted (Gallaspy 2005).

Steinhagen

For example, the Lower Neches Valley Authority has periodically issued plans for raising the height of the Town Bluff dam (which creates the B. A. Steinhagen Reservoir) by 7 to 12 feet. The authority argues that there are national security reasons for it to be able to market its water to Houston's petrochemical refineries (Stewart 2001; Donovan 2006, 6; Hallman 2012). Steinhagen has been gradually losing marketable water over time; silt- ation in the reservoir has caused it to lose 34 percent of its volume since its creation in 1953 (US Army Corps of Engineers 2010). Although raising the dam would not require building a new structure at a new location, the higher pool would have dramatic effects. The elevated dam would create slack water fourteen to twenty river miles upstream on the Neches. The raised water level would enlarge the reservoir property from 13,700 to 21,000 acres and inundate Martin Dies, Jr. State Park and the Angelina-Neches / Dam B Wildlife Management Area (Texas Conservation Alliance 2012).

Rockland

In the reach above Steinhagen, many maps show a dotted line for the out- line of the proposed Rockland Dam. Rockland has been mentioned in water supply plans and appropriations from as early as 1936, and is noted once again in the 1945 federal Rivers and Harbors Act (Lower Neches River Authority 1936; Rivers and Harbors Act of 1945, Sec. 2; Texas Almanac and State Industrial Guide 1945, 169). In the years since, the need for the dam has often been questioned, but never fully dismissed (Angelina and Neches River Authority 2012). While considered "inactive" in 1954, officially de-authorized in 1988, and declined for inclusion on the state's

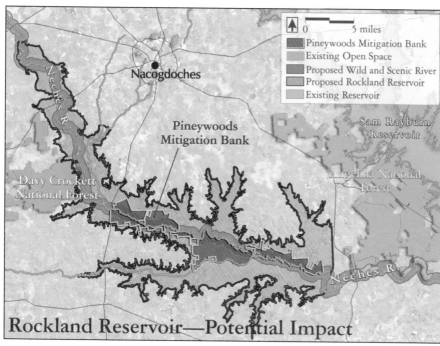

Rockland Reservoir—Potential Impact

The proposed Rockland Reservoir is mapped here, shown with its effect on the Pineywoods Mitigation Bank and the proposed Wild and Scenic River segment (Texas Water Development Board 2005; Lower Neches River Authority 1936).

"unique reservoir list," Rockland nevertheless appeared on the Texas Water Plan in 2001 (Freemantle 2001). If fully restored to life, and built, Rockland Dam would be a $693 million (1987 dollars) structure creating a 126,500-acre lake that would inundate large parts of the Angelina National Forest.

Weches

Then, above Rockland, the so-called Weches Dam has been recommended in the 1968 and 1984 State Water Plans (HDR Engineering et al. 2007, 3–70). Located about ten miles downstream from the dam later proposed at Fastrill, the Weches dam would have been quite tall and long, and its pool would have entirely consumed Fastrill's footprint. In fact, Weches would have been 2.8 times larger than Fastrill, and would have flooded 300 square miles of private timberland, plus portions of Davy Crockett and Angelina National Forests (Bonney 2011, 503). However, along with Fastrill, the Weches reservoir appears to have been blocked by the refuge, or at least is no longer "recommended" for construction.

The Future?

All of these comments should include the caveat, "as of this date." There may well be changes in the Neches's future; in the water business, there is seldom a final word.

Sources

Angelina and Neches River Authority. 2012. Neches Basin Lakes and Rivers. http://www.anra.org/recreation/lakes_and_rivers.html, accessed August 15, 2012.

Bezanson, Janice. 2013. Executive Director, Texas Conservation Alliance. Personal communication, June.

Bonney, Lorraine. 2011. *The Big Thicket Guidebook: Exploring the Backroads and History of Southeast Texas*. Denton: University of North Texas Press.

Bush, Rudolph. 2008. "Judge Blocks Dallas Plans for Fastrill Reservoir in East Texas." *Dallas Morning News*, July 1.

———. 2010. "U.S. Supreme Court Denies Dallas' Lake Fastrill Case." *Dallas Morning News*, February 22.

Carver, Eric, and James Caudill. 2007. *Banking on Nature 2006: The Economic Benefits to Local Communities of National Wildlife Refuge Visitation*, 353, 356. Washington, DC: US Fish and Wildlife Service, Division of Economics. September.

City of Dallas v. Hall, 562 F.3d 712 (5th Cir. 2009), cert. denied, 78 USLW 3479 (U.S. Feb. 22, 2010).

Donovan, Gina, Stephen Lange, and Adrian van Dellen. 2009. *Neches River*

User Guide. College Station: Texas A&M University Press.

Donovan, Richard. 2006. *Paddling the Wild Neches.* College Station: Texas A&M University Press.

Freemantle, Tony. 2001. "Blazing Paddles: Dam Proposal on the Neches Sparks Dispute." *Houston Chronicle,* November 18.

Gallaspy, Beth. 2005. "Water Needs, Landscape Focus of Debate." *Beaumont Enterprise,* July 15.

Gooch, Kelly. 2009. "Nonprofit Group Donates More Than 30 Acres to Neches Refuge." *Tyler Morning Telegraph,* October 23.

Gooch, Thomas. 2010. Memorandum: Errata in the 2011 Region C Water Plan, December 8.

Hallman, Billy. 2012. Neches River Task Force, Texas Conservation Alliance. Personal communication, August.

———. 2013. *Neches River Valley News.* January 13.

HDR Engineering, Freese & Nichols, R. J. Brandes Company. 2007. Reservoir Site Protection Study, February.

Hodge, Larry. 2011. "Can Adversaries Become Partners to Preserve Texas' Wild Waterways?" *Texas Parks and Wildlife* (October).

Holdcamp, Wendee. 2011. "Texas' Thirst for Dams Bucks National Trend." *Pacific Standard,* August 4.

Jones, Andy. 2012. Director, Texas Office, The Conservation Fund. Personal communication, August.

Kagan, Elena, Ignacia Moreno, and Anna Katselas. 2010. City of Dallas v. Gould and Texas Water Development Board v. U.S. Department of the Interior. Brief for Respondents in Opposition, in the Supreme Court of the United States, Nos. 08-1520 and 08-1524.

Lower Neches River Authority. 1936. Lower Neches Valley Authority Irrigation Project, Water Basin Series, Texas Planning Board. December 1. https://www.tsl.state.tx.us/cgi-bin/aris/maps/maplookup.php?mapnum=6685, accessed August 24, 2012.

McCormick, Lacy, Amanda Miller, Jennifer Walker, and Michelle Camp. 2010. "Drop by Drop: How 7 Texas Cities Can Conserve Water." National Wildlife Federation and the Sierra Club. March.

O'Toole-Pitts, Meagan. 2011. "Wildlife Refuge Expansion in Congress' Hands." *Jacksonville Daily Progress,* March 3.

Quarles, Edwin. 2010. "Supreme Court Hands Neches River Refuge a Victory by Declining to Hear Case." *Lufkin Daily News,* February 22.

RefugeWatch. 2011. Partnership Protects 2500 Acres at New Neches NWR, October 14. http://www.refugewatch .org/2011/10/14/partnership-protects-2500-acres-for-new-neches-river-nwr/, accessed August 15, 2012.

Rivers and Harbors Act of 1945. Pub. L. 79-14, 59 Stat. 10, March 2.

Sloan, Robert. 2012. Photograph of Richard Donovan. Provided courtesy of the Donovan family.

Staples, Todd. 2007. "Agricultural Diversification through Nature Tourism: Opportunities for the Rural Business and Land Owner." Texas Department of Agriculture. Report TDA-RED002C (May 2007). http://agecoext.tamu.edu/fileadmin/Rural_Entrepreneurship/Enterprises/Alternatives/NatureTourismBook2007 .pdf, accessed August 15, 2012.

Steinbach, Mark. 2012. Board member, Texas Land Trust Council. Personal

communication, June.

Stewart, Richard. 2001. "Reservoir Expansion Generates Opposition." *Houston Chronicle,* November 10.

Texas Almanac and State Industrial Guide, 1945–1946. 1945. University of North Texas Libraries, the Portal to Texas History, crediting Texas State Historical Association, Denton, Texas. http://texashistory.unt.edu/ark:/67531/metapth117166/, accessed August 16, 2012.

Texas Conservation Alliance. 2012. Reservoirs Proposed for the Neches. http://www.tconr.org/documents/3RESERVOIRS.pdf, accessed August 15, 2012.

Texas Environmental Grantmakers Group. 2007. Pineywoods Protection. http://www.texasegg.org/discussions/piney woods.php, accessed August 15, 2012.

Texas Natural Resources Information System. 2012. StratMap Park Boundaries. http://tg-twdb-gemss .s3.amazonaws.com/d/stratmap_bnd/stratmap_park.zip, accessed August 15, 2012.

Texas Parks and Wildlife. 2012. Pineywoods Wildlife Management: Endangered Species. http://www .tpwd.state.tx.us/landwater/land/habitats/pineywood/endangered _species/, accessed August 15, 2012.

Texas Senate Resolution 6, filed by Sen. Staples, August 16, 2005.

Texas Water Development Board. 2005. East Texas Regional Water Planning Group, Region I. 2005. Initially Prepared Plan, Chapter 8, Appendix B, p. 3. http://www.twdb.state.tx.us/rwpg/2005_1PP/Region%20I/Chapter%208/Appendix%20B.pdf, accessed August 15, 2012.

———. 2006. 2006 Water Plan: East Texas

Region, Appendix B. http://www
.twdb.state.tx.us/rwpg/2005_1PP/
Region%20I/Chapter%208/
Appendix%20B.pdf, accessed August
15, 2012.

———. 2011. State Water Plan: East
Texas Region, Chapter 10, Public
Participation and Adoption of Plan.
http://www.twdb.state.tx.us/wrpi/
rwp/3rdRound/2011_RWP/RegionI/
Word/Ch%2010.doc, accessed August
15, 2012.

———. 2012a. State Water Plan, Plate
1, Existing Major Reservoirs and
Recommended New Major Reservoirs.
http://www.twdb.state.tx.us/publica
tions/state_water_plan/2012/plate_1_
opt.pdf, accessed August 15, 2012.

———. 2012b. State Water Plan, Policy
Recommendations. http://www.twdb
.state.tx.us/publications/state_water_
plan/2012/11.pdf, accessed August 15,
2012.

US Army Corps of Engineers. 2010.
Steinhagen Lake, Civil Works Projects,
Texas Congressional Information
2010: Fort Worth District. http://www
.swf.usace.army.mil/pubdata/ppmd/
issuepaperupdates/indexMainPage
.pdf, accessed September 6, 2012.

———. 2012. National Inventory of
Dams. http://geo.usace.army.mil/
pgis/f?p=397:12:1236137230700301,
accessed August 15, 2012.

US Fish and Wildlife Service. 2005.
North Neches River National
Wildlife Refuge Establishment
Proposal, Environmental Assessment,
Conceptual Management Plan, and
Land Protection Plan. US Fish and
Wildlife Service, National Wildlife
Refuge System, Southwest Region,
Albuquerque, New Mexico. March.

US Forest Service. 1996. Final
Environmental Impact Statement
for the Revised Land and Resource
Management Plan: National Forests
and Grasslands in Texas.

Upper Neches River Wild and Scenic
Study Act, S. 2324, Introduced April
19, 2012. http://www.gpo.gov/fdsys/
pkg/BILLS-112s2324is/pdf/BILLS-
112s2324is.pdf, accessed August 15,
2012.

Van Dellen, Adrian F. 2012. Photographs
of the Neches River at different flow
levels. Personal communications,
August and September.

Wilson, M. R. 2009. "The Proposed
Fastrill Reservoir in East Texas: A
Study Using Geographic Information
Systems." Thesis prepared for the
degree of master of science, University
of North Texas, Denton. http://
digital.library.unt.edu/ark:/67531/
metadc12214/m1/1/high_res_d/thesis
.pdf, accessed September 6, 2012.

Conserving Land and Wildlife

Wildlife is in trouble around the world; recent studies indicate that 10,000 representative populations of mammals, birds, reptiles, amphibians, and fish declined by over 52 percent from 1970 through 2010 (World Wildlife Fund 2014, 8). Texas is not immune from these challenges: scattered throughout the book you will find a number of chapters about the travails of wildlife in the Lone Star State. There are chapters describing both the sad decline and the exciting return of numerous species native to Texas, including the American bison, bighorn sheep, brown pelican, and Kemp's ridley sea turtle. At the same time, other chapters in the atlas touch on the threats posed by exotic creatures, such as tropical sport and forage fish, South American fire ants, and European starlings.

Sources

Schmidly, David. 2002. *Texas Natural History: A Century of Change*. Lubbock: Texas Tech University Press.

Texas Comptroller of Public Accounts. 2013. Texas Ahead: Economic Resources for Growing and Governing Texas: Current Watch Species. http://texasahead.org/texasfirst/species/watch.php#review, accessed January 6, 2013.

Texas Parks and Wildlife. 2013. Texas Natural Diversity Database. http://www.tpwd.state.tx.us/huntwild/wild/wildlife_diversity/txndd/, accessed January 5, 2013.

World Wildlife Fund. 2014. "Living Planet Report 2014: Species and Spaces, People and Places." Edited by R. McLellan, L. Iyengar, B. Jeffries, and N. Oerlemans. Gland, Switzerland.

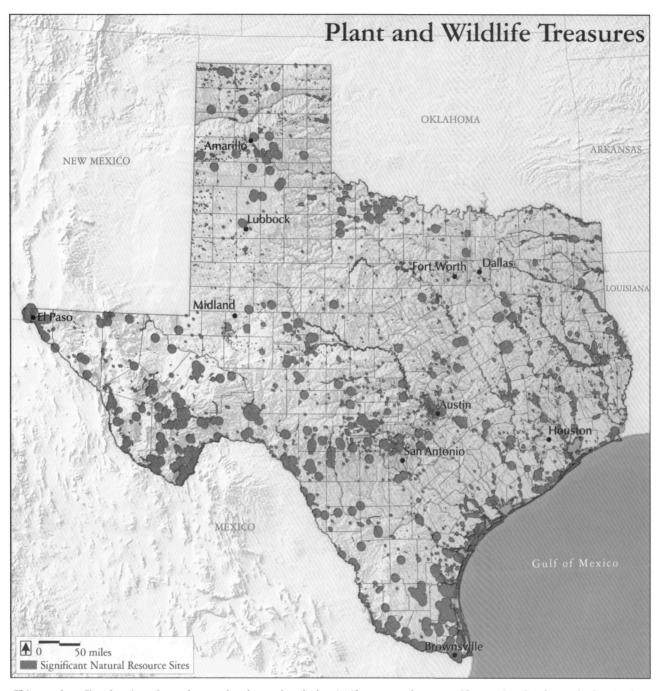

Plant and Wildlife Treasures

NEW MEXICO

OKLAHOMA

ARKANSAS

Amarillo

Lubbock

Fort Worth   Dallas

LOUISIANA

Midland

El Paso

Austin

Houston

San Antonio

MEXICO

Gulf of Mexico

Brownsville

0   50 miles

Significant Natural Resource Sites

This map shows Texas locations of rare, threatened, endangered, and other significant natural resources. These marks reflect thousands of species observations, either for individuals or for entire groups, such as colonial water-bird rookeries or bat roosts. The size and shape of the symbols describe their location, factoring in the uncertainty of their true range. As the map suggests, Texas is fortunate to have an extraordinary wealth of wildlife, including over 540 species of birds (three-quarters of those seen in the United States) and more than 140 animal species. Yet, over ninety species of plants and animals are considered threatened or endangered in Texas. Twenty-nine are under review for possible listing. Already, some species are gone from the state or entirely extinct, including the ivory-billed woodpecker, jaguar, Merriam's elk, passenger pigeon, and red wolf (Schmidly 2002; Texas Comptroller of Public Accounts 2013; Texas Parks and Wildlife 2013).

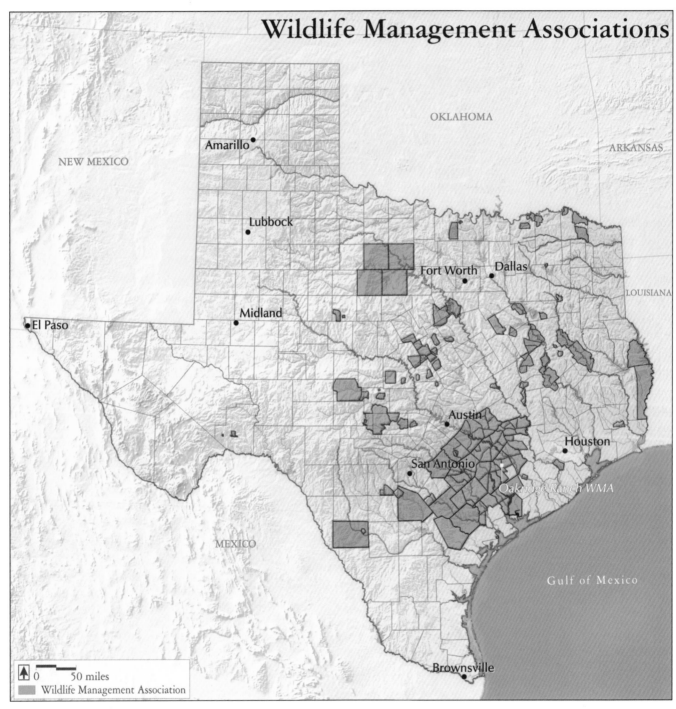

Wildlife Management Associations

This map shows the territories for most of the Wildlife Management Associations in Texas. Currently, there are over 185 co-ops covering more than 2.5 million acres. As you can see, the associations are clustered in the Austin/Houston/San Antonio triangle. This is a region where cooperation is critical because the breakup of large farms and ranches has been rapid, and many rural tracts have shrunk dramatically (Burch 2013; Texas Parks and Wildlife 2013).

Cooperation

No question about it, Texas is a big state. And it is a state rich with diverse habitats and enormous wildlife resources.

But the state's lands have been sliced up and heavily altered to suit human uses. Often those changes have come (albeit unintentionally) at the expense of wildlife.

These man-made changes to Texas habitat started early (Weniger 1989, 176–200). Texas saw thousands of years of manipulation of the land and wildlife by Native Americans removing timber, hunting large herbivores (mammoths, sloths, horses, giant bison, camels, and such), setting fires, and planting crops (Smeins, Fuhlendorf, and Taylor 2013). With generations of subsequent western settlement and effort, conversion of the state's habitat has accelerated. Texas lands have been sown with corn and wheat; planted to fruit and nut orchards; managed for hardwoods and softwoods; and sprigged, broadcast, and drilled for Bermudagrass, kleingrass, buffelgrass, and other forages. These changes have reached broad swaths of the state. As of 2010, 130 million acres of land in Texas were devoted to producing crops and raising livestock (US Census 2012). At the same time, competing, "nonuseful" plants have been treated with herbicides; insect populations have been doused with pesticides; and

predators have been trapped, poisoned, and shot.

With that kind of deep, broad, and long-term habitat change, wildlife needs help to survive and prosper in a modern world. And to make even a modest dent in a land that has been so broadly changed, it needs to be managed widely, on a "landscape" scale. Piecemeal solutions will not work. However, managing habitat on this kind of grand stage is very hard. It is a struggle for many reasons. The factors include the privately owned nature of Texas land, the tectonic shifts in Texas' population, the dwindling size of rural land parcels, and the economic value of the wildlife involved. In recent years, many landowners and wildlife managers have joined together to confront these tough trends with collaborative solutions. By tying together the efforts and pooling the resources and experience of many neighbors, they have had good success.

Private Owners

In some states and countries, land ownership is centralized in the government, allowing habitat decisions to be made in a coordinated way by just a few decision makers. However, Texas is a land that has been split into many privately owned pieces, estimated at 248,000 farms and count-

less urban and suburban tracts (US Census 2012). While state or federal entities own some 3 percent of Texas, hundreds of thousands of farmers, ranchers, and other private individuals own the balance. To manage habitat among so many landowners is daunting. It cannot be done with a single one-size-fits-all remedy; there are simply too many different ecosystems and markets, family circumstances, and financial situations involved. And it cannot be done by edict. Texas has few regulatory tools for land management. Texas counties, for instance, have only the limited authority expressly granted to them in the state constitution or by statutes.

Shifting Populations

The complexity of habitat management in the state has been compounded by the past century of population growth and shift. Inhabited by just three million people in 1900, with 80 percent living in rural areas, Texas has since grown to have more than twenty-six million people, with over 88 percent residing in metropolitan areas. During the same time, financial yields on livestock and crops have varied from flat to poor to volatile. Many farmers and ranchers have migrated to the cities in search of new work and better incomes. As older generations have died out, and younger, more mobile people have left the country, many family farms and ranches have been sold and subdivided, and sometimes resold and redivided time and again (Wilkins et al. 2000).

Shrinking Tracts

With these changes in the state's population and economy, the average size of farms and ranches has steadily slipped. In fact, the mean size of agricultural tracts fell by a full 8 percent from 2000 to 2010. The number of smaller tracts is growing: from 1997 to 2007, the number of Texas land parcels in the range of 1–100 acres grew by 22 percent statewide (Texas A&M Institute of Renewable Natural Resources 2008; Wilkins et al. 2000). The shrinkage in average tract size was particularly quick in the area within the Dallas/Houston/San Antonio triangle, where the median size of a sold tract dropped by 55–60 percent from 1966 to 2012, and now covers just 40 to 65 acres (Real Estate Center 2013).

Tract size is important for wildlife management. With a typical male white-tailed deer roaming across 600 to 1,000 acres, a buck's home habitat might now touch on ten, twenty, or more landowners' property, and even more numerous tracts in the future (Texas Parks and Wildlife 2013). As these tracts have become smaller, it has become essential that neighbors manage their lands in concert to support the wildlife they share.

Game Herds

At the same time that human populations have grown and tract sizes have fallen in Texas, some major game herds in the state have rebounded and increased to huge numbers. During the late 1800s and early 1900s, extensive land clearing and cultivation, market and subsistence hunting, and a lack of game laws cut the Texas white-tailed deer herd to a small remnant of its presettlement size (Higginbotham 1999). The Texas population of white-tailed deer was estimated to have slid to just 232,000 in 1938. However, with game seasons, bag limits, and law enforcement, together with restocking and education, deer herds have recovered and flourished. By 2004, the state's herd size had grown to roughly four million (Graves 2004).

However, increases in the number of white-tailed deer, especially does, have now exceeded what the habitat can support in many places. In parts of Colorado County, roughly 70 miles west of Houston, deer are surveyed at

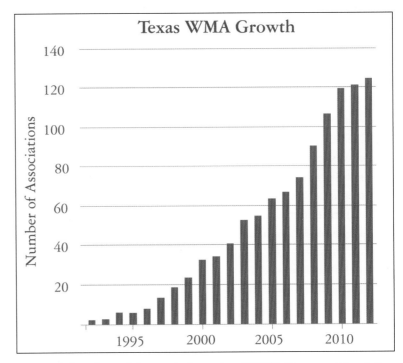

This graph shows the steady increase in the number of Wildlife Management Associations in Texas since the early 1990s. Please note that this chart represents the majority of WMAs, but not all. As private and voluntary associations, data about them are limited (Bailey 2013; Baker 2013; Burch 2013; Campbell 2013; Edwards 2013; Homerstad 2013; Hutchins 2013; Jobes 2013; Lange 2013; Lobpries 2013; Longoria 2013; Pleasant 2013; Siegmund 2013; Texas Parks and Wildlife 2013; Turner 2013; Wagner 2013; White 2013; Witt 2013).

one to every two to three acres. This leaves deer with far less than the ten to fifteen acres of cover and browse that each needs (Lange 2013). With such a large deer population packed into a limited habitat, there have been concerns that both the animals and land will suffer without better management.

Economic Value

These changes in habitat might be more easily ignored if not for the skyrocketing value of wildlife. While many people love nature for its own sake, there is no denying the rising market for wildlife, whether it is for hunting, fishing, or nonconsumptive uses. In fact, while the agricultural value of land has been declining, the leisure price of acreage has risen. By 1998, land's agricultural appraisal had fallen to just 16 percent of its market value (Wagner 1998).

Much of rural land's value is now in its potential for hunting (Wagner 1998). Hunting has indeed become big business in Texas. As of 2006, Texas led all fifty states in the number of hunters (979,000), the amount of spending ($2.2 billion), jobs supported (47,000), and in the size of state and federal tax revenue ($272 and $310 million, respectively) (Adams and Ross 2013; Congressional Sportsmen's Foundation 2008; US Fish and Wildlife Service 2008). In many cases, revenues from hunting leases have begun to outrun income from traditional farming and ranching operations.

Ecotourism for wildlife photography and birding has become another important and rapidly growing business. A 2011 study in the Lower Rio Grande Valley found that nature tourism in just that portion of South Texas contributed $344 million to the local economy (Woosnam 2012). Other research has reported that visits for outdoor experiences are the fastest growing segment of the tourism business, which is already the third largest component in the Texas economy (Lindsay 1996).

Cooperation

A number of converging trends argue for more coordinated and intensive habitat management. The major trends include the high private share of Texas landownership, the growth and movement in the state's population, the decline in tract sizes, the increase in the value of wildlife, and the resurgence of some game populations. Texans have developed a number of tools to do this coordinated work. The approaches have included wildlife management associations, prescribed burn groups, and other landowner organizations. With over 2.5 million acres enrolled in Texas, wildlife management associations (WMAs), originally known as cooperatives, or co-ops, are probably the best-known and largest collaborative effort (Wagner 2013).

Wildlife Management Associations

The origins of WMAs might be traced back, like so many wildlife management ideas, to the noted wildlife biologist Aldo Leopold. Leopold formed a very early association in Wisconsin in 1931, called the Riley Game Cooperative (Silbernagel and Silbernagel 2003). Over time, the idea spread to Texas, where the first WMA began in 1955 and operated in the three-corners region of Bee, Goliad, and Karnes Counties. Named, appropriately, the Tri-County Game Preserve Association, the association had several purposes. Its goals included improving cover and food for wildlife, inventorying game, controlling grazing and stocking rates, planting trees and shrubs, and allowing diverse weeds and forbs to grow. This association was followed in 1973 by the Peach Creek Wildlife Management Co-op, and in 1985 by the Belmont Co-op, both in Gonzalez County (Homerstad 2013).

From this early and small start, WMA chapters spread rapidly across the state. The growth spurt began in 1990 with the organization of associations on Harvey's Creek (in Colorado County) and Caranchua Creek (Jackson County). The next twenty years witnessed the creation of over 185 associations in Texas, as well as a statewide network, the Texas Organization of Wildlife Management Associations (Homerstad 2013; Wagner 2013).

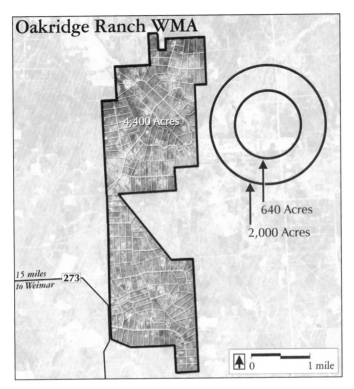

The 4,400-acre Oakridge Ranch Wildlife Management Association is an example of how relatively small tracts (in this case, averaging 25 acres) can be managed for a common goal by a large group of landowners (170, in this instance). The smaller circle represents a square mile (640 acres) of habitat; the larger circle encloses 2,000 acres. This 640–2,000 acre range is considered the average home habitat, or at least a rough figure for management purposes, for a male white-tailed deer in Central and East Texas (Hadash 2013; Hendon 2013; Lange 2013; Maes 2013; Mitchem 2013).

Research

Many new ideas about managing land and wildlife, particularly white-tailed deer, have come out of the joint experience and research of landowners, agency biologists, and academics. The work over the last two generations at the Kerr Wildlife Management Area has been especially helpful. In 1950, the Texas Game, Fish, and Oyster Commission (the predecessor to Texas Parks and Wildlife) acquired the 6,500-acre Kerr tract near Hunt, Texas, in the upper Guadalupe River watershed. By 1954, biologists at Kerr began studying and managing the land and its white-tailed deer herd. In the years since, the work at Kerr has produced a great deal of research on land carrying capacity; habitat management; and deer nutrition, genetics, and behavior (Armstrong and Young 2000).

Teaching

The difficulty has come in spreading these new wildlife management ideas to the many landowners throughout Texas, each with a property that has slightly (or radically) different soils, vegetation, wildlife, and climate. It is a problem of logistics. With about 144 million acres of rural land in Texas, 97 percent of it privately owned, Texas Parks and Wildlife biologists have been stretched thin (Wagner 1998). State biologists have been successful in developing 7,000 wildlife management plans, covering 27 million acres in Texas. However, there is just not enough agency staff or time to give individual landowners enough one-on-one, detailed management advice (Wagner 2013). This is where wildlife management associations have helped. By grouping landowners with similar and nearby lands, the association structure has helped state biologists reach more landowners. Via the WMAs, state biologists have brought like-minded, neighboring landowners together, held joint field days and workshops, and provided a management plan that covers their consolidated association parcels.

Parks and Wildlife biologists have put the experience from Kerr and elsewhere into Managed Land for Deer (MLD) plans for each of the wildlife management association lands. Many MLD plans explain how to provide water, install protein feeders, sow food plots, clear brush stands, defer grazing, conduct burns, plant natives, and take other measures to support deer and other wildlife. The MLD guidelines also serve as the basis for harvesting requirements. Through incentives (bigger bag limits and longer seasons) and targeted hunting regulations, the state's deer herd has been improved. The number of does and genetically inferior spikes have been reduced, while the healthier, larger-rack bucks have been protected and allowed to grow and reproduce for an extra two to three seasons (Lange 2013).

Wildlife

Deer harvest data have shown the impressive gains under modern Texas game laws, especially those worked through the MLD plans and WMA hunting permits. As of 2011, Texas was fourth in the nation among states that have sought to lower the harvest of yearling bucks (21 percent of bucks killed, down from 26 percent in 2001). Texas has also ranked fourth among the fifty states in its efforts to raise the harvest of older bucks. Sixty percent of bucks taken in 2011 were over three and a half years old, up from 48 percent ten years before) (Adams and Ross 2013). This "slot" approach helps protect Texas bucks during their prime reproductive years. Texas hunters have also emphasized doe and spike deer control, reducing the overall herd count, and improving its genetics. This trend has been shown by significant harvest increases for ant-

lerless deer (up 51 percent from 2001 to 2011) (Adams and Ross 2013; Adams, Hamilton, and Ross 2009).

"If you own land in an area where the landownership pattern tends towards small landownerships, and you're interested in wildlife that ranges over more than one landownership, you'd better either join an existing cooperative or be thinking of how you can form a cooperative, and not only paying just lip service to it, but being actively involved in trying to get as much contiguous land into it as possible and developing a good program."
—Al Brothers, 2000

Drawbacks

Despite the success of WMAs in helping manage Texas land and wildlife, there are some remaining cracks in the effort. One major gap involves those who fall outside of the WMA system. For instance, there are perhaps 9 to 10 million acres of land, statewide, that are now under "high fence." These fences are built to be 7 to 8 feet tall, and are designed to keep deer from crossing either in or out (Wagner 2013). As a result, those high-fenced properties cannot be managed together with their traditional, low-fenced neighbors. Other tracts are not engaged with WMAs because their owners or hunting lessees do not care to get involved at the outset, and simply do not join. And there are naturally some WMA members who belong, but as in any vol-

untary organization, choose not to be active, or tire of the work, leaving association chores to others. Finally, WMA involvement can change with the economy, since owning recreational tracts or leasing hunting properties is costly, and people can be forced to drop out just due to financial pressures (Baker 2013).

And for some members and tracts within WMAs, there have been grumblings that a few associations are too focused on white-tailed deer, neglecting other species, the general habitat, and the larger ecosystem issues. Yet supporters point out that the WMAs are grassroots organizations, and their goals simply reflect their members' main interests. Agency officials also note that the excise taxes that deer hunters pay as part of the price of their guns and ammunition are a key source of revenue for Texas Parks and Wildlife. So, indirectly, these hunting taxes do bring funds to benefit the state's other natural resource work. Finally, in some areas, deer are the only major game species that remain, since turkey and quail may have disappeared due to habitat changes (Siegmund 2013).

Nevertheless, some WMAs are evolving beyond a pure focus on deer. There are many associations that now have active programs in bird surveys, cowbird trapping, river otter research, butterfly plantings, native grass restoration, game warden assistance, and feral hog control, reflecting the interests of their members (Baker 2013; Lange 2013).

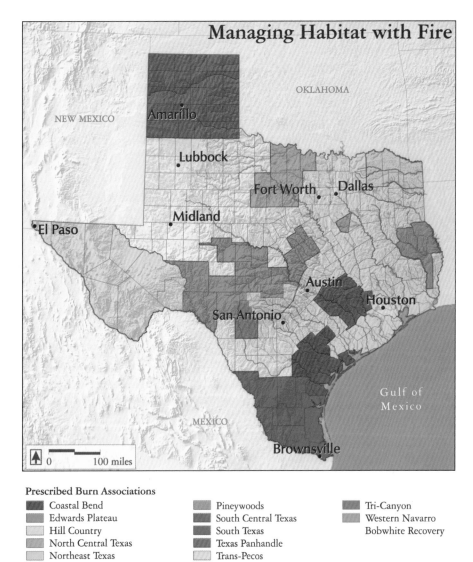

Managing Habitat with Fire

Prescribed Burn Associations
- Coastal Bend
- Edwards Plateau
- Hill Country
- North Central Texas
- Northeast Texas
- Pineywoods
- South Central Texas
- South Texas
- Texas Panhandle
- Trans-Pecos
- Tri-Canyon
- Western Navarro Bobwhite Recovery

The Prescribed Burn Alliance of Texas includes twelve regional associations that help property owners, land managers, extension agents, and contractors in over 110 Texas counties collaborate in using fire to manage habitat (Prescribed Burn Alliance 2013).

Offspring

WMAs' useful role in helping deer, as well as otters, birds, and butterflies, has spawned other efforts in cooperative land management. For instance, in 2012, the Prescribed Burn Alliance of Texas was formed, pulling together twelve multicounty burn associations. The landowners in those associations realized that reintroducing fire to their local landscapes could reduce dangerous wildfire fuel loads, control woody and invasive species, improve water yields, and upgrade wildlife habitats. However, they also understood that managing fire is a hazardous undertaking. They needed their neighbors' help—for advice, volunteer manpower, and borrowed equipment—to make prescribed burns work well, and work safely.

Wildlife management associations grew up, in many parts of the state, due to the problems of having too many deer, more than the habitat could sustain. Other cooperative groups have arisen from the opposite problem. One such organization is the Wildlife Habitat Federation, which recognized the decline in bobwhite quail, Attwater's prairie chickens, and other grassland birds in Texas. The federation linked landowners in the Lower Colorado River basin to rebuild native prairie corridors that would tie in with the Attwater Prairie Chicken National Wildlife Refuge (Willis 2009). Again, as with the wildlife co-ops and burn associations, the federation benefited from the common experience, volunteered time, and shared gear to see their dream come to life (Willis 2013).

Social Capital

Collaborative landowner groups can be described by tallying the number of acres enrolled, miles surveyed, pounds of seed planted, and animals harvested. The associations can also be seen in terms of their organizational work—the raffle tickets sold, barbeque meals served, doe tags distributed, meetings convened, and presentations

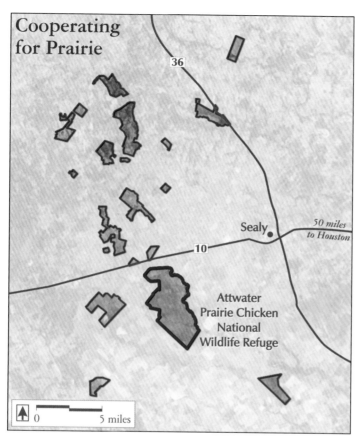

Cooperating for Prairie

36

Sealy

50 miles
to Houston

10

Attwater
Prairie Chicken
National
Wildlife Refuge

0   5 miles

*The Wildlife Habitat Federation has joined a number of private landowners
in a collaborative effort to restore native prairie and the wildlife that depend
on grasslands. This map shows the Attwater Prairie Chicken National Wildlife
Refuge, along with the private tracts participating in the federation's effort, as
of August 2011 (Willis 2013).*

shown. However, these associations' most important asset may be harder to see and touch and understand—their social capital (Wagner 2005).

This social capital is measured in the mutual trust, common values, and shared goals held by members of the associations. Mutual trust is important in any group, but it is essential for long-term neighbors who must deal with natural resources that are commonly held. Members of a landowner group may be separated by fences and legal metes and bounds, but they will always feel the impact of each other's decisions about local habitat and wildlife. The birds and animals do not respect property boundaries! Nor do the impacts of a go-it-alone neighbor. Landowners are always vulnerable to the free-rider problem, to the neighbor who overuses and degrades a common resource. Without trust and mutual compromise, greed can lead to abuse and collapse of a shared resource, in a remorseless process known as the "tragedy of the commons" (Hardin 1968).

These ideas about cooperation are especially relevant now. The modern age of "bowling alone" has seen many social networks fray and many communal efforts stumble. In these times, landowners' mutual support for introducing neighbors, sharing ideas, organizing joint efforts, and building social capital has become all the more important (Putnam 2000). In fact, the "bowling alone" problem may be particularly acute in the countryside. Many rural tracts are owned by absentees (perhaps as many as 75,000 urban Texans own at least 100 acres in a rural county), or are leased to nonlocal tenants who have no close tie to the community (Schmidly 2002). Associations may help unite neighbors over shared natural resource concerns, but more importantly, may also join larger communities together for a variety of common issues. In a sense, these cooperative groups may have started as a way to help land, water, deer, and other animals, but may have come full circle to aid people as well.

Sources

Adams, Kip, and Matt Ross. 2013.
    "QDMA Whitetail Report 2013."
    Quality Deer Management Association.
    http://www.qdma.com/ uploads/pdf/
    WR2013.pdf, accessed April 17, 2013.
Adams, Kip, Joe Hamilton, and Matt
    Ross. 2009. "QDMA Whitetail Report

2009." Quality Deer Management Association. http://www.qdma.com/uploads/pdf/WhitetailReport09.pdf, accessed April 17, 2013.

Armstrong, W. E., and E. L. Young. 2000. "White-Tailed Deer Management in the Texas Hill Country." *Texas Parks and Wildlife* (September).

Bailey, Heidi. 2013. Wildlife Biologist for Anderson County, Texas Parks and Wildlife. Personal communication, April.

Baker, Bob. 2013. Wildlife Biologist for Hardin County, Texas Parks and Wildlife. Personal communication, April.

Brothers, Al. 2000. Oral history interview conducted February 22, in Berclair, Texas. Texas Legacy Project, Conservation History Association of Texas. http://www.texaslegacy.org/, accessed April 17, 2013.

Burch, Cristy. 2013. GIS/TWIMS Specialist, Texas Parks and Wildlife. Personal communications, April and May.

———. 2015. Regional GIS Specialist, Texas Parks and Wildlife. Personal communication, March.

Campbell, Linda. 2013. Program Director, Private Lands and Public Hunting. Texas Parks and Wildlife. Personal communications, April and May.

Chavez, Carmen. 2015. Property Tax Assistance, Texas Comptroller of Public Accounts. Personal communication, March.

Congressional Sportsmen's Foundation. 2008. Hunting and Fishing: Bright Stars of the American Economy. http://www.pafop114.0rg/images/CompleteReport_hunt_fish.pdf, accessed April 14, 2013.

Edwards, James. 2013. Wildlife Biologist for Comanche and Hamilton County, Texas Parks and Wildlife. Personal communication, April.

Graves, Russel. 2004. "Deer World." *Texas Parks and Wildlife* (December).

Hadash, Diane. 2013. Data Entry and Mapping, Colorado County Appraisal District. Personal communication, April.

Hardin, Garrett. 1968. "The Tragedy of the Commons." *Science* 162 (3859): 1243–48.

Hendon, Blake. 2013. Wildlife Biologist for Blanco, Lampasas, San Saba, and Coryell Counties. Texas Parks and Wildlife. Personal communication, April.

Higginbotham, Billy. 1999. "Conservation and Management of the White-Tailed Deer: An East Texas Perspective." Pages II-D-21 to II-D-31. Proceedings of the Symposium on Deer Management. Texas Agricultural Extension Service. September 21–23. College Station, Texas.

Homerstad, Gary. 2013. Retired Wildlife Biologist, Texas Parks and Wildlife. Personal communication, April.

Hutchins, Ashton. 2013. Wildlife Biologist for Dimmit County, Texas Parks and Wildlife. Personal communication, April.

Jobes, Doug. 2013. Wildlife Biologist for Lavaca County, Texas Parks and Wildlife. Personal communication, April.

Lange, Mark. 2013. Wildlife Biologist for Colorado County, Texas Parks and Wildlife. Personal communication, April.

———. 2015. Wildlife Biologist for Colorado County, Texas Parks and

Wildlife. Personal communication, March.

Lindsay, Madge. 1996. The Great Texas Coastal Birding Trail: A Tool for Avitourism. Texas Parks and Wildlife. http://www.birds.cornell.edu/pifcapemay/lindsay.htm, accessed June 27, 2013.

Lobpries, David. 2013. Wildlife Biologist for Fort Bend County, Texas Parks and Wildlife. Personal communication, April.

Longoria, Meredith. 2013. Wildlife Biologist for Bastrop and Caldwell Counties, Texas Parks and Wildlife. Personal communication, April.

Maes, Robert. 2013. Appraiser, Colorado County Appraisal District. Personal communication, April.

Mitchem, David. 2013. Whitetail Deer Chairperson, Oakridge Wildlife Management Association. Personal communication, April.

Pleasant, Greg. 2013. Wildlife Biologist for Fayette and Lee Counties, Texas Parks and Wildlife. Personal communication, April.

Prescribed Burn Alliance. 2013. Counties in Each Prescribed Burn Association. http://pbatexas.org/Associations.aspx, accessed May 14, 2013.

Putnam, Robert. 2000. *Bowling Alone: The Collapse and Revival of American Community*. New York: Simon and Schuster.

Real Estate Center. 2013. "Outlook for Texas Land Markets: Texas Rural Land." Texas A&M University. http://recenter.tamu.edu/data/rland/, accessed April 17, 2013.

Schmidly, David. 2002. *Texas Natural History: A Century of Change*. Lubbock: Texas Tech University Press.

Siegmund, Tim. 2013. Wildlife Biologist for Brazos and Burleson Counties, Texas Parks and Wildlife. Personal communication, April.

Silbernagel, Bob, and Janet Silbernagel. 2003. "Tracking Aldo Leopold through Riley's Farmland: Remembering the Riley Game Cooperative." *Wisconsin Magazine of History* (Summer).

Smeins, Fred, Sam Fuhlendorf, and Charles Taylor Jr. 2013. "Environmental and Land Use Changes: A Long-Term Perspective." Texas Natural Resources Server. texnat.tamu.edu/library/symposia/juniper-ecology-and-management/environmental-and-land-use-changes-a-long-term-perspective/, accessed June 27, 2013.

Texas A&M Institute of Renewable Natural Resources, American Farmland Trust. 2008. Texas Land Trends. http://texaslandtrends.org/10yrtrends.aspx, accessed April 14, 2013.

Texas Organization of Wildlife Management Associations. 2013. "Our History." http://www.towma.org/our_history.html, accessed April 15, 2013.

Texas Parks and Wildlife. 2008. A Guide for Wildlife Management Associations and Co-Ops. Texas Parks and Wildlife, Making Tracts for Texas Wildlife, Private Lands and Habitat Program. http://www.tpwd.state.tx.us/publications/pwdpubs/media/pwd_bk_w7000_0336.pdf, accessed April 13, 2013.

———. 2013. Map of Wildlife Management Associations. http://www.tpwd.state.tx.us/landwater/land/associations/, accessed April 17, 2013.

Turner, Joshua. 2013. Wildlife Biologist for DeWitt County, Texas Parks and Wildlife. Personal communication, April.

US Census. 2012. Statistical Abstract of the United States, Section 17, Agriculture. http://www.census.gov/prod/2011pubs/12statab/agricult.pdf, accessed May 27, 2013.

US Fish and Wildlife Service. 2008. 2006 National Survey of Fishing, Hunting, and Wildlife-Associated Recreation: Texas. FHW/06-TX. May. http://www.census.gov/prod/2008pubs/fhw06-tx.pdf, accessed April 17, 2013.

Wagner, Matt. 1998. "Land Fragmentation in Texas: Meeting the Challenge." *Texas Parks and Wildlife.*

———. 2005. "Wildlife and Water: Collective Action and Social Capital of Selected Landowner Associations in Texas." PhD diss., Texas A&M University.

———. 2013. Deputy Director, Wildlife Division. Texas Parks and Wildlife. Personal communication, April.

Weniger, Del. 1984. *The Explorer's Texas: The Lands and Waters*. Austin: Eakin Press.

White, Ragan. 2013. Wildlife Biologist for Fannin County, Texas Parks and Wildlife. Personal communication, April.

Wilkins, N., R. D. Brown, J. R. Conner, J. Engle, C. Gilliland, A. Hays, R. D. Slack, and D. W. Steinbach. 2000. "Fragmented Lands: Changing Land Ownership in Texas." Technical booklet 15M 9/00. Texas A&M University, College Station.

Willis, Jim. 2009. Founder, Wildlife Habitat Federation. Personal communications, January–October.

———. 2015. Founder, Wildlife Habitat Federation. Personal communication, March.

Witt, Brendon. 2013. Wildlife Biologist for Gonzales and Guadalupe Counties, Texas Parks and Wildlife. Personal communication, April.

Woosnam, K. M., S. An, K. D. Aleshinloye, R. M. Dudensing, and W. Hanselka. 2012. "What's the Value of Nature Tourism in the Lower Rio Grande Valley of Texas?" Texas A&M University, College Station. March.

Wildlife, Land, and Taxes

This is a story of an odd couple—taxes and wildlife. They are a peculiar pair, but seem to have gotten along well in Texas, successfully wedding private property interests and public conservation goals. Much of the plot here has to do with the rather arcane world of ad valorem tax appraisals for rural land, and how those appraisals were adjusted to encourage better wildlife management.

Inflation and Sprawl

The story starts in the post–World War II era, as the American currency started to inflate, and urban centers began to sprawl into the surrounding countryside. As a consequence, rural lands began to go up in price. From 1945 to 1965, US farmland nearly doubled in value, rising from an average of $56/acre to $109, in constant 1960 dollars (Lindert 1988). The increase was far faster for lands near the growing metropolitan areas. At the same time, food prices paid to farmers were declining by about 1 percent per year (Gardner 2010). Facing this squeeze between taxes and income, many farmers and ranchers found it increasingly difficult to afford their property taxes based on the land's market value.

Rural Exodus

During this same period, agriculture became more mechanized and less labor intensive. Jobs tilling soil or herding livestock dried up. Fewer people remained on farms and ranches. Meanwhile, urban factories were booming, beckoning many Texans to leave the countryside and come to the cities. The number of Texas farmers declined by 34 percent from 1935 to 1950 (Bureau of the Census 1952, 5). In 1950, for the first time, the census reported that more Texans were living in the state's cities than in its rural areas (US Census 1995).

Government Services

As the number of agricultural workers dwindled, there were fewer people living on the land and needing town and county government services. Government's cost for rural education (cows don't go to school), fire protection, police work, and other services fell. With time, farmers and ranchers put less burden on local governments. In a nationwide series of studies, the American Farmland Trust found that for every dollar raised in property taxes on ranch or farm acreage, the rural property owner got back far less in public services than his or her suburban counterpart. For example, in Hays County, Hill Country farmers and ranchers received just 33 cents for every local tax dollar they paid in, while residential owners collected $1.26 for every dollar of tax they paid (American Farmland Trust 1999).

Tax Burdens

The mid-twentieth century concern about agricultural land taxes in Texas was not just about dollars and cents. There was also worry that the tradition and culture of rural life were at risk. Some feared that escalating land values and taxes would force ranching and farming families to quit their businesses, sell and break up their land, and leave their communities, taking their folkways and cultural legacy with them (Frentress 2000).

Constitutional Amendments

Out of this background, efforts grew to protect Texas farming and ranching communities and their way of life. There was also pressure to recognize the lower demands that agricultural families put on local government. As a result, property tax structures began to change in Texas. In 1966, Texas voters amended Article VIII of the Texas Constitution, approving an "agricultural appraisal" for property (Texas Proposition 1, 1966). The amended language, "Section 1-d," required county appraisers to assess land differently than before.

Under the Section 1-d approach, appraisers were expected to drop their old assessment process, where a piece of land would be valued based on the amount of money that might get generated from an outright sale of that land. Instead, counties were told to look at the amount of revenue that was actually created from farming or grazing a given piece of land. In other words, appraisers were directed to price the land based on the productive, not the market, value of agricultural land. In the end, these Section 1-d appraisals often provided a deep, 90+ percent discount from market values to use in calculating ad valorem taxes for Texas farmers and ranchers.

In 1978, Texans approved another change ("Section 1-d-1") to the state constitution (Texas Proposition 1, Tax Relief and Reform, 1978). The new amendment extended these reduced appraisal values from just land owned by individuals to also include tracts that were held by partnerships and corporations. Texas voters also agreed to provide discounted appraisals for land owned by those who were not primarily farmers or ranchers.

Even after the amendments of 1966 and 1978, some open, undeveloped lands were still ineligible for the reduced 1-d-1 appraisals. The discount still required that the landowners raise crops or livestock. The property owners needed to show the appraisers that the land had some traditional agricultural use.

Hunting and Fishing

In the years following the 1960s and 1970s, new changes came to the Texas countryside. Rural land use began to shift. More and more open space was being devoted to raising deer, quail, and wild turkey, and less and less to raising cotton, corn, cows, and sheep. More land was used for leisure, and less for commodities. Tim Hixon, a former Texas Parks and Wildlife commissioner, put it this way: "there aren't any ranches in Texas sold today as ranches. They're all sold as hunting places and that's the way of the world right now" (Hixon 2006).

This new kind of recreational use was becoming more popular and

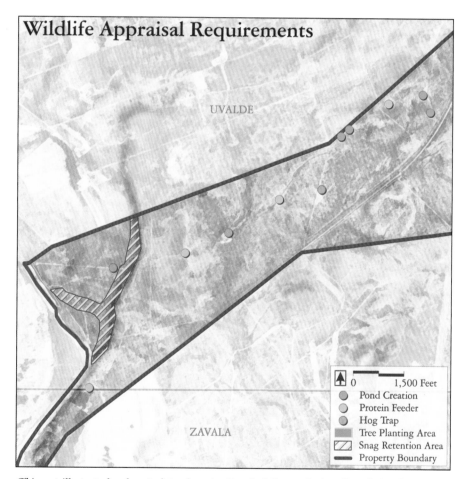

This map illustrates brush control, pond construction, food plots, and other efforts designed to "propagate breeding, migrating, or wintering populations of indigenous wild animals," as required for a successful wildlife management appraisal (Olenick 2012).

more diverse. The new uses certainly involved hunting but also encompassed fishing, birding, and other outdoor pastimes. Plus, this recreation on the land grew to have great financial value. Outdoor fun was generating a good deal of income for Texans, as well as a tax base for the state. Former Parks and Wildlife commissioner Nacho Garza explained: "What is it worth? A billion, two billion a year to the state of Texas. Ecotourism has grown and is the fastest growing . . . segment of the tourism industry in Texas. It is people just coming to view birds, or to hunt or to fish in Texas, or to hike and bike in Texas" (Garza 2000). The income from this "nature tourism" was reflected in Texas land values. For example, in Kleberg County (where the King Ranch is based), a whopping 42 percent of the land's market value was attributed to hunting and outdoor recreation in 1996 (Baen 1997; Garza 2012). Landowners felt that these new wildlife uses, values, and revenues should be given the same protection that had benefited earlier, more agricultural economies.

Conservation

With time, Texas environmentalists joined in to lobby for a change to rural land taxes. Advocates for habitat recognized that many landowners wanted to protect land and wildlife, but could not set aside property without jeopardizing their discounted tax valuations. Perversely,

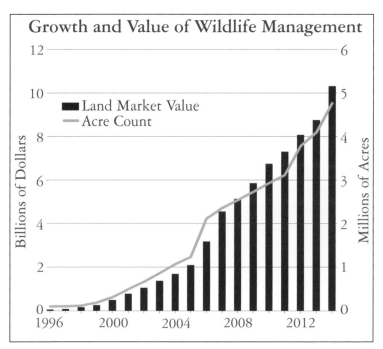

The chart shows the growth of the acreage and market value of Texas land held in the wildlife management program. Acreage in the program included 92,000 acres, with a market price of $31.9 million, in 1997. By 2014, the program had increased to cover more than 4.7 million acres, with a value of over $10.3 billion (Albright 2012; Chavez 2015).

they might have to graze or farm their land simply to maintain its "1-d-1" tax status, regardless of drought, erosion, or other concerns. And from a bottom-line approach, conservation groups reasoned that it was cheaper to have private landowners hold the land and manage the public's wildlife than for the government to carry the cost (Armentrout 1999). Plus, there was recognition that these private land holdings were both immense (some 95–97 percent of open space in Texas) and increasingly precarious. For instance, from 1982 to 2010, over 4.1 million acres of Texas farms, ranches, and timberlands were devel-

oped and converted to other uses (US Department of Agriculture 2013). Texas' population was booming, and there were calculations that each new set of 1,000 residents in the state resulted in the loss of 149 acres of open space (Texas A&M Institute of Renewable Natural Resources 2009).

As a result of these landowner and conservation concerns, the state legislature passed a law in 1991 to acknowledge these changes and extend special valuations to wildlife management (Acts 1991, 72nd Leg., Ch. 560, Sec. 1, eff. January 1, 1992). However, this law raised constitutional concerns with the

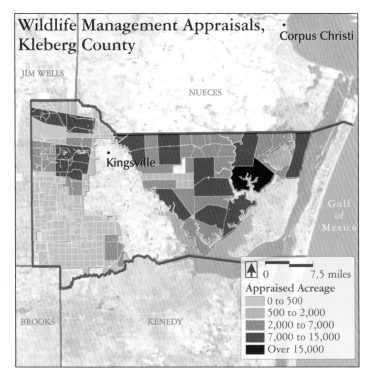

Wildlife Management Appraisals, Kleberg County

JIM WELLS

NUECES

Corpus Christi

Kingsville

BROOKS

KENEDY

Gulf of Mexico

0   7.5 miles

Appraised Acreage
0 to 500
500 to 2,000
2,000 to 7,000
7,000 to 15,000
Over 15,000

Wildlife management appraisals have been popular in hunting areas, such as South Texas. This map shows participating parcels in Kleberg County. Kleberg County has seen more land (over 415,000 acres) set aside for wildlife management than any other county in Texas. Some Kleberg school districts, including Riviera and Santa Gertrudis, have very high participation, with over 44 percent of land, by value, held under a wildlife appraisal (Garza 2012).

Texas attorney general's office, and so the issue was sent to the public for ratification (Ramsey 1996). In 1995, Texans duly went to the voting booth and approved Proposition 11, amending Article VIII, Section 1-d-1 of the Texas Constitution (Texas Proposition 11, 1995). This proposition allowed use of the agricultural land appraisal for properties used to manage wildlife. Coming into force in 1997, House Bill 1358 carried through on the proposition and constitutional amendment by permitting wildlife management to be seen as a

type of agricultural use that would qualify for the discounted appraisal.

Muddle and Fraud

Confusion, and some abuses, arose under the first rules for wildlife management valuations. As David Langford of the Texas Wildlife Association explained, "we found appraisal districts that were not allowing it and giving people grief about applying for it. And we found people on the other end, trying to hang hummingbird feeders and move to the

Cayman Islands and get a tax break, and that wasn't intended either" (Langford 2006). So, in 2001, the state legislature passed H.B. 3123, creating a more structured approach for qualifying agricultural lands for wildlife management use (Texas Tax Code Chapter 23, Subchapter D, and Texas Administrative Code, Chapter 9, Subchapter F).

Rules and Standards

The new standards for wildlife management were quite explicit. They required that qualifying lands "propagate a sustaining, breeding, migrating, or wintering population of indigenous wild animals for human use, including food, medicine or recreation." Landowners had to implement at least three of seven management approaches toward those wildlife goals. The management practices could include controlling habitat, erosion, or predators; supplementing water or food supplies; providing shelters; or making census counts (Texas Comptroller 2007; Texas Tax Code 23.51(2,7)).

Acres

As the program and standards have become better known and understood, use of the wildlife management valuation has grown rapidly in the state. Participating acreage now covers more than 4.7 million acres (Chavez 2015). To give a sense of the huge impact of the wildlife appraisals, its affected acreage amounts to over eight times the 586,000 acres protected by all Texas state parks, historic sites, and natural areas (Texas Comptroller 2012). Without doubt, the wildlife management tax program has helped many landowners afford to keep key habitat intact and wild populations flourishing.

Costs

However, the cost to the public cannot be ignored. The value of the discount is large, and is significant to the school districts and counties that rely on ad valorem taxes. For example, Texas lands within the wildlife program are worth, on the market, $10.3 billion, and the discount for wildlife management amounts to a whopping 97 percent of that value (Chavez 2015). Advocates for the program argue that the wildlife program is revenue neutral, since these lands were originally protected under the livestock and crop appraisals. Still, the cost does make it important that wildlife management be carefully and professionally done, to make sure that the public stake is protected.

Benefits?

It is unclear whether these generous tax discounts are always merited by every parcel's wildlife management activities. There may be some that abuse the system. For instance, Texas Parks and Wildlife standards only require three activities to qualify for

A white-tailed deer poses in the Hill Country of Texas. Will smaller, yet tax-advantaged, parcels protect enough habitat for deer and other wide-ranging animals? (Huntingdesigns 2013).

the discount (Texas Parks and Wildlife 2010, appendix A). While sometimes just the single act of removing livestock from a tract can have a huge habitat benefit, it seems that more proactive efforts could be expected, beyond de minimis fire ant poisoning and bird-house hanging. Could the state ask for more in return for these valuable tax benefits?

Also, there have been ongoing worries about how these management activities, whether they are three, four, or more, are reviewed and approved. There are continuing anecdotes about hostility to the entire 1-d-1 program among some of the more traditionally

agricultural appraisal districts. Some appraisal districts have reputedly rejected wildlife appraisal applications without good cause. These concerns are underscored by the fact that only a handful of the 254 Texas appraisal districts have biologists on staff who are trained to review the validity of wildlife management projects (Braun 2012).

Fragmentation Risk

There are other questions about the appraisals, beyond how well or poorly they are conducted. Some critics have raised broader policy concerns about

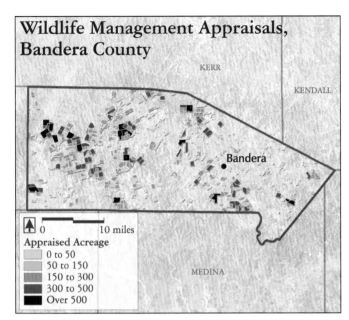

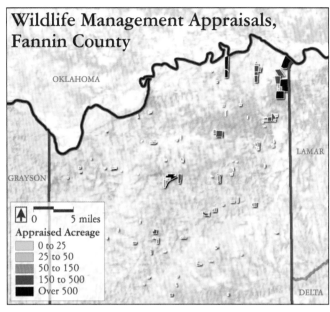

These maps of Bandera and Fannin Counties show how wildlife management appraisals are often used for smaller tracts. This seems especially true for counties that ring major metropolitan areas (Bandera County sits about 25 miles to the northwest of San Antonio, while Fannin County is about 40 miles northeast of Dallas). There are differences though in the impact of these appraisals in cases where tracts under the 1-d-1 program are more (see Bandera County) or less clustered (as in Fannin County) (Garcia 2012; Grams 2012; Kinnaird 2012).

wildlife valuation. For instance, there is a possibility that the wildlife management program has indirectly encouraged fragmentation of large farms and ranches, reducing their value as big-scale habitat (Olenick 2012). The argument is hard to confirm, but goes like this: typically, those with the capital to buy rural land are urban dwellers, and they often do not have enough experience or interest to successfully raise crops or livestock on their own. So, if a large tract were sold to them, they would be reluctant to buy a tract of less than perhaps 100–200 acres. Otherwise, the proud new gentleman or lady farmer would find that his or her new ranch was too small to attract a rural neighbor who would be willing to lease the land for cultivation or for grazing. Of course, under the old, pre-wildlife-valuation regime, a tract without cows or crops would lose its low agricultural appraisal and taxes. The owner would be very disappointed.

However, wildlife management laws now allow subdivision to tracts as small as 12.5 acres (or even as little as 4 acres in isolated, litigated cases). At those small sizes, there are few tenants who would be willing to lease the property for agricultural uses (Grayson CAD 2012; Redmon and Cathey undated). It simply would not be worth their time. However, the wildlife appraisal program might allow the new weekend rancher to avoid the trouble of leasing a small tract of land and simply manage it for wildlife without much local help. In that way, the wildlife tax discount might make it more feasible to subdivide, sell, and manage smaller tracts of land.

On the other hand, the wildlife appraisal minimums of 12.5 to 33.3 acres (they vary with the region of the state) may actually have saved large tracts from even more aggressive subdivision (Texas Administrative Code, Sections 9.2002 and 9.2005). By helping create a "ranchette" market of small yet still rural parcels, the wildlife appraisal program may have discouraged the breakup of ranches and farms down to even smaller, one-quarter- to 1-acre suburban lots. In so doing, the wildlife set-asides of 12.5-acre or

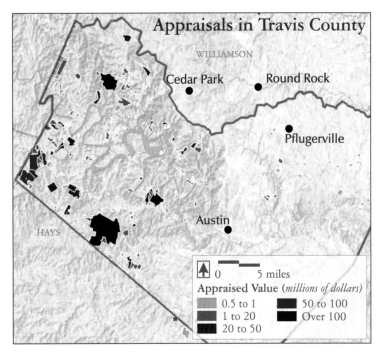

This map shows that, within Travis County, parcels in the wildlife management program are concentrated in the Hill Country toward the western half of the county. Nevertheless, it is not clear that all the wildlife that needs management and protection is so tipped toward the western part of the county (Cortez 2012; Herrera 2015; Michalski 2015).

High Fences

Another issue that has come up is that wildlife appraisals are available for high-fenced tracts, where wildlife, particularly deer, cannot move in and out of the property. Some have challenged the fairness of offering public tax discounts to these parcels, since the tracts offer little public benefit to state wildlife that wander outside of those fences. Defenders might argue that there is indeed a public benefit, although not directly provided to the state's free-roaming wildlife. Supporters might say that the public gain comes from jobs sustained, supplies purchased, and taxes paid by the operators of the high-fenced ranches.

Scenery

The 1-d-1 wildlife use program has also taken its share of criticism on account of where it has been applied. The use of wildlife appraisals sometimes appears to hinge more on a given tract's appeal to their human owners rather than on the parcel's importance to the animals and plants that might be native there. For example, as the map of Travis County shows, wildlife appraisals are much more common in the Hill Country to the west of Austin, and are less frequently found in the Blackland Prairie to the east of Austin (Cortez 2012). People may prefer the hilly vistas and limestone creeks on the west side of Travis County, but does that part of the county really have more intrinsic ecological value than

larger lots may be due some credit for limiting the habitat loss, water pollution, traffic, and costly infrastructure investments associated with more intense development.

All this discussion about the size of an individual parcel in wildlife use may not be so relevant if a small tract were grouped with other, nearby tracts. Consider the cases of Bandera and Fannin Counties (Garcia 2012; Grams 2012; Kinnaird 2012). Both counties have a number of small properties in wildlife management, but their situations are different. In Bandera County, half of the parcels in the wildlife program have fewer than 28 acres, while

in Fannin County, half of its wildlife tracts have fewer than 34 acres. To that degree, they are much the same. Yet while the two counties are quite similar in their 1-d-1 tracts' median acreage, the effect on the ground is very different. In Bandera County the small tracts are clustered together, while in Fannin County, the small tracts are scattered and isolated. If the adjoining tracts in Bandera County can be managed cooperatively, through wildlife management associations or in other, more informal ways, these small tracts may jointly have greater habitat value than those in Fannin County. Size is not everything!

the county's east side? How does one compare an endangered Hill Country cave insect with a rare prairie forb from east of IH-35? Is tax policy biasing the kinds of ecosystems that get protected and restored?

Absentees

Aside from issues about animals and plants, critics of the wildlife management valuations have also had some trouble with the social and political effects on the host counties. They have been concerned that the program raises absentee landownership in rural areas. In earlier days, when a landowner had to run livestock or grow crops to qualify for the discounted agricultural appraisal, many "city slickers" might have decided it was not worth the tractor and the trouble to have a weekend place in the country. However, if a wildlife appraisal is available, without acres to plow or cows to chase, then it becomes more feasible and affordable for an urban owner to buy and, from time to time, visit a country place. If more city people decide to follow this route, some worry that small rural towns may have more neighbors who are like passing tourists, and fewer rooted, resident families to run local businesses, attend local schools, and manage local governments and associations.

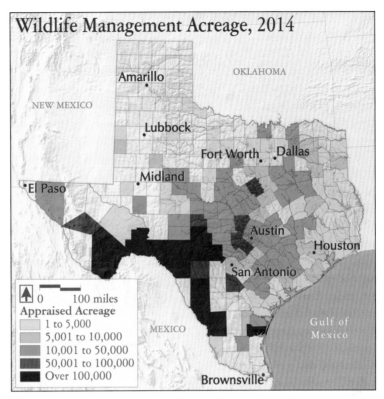

The 1-d-1 wildlife program has been popular statewide, but has not been evenly used in all ecosystems. This map shows the distribution of acreage appraised for wildlife management, as of 2011, by county (Albright 2012; Chavez 2015).

Taxes, Wildlife, and Lessons

These questions about management activities, fragmentation effects, absentee ownership, and ecosystem bias are hard to resolve. The Texas 1-d-1 program is young, and there are many factors involved. Still it appears that the 1-d-1 wildlife management appraisal brings significant conservation benefits that are tough to deny. Some of the changes are tangible, with cattle pens replaced with martin houses, hayfields with food plots, and livestock with wildlife. However, some of the changes

are more subtle and maybe surprising, as landowners begin by focusing on tax law nuances and end up learning and caring more about the state's natural habitats (Braun 2012).

Sources

American Farmland Trust. 1999. Cost of Community Services: The Value of Farm and Ranch Land in Hays County, TX. http://www.farmland.org/programs/states/documents/AFT_COCS_HaysCounty_Texas.pdf, accessed November 25, 1999.

Armentrout, Dede. 1999. Oral history interview conducted on June 22, in San Marcos, Texas. Texas Legacy Project, Conservation History Association of Texas. http://www.texaslegacy.org, accessed May 30, 2015.

Baen, J. S. 1997. "The Growing Importance and Value Implications of Recreational Hunting Leases to Agricultural Land Investors." *Journal of Real Estate Research* 14: 399–414.

Braun, David. 2012. Founder and CEO, Plateau Land and Wildlife Management. Personal communication, December.

Bureau of the Census. 1952. US Census of Agriculture: 1950, vol. 1, part 26, Counties and State Economic Areas: Texas. Table 5: Farm Operators by Color, Residence, Off-Farm Work, Age, and Years on Present Farm: Censuses of 1920 to 1950. Bureau of the Census, US Department of Commerce. Washington, DC: US Government Printing Office.

Chavez, Carmen. 2015. Property Tax Assistance, Texas Comptroller of Public Accounts. Personal communication, March.

Cortez, Oralia. 2012. Information Technology Support Specialist, Travis County Appraisal District. Personal communications, November and December.

Frentress, Carl. 2000. Oral history interview conducted on October 25, in Athens, Texas. Texas Legacy Project, Conservation History Association of Texas. http://www.texaslegacy.org, accessed May 30, 2015.

Garcia, Maria. 2012. Senior Appraiser, Bandera County Appraisal District. Personal communication, December.

Gardner, Bruce. 2010. "U.S. Agriculture in the Twentieth Century." Economic History Association. http://eh.net/encyclopedia/article/gardner.agriculture.us, accessed November 28, 2012.

Garza, Anita. 2012. Agricultural Appraiser/Mapper. Kleberg County Appraisal District. Personal communications, November and December.

Garza, Nacho. 2000. Oral history interview conducted on February 28, in Brownsville, Texas. Texas Legacy Project, Conservation History Association of Texas. http://www.texaslegacy.org, accessed May 30, 2015.

Grams, Wendy. 2012. Chief Appraiser, Bandera County Appraisal District. Personal communications, November and December.

Grayson Central Appraisal District. 2012. Guidelines and Requirements for Agricultural Appraisal Qualification. http://www.graysonappraisal.org/Tax_Info/PDF_links/Guidelines%20&%20Requirements%20for%20Agricultural%20Appraisal%20Qualification.pdf, accessed December 15, 2012.

Herrera, Amie. 2015. IT Support Specialist, Travis Central Appraisal District. Personal communication, March.

Hixon, Tim. 2006. Oral history interview conducted on February 15, in San Antonio, Texas. Texas Legacy Project, Conservation History Association of Texas. http://www.texaslegacy.org, accessed May 30, 2015.

Huntingdesigns. 2013. Hill Country white-tailed deer. Photograph. Digital image. Flickr, Creative Commons. http://www.flickr.com/photos/huntingdesigns/4074051882/sizes/o/in/photostream/, accessed January 31, 2013.

Kinnaird, Mark. 2012. Public Information Officer, Fannin County Appraisal District. Personal communications, November and December.

Langford, David. 2006. Oral history interview conducted on February 13, in San Antonio, Texas. Texas Legacy Project, Conservation History Association of Texas. http://www.texaslegacy.org, accessed May 30, 2015.

Lindert, Peter. 1988. "Long-Run Trends in American Farmland Values." Working Paper 45. Agricultural History Center, University of California at Davis.

Michalski, Richard. 2015. Land/Agriculture and Residential Manager, Travis Appraisal District. Personal communication, March.

Olenick, Keith. 2012. Principal and Senior Biologist, Landmark Wildlife Management. Personal communication, November.

Ramsey, Charles W. 1996. "A Tax Incentive to Encourage Wildlife Management: The Texas Example." Presented at the 8th Triennial National Wildlife and Fisheries Extension Specialists Conference (1996). http://digitalcommons.unl.edu/cgi/viewcontent.cgi?article=1039&context=ewfsc8, accessed November 26, 2012.

Redmon, Larry, and James Cathey. Undated. "Wildlife Management and Property Tax Valuations." AgriLife Extension, Texas A&M System.

Texas A&M Institute of Renewable Natural Resources and American Farmland Trust. 2009. Texas Land Trends. http://irnr.tamu.edu/media/233178/texas_land_trends.pdf, accessed November 25, 2012.

Texas Comptroller. 2007. "Guidelines for Qualification of Agricultural Land in Wildlife Management Use." http://

www.window.state.tx.us/taxinfo/
proptax/agrland/, accessed November
23, 2012.
———. 2012. "Texas State Parks: Natural
Economic Assets." http://www.window
.state.tx.us/specialrpt/parks/overview.
html, accessed November 26, 2012.
Texas Parks and Wildlife. 2010. Wildlife
Management Activities and Practices:
Comprehensive Wildlife Management

Planning Guidelines. Revised April
2010. Texas Parks and Wildlife.
Austin, Texas.
US Census. 1995. Urban and Rural
Population: 1900 to 1990. Release
October 1995. US Census Bureau.
US Department of Commerce. https://
www.census.gov/population/census
data/urpop0090.txt, accessed August
28, 2014.

US Department of Agriculture. 2013.
Summary Report: 2010 National
Resources Inventory, Natural
Resources Conservation Service,
Washington, DC, and Center for
Survey Statistics and Methodology,
Iowa State University, Ames, Iowa.
http://www.nrcs.usda.gov/Internet/
FSE_DOCUMENTS/stel
prdb1167354.pdf.

The iconic Panhandle rancher, trailblazer, and former Texas Ranger, Charles Goodnight, is shown here flanked by a buffalo bull. Goodnight is simultaneously known for rescuing the last of the southern bison and helping introduce their main successor, the cow (Panhandle-Plains Historical Museum 2013; Stricker 2013).

The Fall and Rise of the American Bison

A Crooked-Backed Oxen

An odd sight struck sixteenth-century explorers of the Americas. They saw a new and unusual animal. In Montezuma's menagerie, Hernán Cortés found that "the greatest Rarity was the Mexican Bull; a wonderful composition of divers Animals" with "a Bunch on its Back like a Camel" and "its Neck cover'd with Hair like a Lion" and "its Head armed like that of a Bull" (Fray Gaspar José de Solís 1724, cited in Hornaday 1889). Castaneda, a follower of Coronado, reported seeing these same animals and described them as being like "crooked-backed oxen." They sported a "beard like that of goats," "a frizzled hair like sheep's wool" in the front, a coat in the rear that was "sleek like a lion's mane," all followed by a very short tail that "terminates in a great tuft" that they carried "in the air like scorpions" (Davis 1869, 206, 207).

The Moving Multitude

These beasts were strange to new eyes, but they were not rare. There were huge numbers of these animals. During the 1830s, the artist George Catlin reported seeing crowds of these creatures that were so thick and large that they "literally blacken the prairies for miles together" (Steinberg 2002, 125). In the 1840s, the historian Francis Parkman said that these herds were "like the black shadow of a cloud, passing rapidly over swell after swell of the distant plain (Parkman 1892, 330, 331). Charles Goodnight, the pioneer Texas rancher, tried to give some sense of the herds' size: between 1862 and 1865, he believed that he saw a single group near Fort Belknap that was "125 miles long and probably 25 miles wide." The great explorer Meriwether Lewis tried to assign a number to the "moving multitude which darkened the whole plains"; he wrote that "twenty thousand would be no exaggerated number" (Coues 1893, 1197). And that was a single group. In total, biologists have estimated that this animal's population may have been the greatest of any ungulate on earth, numbering as many as sixty million (Gates et al. 2010, 7). A Native American put it succinctly: in the early days, the "country was one robe" (Steinberg 2002, 125).

The Bison

This animal, of course, came to be called the buffalo, or the American bison. The continent's largest land mammal was a spectacle, an ecological keystone of the prairie landscape, a foundation of Native peoples' culture and life, and an icon of the American West.

This chapter gives a brief account of the decline of the bison during the 1800s, and its gradual recovery over the past century, focusing on the role that Texas played in both its fall and resurgence.

Ecosystems and the Bison

The bison had great value to the ecosystems and peoples of the Great Plains. The buffaloes' hoof action and grazing opened up areas for colonies of pocket gophers and nests for prairie birds, including upland sandpipers, grasshopper sparrows, mountain plovers, and McCown's longspurs. The bison's habit of wallowing dug some 100 million depressions, creating wetland niches for vegetation, frogs, and aquatic insects, and water holes for many prairie animals. And, as bison rubbed their horns against trees, they helped to keep woody species at bay and protected the grasses of the plains. In their migrations with the seasons, the buffalo also had a key, if unwitting, role in carrying seeds in their hair and dung, spreading them throughout the prairies. And even after they died, and their travels were over, the bison's carcasses became an important source of food for grizzly bears, black bears, bald eagles, turkey buzzards, and magpies (Gates et al. 2010, 42, 43; Rinella 2008, 71, 196).

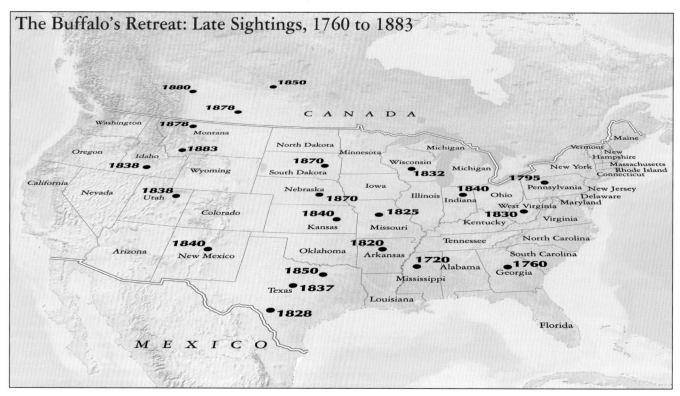

The Buffalo's Retreat: Late Sightings, 1760 to 1883

This map tracks late sightings of the bison during the 1760–1883 period, as the animal retreated from its original, continent-wide range. As early as the 1830s, the buffalo was already seldom seen east of the Mississippi and was also losing ground elsewhere (Allen 1877; Hornaday 1889; Taylor 2011; Scobel 1902).

Native Americans and the Bison

Native peoples, including Apache, Arapaho, Cheyenne, Comanche, Kiowa, Mandan, and Sioux, all relied heavily on the bison not only for food but also for a hundred or more other purposes. Hides became robes, moccasins, drums, shields, and boats. Horns were made into paddles, cups, and ladles. Bones were shaped into knife handles, hoes, and sled runners. Even the dung served a purpose: as fuel for campfires (Geist 2006, 40; Rinella 2008, 221). Native Americans' use of and, indeed, dependence on

the bison date back millennia. Bonfire Shelter, near Langtry, Texas, is the site of the oldest known "buffalo jump" or "sisku." There, some 10,230 years ago, ancient peoples drove bison (actually a now-extinct species, *Bison antiquus* or *Bison occidentalis*) over an 85-foot cliff in a narrow box canyon, killing and using them, much as their descendants would do well into the nineteenth century (Bement 1986).

Early Pressure on the Bison

Buffalo jumps like that at Bonfire Shelter could kill hundreds, if not

thousands, of animals. A jump site near Sundance, Wyoming, holds the remains of roughly 20,000 bison (Bechtel 2012). The Native Americans also took buffalo with bow and arrow and by herding and killing them in surrounds or corrals. In addition, as Indians gained the horse (beginning with the Apache in the mid-1600s, the Mandans in the mid-1700s, and all Plains Indians by 1800), the hunting pressure on the bison grew yet more (Meizner, Sansom, and Roe 2011, 50, 53). Through it all, the bison also had to cope with natural threats: predation, disease, tornadoes, prairie fires, and their greatest enemy, drowning or miring in mud bogs, river bottoms, quicksand, or tar pits (Rinella 2008, 67–71, 145). Nevertheless, the buffalo populations held largely steady until the 1830s, when their world began to change.

Robes, Tongues, and Hooves

During the nineteenth century, subsistence use of the buffalo was overwhelmed by barter and sale of their body parts. Early on, their shaggy winter hides became popular as robes and carriage blankets. In 1815, Indians were killing bison and shipping about 26,000 robes down the Missouri. By 1825, 184,000 robes were reaching New Orleans each year (Baker and Harrison 1986, 3). Their tongues and humps were considered tasty delicacies and were sold by fur traders, prospectors, and Indians. In the 1860s, this meat market scaled up remarkably. Buffalo Bill Cody killed 4,280 bison in just eighteen months to feed workers building the Kansas-Pacific railroad (Gwynne 2011, 260). Bison bones found a market as well: to be stitched onto clothes as buttons, added to clay for chinaware, or ground into bone meal to fertilize poor soils (Rinella 2008, 178–80; Rath 1961). Even their hooves were sold and used as inkwells (Matthews 2002, 65).

Skins, Belts, and Shoes

A huge new market opened in 1871 when a new process for tanning bison leather was invented. This new chemical process allowed the tough bison hide to be used for rugged leather belts to drive the many steam-driven saws,

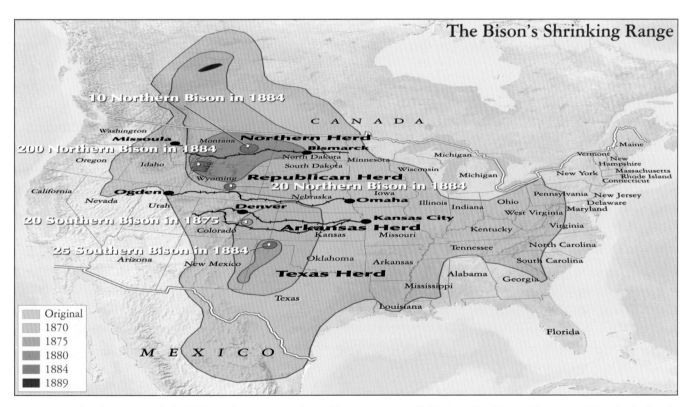

Under extreme hunting pressure, the buffalo's population, once made up of four great groups, the Northern, Republican, Arkansas, and Texas herds, shrank rapidly during the 1870s and '80s. In these two decades, the construction of the Union Pacific, Kansas Pacific, Santa Fe, and Northern Pacific railroads; the development of new weapons and markets; and the control of Native American tribes accelerated the near-extermination of the bison (Hornaday 1889; Oak Ridge National Laboratory 2013).

lathes, mills, and drills of Industrial Revolution factories (Isenberg 2000, 131). As well, the leather found its way into other uses, including army shoe leather, buggy tops, bookbindings, furniture, and wall coverings (Sandoz 2008, 89; Taylor 2011). Tannery demand for "flint," hairless skins, skyrocketed. This allowed the hunt to pursue buffalo into warmer places and seasons, stalking the southern range, and throughout both winter and summer. Hunters and brokers saw huge orders coming in quickly from distant markets. In the winter of 1871/72, the buffalo trader Charles Rath received an order for five hundred hides from a single English tanner. Mere months later, the traders and hunters J. Wright and John Wesley Mooar got an order for two thousand hides from a Pennsylvania tannery (Baker and Harrison 1986, 4). The hide trade grew so valuable that many bison were killed for their skins alone, with their carcasses left to rot.

Railroads

At the same time that demand for buffalo hides, meat, bones, and other parts was growing, the access and the tools for killing bison and moving their remains to market were improving too. After the Civil War, surveying, design, and construction of several railroads began in earnest. Railroad firms laid tracks from Kansas City to Denver (Kansas-Pacific), from Omaha to Ogden (Union Pacific), and from

Bismarck to Missoula (Union Pacific). The new rails opened up vast parts of the High Plains bison range to hunters, skinners, traders, and even sporting tourists (Oak Ridge National Laboratory 2014). For example, when the tracks reached Miles City, Montana, in 1881, that train alone gave access to some 500,000 bison within 150 miles of the railhead (Rinella 2008, 177). And the new tracks made transporting bison products back to eastern and international markets far cheaper and quicker than before. An oxen-pulled wagon might labor over tough trails and across dangerous river fords to bring 150 to 200 hides to market. However, the trains out of Dodge City, Kansas, rolled in with 43,000 hides during just the first three months of operation in 1871 (Holden 1930, 14; Sue 1873). The impact of these new cross-country railroads was so powerful that the great primordial North American herd was torn in two. The bison were split into the southern and northern herds, to either side of the railroad leading from Dodge City, Kansas, to Kansas City, Missouri.

Guns

Technological shifts also brought new, more powerful and accurate weapons to the plains. In 1872, the Sharps 50 rifle, affectionately known as the "Big Fifty," came on the market. The rifle had a long 34-inch barrel that used giant .50 caliber, 600-grain bullets, each powered by 125 grains of black

powder. A Big Fifty could kill a 2,000-pound bull at a great distance, up to hundreds of yards (Gwynne 2011, 270). With new telescopic sights, the rifle's great accuracy allowed hunters to quietly pick off the leaders of a herd, keeping the remaining bison in their sights as calm and close targets (Meinzer, Sansom, and Roe 2011, 62). The quick and lethal nature of the Sharps 50 and other similar new, heavy weapons, is suggested by a few statistics. One famous buffalo hunter, Tom Nixon, shot 120 bison in forty minutes and 3,200 in 35 days; another, J. Wright Mooar, shot more than 20,000 bison during his career (Gwynne 2011, 260; Meinzer, Sansom, and Roe 2011, 72).

The Army

The rigors and horrors of the Civil War had steeled many leaders in the US Army to pursue strategies of total war—tactics to obliterate the food, materiel, and morale of their Confederate enemy. This same philosophy was brought to bear on the Plains Indians during the frontier battles of the 1870s. The military focused on eliminating the bison, the plains commissary that the Indians relied upon so heavily. In 1874, the US secretary of war, Columbus Delano, explained, "the buffalo are disappearing rapidly, but not faster than I desire. I regard the destruction of such game as Indians subsist upon as facilitating the policy of the

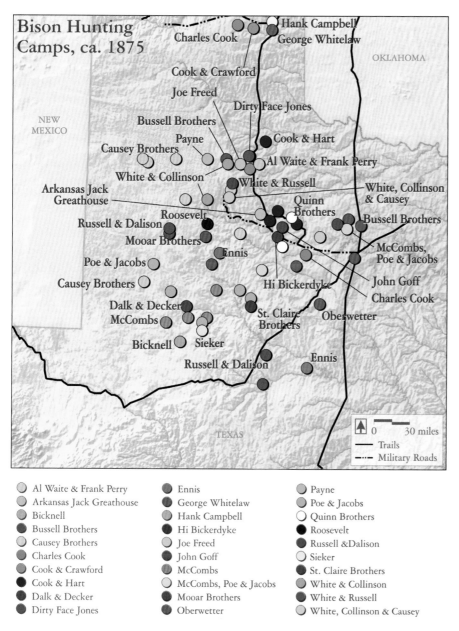

Bison Hunting Camps, ca. 1875

NEW MEXICO

OKLAHOMA

Charles Cook
Hank Campbell
George Whitelaw
Cook & Crawford
Joe Freed
Dirty Face Jones
Bussell Brothers
Payne
Cook & Hart
Causey Brothers
Al Waite & Frank Perry
White & Collinson
White & Russell
White, Collinson & Causey
Arkansas Jack Greathouse
Quinn Brothers
Roosevelt
Bussell Brothers
Russell & Dalison
Mooar Brothers
McCombs, Poe & Jacobs
Poe & Jacobs
Ennis
Causey Brothers
Hi Bickerdyke
John Goff
Charles Cook
Dalk & Decker
McCombs
St. Claire Brothers
Oberwetter
Bicknell
Sieker
Russell & Dalison
Ennis

TEXAS

0   30 miles
— Trails
--- Military Roads

Al Waite & Frank Perry
Arkansas Jack Greathouse
Bicknell
Bussell Brothers
Causey Brothers
Charles Cook
Cook & Crawford
Cook & Hart
Dalk & Decker
Dirty Face Jones

Ennis
George Whitelaw
Hank Campbell
Hi Bickerdyke
Joe Freed
John Goff
McCombs
McCombs, Poe & Jacobs
Mooar Brothers
Oberwetter

Payne
Poe & Jacobs
Quinn Brothers
Roosevelt
Russell &Dalison
Sieker
St. Claire Brothers
White & Collinson
White & Russell
White, Collinson & Causey

From 1874 to 1878, over 99 percent of the southern bison were killed in Texas. This map shows some of the Panhandle hunting camps of the era, populated with shooters, skinners, teamsters, and others who carried out the grisly work (Cook 1907, 114, 126, 158, 178–80; Gilbert, Remiger, and Cunningham 2003, 135, 273).

Government, of destroying their hunting habits, coercing them on reservations, and compelling them to begin to adopt the habits of civilization" (Delano 1874).

Despite this policy, it is not clear that US soldiers directly killed any large part of the buffalo herd. It is known though that the network of federal forts provided ammunition and protection to the lethal private bison hunters and their crews and traders (Lott 2002, 178). Whoever was directly responsible, the attack on the bison worked well as an attack on the Plains Indians. Beyond removing a major source of food, clothing, and tools, the elimination of the bison hit hard at the Indians' morale and tradition. As the Crow chief, Plenty-Coups, lamented, "when the buffalo went away, the hearts of my people fell to the ground, and they could not lift them up again. After this nothing happened. There was little singing anywhere" (Linderman 1962, 311). Sitting Bull felt the same: "a cold wind blew across the prairie when the last buffalo fell—a death-wind for my people" (Steinberg 2002, 124).

The Bison Hunt Comes to Texas

Key chapters in the decline and the revival of the bison, particularly the southern herd, played out in the Texas Panhandle. The story there begins in 1874, when most of the buffalo in Kansas had been shot out. That spring, hunters moved south from Dodge City, crossed the Oklahoma panhandle, and began building camps in Texas along the Canadian River.

The campsites put the great southern herd at close reach.

The hunters who came to the Panhandle were experienced, specialized, and deadly efficient. Some of the larger hunting crews had teams of shooters, skinners, and cooks, supported by teamsters driving as many as sixteen wagons (Meinzer, Sansom, and Roe 2011, 62). These crews killed thousands of bison while in the backcountry, but periodically came

into one of a network of trading posts to sell hides and pick up supplies. The supply sites included operations run by the Cator Brothers, Jones and Plummer, and Jim Springer (Liles 2008, 58).

The Indian Wars

One of these early trading posts in the Texas Panhandle was known as Adobe Walls. On June 27, 1874, two

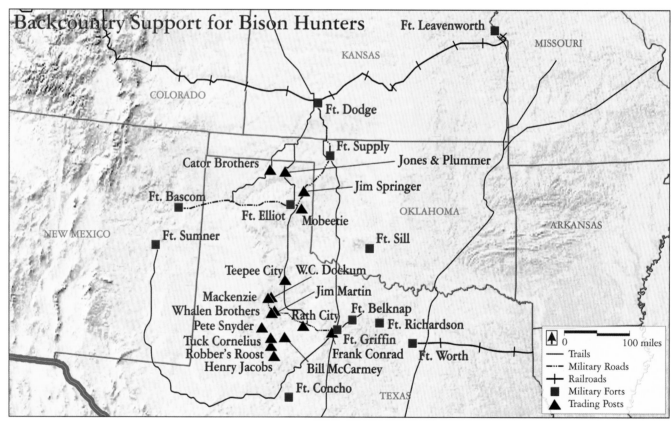

The hunting outfits spent long weeks on their own in the backcountry. Nevertheless, they still required a large network of trading, transport, and protection to support them. There were numerous trading posts (Buffalo Gap, Mobeetie, Rath City, and others), trails (including the Goodnight-Loving, Tascosa/Dodge City, Jones/Plummer, Rath, and Shawnee trails), railroads (the Santa Fe serving Dodge City, and the Texas and Pacific connecting Fort Worth), military roads, and more than ten major forts. The peak of this feverish work of supplying gear and freighting skins ran from 1874 through 1877, and was done by 1880, with the end of the great Texas bison hunt (Dary 1989, 114; Gilbert, Remiger, and Cunningham 2003; Haley 1936; Liles 2008, figs. 3.2 and 3.3, pp. 58 and 63; Sheffield 2002; Tennant 1936; Whitman and Searl 1856).

hundred Comanche, Kiowa, and Cheyenne braves attacked the post (Baker and Harrison 1986, 5–6). The Indians eventually retreated, but lost the lives of fifteen warriors, as well as their confidence in the famous medicine man, Isa-tai, who had predicted an easy victory. They were shaken, but their retreat was temporary. Native Americans counterattacked in a bloody blitz against western settlements in Colorado, Kansas, and Texas.

The Indian attack at Adobe Walls, and Indians' ensuing raids in neighboring states, broke a seven-year peace effort, the "Quaker" policy that had begun with the Treaty of Medicine Lodge in 1867. The treaty had required that the Comanche cede the Texas Panhandle to the United States and stay within a reservation bounded by the 98th meridian and the Washita and Red Rivers (Wooster 1988, 129). However, the treaty had little credibility to begin with, since many Indians did not sign on, and in the ensuing years, the United States had failed to provide the tribes with promised food and supplies.

The Indians had failed to keep their bargain as well. Tribes had often come in the warmth of spring to ransack American settlements and to hunt buffalo in the Panhandle, later retreating from troop reprisals to the protection of the reservation. Nevertheless, the violence at Adobe Walls and in the raids of subsequent weeks broke that very tentative peace. On July 26, 1874, President Grant ordered Sherman to put the reservations under military control and instructed the army to "subdue all Indians who offered resistance to constituted authority" (Gwynne 2011, 273).

A Legislative Pivot

The military policy against the tribes spilled over into an allied legislative attack on the bison. In 1874, dismay at the recent loss of bison in the plains states, and, before that, in eastern areas, had managed to push a bill to protect the animal through the US Congress (H.R. 921, June 23, 1874). However, General Sheridan persuaded President Grant that eliminating the southern bison herd would rob the Comanche and Kiowa of a critical food source. Without the bison to support them, Sheridan said that the tribes would be forced to retreat from the Texas frontier and return to their Oklahoma reservation. Grant bought Sheridan's argument and killed the bill with a pocket veto.

A similar bill seeking to protect the bison reached the floor of the Texas legislature in 1874. Sherman sent General Sheridan to lobby against the bill in Austin. Sheridan told the Texans, "They [the buffalo hunters] are destroying the Indian's commissary; and it is a well-known fact that an army losing its base of supplies is placed at a great disadvantage. Send them powder and lead, if you will; but for the sake of lasting peace, let them kill, skin and sell until the buffaloes are exterminated. Then your prairie can be covered with speckled cattle and the festive cowboy, who follows the hunters as the second forerunner of an advanced civilization" (Cook 1907, 113). The Texas representatives and senators followed Sheridan's advice and rejected the bill.

The Texas Assault

Unfettered by state or federal wildlife laws, and with Native American tribes in retreat, the bison hunters resumed their work in the Panhandle. If anything, they accelerated the pace, pressing the hunt some 200 miles farther south into Texas. In 1876 and 1877, the hunt was large scale, focusing on big herds that had sought to drink at watering holes or to find shelter in river bottoms. During 1877 and 1878, the hunters migrated back into the upper Panhandle to pursue the remnants of the herd. By 1879, the big Texas bison hunt was largely over, barely five years after it began (Liles 2008, 44). Only a few small herds lingered. Perhaps the last herd of any size to be killed was a group of about one hundred, shot in 1882 in the sand hills between Cedar Lake and Midland by George Causey. Causey in turn sold these last bison as meat to feed laborers on the Texas and Pacific Railroad (Liles 2008, 116).

The haul of the hunt was huge. During the peak years of the mid- to late 1870s, crews had succeeded in shooting thousands of buffalo in Texas. In the Fort Concho/Fort Griffin area, from 1874 to 1879, the Russell brothers brought in 6,700 hides, the McCombs 9600, the Mooar brothers 14,700, and the Poe/Jacobs outfit 15,800 (Gilbert, Remiger, and Cunningham 2003, 19). These were just some of the teams of hunters; there were many more. Charles Goodnight and others estimated that there were as many as 3,000 buffalo hunters on the Texas High Plains during the mid-1870s (Holden 1930, 13; Isenberg 2000, 157). Together, the take may have amounted to five or more million animals. A single Texas hide town, Rath City, saw over 1.1 million hides of southern bison brought into trade during its brief boom of 1876–79 (Carlson 2003, 30; Rath 1967, chap. 20).

The Rescue

Not all the bison were killed. A very few were saved. Curiously, some were salvaged by one of the most famous cattlemen to come out of Texas: Charles Goodnight. Goodnight's bison story starts in 1866, when he made his first try at capturing and raising buffalo. He was interested in whether they could be controlled and raised as a commercial herd, either as pure bison or a cattle hybrid (Sandoz 2008, 316). He found that if he chased bison cows and calves, the calves would eventually tire and lag behind. In this way, he managed to catch six buffalo calves, which he paired with domestic cows to nurse and protect.

Unfortunately, his interbreeding efforts were fraught with sterility and miscarriage problems, leading Goodnight to abandon the effort (Meinzer, Sansom, and Roe 2011, 97; Sandoz 2008, 316).

Later, after the great bison hunt had largely decimated the southern herd, Goodnight's wife, Molly, urged him to try once more to capture and protect some of the last survivors. This second effort started in 1878, when he ran across a small group of bison in the Palo Duro Canyon and roped a heifer and bull. Over the years, with more captures and some gifts, the Goodnights' relict herd of bison grew. By 1887, there were thirteen, by 1905, fifty, by 1910, 125, and after the Goodnights' death in the late 1920s, the herd count had grown to 200 (Meinzer, Sansom, and Roe 2011, 90).

The Recovery

The Goodnights contributed in several ways toward restoring the buffalo during the critical precarious years of the late 1800s and early 1900s. First, they were careful in keeping a core herd pure. Over the years, many other bison (admittedly, including some others that the Goodnights had) were interbred with cattle. This contaminated the bison bloodlines and made future restoration difficult. Second, the Goodnight ranch marketed and sold a number of bison to parks, zoos, and private landowners. For instance, some of the Goodnight animals helped build the herd in Yellowstone National Park

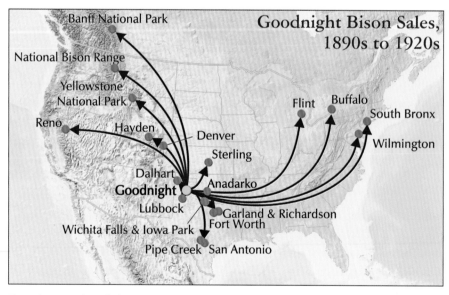

From the 1890s through the 1920s, bison were sold from the Goodnight herd to ranches and refuges across the country, as well as in Canada. Along with just four other small foundation herds, the Goodnight bison formed the basis for much of today's global buffalo population (Barrow 2009; Dratch and Gogan 2010; Geist 1996; Goodnight 1910; Price 2013; Sybert 2013).

in Wyoming (1902) and Banff National Park in Canada (1897) (Dratch and Gogan 2010).

The Goodnights also contributed to bison recovery in a somewhat perverse or at least unintentional way. In 1905, Goodnight bison were killed by Chief Geronimo in a faux hunt staged at the Oklahoma Western Show. The staged "hunt" was met with outrage and gave President Roosevelt courage and/or political cover to create the National Bison Range in Montana. Later, fittingly, the range was stocked with a buffalo from the Goodnight herd (Isenberg 2000, 175).

The last parts of the Goodnights' role in bison restoration came after the couple's death. In 1929, the Texas legislature voted to authorize the Texas Game, Fish, and Oyster Commission to buy the Goodnight bison herd. The commission managed to find the money to buy the herd, and in 1931, a state board was organized to obtain the Goodnight Ranch as well. However, the money for the land purchase could not be raised, and the state effort floundered. In later years, the Goodnight ranch was sold to others. By 1935, Goodnight's bison had broken through their fences and returned to their old haunts on the nearby JA Ranch (Meinzer, Sansom, and Roe 2011, 98).

In 1996, Jay O'Brien, the manager of the JA Ranch, decided that the Goodnight bison were causing too much crop and fence damage on the JA. So he contacted Texas Parks

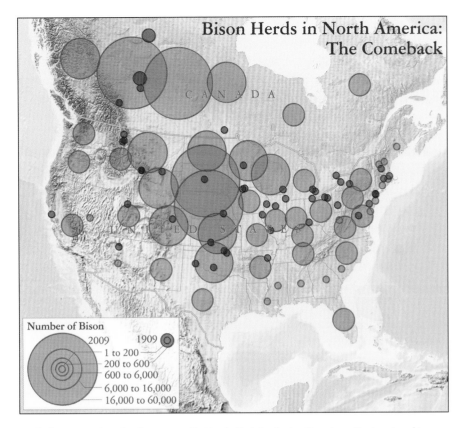

In the first generation after its near eradication in the late nineteenth century, the American bison population gradually grew and spread. Its early recovery relied on support from private ranchers, the American Bison Society, zoos, and the US and Canadian governments. At the turn of the last century, most plains bison survived in small captive herds in US zoos and parks, although some wood bison still roamed wild in northwestern Canada. This map shows the extent of the remnant bison, a total population of just 2,100, as of 1909.

One hundred years later, the bison has returned to most parts of its original habitat. Currently, the total North American population is about 350,000, 175 times what was seen a century before. However, with today's fences, roads, and private lands, it is not the wandering herd of the past. The vast majority of bison, perhaps over 95 percent, are now held in captive herds, including those in commercial ranches, zoos, and for-profit wildlife parks. The fenced bison are concentrated in southern Canada and the northern plains states, although herds are found in nine of the thirteen Canadian provinces, and in all fifty states. Of the 200,000 captive bison in the United States, most are in South Dakota (38,701). However, Nebraska, North Dakota, Colorado, Montana, Wyoming, Oklahoma, and Kansas have over 10,000 buffalo each within their borders. Texas has the most herds (618) in the United States, with 5,890 bison among them. Only 20,500 plains bison are thought to be in sixty-two conservation herds, and just 10,870 wood bison exist in eleven conservation herds (American Bison Society 1909; Gates et al. 2010, 9; Kremeniuk 2013; Matheson 2013; Rinella 2008, 90; US Department of Agriculture 2013).

and Wildlife (TPW) about accepting a gift of the fifty head of bison that made up the descendants of the original Goodnight herd. On Parks and Wildlife's part, there was some reluctance about taking the gift. Like the JA management, the department worried about the buffalo's disdain for fences and crops. The state biologists also worried about disease spread. They knew that some buffalo (mainly the Yellowstone herd) were known to carry brucellosis, a highly dangerous threat to cattle. Critics within the department also pointed out that, since the herd would not be a candidate for hunting, they saw little chance for hunting revenue or support from sportsmen.

Nevertheless, advocates for accepting the herd won out. A TPW team of twenty-five was put together in September 1997 to dart and collect the bison and move them to the Caprock Canyons State Park. Forty-two buffalo were captured. Ten died, but the surviving animals were trucked to their new home at the park. In the early years at Caprock, there were problems with inbreeding. Fortunately, though, in 2003, three bulls arrived from the enormous Turner herd to diversify the bloodlines of the Texas group. As of 2011, the herd had more than doubled in size and appeared to be thriving (McCorkle 2011; Meinzer, Sansom, and Roe 2011, 105–13).

A Review

Looking back, it is startling to see how much damage a well-equipped, determined, and somewhat oblivious society can wreak. It appears that roughly five to six million bison were killed in Texas and perhaps close to sixty mil-

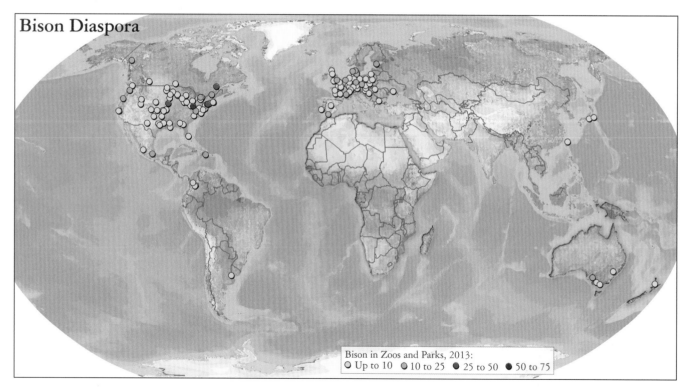

Bison Diaspora

Bison in Zoos and Parks, 2013:
○ Up to 10 ◔ 10 to 25 ◕ 25 to 50 ● 50 to 75

This map excludes the bison that live on commercial ranches and national parks. The figure only shows those places where the public actually tends to see them: in zoos and drive-through wildlife parks. This is a picture of an extraordinary diaspora, extending to South America, Europe, Asia, and Australia. Their careful custody at these exhibits offers a valuable insurance policy for preserving the bison's genetics, and a fine way to educate the public. However, the map raises the question of whether the bison can truly be saved by itself, for its genes alone, without regard to where it is. Some would say that the buffalo's full recovery needs to come through its continued restoration to the North American heartland (International Species Information System 2013).

lion throughout North America. The species was almost extinguished in a matter of a couple of decades. The bison came very close to going the way of the passenger pigeon, Carolina parakeet, and other creatures that have been lost forever.

This is not a murder mystery. The assault on the bison is a very public story. Yet it is difficult to lay the blame on a single culprit. It is tempting to charge the hunters who pulled the triggers, but should we ignore all the others who were involved, including skinners, teamsters, traders, tanners, soldiers, legislators, gun designers, railroad men, and those who bought ink wells made from buffalo hooves? Like many big environmental stories, there is more than enough blame to share. At some level, we are all complicit.

Nevertheless, it is equally remarkable how much good can come from the scattered efforts of just a very few people. Charles and Molly Goodnight's efforts to save a pair of bison in 1878 had immensely far-reaching benefits. Together with a handful of others who intervened to save small parts of the continent's great bison herd (including James McKay and Charles Alloway in Manitoba; Walking Coyote, Michel Pablo, and Charles Allard in Montana; Frederick Dupree in South Dakota; and Charles Jones in Kansas), the Goodnights helped rescue a key part of our ecological wealth and cultural heritage.

Sources

Allen, Joel. 1877. History of the American Bison, extracted from the Ninth Annual Report of the Survey, for the year 1875. United States Geological Survey. Government Printing Office, June.

American Bison Society. 1909. American Bison Census, in Second Annual Report of the American Bison Society, pp. 31–32.

Baker, T. Lindsay, and Billy R. Harrison. 1986. *Adobe Walls: The History and Archeology of the 1874 Trading Post.* College Station: Texas A&M University Press.

Barrow, Mark. 2009. *Nature's Ghosts: Confronting Extinction from the Age of Jefferson to the Age of Ecology.* Chicago: University of Chicago Press.

Bechtel, Stefan. 2012. *Mr. Hornaday's War: How a Peculiar Victorian Zookeeper Waged a Lonely Crusade for Wildlife That Changed the World.* Boston: Beacon Press.

Bement, Leland. 1986. Mammalian Faunal and Cultural Remains in the Late Pleistocene Deposits of Bonfire Shelter, 41VV218, Southwest Texas. University of Texas. http://www.coahuilense.org/modules/pdf/Bonfire_Shelter.pdf, accessed December 2, 2013.

Carlson, Paul. 2003. *The Buffalo Soldier Tragedy of 1877.* College Station: Texas A&M University Press.

Cook, John. 1907. *The Border and the Buffalo, an Untold Story of the Southwest Plains.* Topeka, KS: Printed by Crane.

Coues, Elliott. 1893. *History of the Expedition under the Command of Lewis and Clark.* New York: Francis P. Harper.

Dary, David. 1989. *The Buffalo Book: The Full Saga of the American Animal.* Athens: Ohio University Press.

Davis, William W. H. 1869. *The Spanish Conquest of New Mexico.* Doylestown, PA.

Delano, Columbus. 1874. "Reduction of the Military Establishment." Testimony of January 10, 1874, cited in the Reports of the Committees of the House of Representatives for the First Session of the Forty-Third Congress, p. 99. Washington, DC: Government Printing Office.

Dratch, Peter, and Peter Gogan. 2010. "Bison Conservation Initiative: Bison Conservation Genetics Workshop: Report and Recommendations." Nature Resource Report NPS/NRPC/BRMD/NRR-2010/257.

Gates, C. Cormac, Curtis H. Freese, Peter J. P. Gogan, and Mandy Kotzman, eds. 2010. "American Bison: Status Survey and Conservation Guidelines 2010." IUCN. Gland, Switzerland.

Geist, Valerius. 1996. *Buffalo Nation: History and Legend of the North American Bison.* Stillwater, MN: Voyageur Press.

Gilbert, M., L. Remiger, and S. Cunningham, comps. 2003. *Encyclopedia of Buffalo Hunters and Skinners.* Vol. 1, *A–D.* Union City, TN: Pioneer Press.

Goodnight, Charles. 1910. Letter from Charles Goodnight to H. A. Fleming, 512 Slaughter Building, Dallas, Texas, dated August 18.

Gwynne, S. C. 2011. *Empire of the Summer Moon.* New York: Scribner.

Haley, J. Evetts. 1936. *Charles Goodnight: Cowman and Plainsman.* Boston: Houghton Mifflin.

Holden, W. C. 1930. *Alkali Trails, or Social and Economic Movements of the Texas Frontier, 1846–1900*. Dallas: Southwest Press.

Hornaday, William T. 1889. *The Extermination of the American Bison*. Smithsonian Institution, United States National Museum. Washington, DC: Government Printing Office.

International Species Information System. 2013. *Bison bison*. Holdings at Zoological Institutions.

Isenberg, Andrew. 2000. *The Destruction of the Bison: An Environmental History, 1750–1920*. Cambridge: Cambridge University Press.

Kremeniuk, Terry. 2013. Executive Director, Canadian Bison Association. Personal communication, December.

Liles, Jeff. 2008. "A Historical Geographical Assessment of Bison Hunting on the Southern Great Plains in the 1870s." Thesis submitted in partial fulfillment of the degree of master of science for Oklahoma State University.

Linderman, Frank B. 1962. *Plenty-Coups: Chief of the Crows*. Lincoln: University of Nebraska Press.

Lott, Dale. 2002. *American Bison: A Natural History*. Berkeley: University of California Press.

Martin, Melissa. 2015. Administrative Assistant, Inter Tribal Buffalo Council. Personal communication, March.

Matheson, Jim. 2013. National Bison Association. Personal communication, December.

Matthews, Anne. 2002. *Where the Buffalo Roam: Restoring America's Great Plains*. Chicago: University of Chicago Press.

McCorkle, Rob. 2011. "Home on the Range." *Texas Parks and Wildlife* (November).

Meinzer, Wyman, Andrew Sansom, and Russel Roe. 2011. *Southern Plains Bison: Resurrection of the Lost Texas Herd*. Badlands Blue Star Publications.

Oak Ridge National Laboratory. 2014. Railroad Network. http://cta.ornl.gov/transnet/qn28V.zip, accessed March 14, 2014.

Panhandle-Plains Historical Museum. 2013. Photograph of Charles Goodnight and the bison bull, Skye. Item 425/994. Panhandle-Plains Historical Museum. Canyon, Texas.

Parkman, Francis. 1892. *The Oregon Trail: Sketches of Prairie and Rocky-Mountain Life*. Boston: Little, Brown.

Price, B. Byron. 2013. Coauthor, *Charles Goodnight: A Man for All Ages*. Personal communication, December.

Rath, Ida E. 1961. *The Rath Trail*. Wichita, KS: McCormick-Armstrong.

Rinella, Steven. 2008. *American Buffalo: In Search of a Lost Icon*. New York: Spiegel and Grau.

Sandoz, Mari. 2008. *The Buffalo Hunters: The Story of the Hide Men*. 2nd ed. Lincoln: University of Nebraska Press.

Scobel, A. 1902. Geographisches Handbuch zu Andrees Handatlas. Vierte Auflage. Bielefeld und Leipzig: Velhagen und Klasing.

Sheffield, William T. 2002. *Historic Trails of Texas*. Spring, TX: Absey.

Steinberg, Theodore. 2002. *Down to Earth: Nature's Role in American History*. Oxford: Oxford University Press.

Stricker, Warren. 2013. Director, Research Center, Panhandle-Plains Historical Museum. Personal communication, December.

Sue, Eugene. 1873. "How the Bison Are Slaughtered." *Our Dumb Animals* 6 (1): 2. The Massachusetts Society for the Prevention of Cruelty to Animals.

Sybert, Vicki. 2013. Wildlife Biologist, former Texas Parks and Wildlife employee. Personal communication, December.

Taylor, Scott. 2011. "Buffalo Hunt: International Trade and the Virtual Extinction of the North American Bison." *American Economic Review* 101 (7): 3162–95.

Tennant, H. S. 1936. The Texas Cattle Trails. State Highway Commission, State of Oklahoma. Oklahoma City. http://digital.library.okstate.edu/chronicles/v014/v014p084.html, accessed January 20, 2014.

US Department of Agriculture. 2013. 2007 Census of Agriculture. http://www.agcensus.usda.gov/Publications/2007/index.php, accessed December 1, 2013.

Whitman, E. B., and A. D. Searl. 1856. Map of Eastern Kansas. J. P. Jewett. http://www.kansasmemory.org/item/213048/page/1, accessed December 3, 2013.

Wooster, Robert. 1988. *The Military and United States Indian Policy, 1865–1903*. New Haven, CT: Yale University Press.

Water

John Wesley Powell is famous for many exploits. He rowed the Mississippi from Minnesota to the coast, fought in the Civil War, ran the rapids of the Grand Canyon, explored the West, pioneered cultural anthropology, and led the US Geological Survey (Stegner 1954; Worster 2001).

In 1890, he also offered an odd but prescient proposal for administering the arid lands of the United States. He suggested that the division and governance of lands west of the 100th meridian avoid the traditional Cartesian grid of American boundaries that traced back at least as far as Jefferson's Northwest Ordinance of 1787 (Jackson 1984, 16; Northwest Ordinance, July 13, 1787). Instead, Powell felt that it would be better to divide these territories along wiggling watershed boundaries, to let topography trump geometry and thus ease self-management of critical water problems in those dry lands (Powell 1890; Powell 1879).

Over a century later, Texas is faced with water problems growing from rapid economic and population growth, heavy pollutant loads, cyclical drought, and climate change pressures. To cope with these water challenges, the state appears to be slowly and fitfully morphing into what Mr. Powell might have recommended—reshaping itself in ways that might better fit and manage its water bodies.

In some cases, Texas water districts do track the boundaries of their related water bodies. For instance, Texas river authorities have often taken the shape of their respective watershed, helping them to better balance water supplies and uses within their territory.

However, in other situations, the contours of water districts reflect how hard it can be to mold long-seated political realities and legal traditions to fit the shape of water. This is particularly true of groundwater conservation districts. While these districts are local to the resource and many of their users, their borders have typically followed county boundaries, with little regard to the outlines of the aquifers they seek to manage.

Of course, water debates are often settled far outside the turf of a river authority or a groundwater conservation district, whether it tracks the rectilinear imprint of law and government, or follows the shape of a river basin or aquifer. Often these controversies find their way to a resolution in the state legislature, a state administrative hearing, or judicial court.

Perhaps some of the chapters below will help explain these tensions among water, government boundaries, and powers and private metes, bounds, and demands. In a larger sense, maybe these water controversies show yet again how hard it can be to squeeze environmental realities into political limits and private constraints.

Sources

Anderson, Terry. 1983. "Water Needn't Be a Fighting Word." Wall Street Journal, September 30.

Harris-Galveston Subsidence District. 2015. HGSD KMZ Maps, Subsidence Data. www.hgsubsidence.org/subsidence-data, accessed June 28, 2015.

Jackson, J. B. 1984. *Discovering the Vernacular Landscape.* New Haven, CT: Yale University Press.

Powell, John Wesley. 1879. *Report on the Lands of the Arid Regions of the United States.* Washington, DC: Government Printing Office.

———. 1890. "Arid Region of the United States, Showing Drainage Districts." Eleventh Annual Report, Part II. Plate LXIX. US Geological Survey.

Stegner, Wallace. 1954. *Beyond the Hundredth Meridian: John Wesley Powell and the Second Opening of the West.* New York: Penguin Books.

Texas Water Development Board. 2014. GIS Data: Administrative Boundaries. http://www.twdb.state.tx.us/mapping/gisdata.asp, accessed September 29, 2014.

———. 2015. Administrative Boundaries: Groundwater Conservation Districts, Shapefile. Current as of August 2014, acquired from Texas Commission on Environmental Quality. http://www.twdb.texas.gov/mapping/gisdata/doc/GCD_Shapefiles.zip, accessed March 16, 2015.

Worster, Donald. 2001. *A River Running West: The Life of John Wesley Powell.* New York: Oxford University Press.

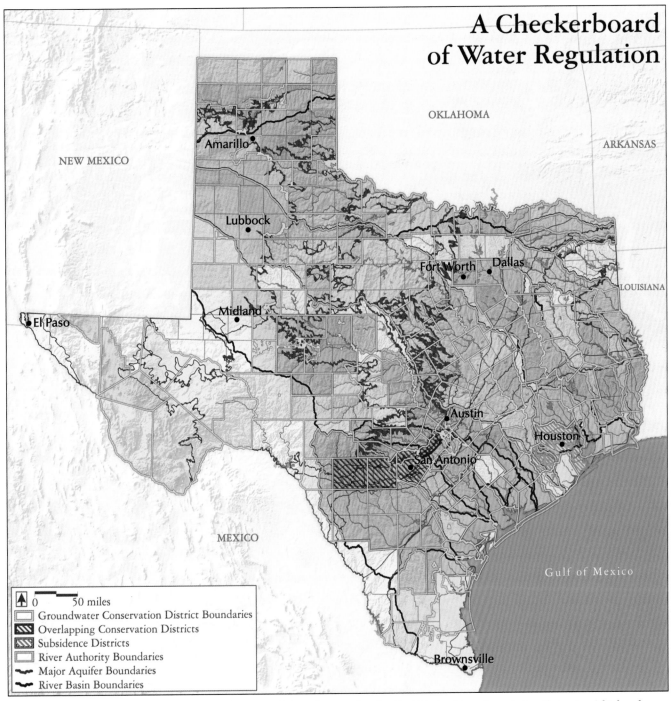

A Checkerboard of Water Regulation

OKLAHOMA

ARKANSAS

NEW MEXICO

Amarillo

Lubbock

Fort Worth   Dallas

LOUISIANA

Midland

El Paso

Austin

Houston

San Antonio

MEXICO

Gulf of Mexico

Brownsville

0   50 miles
☐ Groundwater Conservation District Boundaries
▨ Overlapping Conservation Districts
▨ Subsidence Districts
☐ River Authority Boundaries
〰 Major Aquifer Boundaries
〰 River Basin Boundaries

"Whiskey is for drinking. Water is for fighting" (Anderson 1983). Sometimes attributed to Mark Twain, this quote reminds us that water rights have long been highly contentious. The fights over control of Texas water have become very political, creating a crazy quilt of river authorities and groundwater conservation districts vying to sort out the state's water controversies (Harris-Galveston Subsidence District 2015; Texas Water Development Board 2014, 2015).

Surface Water

This portion of the Texas Landscape Project looks at the diverse signs of change that the past century and a half have brought to Texas surface waters. These years have seen the construction of massive dams and reservoirs, interconnected with vast networks of pumps, gates, canals, and pipelines. However, some of the key signals of change have been more subtle. These markers may only appear on paper, as in the water rights that claim much of the flow in Texas rivers and streams.

Source

US Geological Survey. 2013. Major River Basins of Texas. http://www.twdb.state.tx.us/mapping/gisdata/shapefiles/texas_river_basins/basins_dd.zip, accessed January 1, 2013.

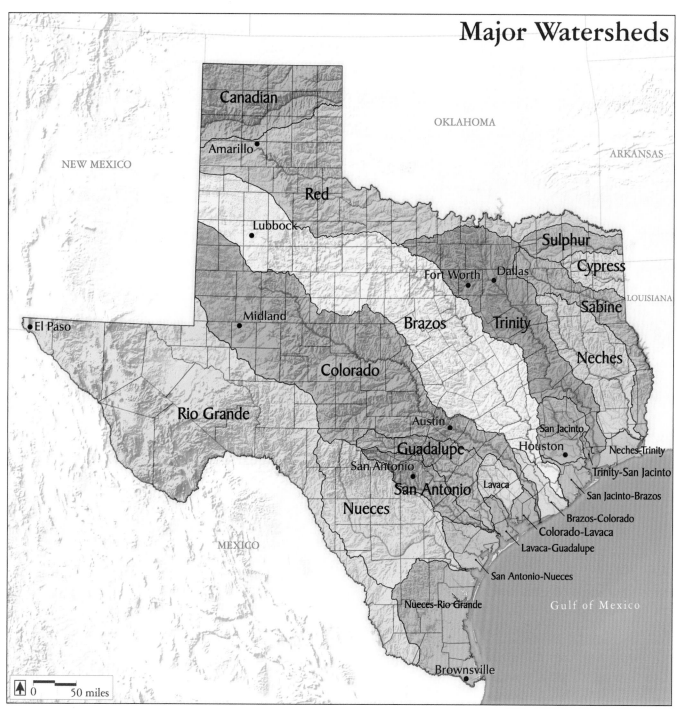

Major Watersheds

This map shows the bounds of the twenty-three major river basins within Texas, ranging from the immense basin of the 1,885-mile Rio Grande to the small watershed of the Lavaca. Its 80,000 miles of waterways include the mighty Sabine, Trinity, and Neches Rivers of East Texas, as well as the clear limestone creeks of the Hill Country and muddy bayous along the coast. Developed for water supply, flood control, and navigation, now threatened by overuse, pollution, and climate change, the state's lakes and streams remain critically vital for Texas residents and wildlife (US Geological Survey 2013).

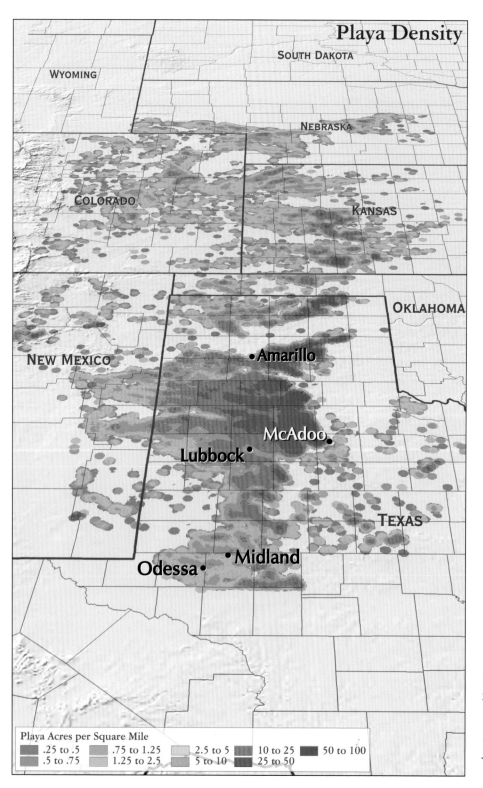

Playa Density

WYOMING

SOUTH DAKOTA

NEBRASKA

COLORADO

KANSAS

NEW MEXICO

OKLAHOMA

•Amarillo

McAdoo•

Lubbock•

TEXAS

Odessa•

•Midland

Playa Acres per Square Mile

.25 to .5	.75 to 1.25	2.5 to 5
.5 to .75	1.25 to 2.5	5 to 10

10 to 25   50 to 100
25 to 50

This figure shows the vast number of playas (30,000 or more) found nationwide, as well as their impressive density in the Panhandle of Texas (Guthrie 2012; McLachlan 2012; Playa Lakes Joint Venture 2014).

High Plains Playas

The American High Plains are pock-marked with an amazing number of playas, perhaps as many as 60,000 (Batzer and Baldwin 2012). These playas are shallow, ephemeral ponds that have been scooped out by wind erosion over the eons (Haukos and Smith 2003, 577; Playa Lakes Joint Venture 2014). Texas has the highest density of playas in North America and is home to most of the playas. It is possible that 20,000 to 30,000 are spread across the Texas Panhandle (Fish et al. 1998, 4; Haukos and Smith 2003, 578; Playa Lakes Joint Venture 2014). Some are quite large, exceeding 800 acres. Most, though, are small—averaging just a yard in depth and nineteen acres in size (Howard et al. 2003, 6).

Water

Playas cover about 385,000 acres in Texas, but only amount to 2 percent of the total land area in the Texas High Plains (Fretwell, Williams, and Redmann 1996, 365; Howard et al. 2003, 6). However, their ecological importance is much greater than that figure might suggest. Since much of the Panhandle receives only fifteen inches of rain in a year's time, the water captured by the playas is critical (Haukos and Smith 2003, 578). It is certainly important for replenishing local water resources. For instance, the playas' water is believed to be the major source of recharge for the Ogallala aquifer (Gurdak and Roe 2009, 21; Smith 2003, 155; Texas Parks and Wildlife 2014).

Visitors

The playas' water is important in another respect. Those shallow ponds support spectacular flocks of birds in the Panhandle. Playas provide key resting and foraging sites for more than 185 types of birds, including a million migrating shorebirds, ducks, geese, and songbirds that pass through the Panhandle each year (Nickens 2011; Haukos and Smith 2003, 579).

American avocets, lesser yellow-legs, long-billed curlews, long-billed dowitchers, stilt sandpipers, and Wilson's phalaropes are some of the more abundant shorebirds that visit playas. Ducks such as blue-winged teal, green-winged teal, gadwall, northern pintails, and mallards are also seen visiting playas. Surveys have found

Here we see images of just a few of the kinds of birds that commonly visit playas. Clockwise from upper left, they include the mallard, Canadian goose, sandhill crane, and American avocet (Fitzgerald 2009; Frankland 2013; Garrett 2013; Hiam 2010).

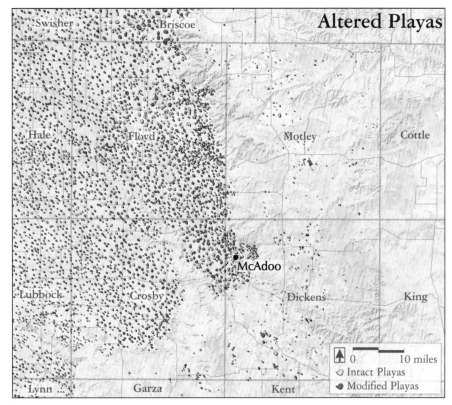

This figure shows the intact (blue) and modified (red) playas in several counties within the central Texas Panhandle. The modified playas have been farmed, excavated, diked, drained, or perhaps affected by road construction. A mark is provided for McAdoo, Texas, to help locate the aerial photographs that follow (Barbato 2014; Texas Tech University 2014).

that 300,000 geese pass through the Playa Lakes region, with Canada geese and snow geese being the most typical geese seen there. Ninety percent of the waterfowl that overwinter in the High Plains inhabit the playa wetlands (Fretwell 1996, 363).

Locals

In addition to the key part they play for birds, playas also host a lush array of 340 plant species, including cattails, bulrush, spikerush, smartweed, dock, and other wetland flora (Haukos and Smith 1992, 3, 6). Playa water and plants also provide a home to some 124 aquatic invertebrates and thirteen types of amphibians (Anderson 1997; Smith 2003, 68–69, 74).

Changes

However, playas exist in a human world. The vast majority of the Panhandle's playas are in highly developed agricultural areas, 99 percent on private lands. They are subject to impacts from many kinds of cultivation and drainage work (Haukos and Smith 1992, 4). Thousands of the playas have been altered. Some estimates hold that over 40 percent of playas in the southern Plains have been disked or cultivated. Seventy percent have been dug out, or "pitted," to collect and concentrate irrigation water (Haukos and Smith 2003, 580). Others have been split by roads or excavated to hold storm water (Haukos and Smith 2003, 581). Many playas have also suffered from sediment flowing in from cultivated fields, wastewater pumped from sewage treatment plants, and polluted runoff coming from feedlots (Haukos and Smith 2003, 578, 582; Smith 2003, 17, 18).

Protecting the Nation's Waters

The appreciation of playas and other wetlands for wildlife habitat, storm flow buffering, and runoff treatment has grown over time. The story reaches back to at least 1972, when the US government passed the Clean Water Act, with the goal of restoring the "chemical, physical and biological integrity" of the nation's waters (Federal Water Pollution Control Act Amendments of 1972). The government implemented the act, in part, through Section 404 regulations. Section 404 limited dredging and filling of navigable waters and adjacent wetlands. In 1975, a federal district court interpreted the legislative history of the Clean Water Act to require that the Corps of Engineers stretch the scope of Section 404 to cover work in "isolated wetlands and lakes, intermittent streams, prairie potholes, and other waters that are not part of a tributary system to interstate waters or to navigable waters of the United States" (*Natural Resources Defense Council, Inc. v. Callaway*, 392 F. Supp. 685 (D.D.C. 1975); 42 Fed. Reg. 37144 (July 19, 1977)). In case the phrases "isolated wetlands" or "prairie potholes" were ambiguous, playas' protection under Section 404 was confirmed under Corps of Engineers regulations issued in 1982. The Corps' 1982 rules clarified that "waters of the United States" did in fact include "playa lakes" (33 CFR 328.3(a)(3)). Further, in 1986 and 1988, the EPA (53 Fed. Reg. 20765) and the Army Corps of Engineers (51 Fed. Reg. 41217) adopted the "Migratory Bird Rule." The rule held that any waters used as habitat by migratory birds should be construed as "waters of the United States" within the ambit of Section 404 protection.

Carrots

Regulatory protections of playas and other wetlands were meant to be complemented by incentives. Rewards for playa protection came primarily through the Swampbuster policy that was passed in 1985, and later tightened in 1990 (Food Security Act of 1985, Public Law No. 99-198, 99 Stat. 1504 (codified, as amended, 16 U.S.C. Sections 3801–23)). The Swampbuster program curtailed Farm

Bill subsidies to farmers who planted crops on drained, leveled, or otherwise converted wetlands. Over 80 percent of Texas playas were covered and protected by the Swampbuster incentives (Haukos and Smith 2003). In its first years, the Swampbuster program was estimated to have lowered the national wetland conversion rate by over 88 percent (Natural Resources Conservation Service 2014).

The 1985 Farm Bill also granted funding through the Conservation Reserve Program for land, including playas, to be set aside from cultivation. More than 1.2 million acres have been enrolled in the Conservation Reserve Program in Texas alone, so the impact on playa protection in the state is substantial (Haukos and Smith 2003). In the 1990 revisions to the Farm Bill, additional incentives to protect playas were also offered through the Wetland Reserve Program (Food, Agriculture, Conservation and Trade Act, Public Law No. 101-624, 104 Stat. 3359, November 28, 1990; Emergency Wetlands Reserve Program, 7 CFR Part 623). Still later, in 1996, the Federal Agriculture Improvement and Reform Act created the Wildlife Habitat Incentive Program (WHIP) and the Environmental Quality Incentive Program (P.L. 104-127), which were also used to help safeguard playas (16 U.S.C. 3839bb-1; 16 U.S.C. 3839aa-5).

Confusion

However, from early on, regulatory crosscurrents and inconsistencies effectively allowed for altering and damaging playas. And, despite regulatory language protecting playas, a playa cannot be well protected if it is not considered to be a legal wetland. Unfortunately, playas are ephemeral. They fill and evaporate and drain. Sometimes they can be seen, and sometimes not. Often, the US Army Corps of Engineers can overlook playas during their wetland surveys. The surveyors may visit a playa site and find that the required water-adapted plants are absent due to drought. Or they may find that the necessary hydric soils are missing, perhaps covered by sediment (Johnson et al. 2012). This soil rule can often undercount playas in agricultural areas, because playas in cropped watersheds may have as much as eight times the amount of sediment as those found in grasslands (Nickens 2011).

Gaps

Some playa damage came from clear openings in government rules, without much nuance or haziness involved. For example, the 1977 Clean Water Act Amendments declared that construction of farm roads, ponds, irrigation ditches, and drainage projects were outside the reach of Section 404 dredge and fill regulation (33 U.S.C. Section 1344(f)(1)(A, C, E)). Since 87 percent of freshwater wetlands lost in the 1950s through the 1970s were the result of

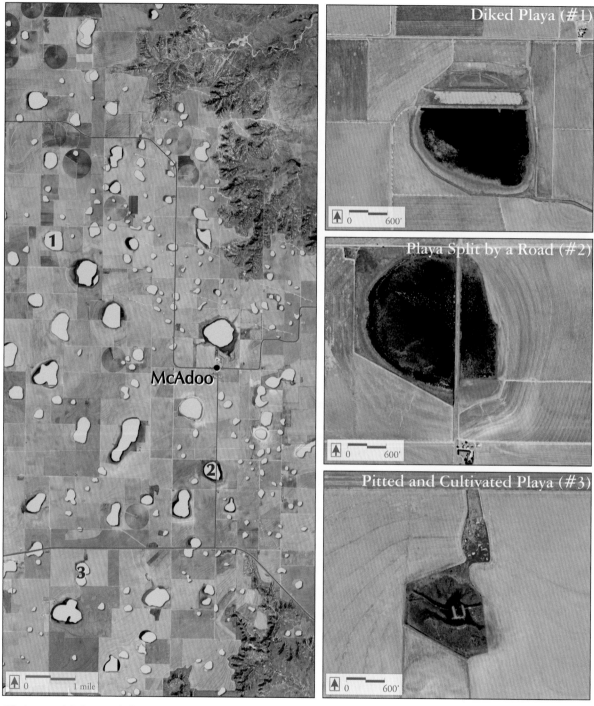

The large aerial photograph shows a playa landscape around McAdoo, in Dickens County, to the east of Lubbock. This high plateau playa landscape with sloped riverine areas is representative of the region. Smaller images show the changes that people have made to playas. From top to bottom there is: (1) a diked playa, (2) a playa split by a road, and (3) a playa that has been pitted and cultivated (Guthrie 2012; McLachlan 2012; Playa Lakes Joint Venture 2011; US Geological Survey 2014).

agricultural conversion, this was certainly a major regulatory gap (McElfish and Adler 1990, 28). Finally, many regulatory and incentive programs have "grandfathered" exemptions allowing maintenance of existing wastewater ponds, dikes, and ditches, despite their ongoing effect on playas or other wetlands (Texas Water Code 26.048(b)).

The year 2001 saw the creation of what is perhaps the largest loophole for playa conversion and damage. In that year, the Supreme Court decided that the "waters of the United States" jurisdiction of the Clean Water Act did not extend to waters isolated from interstate commerce (*Solid Waste Agency of Northern Cook County (SWANCC) v. U.S. Army Corps of Engineers*, 531 U.S. 159 (2001)). The justices rejected the argument that a bird flying an interstate migratory route could make playas, or other isolated wetlands, a "water of the United States" and thus subject to Section 404 regulation. After the SWANCC ruling, the Clean Water Act could generally no longer be used to protect playas. It remains to be seen if the SWANCC language may eventually be reinterpreted to bring playas back within Clean Water Act jurisdiction. The EPA and Corps have recently revised the criteria for "waters of the United States" (80 Federal Register 37054 (June 29, 2015)). The agencies are now pinning the definition on chemical, physical, and biological factors that may pull playas back within the scope of the Clean Water Act (US EPA and US Corps of Engineers 2015, 98, 265).

Tomorrow

It is unclear now what the future will hold for playas. Regulatory and incentive programs have so far had a hard time stemming the decline of playas. However, there is certainly hope that appreciation and voluntary protection for these key wetlands will increase in coming years. Three factors bode well. First, some farmers in the playa region are beginning to earn more from wind energy than from traditional farming of commodity crops, allowing them to reduce cultivation of playas. Second, declines in the Ogallala aquifer are making irrigated agriculture less feasible in the Panhandle, again reducing pressure to plow, drain, or dike a playa. And, last, some farmers are getting curious about the money they can make from birders or hunters who might enjoy, and pay for, the privilege of visiting an intact playa alive with birds.

Sources

Anderson, James. 1997. "Invertebrate Communities in Vegetated Playa Wetlands." PhD diss., Texas Tech University.

Barbato, Lucia. 2014. Center for Geospatial Technology, Texas Tech University. Personal communication, August.

Batzer, Darold, and Andrew Baldwin, eds. 2012. *Wetland Habitats of North America: Ecology and Conservation Concerns*. Berkeley: University of California Press.

Bolen, Eric G. "Playas." Handbook of Texas Online. Published by the Texas State Historical Association. http://www.tshaonline.org/handbook/online/articles/rop07, accessed February 7, 2012.

Clean Water Act, 33 U.S.C. Section 1344(f)(1)(A, C, E).

Federal Agriculture Improvement and Reform Act of 1996, Public Law 104-127 (April 4).

Federal Water Pollution Control Act Amendments of 1972, Public Law 92-500, 86 Stat. 816–903 (October 18).

Fish, Ernest B., Erin L. Atkinson, Tony R. Mollhagen, Christopher H. Shanks, and Cynthia M. Brenton. 1998. "Playa Lakes Digital Database for the Texas Portion of the Playa Lakes Joint Venture Region."

Fitzgerald, Sean. 2009. Avocet. Photograph. Digital image. Flickr. Creative Commons. http://www.flickr.com/photos/sfitzgerald86/3894226351/, accessed August 27, 2014.

Food Security Act of 1985, Public Law No. 99-198, 99 Stat. 1504 (codified, as amended, 16 U.S.C. Sections 3801–23).

Frankland, Colin. 2013. Canada Goose. Digital image. Flickr.com. Creative Commons. https://flic.kr/p/dVXJQW, accessed October 1, 2014.

Fretwell, Judy, John Williams, and Phillip Redmann. 1996. National Water Summary on Wetland Resources. Water Supply Paper 2425. US Geological Survey, Department of the Interior.

Garrett, Brian. 2013. Sandhill Crane. Photograph. Digital image. Flickr.com. Creative Commons. https://flic.kr/p/e2Y7Ug, accessed October 1, 2014.

Gurdak, Jason, and Cassia Roe. 2009. "Recharge Rates and Chemistry beneath Playas of the High Plains Aquifer—A Literature Review and Synthesis." Circular 1333. US Geological Survey, US Department of the Interior.

Guthrie, Ty. 2012. GIS Analyst, Playa Lakes Joint Venture. Personal communication, March.

Haukos, David, and Loren Smith. 1992. "Ecology of Playa Lakes, Waterfowl Management Handbook." Fish and Wildlife Leaflet 13.3.7.

———. 2003. "Past and Future Impacts of Wetland Regulations on Playa Ecology in the Southern Great Plains." *Wetlands* 23 (3).

Hiam, Jerry. 2010. Mallard Drake. Digital image. Flic.kr.com. Creative Commons. https://flickr/p/8Yp5p3, accessed October 1, 2014.

Howard, Teresa, Gordon Wells, Linda Prosperie, Rima Petrossian, Huitang Li, and Amir Thapa. 2003. "Characterization of Playa Basins on the High Plains of Texas." Report 357, August. Texas Water Development Board.

Johnson, Lacrecia, David Haukos, Loren Smith, and Scott McMurry. 2011. "Loss of Playa Wetlands Caused by Reclassification and Remapping of Hydric Soils on the Southern High Plains." *Wetlands* 31 (3): 483–92. http://dx.doi.org/10.1007/s13157-011-0177-4, accessed February 6, 2012.

McElfish, James, and Kenneth Adler. 1990. "Swampbuster Implementation: Missed Opportunities for Wetland Protection," *Journal of Soil and Water Conservation* 45 (3): 383–85.

McLachlan, Megan. 2012. GIS Director, Playa Lakes Joint Venture. Personal communication, February.

Natural Resources Conservation Service. 2014. Wetland Conservation Provisions (Swampbuster). Natural Resources Conservation Service, US Department of Agriculture. http://www.nrcs.usda.gov/wps/portal/nrcs/detailfull/national/programs/alphabetical/camr/?cid=stelprdb1043554, accessed August 27, 2014.

Nickens, T. Edward. 2011. "Here Today, Gone Tomorrow." *Audubon* (June).

Playa Lakes Joint Venture. 2014. Playa Map. Shapefile. http://pljv.org/PPv4_MapBook/probable_playas_v4_shape files.zip, accessed August 27, 2014.

Smith, Loren. 2003. *Playas of the Great Plains*. Austin: University of Texas Press.

Solid Waste Agency of Northern Cook County (SWANCC) v. U.S. Army Corps of Engineers, 531 U.S. 159 (2001).

Texas Parks and Wildlife. 2014. Panhandle Playa Lakes. http://www.tpwd.state.tx.us/landwater/land/habitats/high_plains/wetlands/playa.phtml, accessed August 27, 2014.

Texas Tech University. 2014. Playas/Unclassified Wetlands, Playa Wetland Database. Developed by the Center for Geospatial Technology, Texas Tech University. Data sources include US Fish and Wildlife Service; National Wetlands Inventory Program, Region 2, Albuquerque, New Mexico; and Texas Tech University Department of Natural Resource Management, Lubbock Texas. http://gis.ttu.edu/pwd/DownloadData/ShapeFiles/Playas_UnclassifiedWetlands_Shapefile.zip, accessed August 28, 2014.

Title 33, Navigation and Navigable Waters, Chapter II—Corps of Engineers, Department of the Army, Department of Defense, Part 323—Permits for Discharges of Dredged or Fill Material into Waters of the United States (33 CFR 323.2(a3)).

Tsai, Jo-Szu, Louise Venne, Scott McMurry, and Loren Smith. 2010. "Vegetation and Land Use Impact on Water Loss Rate in Playas of the Southern High Plains, USA." *Wetlands* 30 (6): 1107–16.

———. 2012. "Influences of Land Use and Wetland Characteristics on Water Loss Rates and Hydroperiods of Playas in the Southern High Plains, USA." *Wetlands* 27 (3): 683–92. http://dx.doi.org/10.1672/0277-5212(2007)27[683:IOLUAW]2.0.CO;2, accessed February 6, 2012.

US Environmental Protection Agency and the US Army Corps of Engineers. 2015. Technical Support Document for the Clean Water Rule: Definition of Waters of the United States. May 27. http://www2.epa.gov/sites/production/files/2015-05/documents/technical_support_document_for_the_clean_water_rule_1.pdf, accessed June 29, 2015.

US Geological Survey. 2014. NAIP 2010 Aerial Photography. Earth Explorer. US Department of the Interior. http://earthexplorer.usgs.gov/, accessed August 27, 2014.

Reservoirs

At the beginning of the twentieth century, there were only a handful of lakes in Texas. Most were quite small, many of them seasonal. Included were Caddo Lake, playas in the Panhandle, coastal marshes such as Eagle Lake, and *resacas* and oxbows along Texas rivers. A hundred years later, the state now boasts of 188 major reservoirs, each holding more than 5,000 acre-feet of water. Together they cover a vast area of 1.2 million acres (Texas Water Development Board 2007). How did this happen?

Buchanan Dam and Its Progeny

Many of the now-familiar challenges of raising money and organizing political support for Texas dam construction find their start in 1930s-era Hill Country, with the building of Buchanan Dam. A giant endeavor, Buchanan required the relocation of the entire town of Bluffton and the construction of a huge, two-mile concrete dam stretching across the Colorado River. However, as the Depression settled in, the immense effort and its shaky financing soon overwhelmed the builder. By 1932, only a year into the job, the dam building halted just midway through construction, and its contractor, the nationwide Insull utility, entered bankruptcy under a cloud of fraud accusations. It took until 1935 for the state to charter the Lower Colorado River Authority to pick up the pieces. The Authority became the vehicle to harness millions in federal dollars, bring 1,500 jobs to the Depression-struck state, and finish the dam. By 1938, Buchanan was complete, the biggest reservoir yet built in Texas. Soon it was generating electricity, holding back floodwaters, and providing water deliveries for downstream users (Crisp 2012, 107–11). And its system of using government grants, loans, and bonds, backed by hydroelectricity and water sales and administered by regional river authorities, was repeated time and again throughout the state.

Energy

Some early large Texas dams were built to bring lights and power to isolated plateau ranches and blackland farms in Central Texas. The young congressman Lyndon Johnson and the Lower Colorado River Authority

On June 18, 1937, a construction crew posed at Buchanan Dam, four months before its completion (Lower Colorado River Authority Corporate Archives 1937).

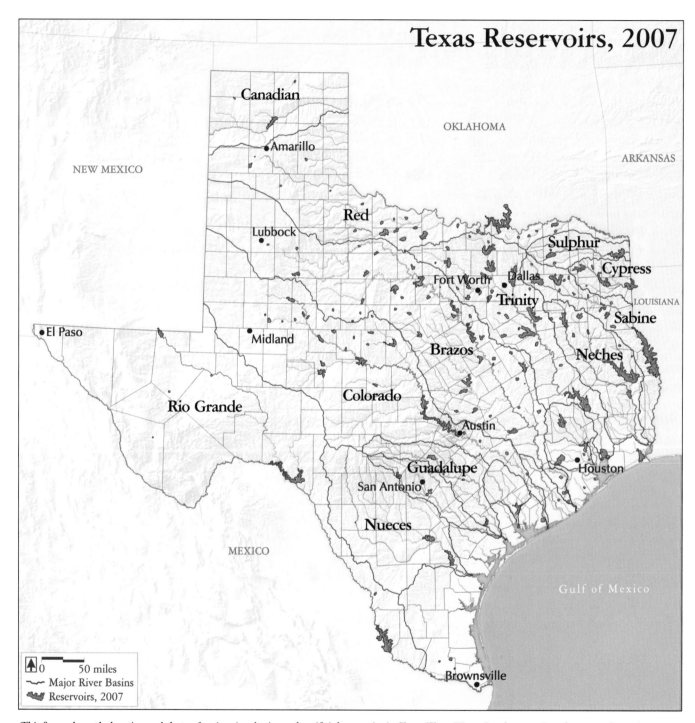

This figure shows the location and shape of major river basins and artificial reservoirs in Texas (Texas Water Development Board 2007 and 2015).

followed the model of the Tennessee Valley Authority and used funding from the Public Works Administration and Rural Electric Administration to build Buchanan and Mansfield Dams and their network of transmission lines (Adams 1990).

Other Texas reservoirs grew out of the desire to produce power thermally, with coal, lignite, natural gas, or nuclear fission. These lakes were built to cool discharge water from the big boilers that spun the plants' steam turbines. Major cooling ponds included Bardwell Lake, Lake Colorado City, Lake Granbury, Lake Hubbard, Lake Limestone, Lake Texana, Martin Lake, and Twin Oaks Reservoir (Scanlon, Duncan, and Reedy 2013, 24).

Flood

The push for building Texas dams also came from flood fears. The memories of lives, homes, and businesses lost in the great floods of Austin (1935), Dallas (1908), Houston (1935), and San Antonio (1921) were very painful. The floods gave Texans great respect for Mother Nature's ability to send great torrents, complete with floating houses, cars, animals, and people, hurtling downstream (Slade and Patton 2003).

After World War II ended, the US Army Corps of Engineers turned its staff and expertise to building dams to control such floods. The Corps built more than twenty major reservoirs in Texas, including some of the largest in the country. Lake Texoma, for

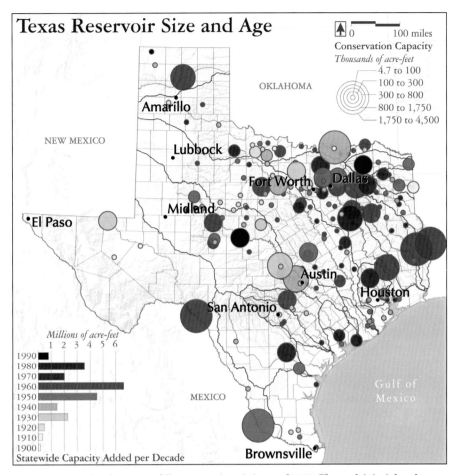

This map shows the relative size of Texas reservoirs existing as of 2007. The marks' size is based on the reservoirs' conservation capacity, while the color is keyed to their impoundment date (lightest for 1900–1909, darkest for 1990–99) (Texas Water Development Board 2007 and 2015).

instance, can hold 5.3 million acre-feet of water and spread flood flows over 144,000 acres (Texas Water Development Board 2007).

While Texans may often look to the Corps' enormous dams as their insurance against these flood risks, there are also many smaller, less obvious structures that work to protect against flood damage. For instance, to reduce flood hazards, the Natural Resources Conservation Service has

built roughly two thousand structures in Texas since the 1930s (authorized by the Flood Control Acts of 1936, Public Law 74-738; Flood Control Act of 1944, Public Law 78-354, December 22, 1944; Flood Control Act of 1954, Public Law 83-566, among many others). Many are dry earthen dams that people might see as a gentle rise or grassy hill, but don't recognize as a flood pool until runoff comes and the lake fills (Owens 2014).

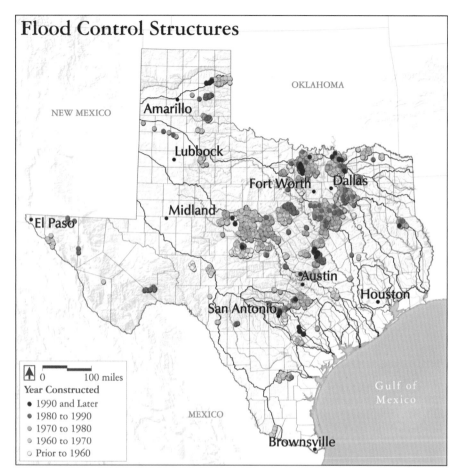

Flood Control Structures

This map shows 2,000 flood control structures that were built by the Natural Resources Conservation Service throughout Texas. At an average size of just 1,950 acre-feet, these NRCS reservoirs are much smaller than the 188 major Texas water supply reservoirs, which all exceed 5,000 acre-feet in capacity. However, it is striking to see how support for the NRCS structures converged so strongly and saw construction through so quickly. Seventy percent were built in the 1960s and 1970s alone. The colors indicate their construction date: before 1960, white; 1960s, yellow; 1970s, light orange; 1980s, orange; and 1990 and later, red (Dean 2014; Owens 2014).

Drought

Recurrent droughts spurred much of the dam construction in the state. The Dust Bowl of the 1930s is still etched deeply into Texans' consciousness. Some remember the stories of John Steinbeck's families uprooted from their homes in the *Grapes of Wrath* (Steinbeck 1939). Others may recall Dorothea Lange's indelible photographs of destitute farmers and abandoned lands (Lange 1938). Drought's bare statistics can be impressive too. The dry years of the 1930s saw an average of 480 tons per acre of topsoil blown away, some of it accumulating in dunes five or more feet in height (Cunfer 2011, 555; Hansen and Libecap 2004). Texans have long remembered the drought of 1950–56 as well. In fact, it was so severe and widespread that it is still used as the worst-case scenario for state water planning.

With the droughts of the 1930s and 1950s in mind, Texas leadership vowed to do what it could to keep fields irrigated, municipal taps flowing, and industrial customers supplied. The state went on a dam-building campaign. In the twenty-five years following the start of the drought in 1950, Texas built over one hundred major water supply dams. Together they held a total conservation storage capacity of more than 30 million acre-feet of water (Texas Water Development Board 2007).

Population

While many factors came into play in the campaign to build dams in Texas over the past century, at its root, the boom owes much to population growth. From 1900 to 2014, the state's population leaped from 3.9 million to over 26 million (Texas Department of State Health Services 2014; Texas State Library and Archives Commission 2014). Guarantees of cheap, plentiful water were needed to both attract and keep residents in the state.

Demands to Meet

The call for more water storage came from the rising population, as well as the climbing expectations of the populace. A new generation of Texans enjoyed new and thirsty domestic appliances. Toilets, hot water heaters, clothes washing machines, dishwashers, and Jacuzzis, some in multiple combinations, became common. Texas settlers also reveled in expansive sprinklered lawns, maybe reminding them of the wetter climes and greener scenery of their homelands.

Reliable water deliveries were also demanded by Texas' new industries, particularly irrigated agriculture (including sugarcane and rice along the coast, fruits and vegetables in the Valley, and grains and fiber in the Panhandle), as well as Gulf Coast refineries and petrochemical plants needing makeup and cooling water.

Support

Financing for the new reservoirs came from bond-issuing agencies such as the Texas Water Development Board and the more than twenty river authorities in Texas, as well as the flows of generous federal cost-share moneys at very low interest rates and water purchase terms. Over time, interests such as engineering firms, construction companies, and a wide variety of real estate, marina, boat, and fishing businesses built a potent lobby for funding the dams.

Opposition

There are winners and losers with any big reservoir project. Reservoirs are essential to meeting the water demands of urban areas. But even the most needed reservoir comes at a price—the huge costs of land acquisition and construction, the flooding of rich agricultural lands and wildlife habitat, and the agony of landowners watching their home place submerged forever.

As the best lake sites were taken in the earlier years of dam building, and as cities developed a more comfortable margin of safety above their immediate needs, grassroots opposition to new reservoirs grew. Sponsors withdrew plans as well. The 1961 State Water Plan laid out plans for forty-five reservoirs (Texas Board of Water Engineers 1961, 2). Roughly fifty years later, the 2012 plan recommended twenty-six new major reservoirs, still a lot but far fewer than earlier (Texas Water Development Board 2012, 190). Furthermore, since the late 1980s, very few reservoirs have actually progressed beyond the planning stage and into construction.

Dollars to Rent

Some of the opposition to dam proposals has come out of the sheer cost of dams. Dams are big, expensive projects, requiring immense amounts of land, steel, concrete, and other materials. For example, the cost of implementing the water supply projects envisioned by the 2012 Texas Water Plan was $53 billion (Texas Water Development Board 2012, 5). Moreover, in recent years, federal cost-shares and low-interest loans have declined, leaving more of the burden for local sponsors. Money has proved hard to come by at the state level too, with referenda on water bonds defeated in 1969, 1976, and 1981 (Texas Proposition 2, 1969; Texas Proposition 1, 1976; Texas Proposition 4, 1981).

Kilowatts to Burn

Generating hydroelectricity has been part of the rationale (and debt service) for some major dams in Texas, such as Toledo Bend, Travis, and Buchanan. However, those kinds of dams are less competitive now in a state richer in natural gas than steep terrain, where fossil fuels can often be a cheaper and more plentiful source of power than falling water. Also, with the recent drought, some dams are not able to generate the amount of hydroelectricity that they had in the past. For instance, in 2014, the Lower Colorado River Authority only produced a third of the hydropower that it did three years earlier (Malewitz 2014).

Water on Tap

Proposals for new dams have also lost out to dams that are already standing. Many existing Texas reservoirs offer a ready supply of unobligated supplies at low prices. For instance, Lake Texoma, Toledo Bend, and Wright Patman Reservoirs all have large amounts of uncommitted water (Bezanson 2014; Freese and Nichols et al. 2010, table 4D.1). Some water users have also found that it may be cheaper, simpler, and closer to pump groundwater. Texas aquifers can be tapped relatively easily under loose rule-of-capture laws, and there is then no need to compete for the more highly regulated, and often quite-distant, state surface waters.

Land to Buy

Another factor in the drop in dam construction is the dwindling number of high-relief, well-watered sites in the state. As mentioned above, many of the best sites were taken in the earlier years of dam building, and those that remain are relatively marginal. Plus, with the real estate boom of the post–World War II era, rural land has become expensive. Purchases of reservoir sites, and the lands to mitigate for related habitat loss, have become very costly. For instance, sponsors of the Waters Bluff reservoir on the Sabine estimated that mitigation costs would exceed $104 million, equal to the cost of the reservoir land itself (Sabine River Authority 1998). This cost estimate is probably quite low, since Texas Parks and Wildlife figured that 141,000 acres would need to be bought to offset the impact of the 31,000-acre lake. This would mean a mitigation level four and a half times as large as the Authority had assumed (LeTourneau 2000; Texas Parks and Wildlife 1998, 9).

Riverine and Estuarine Life

Some of the decline in dam construction can be attributed to a better scientific understanding of the ecological and economic importance of free-flowing river water. The past generation has taught us that water, nutrient, and silt deliveries are critical to Texas' bottomland hardwoods, farmlands, and estuarine fisheries. In fact, this improved grasp of the key role of freshwater inflows has been translated into legal mandates for estuarine releases (Texas Water Code, Sections 11.147, 11.150, 11.152).

Evaporation

The case for reservoir construction has also been undercut by evaporation. In a hot and often dry state like Texas, evaporation can cause huge amounts of water to disappear into the clear blue sky. Recent estimates indicate that long-term mean evaporation from 3,415 of Texas' larger reservoirs represents an annual loss of 6.1 million acre-feet of water. This immense evaporation loss equals 61 percent of the state's agricultural use and 126 percent of municipal use in the state (Wurbs and Ayala 2014).

Siltation

Texas reservoirs are vulnerable to siltation too, the natural process where lakes gradually fill with sediment and decomposed organic matter. With siltation, the average lifespan for a Texas

reservoir may be only 100 to 125 years (Ruesink 1978). Possum Kingdom and Lake Texoma provide a pair of examples of the Texas reservoirs that have struggled with rapid siltation and capacity loss. From its construction in 1941 through a survey in 2005, Possum Kingdom's volume shrank by over 184,000 acre-feet, or more than 25 percent (Texas Water Development Board 2006). Similarly, Lake Texoma's capacity has contracted by 20 percent, dropping from 3.13 million acre-feet in 1942 to 2.52 million acre-feet in 2002 (Texas Water Development Board 2003).

Strife

Even impoundments that manage to successfully run the gauntlet of gathering political backing, garnering financial support, and mastering construction challenges may eventually run into bitter struggles over how the stored water should be managed and used. The confrontations up and down the Colorado River, among lakeside residents of Lake Travis, municipal users in Austin, and irrigators and industrial customers downstream, are one example of the kind of tensions that can arise (Brown 2014).

Citizens

These financial, technical, environmental, and operational problems are serious drawbacks for dams. Often, landowners and conservation advocates have used these arguments when seeking to slow or stop dam construction. Their efforts have succeeded in halting dam proposals at Fastrill, Little Cypress, Paluxy, Shaws Bend, and other sites (Bezanson 2007; Johnson 2008; LeTourneau 2000; McIntire 2000).

Although some opponents succeed in defeating dam proposals, it is never easy. These controversies go on for years, cost thousands of dollars in attorney and expert witness fees, and are deeply upsetting to the residents who see their home, heritage, and livelihood threatened. The kind of passion that drives grassroots opposition is equally clear from those who have successfully opposed local reservoirs, and from those who failed and were evicted (Frentress 2000; McIntire 2000). Perhaps these excerpts from oral histories of two witnesses to dam proposals and construction will help explain.

Carl Frentress remembers his family's reaction to land clearing for the construction of Lake Athens (Frentress 2000):

After he was forced off the land and had to move to town (he didn't live long after that because it just, that was not his kind of lifestyle), this lake was cleared and—and we saw that. We saw the bulldozers absolutely lay bare the ground and the creek itself. Flat Creek itself was just, I mean, it was just a ditch going down through this big couple thousand acre bare cleared area and all those trees were—were

just burned. It was—it was a very shocking experience for everybody who had some sense of connection to that land.

Terry McIntire explains the successful effort by his family and neighbors to defeat the Paluxy Reservoir (McIntire 2000):

The Paluxy River is important to me. I grew up here. We talk about defending the Paluxy River and it was almost as if it wasn't a river or home, it was more like a family member. What do you do to save a family member? Well anything you can. And that's what we've done.

The Future

The drought of the past five years, along with continued growth in the state's population and economy, have kept proposals alive to construct the Marvin Nichols reservoir on the Sulphur River, the Millican Dam on the Navasota, and other impoundments elsewhere. Also, new kinds of off-stem reservoirs that scalp flood flows have recently found favor, including the Pierce Ranch project in the lower basin of the Colorado River.

However, many utilities are realizing that flood control and water supply options that require less infrastructure may be a good deal cheaper and quicker to adopt. Modern thinking about flood control has tended toward moving residents out of risky floodplains instead of building upstream

dams. As a result, federal dollars for flood control lakes have dried up (Devine 1995). Now, instead of dams, planners have often turned to zoning and insurance premiums to steer residents out of flood-prone areas.

Municipal water recycling/reuse is one fast-growing trend for water supply. The North Texas Municipal Water District and Tarrant Regional Water District have developed showcase projects that filter treated wastewater through specially created wetlands (North Texas Municipal Water District 2014; Tarrant Regional Water District 2014). Aquatic plants remove nitrogen, phosphorus, and ammonia so that treated water can be returned to storage reservoirs and used again. Also, the Colorado River Municipal Water District is using reverse osmosis and ultraviolet disinfection to purify treated wastewater to standards much higher than normal drinking water (Wythe 2013). El Paso uses high-tech filters to purify treated wastewater, then injects it into aquifers to store it for water supply (Burge 2012).

Utilities are also looking to existing lakes for water supply. For example, the 2011 Region C Water Plan, for the Dallas–Fort Worth area, identified ten projects that tap underutilized reservoirs or convert existing flood storage to water supply (Region C Water Planning Group 2011). Some of these have the potential to meet huge demands. Toledo Bend, for example, has 600,000 acre-feet per year currently available, and the Sabine River Authority, which operates Toledo

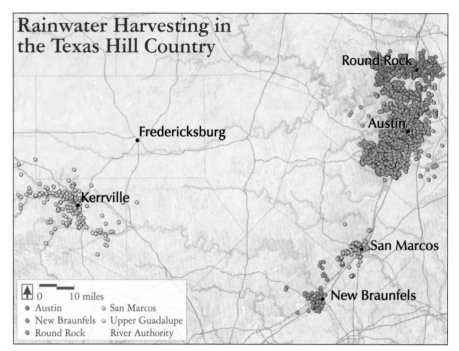

Rainwater Harvesting in the Texas Hill Country

Round Rock

Austin

Fredericksburg

Kerrville

San Marcos

New Braunfels

0   10 miles
- Austin   • San Marcos
- New Braunfels • Upper Guadalupe
- Round Rock   River Authority

This map shows the various rainwater harvesting systems that have been advertised, subsidized, or given away by the cities of Austin, New Braunfels, Round Rock, San Marcos, and by the Upper Guadalupe River Authority (UGRA). They range from many small 25-gallon rain barrels to an immense 29,000-gallon cistern. Some of the catchment programs are well established: Austin has been involved in distributing over 4,100 pieces of equipment since 2003. Others are quite new and still small: the UGRA has helped provide customers with 260 rain barrels since their program began in 2011. Please know that this is by no means a complete map. For instance, it does not include the many systems that have been built privately. However, it does help suggest that rain harvesting is becoming ever more popular (Abbott 2014; Bushnoe 2014; Doeckel 2014; Gilchrist 2014; Klein 2014; Woods 2014).

Bend, is seeking the rights to an additional 293,300 acre-feet.

Pumping brackish groundwater is another alternative to building reservoirs. In 2004, the Texas Water Development Board reported that Texas aquifers held an enormous reserve of 2.7 billon acre-feet of slightly saline groundwater (Kalaswad, Christian, and Petrossian 2004, 1). Brackish groundwater's salt content is only a few thousand parts per million, far less than the ocean's 35,000 ppm,

making it a cost-competitive source of drinking water in some parts of the state. Wichita Falls has already begun to desalinate water from rivers in the Red River Basin that are too salty to drink directly.

Private Efforts

Individual citizens are doing their part too. For instance, many Texans are installing cisterns and rain barrels to capture rainwater for gardening,

washing, and drinking. In addition to reducing our demands somewhat for off-site water, the visibility and sheer finite size of these tanks help remind us of the precious nature of water and encourage us to be more efficient and frugal with our water use.

These ideas are not new. Before western settlement, Mescalero Apaches used natural cisterns, known as tinajas, at Hueco Tanks in West Texas. Anglos took up the notion later. Early Austin residents built a number of them, including tanks at the 1840 French Legation building, the 1877 Smoot House, and the state capitol of the 1880s (Bryce 1995). Many years later, in the 1990s, the Texas Water Development Board, Texas A&M Agricultural Extension Service, and the nonprofit Center for Maximum Potential Building Systems, revisited the rainwater harvesting idea to study and promote it (Vittori and Todd 1997).

The idea took force again as the twenty-first century arrived and as dry weather persisted. Several governments (Austin, New Braunfels, Round Rock, San Marcos, and Sunset Valley) began running advertising, subsidy, and rebate programs to encourage residents to install cisterns and rain barrels (Abbott 2014; Austin Water 2014; Bushnoe 2014; New Braunfels Utilities 2014; City of Round Rock 2014; City of San Marcos 2014, City of Sunset Valley 2014; Doeckel 2014; Woods 2014). Others used more indirect tools to encourage rainwater harvesting, by granting exemptions from the ad valorem tax (Hays County) and offering waivers from storm water regulations (Cities of Dripping Springs and Rollingwood and the Texas Commission on Environmental Quality) (Alexander 2014; Faught 2014; Hays County Development Services 2014; Isley 2014; Lanfear 2014; Thompson 2014).

From enormous reservoirs of millions of acre-feet to small rain barrels of a few gallons, Texans are trying to cope with water in shortage and flood. Gradually, we are beginning to realize water's priceless value in drought and its mortal danger in flood. As the climate grows more volatile, these lessons are becoming ever clearer. In the end, perhaps we are learning how careful and respectful we need to be in all our dealings with water in Texas.

Sources

Abbott, John. 2014. Water Conservation Associate, Austin Water Utility, City of Austin. Personal communications, July and August.

Adams, John. 1990. *Damming the Colorado: The Rise of the Lower Colorado River Authority, 1933–1939*. College Station: Texas A&M University Press.

Alexander, Michael. 2014. Building Official, City of Rollingwood. Personal communication, August.

Austin Water. 2014. Rainwater Harvesting Rebate Program Application. City of Austin. http://austintexas .gov/sites/default/files/Water/ RebateApplications/rainh2orebate.pdf, accessed July 28, 2014.

Bezanson, Janice. 2007. Oral history interview conducted in West Lake, Texas, on January 20. Texas Legacy Project. Conservation History Association of Texas.

———. 2014. Executive Director, Texas Conservation Association. Personal communication, August.

Brown, Kirby. 2014. Chairman, Lower Colorado River Basin Coalition. Personal communication, April.

Bryce, Robert. 1995. "The Brethren of Cisterns." *Austin Chronicle* 15 (41).

Buie, Eugene. 1979. "A History of United States Department of Agriculture Water Resource Activities." Soil Conservation Service, US Department of Agriculture.

Burge, David. 2012. "$16.2 Million Water Treatment Plant Upgrade: Wetland to Be among Places to Benefit from Water." *El Paso Times*, January 16.

Bushnoe, Tara. 2014. Natural Resources Coordinator. Upper Guadalupe River Authority. Personal communication, July.

City of Round Rock. 2014. Rainwater Harvesting Rebate Application. City of Round Rock, Texas.

City of San Marcos. 2014. Rainwater Harvesting Rebate Application Form. City of San Marcos.

City of Sunset Valley. 2014. Rainwater Harvesting System Rebate. City of Sunset Valley.

Crisp, Margie. 2012. *River of Contrasts: The Texas Colorado*. College Station: Texas A&M University Press.

Cunfer, Geoff. 2011. "The Southern Great Plains Wind Erosion Maps of 1936–37." *Agricultural History* 85 (4): 540–59.

Dean, Morgan. 2014. Dam Safety Section, Critical Infrastructure Division, Texas Commission on Environmental Quality. Personal communication, August.

Devine, Robert. 1995. "The Trouble with Dams." *Atlantic Monthly* (August).

Doeckel, Mallory. 2014. Resource Conservation Technician, New Braunfels Utilities. Personal communication, July.

Faught, Ginger. 2014. Deputy City Administrator, City of Dripping Springs. Personal communication, August.

Fisk, Pliny. 1978. "An Appropriate Technology Working Atlas for the State of Texas." Center for Maximum Potential Building Systems. Austin, Texas.

Freese and Nichols, Alan Plummer Associates, CP&Y, Cooksey Communications. 2010. 2011 Region C Water Plan, October 2010. http:// www.regioncwater.org/Documents/ index.cfm?Category=2011+Region+ C+Water+Plan, accessed August 19, 2014.

Frentress, Carl. 2000. Oral history interview conducted in Athens, Texas, on October 25. Texas Legacy Project. Conservation History Association of Texas.

Gilchrist, Suzanne. 2014. Public Information Office, Austin Water Utility, City of Austin. Personal communication, July.

Hansen, Zeynep, and Gary Libecap. 2004. "Small Farms, Externalities, and the Dust Bowl of the 1930s." *Journal of Political Economy* 112 (3).

Hays County Development Services. 2014. Application for Rainwater Harvesting Incentive Program. Hays County.

Isley, Michael. 2014. Edwards Aquifer Protection Program, Texas

Commission on Environmental Quality. Personal communication, August.

Johnson, Pat. 2008. Oral history interview conducted in Fayetteville, Texas, on February 24. Texas Legacy Project. Conservation History Association of Texas.

Kalaswad, Sanjeev, Brent Christian, and Rima Petrossian. 2004. "Brackish Groundwater in Texas, The Future of Desalination in Texas (Volume 3): Technical Papers, Case Studies, and Desalination Technology Resources." Report 363. Texas Water Development Board. December.

Klein, Jan. 2014. Public Services Conservation Coordinator. Electric Utility, City of San Marcos. Personal communication, August.

Lanfear, Zach. 2014. Edwards Aquifer Protection Program, Texas Commission on Environmental Quality. Personal communication, August.

Lange, Dorothea. 1938. Abandoned farm in the Dust Bowl, Coldwater District, Near Dalhart, Texas. Digital photographic file LC-USF34–018260-C. U.S. Farm Security Administration / Office of War Information Collection. Library of Congress. http://www.loc .gov/pictures/resource/fsa.8b32404/, accessed August 14, 2014.

LeTourneau, Richard. 2000. Oral history interview conducted in Longview, Texas, on October 20. Texas Legacy Project. Conservation History Association of Texas.

Lower Colorado River Authority Corporate Archives. 1937. Workers at Buchanan Dam Construction Site, 1937. Photo ID W00081. LCRA Corporate Archives. Flickr Collection.

https://www.flickr.com/photos/lcra_ corporate_archives/3531475791/in/ photostream/, accessed July 23, 2014.

Malewitz, Jim. 2014. "In Central Texas, Drought Threatens Hydropower." *Texas Tribune*, March 10.

McIntire, Terry. 2000. Oral history interview conducted in Paluxy, Texas, on October 16. Texas Legacy Project. Conservation History Association of Texas.

Meredith, Carolyn. 2014. Public Works, City of Sunset Valley. Personal communication, July.

New Braunfels Utilities. 2014. Rainwater Harvesting: Rain Barrel of Cistern Rebate. Form.

North Texas Municipal Water District. 2014. East Texas Wetland Project, John Bunker Sands Wetland Center. http://www.wetlandcenter.com/ waterreuse/default.html, accessed August 21, 2014.

O'Brian, Erik. 2015. GIS/Cartography/ Data, Texas Natural Resources Information System. Personal communication, March.

Owens, Shon. 2014. Engineering Civil Technician, Natural Resources Conservation Service, US Department of Agriculture. Personal communication, August.

Region C Water Planning Group. 2011. Region C Water Plan (Table 4D.1, page 4D.2). http://www.regioncwater.org/ Documents/2011RegionCWaterPlan/ Chapter%204D_final.pdf, accessed August 21, 2014.

Ruesink, Lou Ellen. 1978. "Old Beyond Years." *Texas Water Resources* 4 (1). Texas Water Resources Institute.

Sabine River Authority. 1998. "Comprehensive Sabine Watershed Management Plan Report." Waters Bluff Reservoir:

Appendix F—Opinion of Probable Construction Cost.

Scanlon, Bridget, Ian Duncan, and Robert Reedy. 2013. "Drought and the Water Energy Nexus in Texas: Supporting Information." *Environmental Research Letters* 8.

Slade, R. M., and John Patton. 2003. "Major and Catastrophic Storms and Floods in Texas: 215 Major and 41 Catastrophic Events from 1853 to September 1, 2002." US Geological Survey Open-File Report, 03-193.

Steinbeck, John. 1939. *The Grapes of Wrath*. New York: Viking Press.

Tarrant Regional Water District. 2014. George W. Shannon Wetlands Water Reuse Project. http://www.trwd.com/ wetlands, accessed August 21, 2014.

Texas Board of Water Engineers. 1961. A Plan for Meeting the 1980 Water Requirements of Texas. May. http:// www.twdb.texas.gov/publications/ State_Water_Plan/1961/1961.pdf, accessed July 23, 2014.

Texas Department of State Health Services. 2014. Texas Population, 2010 (Historical Race Ethnicity Categories). https://www.dshs.state.tx.us/chs/ popdat/ST2010.shtm, accessed July 23, 2014.

Texas Parks and Wildlife Department. 1998. "Analysis of Bottomland Hardwood Areas and Assessment of Habitat Quality at the Potential Future Waters Bluff Reservoir Site." Final Report to the Texas Water Development Board, Interagency Agreement No. 97-483-226. April.

Texas State Library and Archives Commission. 2014. United States and Texas Populations, 1850–2012. https:// www.tsl.texas.gov/ref/abouttx/census .html, accessed July 23, 2014.

Texas Water Development Board. 2003. Volumetric Survey of Lake Texoma. Prepared for the US Army Corps of Engineers, Tulsa District. April 14.

———. 2006. Volumetric Survey of Possum Kingdom Lake, December 2004– January 2005 Survey. May.

———. 2007. Existing Reservoirs, Updated December 2007. Shapefile. http://www.twdb.state.tx.us/mapping/gis-data/shapefiles/reservoirs_2001/existing_reservoirs.zip, accessed July 23, 2014.

———. 2012. Water for Texas: 2012 State Water Plan. January 2012. http://www.twdb.texas.gov/publications/state_water_plan/2012/2012_SWP.pdf, accessed July 23, 2014.

———. 2015. Major River Basins. Shapefile. https://www.twdb.texas.gov/mapping/gisdata/doc/Major_River_Basins_Shapefile.zip, accessed May 14, 2015.

Thompson, Jon. 2014. Planning Director, City of Dripping Springs. Personal communication, August.

Vittori, Gail, and Wendy Price Todd. 1997. "Texas Guide to Rainwater Harvesting." Texas Water Development Board in cooperation with the Center for Maximum Potential Building Systems. Austin, Texas.

Woods, Jessica. 2014. Water Conservation Coordinator, City of Round Rock. Personal communication, July.

Wurbs, Ralph, and Rolando Ayala. 2014. "Reservoir Evaporation in Texas, USA." *Journal of Hydrology* 510 (March 14): 1–9.

Wythe, Kathy. 2013. "Reclaiming a Valuable, Clean Resource." TX: H20. Texas Water Resources Institute.

Drought and Water Use

Harsh drought hit Texas in 2011. While low rains have persisted in some parts of the state to the current day, that first year of the dry spell was the most severe and widespread recorded in over one hundred years (Nielsen-Gammon 2011, 35). Although indoor, urban, air-conditioned life has insulated many Texans from the vagaries of much of the natural world, this drought still grabbed our attention and reminded us of the humbling power of Mother Nature.

Any Rain?

There are many ways to measure the brutality of the drought. Statewide rainfall for all of 2011 averaged 15.2 inches, more than 45 percent below the 1895–2012 average (National Climatic Data Center 2012). For Amarillo, El Paso, Lubbock, and Midland-Odessa, 2011 rainfall was under 6 inches for the entire year, putting those West Texas towns on a par with Damascus, Syria; Baghdad, Iraq; and Khartoum, Sudan (Combs 2012, 4). In fact, the entire state was in extreme drought, or worse, by the fall of 2011.

Wildfire

With the low rains and high heat suffered during 2011, wildfires hit record levels in the state, with over 40,700 fires reported. The fires burned 36 million acres and caused

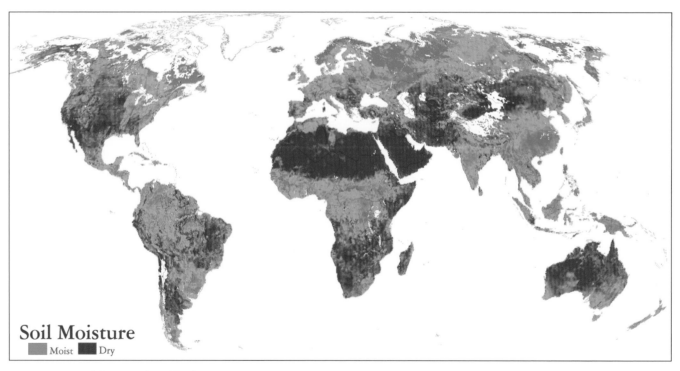

Soil Moisture — Moist / Dry

During 2011, rainfall in West Texas fell to levels seen in the deserts of the Middle East and elsewhere. Global soil moisture levels shown here were detected by satellite-borne microwave sensors in passes made October 1–7, 2011. Red indicates low moisture, green high, ranging from 0 to 0.5 cubic meter per cubic meter (European Space Agency and Tecnische Universitat Wien 2014).

Drought December 2011

Drought Intensity
- Abnormally Dry
- Moderate
- Severe
- Extreme
- Exceptional

The entirety of Texas was in drought during most of 2011, according to a combination of precipitation, streamflow, soil moisture, temperature, and other indicators. The worst of it struck at some point near October 4, when the vast majority of the state was in the grips of the most severe stage of drought, "exceptional" (Nielsen-Gammon 2011, 27; National Drought Mitigation Center 2014).

more than $689 million in damages (Hannemann 2014; Texas Forest Service 2014a and 2014b). One of these, a powerful 32,000-acre blaze, destroyed much of Bastrop State Park in September 2011.

Farm Losses

Without enough rain or irrigation supplies, state agriculture lost $7.62 billion, over 40 percent of typical annual farm and ranch receipts, during 2011. These costs helped rank the 2011 dry spell as the most expensive one in the state's record books (Fannin 2012).

Empty Reservoirs

The shortfalls in rain hit Texas reservoirs hard: Lake Travis, the largest in central Texas, declined to 626.2 msl (mean sea level), 42 feet below average, containing only 35 percent of its capacity (Lower Colorado River Authority 2012; Texas Water Development Board 2012a and 2012b). By November 2011, reservoir storage levels were in the lowest 5 percent on record for twelve of the fourteen major Texas watersheds (other than the Nueces and Lower Rio Grande basins) (Texas Water Development Board 2012a).

Short Deliveries

Rainfall shortages and reservoir declines cut back on municipal water supplies. During 2011, twenty-three municipal utilities believed they were within 180 days of running out of water entirely (Combs 2012, 4). In fact, when the massive E. V. Spence Reservoir ran dry during the fall of 2011, the small town of Robert Lee, north of San Angelo, had to build a 12-mile pipeline for new water supplies (Collier and Galbraith 2011).

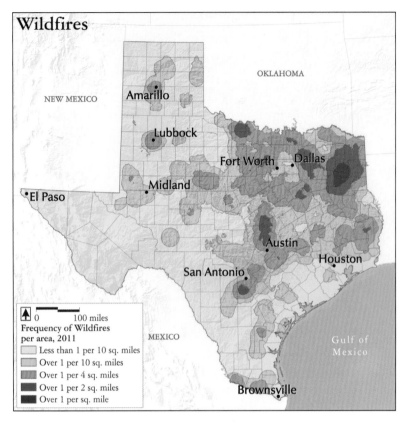

This figure shows the frequency and location of wildfires reported during 2011 to the Texas Forest Service and local fire departments. The map does not weight for the number of acres or casualties (Hannemann 2014; Smith 2015; Texas Forest Service 2014a).

The drought of 2011 exhausted some Texas lakes and undercut many regions' water supplies. On August 3, 2011, Lake O. C. Fisher was essentially empty, with its level 55.91 feet below its conservation storage level (Nottingham 2011).

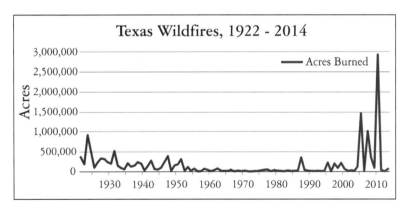

Under pressure from extreme drought and heat, wildfires torched over 2.9 million acres in Texas during 2011. This expanse of acreage had never been approached during nearly ninety years of Texas fire reports (Hannemann 2014; Smith 2015; Texas Forest Service 2014b).

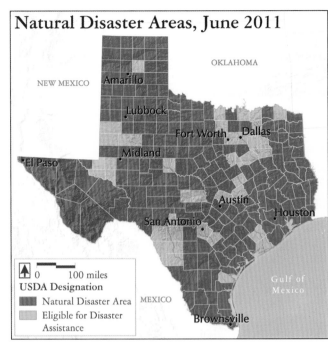

Natural Disaster Areas, June 2011

The severe 2011 drought carried through in massive statewide agricultural losses. On June 27, 2011, the US Department of Agriculture designated the 213 counties shown in red as primary natural disaster areas, and named forty-one contiguous counties (marked in orange) as also eligible for disaster assistance (Farm Service Agency 2011).

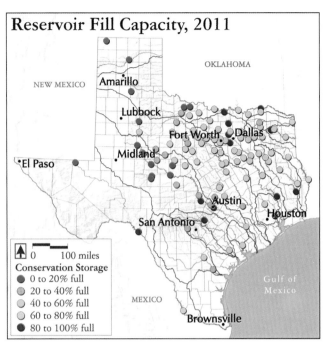

Reservoir Fill Capacity, 2011

This map shows how the drought of 2011 drained many of the reservoirs in Texas. Red markers indicate reservoirs that fell to less than 20 percent of capacity, while orange dots represent lakes that dropped to between 20 percent and 40 percent of capacity (Texas Water Development Board 2012a, 2012b, and 2011).

Conservation

Texans responded to the 2011 drought with strong conservation measures. By early November 2011, nearly 1,000 of Texas' 4,700 public water systems had imposed voluntary or mandatory water restrictions, with fifty-five prohibiting all outside watering. Restrictions are typically triggered by a series of four stages of drought: (1) drought watch, (2) drought warning, (3) drought emergency, and (4) drought disaster. Usually, stage 1 starts public education efforts; stage 2 limits the use of sprinklers and car washes; stage 3 tightens restrictions on sprin-

kling, gardening, car washing, and the filling of pools, and continues with education outreach; stage 4 bans many nonessential outdoor water uses and raises prices on water purchases. Some cities have even developed a fifth stage, "drought catastrophe," when even stronger limits, fees, and penalties are imposed on excessive water use (City of Wichita Falls 2015; San Antonio Water System 2015).

Conservation may become a key long-term strategy that continues through both drought and flood as the state's population and economy grow. A National Wildlife Federation study found that municipal water conserva-

tion could supply 1.6 million acre-feet of water for Texas, far more than the 600,000 acre-feet that are estimated to be needed by 2060 under current projections (Johns 2006). The Texas Water Development Board is more cautious but still believes that an impressive 23 percent of the state's future water needs will be met through water conservation (Vaughan 2011).

While limits on spraying water on lawns, gardens, and cars can have valuable short-range benefits, the state has found other tools that work well for long-term water savings. For example, municipal systems have increased the price of water, replaced leaky waterlines, and given incentives for citizens to buy low-flush toilets, front-loading washing machines, and low-flow showerheads. These measures have certainly driven demand down in big and long-lasting ways.

Huge and durable water conservation advances have also come from rethinking our landscapes. Beginning in the early 1980s, San Antonio became one of the first towns in Texas to encourage residents to reduce thirsty lawn areas, mulch regularly, and plant drought-tolerant, native landscapes (Sinkin 1997).

With these strategies, both in and outside of the home, many Texas communities have been very successful in reducing demand for water. For example, residents of the Alamo City use barely 140 gallons per capita per day, far less than those in Dallas, who use more than 230 gallons/person/day (Johns 2007). The city of Wichita Falls has even gone beyond these conservation measures and has started treating, blending, and reusing its effluent (Campbell 2014).

Opting Out

Challenges remain. While Texas government has relatively strong controls over surface water, loose regulations on aquifer pumpage leave groundwater as a largely private concern. In fact, a recent Texas Supreme Court ruling held that regulation of groundwater use could require state compensation as a "taking" (*Edwards Aquifer Authority v. Day*, 369 S.W.3d 814, 833 (Texas 2012)). As a result, some residents in Texas cities and towns have chosen to drill their own water wells to avoid higher prices and stricter controls on municipal water deliveries, especially for yard watering. In Austin, for example, forty-seven water wells were drilled in 2011, a big jump from the nineteen completed the prior year (Harmon 2012). As shown in the adjoining map, most of the private wells have been drilled in the wealthier areas of central and west Austin, bringing up troubling issues of uneven and unfair sacrifice.

The Long View

While 2011 was a year of severe drought, it is sobering to realize that Texas has experienced similar and even worse spells at other times in its history. Recent studies of tree rings in ancient bald cypress, Douglas fir, and post oak trees scattered throughout the state have revealed that reliable rainfall has skirted Texas repeatedly in the past. For example, particularly harsh and enduring droughts struck

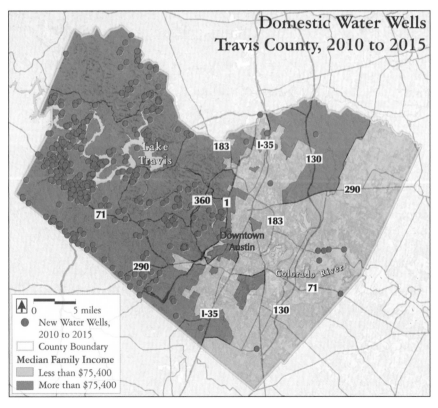

This is a map of 527 new private wells drilled in Travis County from 2010 through April 2015 for domestic use. The well map overlays polygons representing mean household income figures, split at $75,400, the average 2012 level for the Austin / Round Rock SMSA (Texas Water Development Board 2015; Ramirez 2012).

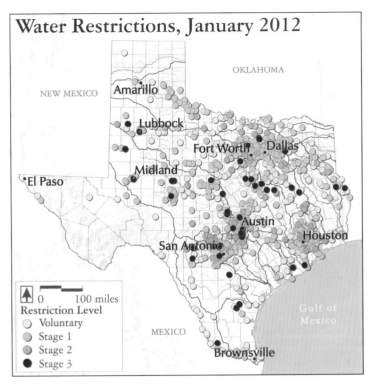

Water Restrictions, January 2012

Restriction Level
- ○ Voluntary
- ○ Stage 1
- ○ Stage 2
- ● Stage 3

As the 2011 drought dragged on, Texans started taking serious measures to cut back their water use. By January 4, 2012, one thousand Texas communities were restricting water uses, including 647 where these limits were mandatory, ranging in severity from Stage 1 to 3 (Hinz 2012).

the state in 1571–80, 1714–16, and 1840–63 (Cleaveland et al. 2011).

The challenge, of course, is that current droughts, such as the dry spell that invaded the state in 2011, now come to a vastly different place than that occupied by Native Americans and western pioneers hundreds of years ago. With over 26 million people and a busy $1.3 trillion economy relying on the fragile and volatile Texas environment, there is less margin for error now (Texas Comptroller of Public Accounts 2014). This is particularly true when we try to factor in the higher temperatures associated with climate change

(Nielsen-Gammon 2011, 42). Going forward, we will need creativity, focus, and perhaps most of all, cooperation, to cope with the droughts and other natural hazards of the future.

Sources

Campbell, Steve. 2014. "Dry Wichita Falls to Try Drinking 'Potty Water.'" *Fort Worth Star-Telegram*, March 20.

City of Wichita Falls. 2015. Water Conservation / Drought Contingency, Water Service, Utilities. Code of Ordinances, Sections 10-185 and 10-186.

Cleaveland, Malcolm, Todd Votteler,

Daniel Stahle, Richard Casteel, and Jay Banner. 2011. "Extended Chronology of Drought in South Central, Southeastern, and West Texas." *Texas Water Journal* 2 (1): 54–96.

Collier, K., and K. Galbraith. 2011. Drought Losses Reach beyond Agriculture. San Antonio *Express News*, November 5. http://www.mysananto nio.com/default/article/Drought-losses-reach-beyond-agriculture-2252384 .php, accessed June 3, 2012.

Combs, S. 2012. "The Impact of the 2011 Drought and Beyond." Texas Comptroller of Public Accounts. Austin. www.window.state.tx.us/specialrpt/ drought/, accessed June 3, 2012.

Edwards Aquifer Authority v. Day, 369 S.W. 3d 814 (Texas 2012).

European Space Agency and Tecnische Universitat Wien. 2014. Soil Moisture CCI Project, European Space Agency Programme on Global Monitoring of Essential Climate Variables. http:// www.esa-soilmoisture-cci.org/ node/145, accessed July 15, 2014.

Fannin, Blair. 2012. Updated 2011 Texas Agriculture Losses Total $7.62 billion. AgriLife Today. http://today.agrilife .org/2012/03/21/updated-2011-texas-agricultural-drought-losses-total-7-62-billion/, accessed June 3, 2012.

Farm Service Agency. 2011. USDA Designates 213 Counties in Texas as Primary Natural Disaster Areas. Release No. 0061.11. Farm Service Agency. US Department of Agriculture. http://www.fsa.usda.gov/FSA/ printapp?fileName=ed_20110628_ rel_0061.html&newsType=ednewsrel, accessed July 16, 2014.

Hannemann, Don. 2014. Coordinator, Emergency Operations Center, Texas

A&M Forest Service. Personal communication, July.

Harmon, Dave. 2012. "More Austinites Drilling Private Wells to Water Lawns." *Austin American-Statesman*, June 2.

Hinz, Alexander. 2012. Drought Coordinator, Texas Commission on Environmental Quality. Personal communication, May.

Johns, Norman. 2006. "The Potential and Promise of Municipal Water Efficiency Savings in Texas." National Wildlife Federation. Austin, Texas. http://www.texaswatermatters.org/projects/save/promise.pdf, accessed June 3, 2012.

Lower Colorado River Authority. 2012. Mansfield Dam and Lake Travis. http://www.lcra.org/water/dams/mansfield.html, accessed June 3, 2012.

Meyer, L. 2012. City of San Antonio Drought Operations Plan. City of San Antonio, Office of Environmental Policy. www.sanantonio.gov/oep/pdf/Drought%200perations%20Plan.pdf, accessed June 3, 2012.

National Climatic Data Center. 2012. Texas Precipitation, January–December 1895–2011. National Oceanic and Atmospheric Administration. http://www.ncdc.noaa.gov/temp-and-precip/time-series/index.php?parameter=pcp&month=12&year=2011&filter=12&state=41&div=0, accessed June 3, 2012.

National Drought Mitigation Center. 2014. GIS Data Archive: Drought Monitor Files. University of Nebraska–Lincoln. http://droughtmonitor.unl.edu/MapsAndData/GISData.aspx, accessed September 8, 2014.

Nielsen-Gammon, John. 2011. The 2011 Texas Drought. Office of the State Climatologist, College of Geosciences, Texas A&M University.

Nottingham, Earl. 2011. Lake O. C. Fisher. Photograph, Digital image. Texas Parks and Wildlife.

Office of the State Demographer. 2012. Demographic Characteristics and Trends: Austin and San Antonio Metro Areas. http://txsdc.utsa.edu/Resources/Presentations/OSD/2012/2012_09_14_Austin_San_Antonio_Growth%20Summit_San_Marcos.pdf, accessed April 28, 2015.

Ramirez, Stephen. 2012. Birdsiview Photography Services. Personal communication, March.

Ripley, Brad. 2012. Meteorologist, US Department of Agriculture. Personal communication, June.

San Antonio Water System. 2015. Drought Restrictions. http://www.saws.org/conservation/droughtrestrictions/, accessed June 1, 2015.

Sinkin, Fay. 1997. Oral history interview, conducted in San Antonio, Texas, August 24. Texas Legacy Project, Conservation History Association of Texas. Austin, Texas. http://www.texaslegacy.org, accessed June 4, 2012.

Smith, Jordan. 2015. Geospatial Specialist, Emergency Operations Center, Texas Forest Service. Personal communication, April.

Texas Commission on Environmental Quality. 2012. List of Texas PWSs Limiting Water Use to Avoid Shortages. http://www.tceq.texas.gov/drinkingwater/trot/location.html, accessed June 4, 2012.

Texas Comptroller of Public Accounts. 2014. Gross State Product and Income. http://www.texasahead.org/economy/indicators/ecoind/ecoind5.php, accessed July 16, 2014.

Texas Forest Service. 2014a. Fire Reports, April 9, 2014. Access database provided by Madelyn Galloway, Public Information Coordinator, July 16.

———. 2014b. Historical Fire Activity. Spreadsheet provided by Madelyn Galloway, Public Information Coordinator, July 16.

Texas Water Development Board. 2011. Reservoir Storage: October 2011. http://www.twdb.state.tx.us/publications/reports/waterconditions/twc_pdf_archives/2011/twcOct2011.pdf, accessed July 15, 2014.

———. 2012a. Reservoir Storage Index by River Basin. Texas Water Development Board. http://www.twdb.state.tx.us/apps/droughtinfo/Animation.aspx, accessed June 3, 2012.

———. 2012b. Reservoir Storage Summary. Texas Water Development Board. http://wiid.twdb.state.tx.us/ims/resinfo/BushButton/lakeStatus.asp, accessed June 3, 2012.

———. 2015. Well Locations from TWDB Submitted Driller's Reports Database (SDRDB), August 24, 2001 through April 21, 2015. https://www.twdb.texas.gov/mapping/gisdata/doc/SDRDB_well_locations.zip, accessed April 28, 2015.

US Census. 2015. Income in the Past 12 Months (in 2013 Inflation-Adjusted Dollars), 2009–2013 American Community Survey 5-Year Estimates. Table S1901. American Fact Finder. US Census. http://factfinder.census.gov/, accessed April 28, 2015.

Vaughan, E. G. 2011. Water for Texas: Summary of the 2011 Regional Water Plans. Texas Water Development Board. Austin. http://www.twdb.texas.gov/wrpi/rwp/documents/2011RWPLegislativeSummary.pdf, accessed June 3, 2012.

Stream Flows and Water Rights

The Rio Grande is a magnificent and storied river, draining more than 11 percent of the continental United States and flowing over 2,000 miles from its source in the southern Rockies to its delta on the Gulf of Mexico.

However, the river is a workhorse, tamed and used by farms and cities throughout its length, on both the Mexican and US sides. In fact, diversions now claim 95 percent of its flows, and parts of the river ran dry in four years during the early 2000s. In 2002, the Rio Grande actually failed to reach the Gulf. As Will Rogers said, the Rio Grande is "the only river I know that is in need of irrigation" (Levings et al. 1998).

The Rio Grande is not alone among Texas rivers in facing serious flow shortages. Water availability models, computer programs that simulate stream flows and water diversions, have dire news for many Texas rivers. The Guadalupe River is one example. If municipalities, farmers, industries, and other users diverted what they typically pump out of the Guadalupe, and these diversions occurred during serious drought conditions, only 9 percent of average flows would remain in the riverbed. Drought conditions during June 2009 were an omen of what the future might hold: the Guadalupe River went dry near Canyon Lake. American Rivers declared it one of America's most endangered rivers in 2002 (Patoski 2004).

How did we get into this situation? The short answer is that there is more water diverted and used than streams such as the Rio Grande and the Guadalupe can support.

How this wide array of large water rights came to be issued is a more complicated story.

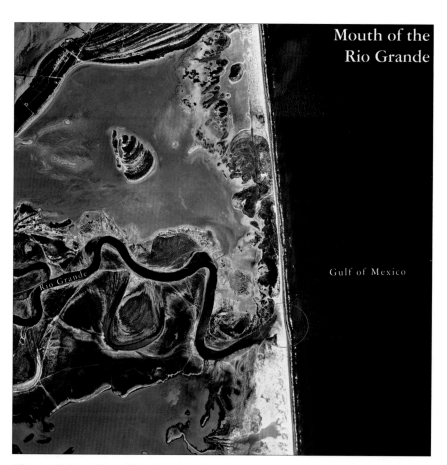

Mouth of the Rio Grande

Gulf of Mexico

Rio Grande

This aerial photo of Boca Chica, the delta of the Rio Grande, was taken on February 8, 2002, during the time that the parched Rio Grande failed to reach the Gulf (US Geological Survey 2014).

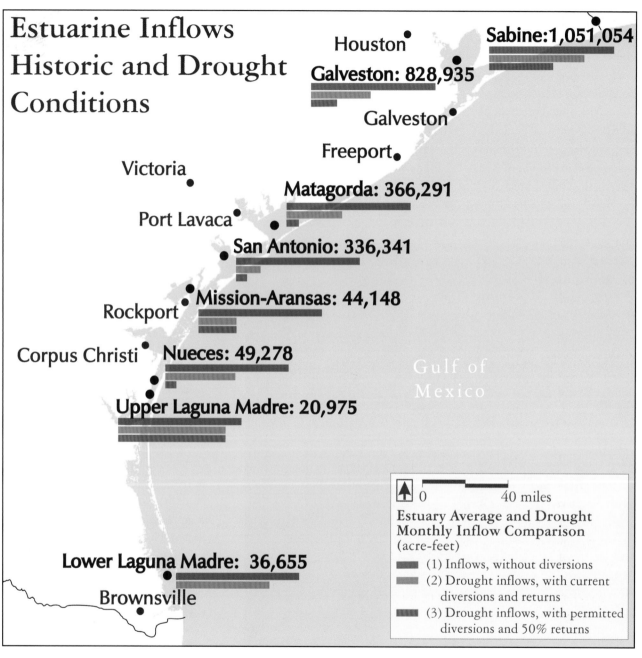

Estuarine Inflows Historic and Drought Conditions

Houston

Sabine: 1,051,054

Galveston: 828,935

Galveston

Freeport

Victoria

Matagorda: 366,291

Port Lavaca

San Antonio: 336,341

Rockport

Mission-Aransas: 44,148

Corpus Christi

Nueces: 49,278

Upper Laguna Madre: 20,975

Gulf of Mexico

Lower Laguna Madre: 36,655

Brownsville

0   40 miles

Estuary Average and Drought Monthly Inflow Comparison (acre-feet)

(1) Inflows, without diversions

(2) Drought inflows, with current diversions and returns

(3) Drought inflows, with permitted diversions and 50% returns

This map of inflows into Texas estuaries shows three sets of conditions:

(1) monthly average (1948–96) flows into Texas bays and estuaries if no human diversions existed (roughly the 1880 situation);

(2) monthly drought-of-record (1950–56) flows into Texas bays and estuaries if actual diversions were deducted and current return flows (the waste-water discharges, cooling and irrigation water returned to a river), were present in the streams; and

(3) monthly drought-of-record flows into Texas bays and estuaries, if all permitted water use were deducted, and only half the return flows were in the stream. It should be noted that the vast majority of water-use permits do not require any return flow (Johns 2012; TCEQ 2012).

International Relations

Some Texas rivers have unique problems. For example, as an international river, the Rio Grande's flows are shared between the United States and Mexico under the Treaty of 1944. Beginning in 1992, Mexico fell behind on its obligations to deliver water to US users, evidently due to drought in Mexico, the construction of five reservoirs along the Rio Conchos (a tributary of the Rio Grande), and increased irrigation in Mexico (Phillips 2002). By 2002, when the Rio Grande failed to reach the Gulf, Mexico owed the United States 450 billion gallons of water (US Water News 2005). In fact, Mexico was not able to catch up on its water debts until October 2005, and only then due to the return of more plentiful rainfall.

Riparian Doctrine

Aside from the Rio Grande's unique challenges, most rivers in Texas share a number of problems. For instance, during the early 1800s, Texian settlers brought with them a fondness and familiarity with the English common law, a tradition that was basically unsuited to managing water in this arid country. The English doctrine of riparian rights allowed for all landowners with river frontage to have rights to stream flow. In the Texas landscape of frequent and severe drought, this competing set of rights to stream flow was only an invitation to contest and controversy.

Since 1913, a stricter and more centralized system of allotting water rights has taken over, based more closely on the "prior appropriation" model that the Spanish and Mexican culture had earlier brought to Texas (Texas Water Rights Adjudication Act of 1967). Still, a 200-acre-feet-per-year exemption for riverside landowners persists, presumably only for home, gardens, and domestic livestock use, but at times stretched to include such imaginative uses as waterskiing (Sansom 2008, 178)!

Groundwater

Another struggle in finding adequate environmental flows hinges on the Texas view of groundwater's connection with surface water. Groundwater use in Texas is governed by the "rule of capture," essentially the law of the biggest pump, where a landowner is presumed to own all the groundwater he can manage to withdraw. There is little concern or liability for subsidence, drawdown, or other impacts the pumper may impose on his neighbors (*Houston & T. C. Railway Co. v. East*, 81 S.W. 279 (1904)). Texas groundwater law is far different from the system of centrally controlled, prior appropriation that applies to Texas surface water. While the Texas legislature recognized the potential for joint or "conjunctive" use of groundwater and surface water in 2001, often the law has seen little connection between the two, allowing essentially unregulated groundwater pumping to reduce, and in some cases,

eliminate spring flows that are essential to streams (Texas Administrative Code, Section 356.52(a)(1)D)).

The Guadalupe basin, where springs provide much of the river's base flow, provides an example of how overuse of groundwater can shortchange surface water supplies. During the drought of 1996, flows from Comal and San Marcos Springs made up 70 percent of the water in the Guadalupe at Victoria, and nearly 40 percent of what reached San Antonio Bay (Guadalupe Blanco River Authority 2012). Clearly, if groundwater withdrawals are excessive, instream and estuarine flows on the surface will suffer.

"Waste was described as a bucket of water that escaped into the Gulf of Mexico. The objective, at that point, was to dam every river in Texas so that there was not a drop of water that went out of a Texas river in to the Gulf of Mexico.... Every river in Texas would be so controlled that no water would be wasted into the Gulf of Mexico."

—Joe Moore Jr., June 22, 1999, San Marcos, Texas

Beneficial Uses and Other Uses

Another challenge for carving out rights for environmental flows lies in what is considered a "beneficial use" in the state. Traditionally, Texas water rights have only been granted for uses seen as "beneficial," such as domestic, municipal, industrial, agricultural, mining, navigation, and other human applications (Texas Water

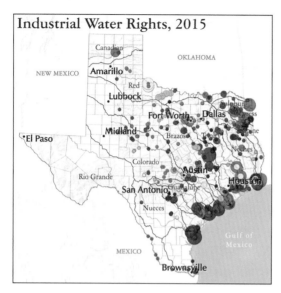

Industrial Water Rights, 2015

This map illustrates where more than 750 rights have been let for industrial process and cooling water. Early rights were issued to the Acme Brick Company (Guadalupe River, 25 acre-feet, 1900), Cemex concrete company (Rio Grande, 178 acre-feet, 1910), and Texas Municipal Power Agency (Navasota, 3,600 acre-feet, 1910). One of the larger rights, for 4.2 million acre-feet from the Brazos River, went to Dow Chemical in 1940 (TCEQ 2015a and 2015b).

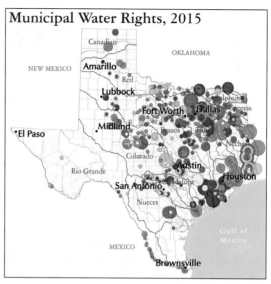

Municipal Water Rights, 2015

This map depicts over 1,050 water rights issued for municipal uses, starting with an 1889 entry by the US government for a diversion from the Rio Grande in El Paso, and ranging as high as the 1.5 million acre-foot permit received by the Lower Colorado River Authority in 1926 (TCEQ 2015a and 2015b).

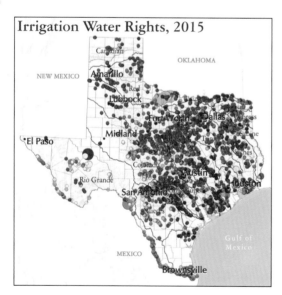

Irrigation Water Rights, 2015

This map shows the size and location of over 6,100 irrigation rights in the state. The history of irrigation rights is long: the first right was granted in 1731, for 1,440 acre-feet from the San Antonio River. The largest right was issued in 1980 for 292,500 acre-feet from the Pecos River (TCEQ 2015a and 2015b).

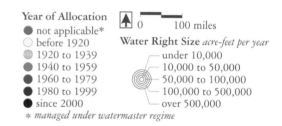

Year of Allocation
- not applicable*
- before 1920
- 1920 to 1939
- 1940 to 1959
- 1960 to 1979
- 1980 to 1999
- since 2000

* *managed under watermaster regime*

0   100 miles

Water Right Size *acre-feet per year*
- under 10,000
- 10,000 to 50,000
- 50,000 to 100,000
- 100,000 to 500,000
- over 500,000

Code, Section 11.023(a)(1)). Stream flow that managed to make it to the bay has typically been considered lost and wasted, since it did not fall within those recognized uses (Moore 1999). Seeing this problem, Texas passed a law in 1985 requiring that all new water rights within 200 river miles of the coast leave enough water to maintain downstream bays and estuaries (Texas Water Code Section 11.147(b)). The legislature attempted to strengthen these environmental flow standards in 2003 and 2007, but roughly 90 percent of Texas water had already been granted, much of it decades before (Texas Water Code Section 11.147(d, e)). Little uncommitted water remained available for fish, wildlife, and other instream uses (Texas Administrative Code, Title 30, Part 1, Chapter 297, Subchapter E, Rule 297.55(c); Johns 2012).

Reuse and Return Flows

Traditionally, some 60 percent of water diverted from Texas rivers for municipal use has been returned to streams from wastewater plants. However, these return flows are not guaranteed. If the municipality continues to use the same discharge location, it is entitled to be more efficient (or more consumptive as the case may be) and return less, much less, to the stream. Technically, Texas water users can decide to return no water to the stream if they have earlier used it "beneficially" (Texas Water Code, Section 11.046).

As stream flows become less plentiful, and rights become more difficult to secure, it is likely that many rights holders will gradually use more and more of the water they have been allocated and return less and less to Texas streams. The estuarine inflows shown in the accompanying map of the coast assume return flows of 50 percent, which may be optimistic. Those returns may turn out to be much less as cities and farmers become more frugal and efficient in their use of water.

Banking and Forfeiture

The state of Texas grants rights not to water per se, but rather to water use. So if the water is not used (under state law, for ten years), the rights are theoretically subject to cancellation (Neuman and Hirokawa 2000; Texas Administrative Code, Rule 297.73). However, the state seldom enforces this forfeiture power, despite the large amount of banked water rights (100,000 acre-feet for the Guadalupe alone) (The Aransas Project 2012). In this way, the state, in effect, encourages rights holders to bank their water licenses, against the possibility that they might need the water in the future.

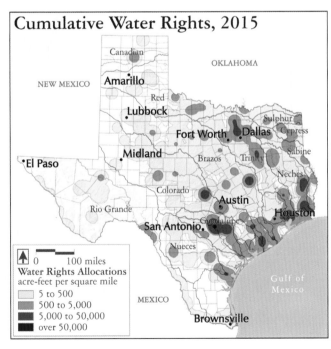

Cumulative Water Rights, 2015

Water Demand

Weather patterns and stream flows vary according to their own rhythm. Those cycles may have nothing to do with human population growth, economic development, and the related water needs. Texas has seen dramatic population growth over the past century, jumping over sixfold from 3.9 million in 1910 to 25.1 million in 2010, and this trend does not seem to be abating (Texas State Library and Archives Commission 2012). To complicate things further, many of these new Texans are finding their homes in the more arid western and southern portions of the state.

Economic increases have been even more rapid. The gross state product for Texas has grown by more than threefold in just the last twenty years, from $450 billion in 1993 to $1.45 trillion in 2013 (Texas Comptroller 2014). Fortunately, despite the growth in the economy and population, we are becoming more efficient in how we use the precious wet stuff. Per-capita water use is actually down slightly, about 13.1 percent from 1974 to 2012 (Texas Water Development Board 2015). However, it is increasingly hard to have natural water supplies and pumped water deliveries follow the dynamic moves of people among many parts of the state and the radical shifts in business among a slew of diverse industries.

Drought of Record

Rain comes and goes. That's particularly true in Texas, which has wide swings in rainfall. To build a buffer against errors, water planning in Texas uses a worst-case scenario of flows that were measured during the so-called drought of record, from 1950 to 1956 (Moore 2005, 8). Unfortunately, historical records in Texas are relatively brief. Earlier droughts, perhaps longer and more severe, may be more useful as a true worst-case scenario. For example, tree-ring studies suggest that Texas went through several twenty- to forty-year droughts in the 1100s and 1200s and faced a serious dry period in the latter half of the 1500s, as well as during the eras of the Revolutionary and Civil Wars (Cleaveland 2006; Cleaveland et al. 2011). The extreme drought of 2011, the most severe one-year dry period on record, reminds us that the threat of a recurring drought is always with us, even one that might possibly be more punishing than the official "drought of record." Harsh droughts can upend the best-laid plans, as when the Lower Colorado River Authority had to seek repeated waivers from its own agreements to deliver flows to Matagorda Bay (Hyde 2014).

Climate Change

As climate changes, rainfall and other weather patterns may not come and go as they did in the past. Past is not always prologue. Projections indicate that Texas will face a warmer and drier climate than what the state experienced in the past. By 2050, scientists expect that the average Texas temperature will increase by 3.6 degrees Fahrenheit, and precipitation will decline, on average, by 5 percent. Predicted growth in population and water demand, factoring in the expected lower rainfall and higher heat and evaporation, gives a dire view of the state's future water situation. Projected stream flows at the Texas coast are predicted to fall by 30 percent under normal conditions, and by 85 percent in drought, compared with the year 2000 (Schmandt, North, and Clarkson 2011, 11). Oddly, so far, the Texas Water Development Board has chosen not to consider climate change in its predictions about future availability of water in the state (Satija 2014).

Interception of Diffused Surface Water

Other water-related factors come into play as well. For example, Texas law gives an exemption for landowners to build stock tanks and farm ponds if they do not exceed 200 acre-feet (Texas Water Code, Section 11.142). However, these ponds' impact is not negligible. Each of these thousands of small ponds diverts and stores runoff, losing significant amounts of water to evaporation and seepage, water that might otherwise reach the main Texas streams and rivers (Templer 1991). Naturally, these same problems also

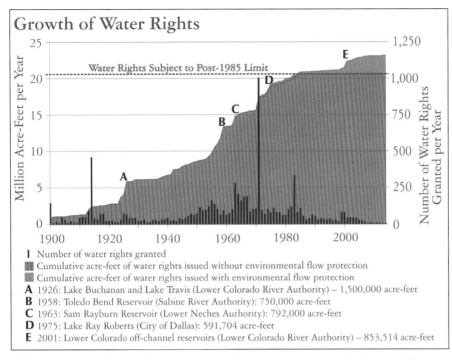

Growth of Water Rights

Water Rights Subject to Post-1985 Limit

I Number of water rights granted
Cumulative acre-feet of water rights issued without environmental flow protection
Cumulative acre-feet of water rights issued with environmental flow protection
A 1926: Lake Buchanan and Lake Travis (Lower Colorado River Authority) – 1,500,000 acre-feet
B 1958: Toledo Bend Reservoir (Sabine River Authority): 750,000 acre-feet
C 1963: Sam Rayburn Reservoir (Lower Neches Authority): 792,000 acre-feet
D 1975: Lake Ray Roberts (City of Dallas): 591,704 acre-feet
E 2001: Lower Colorado off-channel reservoirs (Lower Colorado River Authority) – 853,514 acre-feet

This figure shows the dramatic increase in consumptive water-use rights issued by the state of Texas from 1900 to 2014. While environmental flow conditions were placed on Lake Texana and Choke Canyon Reservoir in 1972 and 1975, most of these rights were exempt from the environmental flow set-asides passed in 1985 (Johns 2004; Johns 2012; Johns 2015; TCEQ 2015a and 2015b).

arise with the major reservoirs in the state, of which there are more than 180 with storage exceeding 5,000 acre-feet (Texas Water Development Board 2012, 159).

Vegetation

Plants catch, absorb, and transpire large amounts of water. However, a long history of overgrazing in Texas has removed many of the native stands of grasses, forbs, and sedges (Weniger 1984, 182–86). Without this groundcover, rains likely evaporate and/or run off more rapidly than before, leaving less to be stored and released gradually during dry times. In some cases, it is the reverse: there is too much vegetation, at least of the wrong kind, intercepting rainfall. For example, tamarisk, a small invasive tree planted for erosion control, has become a significant problem along the banks of the Pecos and Rio Grande, where it absorbs large amounts of water (Sansom 2008, 222).

Time

Perhaps timing is the major problem with water rights and their impact on environmental flow. Most rights were issued in the early part of the twentieth century, before a good deal of the explosive growth in the Texas economy and population. These water rights were also granted before there was a thorough understanding of the key ecological role that stream flows played. Because of the issuance of those early water rights, there is little leeway, little slack, for setting aside water now or in the future for instream and estuarine flows. The water has already been pledged for other uses. Ninety percent of Texas water rights were issued before the initial 1985 agreement to secure flows for environmental needs (Kelly 2004, 28). In the same way, the environmental reallocations promised under Senate Bill 3 of 2007 are limited to the scant flows that have not been previously committed (Texas Water Code, Section 11.1471). Until, or unless, those earlier commitments of water rights can be opened and revised, it will be very difficult to provide sufficient flows to Texas streams, bays, and wildlife.

What Now?

What can be done? A number of solutions have been proposed, several of which might help protect flows in the Rio Grande, Guadalupe, and other threatened Texas rivers.

Groundwater Limits

One step has been to bring some limits to groundwater use. In 1993, the Sierra Club sued to cap withdrawals from the Edwards aquifer on the basis of protecting spring flows that were essential to endangered species, such as the fountain darter. The suit spurred extensive rounds of litigation, statutory interventions, and creation of an entire new agency, the Edwards Aquifer Authority. In the end, caps on groundwater withdrawals from the Edwards did take effect, benefiting spring flows to the Guadalupe and other streams rising in the Hill Country (Votteler 2004; *Sierra Club v. Babbitt*, 995 F2d 571 (1993)).

Water Sales and Leases

Another effort has focused on returning water rights to Texas rivers. In 2005, the Thornton family leased rights for 70 acre-feet of water, or 23 million gallons of flow per year, to the Guadalupe-Blanco River Trust. The family provided those rights to maintain instream flows in the Guadalupe. Although the lease was temporary, for just five years, the arrangement suggests the possibility of other rights being restored to the river (Croteau 2005). There is also hope that water rights might be traded in the lower reaches of the Rio Grande, where the rights do not have the kind of seniority issues that require complex review by the state (Kelly 2004, 18).

Unappropriated Rights

A third approach has been to capture unappropriated water rights and dedicate those to instream flows. In 2000, the San Marcos River Foundation applied for 1.15 million acre-feet of

The whooping crane (Grus americana), and its main food source, the blue crab (Callinectes sapidus), are highly dependent on freshwater inflows to Texas' coastal estuaries (Hagerty 2012).

unclaimed water in the Guadalupe River, for the purpose of insuring that those 40 billion gallons remained in the river and in San Antonio Bay (Bernstein 2002). In a torturous eight-year trip through Texas agency hearings and judicial courtrooms, this claim was ultimately denied by the Texas Supreme Court, which ruled that the claim had been superseded by a process laid out by Senate Bill 3 (SB 3), passed in 2007.

SB 3 provides the major, credentialed approach for protecting estuarine inflows (Texas Water Code, Section 11.1471). However, in streams like the Guadalupe, advocates argue that SB 3 is ineffective, since there is too little spare, unallocated flow for SB 3 to reallot for environmental purposes. They believe the

central problem in the Guadalupe, and perhaps other Texas rivers, is simple overallocation of water. The state water bank has effectively loaned out more than it has.

The Aransas Project

So, some propose skirting SB 3 and pulling from previously appropriated water rights to insure that adequate instream flows remain in Texas rivers. This alternative to SB 3 follows the 1993 example of *Sierra Club v. Babbitt*, where federal protections of the rare fountain darter were used to upend Texas groundwater law and protect spring flows from the Edwards aquifer (*Sierra Club v. Babbitt*, 995 F2d 571 (1993)). In this second instance, another nonprofit group, the Aransas

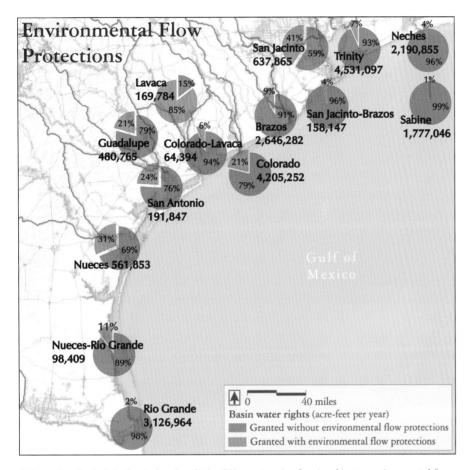

Environmental Flow Protections

San Jacinto 637,865 — 41% / 59%

Trinity 4,531,097 — 7% / 93%

Neches 2,190,855 — 4% / 96%

Lavaca 169,784 — 15% / 85%

San Jacinto-Brazos 158,147 — 4% / 96%

Sabine 1,777,046 — 1% / 99%

Brazos 2,646,282 — 9% / 91%

Guadalupe 480,765 — 21% / 79%

Colorado-Lavaca 64,394 — 6% / 94%

Colorado 4,205,252 — 21% / 79%

San Antonio 191,847 — 24% / 76%

Nueces 561,853 — 31% / 69%

Gulf of Mexico

Nueces-Rio Grande 98,409 — 11% / 89%

Rio Grande 3,126,964 — 2% / 98%

0 — 40 miles

Basin water rights (acre-feet per year)
Granted without environmental flow protections
Granted with environmental flow protections

This map and set of pie charts show how little of Texas estuarine flow is subject to environmental flow conditions. It is estimated that only 12 percent of all consumptive water rights in the state have come under instream protections (Johns 2004; Johns 2015; TCEQ 2015a and 2015b).

Project, has tried to use federal endangered species protection to restructure Texas surface water law. In March 2010, the Aransas Project sued the Texas Commission on Environmental Quality (TCEQ), charging that the agency's overallocation of water rights in the Guadalupe had endangered the rare whooping crane. The drought of 2008–9 had seen the loss of 8.5 percent of the worldwide wild flock of cranes, 42 percent of its juveniles. The Aransas Project alleged that these crane deaths were due to shortages of estuarine inflows, and related declines in the blue crabs that form the core of the cranes' diet.

On March 11, 2013, the court announced its ruling in favor of the Aransas Project, holding that the TCEQ had failed to manage Guadalupe River flows in a way that protected the endangered whooping crane population (*The Aransas*

Project v. Shaw, No. 2:10-cv-075, 2013 WL 943780 (S.D. Texas, March 11, 2013)). However, the ruling was reversed on appeal (*The Aransas Project v. Shaw*, 44 ELR 20146, No. 13–40317 (5th Cir., June 30, 2014)). The circuit court based its opinion on the view that the impact of diversions on the cranes was unforeseeable.

Many environmental advocates hope that there is a silver lining to the much-publicized and very disappointing Aransas Project ruling. Now, these water rights, diversions and shortages, and their dire effect on the natural world have been sufficiently analyzed, briefed, discussed, and reviewed. It seems possible that the impacts of water policy can no longer be considered unforeseeable. Perhaps Texas has finally paid the price for recognition, too long delayed in coming, of the environmental consequences of human water use in the state. Perhaps the state is now aware of the damage that water diversions can cause in the living world and will work harder to protect cranes and all the other wildlife of Texas streams, lakes, and estuaries.

Sources

The Aransas Project. 2012. A Troubled Basin. http://thearansasproject.org/situation/basin-management/, accessed May 31, 2012.

Bernstein, J. 2002. "The Rights of a River: Environmentalists Stake a Radical Claim to the Water in the Guadalupe." *Texas Observer* (June 21).

Christian, Prescott. 2015. Office of Water,

Texas Commission on Environmental Quality. Personal communication, June.

Cleaveland, M. K. 2006. "Extended Chronology of Drought in the San Antonio Area." Revised report. Tree-Ring Laboratory, Geosciences Department, University of Arkansas. Fayetteville.

Cleaveland, M. K., T. H. Votteler, D. K. Stahle, R. C. Casteel, and J. L. Banner. 2011. "Extended Chronology of Drought in South Central, Southeastern, and West Texas." *Texas Water Journal* 2 (1): 54–96. Texas Water Resources Institute.

Croteau, R. 2005. "River Trust Secures Historic Water Rights." *Houston Chronicle*, November 27.

Guadalupe Blanco River Authority. 2012. Edwards Aquifer and the Guadalupe River. http://www.gbra.org/drought/edwardsaquifer.aspx, accessed June 1, 2012.

Hagerty, Ryan. 2012. Whooping Crane. Photograph. US Fish and Wildlife Service. http://www.flickr.com/photos/usfwshq/6777481034/sizes/1/in/photostream/, accessed December 22, 2012.

Hess, Myron. 2015. Counsel South Central Regional Center, National Wildlife Federation. Personal communication.

Hyde, Richard. 2014. An Order Granting an Emergency Authorization to the Lower Colorado River Authority to Amend Its Water Management Plan, Permit No. 5838, pursuant to section 11.139 of the Texas Water Code. Texas Commission on Environmental Quality. January 27.

Johns, Norman. 2004. "Bays in Peril: A Forecast for Freshwater Flows to Texas Estuaries." National Wildlife Federation. October.

———. 2012 and 2015. Water Resources Scientist, National Wildlife Federation. Personal communications, January through December 2012 and May 2015.

Kelly, Mary. 2004. "A Powerful Thirst: Water Marketing in Texas." Environmental Defense.

Levings, G. W., D. F. Healy, S. F. Richey, and L. F. Carter. 1998. "Water Quality in the Rio Grande Valley, Colorado, New Mexico, and Texas, 1992–95." US Geological Survey Circular 1162.

Moore, Joe, Jr. 1999. Oral history interview conducted June 22, in San Marcos, Texas. Texas Legacy Project. Conservation History Association of Texas.

———. 2005. "A Half Century of Water Resource Planning and Policy, 1950–2000." In *Water for Texas*, edited by Jim Norwine, John Giardino, and Sushma Krishnamurthy. College Station: Texas A&M University Press.

National Research Council. 2005. "The Science of Instream Flows: A Review of the Texas Instream Flow Program." Committee on Review of Methods for Establishing Instream Flows for Texas Rivers, Water Science and Technology Board, Division on Earth and Life Studies, National Research Council of the National Academies.

Neuman, J. C., and K. Hirokawa. 2000. "How Good Is an Old Water Right? The Application of Statutory Forfeiture Provisions to Pre-Code Water Rights." *University of Denver Water Law Review* 4 (1).

Patoski, Joe Nick. 2004. "Guad Is Good; Guad Is Great." *Texas Parks and Wildlife* (July).

Phillips, T. 2002. Behind the U.S.-Mexico Water Treaty Dispute, Interim News, April 30, 2002, Number 77-7, House Research Organization, Texas House of Representatives, Austin, Texas. http://www.hro.house.state.tx.us/interim/int77–7.pdf, accessed April 15, 2012.

Sansom, A. 2008. *Water in Texas: An Introduction*. Austin: University of Texas Press.

Satija, Neena. 2014. "Water Planners Focus on Bigger Texas, Not a Hotter One." *Texas Tribune*, July 14.

Schmandt, J., G. R. North, and J. Clarkson. 2011. *The Impact of Global Warming on Texas*. Austin: University of Texas Press.

Templer, O. W. 1991. "Water Rights Issues—Texas Water Rights Law: East Meets West." Water Resources Update, Spring 1991. www.ucowr.org/updates/pdf/V85_A2.pdf, accessed April 10, 2012.

Texas Commission on Environmental Quality (TCEQ). 2012. Water Availability Models. http://www.tceq.texas.gov/permiting/water_rights/wam.html#statewide, accessed April 15, 2012.

———. 2015a. Active Water Rights. https://www.tceq.texas.gov/assets/public/permitting/watersupply/water_rights/applications/wractive.xlsx, accessed June 24, 2015.

———. 2015b. WRAP Input Files and GIS Files by River Basin. https://www.tceq.texas.gov/permitting/water_rights/wr_technical-resources/wam.html/#wrapinput, accessed June 24, 2015.

Texas Comptroller of Public Accounts. 2014. Real Gross State Product, Chained 2005 Dollars, Texas

Economic Forecast: 2012–13. http://www.texastransparency.org/State_Finance/Budget_Finance/Reports/Forecasts/2012–13/rgspcalendar2012–13.csv, accessed August 20, 2014.

Texas State Library and Archives Commission. 2012. United States and Texas Populations, 1850–2010. https://www.tsl.state.tx.us/ref/abouttx/census.html, accessed April 9, 2012.

Texas Water Development Board. 2012. 2012 State Water Plan.

———. 2015. Water Use Summary Estimates, Historical Water Use Estimates. http://www.twdb.texas.gov/waterplanning/waterusesurvey/estimates/index.asp, accessed June 1, 2015.

Texas Water Development Board. 2015. Major River Basins. Shapefile. http://www.twdb.texas.gov/mapping/gisdata/doc/Major_River_Basins_Shapefile.zip, accessed June 25, 2015.

Tischler, Michelle. 2015. Office of Water, Texas Commission on Environmental Quality. Personal communication, June.

US Environmental Protection Agency. 1997. "Climate Change and Texas." Report EPA 230-F-97–008qq. Climate and Policy Assessment Division. Office of Policy, Planning, and Evaluation, US Environmental Protection Agency. Washington, DC. http://nepis.epa.gov/Adobe/PDF/40000IYM.PDF, accessed April 9, 2012.

US Geological Survey. 2014. Rio Grande delta, February 8, 2002. Aerial photograph. Digital image. EarthExplorer. http://earthexplorer.usgs.gov/, accessed August 20, 2014.

US Water News. 2005. Mexico's Rio Grande Water Debt Repaid." *US Water News*, October. http://uswaternews.com/archives/arcglobal/5mexiriox10.html, accessed April 15, 2012.

Votteler, T. H. 2004. "Raiders of the Lost Aquifer? Or, the Beginning of the End to Fifty Years of Conflict over the Texas Edwards Aquifer." *Tulane Law Journal*.

Woodward, C. 2003. "Rio Poco." *E: The Environmental Magazine* (July/August).

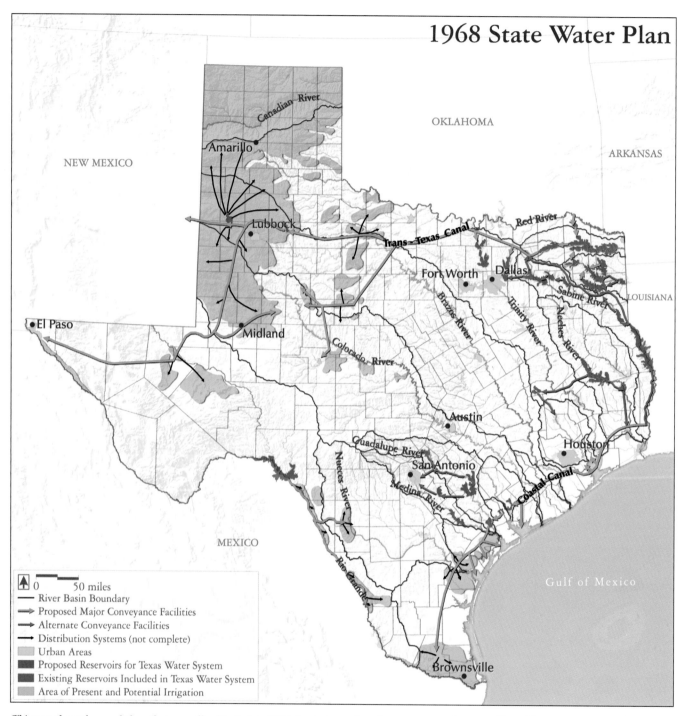

1968 State Water Plan

This map shows the grand plans that were offered in the late 1960s for storing and moving water across the state of Texas (Texas Water Development Board 1968).

Water Planning and Interbasin Transfers

"The Texas Water Plan Calypso
Well, the Texas Water Plan
Oh, the Texas Water Plan
...

When Dalhart is a seaport
And never mind those whiteface steers
There'll be blue lagoons in Hereford
And Venetian gondoliers
There'll be Everglades in Lubbock
And waterfalls so fair"

> —Pete Gunter, Denton,
> Texas, January 18, 1998

Transfers

Six million acre-feet, close to 2 trillion gallons, of water have been authorized for transfer from one watershed to another in the state of Texas (Votteler, Alexander, and Moore 2006, 142). The first major interbasin transfer occurred over one hundred years ago. In 1900, the Garwood Irrigation Company was authorized to use 168,000 acre-feet of Colorado River waters in both the Colorado and Lavaca river basins (Certificate of Adjudication No. 14-5434). The Colorado River is not the only stream involved in these transfers. Excluding Rio Grande transfers (which operate under a different system), there are 103 Texas water rights allowing 156 interbasin transfers (Votteler, Alexander, and Moore 2006, 128).

These transfers of water have grown to be a major part of the state's supply, with 20–25 percent of Texas' total surface water resulting from an interbasin transfer (Texas Water Development Board 1997, 3–31).

Impacts

These transfers are important to the state's water supply, but they are also costly. They are expensive from a financial perspective, on account of the cost to build and operate the canals, pipelines, tunnels, pumps, and other infrastructure required. They can have large impacts environmentally as well. Environmental effects arise from changes in timing and amount of flows, nutrients, and sediments, and the introduction of exotic plants and animals to new watersheds (Geo-Marine, Inc. 1996, V-1-11).

Rain and Stream Flow

There has long been pressure to move water around the state of Texas. In part this is due to natural factors of precipitation and stream flow. Precipitation varies hugely, from nearly 60 inches per year in the Big Thicket, to less than 10 inches annually in El Paso. As a result, stream flow ranges widely from the soggy parts of east and coastal Texas to the drier and more

westerly provinces of the state. For example, the Sabine's average flow, as it comes to the southeastern corner of the state, is 8,310 cubic feet per second, over twenty-two times the flow that arrives at the mouth of the Nueces River, near Corpus Christi (Asquith et al. 2007; Texas Water Development Board 2014a).

Population and Industry

Also, there are contributing factors that have to do with how the state has been settled and developed. Municipal water demands drive much of the pressure for interbasin transfers in Texas (Cai and McCarl 2007, 47). Great distances often separate the areas where people want to live and work, and where the water is. Think of this: 88 percent of the Texas population is urban, yet the vast bulk of water storage is in rural areas (Texas Department of State Health Services 2014). As well, much of Texas surface water supplies are located in East Texas, while many Texans have chosen to live in drier locales to the west and south, including the IH-35 corridor and the Lower Rio Grande Valley.

Another factor to consider is how a great deal of Texas' economy is enmeshed in industries that are heavy, concentrated users of water. Some of these industries, including

From Arid West to Rainy East

OKLAHOMA

NEW MEXICO

15″

Amarillo
17″

Lubbock
19″
21″

Fort Worth   Dallas

Midland
31″   37″   49″
41″   45″
27″   29″   33″   43″   49″
39″

El Paso
9″   17″
11″   11″   35″   51″
13″   25″   Austin   53″ 55″
23″   15″   59″
21″ 17″   23″   Houston

San Antonio

55″

Gulf of
Mexico

MEXICO

↑ 0 _____ 100 miles
Annual Precipitation,
1961 to 1990
59 inches per year

9 inches per year

Brownsville

This map shows how annual precipitation dwindles from over 55 inches in southeast Texas to less than ten inches in the parched deserts of the west. This uneven distribution of rainfall in the state has long driven dreams and plans of water transfers (Texas Water Development Board 2014b).

irrigated farms; petrochemical plants; and coal, gas, or nuclear utilities, may need to draw on distant rivers and lakes, collected from yet more remote tributaries.

Ironically, the transfers to serve these municipal, agricultural, and industrial demands may sometimes lead to moving water for environmental reasons. For instance, surface water exports have been proposed as a way to mitigate groundwater overdraft and decline in the Panhandle's Ogallala,

and to offset overpumping and land subsidence in the Houston Ship Channel region.

Drought

A last factor is a combination of natural and man-made causes. While human needs are quite constant, the state's weather varies widely from year to year. Drought, which visits some part of the state every four years on average, can require por-

tions of the state facing emergency shortfalls to call on their neighbors for water. Particularly sharp pressure for transfers came from the great Texas drought of 1950–56. As a sign of its severity, consider that by 1956, fully 244 of Texas' 254 counties were considered disaster areas for lack of rain! (Sansom 2008, 32). Fear of a return of this "Drought of Record" has driven many communities to seek guarantees of water supplies from near and, often, quite far.

Federal Support

The federal government initiated early efforts to move water across the state. In 1953, the US Bureau of Reclamation developed the Gulf Basins Project, which envisioned a canal from Beaumont to Corpus Christi and on to the irrigated fields of the Lower Rio Grande Valley (US Bureau of Reclamation 1953). A 1964 report from the bureau sought congressional approval for an even more ambitious plan. This grand proposal called for an interbasin canal that would cover two-thirds of the state, move over 2.8 million acre-feet of water, and divert stream flows from the Sabine, Neches, Trinity, Lavaca-Navidad, and Guadalupe–San Antonio river basins that "otherwise would waste into the Gulf of Mexico" (US Bureau of Reclamation 1962, 1, 9). Some of the transfers federal authorities envisioned were even interstate in scope: the Public Works Appropriation Act of 1967 outlined a

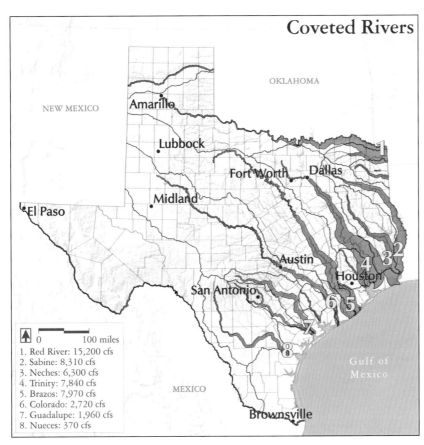

Coveted Rivers

OKLAHOMA

NEW MEXICO

Amarillo

Lubbock

Fort Worth   Dallas

Midland

El Paso

Austin

Houston

San Antonio

0   100 miles
1. Red River: 15,200 cfs
2. Sabine: 8,310 cfs
3. Neches: 6,300 cfs
4. Trinity: 7,840 cfs
5. Brazos: 7,970 cfs
6. Colorado: 2,720 cfs
7. Guadalupe: 1,960 cfs
8. Nueces: 370 cfs

MEXICO

Brownsville

Gulf of Mexico

This map compares historic stream flows in major Texas rivers. Powerful rivers course through East Texas, while stream flows in the southern and western parts of the state are much smaller. This contrast has too many political tensions and water transfer proposals. Nevertheless, please keep in mind that these data can be difficult to parse, as the gauging stations cover different periods of time, western rivers swing wildly from flash flood to low base flow, and reservoirs and diversions have significantly affected many rivers. Also, please note that comparable flow data were not available for the Rio Grande (Asquith, Vrabel, and Roussel 2007; Bezanson 2012, 2014, and 2015; East 2014; Texas Water Development Board 2015a and 2015b; US Geological Survey 2014 and 2015; Wentzel 2014).

$20.49 billion diversion of Mississippi River water from Louisiana to West Texas and New Mexico (Public Law 89-689, Oct. 15, 1966, 80 Stat. 1002).

State Efforts

Lobbying for interbasin transfers often found a good reception among state officials. In May 1961, the Texas Board of Water Engineers issued a report stating that "the Lower Trinity River Basin . . . will supply industrial water to the Houston industrial complex [which falls in the San Jacinto watershed], and a part of the San Antonio water needs would come from the Guadalupe River Basin" (Votteler,

Alexander, and Moore 2006, 133). A 1967 amendment to the state constitution created a source of money, called the Texas Water Development Fund, that would help underwrite transfers of this large scale and cost (Texas Constitution, Article III, Section 49(d)(a-b)). The Texas Water Plan of 1968 proposed how these and other matching funds would be spent. The state's Trans-Texas Canal would convey water from the Cypress, Sabine, Red, and Sulphur river basins westward to Dallas, the High Plains, Trans-Pecos, and New Mexico. Each year, this planned transfer would require lifting 10,034,000 acre-feet of water 3,800 feet in elevation, using seventy-one pumping stations and 50 billion kilowatts of energy to deliver the water 1,400 miles to its final destination (Ross 2006). Meanwhile, the Bureau of Reclamation joined in with its Coastal Plan, also known as Burleigh's Ditch, to bring 4,845,000 acre-feet from the Neches, Trinity, Guadalupe, and San Antonio river basins to the Rio Grande Valley (Votteler, Alexander, and Moore 2006, 135). In 1969, this combined state/federal plan was presented to the Texas public for a related constitutional amendment, but failed by a slim margin (H.J.R. 9, 61st Leg., Reg. Sess., 1969, Proposition 2).

Limits

The 1969 vote by the general public against the transfers reflected both long-standing and more recent statutory and judicial limits on shifting water from one watershed to another. The Burgess-Glasscock Act, also known as the 1913 Irrigation Act, prohibited diversions "to the prejudice of any person or property" (Acts 1913, 33rd Reg. Sess., Chapter 171, General Laws of Texas). A 1966 Texas Supreme Court ruling confirmed the continuing strength of this language (*City of San Antonio v. Texas Water Commission*, 407 S.W. 2d 752 (Tex. 1966)).

Similar pushback was happening in the state legislature during the mid-1960s. Senator Jack Strong represented the East Texas resistance to water exports (Long 1965; Moore 2005, 10). After some horse trading with Governor Connally in 1965, Strong gave his vote for a schoolteacher bill in exchange for statutory language that would bar exports if "the water supply involved will be required for reasonably foreseeable water supply requirements within the basin of origin during the next ensuing 50-year period, except on a temporary, interim basis" (Texas Water Code, Section 16.052).

A public vote in 1985 enshrined this same limiting language in the Texas constitution (Texas Constitution, Article III, Section 49(d)(3)). In 1997, Senate Bill 1 (SB 1) added yet another hurdle for transfers. SB 1 required that transferred waters be ranked as junior in priority to other water rights in the basin of origin. In other words, the imported "junior" water could not be tapped until after the local, in-basin water was used. If one of the available exemptions cannot be found, these transfers of junior rights would be less useful and reliable in times of drought and need (Stowe 2006, section 2, part 2; Texas Water Code, Section 11.085(s)).

Sometimes the opposition to water transfers is not judicial, statutory, or constitutional. Sometimes it is "transactional," one of trust and mistrust. One recent example is the long-brewing project to export Colorado River basin water to San Antonio. First proposed by the Lower Colorado River Authority and the San Antonio Water System (SAWS) in 2002, the idea was to have SAWS invest in agricultural water conservation and groundwater development in the Colorado watershed. In exchange, SAWS would receive 150,000 acre-feet of water per year. There seemed to be benefits for both parties. However, the proposal was mocked as the "San Antone Hose" and generated a great deal of opposition in the Colorado basin, especially for Lake Travis residents (Rowland 1996). The deal finally fell apart in 2009 when the LCRA decided that the project would not generate enough water, and San Antonio determined that it cost too much. Later, the split descended into ugly recriminations and lawsuits (McDonald 2011).

Detours

As some say, water runs uphill to money (Reisner 1993, 10). If there are impediments to water moving from one section of the state to another, often a "work-around," even a costly one, will be found. For instance, the state has witnessed the rise of "water ranching," buying or leasing tracts of land in order to import the groundwater that lies beneath. Groundwater's "Right of Capture" regulations, far looser than the state's surface water laws, allow much more flexibility for those interested in moving water across the state. For example, El Paso Water Utilities purchased land and the connected groundwater rights under 9,200 acres in Dell City, plus 25,000 acres near Valentine and 22,000 acres close to Van Horn (Elder 2003; Texas Center for Policy Studies 2001). West Texas is not the only area involved in water ranching. Central Texas communities (San Marcos, Kyle, and Buda) and private utilities are paying royalties and building pipelines to landowners in order to import their groundwater (O'Rourke and Price 2012).

Current Transfers

Despite the various paper barriers, surface water does continue to flow from basin to basin. However, these transfers do not involve the grand, multibasin, even interstate plumbing systems envisioned by state and federal agencies during the 1960s. While these bold ideas recur in some form from time to time (Gridzilla, a $2 million study of a state water market and conveyance network, got serious consideration during the 2015 legislature), they have not been built (Texas

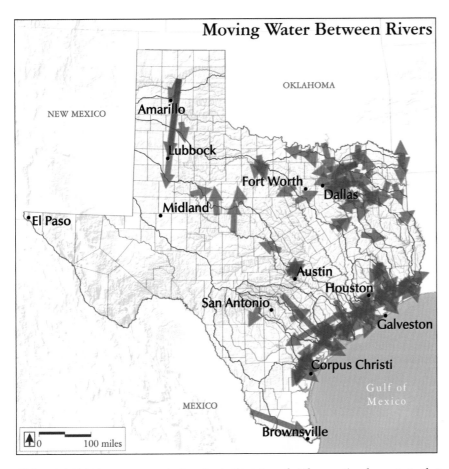

Moving Water Between Rivers

This map depicts the numerous water transfers in the state, and at the same time demonstrates that many of these shifts of water are quite short, from one basin to an adjacent basin, far different from the cross-state transfers that were envisioned fifty years ago (Alexander 2011; Votteler, Alexander, and Moore 2006).

Senate Bill 1907 and Texas House Bill 3298, 84th Legislature, R.S. (2015)). Instead, Texas has woven a crisscross of relatively short diversions among adjoining or close basins, often organized by local river authorities and municipalities. Although they may be shorter and less grandiose, the sheer number and diversity of Texas' approved surface water transfers show their great importance in the state (Votteler et al. 2006, 144–152):

Existing and Approved Transfers:

Brazos River to Brazoria County
Brazos River to BRA service area
Brazos River to City of Freeport
Bringle Lake to City of Texarkana
Calallen Reservoir to South Texas Water Authority
Calallen Reservoir to Corpus Christi industries

Calallen Reservoir to Nueces County WCID #3
Calallen Reservoir to San Patricio MWD and Nueces County WCID #4
City of Taft to Taft Drainage Canal
Colorado River to Corpus Christi and its service areas
Colorado River to Gulf Coast Water Division Service Area
Colorado River to South Texas Reservoir
Colorado River to Colorado-Lavaca and Brazos-Colorado basins
Colorado River and Eagle Lake to Lakeside Irrigation
Cooper Lake to Lake Lavon
Cooper Lake to Lake Lavon to service area
Cooper Lake to Lake Lavon, City of Irving and its service areas
Elm Bayou to San Antonio basin
Freeport Harbor Channel to Brazos River
Guadalupe River to Calhoun County
Guadalupe River to Victoria and its service area
Guadalupe River to Schwings Bayou (discharge point)
Houston County Lake to Highlands Reservoir
Lake Anahuac to Trinity River and Trinity Bay
Lake Athens to Athens WTP
Lake Austin and Lady Bird Lake to Williamson County and possibly others

Lake Clyde to City of Clyde

Lake Corpus Christi to Alice
Terminal Reservoir

Lake Corpus Christi to Beeville

Lake Crook to City of Paris

Lake Cypress Springs to
Mount Vernon WTP

Lake Cypress Springs to City
of Winnsboro

Lake Fork Reservoir to Dallas
via Lake Tawakoni

Lake J. B. Thomas to part of Fisher
County

Lake Kickapoo to City of Olney

Lake Lavon to Royse City and others

Lake Medina and Lake Diversion to
BMA Canals

Lake Meredith to Cities of Lamesa,
O'Donnel, and Brownfield

Lake Meredith to City of Lubbock

Lake Meredith to City of Amarillo

Lake Mexia to City of Mexia and
Mexia State School

Lake O' the Pines to City of
Longview

Lake Palestine to City of Tyler

Lake Palestine to Palestine

Lake Palestine to City of Dallas

Lake Pinkston to Center WTP

Lake Sulphur Springs to City of
Sulphur Springs

Lake Tawakoni to Commerce WTP

Lake Tawakoni to Wills Point

Lake Tawakoni to Dallas WTP or
Lake Ray Hubbard

Lake Tawakoni to Lake Terrell

Lake Texana to Lavaca River and
LNRA service area

Lake Texoma to Lake Lavon

Lake Travis to City of Cedar Park

Lake Travis to City of Leander

Lake Tyler to City of Tyler

Lake Wright Patman to City of
Atlanta

Lake Wright Patman to City of
Texarkana

Lakes Cooper and Olney to City of
Olney

Lakes Livingston and Lake
Houston to City of Houston
service area

Lakes Livingston and Wallisville to
City of Houston service area

Lavaca River to Lavaca-Guadalupe
basin

Mackenzie Reservoir to Cities of
Floydada and Lockney

Megargel Creek Lake and (small
lakes) to City of Megargle and
service area

Moss Reservoir to City of
Gainesville

Neches River to Neches-Trinity
basin

Neches River to Alligator Bayou

Neches River and Pine Island
Bayou to LNVA service area

Nueces River to Rincon Bayou

O. H. Ivie Reservoir to City of
Abilene

Oak Creek Reservoir to Lake
Trammell and Sweetwater

Oyster Creek to Brazos basin

San Antonio River to Elm Creek

SCS Reservoir on Elm Fork Trinity
River to City of St. Jo

Teague City Lake to City of Teague

Trinity River to Devers Rice
Growers

Trinity River to San Jacinto River
Authority

Village Creek to City of Van

Sources

Alexander, Kathy. 2011. Technical
Specialist, Water Rights and
Availability Section, Water Availability
Division, Texas Commission on
Environmental Quality. Personal com-
munication, November.

Asquith, William, Joseph Vrabel, and
Meghan Roussel. 2007. Summary of
Annual Mean, Maximum, Minimum,
and L-Scale Statistics of Daily Mean
Streamflow for 712 U.S. Geological
Survey Streamflow-Gaging Stations in
Texas through 2003. Data Series 248.
US Geological Survey, US Department
of the Interior. In cooperation with the
Texas Commission on Environmental
Quality. http://pubs.usgs.gov/
ds/2007/248/, accessed April 16, 2015.

Bezanson, David. 2012, 2014, and 2015.
Land Protection and Easements
Manager, Texas Chapter, The Nature
Conservancy. Personal communica-
tions, December 2012, December 2014
through May 2015.

Cai, Yongxia, and Bruce McCarl.
2007. "Economic, Hydrologic, and
Environmental Appraisal of Texas
Inter-Basin Water Transfers: Model
Development and Initial Appraisal."
Texas Water Resources Institute.

East, Jeffery. 2014. Surface Water
Specialist, Texas Water Science Center.
US Geological Survey. Personal com-
munication, October.

Elder, Robert, Jr. 2003. "The Battle for
West Texas Water: Landowners Fight
One Another, Outside Investors over
Liquid Gold." *Austin American-
Statesman*, August 24.

Geo-Marine, Inc. 1996. "Final Report:
Potential Aquatic Ecological Impacts of
Interbasin Transfers in the Southeast,

West-Central, and South-Central Study Areas, Plano, Texas."

Gunter, Pete. 1998. "Texas Water Plan Calypso," a song from an oral history interview, January 18, Denton, Texas. Texas Legacy Project, Conservation History Association.

Long, Stuart. 1965. "Water, Water Everywhere—But Whose?" *Victoria Advocate*, April 18.

McDonald, Colin. 2011. "LCRA will Pay SAWs to Settle Suit." *San Antonio Express News*, October 20.

Moore, Joe, Jr. 2005. "A Half Century of Water Resource Planning and Policy, 1950–2000." In *Water for Texas*, edited by Jim Norwine, John Giardino, and Sushma Krishnamurthy. College Station: Texas A&M University Press.

O'Rourke, Ciara, and Asher Price. 2012. "In Central Texas, a Rush to Secure Water Rights." *Austin American-Statesman*, December 7.

Reisner, Marc. 1993. *Cadillac Desert: The American West and Its Disappearing Water*. New York: Penguin.

Ross, Randolph. 2006. The Dust Bowl, Irrigation and the Ogallala Aquifer. Ohio State University. http://people.cohums .ohio-state.edu/roth5/history%20567/ lecture%20°utlines/lectures.htm, accessed November 30, 2011.

Rowland, Cole. 1996. "'San Antone Hose' Could Have a Draining Effect." *PLTA News* 15 (1). Protect Lake Travis Association.

Sansom, Andrew. 2008. *Water in Texas: An Introduction*. Austin: University of Texas Press.

Stowe, Jack. 2006. "Socioeconomic Analysis of Selected Interbasin Transfers in Texas." Draft Report for the Texas Water Development Board, prepared by R. W. Beck, Inc. November.

Texas Center for Policy Studies. 2001. Texas Water Policy Update: Water Ranching in the Lone Star State. December.

Texas Department of State Health Services. 2014. Projected Texas Population by Area, 2013. Center for Health Statistics. http://www.dshs .state.tx.us/chs/popdat/ST2013.shtm, accessed February 8, 2014.

Texas Water Development Board. 1968. 1968 State Water Plan. http://www .twdb.state.tx.us/waterplanning/ swp/1968/, accessed October 30, 2014.

———. 1997. State Water Plan, Water for Texas, Austin.

———. 2014a. River Basins. http://www .twdb.texas.gov/surfacewater/riv-ers/river_basins/index.asp, accessed August 20, 2014.

———. 2014b. Texas Precipitation. http:// www.twdb.state.tx.us/mapping/gis data/shapefiles/precipitation/precipita tion.zip, accessed October 30, 2014.

———. 2015a. GIS Data: Natural Features: Major River Basins. Shapefile. https:// www.twdb.texas.gov/mapping/gisdata/ doc/Major_River_Basins_Shapefile .zip, accessed May 15, 2015.

———. 2015b. GIS Data: Natural Features: Major Rivers. Shapefile. https://www. twdb.texas.gov/mapping/gisdata/doc/ Major_Rivers_dd83.zip, accessed May 15, 2015.

US Bureau of Reclamation. 1953. Water Supply and the Texas Economy: An Appraisal of the Texas Water Problem. Senate Document No. 57, 83rd Congress, 1st Session, January 1953.

———. 1958. Water Development and Potentialities of the State of Texas. Senate Document III, 85th Congress.

———. 1962. The Report of the U.S. Study Commission—Texas, Part I, The Commission Plan. A Report to the President and to Congress by the United States Study Commission on the Neches, Trinity, Brazos, Colorado, Guadalupe, San Antonio, Nueces, and San Jacinto River Basins and Intervening Areas 2–3. US Department of the Interior.

US Geological Survey. 2014. Current Conditions for Texas: Streamflow. National Water Information System. Web Interface. http://waterdata.usgs .gov/tx/nwis/current/?type=flow, accessed April 11, 2014.

———. 2015. USGS Streamgages Linked to the Medium Resolution NHD. http://water.usgs.gov/GIS/dsdl/ USGS_Streamgages-NHD_Locations_ GEODB.zip, accessed May 15, 2015.

Votteler, Todd, Kathy Alexander, and Joe Moore Jr. 2006. "The Evolution of Surface Water Interbasin Transfer Policy in Texas: Viable Options for Future Water, Water Grabs, or Just Pipe Dreams?" *Texas Environmental Law Journal* 36 (3).

Wentzel, Mark. 2014. Instream Flows Team Leader, Surface Water Resources Division, Texas Water Development Board. Personal communication, October.

Dams in the Big Bend

"An unspoiled river is a very rare thing in this Nation today. Their flow and vitality have been harnessed by dams and too often they have been turned into open sewers by communities and by industries. It makes us all very fearful that all rivers will go this way unless somebody acts now to try to balance our river development. So we are establishing a National Wild and Scenic Rivers System which will complement our river development with a policy to preserve sections of selected rivers in their free-flowing conditions and to protect their water quality and other vital conservation values."

—Lyndon B. Johnson, "Remarks upon Signing Four Bills Relating to Conservation and Outdoor Recreation," October 2, 1968

Texas has miles and miles of rivers, 184,797 miles by one count. Yet, there are just 195.7 miles, one-tenth of a percent, that are protected against dams (US Fish and Wildlife Service 2012). All of these protected river segments lie in the Big Bend canyons of the Rio Grande. This is a story of how those canyons came to be saved under the Wild and Scenic Rivers Act.

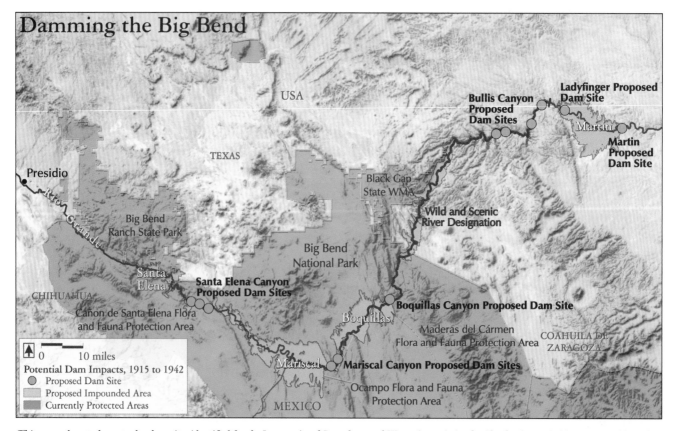

Damming the Big Bend

This general map shows twelve dam sites identified for the International Boundary and Water Commission by Charles Caracristi in 1915, and later by L. H. Henderson in 1942. There were three sites considered for Santa Elena (an upper, middle, and lower location), two for Mariscal (again, an upper and lower siting), one for Boquillas (3,000 feet below the entrance to the canyon), four for Bullis (the Jones, Waters, Madison, and Panther Gulch), one at Martin, and a smaller site at Ladyfinger (Tarabulski 2012).

The Big Bend of the Rio Grande is known as one of the most remote and pristine areas in the country. In fact, for many years, it was barely even known. One long-time Big Bend explorer estimated that fewer than sixty people had seen the entirety of the canyons before 1960 (Baker 2012). While many in the early days felt that the river was impassable, a handful of adventurers made it into the canyons. Some of the visitors were seeking transport routes. Others were trying to survey boundaries or document the natural history of the area. Yet more sought furs from wildlife along the river, while some travelers looked for excitement, beauty, and serenity.

Explorers

One early explorer was Harry Love, a civilian boat captain seeking a supply route for military posts along the Rio Grande. Love is believed to have traveled all the way from Brownsville to the Santa Elena Canyon during 1850, a feat not easily or often matched in later years (Walter 2007). In fact, the surveyor and marine Tyler Chandler ended his 1850 visit to Santa Elena with the remark, "the rapids and falls which occur in quick succession make the descent in boats entirely impracticable" (Tyler 1975, 88). Lieutenant Nathaniel Michler explored the area in 1852 and 1853 to chart the US-Mexico border. Michler managed to report on much of the local geology, vegetation, and wildlife, but traveled upstream only as far as Maravillas Canyon (in

An early and brave technique for running the canyons of the Big Bend is shown here (Duncan 2012; DuPont 1941–60).

Here is a downstream view of Boquillas Canyon, March 2008 (Ogren 2008).

Bob Burleson was a major advocate for appreciation and protection of the Big Bend canyons (Weisman 1999).

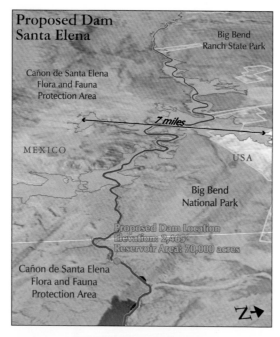
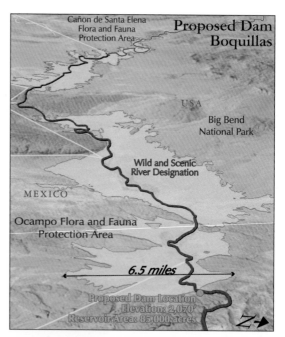
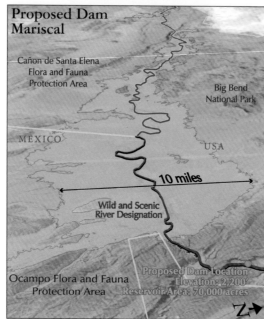

These figures show simulated aerial views, elevations, and dimensions of the major reservoirs proposed for the Santa Elena, Mariscal, Boquillas, and Martin Canyon sites in the Big Bend, based on descriptions in International Boundary and Water Commission documents from 1915 and 1942. Where multiple dam sites were considered for a canyon, we have assumed that the lowest, farthest downstream, site was chosen. Please note the line of the Wild and Scenic River segment authorized in 1978, and how it would block the reservoirs in Mariscal, Boquillas, and Martin Canyons. At this point, Wild and Scenic designation would not protect the Santa Elena Canyon, as the segment does not reach that far upstream (Caracristi 1915; Henderson 1942; Tarabulski 2012).

the vicinity of the modern-day Black Gap State Wildlife Management Area) (Emory 1857; Hill 1901, 374, 375; Aulbach 2007, 12, 73).

A generation later, a beaver trapper, James McMahon of Del Rio, was more successful. He claimed to have floated 300 miles of the Big Bend numerous times (Bentley 1927). However, the first complete and documented trip through the canyons of the Big Bend was not made until 1899, when Robert Hill of the US Geological Survey took a trip of more than a month and 350 miles from Presidio to Langtry. Even then, it was no cakewalk. The river was reputed even then to be "infested with thieves and murderers" and was called "Bloody Bend" in some quarters (Hill 1901).

Dam Proposals

While the canyons remained little understood, interest in damming the Rio Grande in the Big Bend gradually grew. As dam technology improved, prospects for flood control, hydroelectricity, and irrigation drew more attention. For instance, the US and Mexican governments were reported to have spent $1.2 million from as early as the 1870s through 1915 researching dams on the Rio Grande in the Big Bend area (Josten 1915, 1283). Two dam sites were extensively considered for the Big Bend in 1915: first, one in the Lajitas Canyon, and later, and in more detail, a dam in the Santa Elena Canyon (Findley, Cope, and Macon 1915, 667).

The Santa Elena structure was to be a massive dam, 370 feet high and 567 feet wide at its crest. The dam was slated to create the largest reservoir in America, perhaps the world, stretching 49.75 miles upstream and storing 13.6 million acre-feet (Rock Products and Building Materials 1915, 36; Caracristi 1915, 3, 7). Santa Elena's dam was proposed to control flood waters, fix the international boundary (by reducing erosion and accretion), and generate hydroelectricity for smelting iron, lead, silver, copper, and zinc from northern Mexico (Caracristi 1915, 2, 14, 15). This was not a far-fetched proposal for the time and place. The recommendation for a dam in the Big Bend came on the heels of two relatively near and recent Bureau of Reclamation projects. In 1907 and 1912, the bureau had rebuilt the Avalon Dam on the Pecos near Carlsbad, New Mexico. From 1911 through 1916, the bureau was involved in the construction of the Elephant Butte Reservoir farther upstream on the Rio Grande near Truth or Consequences, New Mexico.

The dams proposed in 1915 for the Big Bend canyons were reexamined in 1921 and 1929 but ultimately not pursued (Gilmor 2015; Henny and Walter 1929; Pease and Teeter 1921). The river remained remote and unsettled, with a character that had changed very little since Harry Love ran its rapids in 1850. In fact, its wild nature eventually became an argument for its protection. For example, in April 1937, noted historian and University of Texas profes-sor Walter Prescott Webb lobbied for state political support for the Big Bend National Park. He wrote,

> there is something very precious in this wild country, and that is a place of temporary escape from the world we know. . . . [The Big Bend] is a place where the spirit is lifted up as it must have been when the white man found America and before he had time to mar it with his improvements. . . . There it lies in its gorgeous splendor and geological confusion almost as it fell from the hands of the Creator. (Webb 1937)

River Runners

In May 1937, to give witness to the wild nature of the area, Webb privately organized a trip down the Santa Elena Canyon in two steel rowboats, the *Cinco de Mayo* and the *Big Bend* (Tyler 1975, 198). While the governor ultimately blocked funding of a state park in the Big Bend, the drama of the trip was evident from the breathless coverage in newspapers of the time: "Webb Defying Canyon Perils," "Explorers on Perilous Ride," and "No Word from 4 Explorers" (Welsh 2002).

Other river runners came later, and also worked for the canyons' appreciation and protection. The industrialist Henry DuPont was one pioneer in exploring the river. Through his many journeys down the river beginning in 1941, his early movies of the trips, and his support for new, safer equipment (particularly inflatable rubber rafts),

DuPont helped popularize white-water rafting in the canyons of the Big Bend (Skiles 2007). His adventures on the river opened the door to many who would later follow (some seven to eight thousand people are now estimated to float the canyons of the Big Bend each year) (Henington 2014). And via his photos of the Big Bend, some published in *Big Bend: A Homesteader's Story*, DuPont raised awareness of the long and fascinating story of life in the high desert (Langford and Gipson 1973).

Treaty of 1944

However, in the 1940s, interest still remained high in building a dam along the Rio Grande. In fact, in 1945, the United States and Mexico concluded negotiations on a pact regarding the river's future. The two nations ratified a far-reaching treaty allocating waters and providing for sanitation improvements in the international segment of the Rio Grande, running from Fort Quitman to the Gulf of Mexico (Treaty of February 3, 1944). Known as the Treaty of 1944, Article 5 of this agreement authorized construction of up to three dams on the Rio Grande. Two were eventually built: one at Amistad (dedicated in 1969), another at Falcon (completed in 1954). However, the third, to be sited "in the section between Santa Helena [*sic*] Canyon and the mouth of the Pecos River," mostly falling within the Big Bend, has not yet been built.

This dam in the Big Bend has remained a real possibility for many years. In fact, a 1942 report filed with the International Boundary and Water Commission (IBWC) goes into great detail about twelve possible dam sites in the Big Bend, including locations in Santa Elena, Mariscal, Boquillas, Bullis, and Martin Canyons (Henderson 1942). This was not a superficial or casual study; there were in-depth considerations of leakage through limestone channels; problems with faulting, voids, and caverns; risks of seismic activity; impacts on nearby mercury mines; and tallies of displaced communities. The survey goes on to account for the sourcing and costs of aggregate and concrete, the feasibility and pricing of road and railroad construction, the costs of land acquisition, the estimates of irrigation needs, possible markets for hydroelectricity, and other aspects of dam construction in the region. Nor were these to be small dams or insignificant reservoirs. The two favored sites, in Bullis and Martin Canyons, would have required dams of 435 to 500 feet in height, with crest widths of 850 to 1,000 feet. The dams would have backed up reservoirs covering 60 to 66,000 acres and containing 8 million acre-feet (almost twice the 4.48 million acre-foot capacity of Texas's largest modern-day reservoir at Toledo Bend) (Henderson 1942, 3, 8–9).

Protection

The latest, and presumably final, chapter in the story about a dam in the Big Bend was written from the early 1960s through 1978. In 1963, Bill Thompson, a writer, photographer, and member of the Texas Explorers Club, completed a grueling three-month trip down the Rio Grande, making it all the way from Presidio to the Gulf of Mexico (Koch and Price 2007, 148). Inspired by Thompson's run, a fellow member of the Texas Explorers Club, Bob Burleson, undertook an exploration of the canyons in 1965. Burleson was powerfully impressed by the wildness, isolation, and beauty of these chasms and began a multiyear effort to protect the great canyons (Burleson 1999).

Beginning in the mid-1960s, Burleson recruited many others to run the canyons. From 1965 through 1978, at their own expense and on their own time, Bob Burleson, John Baker, David Riskind, and others took as many as two thousand people, including many influential decision makers, through the canyons. Among the rafters and boaters were local ranchers and landowners; TV crews; and writers and photographers from *Time/Life*, *National Geographic*, the *Christian Science Monitor*, and *Field & Stream*. They also escorted aides from the offices of US senators and representatives, and officials from the Bureau of Outdoor Recreation, the Bureau of Land Management, the Big

Bend National Park, the Texas Sheep and Goat Raisers Association, the Mohair Council, and the International Boundary and Water Commission. In addition, many members of the general public were drawn in when the Sierra Club gave national publicity for promoting a float trip through the lower canyons (Baker 2012). Even Supreme Court justice William O. Douglas came to run the canyons and went on to write about his travels on the river in *Farewell to Texas: A Vanishing Wilderness* (Douglas 1967).

All these river guides sought to persuade the public and the government to protect the canyons from development along the bluffs above the river, and from construction of a dam in the Rio Grande itself. There was a pressing urgency to these trips. The travelers down the canyons were haunted by the concern that a dam would be built in the Big Bend without its glories having been widely seen and appreciated first, much as had happened in Arizona's Glen Canyon, where a massive dam was completed in 1966 (Porter 1963). At the same time, advocates for the Big Bend were troubled by construction on Lake Amistad, just downstream on the Rio Grande near Del Rio. By 1969, this sister reservoir would flood one hundred miles of the river, inundate many ancient cave dwellings and pictographs, and submerge the third-largest set of springs in Texas, the Goodenough Springs (Baker 2012).

The visits to the canyons opened many people's eyes. For some, it was an epiphany. Joe Friedkin, a commissioner for the IBWC, reportedly cried when he saw the Upper Madison Falls from a perch high up on the 1,800-foot cliffs of Burro Bluff. He realized that he had somehow spent a good part of his professional life seeking to dam and submerge these extraordinary canyons, particularly those downstream from Martin Canyon, near Losier Canyon (McNeely 1974; Baker 2012). The stories, photos, movies, and other coverage of the gorges of the Big Bend were also a revelation for the general public. Many Americans who had never been able to visit and see the canyons for themselves were overwhelmed. Thousands were persuaded to join a massive letter-writing campaign to Congress (Baker 2012).

In the end, the efforts by Burleson and his crew were successful. Congress commissioned a 1971 study considering Wild and Scenic protection for the Lower Canyons of the Big Bend. And, with time, the International Boundary and Water Commission became convinced that there would not likely be enough water to fill the reservoir in any case. As a result, the commission concluded that keeping the canyons in a Wild and Scenic state would be a higher and better use (Burleson 1999). Following negotiations with the State Department and the Mexican government, approval for Wild and Scenic

protection was secured. In 1978, a 196-mile reach of the Rio Grande, stretching from Mariscal Canyon down to the Terrell–Val Verde county line (river mile 853.2 to 657.5), was granted protection for its free-flowing and pristine condition (Burleson 1999; Baker 2012).

Postscript

In 2008, a bill was filed to extend Wild and Scenic River designation to an additional sixty miles of the Rio Grande where it passes through the Big Bend (US House of Representatives 2008). This would have stretched protection for the river upstream to the western boundary of Big Bend National Park, as Mexican opposition to the added protection had subsided since the original designation (Whitesell 2008). However, the petition was ultimately unsuccessful (Haas 2015). Nevertheless, the idea of protection first seen in the Rio Grande has happily spread far beyond the canyons to other parts of Texas. There has been a recent effort studying Wild and Scenic protection for the Neches River, located over five hundred miles away in the forests of East Texas (US Senate 2012).

Sources

Aulbach, Louis. 2007. "The Great Unknown of the Rio Grande." Houston, Texas.

Baker, John. 2012. Big Bend explorer. Personal communications, January and July.

Bentley, Max. 1927. "The Old Man of the River." *Dearborn Independent*, June 25, 28, 32.

Burleson, Bob. 1999. Oral history interview conducted June 19, in Temple, Texas. Texas Legacy Project, Conservation History Association.

Caracristi, Charles. 1915. The Proposed Santa Helena International Dam, submitted in August 1915 to John W. Gaines, Water Commissioner, International Boundary Commission, Washington, DC.

Douglas, William O. 1967. *Farewell to Texas: A Vanishing Wilderness*. New York: McGraw-Hill.

Duncan, Samuel. 2012. Library Director, Amon Carter Museum of American Art, Fort Worth, Texas. Personal communication, June.

DuPont, Henry. 1941–60. Running the Rio Grande in the Big Bend. Photograph, Digital image number P1975-153-29. Amon Carter Museum of American Art, Fort Worth, Texas.

Emory, William. 1858. "Report of the United States and Mexican Boundary Survey." Vol. 1, Made under the Direction of the U.S. Secretary of the Interior, Washington, DC.

Findley, A. I., W. Cope, and W. W. Macon, eds. 1915. "Texas." *Iron Age* (September 16): 667.

Gilmor, Sarah. 2015. Reference Librarian, History Colorado. Personal communication, June.

Haas, Dan. 2015. Interagency Coordinating Council, National Wild and Scenic Rivers System, US Fish and Wildlife Service. Personal communication, June.

Henderson, L. H. 1942. Dam Site Possibilities on the Rio Grande in the Big Bend District (Lajitas to Devils River). International Boundary and Water Commission. El Paso, February 2.

Henington, Greg. 2014. Owner, Far Flung Outdoor Center. Personal communication, August.

Henny and Walter. November 22, 1929. Unidentified report on dams in the Big Bend referenced in Henderson (1942) on page 40.

Hill, Robert. 1901. "Running the Cañons of the Rio Grande: A Chapter of Recent Exploration." *Century Magazine* 61 (3): 371–87.

Johnson, Lyndon. 1968. "Remarks upon Signing Four Bills Relating to Conservation and Outdoor Recreation." Washington, DC. October 2. http://www.presidency.ucsb.edu/ws/index.php?pid=29150#axzz1xE20d0br, accessed July 17, 2012.

Josten, Louis. 1915. "Controlling Rio Grande Flood Waters." *Iron Age* 96 (23): 1283.

Langford, Oscar, and Fred Gipson. 1973. *Big Bend: A Homesteader's Story*. Photos by Henry B. DuPont and Joe W. Langford, and drawings by Hal Story. Austin: University of Texas Press.

Koch, Peter, and June Cooper Price. 2007. *Exploring the Big Bend Country*. Austin: University of Texas Press.

McNeely, David. 1974. "Texans Pushing to Save River's Scenic Canyons." Dallas *Morning News*, January 7.

Ogren, Jonathan. 2008. Boquillas Canyon, view looking downstream, March. Photograph, Digital image.

Pease, C. T. and E. E. Teeter. 1921. Lower Rio Grande Project, Texas, 1921. Volume 1. US Bureau of Reclamation,

US Department of the Interior. MSS #1781, Item 42352736, Stephen H. Hart Library and Research Center.

Porter, Eliot. 1963. *The Place No One Knew: Glen Canyon on the Colorado*. San Francisco: Sierra Club.

Rock Products and Building Materials. 1915. "Plan $6,000,000 International Dam." *Rock Products and Building Materials* 16 (12).

Skiles, Raymond. 2007. "Henry B. du Pont: Industrialist and Pioneer Rio Grande River Runner." *Journal of Big Bend Studies* 19: 175–200. Center for Big Bend Studies, Sul Ross State University, Alpine, Texas.

Tarabulski, Michael. 2012. Library Technician, US Section, International Boundary and Water Commission. Personal communications, May through July.

Treaty of February 3, 1944. "Utilization of Waters of the Colorado and Tijuana Rivers and of the Rio Grande."

Tyler, Ronnie. 1975. *The Big Bend: A History of the Last Texas Frontier*. Washington, DC: US Department of the Interior.

US Fish and Wildlife Service. 2012. National Wild and Scenic Rivers System. http://www.rivers.gov/rivers/index.php, accessed July 17, 2012.

US House of Representatives. 2008. "H.R. 6177, To amend the Wild and Scenic Rivers Act to modify the boundary of the Rio Grande Wild and Scenic River (June 4, 2008)." http://www.gpo.gov/fdsys/pkg/BILLS-110hr6177ih/pdf/BILLS-110hr6177ih.pdf, accessed July 20, 2012.

US Senate. 2012. "S. 2324 (112th), Upper Neches River Wild and Scenic Study Act (Introduced April 19, 2012)."

https://www.govtrack.us/congress/
bills/112/s2324, accessed June 2, 2015.

Walter, Matt. 2007. "Love on the Rio
Grande: The 1850 Exploration by
Captain Love." *Journal of Big Bend
Studies* 19: 35–45. Center for Big Bend
Studies, Sul Ross State University.
Alpine, Texas.

Webb, Walter P. 1937. "The Big Bend
of Texas." Press release. April 25,
RG 79, NPS, SWRO, Santa Fe,
Correspondence Relating to National
Parks, Monuments, and Recreational
Areas, 1927–53, Box 1, Folder: Big
Bend International Park, Part 2, DEN
NARA.

Weisman, David. 1999. Bob Burleson.
Photograph. Digital image. June 19.
Texas Legacy Project, Conservation
History Association of Texas.

Welsh, Michael. 2002. "A Dream
Delayed." In *Landscape of Ghosts,
River of Dreams: A History of the
Big Bend National Park*. National
Park Service. US Department of the
Interior. Citing "Webb Defying Canyon
Perils," in *Austin Statesman*, May 17,
1937; "No Word from 4 Explorers,"
Fort Worth Star-Telegram, May 18,
1937; "Explorers on Perilous Ride,"
Oklahoma City Oklahoman, May 19,
1937.

Whitesell, Stephen. 2008. "Statement
before the House Subcommittee on
National Parks, Forests and Public
Lands to amend the Wild and Scenic
Rivers Act (July 10, 2008). http://
www.nps.gov/legal/testimony/110th/
HR6177RioGrandeWSR.doc,
accessed July 20, 2012.

Trinity Barge Canal

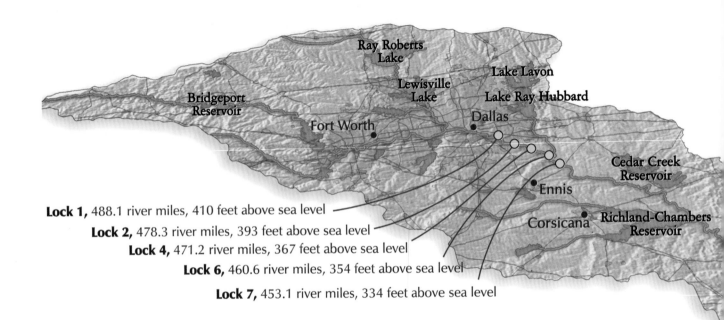

Lock 1, 488.1 river miles, 410 feet above sea level
Lock 2, 478.3 river miles, 393 feet above sea level
Lock 4, 471.2 river miles, 367 feet above sea level
Lock 6, 460.6 river miles, 354 feet above sea level
Lock 7, 453.1 river miles, 334 feet above sea level

Since very early days, Texans have been interested in using the Trinity River as a link to the sea, to allow fast, inexpensive, year-round travel and commerce with the world. Still, navigating the Trinity was never easy. In many places the river was shallow, narrow, crooked, and full of snags and shoals, subject to flood and drought, and impossible to navigate. So, headway was slow.

Rights, Charters, and Surveys

Changes to the Trinity were first proposed in 1831, when surveyor and land commissioner José Francisco Madero asked the legislatures of Coahuila and Texas to give him exclusive rights to navigation on the Trinity, in exchange for his work in improving the river (Raines 1906; Richner, Bagot, and Chaffin-Lohse 1978, 108). While Sr. Madero's plans were interrupted by the War for Texas Independence, his efforts were not the last. In 1866, the Texas legislature chartered the Trinity River Slack Water Navigation Company to establish permanent navigation between Dallas and Galveston. In 1868, Congress joined in authorizing a survey to decide if a navigation channel on the Trinity were feasible (Brown 1979, 84; Gard 2012).

Paddle Wheelers and Railroads

Support for a canal and waterborne freight grew gradually as frustration with the high transport costs on railroads increased, and with the success of a number of paddle wheelers plying long reaches of the river (Sparkman 1999, 119). By 1893, the Trinity River Navigation Company had been formed, selling stock to support the cost of clearing the river and lobbying the state

Lock 2, 1910

Lock 4, 1913

Lock 2, 1913

Lock 7, 1916

These photographs were taken by Army Corps of Engineers staff to document Trinity River locks as they were undergoing construction during the 1910s (Dallas Historical Society 1910a, 1910b, 1910c, 1913a, 1913b, 1916a, 1916b).

Crockett

Trinity

Huntsville

Lake Livingston

Livingston

Lock 20, 265.3 river miles, 193 feet above sea level
Lock 25, 172.2 river miles, 157 feet above sea level
Wallisville, 3.9 river miles, 9 feet above sea level

The map shows the locks that were built to support the proposed Trinity canal. Please notice the impressive length and rise of the proposed channel (Ajemian 2012; American Canal Society 1979; US Army Corps of Engineers 1950).

Trinity Bay

This pair of photographs shows snagboats (ca. 1910) that were used to clear the Trinity River of trees, limbs, and other barriers to navigation (Dallas Historical Society 1910b, 1910c).

and federal governments for assistance. In that same year, a temporary lock and dam at McCommas Bluff, also appropriately known as Lock 1, was completed. In 1899, these private investments attracted a federal grant of $7,000 for a preliminary survey of the Trinity from Dallas to its mouth.

Construction

The survey came back with exciting news for the canal promoters. The US government recommended a set of thirty slack-water dams, and provided $750,000 in 1902, and $500,000 in 1904 to follow through (Durham 1976, 83–87). In 1906, the Army Corps of Engineers began construction of a navigation system, building six new structures by 1922. Made of concrete, with 50 × 140 foot chambers, one Corps structure had steel

gates (Lock 20), while the remainder (Locks 2, 4, 6, 7, and 25) had wooden gates (American Canal Society 1979).

A Pause

In 1921, the Corps conducted a study that concluded that there would be too little navigation to support the project, and progress on the canal ground to a halt. Some charged that lobbying from competing boosters for railroad interests had a role in the decision (Brown 1979, 88, 96).

Resumption

Interest in the canal resumed in 1945, when the Rivers and Harbors Act was amended to support a 9-foot-deep navigable waterway from Galveston Bay to Fort Worth (56 Stat. 703, March 2, 1945). Funding was even

appropriated for construction of reservoirs in the upper Trinity to help stabilize flows in the river. During the 1940s, Congress limited work on the actual channel to the segment from Liberty, Texas, to the bay.

Later, the drought of the 1950s, followed by the 1957 flood, caused a resurgence of interest in the canal idea. The canal's proponents now matched the channel with a set of dams and reservoirs, and in so doing managed to promise water supply, flood control, and soil conservation benefits in addition to the navigation uses (Sparkman 1999, 137–38). Finally, its backers were better organized now, shepherded by the Trinity River Authority (christened in 1955), and complemented by private sector supporters within the Trinity Improvement Association (Gard 2012).

Financial Costs

During the 1960s and '70s, concern had grown about the price of the 23-lock, 19-dam system, with its 12-foot-deep, 150-foot-wide, 362.8-mile channel. Representative Alan Steelman (R) of Dallas referred to the project as the "billion-dollar ditch" (McNeely and Thompson 1973). SMU economics professor Donald Smith calculated that the costs of the project would exceed its benefits, if appropriate interest rates and accurate barge tonnage estimates were used (Durham 1976, 141). Henry Fulcher, a Dallas lumberman, argued that the flood control benefits claimed by the canal's dams could be more cheaply obtained by zoning against construction in the floodplain. Others pointed out that canal barges were being superseded by jet planes that began flying into the Dallas/Fort Worth International Airport in 1973 (Tranchin 2014).

These Texas economic critics were not alone. The Environmental Policy Center in Washington, DC, declared that the Trinity Canal was the number-one boondoggle in the nation (McNeely and Thompson 1973). In fact, there seemed to be widespread suspicion that many similarly questionable infrastructure projects existed throughout the United States. The Trinity project

TOWBOATS ARE COMING TO THE TRINITY

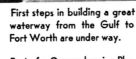

First steps in building a great waterway from the Gulf to Fort Worth are under way.

Part of a Comprehensive Plan to develop water resources of the Trinity Basin, the Trinity Canal will revitalize a great section of the Southwest.

It will mean low-cost water transportation, plus flood control, water supply, soil conservation, and vast new recreational opportunity.

Industries seeking sites along the Trinity Canal may contact:

TRINITY IMPROVEMENT ASSOCIATION
604 Avenue H East
Arlington, Texas 76010

SAVE TAXES AND THE TRINITY

COST 2940 FONDREN DRIVE, DALLAS, TEXAS 75205

CANAL-NO!

YOUR TAXES THEIR CANAL VOTE NO MAR 13

These flyers and bumper stickers advocated for and against the canal during the early 1970s (Fritz 1973a, 1973b, 1973c; Trinity Improvement Association 1973).

had company. A congressional report noted that the federal government was heavily subsidizing too many local canal, aqueduct, and pumping projects that would not stand up to true fiscal scrutiny (National Water Commission 1973, 133).

Environmental Impacts

In the spring of 1972, Ned Fritz, a Dallas environmental lawyer, joined with Mr. Fulcher, Dr. Smith, and others to found a nonprofit group to fight the canal. They called themselves "The Citizens' Organization for a Sound Trinity" (Fritz 1972). With the apt acronym, COST, they pressed financial criticisms, but also raised environmental concerns. They calculated that 200 miles of the Trinity's natural course would be eliminated for the canal, that key estuarine fisheries would be destroyed by the trapping of silt in dams and locks, and that transit of the barge freight on existing railroads would be less damaging to the Trinity's ecosystems (Fritz 1983).

Wallisville

Environmental concerns about the Trinity and the canal project were raised further by the proposal for a 19,700-acre lake at Wallisville, very close to the mouth of the river. The proposal grew out of a temporary saltwater barrier that had been built by rice irrigators in 1956 during a severe drought. Then, from 1962 to 1965, the barrier was adopted for much big-

ger plans when Congress authorized a Wallisville structure as the gateway lock and dam in the Trinity canal system (Rivers and Harbors Act of 1962, Pub. L. No. 87-874, 76 Stat. 1173; Rivers and Harbors Act of 1965, Pub. L. No. 89-298, 79 Stat. 1089). In 1966, the Corps of Engineers moved ahead with construction on the Wallisville project.

Four years later, the Sierra Club, Houston Sportsmen's Club, the Houston Audubon Society, the Texas Shrimp Association, and two fishermen filed suit against Wallisville (Ozmore 1999). They argued that the project should not have proceeded until a full environmental impact statement had been concluded. In addition to the sponsors' procedural mistakes, the plaintiffs pointed out that the Wallisville reservoir would bring substantive harm to the nurseries for shrimp, crabs, and menhaden. The plaintiffs had moral support from state biologists. A Texas Parks and Wildlife representative reported that the project would wreak "wholesale devastation of the existing aquatic and terrestrial plant and animal community" (Proxmire 1973).

Federal judge Carl Bue heard the case. In February 1973, with dam work nearly three-quarters complete, Judge Bue stopped work on the Wallisville project. The judge pinned his ruling on the Army Corps' failure to produce a thorough environmental impact statement, as required by the National Environmental Policy Act (*Sierra Club v. Froehlke*, 359 F.

Supp. 1289 (District Court, Southern District of Texas, 1973)).

"Our Dollars, Their Ditch, Vote No"

Then, barely a month later, at the other end of the river, there was more frustration for canal proponents. On March 13, voters in the seventeen-county domain of the Trinity River Authority went to the ballot to consider a special bond referendum to raise a $150 million local match for the canal (Brown 1979, 115–19). The canal supporters were eager to raise the bond money—this would be the down payment that would bring in a 90 percent federal match. Project backers paid out $500,000 for billboards, brochures, testimonials, and other promotions to swing the vote. COST and its anticanal allies spent just $21,000, but succeeded in using arguments about the canal's financial costs, ecological impacts, and corruption conflicts to persuade voters to vote the bonds down (McNeely and Thompson 1973).

Judges and Eagles

Fourteen years later, there was yet another change of fortune for the canal, or at least the tail end near the Trinity delta. In May 1987, the Fifth Circuit Court lifted Judge Bue's 1973 injunction and allowed construction at Wallisville to resume (*Sierra Club v. Froehlke*, 816 F.2d 205 (5th Circuit 1987)). Even this, though, was not the last word on the project. In November

1989, a pair of bald eagles, a protected endangered species, was discovered nesting near the dam's construction site. Work on the Wallisville impoundment stopped once again. Finally, in 2001, the 39,000-foot dam was breached. Today, only a small remnant of the Wallisville project remains as a set of levees, a salinity barrier, and a lock for river access to Liberty.

The Remnants

With Wallisville's chapter closed, ambitions for navigation on the Trinity died. The old reservoir site is now protected as Cedar Hill Park, Hugo Point Park, and the J. J. Mayes Wildlife Trace. A lock structure at Wallisville remains, as do the ruins of nearly century-old locks near Crockett, Rosser, Combine, Wilmer, Hutchins, and Dallas. Hints of the old canal plans can also be seen in the great height of some of the Trinity River bridges (I-45 downstream from Dallas, and I-10 west of Winnie) that were built to allow the anticipated barge traffic to pass. However, the grand vision of a port at Dallas and a 360-mile-long canal to the sea is no more.

Please see the accompanying map to get a sense of the project as a whole, and imagine what might have been.

Sources

Ajemian, Greg. 2012. Senior Engineer, City of Dallas, Trinity River Corridor Project Office. Personal communication, January.

American Canal Society. 1979. The American Canal Guide, Part 3, p. 14, Canal Index: Trinity River Navigation.

Brown, Clayton. 1979. "Rivers, Rockets, and Readiness: Army Engineers in the Sunbelt, a History of the Fort Worth District, US Army Corps of Engineers." Washington, DC: Government Printing Office, 84–119.

Dallas Historical Society. 1910a. Trinity River: Lock and Dam #2, Photograph, February 1910; digital image. University of North Texas Libraries, The Portal to Texas History. US Army Corps of Engineers Collection. http://texashistory.unt.edu/ark:/67531/metapth3979/, accessed August 26, 2014.

———. 1910b. Trinity River: Snagboat Trinity (port view). Photograph, February 13, 1910; digital image. University of North Texas Libraries, The Portal to Texas History. US Army Corps of Engineers Collection. http://texashistory.unt.edu/ark:/67531/metapth4069/, accessed August 26, 2014.

———. 1910c. Snagboat Guadalupe (aft view). Photograph, February 1910; digital image. University of North Texas Libraries, The Portal to Texas History. US Army Corps of Engineers Collection. http://texashistory.unt.edu/ark:/67531/metapth4072/, accessed August 26, 2014.

———. 1913a. Trinity River: Lock and Dam #2, Photograph, September 3, 1913; digital image. University of North Texas Libraries, The Portal to Texas History. US Army Corps of Engineers Collection. http://texashistory.unt.edu/ark:/67531/metapth3978/, accessed August 26, 2014.

———. 1913b. Trinity River: Lock and Dam #4, Photograph, September 11, 1913; digital image. University of North Texas Libraries, The Portal to Texas History. US Army Corps of Engineers Collection. http://texashistory.unt.edu/ark:/67531/metapth3945/, accessed August 26, 2014.

———. 1916a. Trinity River: Lock and Dam #7, Photograph, August 21, 1916; digital image. University of North Texas Libraries, The Portal to Texas History. US Army Corps of Engineers Collection. http://texashistory.unt.edu/ark:/67531/metapth4134/, accessed August 26, 2014.

———. 1916b. Trinity River: Lock and Dam #7, Photograph, August 21, 1916; digital image. University of North Texas Libraries, The Portal to Texas History. US Army Corps of Engineers Collection. http://texashistory.unt.edu/ark:/67531/metapth4146/, accessed August 26, 2014.

Durham, Floyd. 1976. *The Trinity River Paradox: Flood and Famine*. Wichita Falls, TX: Nortex Press.

Franco, Cynthia. 2012. Librarian, DeGoyler Library, Southern Methodist University. Personal communication, January.

Fritz, Ned. 1972. Agenda from first Meeting of Citizens' Organization for a Sound Trinity, April 13, 1972. Edward C. Fritz Papers, 1950s–2008. Southern Methodist University Digital Collections. http://www.westernwater.org/record/view/123256, accessed August 26, 2014.

———. 1973a. "Canal-No!" Edward C. Fritz Papers, 1950s–2008. DeGolyer Library. Southern Methodist University. http://digitalcollections.smu.edu/cdm/ref/collection/ned/id/342, accessed August 26, 2014.

———. 1973b. "Save Taxes and the Trinity." Edward C. Fritz Papers, 1950s–2008. DeGolyer Library. Southern Methodist University. http://digitalcollections.smu.edu/cdm/singleitem/collection/ned/id/338/rec/3, accessed August 26, 2014.

———. 1973c. "Your Taxes—Their Canal; Vote NO Mar 13." Edward C. Fritz Papers, 1950s–2008. DeGolyer Library. Southern Methodist University. http://digitalcollections.smu.edu/cdm/singleitem/collection/ned/id/341/rec/1, accessed August 26, 2014.

———. 1983. Oral history interview conducted February 7, by J. B. Smallwood. Provided courtesy of University of North Texas Oral History Collection.

Gard, Wayne. 2012. "Trinity River Navigation Projects," Handbook of Texas Online, Texas State Historical Association. http://www.tshaonline.org/handbook/online/articles/ett01, accessed April 04, 2012.

Huseman, Ben. 2012. Cartographic Archivist, Special Collections, University of Texas at Arlington. Personal communication, February.

McNeely, Dave, and Lyke Thompson. 1973. "The Unholy Incident." *Texas Monthly*, June.

Moye, Todd. 2012. Associate Professor of History. Director, UNT Oral History Program. University of North Texas. Personal communication, February.

National Water Commission. 1973. "Water Policies for the Future." Final Report to the Congress of the United States by the National Water Commission. Washington, DC: Government Printing Office.

Ozmore, Keith. 1999. Oral history interview conducted October 8, in Huntsville, Texas. Texas Legacy Project, Conservation History Association of Texas.

Peterson, Anne. 2012. Curator of Photographs, DeGoyler Library, Southern Methodist University. Personal communication, January.

Proxmire, William. 1973. Congressional Record, vol. 199, page 269. Washington, DC: Government Printing Office.

Raines, Cadwell. 1906. Granting to Francisco Madero exclusive right to navigate Trinity river, 1-319-1833. In Analytical Index to the Laws of Texas, 1823–1905. Austin: Von Borckmann-Jones.

Richner, Jeffrey, Joe Bagot, and Margie Chaffin-Lohse. 1978. "A Reconnaissance Survey of the Trinity River Basin, 1976–1977." Dallas: Archaeology Research Program, Department of Anthropology, Southern Methodist University.

Rust, Barbara. 2012. Archivist, National Archives—Southwest Region. Personal communication, February.

Slate, John. 2012. City Archivist, Dallas Municipal Archives. Personal communication, January.

Sparkman, Michael. 1999. "The North Texas Region and the Development of Water Resources in the Trinity River Basin of Texas, 1840–1998." Master's thesis, University of North Texas.

Tranchin, Rob. 2012. Project Director, "Living with the Trinity: A River's Story," KERA, Public Media for North Texas. Personal communication, January.

———. 2014. Cited in Episode 133: Port of Dallas, Time code 11:28. 99% Invisible. September 23, 2014. http://99percentinvisible.org/episode/port-of-dallas/, accessed October 6, 2014.

Trinity Improvement Association. 1973. Towboats Are Coming to the Trinity. Advertisement. Arlington, Texas.

US Army Corps of Engineers. 1950. Abandoned Locks and Dams below Dallas, Texas, Trinity River and Tributaries, Texas. US Army Corps of Engineers, War Department.

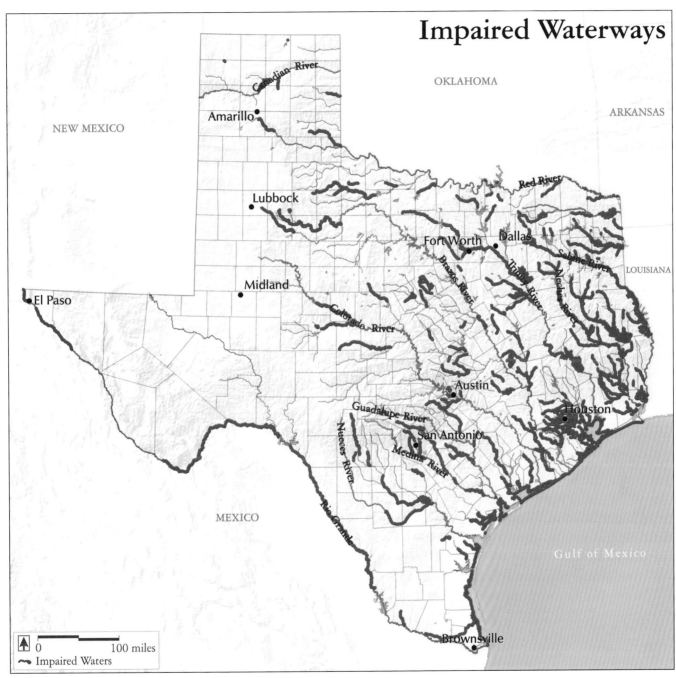

Impaired Waterways

Impaired Waters

"Impaired" streams, bays, and estuaries are listed under Section 303(d) of the Clean Water Act as unable to meet their designated water quality standards based on technology regulations alone (Sullivan 2015; US EPA 2012a).

Fishing, Swimming, and Polluting

"The Neches River, of course, the lower section, is very highly industrialized. And so it was really grossly polluted. In fact, the lower portion of the river was considered a dead river. . . . I started working on the river in '66. . . . When we first started taking samples there were very, very few organisms of any kind that would live in the river. Microorganisms were about the only kind. And there was no measurable dissolved oxygen for maybe six months of the year. When you'd get low river discharge, you would get oxygen depletion occurring. You would occasionally see a fish like a gar moving through that section of the river. But nothing else could live there."

—Richard Harrell, October 11, 1999, Beaumont, Texas

Swill

The pollution in the Neches was not unique. The pattern was repeated throughout Texas and beyond. The Houston Ship Channel suffered from anoxic conditions even into the late 1970s (City of Houston and PBS&J 2003, ii). The highly industrial Cuyahoga River in Ohio regularly caught fire in the 1950s and 1960s (Greenberg 2012). Into the 1970s, a huge expanse of Lake Erie was badly polluted, leading *Saturday Night Live*'s Bill Murray to advertise a new mineral water, called Swill, "the water that's dredged from Lake Erie" (Senate Report 111-361, p. 2). Many other industrial and urban rivers across the country suffered as well, including the Chattahoochee, Hudson, Milwaukee, Buffalo, Merrimack, Monongahela, Niagara, Delaware, Rouge, and more. In Texas, and beyond, there was wide frustration with the ineffective protection of US waters.

The Clean Water Act

Congress took action in 1972. In a powerful vote overriding President Nixon's veto, Congress passed the Clean Water Act, formally known as the Federal Water Pollution Control Act. The act's stated goal was to "restore and maintain the chemical and physical, and biological integrity of the Nation's waters" (118 Cong. Rec. 36,879 and 37060–61; 33 U.S.C. Sec. 1251(a)). Congress was explicit about the act's aims and schedule: to have "fishable and swimmable" waters by 1983 and zero pollution discharge by 1985. Congress declared that "this legislation would clearly establish that no one has the right to pollute" (Senate Report 92-414, 92nd Congress, 1st Sess., 42 (1971)).

Fishable and Swimmable?

While substantial progress has been made toward that goal, many US waters are still not safe for swimming and fishing, and discharges are still numerous and substantial. For instance, in Texas, 44 percent of the rivers, 38 percent of the lakes, and 28 percent of the bays and estuaries were considered impaired by the EPA for the year 2010, thirty-eight years after the passage of the act. Over 7,000 miles, or 42 percent of all assessed Texas rivers, were cited as impaired for use in swimming, while 963 miles of Texas streams that were examined (or 24 percent of the total mileage examined) were considered impaired for fishing (US EPA 2012b).

Pollution

For streams, bacteria have posed the biggest problem in Texas, affecting 30 percent of the rivers that were assessed, largely due to nonpoint source pollution (NPS). For the lakes that were tested, the EPA found mercury contamination to be the greatest threat, affecting 23 percent of the bodies assessed. Mercury came from airborne sources, likely utility emissions. The agency found that the biggest challenge facing the state's bays and estuaries was low dissolved oxygen, affecting 10 percent of these water bodies, with unknown sources making up the largest portion of the cause (US EPA 2012b).

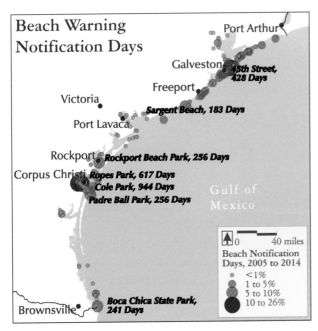

Texas coastal water quality advisories were issued for these areas from 2005 through 2014. This map shows the percentage of days over those ten years for which warning notices were posted. Notices are typically given due to high counts of enterococcus bacteria. Counts rise because of storm-water runoff, sewer overflows, or unknown causes (Davis 2012; Dorfman and Haren 2014; US EPA 2015a).

Current Texas oyster reef harvest zones, including prohibited, restricted, conditionally approved, and approved areas, are shown here. These limits affect not just oysters, but also clams, mussels, and roe-on scallops. Restrictions span November 1, 2014, through October 31, 2015, and are based largely on fecal coliform counts (Heideman 2015; Tennant 2015).

Texas finfish and shellfish consumption advisories and bans are typically linked to contamination with mercury, dioxin, PCBs, or organochlorine pesticides (Tennant 2015; Texas Department of State Health Services 2012b; Texas Parks and Wildlife Department 2015).

These photographs show visitors crabbing and fishing in the industrial waters of the Houston Ship Channel during September 1973 (Pittman 1973a and 1973b).

Progress?

The accompanying maps of impaired waters, beach advisories, restricted oyster beds, and fish consumption warnings suggest the extent to which Texas' waters are not fishable and swimmable, despite forty years of work under the Clean Water Act.

Given the high ambitions for the 1972 Clean Water Act, it seems fair to ask why, over a generation later, so much still needs to be done. There are a number of possibilities.

Costs

The price of improving wastewater discharges, for the capital and operating costs of the equipment, and for the R&D, compliance, and enforcement staffing, has been high. While the benefits have been large (estimated at $11 billion annually, nationwide, in the year 2000), the offsetting costs have been high as well (estimated at $14.1 billion for the United States in 1997) (Bingham et al. 2000, viii; Van Houtven, Brunnermeier, and Buckley 2000, ES-5).

Controls

Plus, there have been undeniable technical challenges for pulling the pollutants out of waste streams. The controls for water pollution have faced a range of increasingly stringent levels of treatment, scaling up from Best Practicable Control Technology, Best Conventional Pollutant Control Technology, to Best Available Control Technology. Each of these treatment strategies offers many complex trade-offs for cost, energy use, and effectiveness (Clean Water Act, Section 304(b)(1, 2, 4)). Pollution control can also create its very own pollution: for instance, sewage treatment may protect a river, but at the expense of creating a toxic sludge with new and distinct disposal problems.

Politics

Water pollution cleanup has struggled with demographic and political obstacles. Many of Texas' metropolitan areas enjoyed sustained booms over many years, especially after the Arab oil embargo of 1972, bringing thousands of new residents to the state. Often, the required improvements and expansions of sewage treatment systems did not keep up with the rapid rise in population, or with the willingness of residents to pay for the new wastewater plants (Melosi 2011, 178).

Paperwork

Administration of the Clean Water Act has presented its own problems. The backbone of the act's water quality protection is its system of discharge permits. These permits have had both good and bad aspects. It has certainly been a benefit to bring thousands of Texas' diverse wastewater discharges into a centrally regulated, monitored, and enforced system.

On the other hand, the regulation of so many outfalls (over 3,700 major discharges by the state's count) has been a large, costly, and complex effort (TCEQ 2015). For instance, permits

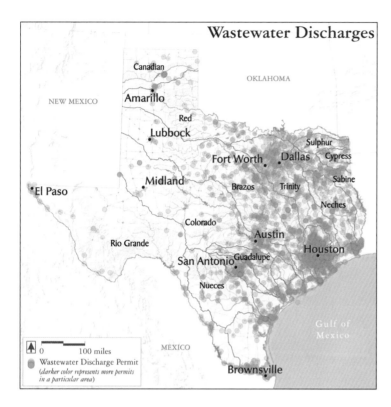

Zero discharge has remained elusive. This map shows 3,764 permitted wastewater discharges in Texas, as reported by the Texas Commission on Environmental Quality, current as of April 21, 2015. The darker and denser the blue, the more discharge permits there are in that area (TCEQ 2015; US EPA 2012c).

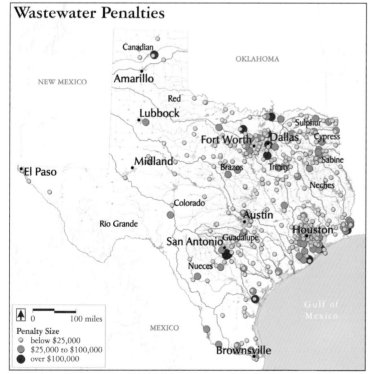

Permits are sometimes broken and discharge limits exceeded. This map shows where penalties were imposed for the more severe Clean Water Act violations prosecuted as federal offenses from 2009 through 2014 (US EPA 2012b).

can become out of date from time to time. In fiscal year 2000, the EPA discovered that about 25 percent of discharger permits for major US facilities had expired (US EPA 2001, 3). Also, even the intact permits require constant monitoring; violation of permit requirements has become a fact of life. One review by the Government Accountability Office found that at least one in six of the nation's major regulated facilities were in significant violation of their wastewater permits (Government Accountability Office 1996, 1). Many are settled administratively on the state level with agreed facility improvements, mitigation projects, and fines. More serious problems can get greater attention and pressure: EPA imposed 163 Clean Water Act penalties in Texas from 2010 through 2014 (US EPA 2015b).

Rights

Despite the complexities and shortcomings of the permit system, it can become heavily entrenched. The full name of the Clean Water Act permit scheme, the "National Pollutant Discharge *Elimination* System," stresses that the goal is to eliminate pollution, and presumably discontinue permits. However, NPDES wastewater permits have tended to survive and prosper and become a protected and long-lasting privilege, almost a property right. The ability to discharge from a sewage treatment plant or industrial facility has become very valuable. As a result, public and

A summer day brings families out to a Hill Country swimming hole in the Pedernales River (McGreevy 2014).

Some Texans retreat to clear, cool swimming holes, many clustered in rural and relatively pristine areas of the Hill Country (Llewellin 2008; Swimming Holes 2012; Texas Outside 2012).

private permit holders lobby to maintain these licenses, manage violations, reduce penalties, minimize mitigation efforts, and generally reduce what are seen as a kind of overhead cost. On their side, agencies must deal with the hazard of "capture," of their staff being drawn into a revolving door with the higher-paying private sector, or of their policies becoming too beholden to their clients, the regulated industries and municipalities.

Hangover

Modern-day efforts to permit, control, and reduce water pollution must also deal with the legacy of past pollution. In many urban and long-industrialized watersheds, pollutants settle out, and contaminated sediments ooze and seep into the water column. Modern improvements in wastewater treatment are sometimes limited by this inheritance of past waste loads that have become part of creek and bay bottoms.

Nonpoint Runoff

While the Clean Water Act has often been impressive in dealing with "point" discharges that come from the end of a pipe, it turns out that much of the impact on the nation's lakes, streams, and bays actually comes from no single, identifiable source that can be easily monitored, regulated, and controlled. Much of this remaining water pollution, including silt, heavy metals, hydrocarbons, bacteria, and nutrients, has come from

These historic photographs show that Hill Country swimming holes have long been popular (Billingsley 2014a and 2014b; Cotton 1940).

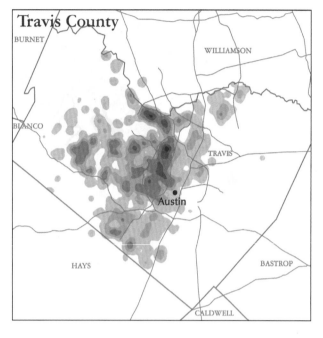

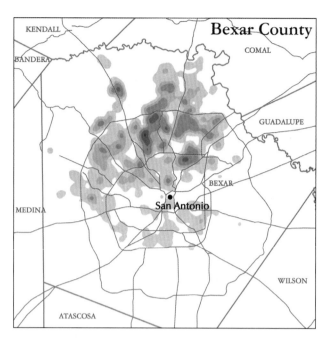

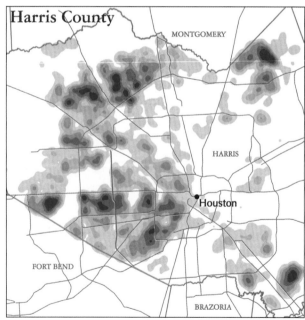

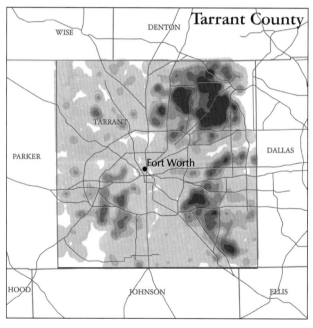

Faced with questionable public and natural waters, many Texas residents have turned to private swimming pools that can be chlorinated, filtered, and fenced. This map shows a sample of pools found in major Texas cities, representing over 200,000 pools within Austin, Fort Worth, San Antonio, and Houston. Even at that large number, this tally represents only a small part of the 770,000 private pools estimated to exist in the state (Association of Pool and Spa Professionals 2012; Carlson 2012; Daam 2012; Nguyen 2012; McCoy 2012).

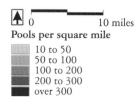

0   10 miles

Pools per square mile

10 to 50
50 to 100
100 to 200
200 to 300
over 300

nonpoint source pollution, with no simple "return address." To give an idea of the scope of the problem, the EPA compiled state Water Quality Inventory reports and found that urban runoff was responsible for large shares of the damage to assessed ocean shorelines (47 percent), estuaries (46 percent), lakes (22 percent), and rivers (14 percent) (Strassler 1999, 4–23).

Property

Even when the origin of NPS pollution can be tracked down, controlling it can run into thorny land use and private property problems. For instance, research has found that polluted runoff from land increases remarkably when impervious cover (rooftops, parking lots, roads, and the like) expands, particularly when it exceeds 10 percent (Strassler 1999, 4–34). In this regard, agencies have struggled with developers and public works departments in efforts to reduce paving and construction. NPS pollution control has gained still more unpopularity from efforts to protect wetlands from filling and draining, to assure their continued role in capturing and filtering out runoff and contaminants. Landowners often criticize these "Section 404" dredge and fill rules, since drying out these playas, swamps, and bottomlands would allow their use as profitable farm fields or building sites.

Monitoring

Just as NPS pollution can be daunting to track and control, it can also be costly and time consuming to adequately monitor the streams that receive the runoff and discharges. In fact, in Texas, only 12 percent of streams have been assessed. In other words, 191,228 miles of Texas streams have not been reviewed for water quality. And for the streams that have been examined and found to be impaired, only 12 percent of those polluted water bodies have a plan (a total maximum daily load) for identifying the kind and amount of waste loads that would need to be removed for the stream to recover (US EPA 2012b).

Accommodations

Forty years after the passage of the Clean Water Act, the political complexity and financial cost of addressing these remaining water problems head-on has been formidable. As a result, it seems that some environmental problems have been met, in the interim, with adaptations to simply guard Texans against exposing themselves to these risks. Through customs and rules, signs and notices, we have steered the public away from contaminated waters.

For instance, if Houston's Buffalo Bayou is too polluted to swim or fish in, it is likely easy to dive into a private swimming pool, drive to a pristine spring in the Hill Country, or fish in a remote bay far south on the Coastal

Bend. The maps included here are an attempt to show how we have adapted to and accommodated water pollution in Texas, marking areas where it is dangerous to swim or fish, and noting safe places that we have agreed to set aside to enjoy. For example, areas of risk are shown in the maps of coastal beach advisories, fishery notices, oyster bed warnings, impaired waters, and wastewater outfalls. On the other hand, places where people can safely enjoy Texas waters are shown in the maps of swimming pools and swimming holes.

In the end, this pragmatic redlining may successfully reduce the public health risks for Texans, but it still raises the question of when we are going to confront the underlying water pollution problems in the state, and how we will reconcile protecting the environment with operating a busy industrial economy.

An Alternative

It is good to remember the original zero-discharge vision for the Clean Water Act of 1972, and know that it is still possible to reach that goal, with collaboration and patience. The story of Diane Wilson is encouraging. Wilson is a fourth-generation shrimper from Seadrift, Texas, and an advocate for the protection of Lavaca Bay. In 1989, she began a series of hunger strikes to press a large local plant, Formosa Plastics, to move toward zero discharge. Media attention, community organizing through the Calhoun

County Resource Watch, pressure from environmental lawyer Jim Blackburn, and a stakeholder process that brought in third-party engineering advice from Jack Matson, all helped move Formosa Plastics toward that elusive zero-discharge goal (Wilson 2003; Blackburn 1999).

By 1994, Formosa was able to find ways to recycle one-third of its waste stream and save 2.6 million gallons of fresh water a day. A 1997 cooperative agreement with Formosa established an ongoing process for dispute resolution, and for moving the plant further toward full recycling and reuse of its wastewater (Schmandt and Ward 2004, 183–97). With Formosa's example, zero discharge may not be here quite yet, but it looks increasingly close and promising.

Jim Blackburn, Houston environmental attorney, and Diane Wilson, Seadrift shrimper, joined forces to negotiate discharge improvements with Formosa Chemical for its 1,600-acre Point Comfort petrochemical complex (Weisman 1999 and 2003).

Sources

Association of Pool and Spa Professionals. 2012. US Swimming Pool and Hot Tub Market 2011.

Billingsley, Claire. 2014a. Camp Waloa girls enjoying "The Narrows," in Blanco County, near Wimberley, Texas, ca. early 1940s. Image contributed by Donna Burdett Cotton. Historic Photo Archive. The Wimberley Institute of Cultures.

———. 2014b. Camp Waloa girls visiting Jacob's Well, in Blanco County, near Wimberley, Texas, ca. early 1940s. Image contributed by Donna Burdett Cotton. Historic Photo Archive. The Wimberley Institute of Cultures.

———. 2014c. Wimberley Institute of Cultures. Personal communication, October.

Bingham, Tayler, Timothy Bondelid, Brooks Depro, Ruth Figueroa, Brett Hauber, Suzanne Unger, and George Van Houtven. 2000. A Benefits Assessment of Water Pollution Control Programs since 1972: Part 1, The Benefits of Point Source Controls for Conventional Pollutants in Rivers and Streams. US Environmental Protection Agency, Office of Water. January.

Carlson, Dianne. 2012. Director of Information Systems, Travis County Appraisal District. Personal communication, September.

Carson, Rachel. 1962. *Silent Spring*. Boston: Houghton Mifflin.

City of Houston and PBS&J. 2003. Houston Ship Channel Water Quality Conditions. Houston-Galveston Area Council and the Texas Commission on Environmental Quality. September.

Cotton, Donna Burdett. 1940. Camp Waloa Campers at Jacob's Well, near Wimberley, Texas. Photograph. Donor to the Historic Photo Archives of the Wimberley Institute of Cultures.

Daam, Barbara. 2012. Bexar County Appraisal District. Personal communication, September.

Davis, Craig. 2012. Texas Beach Watch Coordinator, Beach Watch, Coastal Resources, Texas General Land Office. Personal communication, September.

Dorfman, Mark, and Angela Haren. 2014. Testing the Waters. Natural Resources Defense Council.

Federal Water Pollution Control Act Amendments of 1972, Pub. L. No. 92-500, § 2, 86 Stat. 896 (1972), as amended by Clean Water Act of 1977, Pub. L. No. 95–217, § 2, 91 Stat. 1566 (codified as amended at 33 U.S.C. §§ 1251–1387 (1994)).

Greenberg, Paul. 2012. "The Clean Water Act at 40: There's Still Much Left to Do." *Yale Environment* 360, posted May 21.

Harrel, Richard. 1999. Oral history interview conducted October 11, in Beaumont, Texas. Texas Legacy Project. Conservation History Association of Texas.

Heideman, Gary. 2015. Seafood and Aquatic Life Group, Texas Department of State Health Services. Personal communication, March.

Johnson, Joseph. 2004. "The Cost of Regulations Implementing the Clean Water Act." Mercatus Center, George Mason University.

Llewellin, Charlie. 2008. "Springs Eternal." *Texas Monthly*, August.

McCoy, Mary. 2012. Public Records Officer, Tarrant County Appraisal District. Personal communication, September.

McGreevy, Elizabeth. 2014. Swimming in the Pedernales. Photograph. Digital image.

Melosi, Martin. 2011. *Precious Commodity: Providing Water for America's Cities*. Pittsburgh: University of Pittsburgh Press.

Nguyen, Thang. 2012. GIS Specialist, Harris County Appraisal District. Personal communication, September.

Pittman, Blair. 1973a. Crabbing and Fishing on the Houston Ship Channel. Photograph. Digital image. Documerica Series, US Environmental Protection Agency. National Archives Identifier 542493. Archived at the National Archives and Records Administration.

———. 1973b. Fishing on the Houston Ship Channel. Photograph. Digital image. Documerica Series, US Environmental Protection Agency. National Archives Identifier 1244799. Archived at the National Archives and Records Administration.

Schmandt, Jurgen, and C. H. Ward. 2004. *Sustainable Development: The Challenge of Transition*. New York: Cambridge University Press.

Senate Report 111-361. 2010. Prepared to accompany S. 787, Clean Water Restoration Act. Washington, DC: Government Printing Office. December 10.

Strassler, Eric. 1999. Preliminary Data Summary of Urban Stormwater Best Management Practices. EPA 821-R-99-012.

Sullivan, Andrew. 2015. Team Leader, Surface Water Quality Monitoring Team, Texas Commission on Environmental Quality. Personal communication, March.

Swimming Holes. 2012. http://www.swimmingholes.org/tx.html, accessed September 12.

Tennant, Michael. 2012 and 2015. Seafood and Aquatic Life Group, Texas Department of State Health Services. Personal communications, September 2012 and March 2015.

Texas Commission on Environmental Quality (TCEQ). 2015. Permitted Wastewater Outfalls, GIS Geographic Information Systems. https://www.tceq.texas.gov/assets/public/gis/exports/tceq_wastewater_outfalls_shp.zip, accessed April 21, 2015.

Texas Department of State Health Services. 2012a. Shellfish Classification of Harvesting Areas Maps. http://www.dshs.state.tx.us/seafood/classification.shtm#maps, accessed September 26.

———. 2012b. Survey Information—Current Advisories, Bans, and Rescinded Orders. Seafood and Aquatic Life Group. http://www.dshs.state.tx.us/seafood/survey.shtm#advisory, accessed September 26.

Texas Outside. 2012. Texas Swimming Holes. http://www.texasoutside.com/texasswimmingholes/texasswimmingholes.html, accessed September 11.

Texas Parks and Wildlife Department. 2015. Fishing Consumption Bans and Advisories, General Fishing Rules and Regulations, Fishing, Outdoor Annual. Texas Parks and Wildlife. http://tpwd.texas.gov/regulations/outdoor-annual/fishing/general-rules-regulations/fish-consumption-bans-and-advisories, accessed April 30, 2015.

US Environmental Protection Agency (EPA). 2001. "Water Enforcement: State Enforcement of Clean Water Act Discharges Can Be More Effective." Report 2001-P-00013. Office of Inspector General Audit Report. San Francisco, California. August 14.

———. 2012a. Integrated Data for Enforcement Analysis, EPA Offices of Regional Counsel and Office of Civil Enforcement, compiled in the Integrated Compliance Information System. http://www.epa-echo.gov/echo/compliance_report_water_icp.html, accessed October 7.

———. 2012b. Watershed Assessment, Tracking and Environmental Results: Texas Water Quality Assessment Report. http://ofmpub.epa.gov/waters10/attains_state.control?p_state=TX#total_assessed_waters, accessed September 12.

———. 2015a. Beacon 2.0—Beach Advisory and Closing On-Line Notification. US Environmental Protection Agency. http://watersgeo.epa.gov/beacon2/, accessed April 21, 2015.

———. 2015b. Facility Search— Enforcement and Compliance Data, ECHO Enforcement and Compliance History Online. US Environmental Protection Agency. http://echo.epa.gov/facilities/facility-search/results, accessed April 21, 2015.

———. 2015c. Integrated Compliance System for Clean Water Act Permitted Dischargers (under the National Pollutant Discharge Elimination System). Data Downloads, Enforcement and Compliance History Online. http://echo.epa.gov/files/echodownloads/npdes_downloads.zip, accessed June 9, 2015.

US Government Accountability Office. 1996. Water Pollution: Many Violations Have Not Received Appropriate Enforcement Attention. GAO/RCED-96-23. March.

Van Houtven, George, Smita Brunnermeier, and Mark Buckley. 2000. "A Retrospective Assessment of the Costs of the Clean Water Act: 1972 to 1997." US Environmental Protection Agency, Office of Water, Office of Policy, Economics and Innovation. Washington, DC, October.

Weisman, David. 1999. Jim Blackburn, October 1, 1999. Houston, Texas. Photograph. Digital image. Texas Legacy Project, Conservation History Association of Texas. http://www.texaslegacy.org, accessed April 15, 2015.

Weisman, David. 2003. Diane Wilson, October 23, 2003, Seadrift, Texas. Photograph. Digital image. Texas Legacy Project, Conservation History Association of Texas.

History and Prehistory of Lake Amistad

We all enjoy visiting a lake and relishing the view, the fish and birds, the waves and the breeze. And, of course, the lake provides many benefits for water supply, flood control, and other uses. But, under the water's surface, things of great interest and value may be hidden. Lake Amistad offers an example.

Early Explorations

Lake Amistad covers an enormous complex of very early Native American settlements. Professional archaeological excavations in Val Verde County, along the cliffs of the Rio Grande, Pecos River, and Devil's River, first began in 1932, when the University

of Texas undertook a dig at Fate Bell Shelter (Thomas 1933). The research organization Gila Pueblo (1932), the Witte Memorial Museum (1933), the Smithsonian Institution (1934), and the West Texas Museum (1937) conducted early work in the area as well.

Early digs and surveys found rich, well-preserved signs of early human

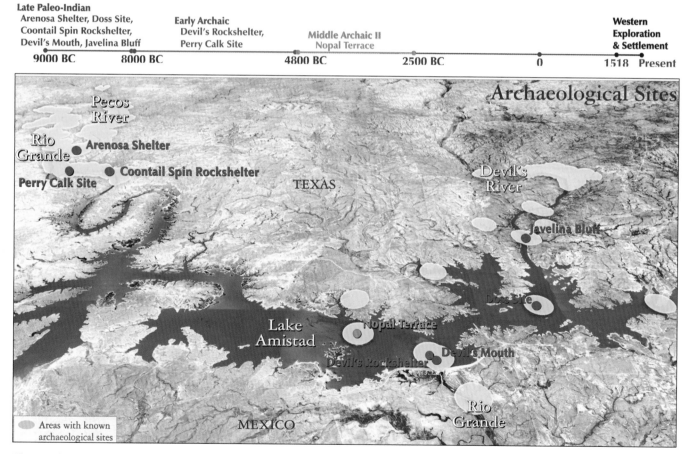

Late Paleo-Indian
Arenosa Shelter, Doss Site,
Coontail Spin Rockshelter,
Devil's Mouth, Javelina Bluff

Early Archaic
Devil's Rockshelter,
Perry Calk Site

Middle Archaic II
Nopal Terrace

**Western
Exploration
& Settlement**

9000 BC   8000 BC   4800 BC   2500 BC   0   1518   Present

The map shows the general areas where archaeological sites have been continuously or periodically flooded in the Rio Grande, Pecos, and Devil's River sections of the Lake Amistad region. The color of those map sites is keyed to the settlement dates given in the timeline (Dering 2002).

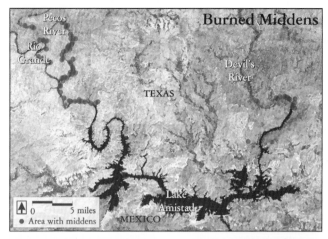

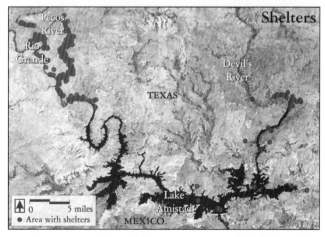

These maps depict three types of continuously or intermittently sub-merged prehistoric sites, including burned rock middens, pictographs, and shelters (caves, overhangs, and rockshelters) in the Lake Amistad region (Dering 2002).

use, dating back to 8000 BC and earlier, millennia before western exploration and settlement (Epstein 1960; Tamers, Pearson, and Davis 1964). The remains included massive bison bones, beautiful cave drawings, elegant necklaces and pendants, and carefully worked tools and weapons, such as nets, scrapers, spear points, and digging tools (Jurgens 2005; Jackson 1938; Lorrain 1965; Story and Bryant 1966).

A Pact and a Flood

However, in 1944, the United States and Mexico entered into a treaty authorizing a 65,000-acre reservoir in this same area (US Department of State 1944). The huge lake was planned to stretch 78 miles up the Rio Grande and to spread far into the canyons of the Pecos and Devil's Rivers. For ten years, the proposal lay dormant. Then, in June 1954, Hurricane Alice hit southern Texas and northern Mexico, bringing a deluge of 35 inches of rain, a 96-foot flood crest on the Pecos, the loss of a highway and three bridges, and at least fifty-five dead.

Salvage

With the authorization of the 1944 treaty, and concerns about those disastrous 1954 floods, plans for Lake Amistad accelerated in the late 1950s. Work began in earnest on the dam in 1960 (US Department of State 1960). From an early date, however, it was clear that Lake Amistad would flood

This photograph gives a view of the Amistad Dam under construction in 1967, with the Devil's Mouth archaeological site in the foreground (Texas Archeological Research Laboratory 1967a).

Archaeologist David Dibble (right) and an assistant are seen here sifting remains collected from the Arenosa shelter (Texas Archeological Research Laboratory 1967b).

many important sites that lay in the river bottoms or in the cliff caves that lined local canyon walls (Graham and Davis 1958; Tunnel 1963). To rescue the history of these sites, their culture and people, there was an impressive and rapid campaign to survey the soon-to-be-flooded area, to document the site and retrieve precious artifacts. From 1958 through 1968, the Texas Archeological Salvage Project, with support from the National Park Service, was busy with bulldozers, backhoes, and teams of archaeologists and laborers recovering what they could from the ancient sites before they were lost to the waters of Amistad (Anderson 1974; Black, Bryant, and Labadie 2008; Black and Dering 2001; Dibble 1967; Johnson 1962; Sorrow 1968).

An early report, dating to 1958, estimated that as many as 188 sites would be affected by Amistad (Graham and Davis 1958). By 1965, that number had risen: one experienced researcher, David Dibble, predicted that Amistad would flood over three hundred sites when all was said and done (Dibble 1965). Even this estimate turned out to be low. In fact, by 1994, J. H. Labadie thought that there were actually nine hundred prehistoric archaeological sites within the immediate flood pool of Lake Amistad (Labadie 1994). Yet Labadie's figure also proved to be too small. In 1998, months of dry weather dropped lake water levels by 56 feet, exposing all but 20 percent of the normally flooded area (Purchase et al. 2001). The drought revealed an additional 150 archaeological sites within Amistad's bounds, boosting the total count of affected sites above one thousand (National Park Service 2012).

The Remains

The map here is based on a thorough 2002 report (Dering 2002). However, it shows only a small fraction of the prehistoric sites that have been identified in the Amistad region. Further, they are shifted and blurred here to protect their location and integrity. Still, this map does show some of the more important and better-understood sites that were affected by the lake, including eight locations: Arenosa Shelter, Coontail Spin Rockshelter, Devil's Mouth, Devil's Rockshelter, Doss Site, Javelina Bluff, Nopal Terrace, and Perry Calk Site.

Since the completion of Amistad Dam in the fall of 1969, flooding has not been kind to these fragile sites. Many had only been preserved into the twentieth century because of the arid and isolated conditions in the area. Given their extreme age and organic makeup, the remains have had little resistance to the changes that came with the new lake. The waters of Amistad have brought wave action from high winds and passing boats, fluctuations of lake levels, tunneling by the Asiatic clam, and just the sheer effects of inundation (Collins and Labadie 1999; Gustavson and Collins 2000; Shaffer et al. 1997). As well, the development of the lake, nearby roads, and other infrastructure has attracted more visitors, not all of whom have respected the sanctity of these ancient sites (Collins 1969).

Gain and Loss

We can certainly be thankful that Lake Amistad brought attention, money, infrastructure, and study to the prehistoric sites of the region (Banks and Czaplicki 2014; Lenihan 1981). Also, we are fortunate that the sites have benefited from government protection (Amistad National Recreation Area, established in 1965, and Seminole Canyon State Park, opened in 1980), and the preservation and archiving of over one million artifacts (National Park Service 2012). However, the question will always remain, as we look out at the lake and imagine the extraordinary sites that lie submerged: at what cost?

Sources

Anderson, Bruce. 1974. An Archeological Assessment of Amistad Recreation Area. US Department of the Interior, National Park Service, Southwest Regional Office, Division of Archeology, Santa Fe, New Mexico.

Banks, Kimball, and Jon Czaplicki, eds. 2014. *Dam Projects and the Growth of American Archaeology: The River Basin Surveys and the Interagency Archeological Salvage Program*. Walnut Creek, CA: Left Coast Press.

Black, Stephen, Vaughn Bryant, and Joe Labadie. 2008. Texas beyond History: Before Amistad. University of Texas at Austin. http://www.texasbeyondhistory.net/pecos/before.html, accessed March 30, 2012.

Black, Stephen, and Phil Dering. 2001. Texas beyond History: Lower Pecos Canyonlands. University of Texas at Austin. http://www.texasbeyondhistory.net/pecos/index.html, accessed March 30, 2012.

Collins, Michael. 1969. "Test Excavations at Amistad International Reservoir, Fall 1967." Papers of the Texas Archeological Salvage Project, No. 16, Austin, Texas.

Collins, Michael, and Joe Labadie. 1999. The 1999 Texas Archeological Society Field School: "Excavation, Rock Art Recordation, Surface Feature Documentation, and Survey at Amistad National Recreation Area." *Texas Archeological Society Newsletter* 43 (1): 3–7. San Antonio.

Dering, Phil. 2002. Amistad National Recreation Area: Archeological Survey and Cultural Resource Inventory. Intermountain Cultural Resource Center, National Park Service. Submitted by the Center for Ecological Archeology, Texas A&M University. Santa Fe, New Mexico.

Dibble, David. 1965. "Bonfire Shelter: A Stratified Bison Kill Site in the Amistad Reservoir Area, Val Verde, Texas," with appendices by Ruben Frank and Dessamae Lorrain. Report submitted to the National Park Service by the Texas Archeological Salvage Project, University of Texas at Austin.

———. 1967. "Excavations at Arenosa Shelter, 1965–66," with an appendix by Vaughn M. Bryant Jr., Report submitted to the National Park Service by the Texas Archeological Salvage Project, University of Texas at Austin.

Dibble, David, and Dessamae Lorrain. 1968. "Bonfire Shelter: A Stratified Bison Kill Site, Val Verde County, Texas." Miscellaneous Papers No. 1, Texas Memorial Museum. University of Texas at Austin.

Epstein, Jeremiah. 1960. "Centipede and Damp Caves: Excavations in Val Verde County, Texas, 1958," with appendices by Curtis D. Tunnell, William A. Davis, Thomas W. McKern, Ernest Lundelius Jr., and LeRoy Johnson Jr. Report submitted to the National Park Service by the Texas Archeological Salvage Project, University of Texas at Austin.

Graham, John, and William Davis. 1958. Appraisal of the Archeological Resources of Diablo Reservoir, Val Verde County, Texas. Archeological Salvage Program Field Office, National Park Service, Austin, Texas.

Gustavson, Thomas, and Michael Collins. 2000. "An Assessment of Flood Damage to Archeological Sites in the San Pedro Drainage, Amistad National Recreation Area, August 1998." University of Texas at Austin, Texas Archeological Research Laboratory.

Jackson, A. T. 1938. "Picture-Writing of Texas Indians." Anthropological Papers, vol. 2, Bureau of Research in the Social Sciences, Study No. 27. University of Texas at Austin.

Johnson, LeRoy, Jr. 1962. "The Archeology of the Devil's Mouth Site, Amistad Reservoir, Texas." Report submitted to the National Park Service by the Texas Archeological Salvage Project, University of Texas at Austin.

Jurgens, Christopher. 2005. "Zooarcheology and Bone Technology from Arenosa Shelter (41VV99), Lower Pecos Region, Texas." Dissertation presented to the Faculty of the Graduate School of the University of Texas at Austin in partial fulfillment of the requirements for the degree of doctor of philosophy, University of Texas, Austin, Texas.

Labadie, Joe. 1994. "Amistad National Recreation Area: A Cultural Resources Study." National Park Service, Southwest Cultural Resources Center. Santa Fe, New Mexico.

Lenihan, Daniel. 1981. "The Final Report of the National Reservoir Inundation Study." Santa Fe, NM: US Department of the Interior, National Park Service, Southwest Cultural Resources Center.

Lorrain, Dessamae. 1965. "Aboriginal Exploitation of Bison at Bonfire Shelter in Trans-Pecos, Texas." Thesis presented to the Faculty of the Graduate School of the University of Texas in partial fulfillment of the requirements for the degree of master of arts, University of Texas at Austin.

National Park Service. 2012. "Geology Fieldnotes: Amistad National Recreation Area, Texas." http://www.nature.nps.gov/geology/parks/amis/index.cfm, accessed February 7.

Purchase, Carol, David Larson, Mark Flora, and John Reber. 2001. "Amistad National Recreation Area, Texas: Water Resources Scoping Report." Technical Report NPS/NRWRD/NRTR-2001/295. Water Resources Division, National Park Service, US Department of the Interior.

Shaffer, Brian, Phil Dering, Joe Labadie, and Frederic Pearl. 1997. "Bioturbation at Submerged Cultural Sites by the Asiatic Clam: A Case Study from Amistad Reservoir, SW Texas." *Journal of Field Archeology* 24 (1): 135–38. Boston.

Sorrow, William. 1968. "The Devil's Mouth Site: The Third Season—1967," with an appendix by Vaughn M. Bryant Jr. and Donald A. Larson. Papers of the Texas Archeological Project, No. 14, Austin.

Story, Dee Ann, and Vaughn Bryant Jr. 1966. "A Preliminary Study of the Paleoecology of the Amistad Reservoir Area." Final Report under the auspices of the National Science Foundation (GS-667).

Tamers, M. A., F. J. Pearson Jr., and F. Mott Davis. 1964. "University of Texas Radiocarbon Dates II." *Radiocarbon* 6: 38–159. Radiocarbon Dating Laboratory, Balcones Research Center, University of Texas at Austin.

Texas Archeological Research Laboratory. 1967a. Amistad Dam and Devil's Mouth Site, Amistad National Recreation Area. Texas Image catalog number 41VV188-113. Archeological Research Laboratory. University of Texas at Austin.

———. 1967b. Archeologist and Assistant at Arenosa Site, Amistad National Recreation Area. Texas Image catalog number 41VV99-C355. Archeological Research Laboratory. University of Texas at Austin.

Thomas, Sidney. 1933. "The Archeological Investigation of Fate Bell Shelter, Seminole Canyon, Val Verde County, Texas." Thesis presented to the Faculty of the Graduate School of the University of Texas in partial fulfillment of the requirements for the degree of master of arts, University of Texas at Austin.

Tunnel, Curtis. 1963. "Salvage Archaeology in Amistad Reservoir." *The Mustang, Newsletter of the Texas Memorial Museum*, Mimeographed Papers No. 9 (5:8). Austin.

US Department of State. 1944. "Treaty Relating to the Utilization of Waters of the Colorado and Tijuana Rivers and of the Rio Grande, and Supplementary Protocol, Signed at Washington, February 3, 1944, and entered into force, November 8, 1945." 59 Stat. 1219; TS 994; 3 UNTS 313.

US Department of State. 1960. "Agreement to Proceed with the Construction of Amistad Dam on the Rio Grande to Form Part of the System of International Storage Dams Provided for by the Water Treaty of February 3, 1944. Signed at Ciudad Acuña, October 25, 1960, entered into force October 24, 1960". 11 UST 2396; TIAS 4624; 401 UNTS 137.

University of Texas at Austin, Division of Natural Resources and the Environment. 1975. Devils River, a Natural Area Survey, Volume Pt. 6.

Falcon Reservoir's Drowned History

The Lower Rio Grande Valley has a very long and rich history, dating to days under the flags of Spain, Mexico, the Republic of Texas, the Confederacy, the United States, and even the little-known Republic of the Rio Grande (Lee and Stambaugh 1954).

Early Settlements

The region was first settled in the mid-eighteenth century as a bulwark against French expansion from their base in Louisiana, and as a buffer against the raids of the Lipan Apache and Comanche. In time, the area grew to be the cradle of the American cattle industry and an important trading post between Mexico and points north.

The Water Treaty of 1944

However, almost two centuries after the first settlement of the Valley, national leaders in Mexico and the United States signed the Water Treaty of 1944 (US Department of State 1944). The treaty authorized the 87,400-acre Falcon Reservoir, slated to be the largest in Texas. The new dam's purpose was to serve the two countries with water supply, hydroelectricity, flood control, recreation, and an international bridge. With these worthwhile goals in mind, construction on the 150-foot-tall, 26,000-foot-long earthen dam began on December 15, 1950, to the south of Zapata, Texas (Kennard 1976, 4–10).

Falcon Dam's Construction

During the dam's construction, the US Sector of the International Boundary and Water Commission elected to dynamite or bulldoze buildings within the reservoir's eventual boundaries. The intention was to minimize risks to boaters from submerged structures. Many old ranch and town structures were lost, and with them much of the colonial heritage along the river disappeared even before the dam was complete.

Floods of 1953

Then, with heavy rains during August 1953, a five-hundred-year flood came roaring down the Rio Grande (George 2008, 4). River flows rose twentyfold in the space of just a few days, and the reservoir began filling rapidly (Jordan and Perez 1953, 38, 82). Many residents were caught off guard and had to flee from low-lying communities along the Rio Grande. Even towns such as San Ygnacio that were hoping for a reprieve from the inundation were flooded (Arreola 2010, 78).

Guerrero Viejo

In short order, many towns and outlying structures were submerged. Guerrero Viejo was hit particularly hard, with its colonial church and Palacio Municipal drowned (Poniatowska and Payne 1997). Graves too were flooded; the rising waters of Falcon affected twenty-one cemeteries in Zapata County alone (Fish 1990, 95). During the evacuation, even livestock and furniture had to be left behind (De la Garza 2013, 175). Some residents had a brief chance to bid farewell to their old communities before leaving for higher ground. A citizen of Guerrero Viejo shuttered the town school with the note, "El día siete de octubre gire por última vez la gran llave de hierro en la cerradura del vetusto portón de madera (On the seventh of October, for the last time, I turned the great iron key in the ancient wooden door's lock)" (De la Garza 2013, 175).

Old Ruins and Current Times

The dam was officially inaugurated on October 19, 1953, with a celebration and joint visit by President Eisenhower and his Mexican counterpart, Adolfo Ruiz Cortines (Sanchez 1994, 201). However, for local residents who had lost their homes, reburied their dead, and abandoned their towns, the

In 1746, the Viceroy of New Spain commissioned Col. José de Escandón to colonize Nuevo Santander. Escandón focused eventually on developing the area around **Old Falcón**, with settlers arriving in 1749, and surveys establishing private property rights in 1767 (Myers 2005, 5).

In 1801, a Franciscan-style mission church, one of the last erected in the United States, was built in **Guerrero Viejo**, to be called Nuestra Señora del Refugio (Doolittle and Maldonado 2008, 14–15; Instituto Tamaulipeco de Vivienda y Urbanismo 2011, 20).

The settlements suffered numerous raids by Lipan Apaches and Comanches. The majority of attacks occurred during the Mexican Revolution (1810–21), when military protection was withdrawn. Violent assaults persisted into later years. For instance, the **Uribeño** site was first settled in 1822 by Doña Ygnacia Uribe, but had to be abandoned in 1830. The family moved on to San Ygnacio, a more settled and safe location (George 2008, 49).

In 1838, Col. Antonio Zapata, a military leader and ranchero, helped organize an insurrection in **Guerrero Viejo** against the Mexican Centralist government. The revolt created the short-lived Republic of the Rio Grande. The Republic had its capital in Laredo and survived from January through March of 1840 (Sanchez 1994, 35–36).

In 1842, the ill-fated 300-man Mier Expedition camped at the **Old Ramireño** site during their march into Mexico to avenge the Dawson Massacre near San Antonio and the Mexican raids along the border (Texas Historical Commission 1988). These attacks had persisted despite the Texan victory at San Jacinto, recognized by the Treaties of Velasco of 1836.

Tradition claims that John James Audubon visited the settlement of **Capitaneño** in April 1848 to help prepare his painting of the roadrunner that later appeared in his opus, Birds of America.

During the First Cortina War of July 1859, the Fifth US Infantry briefly maintained Fort **Lopeño**, seeking to ease friction between Mexican Tejanos and Anglo settlers. Tensions were aggravated by accusations that a group of judges and Brownsville attorneys had expropriated Mexicans' lands since the 1848 Treaty of Guadalupe Hidalgo (Warren 2009).

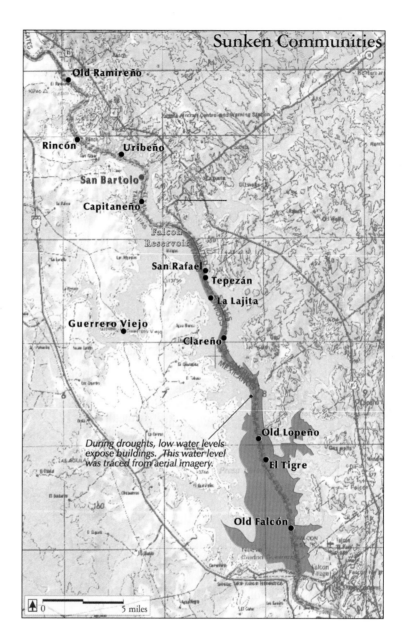

Sunken Communities

During droughts, low water levels expose buildings. This water level was traced from aerial imagery.

On April 15, 1861, an early Civil War skirmish known as the Second Cortina War occurred in the area later submerged by Falcon Reservoir. Just days after the battle of Fort Sumter, Confederates under the command of a Captain Nolan and Sheriff Díaz assaulted the **Clareño** Ranch, attacking Tejanos loyal to General Juan Nepomuceno Cortina (Sanchez 1994, 55–56).

In 1862, Bishop Ignacio Montes de Oca y Obregon came to **Guerrero Viejo**, a town in his diocese. Soldiers of the anticleric Benito Juárez stopped him at the edge of town, asking him to show his belongings. Insulted and angry, the bishop presciently said, "I curse this town. It will end under the waters" (Peña 2006, 309).

In 1916 through 1917, the US military occupied **Old Ramireño**, as the 1911 overthrow of the Mexican President Porfirio Díaz had led to turmoil and associated border raids (Texas Historical Commission 1988).

These photographs depict buildings erected from 1867 through 1876 at the old San Bartolo Ranch near Zapata, Texas. The site is now submerged by Falcon Reservoir. The images were taken by Arthur W. Stewart on June 24, 1936 (Cocke and Lansberry 1936; Stewart 1936a, 1936b, 1936c, 1936d).

event was bittersweet. The damage to their old communities continued into later years. High river flows brought rot, wave damage, and erosion to the remaining artifacts or buildings. In times of drought, goats, squatters, drug runners, and looters visited the old towns (George 2008, xxii).

The map shows a handful of the many significant events that occurred in the settlements that now lie under the waters of Falcon Reservoir (Byfield 1971; Krieger and Hughes 1950; Lott and Martinez 1953; Scott 1970). Perhaps the map also reminds us of how grand policies and big projects can bring welcome benefits, but sometimes at the cost of real pain and cost to a region's historic culture and community.

Sources

Arreola, Daniel. 2010. *Tejano South Texas: A Mexican American Cultural Province.* Austin: University of Texas Press.

Byfield, Patsy Jeanne. 1971. *Falcon Dam and the Lost Towns of Zapata.* Austin: Texas Memorial Museum.

Cocke, Bartlett, and Homer Lansberry. 1936. San Bartolo Ranch, Zapata, Texas. Photographs, Written Historical and Descriptive Data. December 3. District of Texas—3. HABS No. Tex-3113. Historic American Buildings Survey. San Antonio, Texas.

De la Garza, Beatriz. 2013. *From the Republic of the Rio Grande: A Personal History of the Place and the People.* Austin: University of Texas Press.

Doolittle, William, and Oscar Maldonado. 2008. *Guerrero Viejo: Field Guide to a City Found and Lost*. Austin: Casa Editorial Hace Poco.

Fish, Jean. 1990. "Zapata County Roots Revisited." Edinburg, TX: Zapata County Historical Commission and New Santander Press.

George, W. Eugene. 2008. *Lost Architecture of the Rio Grande Borderlands*. College Station: Texas A&M University Press.

Instituto Tamaulipeco de Vivienda y Urbanismo. 2011. Guerrero, Tamaulipas, Registro Estatal Patrimonio Historico y Artistico.

Jordan, David, and Horacio Perez. 1953. "Flow of the Rio Grande and Related Data." Water Bulletin No. 23. Rio Grande Near Zapata, Texas. International Boundary and Water Commission.

Kennard, Don. 1976. Rio Grande–Falcon Thorn Woodland. A Natural Area Survey, No. 13. Lyndon B. Johnson School of Public Affairs, University of Texas at Austin.

Krieger, Alex, and Jack Hughes. 1950. "Archaeological Salvage in the Falcon Reservoir Area: Progress Report No. 1." Typescript. Alex D. Krieger Reports, University of Texas Archives, Austin, Box 2R72.

Lott, Virgil, and Mercurio Martinez. 1953. *The Kingdom of Zapata*. San Antonio, TX: Naylor.

Myers, Terri. 2005. "Historic and Architectural Resources of Rio Grande City, Starr County, Texas." National Register of Historic Places, Multiple Property Documentation Form 10-900-b.

Peña, José. 2006. *Inherit the Dust from the Four Winds of Revilla: A 250-Year Historical Perspective with Emphasis on Ancient Guerrero, Its People and Its Land Grants*. Xlibris.

Poniatowska, Elena, and Richard Payne. 1997. *Guerrero Viejo*. Houston: Anchorage Press.

Sanchez, Mario L., ed. 1994. "A Shared Experience: The History, Architecture, and Historic Designations of the Lower Rio Grande Heritage Corridor." Los Caminos del Rio Heritage Project and the Texas Historical Commission. Austin.

Scott, Florence. 1970. *Historical Heritage of the Lower Rio Grande*. Rio Grande City, TX: La Retama Press.

Stambaugh, Lee, and Lillian Stambaugh. 1954. *The Lower Rio Grande Valley of Texas*. San Antonio, TX: Naylor.

Stewart, Arthur. 1936a. San Bartolo Ranch, near Zapata, Texas, June 24, 1936. Photograph. Historic American Buildings Survey / Historic American Engineering Record. Library of Congress. http://www.loc.gov/pictures/collection/hh/item/tx0289.photos.156526p/, accessed October 1, 2014.

———. 1936b. San Bartolo Ranch, near Zapata, Texas, June 24, 1936. Photograph. Historic American Buildings Survey / Historic American Engineering Record. Library of Congress. http://www.loc.gov/pictures/collection/hh/item/tx0289.photos.156527p/, accessed October 1, 2014.

———. 1936c. San Bartolo Ranch, near Zapata, Texas, June 24, 1936. Photograph. Historic American Buildings Survey/Historic American Engineering Record. Library of Congress. http://www.loc.gov/pictures/collection/hh/item/tx0289.photos.156528p/, accessed October 1, 2014.

———. 1936d. San Bartolo Ranch, near Zapata, Texas, June 24, 1936. Photograph. Historic American Buildings Survey / Historic American Engineering Record. Library of Congress. http://www.loc.gov/pictures/collection/hh/item/tx0289.photos.156529p/, accessed October 1, 2014.

Texas Historical Commission. 1988. Old Ramireño, Texas Historical Markers No. 16600.

US Department of State. 1944. "Treaty Relating to the Utilization of Waters of the Colorado and Tijuana Rivers and of the Rio Grande, and Supplementary Protocol, Signed at Washington, February 3, 1944, and entered into force, November 8, 1945." 59 Stat. 1219; TS 994; 3 UNTS 313.

Warren, Penelope. 2009. "Juan Cortina's War." *Texas Parks and Wildlife* (February).

Exotic Fish in Texas

In recent years, concern has grown about the impact of introduced species on native life. In their new homes, the foreign creatures often outcompete and replace endemic species and upset the overall ecological balance.

Exotic (brought from outside the United States) finfish provide a good example of the invasive problem, and a significant one in Texas. Fifty-two exotic finfish species have been released in Texas, ranking Texas fourth among all states for finfish introductions (Fuller 2015). In some portions of the state, these exotic fish have even overtaken natives. For instance, a survey of the San Antonio River in 2000 found that 61 percent of the species, 17 percent of the individuals, and 62 percent of the biomass of the sample had been introduced (Edwards 2001, 4).

Tank Cars and Milk Cans

Invasives are not a new issue. There has been a long history of fish introductions worldwide, dating back at least to Roman times. During that ancient era, carp were removed from the Danube and brought farther west in Europe for use as a food fish (Balon 1995). The US Bureau of Fisheries continued the tradition of moving fish in more recent times, yet on an industrial scale. For example, in 1885, three specially equipped railway tank cars carried live fish 74,805 miles to streams and lakes across the inland United States. The fish's destinations included a grand total of forty-eight states or territories, 1,348 counties, and 309 congressional districts (McDonald 1886, 385, 392). Often, fish were introduced from the train cars directly into streams at railroad crossings; sometimes they were just distributed with ox carts carrying milk cans of fish (Bean 1881, 205–6). In Texas, the bureau made its first recorded introduction of exotic fish as early as 1874, when it released American shad (*Alosa sapidissima*) and Chinook salmon (*Oncorhynchus tshawytscha*) into the state (Baird 1876). Some of the nineteenth-century introductions went into public waters, while others, such as the "German" (or common) carp (*Cyprinus carpio*), were put into private ponds for propagation and sale ("How Carp Have Grown" 1882).

Barefooted Boys and Weary Toilers

The state government soon became involved as well, passing legislation to create the Texas Fish Commission in 1879 (Chapter 78, 17th Legislature, Regular Session). Two years later, the state went ahead with construction of a fish hatchery at Barton Springs, in Austin, designed to produce common carp (Thompson 1943). By the late 1920s, the state was operating six hatcheries. They had special success in producing black bass (*Micropterus* spp.) and sunfish (*Lepomis* spp.), in order to stock "the 'ole fishin' hole' and the winding streams along whose banks the barefooted boy and the weary toilers of all classes find rest and recreation" (Game, Fish, and Oyster Commission of Texas 1927, 6). During the early twentieth century, federal and state agencies attempted to stock other fish in Texas. Tench (*Tinca tinca*), ide (*Leuciscus idus*), rainbow trout (*Oncorhynchus mykiss*), and brown trout (*Salmo trutta*) were brought in to attract sport fishermen from afar. As the Texas Game, Fish, and Oyster commissioner put it, "we live in a traveling age when something more is demanded than the city boulevard—something to go after and bring back with a story that excites the imagination" (Garrett and Matlock 1991; Howells and Garrett 1992; Game, Fish, and Oyster Commission of Texas 1927, 7).

The Postwar Era

Interest in stocking Texas waters with new species of fish grew further in later years, especially after World War II. This upturn was due to several factors, including the widespread construction of reservoirs, advances in hatchery technology, and the continu-

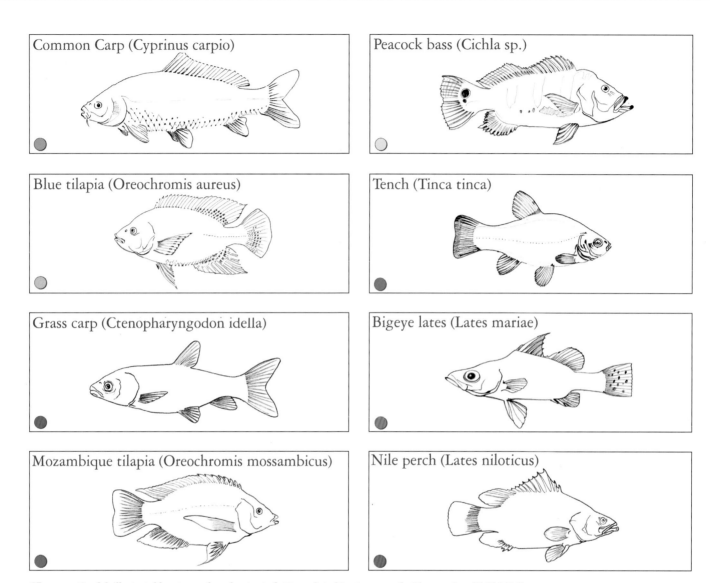

The nonnative fish illustrated here were released as part of approved stocking programs for Texas waters (Todd 2015).

ing development of a leisure industry based on sport fishing. About 50 percent of the species introductions were authorized and made by federal (20 percent) or state agencies (30 percent). However, substantial numbers of fish have moved in via more ad hoc ways. New fish have come from releases by aquarium owners (28 percent), fish farms and bait dealers (7 percent), or other smaller sources, such as ballast water (Howells 2001, ii; Fuller, Nico, and Williams 1999, 11).

Flat Water

The pace of modern, major introductions picked up in the years following the dramatic drought of 1950–57 and the record floods of the late 1950s. In response, Texas decided to manage river flows much more aggressively. In short order, the state erected over 180 major dams to supply water, control flood runoff, and generate electricity. By creating this new flat-water ecological niche, it became

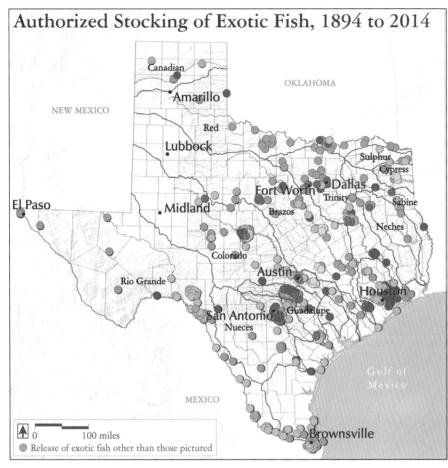

Authorized Stocking of Exotic Fish, 1894 to 2014

● Release of exotic fish other than those pictured

0 — 100 miles

Over the 1880 to 2013 period, exotic fish of numerous species have been intentionally stocked in Texas for sport, food, and biocontrol (Fuller 2015; Fuller 2012; Howells 1992; Howells 2001; Howells and Rao 2003).

possible to introduce a number of new species. In fact, due to booms in lake vegetation and rough native fish species (gar, buffalo, and others), it became important to introduce some new forms of "biocontrol." Also, through improvements in hatchery disease control, feeding, and better understanding of fish physiology, these releases became more practical and successful (Rutledge and Lyons 1976).

Inland Saltwater

With the special conditions in some of the new lakes, such as high salinity in the western and northern areas of the state, state biologists attempted inland introductions of marine species. These ocean fish included red drum (*Sciaenops ocellatus*), black drum (*Pogonias cromis*), Atlantic croaker (*Micropogonias undulatus*), spot croaker (*Leiostomus xanthurus*),

spotted seatrout (*Cynoscion nebulosus*), tarpon (*Megalops atlanticus*) and southern flounder (*Paralichthys lethostigma*) (Fuller et al. 1999; Howells and Garrett 1992). None of these species survived more than a few years, although red drum did have good short-term growth, and was popular with fishermen.

Hot Water

Cooling ponds for power plants offered another unusual situation for stocking. It was thought that these lakes' higher year-round temperatures might allow tropical fish to survive. As a test, in the 1950s and '60s, blue tilapia (*Oreochromis aureus*) were released into state cooling ponds (Howells and Garrett 1992). Later, from 1978 through 1984, Texas Parks and Wildlife put close to 70,000 Nile perch (*Lates niloticus*) and related species, including *L. angustifrons*, *L. mariae*, and *L. microlepis*, into Victor Braunig, Fairfield, and Coleto Creek cooling-water reservoirs (Howells and Garrett 1992). During 1981, 1983, and 1984, the department brought two types of peacock bass (*Cichla* spp.), a fish native to Columbia and Brazil, and introduced them to Alcoa Reservoir, Lake Bastrop, Tradinghouse Creek Reservoir, Coleto Creek, and Wilkes Reservoir. In the years since, these Nile perch and peacock bass populations have evidently died out due to unsuitable temperatures.

Sport Fish

In addition to trying to manage the dynamics of the new reservoirs in the state with introduced fish, there was also an attempt to spur and satisfy sport fishing. At the time, sport fishing was exploding as a popular pastime and as a lucrative business. As well, for government natural resource agencies, the new hobby was a boon for revenues. The Dingell-Johnson Act of 1950 had made taxes on sales of tackle, fish finders, trolling motors, boats, and fuel a major source of agency funding (16 U.S.C. 777). For agencies, restaurants, marinas, and the like, sport fishing began to mean big money. Today, in fact, an estimated 1.8 million anglers fish Texas freshwater bodies, bringing an annual economic impact of $1.49 billion to the state (Texas Parks and Wildlife 2014).

Natives and Exotics

Despite the years of enthusiasm and experiments, intentional stockings of nonnative fish in Texas have declined in the past generation. Direct experiences might help explain the change in attitude. One cautionary tale arose from the release in 1963 of grass carp (*Ctenopharyngodon idella*) in the United States. The carp were brought in to control aquatic plants in Alabama and Arkansas hatcheries, and later to manage vegetation in silt-prone reservoirs. However, the carp quickly escaped into the Mississippi River,

spawned (despite attempts to sterilize them), and turned into a serious problem. They became noted for their ability to outfeed and outbreed rival native fish, to emit barely digested fecal matter that led to algal blooms and oxygen crashes, and to harbor parasites that could attack native species (TexasInvasives.org 2012). Impacts of exotics on endangered fish were especially worrisome. By the mid-1990s, studies estimated that roughly 42 percent of the species listed as rare or endangered under the Endangered Species Act were at risk mostly because of competition with or direct predation by exotic species (Nature Conservancy 1996). Harm from exotic fish was occurring outside the United States as well. The introduction of the Nile perch to the African rift lakes was a prominent case. The perch's release outside its native range in Africa brought the collapse of local fisheries and wide condemnation in the mid-1980s (Howells and Garrett 1992).

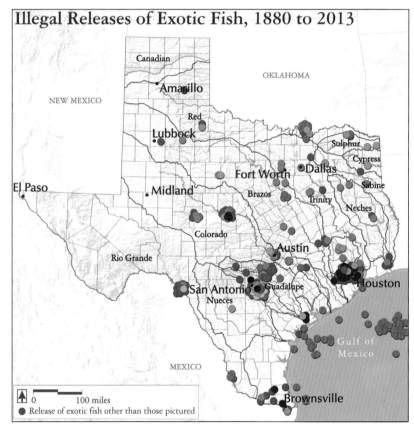

Between 1891 and 2014, exotic fish have been illegally released in many parts of Texas from aquaria, aquaculture farms, bait shops, and zoos (Fuller 2015; Fuller 2012; Howells 1992; Howells 2001; Howells and Rao 2003).

Mesa silverside (Chirostoma jordani)

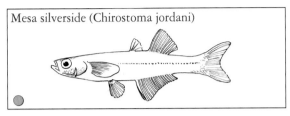

Red lionfish/Devil firefish (Pterois volitans/miles)

Rudd (Scardinius erythrophthalmus)

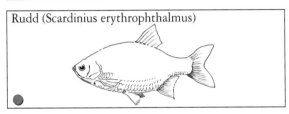

Southern sailfin catfish (Pterygoplichthys anisitsi)

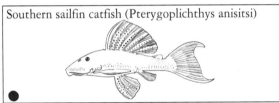

Redbellied pacu (Piaractus brachypomus)

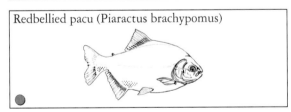

Goldfish (Carassius auratus auratus)

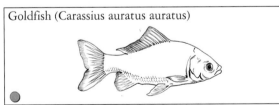

Guppy (Poecilia reticulata)

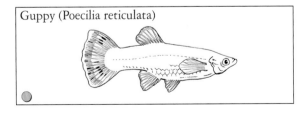

Suckermouth catfish (Hypostomus plecostomus)

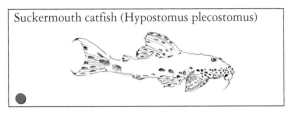

Bighead carp (Hypophthalmichthys nobilis)

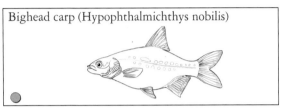

Tiger Oscar cichlid (Astronotus ocellatus)

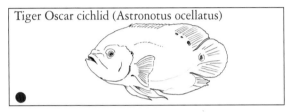

Green swordtail (Xiphophorus helleri)

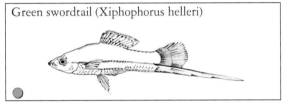

Pike killifish (Belonesox belizanus)

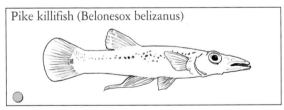

Raphael catfish (Platydoras costatus)

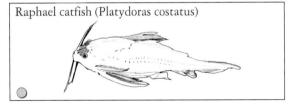

The exotic fish in Texas come in many shapes and sizes. The species shown here were illegally let go in the state (Todd 2015).

Energy

Back in Texas, an industrial problem arose with another exotic, the blue tilapia. There, the fish actually managed to bring down a modern power plant. In 1989, populations of tilapia rose so rapidly in the Victor Braunig cooling pond, south of San Antonio, that water intake screens at the plant were blocked. Fears rose that the power plant could overheat, so the operators were forced to temporarily shut down the utility. Explosives had to be used to remove the tilapia before electricity generation could be restarted (Howells and Garrett 1992).

Pets

Agencies were clearly long engaged in introducing nonnatives. However, recently many exotic fish have been found in Texas waterways due to the popularity of the pet trade among the public (Howells and Rao 2003, 1). The problem has arisen as owners buy tropical fish and then let them go when they tire of the fish, find them too costly to feed and care for, or simply learn that they have become too big for their aquarium tanks. The ability of customers to buy exotic fish over the Internet and get them shipped directly via air transport has made this trade in pet fish very difficult to regulate. Fortunately, however, these fish typically cannot tolerate water below fifty degrees Fahrenheit, so usually they cannot overwinter in much of the United States. However, there is a concern that they could survive the mild winters experienced in the southern third of Texas, or in heated reservoirs statewide (Tompkins 2011).

Food

Some exotic fish may also come to Texas as a food source, even a delicacy in some circles. The northern snakehead (*Channa argus*), a native of southern Asia, is an example. It is sometimes found in Asian live markets; in fact, Texas Parks and Wildlife raids in 2001 found several Houston-area stores selling snakeheads (Howells and Rao 2003, 7; Rauschuber 2002, 4). Tasty as they are, snakeheads are dangerous if released in the wild. A snakehead is an aggressive and mobile predator, capable of surviving winter temperatures and able to live out of water for three days (Texas Parks and Wildlife 2012b). At this point, no snakeheads have yet been found in Texas waters, but they have been discovered in twelve other states, including Arkansas, California, Florida, Illinois, Maryland, Massachusetts, New Jersey, New York, North Carolina, Pennsylvania, Virginia, and Wisconsin (US Geological Survey 2015).

Complications

The past 140 years of fish introductions, both planned and inadvertent, have taught us a number of things. On the one hand, introductions sometimes do not work. Sixty percent of the species released into the state have disappeared entirely, or do not seem to be able to maintain a reproducing population, primarily due to cold temperatures (Howells 1992, i). On the other hand, the common and grass carp that state and federal agencies distributed have taken well to their new home in Texas. Many of the exotic species originating with the pet trade, fish farms, and live bait dealers have also prospered (Howells 2001, ii). If nothing else, this humbling experience of fish introductions has taught us respect for the complexity and delicacy of natural ecosystems, and the power of unintended consequences.

Controls

While the genie is now in a sense "out of the bottle," these concerns about exotic fish in Texas waters have fortunately led to a good deal more caution going forward. The federal and state governments have adopted extensive regulations to control transport and possession of the more dangerous kinds of nonnative species. Arapaima, African pike, various carp, walking catfish, corvinas, Nile perch, snakeheads, and tilapia are just some of the nonnative species subject to limits now (Texas Administrative Code, Title 31, Part 2, Chapter 57, Subchapter A; Executive Order 13112; Nonindigenous Aquatic Nuisance Prevention and Control Act of 1990).

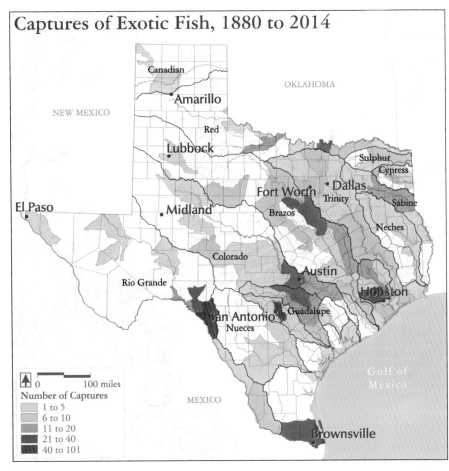

Captures of Exotic Fish, 1880 to 2014

Number of Captures
- 1 to 5
- 6 to 10
- 11 to 20
- 21 to 40
- 40 to 101

This map plots where exotic fish have been collected and reported in Texas, from 1880 to 2014. Please note that the capture counts may reflect where fish are most typically released or surveyed. The data may not indicate where the fish actually exist most commonly over the long term (Cannister 2012; Cannister 2015; Fuller 2012; Howells 1992; Howells, 2001; Howells and Rao 2003).

Springs, the introduction of predatory carp, and local stream poisoning with Rotenone. However, in 1965, the pupfish was rediscovered north of Fort Stockton in Diamond-Y Spring. Still, though, the pupfish remained at risk. The fish was vulnerable to possible spills from the local Gomez oil and gas field and was in peril of hybridizing with the introduced sheepshead minnow (*Cyprinodon variegatus*) (Walker 1976). So, the spring was diked off to protect against spills, the competing fish were seined and removed, and the Leon Springs pupfish was successfully reintroduced in 1976 (US Fish and Wildlife Service 1985, 7).

Sources

Baird, S. F. 1876. "California Salmon Transported to New Waters." Report of the US Commissioner of Fisheries. Part 3: 40–44.

Balon, E. 1995. "Origin and Domestication of the Wild Carp, *Cyprinus carpio*: From Roman Gourmets to the Swimming Flowers." *Aquaculture* 129 (1–4): 3–48.

Bean, T. H. 1881. "Account of a Shipment, by the United States Fisheries Commission, of California Salmon-Fry (*Oncorhynchus chouicha*) to Southern Louisiana, with a Note on Some Collections Made at Tickfaw." Bulletin of the United States Fish Commission. United States National Museum, Washington, DC.

Bowles, D. E., and B. D. Bowles. 2001. "A Review of the Exotic Species Inhabiting the Upper San Marcos

Also, education and marketing efforts have been suggested, particularly to alert aquarium owners of the risks they impose on native ecosystems by releasing exotic fish pets (Bowles and Bowles 2001; Weeks 2012, 10).

Restoration

And, finally, there has been a push to use these same introduction tools for conservation, by bringing endangered species back to old habitats, particularly springs (Minkley and Deacon 1991). One heartening story involves the recovery of the Leon Springs pupfish (*Cyprinodon bovinus*). Once found in Leon Springs, west of Fort Stockton, the pupfish had supposedly been extinct since the 1910s. Its alleged extinction was attributed to the damming and flooding of Leon

River, Texas, U.S.A." *Texas Parks and Wildlife*. Austin.

Cannister, Matt. 2012 and 2015. Nonindigenous Aquatic Species Program, Southeast Ecological Science Center, US Geological Survey. Personal communications, February 2012 and April 2015.

Edwards, Robert 2001. "Ecological Profiles for Selected Stream-Dwelling Texas Freshwater Fishes III." A Report to the Texas Water Development Board, Austin.

Executive Order 13112. 64 Federal Register 25 (February 8, 1999).

Fuller, P. L., L. G. Nico, and J. D. Williams. 1999. "Nonindigenous Fishes Introduced into Inland Waters of the United States." Special Publication 27. American Fisheries Society, Bethesda, Maryland.

Fuller, P. 2011, 2012, and 2015. Nonindigenous Aquatic Species Program, Southeast Ecological Science Center, US Geological Survey. Personal communications, December 2011 through February 2012, March 2015.

Game, Fish, and Oyster Commission of Texas. 1927. Annual Report. Von Boeckmann-Jones, Austin, Texas.

Garrett, G. P., and G. C. Matlock. 1991. "Rio Grande Cutthroat Trout in Texas." *Texas Journal of Science* (November 1).

"How Carp Have Grown in Three Months." 1882. *Galveston Daily News*, March 15, p. 1.

Howells, R. G. 1992. "Annotated List of Introduced Non-Native Fishes, Mollusks, Crustaceans and Aquatic Plants in Texas Waters." Management Data Series, No. 78. Texas Parks and Wildlife, Inland Fisheries Branch. Austin.

———. 2001. "Introduced Non-Native Fishes and Shellfishes in Texas Waters: An Updated List and Discussion." Management Data Series, No. 188. Texas Parks and Wildlife, Inland Fisheries Branch. Austin.

Howells, R. G., and G. P. Garrett. 1992. "Status of Some Exotic Sport Fishes in Texas Waters." *Texas Journal of Science* 44 (3): 317–24.

Howells, R. G., and J. B. Rao. 2003. "Prohibited Exotic Fishes, Shellfishes, and Aquatic Plants Found by Texas Parks and Wildlife Personnel in Harris County, Texas: 1995–1996 and 2001 through mid-2003." Management Data Series, No. 218. Texas Parks and Wildlife, Inland Fisheries Branch. Austin.

McDonald, M. 1886. "Report on Distribution of Fish and Eggs by the U.S. Fish Commission for the Season of 1885–86." Bulletin of the United State Fish Commission, vol. 6, no. 25. Washington, DC.

Minkley, W. L., and J. E. Deacon, eds. 1991. *Battle against Extinction: Native Fish Management in the American West*. Tucson: University of Arizona Press.

Nature Conservancy. 1996. "America's Least Wanted: Alien Species Invasions of U.S. Ecosystems." Arlington, Virginia.

Nonindigenous Aquatic Nuisance Prevention and Control Act of 1990. 16 U.S.C. 4702 et seq.

Rauschuber, C. 2002. "Invasive Species: Texas." Union of Concerned Scientists. Cambridge, Massachusetts.

Rutledge, William, and Barry Lyons. 1976. "Texas Peacock Bass and Nile Perch: Status Report." Vol. 39. Heart of the Hill Fisheries Research Station, Texas Parks and Wildlife Department.

Texas Administrative Code, Title 31, Part 2, Chapter 57, Subchapter A. "Fisheries, Harmful or Potentially Harmful Fish, Shellfish and Aquatic Plants."

TexasInvasives.org. 2012. Invasives Database: *Ctenopharyngodon idella* (Grass carp). http://www.texasinvasives.org/animal_database/detail.php?symbol=13, accessed February 17, 2012.

Texas Parks and Wildlife. 2012. The Snakehead Threat. http://www.tpwd.state.tx.us/huntwild/wild/species/exotic/snakehead.phtml, accessed February 17, 2012.

———. 2014. "Making More Fish for Texas: The TFFC Hatchery." Texas Freshwater Fisheries Center. http://www.tpwd.state.tx.us/spdest/visitorcenters/tffc/hatchery/, accessed February 17, 2012.

Texas State Library and Archives Commission. 2012. "To Love the Beautiful: The Story of Texas State Parks." https://www.tsl.state.tx.us/exhibits/parks/board/page2.html, accessed February 24, 2012.

Thompson, F. D. 1943. "German Carp Responsible for First State Fish Hatchery." *Texas Game and Fish* 2 (1): 8–9.

Tompkins, S. 2011. "Piranhas, Other Dangerous Exotic Species Found in Texas' Waterways." *Houston Chronicle*. September 27. http://www.chron.com/sports/outdoors/article/Piranhas-other-dangerous-exotic-species-found-in2187403.php # photo-1628430, accessed February 17, 2012.

US Commissioner of Fisheries. 1916. "Annual Report of the Commissioner of Fisheries to the Secretary of Commerce, for the Fiscal Year Ended June 30, 1916." Bureau of Fisheries Document

No. 836. Washington, DC: Government Printing Office, 8.

US Fish and Wildlife Service. 1985. Leon Springs Pupfish Recovery Plan. The Rio Grande Fishes Recovery Team. Albuquerque, New Mexico. August 14, p. 7.

US Geological Survey. 2015. Nonindigenous Aquatic Species Database. http://nas.er.usgs.gov, accessed June 3, 2015.

Walker, B. 1976. "The Leon Springs Pupfish . . . A Resurrection Story." *American Currents*, North American Native Fishes Association (November–December).

Weeks, P. 2012. "Freshwater Aquarium Hobbyists and Invasive Species in the Houston-Galveston Region." Houston Area Research Council, submitted to Texas Parks and Wildlife, Austin, Texas. *Houston Chronicle*, September 27, 2011. http://www.chron.com/sports/outdoors/article/Piranhas-other-dangerous-exotic-species-found-in-2187403 .php#photo-1628430, accessed February 17, 2012.

Groundwater

In this part of the atlas, we look at groundwater in Texas, whether in the springs of the Hill Country, the great Ogallala aquifer underlying the Panhandle, or the curiously collapsible aquifers of the Gulf Coast. Tracking changes, especially since they often occur deep underground within aquifer sands, gravels, and rocks, can be difficult. Often, the only indicators of change are technical measurements of fluctuations in well water levels, saturated layers, groundwater contaminants, or in land surface elevations. Sometimes, of course, the signs of change are obvious, as they have been in the subsidence of coastal lands or the disappearance of spring waters as aquifers have been pumped down.

Source

George, Peter, Robert Mace, and Rima Petrossian. 2011. "Aquifers of Texas." Report 380. Texas Water Development Board. 2006. 9 Major Aquifers of Texas. http://www.twdb.state.tx.us/mapping/gisdata/shapefiles/aquifers/major_aquifers.zip, accessed January 1, 2013.

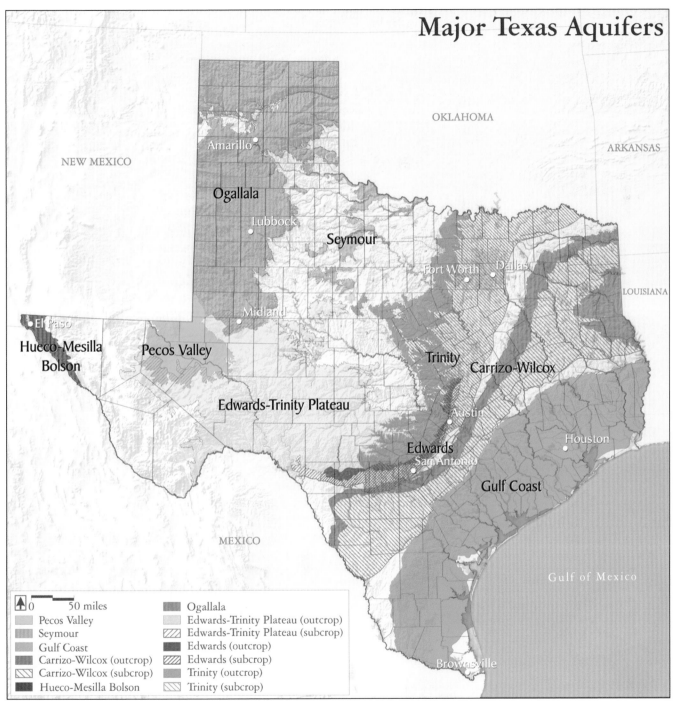

Major Texas Aquifers

NEW MEXICO

OKLAHOMA

ARKANSAS

LOUISIANA

MEXICO

Gulf of Mexico

El Paso

Amarillo

Lubbock

Midland

Fort Worth

Dallas

Austin

San Antonio

Houston

Brownsville

Ogallala

Seymour

Hueco-Mesilla Bolson

Pecos Valley

Edwards-Trinity Plateau

Trinity

Carrizo-Wilcox

Edwards

Gulf Coast

0   50 miles

Pecos Valley
Seymour
Gulf Coast
Carrizo-Wilcox (outcrop)
Carrizo-Wilcox (subcrop)
Hueco-Mesilla Bolson

Ogallala
Edwards-Trinity Plateau (outcrop)
Edwards-Trinity Plateau (subcrop)
Edwards (outcrop)
Edwards (subcrop)
Trinity (outcrop)
Trinity (subcrop)

This map describes the nine major aquifers found within Texas. Drawing on these major aquifers, plus twenty-one minor aquifers, Texas is now heavily dependent on groundwater, using it for close to 60 percent of its agricultural, municipal, and industrial uses. The development of powerful pumps and deep-drilling technology, coupled with near-absolute private title to groundwater, has made protecting aquifers difficult. However, the wider study and monitoring of aquifers, the broader spread of groundwater conservation districts, and the stronger efforts to protect water-reliant endangered species have all helped guard Texas' underground waters (George, Mace, and Petrossian 2011).

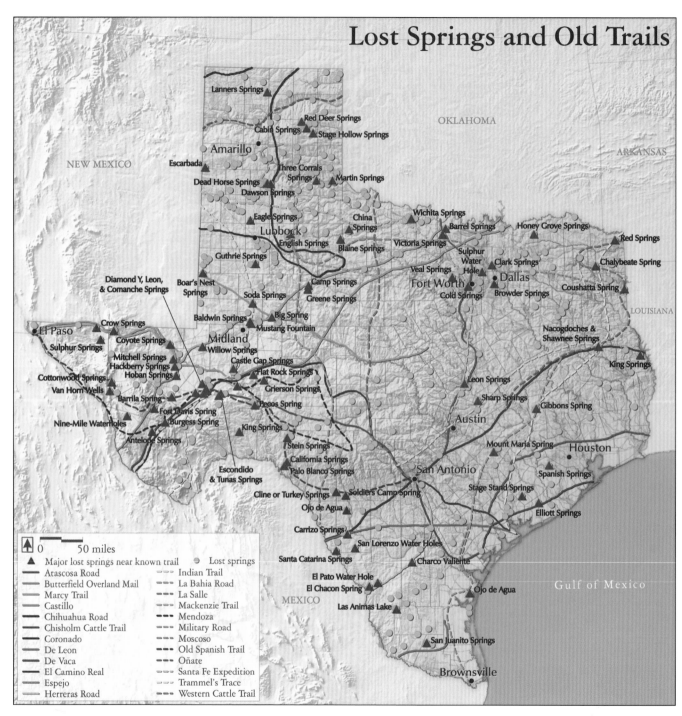

Lost Springs and Old Trails

Legend:

▲ Major lost springs near known trail   ● Lost springs

- Atascosa Road
- Butterfield Overland Mail
- Marcy Trail
- Castillo
- Chihuahua Road
- Chisholm Cattle Trail
- Coronado
- De Leon
- De Vaca
- El Camino Real
- Espejo
- Herreras Road
- Indian Trail
- La Bahia Road
- La Salle
- Mackenzie Trail
- Mendoza
- Military Road
- Moscoso
- Old Spanish Trail
- Oñate
- Santa Fe Expedition
- Trammel's Trace
- Western Cattle Trail

0   50 miles

The map shows the location of more than 410 lost springs that have been cataloged. The eighty-seven major springs marked with blue triangles were on the routes of main trails and roads, and suggest the impact that their loss might have had on the state's early exploration and settlement by humans. The effect on migrating wildlife, local plants, and endemic fish of past years can only be guessed at (Besse 2011; Brune 1975, figures 2 and 18; Hopkins 2011).

Lost Springs and Old Trails

First Sights

Early travelers to Texas frequently noted the number, purity, and power of springs in the area (Weniger 1984, 95–110). Often under intense artesian pressure, many were not even called springs, but instead were described as "founts" or "fountains." It is estimated that there were originally at least two thousand springs in Texas, with 281 considered major and historically important, and four, Comal, San Marcos, Goodenough, and San Felipe, ranked as very large (in excess of 100 cubic feet per second flow) (Brune 1975, 2, 9; Heitmuller and Williams 2006, 4).

Animals and Plants

Early visitors to the springs saw how important they were to animals of all kinds, even naming them for what they saw there. Old Texas maps, travel logs, and surveys mention Antelope Springs, Bear Springs, Beaver Springs, Bird Springs, Boar's Nest Springs, Buffalo Creek Springs, Coyote Springs, Crow Springs, Deer Springs, Duck Water Hole, Eagle Springs, Lizard Springs, Mustang Springs, Panther Springs, Red Deer Springs, Thrasher Springs, and Turkey Springs. Their rich vegetation was noted as well, with springs named for cedar, cottonwood, gum, hackberry, live oak, mulberry, pecan, prickly pear, shin oak, walnut, and willow (Brune 2002; Weniger 1984, 95–110). They were literally the oases of the state, valuable for life of all kinds, particularly in the arid west.

"The next water that the traveler finds is in the Sand Mountains, and sand alone, and on approaching it seems that nothing but sand is to be seen, until winding through a circuitous route you can see the tops of the Lonely Willow; there is that pure beverage God gave to man, and that too found plentifully in that portion of the great desert for man and animals; what a blessing and comfort."

—Brad Fowler, speaking in 1853 of Willow Springs.

The springs, formerly in Winkler County, southeast of Kermit, are now dry.

Trails, Camps, and Forts

The springs were not only havens for wildlife, but were also vital as watering sites for early explorers, travelers, Native Americans, soldiers, farmers, and ranchers who played a founding role in Texas history. Many western explorers stopped at the springs, including Cabeza de Vaca, 1532–36; Coronado, 1541–42; Moscoso, 1542; Espejo, 1562; Oñate, 1601; Castillo, 1650; Bosque, 1675; Mendoza, 1683–84; La Salle, 1686; and De Leon, 1687–89 (Brune 1975, 30, 35, 36, 37, 41, 42, 48, 53). Many of these sixteenth- and seventeenth-century explorers followed routes that were based on still more ancient Native American trails. With time, these routes were developed into more widely recognized tracks and roads, including El Camino Real, La Bahia Road, the Old Spanish Trail, the Atascosa Road, the California gold-miners trail, the Butterfield Overland Mail route, and the Chisholm Cattle Trail (Brune 2002; Pool 1975; Sheffield 2002). Many early Texas forts built to guard these travelers were established close to reliable springs, including Fort Davis, Fort Elliott, Fort Richardson, and Fort Terrett (Brune 2002, 261, 249, 414, 468).

Cities, Farms, Mills, and Spas

As the state became more settled, and its economy more developed, springs played a major role in anchoring towns and cities; in locating gins, mills, and factories; in irrigating farms and orchards; and in simply providing places for swimming, picnicking, and baptizing. Roughly 200 Texas towns relied on springs for their water supply, including San Antonio (the San Pedro Springs, among perhaps 100 others), Dallas (Browder Springs), Nacogdoches (La Nana and El Bañito), and New Braunfels (Hueco Springs) (Brune 2002, 70, 133, 152;

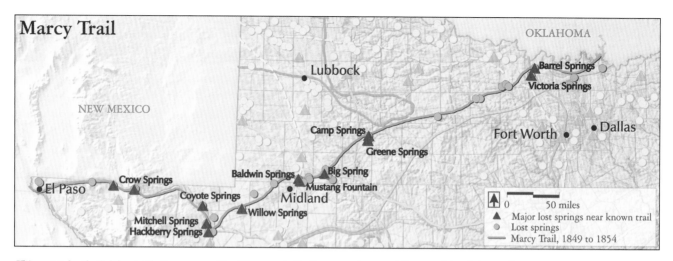

This map takes the California Trail as an example of the many paths that once crisscrossed Texas, making their way from spring to spring. Sadly, the map also shows that many of these springs are now dry (Brune 1975, figure 18; Brune 2002; Hopkins 2011).

Ruesink 1980; Weniger 1998, 104, 109). Important agricultural areas were organized around significant springs: Comanche Springs, near Fort Stockton, was the source for irrigating more than 6,000 acres of farmland in Pecos County. Major ranches were also centered on the water from springs, including Buffalo Springs in Dallam County, at the heart of the 3-million-acre XIT Ranch (Brune 2002, 151). As well, springs played a part in the early development of industry in the state. For example, Riley Spring, in Van Zandt County, powered a gristmill, cotton gin, and furniture factory (Brune 2002, 458). A number of hot and mineral springs became famous as therapeutic spas. For instance, Sam Houston reputedly treated an old wound at Sour Springs, in deep East Texas' Hardin County (Brune 2002, 210).

Goats, Wells, and Laws

Unfortunately, many of these historically important springs have dried up in the century and a half since western settlement. Due to the introduction of cattle, sheep, and goats, and the subsequent overgrazing and compaction of soils, the recharge to aquifers that fed these springs declined (Brune 1975, 2; Brune 2002, 88; Ruesink 1980). And the invention of rotary well-drilling, submersible-pump, diesel, and electric power technologies made it possible to rapidly pump out the groundwater in these aquifers, reducing both the supply and the pressure that had fed these springs. Texas' governing law of groundwater ownership was another factor in the loss of Texas springs (*Houston & Texas Central Railroad Co. v. East*, 81 S.W. 279 (Texas 1904); *Denis v. Kickapoo Land Co.*, 771 S.W.

2d 235 (Tex. App.—Austin 1989, writ denied)). Known as the rule of capture, this legal tradition has made it very difficult to bring claims against pumpers for draining aquifers and any dependent springs.

People

Perhaps a final reason for the loss of so many Texas springs goes back beyond ranching practices, technology, and law. Perhaps this factor goes back to more basic, ingrained human nature. As many have pointed out, people often have a very hard time managing resources that are commonly held. Most of us naturally tend to think first, and most, about what we need and want individually. Sometimes our thoughts about the community's needs come only later (Hardin 1968). Often we may think first of our goat,

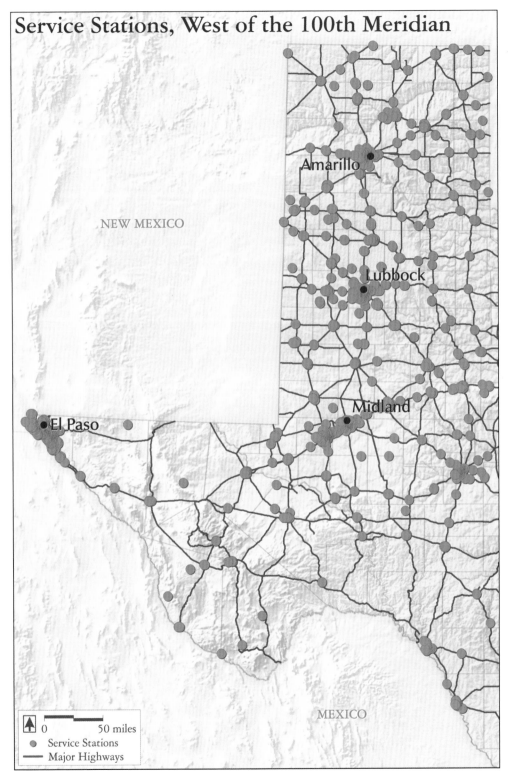

Service Stations, West of the 100th Meridian

NEW MEXICO

Amarillo

Lubbock

Midland

El Paso

MEXICO

0　　　　50 miles
Service Stations
Major Highways

In much the way that springs once provided rest, water, and food for early explorers and pioneers, service stations now provide fuel, sodas, and chips for today's drivers. This map shows over 1,780 gas stations located in the arid lands to the west of the 100th meridian, where springs were once such a critical, life-saving part of travel and community (TCEQ 2014).

our well, or our legal rights, and only remember the shared springs somewhat later, and maybe too late to save them.

Modern Times

For a variety of reasons, we have lost many local springs and watering holes in Texas. Fortunately, though, we are resilient and resourceful and have found substitutes. We now have filtered, chlorinated, trucked-in bottled water waiting for us in the refrigerated cases at many service stations. Perhaps this is the modern and convenient way. Still, it does seem that something has been lost. Maybe we miss something poetic about the old springs' beauty, or feel the absence of the wildlife watering in the old pools. Or perhaps we have lost the confidence that we can rely on local resources and must now trust that there is still a reliable supply of water coming somehow from somewhere else.

Sources

Besse, Helen. 2011. President, Ecological Recovery Foundation. Personal Communication. October.

Brune, Gunnar. 1975. "Major and Historical Springs of Texas." Report 189, Texas Water Development Board, Austin, March.

———. 1981. *Springs of Texas*, vol. 1. Fort Worth, TX: Branch-Smith.

Brune, Gunnar, with an introduction by Helen Besse. 2002. *Springs of Texas*, vol. 1. College Station: Texas A&M University Press.

Fowler, Brad. 1853. "The Rhine Party, 1853." *The Standard*, Clarksville, Texas, October 1. Reprinted in "Wagon Trails and Cattle Herds on the Trail in the 1850s," West Texas Historical Association Year Book, vol. 30 (October 1954), 141–48.

Hardin, Garrett. 1968. "The Tragedy of the Commons." *Science* 162 (3859): 1243–48.

Heitmuller, Franklin, and Iona Williams. 2006. "Compilation of Historical Water-Quality Data for Selected Springs in Texas, By Ecoregion." US Geological Survey, in cooperation with the Texas Parks and Wildlife Department. http://pubs.usgs.gov/ ds/2006/230/pdf/ds230.pdf. Related database available at http://pubs.usgs .gov/ds/2006/230/QW_TXSprings .zip, accessed June 3, 2015.

Hopkins, Janie. 2011. Manager, Groundwater Monitoring, Texas Water Development Board. Personal communication, October.

Pool, William. 1975. *A Historical Atlas of Texas*. Austin: Encino Press.

Ruesink, Lou Ellen. 1980. "Texas Treasure," vol. 6, no. 10. Texas Water Resources Institute, Texas A&M University. December.

Sheffield, William. 2002. *Historic Texas Trails: How to Trace Them*. Spring, TX: Absey.

Texas Commission on Environmental Quality. 2014. Underground Storage Tank Extract, Tank Data, Petroleum Storage Tank (PST) Datasets. https:// www.tceq.texas.gov/assets/public/ admin/data/docs/pst_ust.txt, accessed August 24, 2014.

Texas Department of Transportation. 2014. TXDOT Roadways. http:// tg-twdb-gemss.s3.amazonaws.comd/ transportation/txdot_roadways2014. zip, accessed August 25, 2014.

Weniger, Del. 1984. *The Explorers' Texas: The Lands and Waters*. Austin: Eakins Press.

Barton Springs, Austin, and Nonpoint Source Pollution

"Why do people worry so
about Barton Springs Eternal?
They holler out "look out below"
in Barton Springs Eternal.
It's a little twist on down and up
when your aquifer's an aqueduct.
What goes down and then comes up
in Barton Springs Eternal.
How many times we read and weep,
Barton Springs Eternal.
Watch development as it creeps
up Barton Springs Eternal.
This piecemeal progress and grand
    demise
been mauled and golfed and
    condo-ized,
We don't want no consolation prize.
We want Barton Springs Eternal,
    Barton Springs Eternal!"

    —"Barton Springs Eternal,"
        Bill Oliver, 2002

"Barton Springs Eternal," Bill Oliver, 2002 (Weisman 2002)

The Big Spread

Austin is a boomtown, doubling in population roughly every twenty years (Imagine Austin 2009). And as the center city has grown, residents and businesses have moved to the outskirts, driven by cheaper land, larger lots, less traffic, white flight, beautiful scenery, and other factors. Much of this suburban growth has funneled into the lands southwest of Austin. Homes, stores, and offices have spread far into the contributing and recharge zones for the Edwards aquifer and Barton Springs (jumping by 45,000 people, or 80 percent, from 1990 to 2000 alone). In this way, Austinites have hurtled straight into a political collision and an environmental wreck (Herrington 2012).

The Springs

Barton Springs pumps out 40 million gallons per day of cool, clear 70-degree water from the northern arm of the Edwards aquifer. The water emerges from fissures in the limestone bed of Barton Creek, less than two miles southwest of downtown Austin and the state capitol. Barton Springs served as a source of reliable, clean drinking water long before western settlement, and became a major place for industry and recreation during the 1800s (Brune 2002, 430–32). Many consider the springs, particularly the 1920s-era 900-foot-long pool that it feeds in Zilker Park, as the social and cultural center of Austin. Some even call it the "Soul of the City" (Swearingen 2010, 164). So there has been a long-lasting love for the springs and a concern about its protection (Pipkin and Frech 1993).

The Aquifer

Unfortunately, the aquifer and the springs themselves are vulnerable in

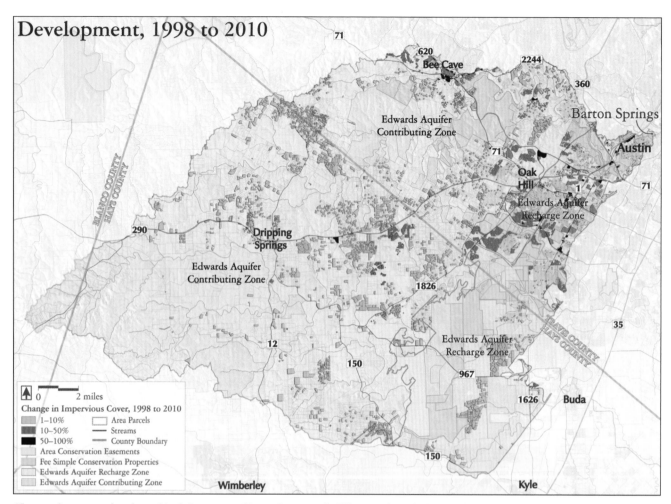

Development, 1998 to 2010

The map shows tracts that changed in their amounts of impervious cover (buildings, roads, and other paved surfaces) from 1998 to 2010. The percentages mentioned here represent the increment of change; in other words, an increase from 15 percent to 35 percent impervious cover for a given property would be reported as a net 20 percent change (Herrington 2012).

subtle and remote ways to the kind of growth that has been occurring in the lands to the southwest of Austin. Studies dating back as early as 1922 identified the risk for contamination of Barton Springs from diffuse sources located far away from the springs in the contributing zone (Burns and McDonnel Engineering Company 1922). Research from the 1970s and later established that nonpoint source pollution, diffuse storm runoff of oil, sediment, nutrients, pesticides, fertilizers, and other contaminants from developed lands, could cause serious water pollution problems (Espey, Huston & Associates 1979; City of Austin and Engineering Sciences 1982; City of Austin 2006).

The Brakes

As a result, there has been a generation-long public effort to restrain growth and development in Austin's suburbs, particularly this sensitive southwestern quadrant of the city. The organizing, education, and advocacy have been led by a variety of groups, including the Austin Neighborhood Council, Austin

Here is a 1925 view of the diving board area at Barton Springs Pool (Ellison Photo Company 1925).

These two 1947 images show Barton Springs Pool, as seen from the upstream end of the pool (Barton Springs Pool 1947a and 1947b).

Sierra Club, Citizens for the Protection of Zilker Park and Barton Springs, Save Barton Creek Association, the City of Austin's Environmental Board, the Save Our Springs Alliance, and the Zilker Park Posse.

Money, Plans, and Rules

One early protection effort was financial. In 1975, advocates organized to defeat a package of city bonds that would have paid for streets, sewers, and other projects that were seen as furthering sprawl (Swearingen 2010, 91). Another conservation measure involved planning: the Austin Tomorrow Plan, adopted by Austin's city council in 1979, was one such venture. The plan laid out a vision for a more compact city, reducing sprawl in protected areas, such as the Barton Springs district. At the same time, the plan sought to direct growth into areas where municipal infrastructure and services already existed, largely along a north–south axis that followed IH-35 (Swearingen 2010, 82). A third move was regulatory: in 1980, the council passed the innovative Barton Creek Watershed Ordinance, with extensive water quality protections and development density limits (City of Austin Ordinance No. 800417-I, adopted April 17, 1980).

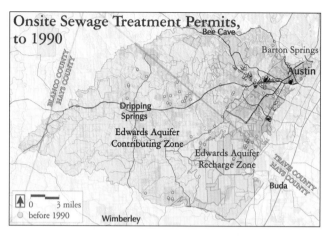

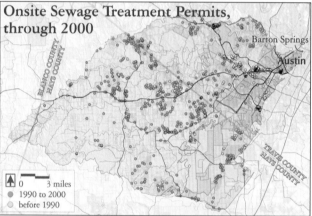

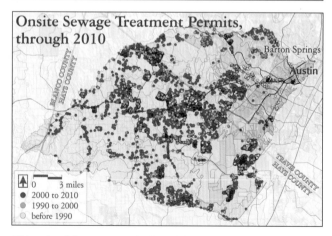

This series of three maps tracks the proliferation of septic tank systems in the contributing and recharge zone. Records for 2010 show that at least 9,470 septic tank systems have been permitted by local authorities within the Barton Springs Zone, with the highest density found in the Bear Creek watershed (City of Austin 2015; Herrington 2012).

The Gaps

Nevertheless, development in the Austin suburbs has continued to be difficult to control, for a variety of reasons, often, ironically, spurred by initial environmental successes.

MUDs

For example, the defeat of the 1975 bonds left the city with little money to buy parkland in sensitive suburban areas, exposing that acreage to development. Also, development interests rebounded from the defeat of the 1975 city bonds to successfully lobby the legislature to authorize Municipal Utility Districts. These districts allowed builders to operate in suburban areas largely independently of municipal or county control or financing. The "MUDs" could issue bonds to pay the high, upfront costs of subdivisions' infrastructure, later to be repaid by taxes on future residents within the districts. The city was reluctant to annex these MUDs until growth within each district generated enough in ad valorem taxes to offset the bond interest. That financial tipping point usually came long after much of the construction was complete, and when few ways to mitigate the impact remained (Swearingen 2010, 94).

Ordinances

Similarly, when the stringent impact of the 1980 Barton Creek Watershed Ordinance became apparent, builders became more involved in the drafting of ordinances in other parts of the contributing and recharge zones during the 1980–82 period. These new city ordinances permitted higher building densities in the watershed. The municipal rules also relied more on detention ponds and other technological fixes to the nonpoint runoff problem. With time, it became apparent that these technical solutions, largely settling ponds, do a reasonable job of trapping some 80 percent of total suspended solids in runoff. However, they filter only 30–50 percent of the dissolved nutrients, such as nitrogen and phosphorus. Plus, the devices are often subject to design, construction, and maintenance shortfalls (Swearingen 2010, 145).

Politics

Citizen organizing and support were often effective in doing the initial, public work of electing sympathetic officials, passing ordinances, and crafting bond packages in Austin. However, it became more difficult for the general public to influence the inner workings of council and its agencies that actually implemented policies, enforced ordinances, and distributed bond funds. For instance, the benchmark Barton Creek Watershed Ordinance of 1980 was loosened as the years went by, with 80 percent of covered projects receiving some kind of variance (Swearingen 2010, 145). Similarly, the Save Our Springs ordinance of 1992

was undermined by a three-month delay in its referendum and implementation, allowing 12,000 acres in development plats to be filed, grandfathered, and exempted (Smith 2012).

Another obstacle for those arguing for protection of the outlying areas of Austin came in the ability of other levels of government to become involved. While local neighborhood councils, municipal boards, and nonprofit groups could compete well within Austin city politics, they were often unable to compete with the more powerful forces that vied at the state level, federal realm, or in judicial courts.

For instance, at the state level, in 1987, the legislature passed HB 4 (later recreated as SB 1704 in 1995 and reenacted as HB 1704 in 1999). This series of statutes barred the city from altering a water quality ordinance once a construction project had been approved (Austin Chronicle 2002; Ankrum 2010). This gave grandfathered protection to developments, even those that had been merely sketched out in very rough, preliminary drafts. These "vested" development rights provided a shield against a battery of tightening regulations for many years to come.

At the federal level, the US Fish and Wildlife Service was slow to grant endangered species status to the Barton Springs salamander. The salamander is vulnerable to habitat alteration, increased sediment, decreased dissolved oxygen from lowered spring flows, and the possibility of a catastrophic toxic chemical spill or sewer

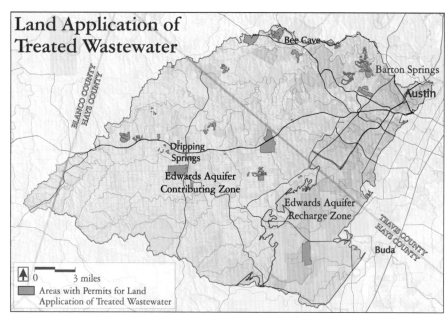

As of 2010, there were twenty-seven active permits in the Barton Springs Zone for 3.8 million gallons per day of wastewater disposal via land application (Herrington 2012).

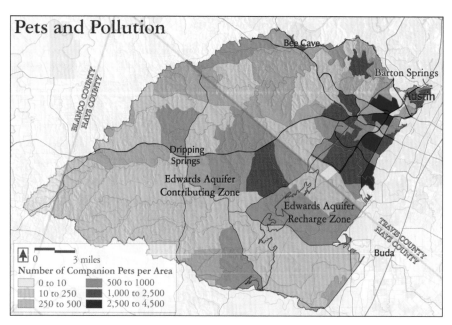

It is estimated that there were 48,000 dogs and 54,000 cats in the Barton Springs Zone in 2010, not all with a careful human picking up after them (Herrington 2012).

line break upstream (US Fish and Wildlife Service 2005). In that sense, conservationists saw the salamander as the proverbial canary in the coal mine for the Barton watershed. The Fish and Wildlife Service only approved the listing after being ordered to by US District Court judge Lucius Bunton in 1997, more than five years after listing had been initially petitioned. Further, the service granted the status only with the broad caveat that development within state and local water quality rules, would, per se, pose no hazard to the salamander and, thus, not violate the Endangered Species Act (62 FR 23377–23392, May 30, 1997; 57 FR 58779, December 11, 1992).

Rulings

Court challenges also went against conservation interests. In 1992, the Fifth Circuit Court of Appeals ruled against environmentalists who had challenged the Texas Department of Transportation in its bid to construct the southern extension of MoPac. This highway building project provided major access to the heart of the Barton Springs contributing and recharge zone, accelerating development there (*Save Barton Creek Association v. Federal Highway Administration and Texas State Department of Transportation*, 950 F.2d 1129 (5th Cir. 1992)). Similarly, in 1994, a Hays County court rejected the Save Our Springs ordinance as "unreasonable, arbitrary, and inefficient." The court ruled that the ordinance was void and ineffective from its original date of passage, and so allowed many developments to proceed without strict control (confirmed on appeal in *City of Austin v. Quick*, 930 S.W.2d 678 (1996)).

Splits

Some of the difficulty in regulating development in Barton Springs's contributing and recharge zones has also, admittedly, been due to conflicts within the environmental community. For example, some groups, such as PODER (People Organized in Defense of Earth and her Resources), have argued that too much attention

has been paid to protecting natural resources on the west, predominantly upper-income, white side of town, and too little to protecting public health in poor and minority neighborhoods to the east of IH-35. This tension became evident in controversies about the fuel storage tank farm (1993), BFI recycling facility (1997), and the Holly power plant (2007) (PODER 2012). Another division among various environmental factions appeared in the 2006 debate over the Open Government Amendment, a proposed city charter change that grew out of concerns over secret dealings between the city and private developers. Veteran environmental activists

found themselves on opposite sides of the amendment. Some advocates supported the amendment on transparency grounds, while opponents argued that some features (posting schedules for all agency and elected official meetings online) would be unworkable in practice (Swearingen 2010, 207, 208).

Whack-a-Mole

The challenge of regulating nonpoint source pollution in Austin, or for that matter anywhere, boils down to its essential nonpoint, diffuse character. Controlling runoff involves regulating many people's diverse decisions about many uses on many tracts over

Circle C Development, in southwest Austin, is an example of development over the recharge zone in the Barton Springs segment of the Edwards aquifer (US Geological Survey 2012).

a large and varied landscape. There will undoubtedly be divisive political problems and high financial costs and complex administrative headaches involved.

As a result, some of the recent responses have turned to more laissez-faire, market-based solutions. For example, in 1999, the Hill Country Conservancy was formed to simply buy fee-simple interests and conservation easements on sensitive land within the Barton contributing and recharge zones, and beyond. Often, the conservancy uses money from development and other business interests to pay for these purchases, in some cases as mitigation for construction projects. Some feel this is practical, quick, efficient, and less polarizing; others feel it is too expedient.

The Future

As time passes, as shown in the maps, living among Barton's limestone draws and wooded hills remains as popular as ever. New subdivisions, shopping centers, and office buildings continue to spread in the watershed. At the same time, related septic tanks, wastewater irrigation fields, treatment plants, and sewer lines scatter throughout the recharge and contributing zones. And, unfortunately, nutrient levels climb, algal blooms happen, bacterial outbreaks occur, and the springs are periodically closed to the community that loves it (Mahler et al. 2011; Herrington, Menchaca, and

Westbrook 2010). With that in mind, most would likely join Bill Oliver's refrain and keep working on all options to truly keep Barton Springs eternal.

Sources

Ankrum, Nora. 2010. "Before Save Our Springs." http://www.austinchronicle.com/news/2010-04-23/1018733/print/, accessed March 29, 2012.

Austin Chronicle. 2002. "The Battle for the Springs." August 9.

Barton Springs Pool. 1947a. Barton Springs Pool, seen from the south bank looking east, July 1947. Photograph, digital image. The Portal to Texas History. University of North Texas Libraries, crediting Austin History Center, Austin Public Library. Austin, Texas. http://texashistory.unt.edu/ark:/67531/metapth125207/, accessed August 31, 2014.

———. 1947b. Barton Springs Pool, looking east, July 1947. Photograph, digital image. The Portal to Texas History. University of North Texas Libraries, crediting Austin History Center, Austin Public Library. Austin, Texas. http://texashistory.unt.edu/ark:/67531/metapth125206/, accessed August 31, 2014.

Brune, Gunnar, with an introduction by Helen Besse. 2002. *Springs of Texas*, vol. 1. College Station: Texas A&M University Press.

Burns and McDonnell Engineering Company. 1922. Report on Water Supply Development and Water Works Improvements for Austin, Texas.

City of Austin. 2015. Watersheds, April 15, 2013. Shapefile. GIS/Map Downloads. Information Technology, City of Austin. https://data.austintexas.gov/Environmental/Watershed-Floodplain-Model/uphq-h3jn, accessed May 17, 2015.

City of Austin and Engineering Sciences, Inc. 1982. Final Report of the National Urban Runoff Program in Austin, Texas.

City of Austin Watershed Protection Department. 2006. "Stormwater Runoff Quality and Quantity from Small Watersheds in Austin, Texas." Water Quality Report Series COA-ERM/WQM 2006-1. City of Austin, Watershed Protection Department, Environmental Resources Management Division.

Ellison Photo Company. 1925. Barton Springs Pool, seen from the north bank, looking southeast, June 17, 1925. Photograph, digital image. The Portal to Texas History. University of North Texas Libraries, crediting Austin History Center, Austin Public Library. Austin, Texas. http://texashistory.unt.edu/ark:/67531/metapth125201/, accessed August 31, 2014.

Espey, Huston & Associates. 1979. Barton Creek Watershed Study.

Herrington, Chris. 2012. Manager, Water Resource Evaluation Section, Watershed Protection Department, City of Austin. Personal communication, April.

———. 2015. Watershed Protection Department, City of Austin. Personal communication, April.

Herrington, Chris, Matthew Menchaca, and Matthew Westbrook. 2010. Wastewater Disposal Practices and Change in Development in the

Barton Springs Zone. City of Austin, Watershed Protection Department, Environmental Resources Management Division.

Imagine Austin. 2009. Demographic and Household Trends, City of Austin Community Inventory Report. Draft, December 11. ftp://ftp.ci.austin.tx.us/GIS-Data/planning/compplan/community_inventory_Demographcs_v1.pdf, accessed June 3, 2015.

Mahler, Barbara, MaryLynn Musgrove, Chris Herrington, and Thomas Sample. 2011. "Recent (2008–10) Concentrations and Isotopic Compositions of Nitrate and Concentrations of Wastewater Compounds in the Barton Springs Zone, South-Central Texas, and Their Potential Relation to Urban Development in the Contributing Zone." US Geological Survey Scientific Investigations Report 2011-5018.

Oliver, Bill. 2002. "Barton Springs Eternal." Oral history interview, conducted April 11, in Austin, Texas. Texas Legacy Project, Conservation History Association of Texas.

Pipkin, Turk, and Marshall Frech, eds. 1993. *Barton Springs Eternal: The Soul of a City*. Austin: Softshoe Publishing.

PODER. 2012. Victories. http://www.poder-texas.org/victories.html, accessed March 29, 2012.

Smith, Amy. 2012. "The SOS Ordinance Turns 20." *Austin Chronicle*, August 3.

Swearingen, William Scott. 2010. *Environmental City: People, Place, Politics, and the Meaning of Modern Austin*. Austin: University of Texas Press.

US Fish and Wildlife Service. 2005. "Barton Springs Salamander (*Eurycea sosorum*) Recovery Plan." US Fish and Wildlife Service, Albuquerque, NM.

US Geological Survey. 2012. Circle C subdivision view. Aerial photograph. Digital image. Earth Explorer. http://earthexplorer.usgs.gov/, accessed March 15, 2012.

Weisman, David. 2002. Bill Oliver, April 11, Austin, Texas. Photograph. Digital image. Texas Legacy Project, Conservation History Association of Texas.

Ogallala Aquifer

There are some very big and magnificent things in the natural world. The Ogallala aquifer is certainly one of them. It is almost unimaginably vast. The aquifer is like an immense underground lake, containing in its sands and gravels as much water as nine Lake Eries (Ashworth 2007; Opie 2000, 3). The aquifer underlies forty seven Texas counties and stretches north under the High Plains, through New Mexico, Oklahoma, Colorado, Kansas, Nebraska, South Dakota, and Wyoming (Gutentag et al. 1984). The Ogallala is an especially significant source of water in Texas, fulfilling roughly 40 percent of the state's demands (Galbraith 2013).

Groundwater Use

As big as it is, the aquifer is also finite. It is essentially a fossil aquifer, receiving recharge of just one-half inch per year (Bell and Morrison 1982, 8; Reedy et al. 2009; Wyatt, Bell, and

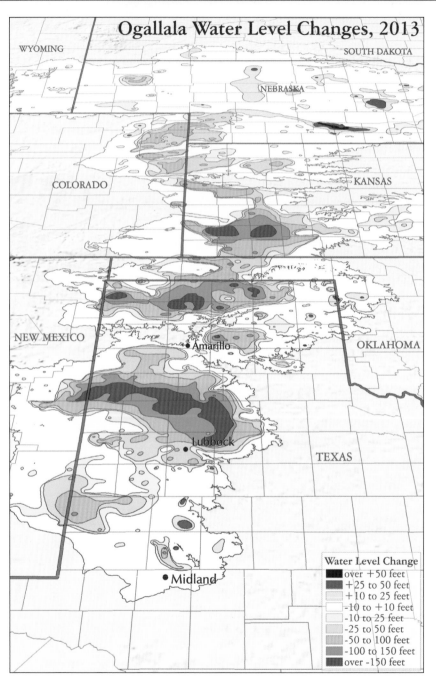

Water level changes in the Ogallala show large declines, from the pre-development period (roughly prior to 1950) through 2013 (McGuire 2007; 2009; 2011; 2014a; 2014b).

Morrison. 1976, 7). At the same time, it is being rapidly pumped by more than 170,000 wells, and is shrinking at a rapid rate (Magnuson 2013, 86).

Withdrawals from the Ogallala are made for the typical mix of agricultural, municipal, and industrial uses. However, the vast majority of the groundwater use, roughly 95 percent, goes to irrigating 3.3 million acres of the Panhandle (Gollehon and Winston 2013, 4). Gigantic amounts have been used in that way. Between 1900 and 2008, Texans removed 147 million acre-feet of water from the aquifer (Konikow 2013, 4). Recent pumping rates in the Texas section of the Ogallala remain high. Aquifer pumpage in Texas, during just the 2001 to 2008 period, amounted to 17 million acre-feet (Konikow 2013, 7).

Water Table Declines

Pumpage can now exceed recharge in the Ogallala by as much as 160 percent (Anderson and Snyder 1997, 162). With the pressure from these withdrawals, dramatic drawdowns in the Ogallala's water table have occurred, exceeding 150 feet in some Texas locations (McGuire 2009). Declines now average ninetenths of a foot per year and move as fast as three feet per year in certain areas (True 2007). The High Plains Underground Water Conservation District No. 1 reported remarkably fast drawdown during the recent drought. The sixteen-county district, which stretches from Amarillo

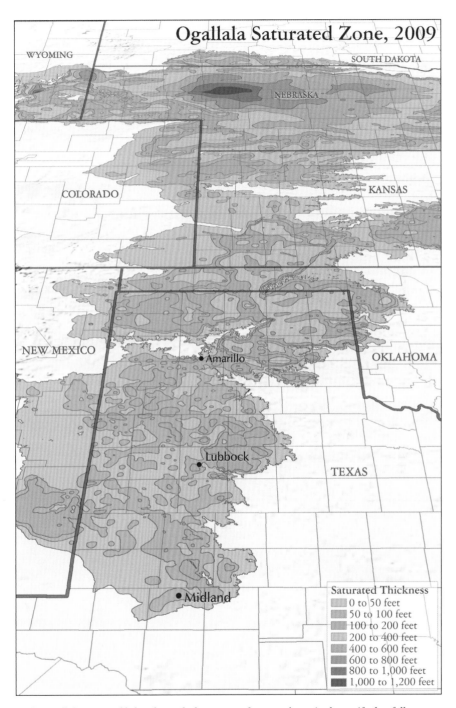

As the Ogallala water table has dropped, the amount of saturated zone in the aquifer has fallen as well. In some of the areas to the south of Amarillo, the saturated zone has grown quite thin, measuring less than 50 feet. If pumping continues for long at historic rates, groundwater withdrawals in those thin zones will no longer be economically viable (Houston 2011; Houston, Garcia, and Strom 2003; McGuire, Lund, and Densmore 2012a and 2012b.

south to Lubbock, recorded an average decline of 1.87 feet per year (Mullican 2013).

Farming and Ranching

A short historical review may help explain the southern Ogallala's current-day situation. Groundwater use in the Panhandle increased gradually in the late nineteenth century with the arrival of new settlers intent on farming. Raising crops grew yet more attractive as the ranching business collapsed following years of overgrazing, a glut of cattle, and the harsh winters of 1886 and 1887. Irrigated farming increased as the introduction of the windmill made pumping water from substantial depths far easier.

Dust Bowl

After more than a generation of farming, aggressive cultivation of marginal lands and extended drought in the Panhandle left little groundcover. By the early 1930s, the stage was set for the Dust Bowl. With the land's protective hide of grasses and crops gone, wind erosion peeled away frightening amounts of soil. Many farmers and their families simply abandoned their barren fields and left the area. The farmers who remained behind sought to hedge their bets on rainfall by more fully developing groundwater-based irrigation systems (Gutentag et al. 1984, 7).

Pumpage accelerated in the post–World War II era. A number of factors helped speed the Ogallala's use. New technology (rotary drills, submersible pumps, and pivot sprinklers), government subsidies (for commodities such as cotton, corn, peanuts, and soybeans), tax depreciation allowances, and plentiful supplies of cheap energy all had a role (Aillery 2014; Internal Revenue Service 1966). It also helped that there were few legal limits to the pumping. Texas' long-standing "rule of capture" allowed near-absolute private ownership of groundwater and limited pumpers' liability for drying up any neighbors' wells (*Houston & Texas Central Railroad v. East*, 81 S.W. 279 (1904)).

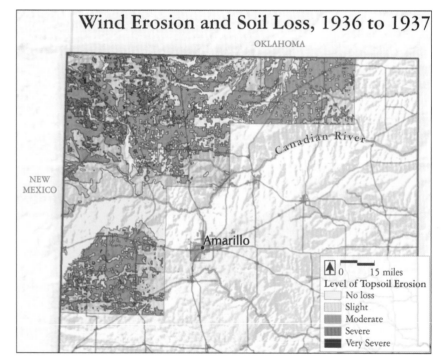

To understand the drive that many Texans might have felt to develop the Ogallala, it is important to remember the scar that the drought of the 1930s left. This map is based on a survey of the southern Great Plains conducted from 1936 through 1937, during the worst of the Dust Bowl. The data represent several levels of soil erosion, including no removal of soil (white), slight or less than 25 percent of topsoil lost (yellow), moderate or 25 percent to 75 percent of topsoil lost (orange), severe or over 75 percent of soil lost (red), and very severe removal or wind erosion into the lower subsoil (magenta) (Cunfer 2011; Cunfer 2014; Beamon 1937).

Pending Changes

Over a century of withdrawals has greatly diminished saturated thickness in the aquifer. Less than fifty feet of saturated sands and gravels remain in many chunks of the Ogallala between Amarillo and Midland (McGuire et al. 2012a, 6). Some saturated zones have been wrung out yet further. As

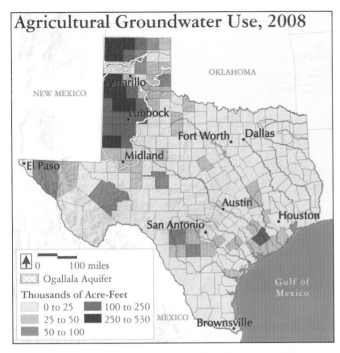

This map of agricultural groundwater use shows that the Ogallala has seen heavy pumpage for irrigating crops (2008 data are represented in shades of blue) (Texas Water Development Board 2014a).

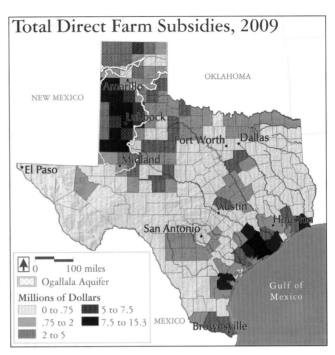

A good deal of irrigation and cultivation surely follows private market trends. However, at least some of the pumpage is likely accelerated by government farm subsidies. Total direct payments from the US government are shown here in shades of purple for 2009 (US Department of Agriculture 2012).

little as twenty-eight feet remain in the aquifer underlying Oldham County, to the west of Amarillo (Texas Tech University 2014). Major changes to Panhandle water wells, and the dependent economy, will come soon, as most pumps' efficiency drops dramatically when the saturated thickness falls below twenty to thirty feet (Bell and Morrison 1980, 9). This is likely to occur within ten years in some areas (McGuire 2011).

Ethanol, Dairies, and Exports

Concerns about the Ogallala's sustainability extend beyond the effects of a century of pumping and farming. These new issues include the rise of the ethanol market, the influx of confined dairies, and the proposals to pump and export groundwater to large cities (Amosson et al. 2011).

There are currently four ethanol plants overlying the Texas portion of the Ogallala—one each in Levelland and Plainview, and two located in Hereford (Ethanol Producer Magazine 2015). Critics have charged that brew-

ing a gallon of ethanol requires up to 16,000 gallons of water and ultimately consumes more energy than produced (Lacewell, Taylor, and Rister 2012; Seawright et al. 2010). However, this may not be a major debate in the Texas Ogallala's future, since ethanol production is capped by current fuel mixture rules (Jones 2013). Also, some of these refineries are already struggling: a plant in Hereford and the one in Levelland entered Chapter 11 bankruptcy in 2009 and 2011, respectively (Neff 2012; Prozzi et al. 2011, 8).

The early twenty-first century has also seen many large confined dairy

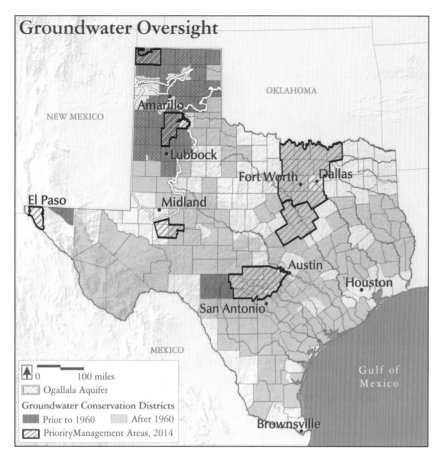

Groundwater Oversight

This map shows local- and state-level efforts to focus attention on protecting groundwater resources in the state. Some portions of the state, primarily the Ogallala region, saw the need to start work on these issues as early as the 1950s. Groundwater Conservation Districts that were established before 1960 are shown in dark blue. Some critical aquifers in the state have also attracted the state's involvement through designation of Priority Groundwater Management Areas, as marked with hatching (O'Brian 2014; Petrossian 2014; Texas Water Development Board 2014b).

operations come into the Panhandle from California and elsewhere. These dairies bring with them substantial demands for irrigated silage, and in turn, water from the Ogallala. The number of new dairy cows in the Ogallala region is impressive. From 1993 to 2013, dairy cattle numbers have soared by more than twenty-fold in seven counties located atop the Ogallala (National Agricultural Statistics Service 2014). However, the 2013 drought-related closure of a major Cargill beef processing plant in Plainview suggests that these dairies may not be immune to water shortages (Fernandez 2013).

Recent years have also seen the promotion of "water ranching" ventures to tap the Ogallala. T. Boone Pickens and Mesa Water were perhaps the most active marketers, hawking plans to build a $3 billion, 350-mile pipeline, and export Ogallala water to Dallas (Mildenberg 2011). Yet the prospect of immediate development and large-scale exports died in 2011, when Pickens sold 211,000 acre-feet of rights to a local water provider, the Canadian River Municipal Water Authority (Welch 2011). While the water may still be pumped, it is less likely to be hitched to the meteoric growth of the big downstate metropolises.

Districts and Management Areas

Several trends suggest that there may be good news for protecting the Ogallala. For instance, there is an increased awareness of aquifer limits, as shown by the statewide rise in groundwater conservation districts. Ninety-nine districts now exist in the state (Texas Water Development Board 2015). Early on, Ogallala users recognized their vulnerabilities and created many of the state's first districts, including the High Plains Underground Water Control District No. 1 (1951), the North Plains Groundwater Conservation District (1955), and the Panhandle Groundwater Conservation District (1956) (O'Brian 2014; Petrossian 2014). The North Plains District was one of the first in the Panhandle to begin serious regulation, phasing in well meters in 2003 and pumping limits in 2005 (Galbraith 2013; Kaiser 2006, 481; North Plains Groundwater

Conservation District 2014). However, controls are still relatively light and districts retain the right to exempt wells from all regulation if they choose (Texas Water Code, Section 36.117(a)).

While much of the day-to-day management of Ogallala resources occurs at the district level, the Texas Water Development Board coordinates the various districts' efforts through large Groundwater Management Areas. Within those areas, the board has calculated sustainable pumping levels for local districts to maintain what those communities envision for a fifty-year "desired future condition" (Texas Water Code, Section 36.108). The improved monitoring, modeling, and projections help with understanding the Ogallala's limits. However, it is important to remember that some districts have nevertheless chosen a "future condition" that would allow them to drain as much as half of the aquifer in the next fifty years (Wilder 2010).

In 1990, Texas went further in efforts to protect aquifers threatened by overuse. The state designated four Panhandle counties—Briscoe, Dallam, Hale, and Swisher—as Priority Groundwater Management Areas (PGMA) (Texas Commission on Environmental Quality and the Texas Water Development Board 2011, 19). The Texas Commission on Environmental Quality can require portions of those PGMA counties to come under the regulation of a Groundwater Conservation District (Texas Water Code, Sections 35.013 and 36.0151). This helped bring some of the more freewheeling regions within the ambit of a district (Shaw 2012).

Efficiencies and Cutbacks

With regulatory and market pressures, there have been signs that Panhandle farmers are becoming more efficient with their water use by turning to no-till cultivation, subsurface drip irrigation, and other conservation methods (Gollehon and Winston 2013). Some irrigated fields are simply being converted straight to dryland farming. In fact, research suggests that irrigated farmland acreage in the Texas High Plains has plummeted 45 percent below its peak in the mid-1970s (Amosson et al. 2011, 6). In a related trend, federal data show the entry of more acreage into the federal "Conservation Reserve" program, returning croplands to less-thirsty native grasses and other perennial groundcover (Food Security Act, P.L. 99-198, December 23, 1985; US Department of Agriculture 2012).

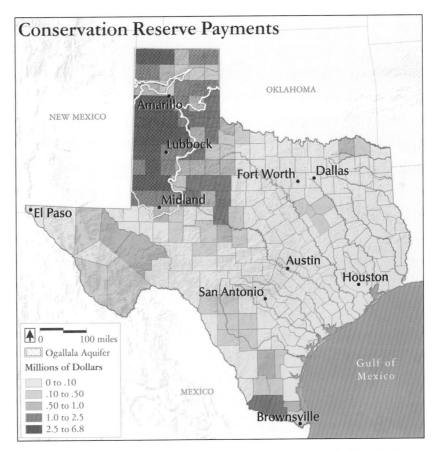

This map shows total Conservation Reserve Program payments per county for Texas, for the year 2009. The large payments to Panhandle counties suggest that landowners may be trying to shift away from irrigated crops to dryland range (US Department of Agriculture 2012).

Desired Future Conditions

State water agencies, local groundwater conservation districts, and Panhandle farmers are trying to reduce water use and conserve the remaining water in the Ogallala. However, this will mean wrenching change for irrigators, with nearly 60 percent water cutbacks projected from 2020 to 2070 (Almas, Colette, and Wu 2004, 9; Blandford et al. 2003; Texas Water Development Board 2014c). Development of stingier irrigation techniques and introduction of drought-tolerant sources of grain (including milo and eastern gamma) may help ease farmers' lives. Still, the farming families on the High Plains will definitely confront major changes (Anderson 2002).

The Ogallala itself will change as well. Many groundwater districts have already conceded that the "desired future condition" for the Ogallala will be quite unlike today's, and certainly different from a century ago. The extent of change is still unclear. In the coming years, the aquifer might see a definite yet gradual shift. Or it could face a severe and dramatic swing. It is important that we all remember that existing Texas statutes do authorize the Ogallala's "managed depletion." In other words, the aquifer's calculated and intentional draining remains a possible and legal option (Texas Water Code, Section 36.116(a)(1)(E)). Now though, there are still a few years and choices remaining. We can still decide if the Ogallala will be protected or depleted, and whether the "sandstone champagne" will indeed run out.

Sources

Aillery, Marcel. 2014. Agricultural economist. Economic Research Service, US Department of Agriculture. Personal communication, July.

Almas, Lal, W. Arden Colette, and Zhen Wu. 2004. "Declining Ogallala Aquifer and Texas Panhandle Economy." Presented at the Southern Agricultural Economics Association meeting, Tulsa, Oklahoma, February 14–18.

Amosson, Steve, Bridget Guerrero, Jackie Smith, Jeffrey Johnson, Phillip Johnson, Justin Weinheimer, Lal Almas, and Jacob Roberts. 2011. "Water Use by Confined Livestock Operations and Ethanol Plants in the Texas High Plains." Texas AgriLife Extension. Texas A&M System.

Anderson, Jim Bill. 2002. Conservation history interview, conducted in Canadian, Texas, on October 8. Texas Legacy Project. Conservation History Association of Texas.

Anderson, Terry, and Pamela Snyder. 1997. *Water Markets: Priming the Invisible Pump*. Washington, DC: Cato Institute.

Ashworth, William. 2007. *Ogallala Blue: Water and Life on the Great Plains*. New York: W. W. Norton.

Barbato, Lucia. 2014. Texas Tech University, Center for Geospatial Technology. Personal communication, August.

Beamon, W. F. 1937. Soil Conservation Survey Maps and Summarized Erosion Map of the Southern Great Plains Wind Erosion Area, for Use with US Department of Agriculture Technical Bulletin 556. Map. US Soil Conservation Service.

Bell, Ann, and Shelly Morrison. 1982. "Analytical Study of the Ogallala Aquifer in Hemphill County, Texas." Report 267. Texas Water Development Board.

Blandford, T. N., D. J. Blazer, K. C. Calhoun, A. R. Dutton, Thet Naing, R. C. Reedy, and B. R. Scanlon. 2003. "Groundwater Availability of the Southern Ogallala Aquifer in Texas and New Mexico: Numerical Simulations through 2050." Final report prepared for the Texas Water Development Board by Daniel B. Stephens and Associates.

Cunfer, Geoff. 2011. "The Southern Great Plains Wind Erosion Maps of 1936–1937." *Agricultural History* 85 (4): 540–59.

———. 2014. Associate Professor, Department of History and School of Environment and Sustainability, University of Saskatchewan. Personal communication, August.

Ethanol Producer Magazine. 2015. "U.S. Ethanol Plants." Last modified on May 8, 2015. http://www.ethanolproducer.com/plants/listplants/US/Existing/All, accessed June 3, 2015.

Fernandez, Manny. 2013. "Drought Takes Its Toll on a Texas Business and a Town." *New York Times*, February 27.

Galbraith, Kate. 2013. "In Texas, a Push to Show Farmers How to Save Water." *Texas Tribune*, June 30.

Gollehon, Noel, and Bernadette Winston. 2013. "Groundwater Irrigation and Water Withdrawals: The Ogallala

Aquifer Initiative." *Economic Series Number 1.* Resource Economics, Analysis and Policy Division, Natural Resources Conservation Service, US Department of Agriculture. August.

Gutentag, Edwin, Frederick Heimes, Noel Krothe, Richard Luckey, and John Weeks. 1984. "Geohydrology of the High Plains Aquifer in Parts of Colorado, Kansas, Nebraska, New Mexico, Oklahoma, South Dakota, Texas, and Wyoming." Professional Paper 1400-B. US Geological Survey.

Houston, Natalie. 2011. Hydrogeologist, Texas Water Science Center, US Geological Survey. Personal communication, October.

Houston, Natalie, Amanda Garcia, and Eric Strom. 2003. "Selected Hydrogeologic Datasets for the Ogallala Aquifer, Texas." Open File Report 2003-296. August.

Internal Revenue Service. 1966. Revenue Procedure 66-11, Cumulative Bulletin 1966-1. Internal Revenue Service, US Treasury.

Jones, Ernesta. 2013. News Release: EPA Proposes 2014 Renewable Fuel Standards. US Environmental Protection Agency, Washington, DC.

Kaiser, Ronald. 2006. "Groundwater Management in Texas: Evolution or Intelligent Design?" *Kansas Journal of Law and Public Policy* 15 (3): 467–86.

Konikow, Leonard. 2013. "Groundwater Depletion in the United States (1900–2008)." Scientific Investigations Report 2013-5079. US Geological Survey, US Department of the Interior.

Lacewell, Ronald, Robert Taylor, and Edward Rister. 2012. "Irrigation Water Consumed per Gallon of Corn Ethanol Produced in the Texas High Plains."

BioEnergy Policy Brief, November. Auburn College of Agriculture and Texas A&M AgriLife.

Magnuson, Joel. 2013. "The Growth Imperative: Prosperity or Poverty." In *Debt: Ethics, the Environment, and the Economy,* edited by Peter Paik and Merry Wiesner-Hanks. Madison: University of Wisconsin Press.

McGuire, Virginia. 2009. "Changes in Water Levels and Storage in the High Plains Aquifer, Predevelopment to 2007." US Geological Survey Fact Sheet 2009-3005, 2 pp. http://pubs .usgs.gov/fs/2009/3005/, accessed July 14, 2014.

———. 2011. US Geological Survey. Personal communications, September and October.

———. 2014a. Water-Level Changes and Change in Water in Storage in the High Plains Aquifer, Predevelopment to 2013 and 2011–13. US Geological Survey Scientific Investigations Report 2014-5218. http://pubs.usgs.gov/ sir/2014/5218/, accessed April 14, 2015.

———. 2014b. Water-Level Changes and Change in Water in Storage in the High Plains Aquifer, Predevelopment to 2013 and 2011–13. US Geological Survey Scientific Investigations Report 2014-5218. ESRI grid format file. http://water.usgs.gov/GIS/dsdl/ sir2014-5218_hp_wlcpd13g.zip, accessed April 14, 2015.

McGuire, Virginia, Karen Lund, and Brenda Densmore. 2012a. "Saturated Thickness and Water in Storage in the High Plains Aquifer, 2009, and Water-Level Changes and Changes in Water in Storage in the High Plains Aquifer, 1980 to 1995, 1995 to 2000,

2000 to 2005, and 2005 to 2009." US Geological Survey Scientific Investigations Report 2012-5177. http://pubs.er.usgs.gov/publication/ sir20125177, accessed April 14, 2015.

———. 2012b. "Saturated Thickness and Water in Storage in the High Plains Aquifer, 2009, and Water-Level Changes and Changes in Water in Storage in the High Plains Aquifer, 1980 to 1995, 1995 to 2000, 2000 to 2005, and 2005 to 2009." US Geological Survey Scientific Investigations Report 2012-5177. ArcInfo Workstation GRID file. http:// water.usgs.gov/GIS/dsdl/hp_satthk 09a.zip, accessed April 14, 2015.

Mildenberg, David. 2011. "Pickens Water-to-Riches Dream Unravels as 11 Texas Cities Scoop Up Rights." *Bloomberg News,* July 13.

Mullican, William. 2013. "Rate of Groundwater Level Decline Slows Despite Continuation of Drought." *Cross Section,* vol. 59, no. 5. High Plains Underground Water Conservation District, No. 1. Lubbock, Texas.

National Agricultural Statistics Service. 2014. QuickStats. US Department of Agriculture. Accessed August 11, 2014.

Neff, Walt. 2012. "Bankruptcy Judge Approves Schedule for Levelland Ethanol Plant Auction." *Lubbock Avalanche-Journal,* April 2.

North Plains Groundwater Conservation District. 2014. Rules of North Plains Groundwater Conservation District, Rules Adopted by the Board on July 14.

O'Brian, Erik. 2014. Senior Cartographer and Data Analyst. Data and Mapping Solutions, Texas Natural Resources

Information System. Texas Water Development Board. Personal communication, August.

Opie, John. 2000. *Ogallala: Water for a Dry Land*. Lincoln: University of Nebraska Press.

Petrossian, Rima. 2014. Manager, Groundwater Technical Assistance. Texas Water Development Board. Personal communication, August.

Prozzi, Jolanda, Ashley Dumais, Mike Cline, Lisa Loftus-Otway, and Eleanor Seaborne. 2011. "Texas Energy Sector: Past and Future." Center for Transportation Research Technical Report 0-6513-1B. University of Texas at Austin.

Reedy, Robert, Sarah Davidson, Amy Crowell, John Gates, Osama Akasheh, and Bridget Scanlon. 2009. "Groundwater Recharge in the Central High Plains of Texas: Roberts and Hemphill Counties." Panhandle Water Planning Group. Texas Water Development Board.

Seawright, Emily, Ron Lacewell, Naveen Adusumilli, Robert Taylor, and Edward Rister. 2010. "Net Energy Balance for Ethanol from Irrigated Corn in the High Plains of Texas." BioEnergy Policy Brief, April. Auburn College of Agriculture and Texas A&M AgriLife.

Shaw, Bryan. 2012. Order Granting the Petition for Addition of Dallam County Priority Groundwater Management Area to the North Plains Groundwater Conservation District. TCEQ Docket No. 2008-1940-WR, August 7. Texas Commission on Environmental Quality.

Texas Commission on Environmental Quality and the Texas Water Development Board. 2011. "Priority Groundwater Management Areas and Groundwater Conservation Districts, Report to the 82nd Texas Legislature." Report SFR-053/07, January.

Texas Commission on Environmental Quality. 2015. Contact List for Created and Confirmed GCDs, current as of February 2015. https://www.tceq.texas .gov/assets/public/permitting/water supply/groundwater/gcd/gcdcontact list.pdf, accessed June 3, 2015.

Texas Tech University. 2014. Texas Ogallala Summary. Center for Geospatial Technology, Texas Tech University. http://www.gis.ttu.edu/ ogallalaaquifermapsTXOgallala Summary.aspx, accessed August 11, 2014.

Texas Water Development Board. 2014a. "Historical Agricultural Irrigation Water Use Estimates." http://www .twdb.texas.gov/conservation/agricul ture/irrigation/Present-IrrEstimates .asp, accessed July 14, 2014.

———. 2014b. "Priority Groundwater Management Areas." Shapefile. http:// www.twdb.state.tx.us/mapping/ gisdata/shapefiles/priority_ground water_management_areas/pgmas_DD_ NAD83.zip, accessed August 11, 2014.

———. 2014c. "2016 Regional Water Plan: Population & Water Demand Projections." http://www.twdb.state .tx.us/waterplanning/data/projections/ 2017/doc/Demand/2RegionalDemand ByCategory.pdf, accessed August 11, 2014.

Texas Water Development Board. 2015. Administrative Boundaries: Groundwater Conservation Districts. Shapefile. Current as of August 2014, acquired from Texas Commission on Environmental Quality. http://www .twdb.texas.gov/mapping/gisdata/doc/ GCD_Shapefiles.zip, accessed March 16, 2015.

True, Larissa. 2007. "Beneath the Surface: Mapping the Ogallala." *Archway*, Texas Tech University.

US Department of Agriculture. 2012. "Farm Program Atlas." http://www.ers .usda.gov/media/622947/farmprogram atlasdata.xls, accessed July 14, 2014.

Welch, Kevin. 2011. "Group Buys Mesa Water Rights." *Amarillo Globe-News*, June 24.

Wilder, Forrest. 2010. "Cash Flow: A Tiny Texas Town Takes on T. Boone Pickens—and Tries to Save Its Water." *Texas Observer*, September 9.

Wilkinson, Andy. 2002. Oral history interview conducted on October 11, in Lubbock, Texas. Texas Legacy Project. Conservation History Association of Texas.

Wyatt, Wayne, Ann Bell, and Shelly Morrison. 1976. "Analytical Study of the Ogallala Aquifer in Castro County, Texas." Report 206. Texas Water Development Board.

Comal, San Antonio, and the Edwards

The Edwards aquifer is well known today as the huge water-bearing strata that stretch across 3,500 square miles and six counties in the Hill Country of Central Texas. However, the aquifer was hidden from early Texans and only known by the springs it fed, such as Comal Springs. Comal consists of a collection of seven major springs near New Braunfels, and they make up the major outlet for the Edwards aquifer. As the largest set of springs in Texas, and perhaps the greatest in the entire Southwest, Comal's waters have drawn explorers, settlers, and visitors for generations (Brune 2002, 10, 129–31).

Native Americans

In 1691, the Spanish explorer Damián Massanet was likely the first westerner to come across the springs. He discovered a large settlement of Tonkawas and other Native Americans there, some who had traveled from

Pollutant risks for the Edwards aquifer area include: (A) Spills (accidental releases, 2005–12, of sewage, fuel, and other contaminants in the contributing or recharge zone); (B) Regulated Storage Tanks (both underground and above ground, typically containing gasoline and diesel); (C) VOCs (volatile organic compounds, including PCE, trans-1,2-dichloroethene, 1,2-dichloroethane, TCE, toluene, carbon tetrachloride, and chloroform found in area wells, 1983–2006) (Cunningham 2015; Johnson 2012 and 2015; Thompson 2012 and 2015).

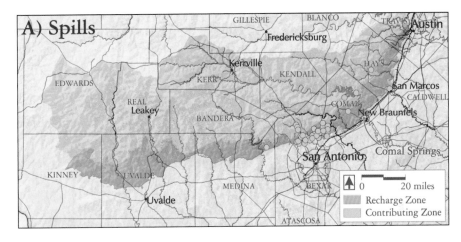

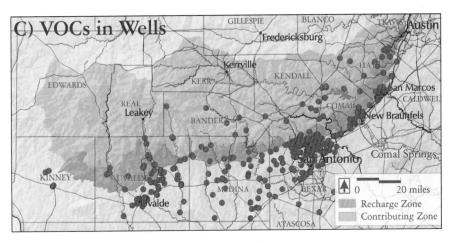

as far away as New Mexico, and Parral, Mexico. They called the place "Conaqueyadesta," meaning, "where the river [the Comal, and then the Guadalupe] has its source" (Ximenes 1963).

Spaniards

Massanet was followed by other western visitors to the springs. Fray Isidro Félix de Espinosa, a part of the 1716 expedition led by Domingo Ramón, wrote, "the waters are clear, crystal, and so abundant." In view of the springs' immense pressure (over 310 cubic feet per second), they dubbed them, "Las Fontanas," the fountains (Brune 2002, 129–30). In 1756, the Spaniards built a mission at the springs called La Señora de Guadalupe (Reid 2002).

Germans

For early German settlers, the Adelsverein, the clean, plentiful waters of Comal were a lifesaver. In 1845, Prince Carl of Solms-Braunfels bought 1,265 acres surrounding the springs to act as a waystation for thousands of immigrants headed inland to the 3.8-million-acre Fisher-Miller land grant in the Hill Country. These immigrants had been stranded at the coastal port of Indianola, where roughly three-quarters had died of cholera, malaria, yellow fever, or starvation (Galveston Weekly News 1877; Biesele 1946, 90).

Wood, Flour, and Fun

By 1849, the Comal Springs were powering two saw- and gristmills, and as early as 1860 were hosting seven grist-, flour, and sawmills. By that time, Comal was also supporting a paper mill, brewery, ice plant, and cotton and wool factories. Beginning in 1890, the springs also were developed for hydro-electricity, and as Landa's Pasture and Park, for picnicking and recreation (Brune 2002, 129; Haas 1968). By the late 1800s, the development of the springs was paired with a better understanding of the springs' connections with the geology and hydrology of the Edwards Plateau (Hill and Vaughan 1898).

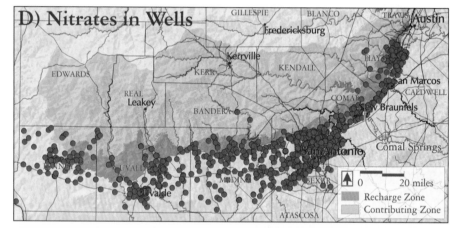

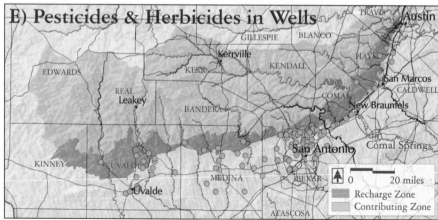

Additional risks to the Edwards Aquifer include: (D) Nitrates (samples above 2 milligrams/liter found in local wells, 1913–2006) and (E) Pesticides and Herbicides (samples found in area wells, 1986–2006, including atrazine, simazine, diazinon, 4,4 -DDE and 4,4 -DDT) (Thompson 2012 and 2015; Johnson 2012 and 2015; Johnson, Schindel, and Hoyt 2009).

Flows and Purity

For all its long-lived history, beauty, recreation, and industry, the Comal Springs have not been invulnerable. Drought and excessive withdrawals are one threat; from June to November of 1956, and again during a dry spell in the 1980s, the springs ran completely dry (Miller 2004, 32). Aside from flow, its water quality has grown to be another concern, due to upstream use of various chemicals. Nitrates in the springs, likely from agricultural fertilizer use, have gradually grown over time. Nitrate levels are now roughly twice what measurements first showed in the late 1930s. As well, a number of volatile organic compounds used in dry cleaning and degreasing and other applications (benzene, chloroform, chloromethane, tetrachloroethene, and trichloroethene) have turned up in the springs (Johnson, Schindel, and Hoyt 2009, 18, 38).

The Edwards Aquifer

Comal has become a barometer for change in the Edwards aquifer. It is just one example of how so many diverse activities across thousands of square miles of land surface can affect the Edwards aquifer far below. These aquifer impacts are seen in flow rates and pollutant levels in the Comal and other springs and wells that feed San Antonio, New Braunfels, San Marcos, and other communities.

San Antonio

San Antonio, and Bexar County, are bound especially tightly with the Edwards. Bexar accounts for a 54 percent share of all withdrawals from the Edwards, and over 88 percent of San Antonio's water comes from the Edwards (Donahue and Sanders 2001, 184; Evanson and Bailey 2014, 149). San Antonio's fate is tied to the Edwards. The city has few options beyond the 116 wells that the San Antonio Water System has developed (Mills, Rathburn, and Martinez 2014, 477). The city has rejected constructing surface water sources, such as the aborted Applewhite reservoir on the Medina (Putnam and Peterson 2003, 135). Likewise, it has backed out of connecting to existing lakes such as Canyon Dam on the Guadalupe, and the city has been denied supplies from the Colorado River by the Lower Colorado River Authority (Donahue 1998, 199–200; Mashhood 2011). San Antonio has become the largest American city to be entirely dependent on groundwater (Ashworth and Hopkins 1995, 16).

Geology

The purity of the Edwards groundwater that San Antonio and other Central Texas towns enjoy is at risk due to the geology of the area, the nature of rainfall in that region, and the pace and scope of local development. The aquifer underlies a landscape of thin soils, steep slopes, and a porous and fractured limestone substrate. This geologic structure allows water to move quickly (as fast as 12,000 feet per day) from the surface, through the underground, and toward springs and wells with very little filtration (Johnson, Schindel, and Hoyt 2009, 7).

Rainfall

The Hill Country receives some of the most intense precipitation ever recorded, causing rapid runoff, flash floods, and extreme erosion. For example, Medina County, west of San Antonio, was drenched by 22 inches of rain in 2 hours and 45 minutes—the greatest rainfall ever measured for that span of time in the world (Caran and Baker 1986). With all this gushing water, many contaminants are swept downstream and into the aquifer.

Urban Development

The impacts of local geology and rainfall are worsened by rapid urban development in the aquifer's contributing and recharge zones. The suburbs and exurban areas to the west and northwest of IH-35 are building out rapidly. Sedimentation from construction projects, long-term contaminant runoff from roads, parking lots, and urban yards, and the chance of a catastrophic spill of sewage, fuel, or other toxic materials, put the aquifer at risk.

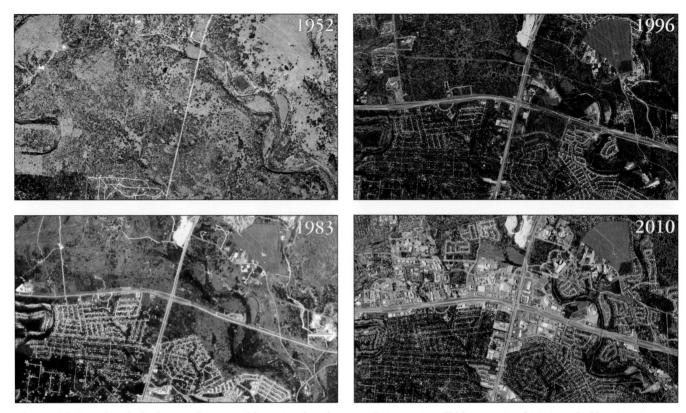

These aerial photos show the development that occurred from 1952 through 2010 at the intersection of highways 281 and 1604, north of San Antonio. The photographs show the rapid construction of roads, educational buildings, shopping areas, and residential neighborhoods during that period (US Geological Survey 2014a).

It's San Antonio's sole source of water. . . . And therefore, it's absolutely essential that we do two things. That we allow as much recharge as we possibly can and that we worry to death about the quality of the water, particularly from the development with all the pesticides and insecticides, the gasolines and the oils that leak from cars.

—Fay Sinkin, August 15, 1997, San Antonio, Texas

Conservation

To protect the high quality of the water in the Edwards aquifer, several strategies have been followed. One tactic has involved regulating development in the sensitive recharge zone that feeds the aquifer. A second approach has undertaken purchases of lands in the aquifer's recharge and contributing zone, to guard against nonpoint source pollution from the tracts' development.

Federal Rules

In 1974, local congressional representative Henry Gonzalez was successful in amending the Safe Drinking Water Act to block federal assistance to any project that might pollute urban groundwater supplies (Safe Drinking Water Act of 1974, Section 1424(e) (Public Law 93-523, 42 U.S.C. 300 et seq.)). The amendment was likely fueled by opposition to a HUD-supported development in the recharge zone called "San Antonio

Ranch New Town" (Wimberley 2001, 174). The next year, the EPA designated the Edwards aquifer as the first "sole source aquifer" under the Safe Drinking Water Act, empowering review of road construction, public wells, wastewater treatment plants, and block-grant–funded projects (Notice of Determination, 40 Fed. Reg. 58344 (December 16, 1975); Review of Projects Affecting Sole Source Aquifers—Edwards Aquifer, San Antonio, Tex., *Code of Federal Regulations*, Title 40 CFR Part 149, Subpart A (1977)). However, the act's scope was expressly limited; it did not reach to nonfederal landfills, treatment plants, or a variety of private facilities.

State Policies

The state legislature made an early regulatory effort to protect the aquifer through creation of the Edwards Underground Water District (EUWD) in 1959 (Boadu, McCarl, and Gillig 2007). However, it soon became clear that weak enforcement authority hampered the district's impact. In 1970, the state took stronger measures. The Texas Water Quality Board issued regulations intended to control sewer lines and storage tanks in the recharge and buffer zones within Bexar, Comal, Hays, Kinney, Medina, and Uvalde Counties (Texas Water Quality Board, Order No. 70-0731-12, July 31, 1970). Although strengthened in 1977, these state rules had worrisome gaps. By ignoring the diffuse but major aquifer threats posed by wide-scale development and impervious cover increases, the new laws remained quite ineffective.

Litigation

State and regional efforts to protect the aquifer, particularly its spring flows, were boosted a great deal in 1991. In that year, the Sierra Club and the Guadalupe-Blanco River Authority filed a federal suit to protect endangered species in Comal Springs (*Sierra Club v. Babbitt*, 995 F.2d 571 (5th Cir. 1993)). The lawsuit culminated in the state's replacement of the EUWD with a stronger agency, the Edwards Aquifer Authority. The authority has been particularly focused on pumpage controls and on monitoring water quality. The local water utility, the San Antonio Water System (SAWS), has also been active in assuring adequate supplies of water from the Edwards through metering, modeling, impact fees, water-reuse rebates, contractor bonding and licensing, and various other restrictions and incentives (San Antonio Water System 2012). Again, though, like the Edwards Aquifer Authority, SAWS has been reluctant to implement water quality controls, given the sensitivity of private property rights and development limits (Donahue and Sanders 2001, 195).

Grassroots

Much of the effort to protect the aquifer's water quality has reverted to local citizen work. Public concerns about the aquifer grew out of the proposal of a number of Edwards-area subdivisions (Ranch Town and PGA Village), stores and shopping centers (the Northwoods Shopping Center,

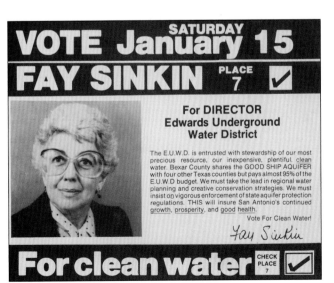

This postcard shows Fay Sinkin during her 1983 campaign for a seat on the board of the Edwards Underground Water District (Sinkin 1928–2008).

the Shops at La Cantera, and the Wal-Mart near Helotes), and educational complexes (the University of Texas at San Antonio) (Miller 2004, 83–85). These proposals galvanized opposition from community leaders, such as Merry Baker, Bill Bunch, Ernie Cortes, Susan Hughes, George Rice, Fay and Lanny Sinkin, Enrique Valvidia, Tom Wassenich, and many others, who led nonprofit groups to improve groundwater management (Cortes 2002; Hughes 2006; Rice 2006; Sinkin 1997; Sinkin 2008). These groups included the Aquifer Protection Association, Citizens for a Better Environment, League of Women Voters, and Citizens Organized for Public Service, followed later by Aquifer Guardians in Urban Areas, METRO Alliance, and the Greater Edwards Aquifer Alliance.

Voters

Grassroots power grew with changes in San Antonio's at-large electoral system mandated by the Voting Rights Act (Cotrell and Stevens 1978; Voting Rights Act of 1965, Public Law 89-110, August 6, 1965). As a result, the city council makeup changed dramatically in April 1977. This shift undercut the traditional development-friendly clout of the Good Government League and the Independent Team and gave more say to conservation interests. The first sign of the interests and concerns of the new council was seen on June 10, 1977, when the council passed

an eighteen-month ban on construction over the Edwards recharge zone, pending completion of a study by the consultants at Metcalf & Eddy (Plotkin 1987, 142).

Pushback

However, this first effort to limit growth over the Edwards was almost immediately aborted by a pair of lawsuits. Developers filed $750 million takings claims in federal and state courts. They argued that the city's regulations amounted to an unconstitutional appropriation of their property without due compensation. The suits carried the day and resulted in temporary injunctions against the construction moratorium (Plotkin 1987, 143).

Later, in early 1979, Metcalf & Eddy filed its report advising the city on the few feasible strategies it could see to protect the Edwards (Walden 1979). Given the immense size and multijurisdictional extent of the recharge zone, the consultants conceded that the "municipalities and counties may be helpless in protecting the health, welfare, and safety of their citizens." The firm recommended that the state take the lead, and felt that local governments would be limited to post hoc and relatively tepid responses. These remedies might include concrete-lining streambeds crossing the recharge zone, or simply pumping drinking water into the area once Edwards groundwater became too polluted to drink.

Recent Controls

In the thirty years since, direct development controls and impervious cover limits have remained slow and difficult to enact in the Edwards area. Most of the attention has instead focused on collecting information, preparing plans, or on mandating structural solutions for treating and controlling runoff after development has already occurred. In 1977, the state mandated double walls and leak detection systems for storage tanks in the Edwards aquifer area. In 1984, the state compelled Water Pollution Abatement Plans for residential, commercial, and industrial construction. Additionally, a geologic study was mandated for housing and industrial developments. In the same year, testing requirements for leakage from sewer lines were passed. In 1988, fees for development were imposed to recover the costs of regulation (Eckhardt 2014).

In 1995, some of the first prospective development rules and guidelines were enacted for the recharge zone. Unfortunately, state-grandfathered exemptions allowed numerous plats, estimated to cover 30 percent of the 82,000 acres within Bexar County's portion of the recharge zone, to be filed before the rules could take effect (Donahue and Sanders 2001, 187). In 1999, the state returned to using technological solutions to curb impacts from the rapid development. For instance, the state passed design performance standards for sand filters, detention basins, and retention ponds, and extended regulation to cover parts of the contributing zone. In 2008, the Edwards Aquifer Authority imposed spill containment rules for businesses that stored large amounts of hazardous materials (Texas Commission on Environmental Quality 2012). While all of these measures have been useful and helpful, a nagging concern remains that government has ignored the 800-pound gorilla of rampant growth in the Edwards area.

Referenda

Local, regional, and state governments have focused on mitigating, but seldom seriously restricting construction over the Edwards. However, the public has taken a different route. Over the past fifteen years, the San Antonio electorate has made impressive commitments of over $376

million to set aside land that might otherwise be developed. The referenda have included approvals for sales tax increases generating $65 million (2000), $135 million (2005), and $135 million (2010). Bonds have been issued too, covering $2.8 million (1999), $3.9 million (2003), and $34.9 million (2007) (Trust for Public Land 2014). These funds have allowed almost 100,000 acres to be safeguarded in the first dozen years of this acquisition campaign (Texas Land Trust Council 2012).

Government Canyon

The history of the work to protect Government Canyon State Natural Area can give a good example of the wider efforts to acquire land over the aquifer's contributing and recharge zones. Originally planned for devel-

opment in the 1970s and '80s as the "San Antonio Ranch," or "Ranch Town" subdivision, the future park land reverted on bankruptcy to the Resolution Trust Corporation in the early 1990s. The bankruptcy kept the price low and the land available for protection (Chapman 2005).

However, there were other special aspects that attracted an extraordinary team of more than three dozen agencies and nonprofits interested in Government Canyon's purchase and management. This conservation alliance included Texas Parks and Wildlife, the US Fish and Wildlife Service, the Trust for Public Land, the Edwards Aquifer Authority, and the San Antonio Water System. Each agency saw Government Canyon in a slightly different light. For example, Texas Parks and Wildlife viewed it as a large tract of open space within twenty miles of over a million potential visitors. Fish and Wildlife recognized a piece of critical habitat that would harbor eight endangered invertebrate species as well as the rare golden-cheeked warbler. For the Edwards Aquifer Authority and San Antonio Water System, the tract provided a key opportunity to protect the flows and quality of the Edwards aquifer. Tim Hixon, chair of the Texas Parks and Wildlife Commission at the time, summed it up: "it's a pretty special place, and as I said, we have all these different factors—historical, environmental—protecting our water system. There is just an unbeatable combination" (Hixon 2006).

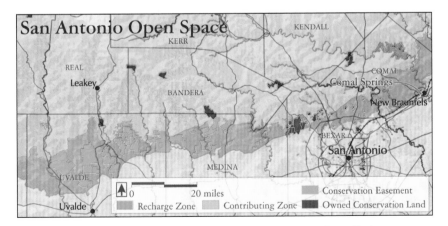

Edwards Aquifer Protection Program lands located over the recharge and contributing zones west and north of San Antonio are held under conservation easements (shown in light green) and in fee simple (shown in dark green). These lands help guard the water quality and recharge flows for the Edwards aquifer. Over 96,000 acres are held by the city of San Antonio, Texas Parks and Wildlife, the Texas Nature Conservancy, and other partners (Bezanson 2012 and 2014–15; Olson 2015; Steinbach 2011 and 2012; Texas Land Trust Council 2012).

Government Canyon is a wonderful example of the kind of collaborative effort that can protect the Edwards aquifer and preserve the springs at Comal and throughout the Hill Country. Perhaps as we understand more about all that we gain from protecting the aquifer, from open space to rich habitat to pure plentiful water, there will be more widespread and diverse support for the work. In that way, maybe we can ensure that future explorers can visit Comal Springs and splash in its waters, much as Native Americans did five hundred years ago.

Sources

Ashworth, John, and Janie Hopkins. 1995. "Aquifers of Texas." Report 345. Texas Water Development Board. November.

Barron, Patty. 2012. Records Associate, Edwards Aquifer Authority. Personal communication, May.

Bezanson, David. 2012, 2014, and 2015. Land Protection and Easements Manager, Texas Chapter, The Nature Conservancy. Personal communications, December 2012, December 2014 through May 2015.

Biesele, Rudolph. 1946. "Early Times in New Braunfels and Comal County." *Southwestern Historical Quarterly* 50 (1).

Boadu, Fred, Bruce McCarl, and Dhazn Gillig. 2007. "An Empirical Investigation of Institutional Change in Groundwater Management in Texas: The Edwards Aquifer Case." *Natural Resources Journal* 47: 118–63.

Brune, Gunnar. 2002. *The Springs of Texas,* vol. 1. College Station: Texas A&M University Press.

Caran, Christopher, and Victor Baker. 1986. "Flooding along the Balcones Escarpment, Central Texas." In *The Balcones Escarpment*, edited by P. L. Abbott and C. M. Woodruff. San Antonio: Geological Society of America.

Chapman, Carol. 2005. "Government Canyon's Big Debut." *Texas Parks and Wildlife* (October).

Cortes, Ernie. 2002. Oral history interview conducted on April 12, in Austin, Texas. Texas Legacy Project. Conservation History Association of Texas.

Cotrell, Charles, and Michael Stevens. 1978. "The 1975 Voting Rights Act and San Antonio, Texas: Toward a Federal Guarantee of a Republican Form of Local Government." *Publius* 8 (1): 79–99. The State of American Federalism, 1977. Oxford University Press.

Cunningham, Nichelle. 2015. Records Associate, Records, Edwards Aquifer Authority. Personal communication, May.

Donahue, John. 1998. "Water Wars in South Texas." In *Water, Culture, and Power: Local Struggles in a Global Context*, edited by John Donahue and Barbara Johnston. Washington, DC: Island Press.

Donahue, John, and Jon Sanders. 2001. "Sitting Down at the Table: Mediation and Resolution of Water Conflicts." In *On the Border: An Environmental History of San Antonio*, edited by Char Miler. Pittsburgh: University of Pittsburgh Press.

Eckhardt, Greg. 2014. San Pedro Springs. Edwards aquifer website. http://www.edwardsaquifer.net/spspring.html, accessed August 15, 2014.

Evanson, Douglas, and Mary Bailey. 2014. "Comprehensive Annual Financial Report of the San Antonio Water System, A Component Unit of the City of San Antonio, Texas, for the Years Ended December 31, 2013 and 2012." http://www.saws.org/who_we_are/Financial_Reports/CAFR/docs/CAFR_2013.pdf, accessed August 14, 2014.

Galveston Weekly News. 1877. Untitled, *Galveston Weekly News*, November 12.

Haas, Oscar. 1968. *History of New Braunfels and Comal County, Texas, 1844–1946*. Austin: Steck.

Hill, Robert, and Thomas Vaughan. 1898. "Geology of the Edwards Plateau and Rio Grande Plain Adjacent to Austin and San Antonio, Texas, with Reference to the Occurrences of Underground Waters." 18th Annual Report of the Director of the U.S. Geological Survey for the Year 1896–1897, Part II.

Hixon, Tim. 2006. Oral history interview conducted on February 15, in San Antonio, Texas. Texas Legacy Project. Conservation History Association of Texas.

Hoyt, John. 2012. Assistant General Manager—Aquifer Management, Edwards Aquifer Authority. Personal communication, May.

Hughes, Susan. 2006. Oral history interview conducted on February 17, in San Antonio, Texas. Texas Legacy Project. Conservation History Association of Texas.

Johnson, Steve. 2012 and 2015. Hydrogeologist Supervisor, Aquifer Science Team, Edwards Aquifer Authority. Personal communications, May 2012 and April 2015.

Johnson, Steven, Geary Schindel, and

John Hoyt. 2009. "Water Quality Trends Analysis of the San Antonio Segment, Balcones Fault Zone, Edwards Aquifer, Texas." Edwards Aquifer Authority, San Antonio, Texas.

Mashhood, Farzad. 2011. "LCRA Settles Suit over Canceled Water Deal, Approves Drought Plan." *Austin American-Statesman*, October 19.

Miller, Char. 2004. *Deep in the Heart of San Antonio: Land and Life in South Texas*. San Antonio: Trinity University Press.

Mills, Samuel, Dwayne Rathburn, and Felipe Martinez. 2014. "Water Statistics, Year Ending December 31, 2013." San Antonio Water System.

Olson, Lori. 2015. Executive Director, Texas Land Trust Council. Personal communication, March.

Plotkin, Sidney. 1987. *Keep Out: The Struggle for Land Use Control*. Berkeley: University of California Press.

Putnam, Linda, and Tarla Peterson. 2003. "The Edwards Aquifer Dispute: Shifting Frames in a Protracted Conflict." In *Making Sense of Intractable Environmental Conflicts: Concepts and Cases*, edited by Roy Lewicki, Barbara Gray, and Michael Elliott. Washington, DC: Island Press.

Reid, Jan. 2002. "The Fount." *Texas Parks and Wildlife* (July).

Rice, George. 2006. Oral history interview conducted on February 16, in San Antonio, Texas. Texas Legacy Project. Conservation History Association of Texas.

San Antonio Water System. 2012. San Antonio Water System Utility Service Regulations, Adopted Version, Current as of December 4, 2012. San Antonio Water System.

Sinkin, Fay. 1997. Oral history interview conducted on August 15, in San Antonio, Texas. Texas Legacy Project. Conservation History Association of Texas.

Sinkin, Lanny. 2008. Oral history interview conducted on April 10, in San Antonio, Texas. Texas Legacy Project. Conservation History Association of Texas.

Sinkin, William, and Fay Sinkin. 1928–2008. William and Fay Sinkin Papers, MS 64, University of Texas–San Antonio, Libraries Special Collections, Box 6, Folder 7.

Steinbach, Mark. 2011, 2012, and 2014. Executive Director, Texas Land Conservancy. Personal communications, April 2011, July 2012, and 2014.

Texas Commission on Environmental Quality. 2012. "Regulatory History of the Edwards Aquifer." http://www.tceq.texas.gov/field/eapp/history.html, accessed May 29, 2012.

Texas Land Trust Council. 2012. Land Protection Database.
———. 2015. Conservation Lands Inventory, Shapefile.

Texas Natural Resources Information System. 2015. StratMap Park Boundaries, Boundaries, Texas Statewide Datasets, Data Search and Download. Geographic Information Office, Texas Natural Resources Information System, Texas Water Development Board. https://tg-twdb-gemss.s3.amazonaws.com/d/stratmap_bnd/stratmap_park.zip, accessed May 1, 2015.

Texas Parks and Wildlife. 2012. Land and Water Resources Conservation and Recreation Plan Statewide Inventory 2012, Geodatabase. http://tpwd.texas.gov/gis/apps/lwrcrp/, accessed May 1, 2013.

Thompson, Emily. 2012 and 2015. Senior Water Quality Program Coordinator, Edwards Aquifer Authority. Personal communications, July 2012 and April 2015.

Trust for Public Land. 2014. LandVote Database. http://www.tpl.org/landvote, accessed August 14, 2014.

US Fish and Wildlife Service. 2015. USFWS Interest Shapefile, Boundaries Showing USFWS Acquired Lands (March 1, 2015). http://ecos.fws.gov/ServCatFiles/Reference/Holding/45000, accessed May 1, 2015.

US Geological Survey. 2014a. Earth Explorer. http://earthexplorer.usgs.gov/, accessed August 15, 2014.

US Geological Survey. 2014b. Protected Areas Database of the United States (PAD-US). http://gapanalysis.usgs.gov/padus/data/download/, accessed August 8, 2014.

US Safe Drinking Water Act, 42 U.S.C. 201, 300 et. seq. and 21 U.S.C. 349, Section 1424(e).

Walden, Don. 1979. "Study: Only State Can Protect Aquifer." *San Antonio Express-News*, January 6.

Wimberley, Laura. 2001. "Establishing 'Sole Source Protection': The Edwards Aquifer and the Safe Drinking Water Act." In *On the Border: An Environmental History of San Antonio*, edited by Char Miller. Pittsburgh: University of Pittsburgh Press.

Winterle, Jim. 2015. Director, Data Management and Modeling. Edwards Aquifer Authority. Personal communication, March.

Ximenes, Ben. 1963. *Gallant Outcasts: Texas Turmoil, 1519–1734*. San Antonio, TX: Naylor.

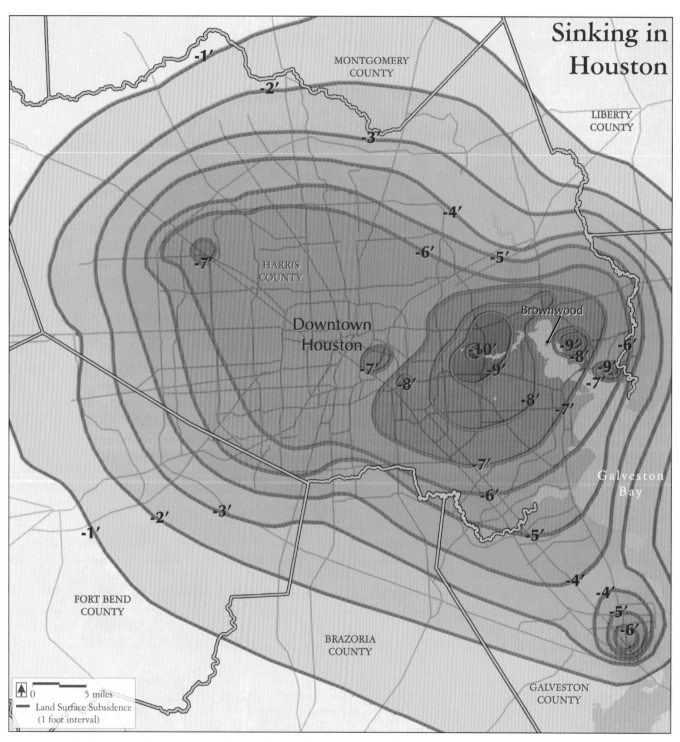

Large parts of the Houston area have seen land surface subsidence in the 1906–2000 period (Gabrysch and Neighbors 2005; Harris Galveston Subsidence District 2013; Kasmarek 2013).

Houston Subsidence

When we think of the land, many of us probably think of something stable, permanent, and strong. We may cast our mind back to the old Latin term, "terra firma," meaning "solid earth."

Nevertheless, sometimes the land moves. Headlines often tell us of the abrupt and catastrophic tremors along the globe's many fault lines. Yet the gradual, but still serious, movements of land subsidence are perhaps not as well known.

Land-surface subsidence is tied to the withdrawal of underground fluids that then allow the sedimentary substrates to settle and collapse. The problem affects a number of major cities around the globe, including Bangkok, Osaka, Shanghai, San Jose, and Venice (Holzer and Johnson 1985). Impacts have struck as many as 15,000 square miles of land surface in the United States, scattered across forty-five states (Galloway, Jones, and Ingebritsen 1999). Subsidence has long been a particular hazard in coastal Texas.

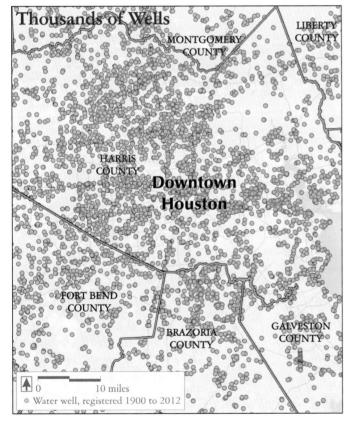

The Houston area is pockmarked with many groundwater wells, showing the area's heavy historic reliance on the local aquifer. The location of over 10,900 known Houston-area water well sites, dating from 1900 through 2012, are shown here (Texas Water Development Board 2014).

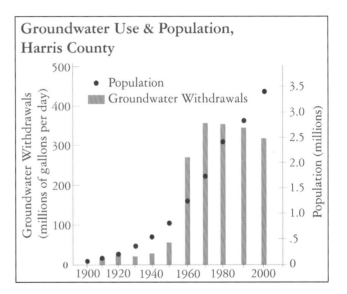

This chart comparing population and pumpage trends in Harris County shows a declining per-capita reliance on groundwater (Kasmarek, Gabrysch, and Johnson 2009).

Oil, Gas, and Sulfur

The story of this subsidence in southeast Texas stretches back to the early 1900s. Some of the earliest-measured subsidence was associated with oil and gas extraction in the Goose Creek field (3.25 feet, as early as 1925), Spindletop Dome (4.9 feet, from 1925 through 1977), and Port Acres Gas Field (3.3 feet, 1959–77) (Gabrysch and Bonnett 1977, 10; Ratzlaff 1982, 2, 10, 11; Pratt and Johnson 1926). Solution mining of sulfur, such as at the Moss Bluff Salt Dome (15.1 feet) and Boling Dome, has also caused declines in land elevation (Mullican 1988; Ratzlaff 1982, 2, 6, 10).

Groundwater

However, the largest part of the area's subsidence has been attributed to groundwater withdrawals for industrial processes and municipal supplies or associated with oil and gas production (Holzer and Bluntzer 1984). While oil, gas, and sulfur extraction has mostly affected land elevations in the area immediately around the mined zone, groundwater-related subsidence has been felt across large regions. Until 1942, groundwater supplied virtually all industrial and municipal users in the Houston area (Galloway, Jones, and Ingebritsen 1999, 40). Pumpage in the Houston-Galveston region appeared to have peaked by 1974 at over 530 million gallons a day (Gabrysch 1984, 60). As a consequence, by 1979, close to

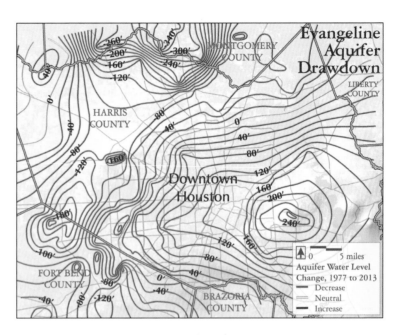

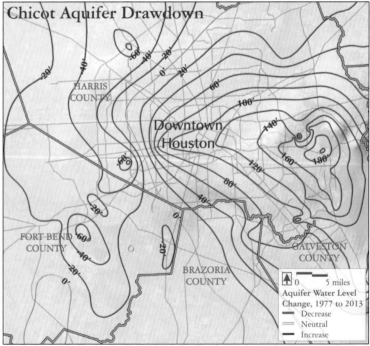

Aquifer drawdown can lead to land subsidence. These map contours depict Houston area groundwater level changes in the Evangeline and Chicot aquifers, from 1977 through 2013. The figures show the rebound of water levels in the southeastern portion of Houston, as groundwater pumpage has declined. At the same time, accelerating drawdown in the northwestern region can now be seen (Kasmarek, Johnson, and Ramage 2010; Kasmarek 2012; Johnson 2015; Johnson and Linard 2014).

3,200 square miles of the area around the Houston Ship Channel had subsided by more than one foot, and as much as ten feet in places (Coplin and Galloway 2001, 132).

Impacts

The impacts of subsidence and related faulting have been diverse. The ecological aspects of subsidence have been significant: 26,000 acres of emergent wetlands that fringe Galveston bay have been lost to subsidence (White et al. 1993, 92). Aside from the loss of this important bird habitat and aquatic nursery ground, the disappearance of the wetlands has created a worrisome public safety risk as well, given marshes' ability to buffer storm surge (White and Tremblay 1995). Subsidence impacts have even been historical and cultural; as many as 100 acres of the San Jacinto site commemorating the 1836 independence of Texas have subsided and dropped under Galveston Bay (Coplin and Galloway 1999, 35). And, of course, the financial cost of subsidence has been immense, including the private expense coastal industries have faced in building levees, moving docks, and replumbing drainage systems.

Brownwood

However, perhaps the most traumatic experiences have occurred with the abandonment of whole communities, such as the Brownwood neighborhood of Baytown. The remains of Brownwood can be found on a peninsula that lies between Burnet Bay, Crystal Bay, and Scott Bay. Formerly a cattle ranch, Brownwood was built out on lands subdivided and sold in 1937 to Humble Oil executives and engineers for homes along the shore. In time, the Brownwood subdivision grew to become an exclusive area of some 360 homes, called the "River Oaks of Baytown," where residents enjoyed fishing, sailing, and cool coastal breezes (Snyder 2001).

Submarine Acres

Unfortunately, the community began to sink not long after its founding. Groundwater withdrawals in the Baytown area had begun as early as 1918 (Gabrysch and Bonnet 1977, 5). By 1943, the area had sunk by about 2.4 feet with withdrawal of oil, gas, and, mainly, massive amounts of groundwater for nearby agricultural and industrial use (Gabrysch and Bonnet 1977, 14). By 2000, records indicated that the land surface in the Brownwood area had declined by about nine feet. Aerial images from 1944 through 2005 show that shorelines surrounding the bay had retreated dramatically (US Geological Survey 2014).

As subsidence took effect, the area began to flood periodically from rain events and storm surge from the surrounding bays. Hurricane Carla struck particularly hard in 1961, rushing in with an 11-foot storm surge. Many homes were swept away; others were luckier but were left with ruined sheetrock and mud and crabs in bathtubs (Baker 2003, 20; Sherwood 2008). Carla largely stopped further construction in the subdivision, but she did not end the risk of continued flooding. Between 1967 and 1981, there were twenty-six reports of flooding or evacuations in Brownwood. With time, the area got a new nickname, "Submarine Acres" (Baker 2003, 20–22).

Residents tried to live with the periodic slosh of high water. They learned to watch the weather reports for incoming storms. They kept their electric appliances balanced on top of concrete blocks, clothes dryers perched on tables, and important papers stowed on second floors. They used portable toilets in their yards as sewage lines failed. And, as floodwaters came in, they warily watched for water moccasins, fire ants, and looters (Albert 2000; Gray 2013). Still, there was the sense that these stoic efforts were not permanent solutions.

Levees and Ring Roads

There were attempts to protect Brownwood. As early as 1961, following the damage inflicted by Hurricane Carla, a long $10-million levee was proposed to protect Brownwood and its neighboring communities (Houston Post 1961). Engineers planned a levee that would tie together spoil islands created from dredging in the nearby reaches of the Houston Ship Channel. Yet no progress was made on the levee for over a decade.

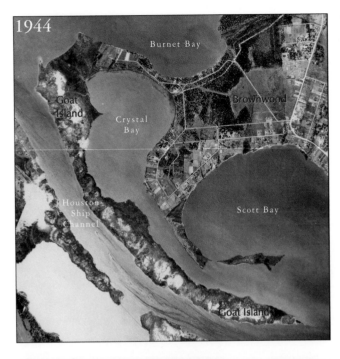
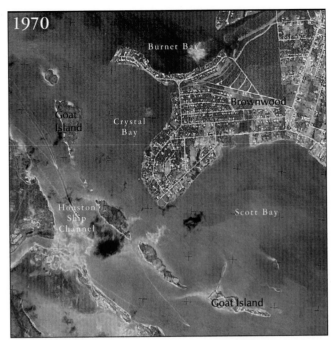
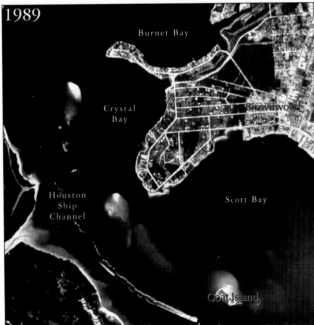

These aerial photographs track the marked land surface subsidence and coastal retreat in the Brownwood area of Baytown, Texas, that occurred from 1944 through 1989. The aerial photograph from 2010 shows the canals and ponds constructed for the Baytown Nature Center, overlaid with the roads that remain from the now-abandoned Brownwood subdivision. It is also interesting to note how 210 acres of new land were created in 2003 and 2004 in the midst of the areas lost to subsidence, as dredged materials from the Houston Ship Channel were diked and deposited on the site of the old Goat Island (Smith 2012; US Geological Survey 2014).

Finally, by 1973, the city of Baytown erected a more modest, seven-foot-tall ring road and levee to protect the area immediately around Brownwood, with old rice irrigation pumps installed to dewater the region within the levee (Pilgrim 1974). Unfortunately, two months after completion of the levee, storm surge from Tropical Storm Delia overtopped the levee, and water poured into the neighborhood. The levee was evidently a foot and a half lower than expected because contractors had used benchmarks that had subsided since they had been set.

Suits and Pumps

While engineers sought to plug the flows into Brownwood, there was little mystery about the causes behind the rising waters. Scientists had long known that subsidence around Galveston Bay could be traced back to groundwater withdrawals (Pratt and Johnson 1926; Winslow and Doyel 1954). And, in fact, some of the flooding victims did bring legal efforts to stop, slow, or at least seek costs against nearby pumpers. At the outset, the claimants certainly faced practical problems of how they might get satisfaction in the courts from so many hundreds, indeed thousands, of pumpers. However, the plaintiffs did not manage to reach the courts with those issues. Their suit quickly ran up against the Texas "right of capture," with its near-absolute rights to use groundwater under one's prop-

erty (Reuter 1980). Litigation seeking remedies for subsidence caused by groundwater withdrawals was ultimately unsuccessful (*Friendswood Development Co. v. Smith-Southwest Industries*, 546 S.W. 2nd 890 (Tex Civ. App. 1977), rev'd 576 S.W. 2d 21 (Texas. 1978)).

A Bond and a Buyout?

During the late 1970s, there was increasing skepticism that structural solutions could save Brownwood. Litigation to mitigate the problem also seemed to be at a dead end. Buyouts of the flood-prone areas appeared to be the only practical option that remained. Members of the Brownwood Homeowners Association took their case to Washington and were successful in getting a multi-million-dollar federal buyout commitment in 1976 (Associated Press 1984; Halff Associates 2005, 74). However, the US government required that the city of Baytown provide a 20 percent match to the federal dollars, and many local residents resented paying the proposed cost of the real estate and moving expenses for their Brownwood neighbors. Baytown voters turned down a buyout bond referendum in 1979, and again in 1980.

Hurricane Alicia

Where voters may have been conflicted and unsure, the issue was soon decided by nature. In August 1983, Hurricane Alicia sealed Brownwood's

fate. The hurricane brought storm tides over ten feet tall that demolished or severely damaged three-quarters of the homes in the neighborhood. The city of Baytown declared the area unfit for human habitation and required abandonment of Brownwood. In 1984, the city of Baytown and FEMA began buyouts of the remaining Brownwood residents and initiated planning for a nature center (Albert 2000; Associated Press 1984; Property Purchase Program, Section 1362, of the Flood Disaster Protection Act of 1973, PL 93-234 (approved December 31, 1973)).

A Nature Center

Progress was slow. However, by 1994, money had been raised for a kind of metamorphosis of the abandoned Brownwood subdivision. Some funds came from a Baytown bond issue. Other cash came from corporate contributions intended to mitigate damage from the nearby French Limited Superfund waste site. With this money in hand, recovery of the 450-acre Brownwood site began. Flooded areas were drained, and roads, houses, and utilities were removed. Later, three 60-foot-wide channels were dug through the peninsula to improve tidal exchange among wetlands and brackish pools, with spoil used to create elevated areas for freshwater ponds, islands, and mature trees. A visitors' center was constructed, and fishing piers, picnic tables, walking trails, observation platforms, and a children's

Darrell Davidson/©Houston Chronicle. Used with permission.

Othell O. Owensby/©Houston Chronicle. Used with permission.

These photographs from the mid-1970s show a series of abandoned and half-submerged homes in the Brownwood subdivision of Baytown, Texas, all casualties of subsidence (Michel 2012).

discovery area were added (Friends of the Baytown Nature Center 2012). In 1995, the Baytown Nature Center was open for business on the old Brownwood site (Snyder 2001).

The area remains low lying, and the Nature Center is still vulnerable to storm surges. In fact, Hurricane Ike damaged the complex in 2008. Still, the site's ecological recovery has been remarkable, providing habitat for 317 species of resident and neotropical migratory birds; nursery grounds for shrimp, crab, and a variety of fish; and a wonderful educational site for visitors on the Great Texas Coastal Birding Trail (Friends of the Baytown Nature Center 2012).

New Water Supplies

The solution for Brownwood, of a community's desertion and a marsh's restoration, may have worked there, but it is clear that that route would be costly and impractical for many areas of Houston. Gradually, community leaders have come to believe that traditionally heavy groundwater reliance has simply become unsustainable. Actually, efforts to mitigate subsidence began a good while before the difficulties facing Brownwood became apparent in the early 1960s. Surface water deliveries to Galveston, Pasadena, and Texas City began as early as the 1940s. The new source of water allowed these communities to ease off of groundwater use.

Groundwater Limits

Regulation was part of the solution too. Water well limits and fees began with the creation of the Harris-Galveston Coastal Subsidence District (HGCSD) in May 1975 (1975 Tex. Gen. Laws Ch. 284). The establishment of the HGCSD was followed by creation of its sister agencies, the Fort Bend Subsidence District in 1989, and the Lone Star (for Montgomery County) Groundwater Conservation District in 2001 (1989 Tex. Gen. Laws 4251; 2001 Tex. Gen. Laws 1991). These efforts to reduce groundwater use, together with the shifts to surface water, have already shown remarkable success in Houston's eastern side. Aquifer levels have rebounded, and there is promise that compaction and subsidence will slow as well (see the water table maps for the period of 1977 through 2013) (Gabrysch 1984, 62; Stork and Sneed 2002).

Recent Times

However, even these solutions to subsidence have not come without cost. The new reservoirs, canals, and treatment and distribution facilities have been expensive. Also, construction of these new reservoirs, including Lakes Houston, Livingston, and Conroe, has a variety of environmental impacts. The new lakes have reduced critical sediment and nutrient supplies to Galveston and Trinity Bays, have changed the location and timing of freshwater releases to the bays, and have had severe impacts on fisheries and coastal erosion. Finally, the reservoirs' construction has not solved all drawdown and subsidence problems. Groundwater levels continue to decline in the western portion of Houston, signaling ongoing subsidence in these areas where surface water supplies are still lacking (Stork and Sneed 2002).

Nevertheless, there are some silver linings. The old Brownwood residents have moved to safer, higher ground. Students now visit and enjoy the Baytown Nature Center, and herons, pelicans, ibis, and spoonbills call the old Brownwood site home. As with many conservation challenges, there are often no easy or quick answers, but there are rewards for resilience and creativity.

Sources

Albert, Larry. 2000. "Houston Wet: A Sprawl Ecology." Rice University, Houston, Texas. http://www.rice.edu/~lda/wet/index.htm, accessed May 9, 2012.

Associated Press. 1984. "Baytown Families Fighting Ordinance." *Victoria Advocate*. August 28.

Baker, Lindsay T. 2003. *More Ghost Towns of Texas*. Norman: University of Oklahoma Press.

Coplin, Laura, and Devin Galloway. 2001. "Historical Subsidence in the Houston-Galveston Area, Texas." Virtual Proceedings for the State of the Bay Symposium V, January 31–February 2. Texas A&M University–Galveston.

Friends of the Baytown Nature Center. 2012. "Friends of the Baytown Nature Center." http://www.baytownnaturecenter.org/, accessed May 9, 2012.

Gabrysch, R. K. 1984. "Ground-Water Withdrawals and Land-Surface Subsidence in the Houston-Galveston Region, Texas, 1906–80." Report 287. Texas Department of Water Resources, Austin.

Gabrysch, R. K., and C. W. Bonnet. 1977. "Land Surface Subsidence in the Houston-Galveston Region, Texas." Report 188, second printing. Texas Department of Water Resources, Austin.

Gabrysch, Robert, and Ronald Neighbors. 2005. "Measuring a Century of Subsidence in the Houston-Galveston Region, Texas, USA." Seventh International Symposium on Land Subsidence. Shanghai, China, October 23–28, Proceedings, 379–87.

Galloway, Devin, David Jones, and S. E. Ingebritsen. 1999. "Land Subsidence in the United States." Circular 1182. US Geological Survey, US Department of the Interior.

Gray, Lisa. 2013. "Brownwood: The Suburb That Sank by the Ship Channel." *Houston Chronicle*, March 23.

Halff Associates. 2005. City of Baytown Flood Mitigation Plan, February 28. City of Baytown Floodplain Mitigation Planning Committee.

Harris-Galveston Subsidence District. 2013. Subsidence, 1906–2000. Map contoured in 1-foot intervals. Data Source: National Geodetic Survey. Contour interpretation by Harris-Galveston Subsidence District. http://hgsubsidence.org/ wp-content/uploads/2013/07/SubsidenceMap1906-2000.pdf, accessed April 29, 2015.

Holzer, Thomas, and Robert Bluntzer. 1984. "Land Subsidence Near Oil and Gas Fields, Houston, Texas." *Groundwater* 22: 450–59.

Holzer, Thomas, and Ivan Johnson. 1985. "Land Subsidence Caused by Ground Water Withdrawal in Urban Areas." *GeoJournal* 11 (3): 245–55.

Houston Chronicle. 1976. Darrell Davidson, Brownwood addition. Photo 117237823 19761008_Brownwood addition_dd.

———. 1977. Othell O. Owensby, Brownwood addition. Photo 117237827 19770831_Brownwood addition_ooo.

Houston Post. 1961. "Brownwood Looks to Channel for Help: Spoil from Enlarging Job Could be Used to Build Flood Levee." October 12.

Johnson, Michaela. 2014 and 2015. Hydrologist, USGS Texas Water Science Center—Gulf Coast Program Office. Personal communications, March 2014 and March 2015.

Johnson, Michaela, and Joshua Linard. 2014. "Geospatial Compilation of Historical Water-Level Changes in the Chicot and Evangeline Aquifers 1977–2013 and the Jasper Aquifer 2000–13." Gulf Coast Aquifer System, Houston-Galveston Region, Texas. Data Series 900. http://pubs.er.usgs.gov/publication/ds900, posted December 11, 2014.

Kasmarek, Mark. 2012. Groundwater Hydrologist, US Geological Survey. Personal communications, October 2011 through May 2012.

———. 2013. "Hydrogeology and Simulation of Groundwater Flow and Land-Surface Subsidence in the Northern Part of the Gulf Coast Aquifer System, Texas, 1891–2009." Scientific Investigations Report 2012-5154, Version 1.1, December. Prepared in cooperation with the Harris-Galveston Subsidence District, the Fort Bend Subsidence District, and the Lone Star Groundwater Conservation District. US Geological Survey, US Department of the Interior.

Kasmarek, Mark, Robert Gabrysch, and Michaela Johnson. 2009. Estimated Land-Surface Subsidence in Harris County, Texas, 1915–17 to 2001. Scientific Investigations Map 3097. US Geological Survey, in cooperation with the Harris-Galveston Subsidence District.

Kasmarek, Mark, Michaela Johnson, and Jason Ramage. 2010. Water-Level Altitudes 2010 and Water-Level Changes in the Chicot, Evangeline, and Jasper Aquifers and Compaction 1973–2009 in the Chicot and Evangeline Aquifers, Houston-Galveston Region, Texas. Scientific Investigations Map 3138. US Geological Survey. US Department of the Interior.

Michel, Tom. 2012. Deputy General Manager, Harris-Galveston Subsidence District. Personal communication, May.

Mullican, W. F. 1988. Subsidence and Collapse at Texas Salt Domes. Report GC8802. Bureau of Economic Geology, University of Texas at Austin.

Pilgrim, Lee. 1974. "Sinking $$$$ into Sinking Land." *Texas Water Resources Institute* 1 (2): 1–4.

Pratt, Wallace, and Douglas Johnson. 1926. "Local Subsidence of the Goose

Creek Oil Field." *Journal of Geology* 34 (7, pt. 1): 577–90.

Ramage, Jason. 2015. Hydrologist, Texas Gulf Coast Program Office, Texas Water Science Center, US Geological Survey, US Department of the Interior. Personal communication, May.

Ratzlaff, Karl. 1982. "Land-Surface Subsidence in the Texas Coastal Region." Report 272. Texas Department of Water Resources, Austin, November.

Reuter, Joanne. 1980. "Sinking Fortunes: Texas Remedies for Victims of Land Subsidence." *Natural Resources Journal* 20 (2): 375–86.

Sherwood, Ronnie. 2008. "J. R. Gonzales, Comment on 'Remembering Carla,'" *Houston Chronicle*, September 26, 2007. http://blog.chron.com/bayou cityhistory/2007/09/remembering-carla/, accessed June 4, 2015.

Smith, Philip. 2012. Director of Conservation, Galveston Bay Foundation. Personal communication, May.

Snyder, Mike. 2001. "Nature Center Owes Birth to Subdivision's Ruin." *Houston Chronicle*, July 29.

Stork, S. V., and M. Sneed. 2002. "Houston-Galveston Bay Area, Texas, from Space: A New Tool for Mapping Land Subsidence." USGS Fact Sheet 110-02. December.

Texas Water Development Board. 2014. Well Data from TWDB Groundwater Database. http://www.twdb.state.tx.us/mapping/gisdata/shapefiles/GWDB_well_locations.zip, accessed August 20, 2014.

US Geological Survey. 2014. Earth Explorer. Aerial Images. http://earth explorer.usgs.gov/, accessed August 19, 2014.

White, W. A., and T. A. Tremblay. 1995. "Submergence of Wetlands as a Result of Human-Induced Subsidence and Faulting along the upper Texas Gulf Coast." *Journal of Coastal Research* 11 (3): 788–807.

White, W. A., T. A. Tremblay, E. G. Wermund, and L. R. Handley. 1993. Trends and Status of Wetland and Aquatic Habitats in the Galveston Bay System. GBNEP-31. Galveston Bay National Estuary Program. Webster, Texas. April.

Winslow, A. G., and W. W. Doyel. 1954. "Land Surface Subsidence and Its Relation to the Withdrawal of Groundwater in the Houston-Galveston Region, Texas." *Economic Geology* 49 (4): 413–22.

Gulf of Mexico

Different readers can interpret this map differently, as with all maps. It is like looking at clouds—some see rabbits, some see sheep, some see vapor in the sky. One person might look at the map and think of the long distances these ships travel. Another user might be impressed at the technology that allows these vessels to find their way across this great sea in such straight and efficient courses from one port to the next.

The map might evoke other thoughts for other users, beyond the distance and trajectory of the vessels. These people might think mostly of the cargo of these trawlers and tankers. They might feel grateful for the many tons of fish and barrels of crude oil offered up by the Gulf waters and its deep sediments. Another viewer might look at this snarl of busy traffic and worry about the oil spills, fishing nets, and other risks the Gulf and its creatures face.

A last reader might look at the tracery of travel and think more of the connections that bind us and the communications that teach us. He or she might look at the map and think of how, at some level, we are all linked to the productivity and the vulnerability of the Gulf. The map might also suggest how solutions that appear in one inlet of the Gulf quickly travel far to other parts of the Gulf. We hope the chapters in this section about sea turtle recovery, coastal storm protection, and artificial reef construction provide examples of how we can all share the Gulf and her conservation.

Source

Office of Coast Survey. 2014. "2009–2010 Commercial Vessel Density (October—AIS)." National Oceanic and Atmospheric Administration. ftp://ftp.csc.noaa.gov/pub/MSP/AIS/CommercialVesselDensity October2009_2010National.zip, accessed August 23, 2014.

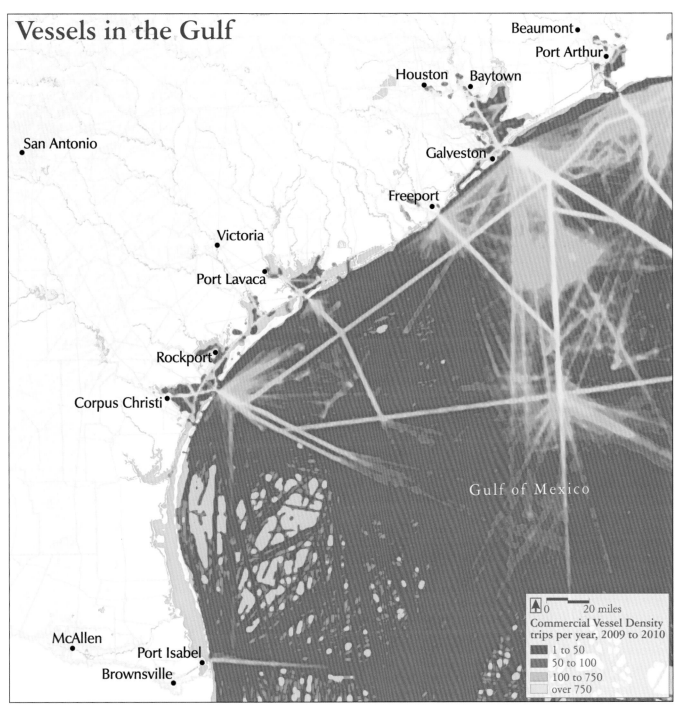

Vessels in the Gulf

Beaumont•
Port Arthur•

Houston• Baytown•

San Antonio•

Galveston•

Freeport•

Victoria•

Port Lavaca•

Rockport•

Corpus Christi•

Gulf of Mexico

McAllen•

Port Isabel•

Brownsville•

▲ 0   20 miles
Commercial Vessel Density
trips per year, 2009 to 2010
☐ 1 to 50
☐ 50 to 100
☐ 100 to 750
☐ over 750

Here is a map showing the density of commercial vessels traveling across the Gulf of Mexico from October 2009 through October 2010. The National Oceanic and Atmospheric Administration's Office of Coast Survey provided the data and tallied each point as a unique ship crossing a 1-kilometer-square cell each day. The information was collected from the Automatic Identification System, a shipborne tracking network that reports position, course, and speed. That is the meaning of the map and the underlying data in a literal sense (Office of Coast Survey 2014).

Reefs

Many parts of the world are known for their colorful coral reefs, busy with schools of fish spawning, feeding, hiding, and hunting. The Gulf Coast of Texas is different though. Most of the coast has a soft, nearly featureless seabed of sand or mud, not known for reefs.

Coral in the Gulf

However, for decades into the early twentieth century there were rumors among offshore fishermen and shrimpers that a reef lay hidden in the northwestern waters of the Gulf. Many dismissed these tales, thinking this area was simply too far north, too cold, and too turbid to support a coral reef. Yet in 1936, a US Coast and Geodetic Survey mapped curious pinnacles in the northwestern Gulf, about 105 miles south of Sabine Pass, Texas (Shepard 1937). In 1953, H. C. Stetson confirmed the existence of corals at what were eventually known as the Flower Gardens and Stetson Banks (Stetson 1953). During the 1960s, teams from the Houston Museum of Natural Science and the Flower Gardens Ocean Research Center confirmed that the Gardens and Banks did indeed support extensive reefs of twenty-one types of coral, along with over three hundred species of fish, numerous crustaceans, sponges, and sea turtles. With lob-bying from the Houston Underwater Club and others, the Flower Gardens were declared a National Marine Sanctuary on January 17, 1992, joined in 1996 by the Stetson Banks (Bright et al. 1985).

Artificial Reefs

While the Flower Gardens and Stetson Banks are extraordinary places, they are no longer the only sites where reefs are found in the Gulf. Sunken oil

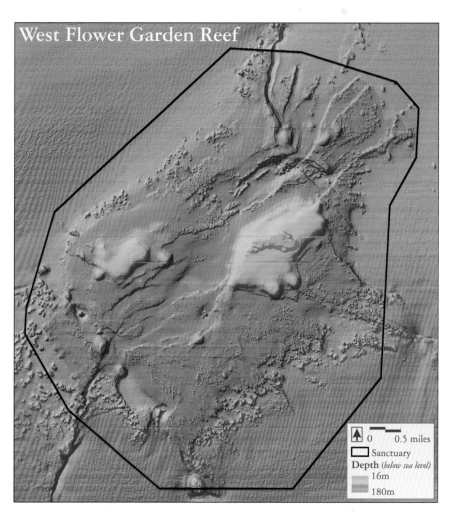

West Flower Garden Reef

0   0.5 miles
☐ Sanctuary
Depth (*below sea level*)
16m
180m

This is a bathymetric survey of the natural reefs of the West Flower Garden, based on 1997 and 2002 multibeam sonar surveys. The boundaries for the National Marine Sanctuary, which are also shown here, help protect the reef from anchoring and fishing (US Geological Survey 2002; Nuttall 2013; O'Malley 2013).

Artificial Reefs in the Gulf and Atlantic

● Artificial Reefs, 2013

This map shows more than six thousand artificial reef sites on the soft-bottom Atlantic and Gulf Coast. There are also close to two hundred artificial reef sites off the Pacific coast, mostly near the southern California shore. However, the majority of the western US coast has few constructed reefs, since the coastline is rocky, with plenty of natural sites for reef attachment (Alabama Department of Conservation and Natural Resources 2007; Barsky 2013; Berman 2013; California Department of Fish and Game 2001; Evans 2013; Florida Fish and Wildlife Commission 2011; Francesconi 2013; Georgia Department of Natural Resources 2012a and 2012b; Ledford 2013; Martore 2013; Meier 2013; Mississippi Department of Natural Resources 2012; New Jersey Department of Environmental Protection 2013; National Oceanic and Atmospheric Administration 2013; North Carolina Department of Environment and Natural Resources 2013; Rousseau 2008; Shipley-Lozano 2013; South Carolina Marine Resources Research Institute 2013; Rhode Island Department of Environmental Management 2010; Texas Parks and Wildlife 2013; Tinsman 2013; Virginia Marine Resources Commission 2013).

and gas platforms, naval vessels, and a diverse and growing array of other man-made structures have become an enormous artificial reef complex along much of the American coast (Stanley and Wilson 2000). In fact, man-made reefs cover more than 4,000 acres off the Texas shore (Biermann 2013).

History

Artificial reefs are not an entirely new idea. The Japanese have sunk old ships and rocks offshore to attract fish since roughly 1650 (Ito 2011, 240). And there are records of South

Carolina fishermen piling up logs to use as simple reefs in the 1830s (United Nations Environmental Program 2009, 1). A formal Texas program was established in 1990, but the state's constructed reefs can actually be dated back to at least the early 1960s. In 1962 and 1963, the Texas Game and Fish Commission cabled together 330 sections of concrete pipe, 30 inches to 60 inches in diameter, and dropped them in "Pipe Reef," eleven miles offshore from Galveston (Lukens and Selberg 2004). In the early days, some do-it-yourself reef architects even sank refrigera-

tors, shopping carts, and old vending machines (Harrigan 2011).

Reef Life

Whatever their shape and size, these structures work by giving a hard surface that allows corals, barnacles, sponges, and clams to attach, eventually creating a reef-like structure. Reefs, whether natural or man-made, are magnets for aquatic life. They channel ocean currents, funneling plankton and attracting sardines, minnows, and other small fish, which in turn pull in predators such as snapper, grouper and shark. The reefs also often contain slots and holes and other crevices that appeal to eel, triggerfish, and squirrelfish, or that provide protection for spawning and for young fish (Texas Parks and Wildlife 2013).

Reef Fishing

Fish begin to appear around the reefs, and this in turn provides diving and fishing opportunities for the public. Research on the fishery impact of oil and gas platforms gives an idea of the value of all kinds of artificial reefs. For example, there is evidence that fish densities are twenty to fifty times higher at platforms than in nearby open water. Single platforms can each create as many as three to four acres of

rich habitat with 10,000 to 20,000 fish weaving among the steel legs of the structure (Stanley and Wilson 2000). In fact, studies suggest that 30 percent of the sport fish caught off the coasts of Texas and Louisiana (about fifteen million fish) are reeled in near platforms (Dauterive 2000; Texas Parks and Wildlife 2013). And as these built reefs multiply, the fishing pressure on each individual reef drops, creating relatively protected areas.

Rig Reefs

However, many of these artificial reefs are actually operating offshore platforms that have a limited lifespan. As petroleum reserves are withdrawn, technology progresses, laws

are refined, or markets shift, platforms may be retired after just fifteen to thirty years. Federal law has long required that obsolete platforms be removed from the seabed after their useful life has ended, and in fact, at least 4,100 have been removed from the Gulf of Mexico since 1973 (Louisiana Department of Wildlife and Fisheries 2013a; Pulsipher et al. 2001). Removal is costly. Since there are some 6,500 installations globally, disposal estimates range as high as $40 billion (Salcido 2005, 865).

Reef Incentives

The National Fishing Enhancement Act (NFEA) of 1984 took these costs into account and also recognized that offshore platforms offered a valuable kind of marine habitat (33 U.S.C. 2101). The act created an exemption for platform removal if a partner state agreed to develop the platform as an artificial reef. State laws followed, setting up arrangements for recycling platforms and other salvaged materials to use as reefs (Louisiana Fishing Enhancement Act of 1986, Acts 1986, No. 100, effective June 23, 1986). In addition to making the rig-to-reef conversions legal, the federal law also helped create economic incentives. Typically, the platform owner saved $1 million in costs by avoiding the retired platform's long tow to shore. Instead, the firm wrote a $500,000 check to the state to convert and maintain the platform as a reef. Under these new federal and state reef laws, other

Elizabeth Foster, a volunteer scientific diver from Moody Gardens Aquarium, is seen here monitoring aquatic life at the HI-A-492 artificial reef in Texas waters. HI-A-492 consists of oil and gas platform materials donated by McMoRan Oil and Gas, Newfield Exploration, and Transco that sit in 195 feet of water, about 80 miles offshore from Galveston (Ledford 2013).

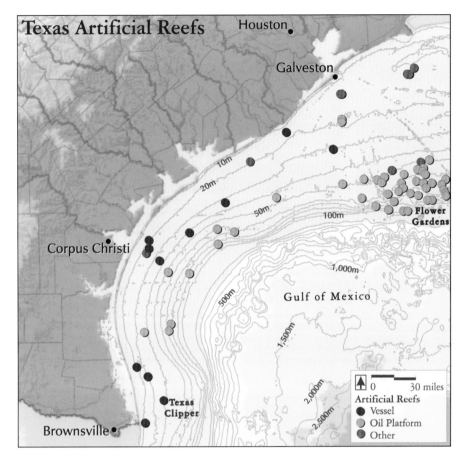

Texas Artificial Reefs

Houston

Galveston

Corpus Christi

10m
20m
50m
100m

Flower
Gardens

1,000m

Gulf of Mexico

500m

1,500m

2,000m

2,500m

Texas
Clipper

Brownsville

0   30 miles

Artificial Reefs
- Vessel
- Oil Platform
- Other

This map offers a closer view of artificial reefs off the Texas coast, showing the wide variety of materials used for these reefs, including over 140 oil and gas platforms, as well as purpose-made reef balls, plus quarry blocks, culverts, barges, tugs, and ships (please note the final resting place of the Liberty ship, the Texas Clipper*) (Ledford 2013; Shipley-Lozano 2013; Texas A&M University 2013).*

kinds of reef materials could also be given to the state and could generate a tax deduction and good press for the donor. And as part of the bargain, the donor got a full or partial release of liability, as responsibility shifted to the state (Texas Parks and Wildlife Code, Section 89.061).

Reefs of Many Kinds

As mentioned above, the oil and gas platforms became some of the larger items in these artificial reefs, but they had lots of mixed company. The biggest structures, next to the offshore oil platforms, were old vessels that had been retired by the US Navy and US Maritime Administration. The Liberty Ships Act of 1972 and the NFEA authorized the use of these

ships as reefs, and many were cleaned, stripped, and dropped off the US coast (Public Law 92-402, 16 U.S.C. Section 1220). In fact, forty-five of these World War II–era Liberty ships have been sunk offshore, including fourteen in Texas coastal waters (Self 2011; Texas Parks and Wildlife 2013).

Some of the reefs also contain specially designed reef balls. Other reefs are made in a more ad hoc way using a variety of waste materials. Reef building blocks include many surprising things, including mailboxes, concrete culverts, blocks and rubble, tires, sulfur mine bridgework, car bodies, army tanks, train boxcars, sailboats, barges, ferries, tugboats, and old luxury liners. In some states, including Texas and North Carolina, entrepreneurs have sold the idea of mixing cremated human remains into cast concrete shells to lay down on the sea floor as "eternal reefs" (Francesconi 2013).

Idle Iron

In the years to come, there may be many more materials, especially platforms, reborn as reefs. In 2010, the Department of the Interior issued its "Idle Iron" policy, ordering oil producers to remove nonperforming platforms within five years (US Department of the Interior 2010). Spurred by damage associated with Hurricane Katrina and the Deepwater Horizon spill, the agency grew concerned that inactive wells and platforms jeopardized shipping traffic and presented a risk of leaks and accidents,

The 473-foot Texas Clipper, *stripped of her masts and stack, is shown here leaving the Port of Brownsville in November 2007, and later as she sank in 132 feet of water about 17 miles northeast of South Padre Island. The* Texas Clipper *had a long career before its final journey, serving first as a Windsor-class attack transport during World War II, and later as an ocean liner and merchant marine officer training ship (Fountain 2007; Murphy 2007).*

particularly during storms. This federal rule could force oil companies to remove as many as 650 platforms from the Gulf (Eaton 2012). While only 13 percent of nonproducing rigs in the Gulf have so far been repurposed as reefs, the Idle Iron policy may change that. It could be cheaper and simpler to redesignate them as reefs, toppling them or cutting off their upper portions and leaving them in place, rather than towing them to shore, chopping them up, and selling them for scrap (Gaskill 2012).

Cautions

The prospect of the conversion of more platforms as reefs, and the continued creation of other kinds of artificial reefs, does not mean that reef programs are without critics. There are those who feel that the benefits of artificial reefs have been oversold, and their risks and shortcomings underestimated.

For instance, some find that the biological claims for artificial reefs are exaggerated; they argue that reefs tend to concentrate schools of fish, but do not actually build up overall populations (Bohnsack 1989; Lukens and Selberg 2004). Critics object as well that the reefs can become an easily accessed and abused target for catching popular fish, such as red snapper (Harrigan 2011).

There have also been financial criticisms of artificial reefs. Opponents charge that oil companies, the armed forces, municipal transit authorities, and other donors are merely avoiding short-term salvage and moving costs and are offloading significant long-term liabilities. And whoever absorbs the costs, there are worries that the price of adequately cleaning vessels, or the expense of foregoing their salvage value, can be too high to allow for reefing (Self 2011). Others worry that there will be costs to shrimpers who wander into the reef zones and find their nets tangled or torn in the submerged structures (Alexander-Bloch 2011).

Artificial reefs can cause pollution problems, litter on a large scale, and toxicity at an invisible yet lethal level (Interlandi 2008). Some constructed reefs get off to a bad start. For example, the *Texas Clipper* ship rolled to its side after it was sunk, blocking many of the openings that would have made it a better reef (Curley 2011, 176). Other artificial reefs develop problems later in life. For instance, in 1972, two million used tires were deployed off the east Florida coast. Unfortunately, they soon lost their tie-downs and moorings to corrosion and storms, and then became flotsam that damaged real reefs and spoiled popular beaches (Trenton 2006). Even the constructed reefs that stay in place may not last as long as might be hoped. Auto and tram bodies may only last thirty years or less before they rust and disintegrate, while some structures simply get buried in sand and mud.

Reports of PCBs leaching from sunken ships, such as the US aircraft carrier *Oriskany*, have also raised concern. Despite extensive and costly (estimated at $23.6 million) cleaning and preparation of the *Oriskany*, PCB concentrations increased dramatically in red snapper caught near the vessel within just three years of the carrier's sinking (Florida Fish and Wildlife Commission 2011). Challenges to the navy's practice of scuttling ships with PCBs and heavy metals onboard have raised complex problems of statutory power and national defense exemptions (Self 2011; Zippel 2013).

Review and Support

Overall, though, artificial reefs do seem to have won wide praise from a diverse community of environmentalists, fishermen, and business interests as an economical way to get new life out of old equipment, and, at the same time, create new expansive and diverse habitat in the ocean. A good deal of the support for the artificial reef program is due to the gauntlet of protective federal and state reviews that new zones, individual sites, and materials must

undergo. Also, these constructed reefs need to still be seen as a work in progress with many openings for improvement. For instance, the Environmental Defense Fund suggests that the artificial reefs could help fish populations more if they were treated as permanent or rotating sanctuaries, kept off limits to anglers (Baker 2013).

Still, the problems with costs, liabilities, corrosion, and leaks suggest how complicated it can be to create a successful and long-lasting artificial reef. Perhaps, though, these hurdles serve as a good impetus to continue research on reef materials and biological impacts, and to improve constructed reefs to meet their great promise. And the flaws in artificial reefs may remind us of the value of the natural reefs that we need to protect at the Flower Gardens, Stetson Banks, and elsewhere.

Sources

Alabama Department of Conservation and Natural Resources. 2007. Alabama artificial reef map dataset (latest entry dated 2007). http://www.outdoor alabama.com/fishing/saltwater/fisheries/artificial-reefs/, accessed February 6, 2013.

Alexander-Bloch, Benjamin. 2011. "Louisiana's Largest Inshore Artificial Reef Completed Northeast of Grand Isle." *Times-Picayune*, June 13.

Baker, Pam. 2013. Gulf and Southeast Oceans Program, Environmental Defense Fund, Gulf of Mexico and Southeast Oceans Program. Personal communication, March.

Barsky, Steven. 2013. Board member, Ships to Reefs International. Personal communication, February.

Berman, Dan. 2013. US Department of Transportation, Rhode Island Division. Personal communication, February.

Biermann, Bruce. 2013. "Mysteries of the Deep." *Texas Parks and Wildlife* (June).

Bohnsack, James. 1989. "Are High Densities of Fishes at Artificial Reefs the Result of Habitat Limitation or Behavioral Preference?" *Bulletin of Marine Science* 44 (2): 631–45.

Bright, Thomas, David McGrail, Richard Rezak, Gregory Boland, and Anita Trippett. 1985. "The Flower Gardens: A Compendium of Information." OCS Studies, MMS 85-0024. Minerals Management Service, US Department of the Interior.

California Department of Fish and Game. 2001. California artificial reef map dataset. http://www.dfg.ca.gov/marine/artificialreefs/index.asp, accessed February 6, 2013.

Curley, Stephen. 2011. *The Ship That Would Not Die: USS* Queens, SS Excambion, *and USTS* Texas Clipper. Austin: Texas Parks and Wildlife Department.

Dauterive, Les. 2000. "Rigs-to-Reefs Policy, Progress, and Perspectives." OCS Report MMS 200-073. US Department of the Interior, Minerals Management Service, Gulf of Mexico OCS Region.

Eaton, Tim. 2012. "Texas Rig Program at Risk." *Houston Chronicle*, May 14.

Evans, Barry. 2013. National Geophysical Data Center, NESDIS, NOAA, US Department of Commerce. Personal communication, February 14.

Florida Fish and Wildlife Commission. 2011. Florida artificial reef map dataset. http://myfwc.com/conservation/saltwater/artificial-reefs/export-reef-data/, accessed February 6, 2013.

Fountain, Chase. 2007. *Texas Clipper* in transit to scuttling site for use as an artificial reef, November 16. Photographic image. Texas Parks and Wildlife. http://imagesbychase.wordpress.com/2008/05/, accessed February 13, 2013.

Francesconi, Jim. 2013. North Carolina Department of Environmental and Natural Resources. Personal communication, February.

Gardner, James V. 2002. Multibeam Mapping of Selected Areas of the Outer Continental Shelf, Northwestern Gulf of Mexico. US Geological Survey, Coastal and Marine Geology. http://pubs.usgs.gov/of/2002/0411/data.html and http://pubs.usgs.gov/of/2003/of03–002/html/GISData.htm#FGBdata, accessed February 12, 2013.

Gaskill, Melissa. 2012. "In Its First Life, an Oil Platform; in Its Next, a Reef?" *New York Times*, June 12.

Georgia Department of Natural Resources. 2012a. Georgia inshore artificial reef map dataset. Georgia Department of Natural Resources, Coastal Resources Division. http://www.coastalgadnr.org/node/2089, accessed February 7, 2013.

———. 2012b. Georgia offshore artificial reef map dataset. Georgia Department of Natural Resources, Coastal Resources Division. http://www.coastalgadnr.org/node/2089, accessed February 7, 2013.

Harrigan, Stephen. 2011. "Relics to Reefs." *National Geographic*, February.

Interlandi, Jeneen. 2008. "Are Artificial Reefs Good for the Environment?" *Newsweek*, June 19. http://www.thedailybeast.com/newsweek/2008/06/19/are-artificial-reefs-good-for-the-environment.html, accessed February 11, 2013.

Ito, Yasushi. 2011. "Artificial Reef Function in Fishing Grounds off Japan." In *Artificial Reefs in Fisheries Management*, edited by Stephen Bortone, Frederico Brandini, Gianna Fabi, and Shinya Otake, 239–64. Boca Raton, FL: CRC Press.

Ledford, Chris. 2013. Artificial reef and diver, October 5, 2011. Photographic image. Texas Parks and Wildlife. http://www.flickr.com/photos/67774715@N07/6360680001/sizes/o/in/set-72157628223160285/, accessed February 19, 2013.

Louisiana Department of Wildlife and Fisheries. 2013a. Artificial Reef Program. http://www.wlf.louisiana.gov/fishing/artificial-reef-program, accessed June 5, 2015.

———. 2013b. Louisiana Artificial Reef Program, Inshore Reefs. http://www.wlf.louisiana.gov/sites/default/files/pdf/page_fishing/32430-Artificial%20Reef%20Program/ldwf_inshore_artificial_reefs_11.14.12.pdf, accessed February 14, 2013.

Lukens, Ronald, and Carrie Selberg. 2004. "Guidelines for Marine Artificial Reef Materials." 2nd ed. A Joint Publication of the Gulf and Atlantic States Marine Fisheries Commissions. Ocean Springs, Mississippi. http://www.gsmfc.org/publications/GSMFC%20Number%20121.pdf, accessed February 11, 2013.

Martore, Bob. 2013. Office of Fisheries Management, South Carolina Department of Natural Resources. Personal communication, February.

Meier, Mike. 2013. Director, Artificial Reef Program, Virginia Marine Resources Commission. Personal communication, February.

Mississippi Department of Natural Resources. 2012. Mississippi artificial reef map dataset. http://www.dmr.ms.gov/marine-fisheries/artificial-reef, accessed February 6, 2013.

Murphy, Lauren. 2007. Scuttling of the *Texas Clipper* for use as an artificial reef, November 16. Photographic image. Texas Parks and Wildlife. https://www.flickr.com/photos/25908390@N00/2047277855, accessed February 19, 2013.

National Fishing Enhancement Act of 1984, 33 U.S.C. Section 2101 et seq., P.L. 98-623.

National Oceanic and Atmospheric Administration. 2013. ETOP01 Global Relief Model. National Oceanic and Atmospheric Administration, National Geophysical Data Center. http://www.ngdc.noaa.gov/mgg/global/global.html, accessed February 14, 2013.

National Oceanic and Atmospheric Administration, National Oceanic Service, Office for Coastal Management. 2014. Artificial Reefs for US Waters as of February 2014. ftp://ftp.coast.noaa.gov/pub/MSP/ArtificialReefs.zip, accessed May 8, 2015.

New Jersey Department of Environmental Protection. 2013. Artificial Reef Site Locations in DGPS. http://www.nj.gov/dep/fgw/refloc00.htm, accessed February 12, 2013.

North Carolina Department of Environment and Natural Resources. 2013. Artificial reef dataset (last entry dated June 2012).

Nuttall, Marissa. 2013. Research Specialist, Flower Gardens National Marine Sanctuary. Personal communication, February 11.

O'Malley, John. 2013. Woods Hole Coastal and Marine Science Center, US Geological Survey. Personal communication, February 12.

Pulsipher, Allan, Omowumi Iledare, Dmitry Mesyanshinov, Alan Dupont, and Quiaozhen Zhu. 2001. "Forecasting the Number of Offshore Platforms on the Gulf of Mexico OCS to the Year 2023." OCS Study MMS 2001-013. Minerals Management Service, US Department of the Interior.

Rhode Island Department of Environmental Management. 2010. *Wild Rhode Island 3* (2). Rhode Island Department of Environmental Management, Division of Fish and Wildlife. http://www.dem.ri.gov/programs/bnatres/fishwild/pdf/wrispr10.pdf, accessed February 14, 2013.

Rousseau, M. A. 2008. Massachusetts Marine Artificial Reef Plan. Massachusetts Division of Marine Fisheries, Department of Fish and Game, Executive Office of Energy and Environmental Affairs, Commonwealth of Massachusetts. http://www.mass.gov/dfwele/dmf/programsandprojects/artificial_reef_policy.pdf, accessed February 12, 2013.

Salcido, Rachael. 2005. "Enduring Optimism: Examining the Rig-to-Reef Bargain." *Ecology Law Quarterly* 32 (4): 863–938.

Self, Colby. 2011. "Dishonorable Discharge: The Case against Dumping U.S. Naval Vessels at Sea." Basel Action Network. Seattle, Washington. http://ban.org/library/Dishonorable%20Disposal_BAN%20Report.pdf, accessed February 11, 2013.

Shepard, F. P. 1937. "Salt Domes Related to Mississippi Submarine Trough." *Geologic Society of America Bulletin* 48: 1349–61.

Shipley-Lozano, Brooke. 2013. Chief Scientist and GIS Analyst, Texas Parks and Wildlife. Personal communications, June 2010 and February 2013.

South Carolina Marine Resources Research Institute. 2013. Artificial reef dataset.

Stanley, David R., and Charles A. Wilson. 2000. "Seasonal and Spatial Variation in the Biomass and Size Frequency Distribution of the Fish associated with Oil and Gas Platforms in the Northern Gulf of Mexico." OCS Study MMS 2000-005. Coastal Marine Institute.

Stetson, H. C. 1953. "The Sediments of the Western Gulf of Mexico, Part 1—The Continental Terrace of the Western Gulf of Mexico: Its Surface Sediments, Origin, and Development." *Papers in Physical Oceanography and Meteorology* 12 (4): 1–45. Massachusetts Institute of Technology / Woods Hole Oceanographic Institute.

Texas A&M University. 2013. "Derived Products of the STRM30 Plus V6: Estimated Seafloor Topography." Texas A&M University, Gulf of Mexico Coastal Ocean Observing System. http://gcoos.tamu.edu/products/topography/SRTM30PLUS.html, accessed February 14, 2013.

Texas Parks and Wildlife. 2013. Artificial Reef Program Overview. http://www.tpwd.state.tx.us/landwater/water/habitats/artificial_reef/overview.phtml, accessed February 19, 2013.

Tinsman, Jeff. 2013. Manager, Reef Program. Fisheries Section, Delaware Division of Fish and Wildlife. Personal communication, February.

Trenton, Daniel. 2006. "Artificial Reef Made of Tires Becomes Ecological Disaster." *Miami Herald*, September 20.

United Nations Environmental Program. 2009. "Guidelines for the Placement of Artificial Reefs." London Convention and Protocol / UNEP. International Maritime Organization. London, United Kingdom.

US Department of the Interior. 2010. "Decommissioning Guidance for Wells and Platforms." NTL No. 2010-G05. September 15. Bureau of Ocean Energy Management, Regulation and Enforcement, Gulf of Mexico OCS Region. US Department of the Interior.

US Geological Survey. 2002. Multibeam Mapping of Selected Areas of the Outer Continental Shelf, Northwestern Gulf of Mexico, Multibeam Bathymetry and Acoustic Backscatter Data. http://pubs.usgs.gov/of/2002/0411/data.html, accessed 23 March 2015.

Virginia Marine Resources Commission. 2013. VMRC Artificial Reefs. https://www.vasaltwaterjournal.com/maps/reef_map.php, accessed February 13, 2013.

Zippel, Laura. 2013. "A Sinking Ship: EPA Regulation of the Navy Training Program SINKEX under the Ocean Dumping Act and the Toxic Substances Control Act." *Washington Journal of Environmental Law and Policy* 3: 267–95.

Storms and the Texas Coast

Natural Hazards

From simple footprints to immense pit mines, people leave diverse signs and impacts of their lives on the earth. Sometimes though, the tables are turned, and the earth can leave a mark on people and their homes. The Texas coast is an example of the sort of place that can carry such risks—serious and surprising ones at that.

Many visitors to the Texas shore have happy memories of swimming and sailing and sunning in mild breezes and calm warm seas. However, a peaceful Gulf can be quickly roiled by fierce winds and powerful storm surges. The history of the Texas coast is rife with records of potent hurricanes and tropical storms. For example, from 1851 through 2009, one tally showed

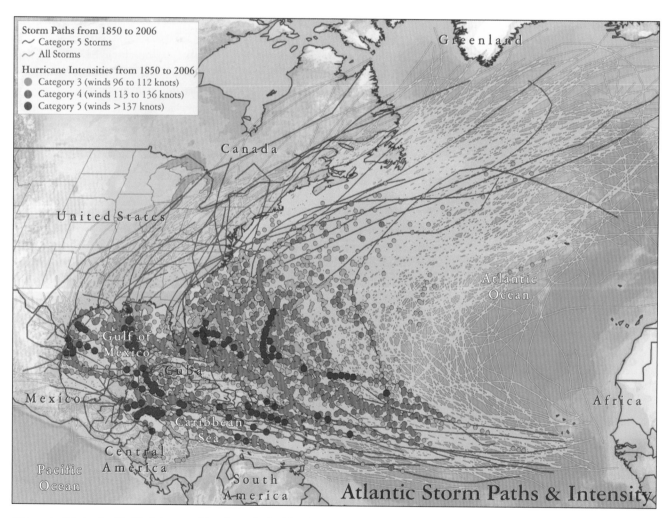

This map of the tracks of tropical storms and hurricanes in the Atlantic, 1850–2006, shows how cyclones have repeatedly battered the eastern seaboard of the United States (National Weather Service 2013b).

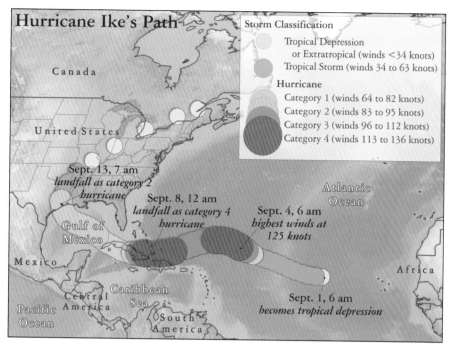

Hurricane Ike's Path

Storm Classification

Tropical Depression
or Extratropical (winds <34 knots)
Tropical Storm (winds 34 to 63 knots)

Hurricane
Category 1 (winds 64 to 82 knots)
Category 2 (winds 83 to 95 knots)
Category 3 (winds 96 to 112 knots)
Category 4 (winds 113 to 136 knots)

Canada

United States

Atlantic
Ocean

Sept. 13, 7 am
*landfall as category 2
hurricane*

Sept. 8, 12 am
*landfall as category 4
hurricane*

Sept. 4, 6 am
*highest winds at
125 knots*

Gulf of
Mexico

Mexico

Africa

Central America

Caribbean
Sea

Sept. 1, 6 am
becomes tropical depression

Pacific
Ocean

South
America

This is the track of Hurricane Ike, a Category 2 storm that surged out of the mid-Atlantic in September 2008, struck the Houston-Galveston area, and then wound its way through the Midwest and into Canada (National Weather Service 2013a).

that the Texas coast was hit by fifty-six tropical storms and sixty-nine hurricanes. Ten of those were truly devastating category 4 (winds of 130–56 mph) storms and twelve were category 3 storms (111–29 mph) (Collins and Lowe 2001; Roth 2010).

Historic Coastal Storms

With that kind of force, some of these storms have caused vicious damage in Texas and neighboring states. A few inflation-adjusted examples may give an idea of the scale of harm involved: Hurricane Celia (1970) brought losses of $12.1 billion, and Hurricane Carla (1961) left casualties of $14.9 billion. The long-ago storms of 1900 and 1915 were actually some of the most damaging of all: leaving losses of $104.3 and $71.4 billion, respectively (Blake and Gibney 2011). For some towns, the damage was fatal. Indianola, once the major rival Texas seaport to Galveston, was pummeled by a series of three hurricanes in 1875 and 1886 that killed close to three hundred residents and gave the death knell to the town (Roth 2010; Wolff 1999). The remains of its courthouse now sit under Matagorda Bay, some 100 yards offshore.

Hurricane Ike

More recent storms should not be discounted; many have been severe as well. Hurricane Ike, which swept across the northeastern Texas coast in September 2008, was certainly one for the record books. The Harris County Flood Control District reported that Ike brought 110-mph sustained winds at landfall, kicked up 12- to 17-foot storm surges (reportedly the highest on Galveston Island since 1915), and spurred an evacuation of 1.2 to 1.5 million people. When the winds died down and the surge abated, damages ran to $27 billion, and federal disaster payments in Texas topped $5.4 billion (Federal Emergency Management Agency 2013). Harris County was particularly hard hit, with eleven fatalities, 92,000 damaged homes, and 7,100 affected businesses (Harris County Flood Control District 2013).

Hurricane Ike offers just one example of the kind of damage that tropical storms and hurricanes have brought to the Texas coast. However, Ike is also an omen of the scale of harm that can be expected as time goes on, especially as the population grows, sea level rises, and the coast erodes (Parris 2012; Tebaldi et al. 2012).

Coastal Protection

The dangers of building and living on the Texas coast are not new, but our love of these Gulf shores continues to bring us ever closer to the dangers of

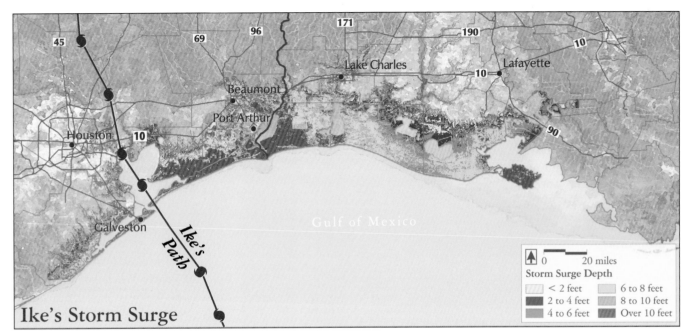

Ike's Storm Surge

Storm Surge Depth
- < 2 feet
- 2 to 4 feet
- 4 to 6 feet
- 6 to 8 feet
- 8 to 10 feet
- Over 10 feet

As Hurricane Ike hit the Gulf Coast in the morning of September 13, 2008, it pushed heavy storm surge waters into much of Texas and Louisiana, reaching 17-foot depths in some places (Harris County Flood Control District 2009; National Weather Service 2013c).

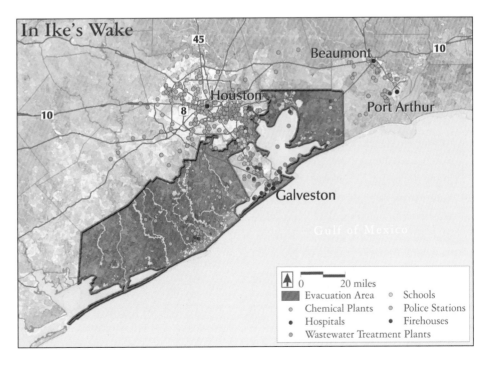

In Ike's Wake

- Evacuation Area
- Chemical Plants
- Hospitals
- Wastewater Treatment Plants
- Schools
- Police Stations
- Firehouses

Hurricane Ike also had an impact on industrial and institutional sites throughout the Houston-Galveston area. FEMA's HAZUS-MH software estimated that Hurricane Ike affected numerous chemical plants, wastewater facilities, hospitals, firehouses, police stations, and schools, as of September 13, 2008. With infrastructure and emergency services crippled by Hurricane Ike, the authorities called for a wide evacuation of residents in Brazoria, Chambers, Fort Bend, Galveston, Harris, and Liberty Counties (Bass 2013; Federal Emergency Management Agency 2009; Houston-Galveston Area Council 2013).

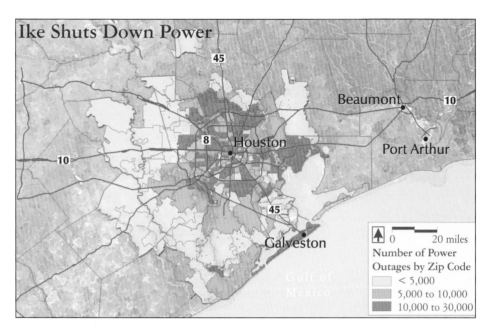

Winds and floods from Hurricane Ike led to widespread power outages in Texas, Louisiana, and Arkansas. Houston was especially hard-hit, with over 1.5 million customers losing power (over two-thirds of those served), as shown in this map of outages reported by the local utility on September 14, 2008 (CenterPoint Energy 2008).

Hurricane Ike presents one instance of the kind of natural hazards that Texans can face. Here we see the devastation that Hurricane Ike brought to Gilchrist, Texas, on the Bolivar Peninsula, as seen on September 22, 2008, eight days after landfall. Eighty-five percent of structures on the eastern three-quarters of Bolivar Peninsula, from Crystal Beach to High Island, were destroyed or badly hurt during Ike's passage (Augustino 2008).

flood and wind. Fortunately, there have been a number of efforts over the years to protect against the risks to homes, businesses, and even lives. Five major efforts have been pursued: raising and armoring the coast, legislating setbacks from the water's edge, setting aside coastal areas as parks or preserves, improving storm alerts and evacuation planning, and using market and insurance tools to realistically price the risks of living on the Texas coast.

Earth Moving

The first tool, filling and raising coastal lands to bring them out of the reach of storm surge, was used in a grand and powerful way in Galveston. When the great hurricane of 1900

Representative Bob Eckhardt, the father of the Open Beaches Act, as seen at the Texas legislature, circa 1960 (Lee 1963).

hit Galveston, much of the town was obliterated, and over six thousand of its residents were killed. Recalling the series of storms that had hit, and eventually drowned, Indianola, Galveston's leaders realized they needed to quickly prepare for the next storm. Galveston used jacks, screws, and over sixteen million cubic yards of sand to raise five hundred city blocks by as much as sixteen feet, and to guard it with a seventeen-foot, three-mile-long oceanside seawall. This was a costly means to protect a small part of the Texas coast and its residents, but it proved its mettle in the 1915 hurricane, when sixteen-foot swells failed to breach the seawall and flood the city (US Army Corps of Engineers 1981).

Open Beaches

The Open Beaches Act of 1959 created a second way to protect the Texas coast. Representative Bob Eckhardt led passage of this state law in order to recognize a public easement on Texas' Gulf shores. He based the easement on English common law precedents and Spanish and Roman civil law. Eckhardt also grounded the legislation on traditional public uses of the beach for landing boats, drying nets, collecting shellfish, traveling on smooth and hard sands, and enjoying the sun and surf (Keith 2007, 157–58). The act, with judicial backing, confirmed that the "public shall have the free and unrestricted right of ingress and egress to and from the state-owned beaches bordering on the

seaward shore of the Gulf of Mexico . . . extending from the line of mean low tide to the line of vegetation bordering on the Gulf of Mexico" (*Seaway Co. v. Attorney General*, 375 S.W.2d 923 (Tex. Civ. Appl.—Houston 1964, writ ref'd n.r.e.); Texas Natural Resources Code: Title 2, Subtitle E: Chapter 61: Subchapter B. Access to Public Beaches). In other words, the state of Texas held the "wet beach" in trust for the public, limiting the shore's fencing and development for private purposes.

Parks and Refuges

There have been other efforts to set aside lands along the coast, in this case, by buying them as parks or refuges. The largest park, the Padre Island National Seashore, provides wildlife habitat and public recreation across the 70-mile beach and 130,000-acre expanse of the barrier island. Padre Island had been considered a prime candidate for park acquisition by the city of Corpus Christi, the Texas State Parks Board, and the federal government as early as 1924. However, park proposals had been repeatedly slowed, shelved, and restarted, as biological opinions of the land's value waxed and waned; as ferries, causeways, and highways were proposed and canceled and reborn; and as tourist proposals were launched and scuttled. Park prospects also swung back and forth as surface title and mineral rights were explored and litigated, naval bombing ranges were withheld and released, rocket launch-pad proposals were circulated, and as the recreational possibilities of national parks were debated (Sheire 1971).

Finally, a 1955 federal survey of the Atlantic and Gulf Coasts spurred action. The National Park Service report showed that public protection of US shores was seriously lagging, and that much of the open coast was quickly disappearing into private ownership. At the time, only 6.5 percent of the eastern seaboard was in state or federal hands for public recreation. Eleven of the twelve seaside tracts identified for acquisition in 1935 had already been privately developed, and remaining open parcels were soaring to prohibitive prices (National Park Service 1955).

At last, with persistent pressure from senator Ralph Yarborough, the Padre Island National Seashore was created in 1962 (Public Law 87-12, September 27, 1962). Over the next two decades, a number of other major coastal tracts were protected in Texas. The new preserves included Big Boggy National Wildlife Refuge (4,526 acres, established in 1983),

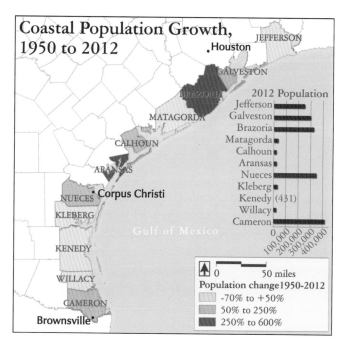

It is likely that the impacts from tropical storms and hurricanes will only increase with time as near-coast populations grow. People are flocking to the Texas coast. This map shows the population trends during the post–World War II period, from 1950 through 2012, with particularly dramatic jumps in resident counts in Brazoria (7x), Aransas (5.6x), Cameron (3.3x), and Galveston Counties (2.7x) (these year-round numbers are low: they neglect the thousands of seasonal visitors). With the population growth, the number of homes at risk has increased too. In 2011, the number of housing units in Texas coastal counties was 3.3 times what there was in 1950, with the highest growth in Brazoria (8.4x), Aransas (8.4x), Cameron (4.2x), and Galveston Counties (3.6x) (US Census Bureau 2013; US Census Bureau 2003; US Census Bureau 1992; US Census Bureau 1951).

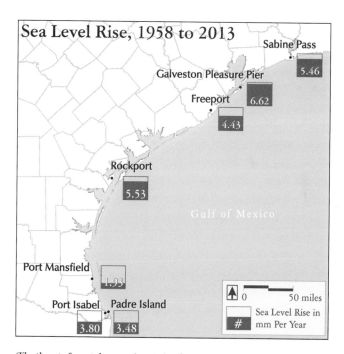

The threat of coastal storms is growing from natural factors, aside from the increase in population and structures along the shores. The Texas coast is simultaneously experiencing sea level rise and, in places, severe erosion. Due to glacial melt, ocean expansion, and local land subsidence, NOAA is reporting sea level rise in the upper Texas coast of four to six millimeters per year, or seven to eleven inches over a shared 1958–2006 period of record. Considering that much of west Galveston Island lies at just three to six feet above sea level, these changes in the sea's surface already pose a very real threat. Climate change will only compound the problem: additional sea level increases of 1–1.5 feet are predicted for the year 2050, with as much as 6.6 feet of rise projected for the year 2100 (Karl, Melillo, and Peterson 2009; National Oceanic and Atmospheric Administration 2009; National Oceanic and Atmospheric Administration 2015; Parris et al. 2012; Tebaldi, Strauss and Zervas 2012).

Brazoria National Wildlife Refuge (44,413 acres, 1966), Matagorda Wildlife Management Area and State Natural Area (56,688 acres, managed by the state since 1983), Mustang Island State Park (3,954 acres, 1972), San Bernard National Wildlife Refuge (54,000 acres, 1969), and Sea Rim State Park (4,141 acres, 1972) (Miller 1984; US Fish and Wildlife Service 1975, A-11).

Flood and Wind Insurance

The fourth concept for protecting coastal residents has involved insurance markets. The thought has been that fully pricing the risk of living in the crosshairs of major storms might discourage some from settling in dangerous areas along the coast, or at least persuade residents to take precautions.

In the early days, private insurers had offered flood and wind policies. However, storm impacts became so costly and predictable that private underwriters dropped these policies. As a result, the costs of rebuilding after a storm shifted to public disaster assistance, with taxpayers picking up the tab. To move the costs back to property owners in risky areas, the government created public insurance programs.

The United States established a voluntary federal program in 1968, with reforms in 1973 to require flood insurance for properties in Special Flood Hazard Areas (National Flood Insurance Act of 1968 and Flood Disaster Protection Act of 1973, 42 U.S.C. 4001 et seq.). In some high-risk sections of the coast, commonly known as "COBRA zones," federal flood coverage was later banned (Coastal Barrier Resources Act, P.L. 97-438, October 18, 1982). Homeowners in these COBRA zones were forced to turn to the much more costly private flood insurance market.

Floods were not the only risk coastal residents faced; winds could wreak terrible havoc as well. However, private insurance had become unavailable. In 1970, high winds (180 mph in some areas!) and the staggering costs of Hurricane Celia had run off private Texas carriers. So the state of Texas followed FEMA's example by offering public wind insurance, principally for the state's fourteen coastal counties (Roth 2010; Texas Insurance Code 2210). In 1987, to protect coastal citizens and to reduce the risk to the wind insurance underwriters, the state mandated that covered homes be sturdy enough to pass a wind insurance inspection (Texas Insurance Code, Title 10, Subtitle G, Chapter 2210, Subchapter F).

Forecasts and Alerts

Still, despite these precautions, there were many vulnerable parts of the Texas coast where people lived, worked, and played. For these residents and visitors, the best remaining option has been to make sure they receive early, accurate warnings of impending storms and truly understand the risk they face. Many people are unaware of the damage a coastal storm can bring: roughly 80–90 percent of people living in hurricane-prone areas have never experienced the full fury of a major hurricane (Nagle 1999, 80). The lack of prior warning before the destruction of Indianola led to the creation of the Weather Bureau in 1890. Funding and support for the bureau rose when the navy had to sail the storm-ridden Caribbean during the Spanish-American War of 1898. With time and new technology, the bureau's ability to accurately predict storms increased. Reports of storms by wireless telegraph (1905) and radio (mid-1930s) helped give better advance notice. Aircraft began scouting cyclones in 1943, when Colonel Duckworth flew from Galveston to investigate a storm, leading to the development of the Hurricane Hunters of the 53rd Weather Reconnaissance Squadron. Coastal radar in the mid-1950s and satellites in the 1960s gave forecasters yet more tools to track and understand hurricanes. The ability to forecast storms increased from a day in 1954, to two days in 1961, to three days in 1964, to as much as five days by 2003 (Lepore 2003; Sheets 1990).

Recent Steps

There have been a number of new responses to Texas coastal storm threats. These efforts include: bulwarking the coast, buying up flood-prone areas along the shore, interpreting the Open Beaches Act, and insuring against damaging wind and surge.

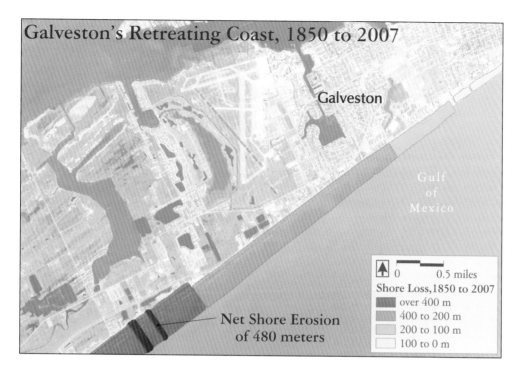

Galveston's Retreating Coast, 1850 to 2007

Galveston

Gulf
of
Mexico

0   0.5 miles

Shore Loss, 1850 to 2007

- over 400 m
- 400 to 200 m
- 200 to 100 m
- 100 to 0 m

Net Shore Erosion
of 480 meters

Just as average sea level is moving, so is the shore. Based on surveys dating back as early as 1838, measurements show that 64 percent of the Texas coast is eroding, with a mean shoreline change of -2.3 feet per year. Heavily settled portions of west Galveston Island and Bolivar Peninsula are seeing even higher erosion rates of three to seven feet per year and, cumulatively, over 1,575 feet from 1850 to 2007. In parts of the shore, that is fast enough to swallow a typical beachfront lot in just ten to twenty years (Bureau of Economic Geology 2013; McKenna 2009; Paine 2013).

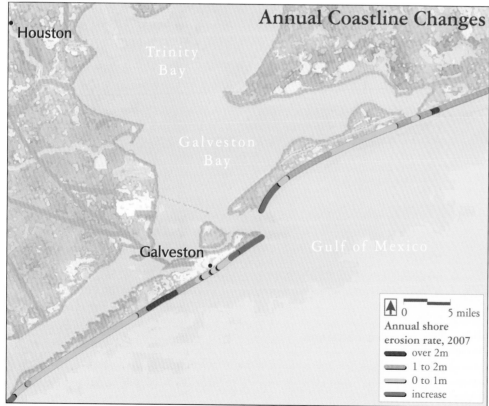

Annual Coastline Changes

Houston

Trinity
Bay

Galveston
Bay

Gulf of Mexico

Galveston

0   5 miles

Annual shore
erosion rate, 2007

- over 2m
- 1 to 2m
- 0 to 1m
- increase

Buildings and Shorelines

There has been no grand effort to raise low-lying areas up and out of surge levels akin to Galveston's heroic endeavor at the turn of the last century. However, there have been other attempts to buttress buildings in the coastal areas of Texas. For instance, the state has pressed for stronger construction rules including many requirements for slab reinforcement, anchor bolt and fastener use, pier burial, wall bracing, joist spans, wood treatment, impact-resistant windows and doors, and other measures. These structural standards are drawn from storm damage observations, model building codes, and the requirements of the National Flood Insurance Program (Federal Emergency Management Agency 2009; International Building Code; International Residential Code; National Fire Protection Association's Building Construction and Safety Code, NFPA 500; National Flood Insurance Act of 1968, 42 USC 4001 et seq.; Texas Administrative Code Title 28, Part 1, Chapter 5, Subchapter E, Division 1, Rule 5.4008(a)).

Modern coastal protection has also looked to "living shoreline" solutions. Nonprofits, agencies, and volunteers have restored coastal marshes, oyster reefs, and coastal dunes to help absorb the blows of tropical storms and hurricanes. Less concrete is poured and fewer pilings are sunk. Fewer levees, seawalls, jetties, and rock groins are built. Instead, more spartina is

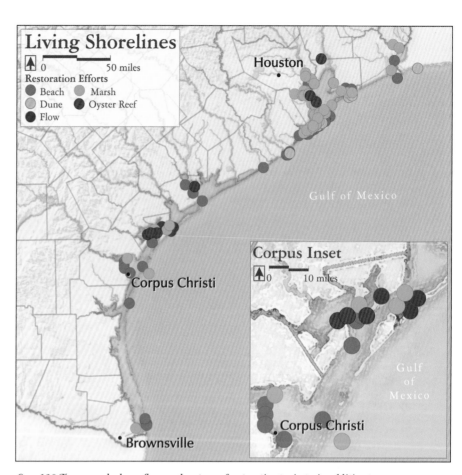

Over 130 Texas marsh, dune, flow, and oyster reef restoration projects, in addition to numerous beach nourishment efforts, are shown here, reported for 1973 through 2013. The projects should help bolster the coast, although likely sea level rise, coastal erosion, and storm impacts will be powerful foes (Coastal Conservation Association of Texas 2013; Gulf of Mexico Foundation 2015; National Oceanic and Atmospheric Administration 2013b; McKenna 2009; White, Calnan, and Morton 1998; Williams 2013).

plugged in the marshes, more sea oats are planted in the dunes, and more oyster shell is laid on the bay bottoms.

Severance v. Patterson

The Open Beaches Act remains on the books in Texas over fifty years after its passage, but it has faced a number of efforts to limit or repeal it, both in the legislature and in the courts. In 2010, the Texas Supreme Court certainly muddied interpretation of the act and likely severely undermined its strength (*Severance v. Patterson*, 345 S.W.3d 18 (Texas 2010, reh'g granted), 370 S.W.

3d 705 (Texas 2012)). The court basically ruled that the public portion of the beach does not roll landward if erosion is "avulsive" (in other words, if the shore is cut back due to a storm rather than by gradual erosion). Many critics are now unsure how to distinguish between storm-related and gradual erosion of the Texas shores. They feel that the ruling upends hundreds of years of common law precedent and traditional public beach use and access. Given this added confusion over title, it is not clear how property owners will respond, if they will move to build more and closer along the coast, or retreat to higher and safer places.

Flood Costs

Over the years, insurance rates under the National Flood Insurance Program were found to be unrealistically low, and areas that regularly flooded were not included in the flood zone maps. Many of the losses came from properties that had repeatedly and predictably flooded. Just 1 percent of NFIP-covered properties had repetitive losses, but they carried grandfathered policies and pulled in a full 30 percent of federal payouts (King 2005, CRS-20). In Texas alone, over $1.8 billion has been paid out for repetitive losses (Bowman 2013). As a result, the flood insurance program racked up some $30 billion in debt nationally, and it became clear that changes were needed. One route has involved buyouts of structures that have a high risk of flooding,

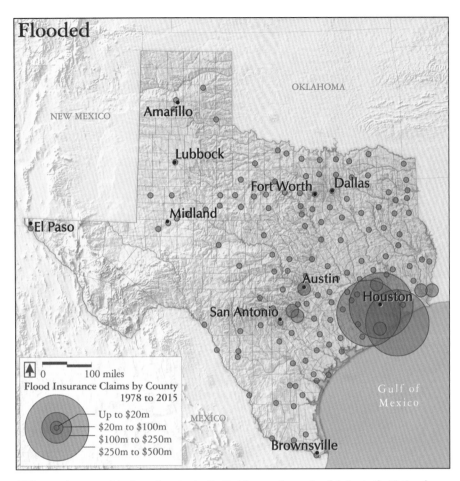

This map shows repetitive losses from properties that have made a series of claims to the National Flood Insurance Program over the 1978–2013 period, summed by county. A large portion of these losses occurs along the upper Texas coast (Bowman 2013 and 2015; FEMA 2015).

using funds from the federal government (National Flood Insurance Reform Act of 1994, 42 U.S.C. 4101, Flood Mitigation Assistance, Hazard Mitigation Grant Program, Pre-Disaster Mitigation Grant Program, Severe Repetitive Loss Program). Also, reforms in 2012 revised flood mapping and insurance premiums to more accurately reflect the liabilities (Biggert-

Waters Flood Insurance Reform Act of 2012, H.R. 4348-512). The higher premiums and wider flood maps may well discourage some development of high-risk coastal areas (Collier 2013).

Wind Expenses

The Texas Wind Insurance Association (TWIA) ran into challenges similar

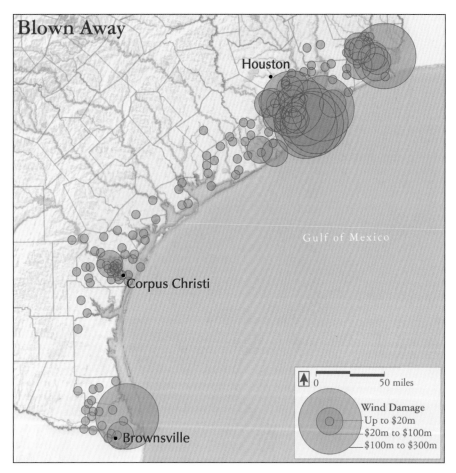

Blown Away

Houston

Gulf of Mexico

Corpus Christi

0   50 miles

Wind Damage
—Up to $20m
—$20m to $100m
—$100m to $300m

Brownsville

Wind damage and associated losses (sorted and summed by zip code) have been severe along the Texas coast. Paid losses amounted to over $3 billion from 2002 through March of 2015, largely clustered in the "Golden Triangle" of Houston, Galveston, and Beaumont (Resnick 2015; US Census Bureau 2015).

However, the association currently carries only $500 million in its coffers for future storms. In addition, it has struggled with thousands of lawsuits and has learned that the state will not back TWIA if the fund runs out of money (Abbott 2013). Some have argued that TWIA should declare bankruptcy (Aaronson and White 2013). Others have recommended that the association take less drastic measures to restore itself. These observers urge that the agency use more conservative estimates of future storms, float bonds, charge private insurers, raise premiums, and enforce better compliance with building codes (Purdy and Sourtis 2012; Texas Wind Insurance Association 2011). In any outcome, though, it appears that wind insurance will become more expensive, and more in line with the real risks of building on the coast.

Industrial Losses

There is concern that building codes, marsh plantings, beach setbacks, and insurance policies, while well intentioned, may not be enough to protect Texans along the coast. Researchers are especially alarmed by the vulnerability of the valuable, and toxic, industries in Beaumont and Port Arthur, and especially along the Houston Ship Channel. After Hurricane Ike's strike, the Gulf Coast saw over 440 releases of oil, gasoline, and other substances reported, and 1,500 sites requiring cleanup. The Coast Guard noted

to those that FEMA faced with its flood policies. TWIA was originally designed as an insurer of last resort, a backstop of a sort when private insurance was hard to come by. However, in 2006 and 2007, in the aftermath of Hurricane Katrina, private insurers largely abandoned insuring coastal properties. In 2001, TWIA wrote only 77,000 policies; ten years later, it issued 255,945 policies (Texas

Wind Insurance Association 2012). In 1992, TWIA had $5 billion in exposure; by the end of 2011, it covered $71.1 billion (Southwestern Insurance Information Service 2011).

TWIA had essentially become the state's default wind insurer, and a grossly undercapitalized one. In 2008, policyholders claimed $2.8 billion against TWIA for damages from Hurricanes Ike and Dolly alone.

that damaged, destroyed, and missing tanks were leaking isopropyl alcohol, benzene, propylene oxide, ammonia, diesel, jet fuel, and crude oil (National Response Center 2013). And yet Ike was only a category 2 storm. Nor did Ike make a direct hit on the most exposed areas around the Houston Ship Channel. It could have been worse, much worse, if Ike had been a more powerful storm, or if it had made landfall just 30 miles to the southwest. SSPEED (Severe Storm Prediction, Education, and Evacuation from Disasters), a consortium of universities led by Rice, has recommended two major answers to this threat question: a $1.5 billion, 25-foot-tall retractable sea gate to guard the Houston Ship Channel, and a National Recreation Area to help protect and restore the marshes and dunes that offer natural protection for the coast (Sheehy 2013).

Risks and the Environment

The efforts to deal with coastal storms in Texas may provide a good window into thinking about a number of recurring environmental problems. First, people are often not good at coping with low-frequency, high-damage events, whether they are hurricanes or nuclear meltdowns or car accidents. Perhaps we have a short memory, or a hopeful attitude.

Also, private individuals have a tendency to take advantage of the commons, whether it is the NFIP flood insurance pool, the TWIA wind insurance fund, or the Open Beaches easement. We like to take what is ours, and maybe a little of what is yours too (as state senator Babe Schwartz put it, we enjoy "private leisure at public expense") (Schwartz 2006).

And, last, we have a tough time understanding growing risks from gradual changes, such as beach erosion, marsh loss, or sea level rise. These changes may be slow, but they are relentless, and as some wag once said, "Remember, Mother Nature bats last!"

Sources

Aaronson, Becca, and Audrey White. 2013. "Board Tables Proposal to Put TWIA into Receivership." *Texas Tribune*, March 25.

Abbott, Greg. 2013. Whether the State of Texas has a legal obligation to pay unfunded losses that exceed the Texas Windstorm Insurance Association's ability to pay. Texas Attorney General Opinion No. GA-1012, dated July 1.

Augustino, Jocelyn. 2008. "Gilchrist, Texas, as Seen on September 22, 2008, Nine Days after Hurricane Ike Struck." Federal Emergency Management Agency. https://share.sandia.gov/news/resources/news_releases/images/2013/fema.jpg, accessed October 10, 2014.

Bass, Bill. 2013. Chief GIS Specialist, Community and Environmental Planning, Houston-Galveston Area Council. Personal communication, November.

Blake, Eric, and Ethan Gibney. 2011. The Deadliest, Costliest, and Most Intense United States Tropical Cyclones from 1851 to 2010 (and Other Frequently Requested Hurricane Facts). NOAA Technical Memorandum NWS NHC-6. National Hurricane Center, National Weather Service. August.

Bowman, John. 2013 and 2015. Natural Hazards Program Specialist, Federal Emergency Management Agency. Personal communications, November 2013 and March 2015.

Bureau of Economic Geology. 2013. Shoreline Change Rates: Gulf of Mexico Shorelines." Coastal Studies. Bureau of Economic Geology. Jackson School of Geosciences. University of Texas. http://www.beg.utexas.edu/coastal/download.php, accessed November 11, 2013.

CenterPoint Energy. 2008. CenterPoint Energy Customer Outages by Zip Code, as of September 14, 2008. http://www.centerpointenergy.com/static files/CNP/Common/SiteAssets/doc/Ike%20°utage%20map_9.14_8pm.pdf, accessed January 21, 2014.

Coastal Conservation Association of Texas. 2013. Habitat Today for Fish Tomorrow Projects. http://www.cca texas.org/where-we-work/habitat-projects/, accessed November 15, 2013.

Collier, Kiah. 2013. "Residents Could See Massive Insurance Rate Hikes." *Houston Chronicle*, August 12.

Collins, Douglas, and Stephen Lowe. 2001. "A Macro Validation Dataset for U.S. Hurricane Models." Casualty Actuarial Society Forum. Casualty Actuarial Society, Arlington, Virginia, pp. 217–51.

Federal Emergency Management Agency (FEMA). 2009. "Hurricane Ike in Texas and Louisiana: Building

Performance Observations, Recommendations and Technical Guidance." Report FEMA P-757, April.

———. 2013. Texas Hurricane Ike (DR-1791). http://www.fema.gov/disaster/1791, accessed November 11, 2013.

———. 2015. Loss Statistics: Texas: January 1, 1978 through January 31, 2015. http://bsa.nfipstat.fema.gov/reports/1040.htm#48, accessed March 25, 2015.

Gulf of Mexico Foundation. 2015. Category Archives: Gulf of Mexico Community-Based Restoration Partnership Projects. http://www.gulfmex.org/category/projects/conservation-and-restoration-projects/gom-community-based-restoration-partnership-projects/, accessed May 18, 2015.

Harris County Flood Control District. 2009. Ike Storm Surge Inundation Map. https://www.hcfcd.org/media/1242/ike_stormsurge-inundation_maps.pdf, accessed November 1, 2013.

———. 2013. "Hurricane Ike: The Storm; the Facts." http://www.hcfcd.org/tropicalweather/ike.html, accessed October 23, 2013.

Houston-Galveston Area Council. 2013. Hazards Related Data. Houston-Galveston Area Council, Community and Environmental Planning. https://www.hgac.com/rds/gis_data/clearinghouse/default.aspx, accessed November 19, 2013.

Karl, Thomas, Jerry Melillo, and Thomas Peterson, eds. 2009. *Global Climate Change Impacts in the United States*. New York: Cambridge University Press.

Keith, Gary. 2007. *There Once Was a Congressman from Texas*. Austin: University of Texas Press.

King, Rawle. 2005. "Federal Flood Insurance: The Repetitive Loss Problem." CRS Report for Congress, Order Code RL32972. June 30.

Lee, Russell. 1963. Bob Eckhardt at the Close of the Legislature, circa May 1963. Photograph. Digital image. Russell Lee Photograph Collection, 1935–77. Briscoe Center for American History, University of Texas.

Lepore, Frank. 2003. "NOAA Extends Hurricane Forecasts from Three to Five Days." *U.S. Department of Commerce News*, March 10.

McKenna, K. K. 2009. "Texas Coastwide Erosion Response Plan, 2009 Update." Texas General Land Office, GLO Contract No. 06-076-000, Work Order No. 3963.

Miller, Ray. 1984. *Ray Miller's Texas Parks: A History and Guide*. Houston: Cordovan Press.

Nagle, Garrett. 1999. *Hazards*. Oxford: Nelson Thornes.

National Oceanic and Atmospheric Administration. 2009. "Sea Level Variations of the United States, 1854–2006." Technical Report NOS CO-OPS 053. National Ocean Service, Center for Operational Oceanographic Products and Services, National Oceanic and Atmospheric Administration, US Department of Commerce. Silver Spring, Maryland. December, table 4, pp. 22, 23.

———. 2013. Restoration Atlas. National Oceanic and Atmospheric Administration, US Department of Commerce. https://restoration.atlas.noaa.gov/src/html/index.html, accessed November 14, 2013.

———. 2015. "Sea Level Trends." National Water Level Observation Network. Center for Operational Oceanographic Products and Services, National Water Level Observation Network, National Oceanic and Atmospheric Administration, US Department of Commerce. tidesandcurrents.noaa.gov/sltrends/sltrends.html, accessed March 24, 2015.

National Park Service. 1955. "A Report on Our Vanishing Shoreline." National Park Service, US Department of the Interior. Washington, DC.

National Response Center. 2013. NRC Data. US Coast Guard. http://www.nrc.uscg.mil, accessed November 21, 2013.

National Weather Service. 2013a. "Atlantic Hurricane Season (2007–2013)." National Hurricane Center, National Weather Service, National Oceanic and Atmospheric Administration, US Department of Commerce. http://www.nhc.noaa.gov/ 2013atlan.shtml, accessed October 8, 2013.

———. 2013b. "Past Atlantic Storm Tracks, 1851–2006." National Hurricane Center, National Weather Service, National Oceanic and Atmospheric Administration, US Department of Commerce. http://www.srh.noaa.gov/gis/kml/hurricanetrack/Atlantic%20Hurricanes.kmz, accessed October 7, 2013.

———. 2013c. "Probabilistic Hurricane Storm Surge." Meteorological Development Laboratory. National Oceanic and Atmospheric Administration, US Department of Commerce. Silver Spring, Maryland. http://www.nws.noaa.gov/md/psurge/download.php, accessed November 11, 2013.

Paine, Jeffrey. 2013. Senior Research Scientist. Bureau of Economic Geology, Jackson School of Geosciences, University of Texas at Austin. Personal communication, November.

Parris, Adam. 2012. Global Sea Level Rise Scenarios for the US National Climate Assessment. NOAA Technical Memo OAR CPO-1. NOAA Climate Program Office. http://cpo.noaa.gov/sites/cpo/Reports/2012/NOAA_SLR_r3.pdf, accessed May 18, 2015.

Purdy, Ryan, and Peter Scourtis. 2012. "Actuarial Rate Level Analysis— Commercial and Residential Property Programs." April 17 correspondence with James Murphy at Texas Wind Insurance Association.

Resnick, Greg. 2015. Compliance Specialist, Texas Windstorm Insurance Association. Personal communication, April.

Roth, David. 2010. "Texas Hurricane History." National Weather Service, National Oceanic and Atmospheric Administration, US Department of Commerce. Camp Springs, Maryland. http://www.hpc.ncep.noaa.gov/research/txhur.pdf, accessed October 8, 2013.

Schwartz, Babe. 2006. Oral history interview conducted by Jessica Schoenbaechler, January 20, in Austin, Texas. Texas Legacy Project, Conservation History Association of Texas.

Sheehy, Sandy. 2013. "One Wild Idea." *Rice Magazine* (Fall).

Sheets, Robert. 1990. "The National Hurricane Center—Past, Present, and Future." *Weather and Forecasting* 5 (2).

Sheire, James. 1971. Padre Island National Seashore: Historic Resource Study. Office of History and Historic Architecture, Eastern Service Center, National Park Service.

Southwestern Insurance Information Service 2011. "The Texas Windstorm Insurance Association: Challenges and Solutions." http://www.siisinfo.org //files/twia-december-2011.pdf, accessed November 20, 2013.

Tebaldi, Claudia, Benjamin Strauss, and Chris Zervas. 2012. "Modelling Sea Level Rise Impacts on Storm Surges along US Coasts." *Environmental Research Letters*, 7 014032, March 14.

Texas Natural Resources Code. 2013. Title 2, Subtitle E, Chapter 61, Subchapter B, Access to Public Beaches.

Texas Wind Insurance Association. 2011. Texas Wind Insurance Association Residential Property Rate Level Review, 2012. June 2011.

———. 2012. Texas Wind Insurance Association Board of Directors' Biennial Report to the Commissioner of Insurance, House Committee on Insurance, Senate Committee on Business and Commerce, and Sunset Advisory Commission.

US Army Corps of Engineers. 1981. "Galveston's Bulwark against the Sea: History of the Galveston Seawall." October.

US Census Bureau. 1951. "US Census of Population: Vol. 1, Characteristics of the Population. Part A, Number of Inhabitants." Washington, DC: Government Printing Office.

———. 1992. "1990 Census of Population and Housing, Population and Housing Unit Counts, United States." Report 1990 CPH-2-1. US Census Bureau, US Department of Commerce.

———. 2003. "Texas: 2000, Population and Housing Unit Counts, 2000 Census of Population and Housing." Report PHC-3-45. Issued October. US Census Bureau, US Department of Commerce.

———. 2013. American Fact Finder. US Census Bureau, US Department of Commerce. http://factfinder2.census.gov/faces/nav/jsf/pages/searchresults.xhtml?refresh=t, accessed November 11, 2013.

———. 2015. Zip Code Tabulation Areas Gazetteer File, Census 2000 Gazetteer Files, Geography. US Census Bureau, US Department of Commerce. http://www2.census.gov/geo/docs/maps-data/data/gazetteer/zcta5.zip, accessed April 2, 2015.

US Fish and Wildlife Service. 1975. "Operation of the National Wildlife Refuge System, DES 75-57." Draft Environmental Statement. Department of the Interior.

White, W. A., T. R. Calnan, and R. A. Morton. 1998. "Evaluation of Marsh Creation and Restoration Projects and Their Potential for Large-Scale Application, Galveston-Trinity Bay System." Unnumbered report from the University of Texas at Austin, Bureau of Economic Geology and the Texas General Land Office, Coastal Division.

Williams, Deidre. 2013. Conrad Blucher Institute for Surveying and Science, Texas A&M University–Corpus Christi. Personal communication, November.

Wolff, Linda. 1999. *Indianola and Matagorda Island, 1837–87: A Local History and Visitor's Guide for a Lost Seaport and a Barrier Island on the Texas Gulf Coast*. Austin: Eakin Press.

Kemp's Ridley Sea Turtle

The Race

Recent years have seen an explosion of knowledge about the bewildering, rich diversity of wildlife on the planet. Just the year 2011 saw the discovery of a monkey, nematode, tarantula, orchid, wasp, mushroom, and even a walking cactus! (International Institute for Species Exploration 2011).

Ironically, at the same time, we are witnessing a rapid die-out among our newly appreciated fellow creatures. Some are calling the modern era "the Sixth Great Extinction," akin to the Cretaceous demise of the dinosaurs (Kolbert 2014). The International Union for Conservation of Nature has estimated that 36 percent of all species assessed globally are threatened with extinction (International Union for Conservation of Nature 2009). The noted biologist David Wilcove figured that 16 percent of US flora and fauna are in immediate danger of extinction, and another 15 percent are considered vulnerable (Vie, Hilton-Taylor, and Stuart 2009; Wilcove 1994).

This race between discovery and loss is exemplified by the roller-coaster

A Kemp's ridley sea turtle lays her eggs on Padre Island National Seashore (National Park Service 2013).

fortunes of the Kemp's ridley sea turtle (*Lepidochelys kempii*) during the past sixty-five years. The Kemp's ridley, a 100-pound, 2-foot-long creature native to the Gulf of Mexico and North Atlantic, was barely known in the first half of the twentieth century. Spending the vast majority of its life at sea, often underwater, its life and origins were little understood. For years it was known as the "bastard turtle," thought to be just a sterile hybrid of the loggerhead and either the hawksbill or green sea turtle, or perhaps only a subspecies of the olive ridley (Plotkin 2007; Safina and Wallace 2010; Sharpe 1988).

Henry Hildebrand was a marine biologist deeply involved in the early work to protect and restore the Kemp's ridley sea turtle (Weisman 2000).

Discovery

Then, in 1947, a young road engineer, Andres Herrera, saw an amazing event. He filmed an arribada, a great synchronized nesting of thousands of Kemp's ridleys clambering up a remote shore on the western edge of the Gulf of Mexico. Herrera described the hordes of turtles coming aground at the Rancho Nuevo beach as like "blotches of confetti floating on the water" (Kemp's Ridley Sea Turtle Nesting 2007). Henry Hildebrand, a marine biologist from Corpus Christi State University, saw Herrera's film in 1960 and estimated that this huge arribada involved 40,000 female Kemp's ridleys coming ashore along just a mile of beach in a single day. Until then, the great size of this nesting flotilla had been unknown. Only small scattered laying sites had been identi-

fied. One was found at Little Shell (on Padre Island in Texas), while some nesting sites were suspected to exist on Veracruz beaches at Nautla, Anton Lizardo, Alvarado, and Montepio (Carr 1961; Carr and Caldwell 1958; Hildebrand 1963).

Decline

However, in a kind of cruel joke, researchers found that Kemp's ridleys were disappearing just as they were being discovered. By 1966, the Rancho Nuevo arribada comprised only 1,300 female turtles, and by the 1980s, seldom included more than 200 (Committee on Sea Turtle Conservation 1990; Witherington 2006). As the arribadas shrank, so

did the nest counts. Ridley nests fell from over 40,000 in 1947 to 6,000 in 1966 to only 700 in 1985 (Turtle Expert Working Group 1998). In 1977, the sea turtle expert Archie Carr extrapolated from the nesting data and estimated that the total mature population of Kemp's ridleys had fallen from 162,000 in 1947, to 10,150 in 1970, to only 4,872 in 1974 (Carr 1977). The US government listed the Kemp's ridley as endangered in 1970. The turtle's extreme global rarity was recognized by the 1973 International Convention on Commerce in Threated Species of Flora and Fauna (Endangered Species Act Listing, 35 Federal Register 18319–18322 (December 2, 1970)); International Union for Conservation of Nature

1973; Marquez 1994, 61–62; Turtle Expert Working Group 1998, 2). Prospects were not good.

The species is clearly on the skids, and if present conditions continue it will shortly—in two years perhaps, or three, or five—be gone.

—Archie Carr, 1977

Threats, Old and New

After a history of more than 2.5–3.5 million years, why had the Kemp's ridley population fallen so far and so fast during the post–World War II years? (Bowen, Meylan, and Avise 1991). The turtle had long had natural enemies, such as coyotes, skunks, raccoons, and ghost crabs that raided recently laid eggs. Black vultures, blackbirds, and coatis later attacked hatchlings as they made their way to the sea. And once in the ocean, gulls and frigate birds might grab young turtles. Certain fish, including crevalle jack and red drum, gobbled young hatchlings as well (Pritchard and Marquez 1973; Marquez 1994).

However, the collapse in turtle numbers was more likely due to several recent human causes. First, beginning in the late 1950s, Mexican *hueveros* collected the turtle's eggs and brought them to market, where they were bought as an aphrodisiac and as a medicine for lung and skin diseases (Hildebrand 1963; Witherington 2006). The turtle's decline was also likely due to the post–World War II growth in the brown shrimp (*Penaeus*

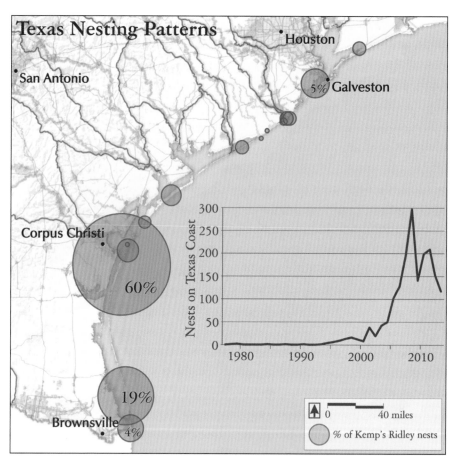

Nesting sites of the Kemp's ridley sea turtle in Texas, 1978–2014, are shown here. While nesting is gradually moving north, 87 percent of Kemp's ridley nests in the state have been clustered at Mustang Island and southward. The historic trend chart shows the remarkable resurgence in the turtle's numbers through 2009, and the worrisome, as-yet-unexplained dip beginning in 2010 (Burchfield 2013; Peña 2013 and 2015; Shaver 2010–15; Shaver and Caillouet 1998).

aztecus) fishery, as diesel-powered trawlers plied their trade and accidentally scooped up turtles in the western Gulf of Mexico (Turtle Expert Working Group 1998). The turtle also faced other dangers, including dredging, beach manipulation, oil rig removal, power plant entrainment, and ingestion of plastics and toxic materials (Committee on Sea Turtle Conservation 1990; National

Marine Fisheries Service, US Fish and Wildlife Service, and SEMARNAT 2011).

Rookeries, Old and New

Mexico had begun turtle conservation work as early as 1922, with closed seasons, harvest sizes, egg sale bans, and nest protections, but these measures were hampered by weak enforcement

(Marquez 1994, 62). Efforts to protect the Kemp's ridley in earnest began in 1966, when the Mexican government posted armed marines on the Rancho Nuevo beach to protect the turtle nests from the *hueveros*. The Programa Nacional de Marcado de Tortugas Marinas began tagging and releasing ridleys at this time as well (Sweat 1968). In 1977, the Mexican government declared fifteen kilometers of the beach, stretching out to four kilometers offshore, to be a Natural Reserve (Diario Oficial 1977). By 1997, turtle protection and monitoring grew to span 200 kilometers of the Tamaulipan coast and pulled in many years of help from the Florida Audubon Society and the Gladys Porter Zoo in Brownsville (Burchfield 2013; Marquez 1999).

Still, despite the guards at Rancho Nuevo, the Kemp's ridley population remained vulnerable. Too much of the ridley's future rested on the precarious fate of this small nesting site. Hurricanes or oil spills could strike a knockout blow to the small beach at Rancho Nuevo. Indeed, with time, the fears have been shown to be well founded: a huge blowout at the Pemex well, Ixtoc I, sent oil to Rancho Nuevo in 1979, and just a year later, Hurricane Allen flooded the beach (Jernelov and Linden 1981; Marine Turtle Newsletter 1981).

Some of the first efforts to create a backup rookery began when a Brownsville-area nonprofit, the Valley Sportsman Club, voted to restore sea turtles to South Padre Island. The club decided to focus on the Kemp's ridley due to its extreme rarity, and the proximity of Rancho Nuevo. A club volunteer, Dearl Adams, took the lead and secured permission from the Mexican government to transplant ridley eggs collected at Rancho Nuevo. By 1966, the Adams family and a fellow helper, Ila Loetscher (eventually dubbed the "Turtle Lady"), were bringing two thousand eggs annually to South Padre Island, where they buried them in the sand and guarded them against coyotes and other predators. In 1967, they saw the first hatch at their "Ranchito Tortugo," and seven years later, witnessed the return of the first of the 1967 brood, a female fittingly called "Alpha" (Bigony 2004).

Captive Rearing

With time, and support from the Endangered Species Act's passage, professional interest rose for reestablishing a nesting population north of the US-Mexico border (35 FR 18320, December 2, 1970). In 1974, Dr. Hildebrand and Robert Whistler, the chief naturalist at Padre Island National Seashore, proposed that a breeding colony of Kemp's ridleys be created on Padre Island (Jones 1999). There was initial reluctance to try the idea, but in 1978, the National Park Service began a ten-year partnership with the US Fish and Wildlife Service, Texas Parks and Wildlife, National Marine Fisheries Service, and the Instituto Nacional de Pesca in Mexico to build this new rookery (Bowen, Conant, and Hopkins-Murphy 1994).

In the late 1970s, this team began two experiments to help boost the chances of Kemp's ridley eggs making it to maturity. From 1978 through 1988, up to two thousand eggs were brought annually from Rancho Nuevo to Padre Island, where they were incubated in the sands of the National Seashore and hatched. Hatchlings were allowed to crawl down the island's beach to the surf, in hopes that they might imprint on the site and later return as adults. The young turtles were then netted and passed on to the National Marine Fisheries Service laboratory in Galveston. Lab staff raised them to an age of nine to eleven months, large enough to allow tagging and to avoid most predators, and then released them in the Gulf. A second program ran from 1978 through 1992, where up to two thousand hatchlings were first imprinted at Rancho Nuevo and then brought to the service lab in Galveston. At the laboratory, they were captive-reared, tagged, and released, with the goal of leapfrogging the most vulnerable early days of their lives (Byles 1993; Caillouet 2013; Manzella et al. 1988; Williams 1993).

As the program wound down in the early 1990s, many were sad to see the end of the captive rearing, tagging, and release programs. The ridley program had caught the public's imagination and support. For instance, thousands of turtle-besotted children had collected and funneled money through Carole Allen's group, Help Endangered Animals—Ridley Turtles, to feed and support the captive-grown

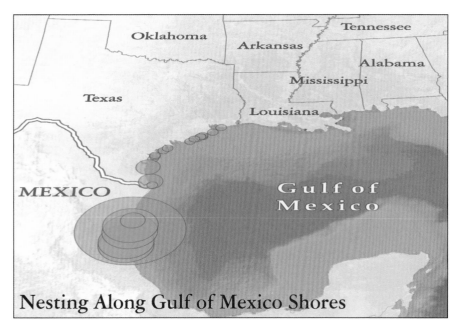

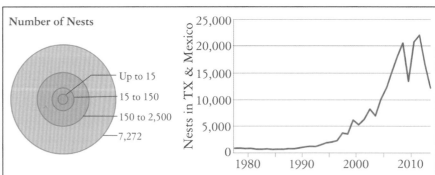

The map shows the 2014 nesting pattern of the Kemp's ridley sea turtle in the Gulf of Mexico. While more Kemp's ridleys have begun nesting in Texas during recent years, over 99 percent of the ridley population continues to nest in an 80-mile stretch of Mexican beach, peaking in the Rancho Nuevo area, 200 miles south of Brownsville. The charted trend combines both Texas and Mexican nest counts for the 1978–2014 period. Please note that nesting data may be skewed by early misidentification or varying search efforts over time (Burchfield 2013; Peña 2013 and 2015; Shaver 2010–15).

hatchlings from Mexico to the United States, with captive rearing, tagging, and release, was continued through the year 2000 (Gallaway et al. 2013).

Shrimp, Trawlers, and TEDs

Despite the work to protect and expand nesting areas and to ensure the turtles' early survival through captive-rearing, the Kemp's ridleys have long faced threats offshore. Kemp's ridleys spend much of their time traveling through the shallow waters of the continental shelf of the Gulf of Mexico. There, the turtles forage for some of their favorite foods, including blue, calico, stone, and horseshoe crabs (Servis, Lovewell, and Tucker 2013). Unfortunately, their routes in the Gulf of Mexico intersect with the shrimp trawling nets of a large commercial fishing fleet based out of US and Mexican ports. Many Kemp's ridleys, along with loggerhead and hawksbill sea turtles, have been snared as "bycatch" and drowned in shrimp nets (Wallace et al. 2013). In 1990, the National Research Council estimated that five thousand Kemp's ridleys were killed annually in shrimp trawls (Committee on Sea Turtle Conservation 1990).

To limit the bycatch drownings, the National Marine Fisheries Service promoted use of a turtle excluder device (TED), a trapdoor at the trawl net throat that released turtles and other larger creatures and debris (50 CFR 223.205; Federal Register Vol. 68, No. 35, pp. 8456–71, February 21, 2003). There was controversy among shrimp-

turtles (Allen 2013). However, many scientists felt the programs had failed to produce any nesting turtles, and moreover, might be diverting attention from more serious threats to the turtle (Eckert et al. 1994; Woody 1990). Then, in 1996, there was late but

good news. Dr. Donna Shaver, a noted National Park Service turtle biologist, found the first of the program's headstarted turtles nesting on Padre Island (Safina and Wallace 2010; Shaver 1996). With this encouragement, a reduced annual transfer of 200

This map, based on NOAA satellite-based telemetry data for 1989 through 1996, gives some idea of how far Kemp's ridley sea turtles can roam from their major nesting sites. In fact, the turtle is even known to visit the west coast of Europe and north Africa (Manzella, Caillouet, and Fontaine 1988; Williams 2013).

ers who objected to the cost of the TED ($100–$300), the extra weight and fuel cost for pulling the TED, and the risk of handling the heavy TED. However, other shrimpers found that TEDs reduced bycatch weight and saved shrimp from being crushed by the sea turtles or other large objects.

While the controversy raged on, the United States proceeded to require TEDs on offshore shrimp boats in limited circumstances in June 1987, and region-wide in May 1990 (Renaud et al. 1990). In 1989, the federal government prohibited shrimp imported from

countries that did not require TED use (Public Law 101-162, Section 609; 6 U.S.C. 1537; 78 Federal Register 45285). By April 1993, TEDs became compulsory for the Mexican fleet (Marquez 1994, 102).

All these measures have helped reduce Kemp's ridley bycatch and mortality, down by about 37 percent from 1990 through 2007. Still, the sheer numbers of trapped (4,200 per year) and dead ridleys (2,700 annually) have stayed stubbornly high (Caillouet 2012; Finkbeiner et al. 2011; Karp, Desfosse, and Brooke 2011).

Shrimp Seasons

Even after TEDs were widely adopted, dead adult ridleys continued to be found stranded on South Texas Gulf shores, most within the shrimp trawling season. Of 104 stranded Kemp's ridleys collected from 1995 through 2000, 101 were found during the times when the waters were open to trawling (Shaver 2001). There have been hints that repeated captures in shrimp nets, even with release through TEDs, could ultimately kill sea turtles (Caillouet et al. 1996). So in the year 2000, Texas

Parks and Wildlife banned shrimpers from waters out to five nautical miles off North Padre Island, South Padre Island, and Boca Chica. The closure ran from December 1 through mid-May, stretching out the regular mid-May to mid-July "Texas Closure" that had protected the brown shrimp industry since 1959 (Fisher 2013; Gulf of Mexico Fishery Management Council 2002). In 1978, the Mexican government closed its territorial waters to American shrimpers entirely (Turtle Expert Working Group 1998). The trawling seasons and closures seem to have helped protect the Kemp's ridleys in South Texas (Lewison, Crowder, and Shaver 2003; Shaver and Rubio 2007).

Oil Spills

Shrimping has not been the only threat to the Kemp's ridley's habitat. In April 2010, the Deepwater Horizon oil rig exploded and released roughly 210 million gallons of crude near some of the turtle's most important foraging waters. NOAA reported that 481 dead Kemp's ridleys were found in the eleven months following the spill (National Oceanic and Atmospheric Administration 2013a). NOAA and the US Fish and Wildlife Services are working through a Natural Resource Damage Assessment to determine the restoration effort required (Oil Pollution Act of 1990, 101 H.R. 1465, P.L. 101-380).

This map shows the locations of over 4,400 Kemps ridley sea turtle strandings for the verified years of 1998 through 2006 (the color of the counties reflects the relative number of strandings). Given the extreme rarity of Kemps ridleys, every loss is critical, but the numbers and possible causes are difficult to interpret. Some of the losses are due to natural reasons (for instance, many turtles are stunned or die from cold in the northern part of their range), while others die due to human factors, such as trawl seines and oil spills (Stacy, Innis, and Hernandez 2013; Sea Turtle Stranding and Salvage Network 2013).

Habitat

In February 2010, the nonprofit group WildEarth Guardians filed a petition with the Fish and Wildlife Service and the National Oceanic and Atmospheric Administration seeking to designate critical habitat for the Kemp's ridley (WildEarth Guardians 2010). The petition was rejected by the agencies in May 2011, with support from the courts in March 2013 (Jones 2013). However, a new recovery plan for the Kemp's ridley was developed in 2010 that sought to upgrade understanding and protection for the turtle (National Marine Fisheries Service, US Fish and Wildlife Service, and SEMARNAT 2011).

Progress and Challenges

As we have seen, many have worked to help the Kemp's ridley. There have been impressive joint efforts in the United States and Mexico, and by nonprofits, academics, and government researchers. Scientists have undertaken in-depth studies to understand the turtle's nesting and foraging patterns. Agencies have protected nesting beaches and near-shore waters, while working hard to move eggs and headstart hatchlings. Fishermen have installed turtle excluder devices on shrimp trawls. Good progress has been made, and the numbers show it. From 2002 to 2009, 771 Kemp's

In their wide travels, Kemp's ridleys run the gauntlet of natural and man-made dangers, including shrimp trawls, oil spills, and simple cold water. The purple shading shows the 2008 habitat range of white, brown, and pink shrimp. Offshore oil spills from tankers, pipelines, and platforms (1957 through 2015) are shown by brown markers. Turquoise markers off the mid-Atlantic and New England coast denote areas that can see coastal sea temperatures below 10°C, the level that can stun and immobilize turtles (National Oceanic and Atmospheric Administration 2013b; National Oceanic and Atmospheric Administration 2015; Northern Gulf Institute 2008; South Atlantic Fishery Management Council 2008; Dasa 2012).

ridley nests were found on the Texas coast, more than nine times the eighty-one discovered during the previous fifty-four years (1948–2001) (National Marine Fisheries Service 2012). Nesting Kemp's ridleys are now found on many Texas beaches, including Bolivar, Galveston, Surfside, Quintana, Bryan, Sargent, Matagorda, San Jose, Mustang, Padre, and Boca Chica. And nests in Mexico have grown twenty-fold, from 800 to more than 16,000, in just the past thirty years (Burchfield 2013; Peña 2013 and 2015).

Still, looking forward, the Kemp's ridley continues to face significant threats, both on- and offshore. For instance, development near its nesting beaches is a concern. A SpaceX rocket launch pad is under construction at Boca Chica, and more typical coastal developments have also been built or suggested (Perez-Treviño 2015; Federal Aviation Administration 2013). A commercial fishing complex was built in 1987 close to the major Rancho Nuevo turtle camp. There are recurring proposals to develop the turtle beaches of La Pesca as a marina of some kind, or to dredge the Gulf Intracoastal Waterway from Brownsville south to Barra del Tordo. Artificial lights from existing beach developments can confuse and disorient nesting sea turtles. And, over the longer term, there are concerns about climate change and sea-level rise, which might flood low-lying nesting beaches (National Marine Fisheries Service and US Fish and Wildlife Service 2007).

Kemp's ridleys face challenges while they are in the deep sea as well, especially from floating debris now commonly found in the Gulf of Mexico. Plastics, monofilament line, or fragments of netting can entangle and drown the turtles. Ridleys can also suffer and die from ingested plastic, Styrofoam, balloons, tar, glass, paper, aluminum, hooks, and other waste (Plotkin and Amos 1989).

Nevertheless, interest and care for the Kemp's ridley continue to grow at the grassroots level and in the halls of power. Down on the Texas beach, scores of volunteers regularly help monitor nestings and collect eggs for headstart work. Hatchling releases have become celebrity events, attracting hundreds of onlookers and supporters (Shaver 2013–15). Sea Turtle Inc. operates a veterinary and educational program for the ridleys on South Padre Island (Burchfield 2013). Progress is being seen statewide too: the Texas Senate unanimously declared the Kemp's ridley to be the official state sea turtle (HCR 31, April 29, 2013). Even a brewery has joined the cause, and now sells a Kemp's Ridley Bock with proceeds going to the recovery work (Clark 2013). The wide attention and varied efforts all bode well for the ridley's continued protection and restoration in Texas and beyond.

Sources

Allen, Carole. 2013. "Guest Editorial: The Kemp's Ridley Sea Turtle Is Recognized in Texas!" *Marine Turtle Newsletter* 138: 1–2. http://www .seaturtle.org/mtn/archives/mtn138/ mtn138–1.shtml, accessed October 18, 2013.

Bigony, Mary-Love. 2004. "Solving the Riddle of the Ridley." *Texas Monthly*, March.

Bowen, B. W., T. A. Conant, and S. R. Hopkins-Murphy. 1994. "Where Are They Now? The Kemp's Ridley Headstart." *Conservation Biology* 8 (3).

Bowen, B. W., A. Meylan, and J. Avise. 1991. "Evolutionary Distinctiveness of the Endangered Kemp's Ridley Sea Turtle." *Nature* 352: 709–11.

Burchfield, Pat. 2013. Director, Gladys Porter Zoo. Personal communications, August through October.

Byles, Richard. 1993. "Head Start Experiment No Longer Rearing Kemp's Ridleys." *Marine Turtle Newsletter* 63 (1–2). http://www.seaturtle.org/ mtn/archives/mtn63/mtn63p1.shtml, accessed October 18, 2013.

Caillouet, Charles. 2012. "Editorial: Does Delayed Mortality Occur in Sea Turtles That Aspirate Seawater into Their Lungs during Forced Submergence or Cold Stunning?" *Marine Turtle Newsletter* 135 (1–4). http://www .seaturtle.org/mtn/archives/mtn135/ mtn135p1.shtml.

———. 2013. Marine fisheries volunteer and scientist, retired, National Oceanic and Atmospheric Administration, Marine Fisheries Service, Galveston Laboratory. Personal communications, September through October.

Caillouet, Charles, Donna Shaver, Wendy Teas, James Nance, Dickie Revera, and Andrea Cannon. 1996. "Relationship between Sea Turtle Stranding Rates and Shrimp Fishing Intensities in the

Northwestern Gulf of Mexico: 1986–1989 versus 1990–1993." *Fishery Bulletin* 94 (2): 237–49.

Carr, Archie. 1961. "The Ridley Mystery Today." *Animal Kingdom* 54 (1): 7–12.

———. 1977. "Crisis for the Atlantic Ridley." *Marine Turtle Newsletter* 4: 2–3. http://www.seaturtle.org/mtn/archives/mtn4/mtn4p2.shtml, accessed October 18, 2013.

Carr, Archie, and D. K. Caldwell. 1958. "The Problem of the Atlantic Ridley (*Lepidochelys kempii*) in 1958." *Review Tropical* 6 (3): 245–62.

Clark, Steve. 2013. "Kemp's Ridley Bock Raises Conservation Funds." *Brownsville Herald*, March 21.

Committee on Sea Turtle Conservation. 1990. "Decline of the Sea Turtles: Causes and Prevention." National Research Council. Washington, DC: National Academy Press.

Dasa, Venkata. 2012. Continents. Shapefile. http://www.arcgis.com/home/item.html?id=3c4741e22e2e4af2bd4050511b9fc6ad, accessed March 26, 2015.

Diario Oficial. 1977. "Acuerdo que establece la Zona de Refugio y Veda para la protección de la Tortuga Lora." Departamento de Pesca. Diario Oficial de la Federación, México. Julio 4.

Eckert, Scott, Deborah Crouse, Larry Crowder, Michael Maceina, and Arvind Shah. 1994. "Review of the Kemp's Ridley Sea Turtle Headstart Program." NOAA Technical Memorandum NMFS-OPR-3. August.

Federal Aviation Administration. 2013. "Draft Environmental Impact Statement for the SpaceX Texas Launch Site, Vol. 1, Executive Summary and Chapters 1–14." April.

Finkbeiner, Elena, Bryan Wallace, Jeffrey Moore, Rebecca Lewison, Larry Crowder, and Andrew Read. 2011. "Cumulative Estimates of Sea Turtle Bycatch and Mortality in USA Fisheries between 1990 and 2007," *Biological Conservation* 144 (11): 2719–27.

Fisher, Mark. 2013. Science Director. Coastal Fisheries, Texas Parks and Wildlife. Personal communication, August.

Gallaway, Benny, Charles Caillouet, Pamela Plotkin, William Gazey, John Cole, and Scott Raborn. 2013. "Kemp's Ridley Stock Assessment Project: Final Report." Gulf States Marine Fisheries Commission. Ocean Springs, Mississippi. June. http://www.gsmfc.org/publications/Miscellaneous/Kemp%20Ridley%20Stock%20Assessment%20Report%20Final%20June%2027%202013.pdf, accessed August 20, 2013.

Gulf of Mexico Fishery Management Council. 2002. "Environmental Sites of Special Interest: Gulf of Mexico Marine Protected Areas Established by the Council, 1979–2002." http://www.gulfcouncil.org/Beta/GMFMCWeb/Aquaculture/Environmental%20Sites%20of%20Special%20Interest.doc, accessed October 3, 2013.

Hildebrand, Henry. 1963. "Discovery of the Area of Nesting of the Marine Turtle 'lora,' *Lepidochelys kempii* (Garman), in the West Coast of the Gulf of Mexico." *Ciencia* 22 (4): 105–12.

———. 2000. Oral history interview conducted on February 21, in Flower Bluff, Texas. Texas Legacy Project, Conservation History Association of Texas.

International Institute for Species Exploration. 2011. "State of Observed Species." International Institute for Species Exploration. Arizona State University. Tempe, Arizona.

International Union for Conservation of Nature. 1973. Convention on International Trade in Endangered Species of the Wild Fauna and Flora. Plenipotentiary Conference to Conclude an International Convention on Trade in Certain Species of Wildlife. Washington, DC, February 12–March 2, 1973. *IUCN Bulletin* 4 (3) (Special Supplement): 12 pp.

International Union for Conservation of Nature. 2009. Extinction Crisis Continues Apace. http://www.iucn.org/?4143/Extinction-crisis-continues-apace, accessed June 5, 2015.

Jernelov, Arne, and Olof Linden. 1981. "Ixtoc I: A Case Study of the World's Largest Oil Spill." *Ambio* 10 (6) (The Caribbean): 299–306.

Jones, Taylor. 2013. Endangered species advocate, WildEarth Guardians. Personal communication, August.

Jones, W. Dwayne. 1999. "Padre Island National Seashore: An Administrative History, Chapter 8: Natural Resource Issues." http://www.nps.gov/history/history/online_books/pais/adhi8.htm, accessed August 16, 2013.

Karp, William, Lisa Desfosse, and Samantha Brooke. 2011. "U.S. National Bycatch Report." National Marine Fisheries Service. National Oceanic and Atmospheric Administration.

Kemp's Ridley Sea Turtle Nesting. 2007. 1947 Kemp's Ridley Sea Turtle Nesting. http://www.youtube.com/watch?v=W4u3GL9SyyM, accessed August 16, 2013.

Kolbert, Elizabeth. 2014. *The Sixth Extinction: An Unnatural History*. New York: Henry Holt.

Lewison, Rebecca, Larry Crowder, and Donna Shaver. 2003. "The Impact of

Turtle Excluder Devices and Fisheries Closures on Loggerhead and Kemp's Ridley Strandings in the Western Gulf of Mexico." *Conservation Biology* 17: 1089–97.

Manzella, Sharon, Charles Caillouet, and Clark Fontaine. 1988. "Kemp's Ridley, *Lepidochelys kempii*, Sea Turtle Head Start Tag Recoveries: Distribution, Habitat and Method of Recovery." *Marine Fisheries Review* 50 (3): 24–32.

Marine Turtle Newsletter. 1981. "Kemp's Ridley: The 1980 Season at Rancho Nuevo." *Marine Turtle Newsletter* 17 (7). http://www.seaturtle.org/mtn/ archives/mtn17/mtn17p7.shtml, accessed October 18, 2013.

Marquez, Rene. 1994. "Synopsis of Biological Data on the Kemp's Ridley Turtle, *Lepidochelys kempii* (Garman, 1880)." Southeast Fisheries Science Center, National Marine Fisheries Service, National Oceanic and Atmospheric Administration. Miami, Florida. January.

———. 1999. "Status and Distribution of the Kemp's Ridley Turtle, *Lepidochelys kempii*, in the Wider Caribbean Region." Proceedings of the Regional Meeting. "Marine Turtle Conservation in the Wider Caribbean Region: A Dialogue for Effective Regional Management," edited by K. L. Eckert and F. A. Abreau Grobois. Santo Domingo, November 16–18, 1999.

National Marine Fisheries Service. 2012. "Draft Environmental Impact Statement to Reduce Incidental Bycatch and Mortality of Sea Turtles in the Southeastern U.S. Shrimp Fisheries." http://www.nmfs.noaa.gov/pr/pdfs/ species/deis_seaturtle_shrimp_ fisheries_interactions.pdf, accessed August 26, 2013.

National Marine Fisheries Service and US Fish and Wildlife Service. 2007. "Kemp's Ridley Sea Turtle, 5-Year Review: Summary and Evaluation." National Marine Fisheries Service, Office of Protected Resources and US Fish and Wildlife Service. August.

National Marine Fisheries Service, US Fish and Wildlife Service, and SEMARNAT. 2011. "Bi-National Recovery Plan for the Kemp's Ridley Sea Turtle, Second Revision." National Marine Fisheries Service. Silver Spring, Maryland.

National Oceanic and Atmospheric Administration. 2013a. "Sea Turtles and the Gulf of Mexico Oil Spill: Turtles Documented by Species, through February 15, 2011." http:// www.nmfs.noaa.gov/pr/health/oilspill/ turtles.htm, accessed August 27, 2013.

———. 2013b. "Water Temperature Table of all Coastal Regions." http://www .nodc.noaa.gov/dsdt/cwtg/all_meanT .html, accessed October 10, 2013.

———. 2015. Raw Incident News, Raw Incident Data. Table. http://incident news.noaa.gov/raw/incidents.csv, accessed March 25, 2015.

National Park Service. 2013. "Kemp's Ridley Sea Turtle Nesting on Padre Island National Seashore." http:// www.nps.gov/media/photo/gallery .htm?tagID=15446, accessed November 19, 2013.

Northern Gulf Institute. 2008. Shrimp Essential Fish Habitat, Gulf of Mexico Fisheries Data. http://www.northern gulfinstitute.org/edac/gulfOfMexico Data/fisheries/Essential_Fish_Habitat/ SHP/GOM_EFH_Shrimp.zip, accessed September.

Peña, Luis Jaime. 2013 and 2015. Curator of Conservation Programs, Gladys

Porter Zoo. Personal communications, October 2013 and March 2015.

Perez-Treviño, Emma. 2015. "Activity Picks Up in SpaceX's Boca Chica Area." *The Monitor*. May 11.

Plotkin, Pamela, ed. 2007. *Biology and Conservation of Ridley Sea Turtles*. Baltimore: Johns Hopkins University Press.

Plotkin, Pamela, and Anthony Amos. 1989. "Effects of Anthropogenic Debris on Sea Turtles in the Northwestern Gulf of Mexico." Proceedings of the Second International Conference on Marine Debris, April 2–7, 1989, Honolulu, Hawai'i. US Department of Commerce, NOAA Technical Memo NOAA-NMFS-SWFSC-154.

Pritchard, P. C. H., and Rene Marquez. 1973. "Kemp's Ridley Turtle or Atlantic Ridley: *Lepidochelys kempii*." IUCN Monograph No. 2: Marine Turtle Series. International Union for Conservation of Nature and Natural Resources. Morges, Switzerland. http:// data.iucn.org/dbtw-wpd/edocs/Mono-002.pdf, accessed August 20, 2013.

Renaud, Maurice, Gregg Gitschlag, Edward Klima, Arvind Shah, James Nance, Charles Caillouet, Zoula Zein-Eldin, Dennis Koi, and Frank Patella. 1990. "Evaluation of the Impacts of Turtle Excluder Devices (TEDs) on Shrimp Catch Rates in the Gulf of Mexico and South Atlantic, March 1988 through July 1989." NOA Technical Memorandum NMFS-SEFC-254. May. http://www.st.nmfs .noaa.gov/tm/sefc/sefc254.pdf, accessed August 18, 2013.

Safina, Carl, and Bryan Wallace. 2010. Solving the "Ridley Riddle." SWOT Report. http://seaturtlestatus.org/sites/

swot/files/SWOT5_p26_Ridleys.pdf, accessed August 25, 2013.

Sea Turtle Stranding and Salvage Network. 2013. Online Stranding Reports. http://www.sefsc.noaa.gov/STSSN/ STSSNReportDriver.jsp, accessed October 18, 2013.

Servis, Jennifer, Gretchen Lovewell, and Tony Tucker. 2013. "Diet Analysis of Stranded Kemp's Ridley Sea Turtles." https://dspace.mote.org/dspace/bit stream/2075/3039/1/Servis.pdf.

Sharpe, Rebecca. 1988. "Swimming to Oblivion." *Texas Monthly*, June.

Shaver, Donna. 1990. "Kemp's Ridley Project at Padre Island Enters a New Phase." *Park Science* 10 (1).

———. 1996. "Head-Started Kemp's Ridley Turtles Nest in Texas." *Marine Turtle Newsletter* 74: 5–7. www.seaturtle .org/mtn/archives/mtn74/mtn74p5 .shtml, accessed November 24, 2013.

———. 2001. "Crossing Boundaries to Increase Nesting by Kemp's Ridley Sea Turtles at Padre Island National Seashore." Parks and on Public Lands, 2001 GWS Biennial Conference.

———. 2010–15. Chief of Sea Turtle Science and Recovery, Padre Island National Seashore, US National Park Service. Personal communications, March 2010–2015.

Shaver, Donna, and Charles Caillouet. 1998. "More Kemp's Ridley Turtles Return to South Texas to Nest." *Marine Turtle Newsletter* 82: 1–5. http://www .seaturtle.org/mtn/archives/mtn82/ mtn82p1b.shtml, accessed October 18, 2013.

Shaver, Donna, and Cynthia Rubio. 2007. "Post-Nesting Movement of Wild and Head-Started Kemp's Ridley Sea Turtles *Lepidochelys kempii* in the Gulf of Mexico." Inter-Research Symposium, "Satellite Tracking for the Conservation of Migratory Vertebrates," Myrtle Beach, South Carolina. February.

South Atlantic Fishery Management Council. 2008. Shrimp EFH, Essential Fish Habitat, SAFMC GIS data. http:// ocean.floridamarine.org/efh_coral/zip/ shrimp_efh.zip, accessed October 1, 2013.

Stacy, N. I., C. J. Innis, and J. A. Hernandez. 2013. "Development and Evaluation of Three Mortality Prediction Indices for Cold-Stunned Kemp's Ridley Sea Turtles." *Conservation Physiology* (1).

Sweat, Donald. 1968. "Capture of a Tagged Ridley Turtle." *Quarterly Journal of the Florida Academy of Sciences* 31 (1): 47–48.

Turtle Expert Working Group. 1998. "An Assessment of the Kemp's Ridley (*Lepidochelys kempii*) and Loggerhead (*Caretta caretta*) Sea Turtle Populations in the Western North Atlantic." US Department of Commerce, National Oceanic and Atmospheric Administration, National Marine Fisheries Service, Southeast Fisheries Science Center. March. Miami, Florida.

Vie, Jean-Christophe, Craig Hilton-Taylor, and Simon Stuart, eds. 2009. "Wildlife in a Changing World: An Analysis of the 2008 IUCN Red List of Threatened Species." IUCN. Gland, Switzerland. http://data.iucn.org/dbtw-wpd/edocs/ rl-2009-001.pdf, accessed August 27, 2013.

Wallace, B. P., C. Y. Kot, A. D. DiMatteo, T. Lee, L. B. Crowder, and R. L. Lewison. 2013. "Impacts of Fisheries Bycatch on Marine Turtle Populations Worldwide: Toward Conservation and Research Priorities." *Ecosphere* 4 (3): 40. http:// dx.doi.org/10.1890/ES12–00388.1.

Weisman, David. 2000. Henry Hildebrand, February 21, Flower Bluff, Texas. Photograph. Digital image. Texas Legacy Project, Conservation History Association of Texas.

Wilcove, David. 1994. *The Condor's Shadow*. New York: W. H. Freeman.

WildEarth Guardians. 2010. Petition to Designate Critical Habitat for the Kemp's Ridley Sea Turtle (*Lepidochelys kempii*). Submitted to the US Secretary of the Interior. Santa Fe, New Mexico. February 17, 2010. http://www.nmfs .noaa.gov/pr/pdfs/petitions/kemps ridley_critical habitat_feb2010.pdf, accessed August 20, 2013.

Williams, Jo. 2013. Research Fishery Biologist, National Oceanic and Atmospheric Agency Fisheries. Personal communication, September.

Williams, Phil. 1993. NMFS to Concentrate on Measuring Survivorship, Fecundity of Head-Started Kemp's Ridleys in the Wild." *Marine Turtle Newsletter* 63 (3–4). http://www.seaturtle.org/mtn/archives/ mtn63/mtn63p3.shtml, accessed October 18, 2013.

Witherington, Blair. 2006. *Sea Turtles: An Extraordinary Natural History of Some Uncommon Turtles*. St. Paul, MN: Voyageur Press.

Woody, Jack. 1990. "Guest Editorial: Is 'Headstarting' a Reasonable Conservation Measure? On the Surface, Yes; In Reality, No." *Marine Turtle Newsletter* 50: 8–11. www.seaturtle.org/ mtn/archives/mtn50/mtn50p8.shtml, accessed November 24, 2013.

Air

This section of the atlas looks at those issues and parts of our landscape that affect our atmosphere. As the garage for millions of cars, and the home for major petrochemical industries and utility complexes, the Lone Star State has a challenge in protecting the air Texans breathe. Since these same vehicles and facilities emit copious amounts of CO_2, carbon black, and methane, Texas also needs to confront how its residents' lifestyles and economy risk warming and destabilizing the climate.

Sources

Carman, Neil. 2015. Clean Air Director, Sierra Club, Lone Star Chapter. Personal communication, May.

Texas Commission on Environmental Quality. 2012. Nonattainment Areas. www.tceq.texas.gov/assets/ public/permitting/air/factsheets/factsheets-psd-na-maparea.pdf, accessed May 8, 2015.

US Census. 2014. Annual Estimates of the Resident Population: April 1, 2010, to July 1, 2013. http:// factfinder2.census.gov/faces/tableservices/jsf/pages/productview.xhtml?src=bkmk, accessed August 3, 2014.

US Environmental Protection Agency (EPA). 2015. Green Book, Downloads: GIS: Shapefiles Containing all Designated Nonattainment Areas (compressed, various files, last updated January 30, 2015). US Environmental Protection Agency. http://www.epa.gov/airquality/greenbook/gis_download.html, accessed May 8, 2015.

Williamson, Walker. 2015. SIP Team Leader, Air Quality, Texas Commission on Environmental Quality. Personal communication, May.

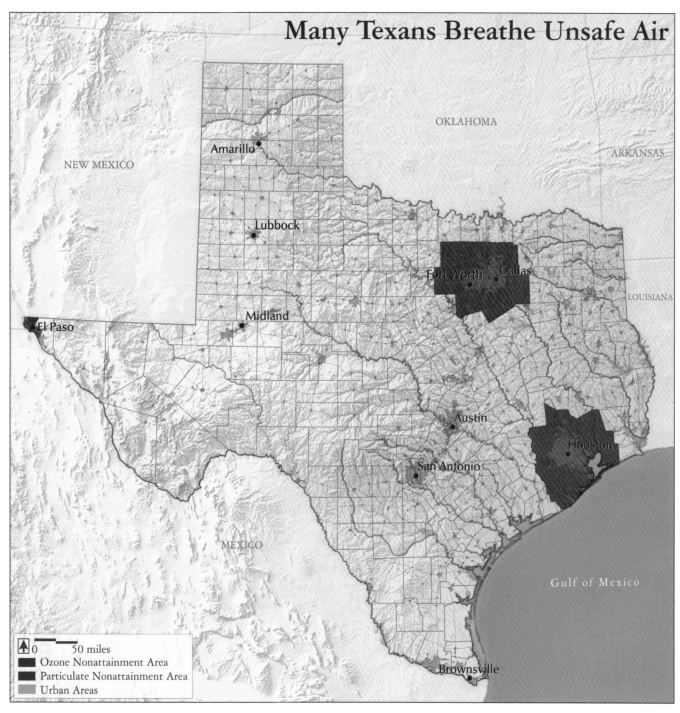

Many Texans Breathe Unsafe Air

This map shows that large parts of Texas fail to meet federal air quality rules. The state's two largest metropolitan areas, Houston and Dallas–Fort Worth, break eight-hour ground-level ozone standards, while El Paso fails to comply with particulate matter standards, and parts of Frisco violate lead requirements. Close to fourteen million Texans live in areas that violate air quality standards. In more stark terms, over one-half of the state's population breathes air that the US government considers unsafe (US Census Bureau 2014; TCEQ 2012; US EPA 2015; Williamson 2015).

Lead, Smeltertown, and the Family Car

"There could be no more efficient way of spreading lead across the US countryside than to put it in fuel, pump it into automobile tanks, and burn it in car engines that move around our cities and towns."

— John A. S. Adams,
Rice University

Lead is a very useful metal, but also a long-lasting and subtle poison widely spread in twentieth-century America. The removal of lead from gasoline, and from air, soil, and blood, is considered one of the great public health accomplishments, but it was neither quick nor easy (Needleman 1998). Eliminating its major ambient source, leaded gasoline, from the American

market took nearly fifty years. An important tipping point in the fight against leaded gas can be traced to a tragedy that struck a settlement of 250 Mexican American families in Smeltertown, near El Paso, Texas.

Knocking

The story begins over ninety years ago with an engineering problem. Gasoline can auto-ignite in high-compression engines, causing a "knocking" sound, damaging exhaust valve seats and cutting engine performance. To fix this, Henry Ford and allied researchers recommended using alcohol blends and fuels refined from corn, sugarcane, and other crops. These alcohol-based

fuels did not generate a knock, and furthermore, they were drawn from a reliable, renewable source. As Ford said, "the fuel of the future is going to come from fruit like that sumac out by the road, or from apples, weeds, sawdust—almost anything. There is fuel in every bit of vegetable matter that can be fermented. There's enough alcohol in one year's yield of an acre of potatoes to drive the machinery necessary to cultivate the fields for a hundred years" ("Ford Predicts" 1925).

Leaded Gasoline

However, there was concern that the burgeoning fleet of US vehicles would quickly outrun the amount of alcohol that could be produced with known technology from American farm fields. In 1921, Thomas Midgley and researchers at General Motors found a substitute. They learned that lead compounds, particularly tetraethyl lead, could work as an antiknock additive that increased gasoline's octane level and allowed use of more powerful, high-compression engines. And lead could do all this at a cheap price, just a penny a gallon. In 1923, GM, DuPont, and Standard Oil created the Ethyl Corporation to introduce leaded gasoline to the market as a bridge fuel until alcohol's supply shortages and distillation problems could be resolved (Kovarik 1998).

Leaded gasoline was the dominant fuel at US service stations for over fifty years (Seigle 2013).

With time, leaded gasoline became the fuel of choice for the US market, in large part because it historically cost roughly two-thirds the price of alcohol, but also because of shrewd lobbying and political wrangling. As the American auto fleet grew, and the US road network expanded, US citizens drove more and more, and burned more and more of the leaded gasoline. By 1970, Americans had 89.2 million cars and were traveling 916 billion miles and burning 67.8 billion gallons of fuel each year. Most of that fuel had been treated with lead, resulting in the release of 171,961 tons of lead into the atmosphere each year, 78 percent of the total lead emissions in the nation (US EPA 2000). In 1970, an estimated 11,500 tons of lead were discharged from Texas vehicles alone; the cumulative load over decades of emissions was clearly much higher.

"Hence gout and stone afflict
    the human race;
Hence lazy jaundice with her
    saffron face;
Palsy, with shaking head and
    tott'ring knees.
And bloated dropsy, the staunch
    sot's disease;
Consumption, pale, with keen but
    hollow eye,
And sharpened feature, shew'd
    that death was nigh.
The feeble offspring curse their
    crazy sires,
And, tainted from his birth, the
    youth expires."

    —Description of lead poisoning
    from the Roman era. Translated by
    Humelbergius Secundus, 1829

Here we see an early view of the ASARCO smelter, the Smeltertown settlement, and a burro, circa 1899 (Aultman 1910).

Lead in History

It was known from Greek and Roman times that lead was harmful. US medical authorities had first diagnosed childhood lead poisoning as early as 1887. Lead's particular role in the twentieth-century automobile industry raised serious early concerns as well. Thomas Midgley, the GM developer of leaded fuel, suffered from lead poisoning in 1923, and the next year, there were seventeen deaths and over thirty hospitalizations among workers at Standard Oil and DuPont facilities where leaded gasoline was being made. A DuPont refinery in Deepwater, New Jersey, became known as the "House of Butterflies" because hallucinating workers there felt driven to brush off the imaginary insects. Journalists dubbed leaded gasoline "loony gas" (Skloot 2001). A two-year ban on leaded gasoline and a Public Health Service inquiry ensued, but the brief study determined that diluted use of lead in gasoline posed no immediate threat to the wider public. Production resumed in 1926 (Kovarik 1998). Questionable research, industry lobbying, and the distractions of the Great Depression and World War II kept lead in gasoline (as well as paint, plumbing, and other products) for decades to come (Kovarik 2005; Reich 1992).

Lead and ASARCO

While health concerns about lead exposure persisted, it was not until the early 1970s that lead got strong

Dust fallout's lead content decreased with greater distance from the ASARCO smelter. Readings were taken at eleven locations from October 1970 through July 1971, measured in milligrams/square meter/month, and reported here as ten-month mean values. The highest value (a ten-month mean of 204 milligrams lead per square meter per month) was recorded at the smelter, with lower readings found in areas shielded by the mountains to the northeast of ASARCO (Landrigan et al. 1975; Rosenblum, Shoults, and Candelaria 1976).

the course of the litigation, the El Paso City-County Health Department discovered serious lead contamination in local children's bloodstreams, and in soils near the plant. The department also found that the smelter had emitted 1,012 metric tons of lead from 1969 through 1971 and was the likely source of the lead in local soils (Rosenblum, Shoults, and Candelaria 1976).

"Lead poisoning is flowing through the blood of our city."

—Bert Williams, mayor of El Paso, 1972 (Perales 2010)

With this new information, the focus of the ASARCO plaintiffs switched to hone in on lead pollution. The suit ultimately resulted in a 1972 settlement, with the company providing improved emission controls, medical payments, and resettlement. The parties agreed that ASARCO would provide $750,000 in new emission control equipment as well as medical payments for 134 affected children, including painful chelation treatments for thirty-five youngsters. A subsequent injunction in 1975 forced ASARCO to invest $120 million in modernizing the smelter and reducing emissions, resulting in a two-thirds drop in air pollution from pre-1970 levels. In 1990, the plant was revamped again, at a cost of $81 million, resulting in still higher pollution capture, including 98 percent or more of sulfur emissions (Shapleigh 2008; Valdez 2013).

regulatory attention (Bridbord and Hanson 2009). The newfound focus on lead was crystallized in a health problem that arose near the ASARCO smelter in El Paso, Texas. First founded in 1887, ASARCO employed as many as 1,500 workers in refining zinc, copper, lead, and other minerals mined in Mexico and the American Southwest. While ASARCO jobs and company dining halls, schools, hospitals, and shops in the nearby worker community of Smeltertown were wel-

comed, there was also long-brewing resentment of the smoke that streamed from the smelter's stacks.

Complaints about dust and sulfur dioxide from the smelter prompted the city of El Paso to file a $1 million lawsuit in April 1970 against ASARCO, joined later by the state of Texas, charging violations of the Texas Clean Air Act (*City of El Paso v. American Smelting and Refining Co.*, Civil No. 70-1701 (41st District Court, El Paso County, filed April 17, 1970)). During

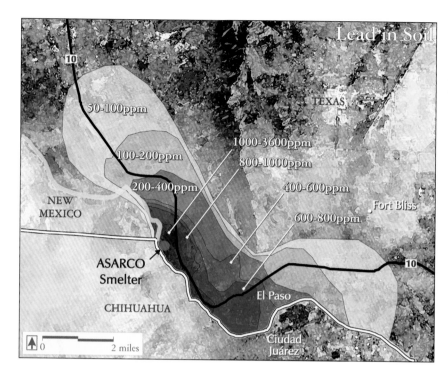

Lead was found in surface soil near the ASARCO smelter. Readings were taken at 102 locations from March 1972 through June 1973, measured in parts per million. Soil lead levels declined with distance from the smelter and in the lands blocked by mountains to the northeast (Landrigan et al. 1975; Rosenblum, Shoults, and Candelaria 1976).

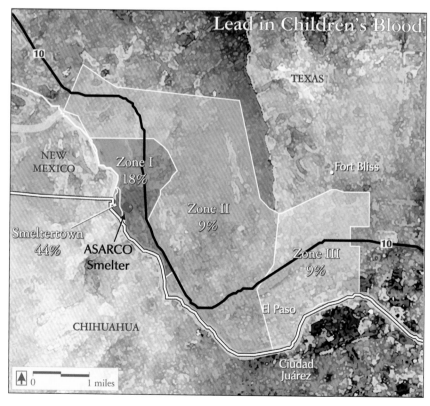

Lead found in blood tests declined with the distance from the ASARCO smelter. In August 1972, 44 percent of Smeltertown's young people, from one to nineteen years of age, had lead concentrations of 40–59 micrograms per 100 milliliters. In zone I, outside of Smeltertown, the percentage fell to 18 percent; while in zones II and III, the proportion dropped still more, to 9 percent. While 40 micrograms was considered a level of concern in 1970, the Centers for Disease Control hazard threshold has dropped dramatically as the agency's understanding of lead's severe health impact has grown. The threshold was 100 to 120 micrograms in 1943, fell to 30 by 1978, and now rests at 5 (Centers for Disease Control and Prevention 2013; Landrigan et al. 1975; Marshall 1984; Rosenblum, Shoults, and Candelaria 1976).

Smeltertown

While the environmental safety of the smelter improved, the consequences for the tight community of Smeltertown were severe. Smeltertown was a company town. The residents of Smeltertown had built their own homes and had lived there for three or more generations, but they only rented the ground that the houses were built on. After the lead dispute, neighbors tried to buy the underlying land from ASARCO, but the local housing agency condemned the town as unsafe for habitation. In January 1973, ASARCO issued eviction notices for the families in Smeltertown, a small settlement was paid, and their buildings were bulldozed. Where the adobe houses, pool halls, and barber shops had once stood, loads of polluted soil were excavated and trucked away, and Smeltertown was abandoned (Perales 2010; Romero 1998).

This photograph provides a 1972 view of the ASARCO smelter and the cemetery for Smeltertown, a part of El Paso, Texas. By early 1973, the cemetery was most all that remained after eviction and razing of the community (Lyons 1972).

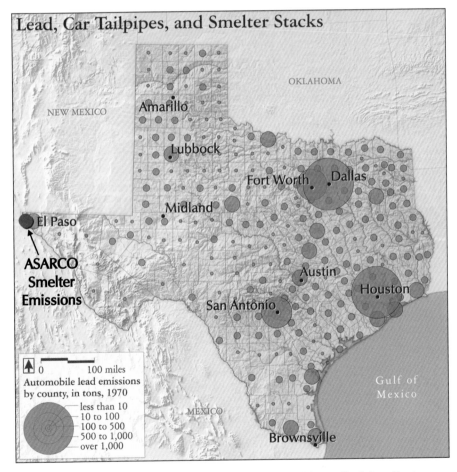

This map shows the estimated lead emissions in Texas from automobile use of leaded gasoline in 1970. Calculations are based on population census figures, national fuel/capita use data, and a 2.4 grams/gallon lead additive rate. The family sedan's exhaust pipe would seem far less imposing than the ASARCO smelter stack. However, the 11,500 tons of lead emitted annually by Texas vehicles of that era dwarfed the roughly 300 tons per year discharged then by ASARCO in El Paso (Davis, Diegel, and Boundy 2011; Texas State Library and Archives 2011; Alternative Fuels Data Center 2013.

Lead, Children, and Health

However, Smeltertown survived in another, and very important, way—in the public health research and national legislation that followed the case. In 1970, young Centers for Disease Control (CDC) doctors and epidemiologists, including Julian Chisolm, George Gelbach, and Philip Landrigan, had come to El Paso and soon discovered that 60 percent of the children living within one mile of the smelter had elevated blood lead levels (Landrigan et al. 1975). While lead had long been known to be dangerous at high concentrations, causing convulsions and death, the Smeltertown case showed that even relatively low childhood exposure to lead dust had significant impacts on blood concentrations, and in turn, IQ, hyperactivity, and lifetime learning difficulties (Bridbord and Hanson 2009).

As sad as the situation in El Paso was, the case helped scientists connect the dots between lead emissions, dispersion, dust fallout, blood contamination, and long-term health damage. The CDC's early investigations and concerns were expanded by later research on airborne sources. Scientists conducted lead studies at other smelters, including ones in Bartlesville, Oklahoma; Helena, Montana; Kellogg, Idaho; Palmerton, Pennsylvania, and elsewhere. They also tested emission impacts from vehicles on nearby traffic policemen, parking garage attendants, and highway neighbors (Mushak 2011). In 2000, research connecting lead and violence came out, showing a disturbing relationship between lead exposure among children and violent crime, including rapes, robberies, aggravated assaults, and murders that they perpetrated years later (Nevin 2000).

Lead Regulation

Because of the early health concerns and research, later confirmed and strengthened, standards to phase out the use of lead in gasoline were first enacted in 1973 (38 Federal Register 33734 (December 6, 1973)). The rules were issued under the Clean Air Act and called for a gradual decline

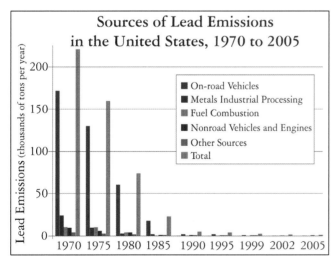

National trends in lead emissions, for all sectors, dropped remarkably from 1970 through 2005. The trend shows a 99 percent decline from a total release of more than 220,000 tons to less than 1,300 tons per year (US EPA 2013b).

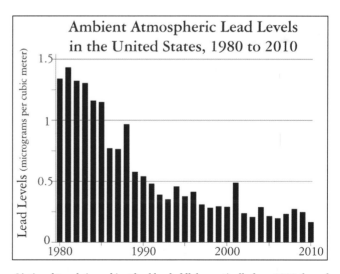

National trends in ambient lead levels fell dramatically from 1980 through 2010. The data are drawn from sampling at thirty-one sites throughout the United States, and summarized as annual maximum three-month averages. The data are presented here in terms of micrograms per cubic meter (US EPA 2013a).

in lead content from four grams per gallon to one-half of a gram per gallon by 1985, and to one-tenth of a gram by 1986. Total lead emissions from vehicles followed suit, dropping from more than 170,000 tons of lead per year in 1973 to less than 2,000 tons of lead in 1995. In 1995, leaded fuel amounted to only 0.6 percent of total gasoline sales in the United States, and its use was banned in all on-road vehicles (US EPA 1996). The restrictions on lead in fuel were followed by other measures, including the 1978 banning of lead-based paint by the Consumer Product Safety Commission, the 1986 ban on lead in plumbing, and a 1995 ban on lead solder in food cans (Lead-Based Paint Poisoning Prevention Act of 1971, P.L. 93-151. 42 U.S.C. 63, Section 4831; Lead Contamination Control Act of 1988, P.L. 100-572, 42 U.S.C. Part F, Section 300; Residential Lead-Based Paint Hazard Reduction Act of 1992, P.L. 102-550. 42 U.S.C. Section 4851; Lead-Safe Housing Rule of 1999, 24 CFR Part 35; Standards for Hazardous Levels of Lead in Paint, Dust and Soil, Toxic Substances Control Act, P.L. 94-469, 15 U.S.C. 2683).

Lead Declines

With these regulatory efforts, lead emissions, ambient lead levels, and blood concentrations all fell sharply. Total US lead emissions dropped by 98 percent from 1970 to 1998 (US EPA 2000). Lead concentrations in the air, measured at 138 sites around the country, dropped by 67 percent from 1975 to 1981 (US EPA 1985). These emission and ambient declines played out in a dramatic 77 percent fall in lead levels in American children from 1977 to 1991 (Pirkle et al. 1994).

Much progress has been made in controlling lead exposure, but legacies from the past and challenges in the future remain. The long history of US lead emissions from gasoline combustion released some seven million tons of lead into the environment, much of it now mixed in the nation's soil (Iskandar and Kirkham 2001). Part of the lead burden is also carried in our bodies. A geochemist, Clair Patterson, found that modern bodies carry 700 to 1,170 times more lead than the 1,600-year-old corpses of Peruvian Indians (Ericson, Shirahata, and Patterson 1979).

Still, step by step and sector by sector, lead is being reduced. The remaining leaded gasoline sold in the United States is used in off-road vehicles, racing cars, farm equipment, marine engines, and, primarily, 167,000 piston-driven aircraft. Friends of the Earth filed a petition in 2006 requesting that the EPA regulate aviation gas lead emissions. The EPA denied the request in 2012, but the Federal Aviation Administration is nevertheless planning to find a substitute for leaded avgas by 2018 (Kessler 2013; US EPA 2012; US FAA 2012). And, back in El Paso, the ASARCO smelter was mothballed in 1999, and its smokestacks were demolished on April 13, 2013. The city envisions the site's redevelopment with sports facilities and residential buildings (Roberts 2012). A chapter of pollution and tragedy will be paved over, but with hope, will still be remembered for its lessons and cautions.

Sources

Adams, John A. S. 1982. Professor of Geochemistry, Rice University. Personal communication, July.

Alternative Fuels Data Center. 2013. US Light-Duty Fuel Consumption and Vehicle Miles Traveled. http://www .afdc.energy.gov/data/tab/all/data_ set/10307, accessed March 23, 2013.

Aultman, Otis A. 1910. View of ASARCO smelter. El Paso Public Library, Aultman Collection.

Bridbord, Kenneth, and David Hanson. 2009. "A Personal Perspective on the Initial Federal Health-Based Regulation to Remove Lead from Gasoline." *Environmental Health Perspectives* 117 (8).

Centers for Disease Control and Prevention. 2013. Lead. http://www .cdc.gov/nceh/lead/, accessed April 2, 2013.

City of El Paso v. American Smelting and Refining Company, et al., Cause No. 70-1701, Original Petition (El Paso County, Texas, 41st District Court, April 24, 1970).

Clean Air Act. 1970. 84 Stat. 1676. P.L. 91-604. 42 U.S.C. 7401, 7545.

Davis, Stacy, Susan Diegel, and Robert Boundy. 2011. Transportation Energy Data Book, Edition 30. Table 4.1. US Department of Energy, Office of Energy Efficiency and Renewable Energy, Vehicle Technologies Program,

June 2011. http://info.ornl.gov/sites/publications/files/Pub31202.pdf, accessed March 18, 2013.

Ericson, J. E., H. Shirahata, and C. C. Patterson. 1979. "Skeletal Concentrations of Lead in Ancient Peruvians." *New England Journal of Medicine* 300 (17): 946–51.

"Ford Predicts." 1925. "Ford Predicts Fuel from Vegetation." *New York Times*, September 20.

Humelbergius Secundus, Dick. 1829. *Apician Morsels; or, Tales of the Table, Kitchen, and Larder*. London: Whittaker, Treacher.

Iskandar, I. K., and M. B. Kirkham, eds. 2001. *Trace Elements in Soil: Bioavailability, Flux, and Transfer*. Boca Raton, FL: Lewis; CRC Press, 262.

Kessler, Rebecca. 2013. "Sunset for Leaded Aviation Gasoline?" *Environmental Health Perspectives* 121 (2): A54–A57

Kovarik, Bill. 1998. "Henry Ford, Charles Kettering, and the Fuel of the Future." *Automotive History Review* 32 (Spring): 7–27.

Kovarik, William. 2005. "Ethyl-Leaded Gasoline: How a Classic Occupational Disease Became an International Public Health Disaster." *International Journal of Occupational Environmental Health* 11 (4): 384–97.

Landrigan, P. J., S. H. Gelhlbach, B. F. Rosenblum, J. M. Shoults, R. M. Candelaria, W. F. Barthel, J. A. Lidle, A. L. Smrek, N. W. Staehling, and J. F. Sanders. 1975. "Epidemic Lead Absorption Near an Ore Smelter: The Role of Particulate Lead." *New England Journal of Medicine* 292 (3): 123–29.

Lyons, Danny. 972. ASARCO copper smelter, Smeltertown, El Paso, Texas.

Photograph. Digital image. Documerica Project. US Environmental Protection Agency. National Archives, Agency-Assigned Identifier: 048/50/002870, NAIL Control Number: NWDNS-412-DA-2870. Record Group 412. https://flic.kr/p/6VAqWd or http://arcweb.archives.gov/arc/action/ExternalIdSearch?id=545363, accessed April 24, 2013.

Marshall, E. 1984. "Senate Considers Lead Gasoline Ban." *Science* 225 (4657): 34–35.

Mushak, Paul. 2011. *Lead and Public Health: Science, Risk and Regulation*. Boston: Elsevier.

Needleman, H. L. 1998. "Childhood Lead Poisoning: The Promise and Abandonment of Primary Prevention." *American Journal of Public Health* 88 (12): 1871–77.

Nevin, Rick. 1999. "How Lead Exposure Relates to Temporal Changes in IQ, Violent Crime, and Unwed Pregnancy." *Environmental Research* 83 (1): 1–22.

Perales, Monica. 2010. *Smeltertown: Making and Remembering a Southwest Border Community*. Chapel Hill: University of North Carolina Press.

Pirkle, James, et al. 1994. "The Decline in Blood Lead Levels in the United States." *Journal of the American Medical Association* 272 (4): 284–91.

Reich, Peter. 1992. "The Hour of Lead." Environmental Defense Fund. http://m.edf.org/sites/default/files/the-hour-of-lead.pdf, accessed April 3, 2013.

Roberts, Chris. 2012. "Asarco Smokestacks Will Be Demolished." *El Paso Times*, December 5.

Romero, Mary. 1984. "The Death of Smeltertown: A Case Study of Lead Poisoning in a Chicano Community." In *The Chicano Struggles: Analyses of Past and Present Efforts*, edited by John García, Juan García, and Teresa Cordova, 26–41. Binghamton, NY: Bilingual Press.

Rosenblum, B. F., J. M. Shoults, and R. Candelaria. 1976. "Lead Health Hazards from Smelter Emissions." *Texas Medicine* 72: 44–56.

Seigle, Cindy. 2013. For Use as a Motor Fuel Only. Flickr, Creative Commons. www.flickr.com/photos/cindy47452/58942034/sizes/m/in/photostream, accessed April 24, 2013.

Shapleigh, Elliot. 2008. ASARCO in El Paso. Texas State Senate. September.

Skloot, Rebecca. 2001. "House of Butterflies." *Pittmed*. University of Pittsburgh School of Medicine. January.

Texas State Library and Archives. 2011. Texas County Population Estimates, 1971–74. https://www.tsl.state.tx.us/ref/abouttx/popcnty71–74.html, accessed March 19, 2013.

US Environmental Protection Agency (EPA). 1985. National Air Quality and Emissions Trends Report, 1983. US Environmental Protection Agency, April.

———. 1996. EPA Takes Final Step in Phaseout of Leaded Gasoline. January 29. http://www.epa.gov/oms/regs/fuels/additive/lead/pr-lead.txt, accessed March 17, 2013.

———. 2000. National Air Pollutant Emission Trends, 1900–1998. Table ES-4. US Environmental Protection Agency, Office of Air Quality. EPA-454/R-00-002, March.

———. 2012. EPA Response Letter and Memorandum to the 2006 Petition from Friends of the Earth Regarding Lead Emissions from Piston-Engine Aircraft. July 18. http://www.epa

.gov/otaq/regs/nonroad/aviation/ltr-response-av-ld-petition.pdf, accessed March 17, 2013.

———. 2013a. National Trends in Lead Levels. http://www.epa.gov/airtrends/lead.html ; http://www.epa.gov/cgi-bin/broker?_service=data&_program=dataprog.aqplot_data_2010.sas&parm=12128&stat=rqmax&styea

r=1980&endyear=2010&pre=val&query=csv, accessed April 3, 2013.

———. 2013b. Report on the Environment: Lead Emissions. http://cfpub.epa.gov/eroe/index.cfm?fuseaction=detail.viewInd&lv=list.listbyalpha&r=216603&subtop=341, accessed April 3, 2013.

US Federal Aviation Administration (FAA). 2012. FAA Creates Fuels Program Office to Facilitate General Aviation Transition to Unleaded Avgas. June 27. http://www.faa.gov/about/initiatives/avgas/, accessed March 17, 2013.

Valdez, Diana. 2013. "Doomed Smokestacks Symbolize ASARCO's Legacy." *El Paso Times*, April 12.

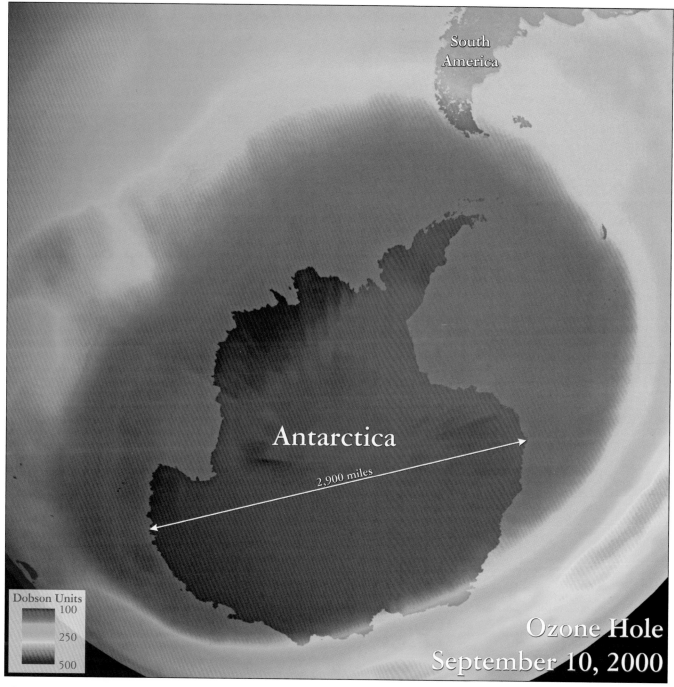

Dobson Units
100
250
500

South
America

Antarctica

2,900 miles

Ozone Hole
September 10, 2000

This is a color-adjusted image of the stratospheric ozone hole (indicated by lower Dobson Units) gauged in September 2000 by the TOMS instrument aboard NASA's Earth Probe satellite. At nearly 29 million square kilometers in size, it is considered one of the largest ozone holes witnessed to date. The hole covers nearly the entirety of Antarctica, a continent over twenty times the size of Texas (British Antarctic Survey 2014; National Aeronautics and Space Administration 2002; US Census Bureau 2012).

The Ozone Hole

Deodorant, hair spray, shaving cream, Reddi-Whip, Silly String, and air conditioning refrigerants have something in common. Forty years ago, each of these products contained chlorofluorocarbons, or CFCs for short. CFCs are nontoxic, nonflammable, noncorrosive, and very useful chemicals, valuable as aerosol propellants, solvents, and refrigerants (Hansen 2013, 28). They are also odd pieces of an international puzzle of science, diplomacy, and environmental protection, with encouraging lessons about bipartisan and international partnership, and innovations in chemistry and market incentives.

CFCs' environmental role came about due to their impact on the stratospheric ozone layer. Floating ten miles above our heads, the Earth's stratosphere holds a thin layer of ozone that screens out some 95–98 percent of the ultraviolet UVB rays that come from the sun. The ozone layer's filtering action protects against skin cancers, cataracts, genetic mutations, and immune system breakdowns; it also guards against diverse damage to crops, plankton, and even cloud cover (Litfin 1994, 163). Millennia ago, this same ozone shielded primordial creatures from solar radiation, allowing life to evolve and emerge from the sea. Yet in modern times, this crucial ozone layer was under threat from the seemingly innocuous CFCs.

International Research

The links between CFCs and ozone were first uncovered in 1970, when James Lovelock, a wide-ranging researcher (and originator of the Gaia hypothesis) wondered about the origins of haze along the isolated western shores of Ireland. Lovelock decided to use CFCs as a tracer to test whether the haze could be due to pollutants that had traveled hundreds, or even thousands, of miles from some faraway urban area. He confirmed that indeed CFCs had arrived on the Irish shores from some distant source, and later found CFCs were ubiquitous, even in remote areas of the south Atlantic (Lovelock 1973).

In 1972, a chemist named Sherwood Rowland learned of Lovelock's discovery of the persistence of CFCs and began to puzzle over their ultimate fate. Mario Molina joined Rowland in his research, and they came to believe that the CFCs

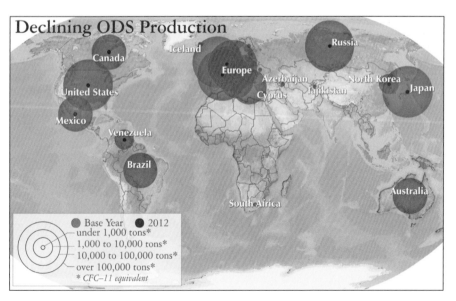

This map displays the precipitous drop (over 99 percent) in global production of ozone over the past two decades. We can also see that ODS production was a global issue, yet dominated by a handful of countries. The decline in ODS manufacture shown here is based on a comparison of production in a "base year" (the larger circles) and 2012 (the smaller dot within each circle). The base-year figure is the average of 1995–97 production for smaller, less-developed "Article 5" nations, and 1986 levels for more industrialized "Non-Article 5" countries (United Nations Environment Programme 2013, Annex 1b and 1c, pp. 17–28).

were ultimately degraded when they floated high in the atmosphere over the course of forty to 150 years. At the great heights of the stratosphere, solar radiation could succeed in slicing off chlorine atoms from the CFC molecules. It was these liberated chlorine atoms that were so lethal to stratospheric ozone. Amazingly, a single chlorine atom could destroy roughly 100,000 ozone molecules (Ahrens 2012, 57).

Molina and Rowland published the results of their initial findings in 1974 and triggered a wider search among many scientists to confirm their estimates and find a solution to protect the ozone layer (Molina and Rowland 1974). In 1985, atmospheric readings showed that ozone concentrations over Antarctica were indeed dropping (Farman, Gardiner, and Shanklin 1985). By 1987, additional measurements by the National Ozone Expedition confirmed Rowland and Molina's idea that the ozone loss was caused by chlorine (Solomon et al. 1986; Solomon et al. 1987). In 1996, satellite data established that CFCs were the chief source of this ozone-depleting chlorine (Russell et al. 1996).

Bipartisan and Global Politics

Throughout this time, regulatory work geared up to shrink CFC emissions, or at least cut back on CFC's more trivial uses. In March 1978, the EPA, using the Toxic Substances Control Act introduced by representative Bob Eckhardt (D-Texas), together with the FDA, banned the use of CFCs as a propellant in spray cans (Toxic Substances Control Act, 15 U.S.C. Sections 2601–2692; Keith 2007, p. 259; Federal Food, Drug and Cosmetic Act, 21 U.S.C. Section 321 et seq.; 43 Federal Register 11301, 11318, March 17, 1978). This single rule had a huge impact, since aerosol propellants made up over half of the total CFC use in the United States (58 Federal Register 4768, January 15, 1993).

Progress on controlling CFCs next moved to the international level. In September 1987, President Reagan and a Republican-controlled Senate, along with the leaders of twenty-two other nations, joined the Montreal Protocol on Substances That Deplete the Ozone Layer (1522 UNTS 3; 26 ILM 1550 1987). The Montreal Protocol committed signatories to lowering production and import of CFCs to half that of 1986 by 1998. In June 1990, the parties to the Montreal Protocol met again, this time in London, and called for complete phaseout of CFCs by 2000 (The London Amendment 1990).

These international agreements were reflected in domestic law here in the United States. In August 1988, the EPA issued rules on ozone-depleting chemicals, cutting their production and import by 50 percent, using an innovative market in tradable allowances (42 U.S.C. Section 7671f; 53

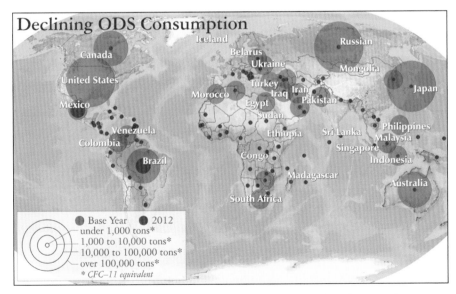

ODS regulators worried about black and gray markets developing as legal producers cut the manufacture of ODS. Fortunately, though, wide consumption declines tracked the production cuts. This map shows the dramatic (typically 99+ percent) declines in global ODS consumption from a base year (described above) through 2012. Base-year consumption is shown by the larger circle, while 2012 consumption is represented by the smaller dot within each circle (United Nations Environment Programme 2013, Annex 1b and 1c, pp. 17–28).

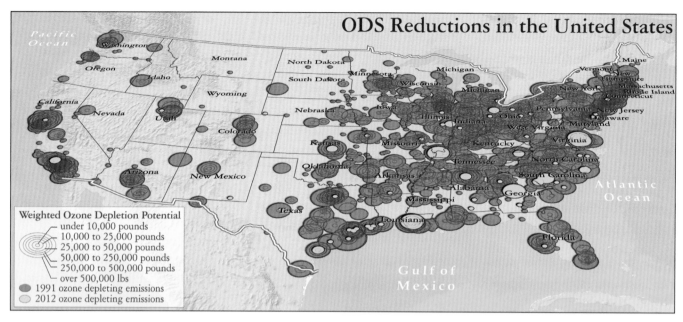

As production and use of ODS fell in the United States, related emissions declined remarkably. This map compares 1991 and 2012 emissions of a variety of chemicals, weighted for their ozone-depletion potential. Releases dropped by 98.4 percent, and the number of affected facilities fell from 4,054 to seventy-six (US EPA 2014a).

Federal Register 30566 (August 12, 1988)). The following year, President Bush, joining with a Democratically led Congress, carried this market-based idea further by levying excise taxes on sales of CFCs and other ozone-depleting chemicals (Omnibus Budget Reconciliation Act of 1989; Internal Revenue Code Sections 4681, 4682). Congress also passed major legislation in 1990, in which the Clean Air Act Amendments put the London Protocol into force, with CFC, halon, and carbon tetrachloride phaseout by 2000 (42 U.S.C. Section 7671).

In the early 1990s, with new and more alarming evidence of ozone deterioration, international diplomats returned to their negotiations with a heightened sense of urgency. A new agreement, the Copenhagen Protocol, came out in November 1992 and accelerated phaseout of CFCs, carbon tetrachloride, and methyl chloroform to January 1996, and halons to January 1994. This latest protocol had a greatly expanded reach, binding 107 nations, far more than the original group of twenty-three that had signed on to the Montreal Protocol just five years before (US Environmental Protection Agency 1993).

Ties That Bind

Many thoughts can come from this history of Texas, the ozone hole, and CFC control and replacement.

First, in all of this, Texas had a role, but as more a peer and partner than as a great leader or terrible villain. Like most industrial economies, its factories produced and its customers used CFCs, and in that way had been responsible for some portion of the chlorine floating high in the atmosphere. But, CFCs were not Texas' problem alone. And that point is not a small one. Perhaps the key part of the CFC issue is that many environmental problems are widely shared and cannot be solved alone. Every partner's role is important, and every partial solution counts.

Just as Texas' industrial facilities and consumer tastes are tied to those in much of the rest of the world, so are

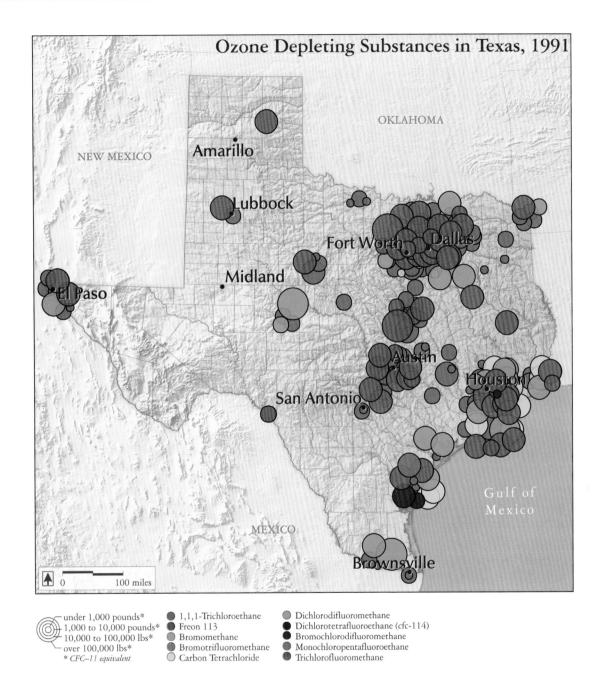

Ozone Depleting Substances in Texas, 1991

Legend:
- under 1,000 pounds*
- 1,000 to 10,000 pounds*
- 10,000 to 100,000 lbs*
- over 100,000 lbs*
  * CFC–11 equivalent

- 1,1,1-Trichloroethane
- Freon 113
- Bromomethane
- Bromotrifluoromethane
- Carbon Tetrachloride
- Dichlorodifluoromethane
- Dichlorotetrafluoroethane (cfc-114)
- Bromochlorodifluoromethane
- Monochloropentafluorethane
- Trichlorofluoromethane

The reductions in ozone-depleting chemical use were all the more remarkable because of the wide variety of changes that needed to be made in the compounds' chemistry, manufacture, use, and customer base. This map shows the many and diverse ozone depleting-compounds (marked by color) emitted in Texas during 1991, including 1,1,1-Trichloroethane, Bromochlorodifluoromethane, Bromomethane, Bromotrifluoromethane, Carbon Tetrachloride, Dichlorodifluoro-methane, Dichlorotetrafluoroethane, Freon 113, Methyl Bromide, Monochloropentafluorethane, and Trichlorofluoro-methane (US EPA 2014a).

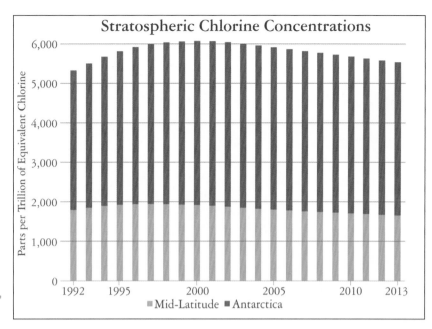

As the use of ozone depleting substances has fallen around the world, chlorine levels have slowly but steadily declined, helping restore the stratospheric ozone layer (Montzka, Dutton, and Butler 2013).

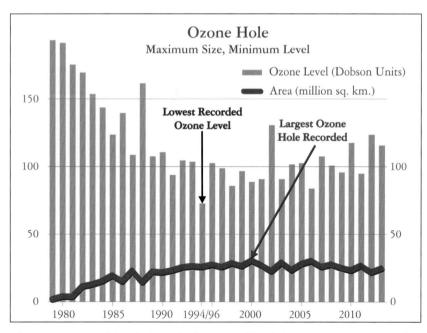

The Antarctic ozone hole's daily size peaked in 2000, and its minimum concentration troughed in 1994 (please note that no data are available for 1995). Since then the ozone layer has gradually stabilized (National Aeronautics and Space Administration 2002).

the photochemical reactions and diffusion patterns over Texas skies. CFC emissions in Texas float and drift and mix with those from other lands without any respect for political boundaries, dropping chlorine atoms and splintering ozone molecules far and wide. In a slow and circuitous but still clear and sure way, the Texas emissions join their kindred pollutants from around the world to erode the stratospheric ozone layer.

Patience

Fortunately, with cutbacks in CFC use in Texas and around the globe, the ozone layer is gradually recovering. The drastic reductions in production, use, and release of CFCs and other ozone-depleters over the past quarter century have had a definite, good impact on chlorine levels in the atmosphere. However, the decline has been slow, and ozone layer damage persists. Scientists expect that ozone levels of 1980 will not return until 2045 to 2060 (World Meteorological Organization / United Nations Environment Programme 2010, 25). Considering that CFCs were only developed as recently as the 1930s, this is a sobering reminder of how rapidly billion-year-old natural systems can be disturbed, and how long it can take to rebalance.

Resilience

There are also lessons here of the need to be flexible and resourceful. CFCs were once celebrated as a sign of great creativity and progress. DuPont and General Motors introduced chlorofluorocarbons as a class of nontoxic, nonflammable refrigerant chemicals to replace highly flammable butane and corrosive and toxic compounds such as ammonia, methyl chloride, and sulfur dioxide. CFCs were indeed nonreactive, nontoxic, and nonflammable and brought the many public health benefits of refrigeration. They were good in many ways, and were soon used and relied on widely. However, they also turned out to cause very serious damage to the environment, and industry, government, and society had to have the resilience to drop CFCs and find safe and effective substitutes.

A side note: CFC's inventor, Thomas Midgley, was a very talented chemist. Tragically, in a strange echo of the CFC and ozone story, he was also a crucial part of the team that brought the world safer, more efficient motors and generations of lead poisoning with the fuel additive tetraethyl lead (Kettering 1947, 361).

Struggles have persisted for formulating effective compounds that are still friendly to the natural chemistry of the environment. In the past two decades, a group of synthetic chemicals, HFCs and PFCs, were introduced to replace CFCs and thus protect the stratospheric ozone layer. Unfortunately, these new substances turned out to be potent, long-lived greenhouse gases. Impacts on one aspect of the atmosphere had been traded for another. While the effect of substituting this new family of chemicals for the old ozone-depleting substances has been slight in the overall picture (representing only 2.5 percent of all US greenhouse gases in 2012), their release has grown rapidly—by over 41 percent since 1990 (US EPA 2014b, table ES-4). The diverse challenges of protecting our atmosphere continue.

Facing Doubt

The story of CFC and ozone research is simpler to tell in hindsight. Along the way, though, there were misgivings, uncertainties, and surprises. Not everyone believed the ozone-depletion theory. In 1975, one air-pollution expert, Richard Scorer, argued CFCs' reputed role was "a science fiction tale . . . a load of rubbish . . . utter nonsense" (Schneider 2009, 110). Nor were CFC controls easily accepted within industry. As late as 1992, DuPont, the major manufacturer of CFCs, continued to fight shareholder resolutions asking for a more rapid phaseout of the chemicals (*Roosevelt v. E. I. DuPont*, 958 F.2d 416 (1992)). Political minds were slow to change too. In 1995, more than a decade after CFCs' devastating role in ozone depletion was understood, Congressman Tom DeLay (R-Texas) introduced legislation to pull back on CFC regulation, asserting that "the benefits EPA attributes to banning CFCs at the close of this year have been grossly overstated . . . instead of responding with scientific facts, some NASA scientists, EPA officials, and extreme environmental organizations have forced this imminent CFC phase-out on the American people using fear and doomsaying" (US Congress 1995). His bill failed. Still, Mr. DeLay's effort reminds us all that conservation work needs partnerships, patience, and resiliency to resolve doubts and uncertainties and win a high-stakes race against ecological damage.

Sources

Ahrens, C. Donald. 2012. *Meteorology Today: An Introduction to Weather, Climate, and the Environment.* 10th ed. Belmont, CA: Brooks/Cole/Cengage Learning.

British Antarctic Survey. 2014. Antarctic Factsheet: Geographical Statistics. British Antarctic Survey, Natural Environment Research Council.

Farman, J. C., B. G. Gardiner, and J. D. Shanklin. 1985. "Large Losses of Total Ozone in Antarctica Reveal Seasonal ClO_x/NO_x Interaction." *Nature* 315 (May 16): 207–10.

Hansen, Paul W. 2013. *Green in Gridlock: Common Goals, Common Ground, and Compromise.* College Station: Texas A&M University Press.

Kettering, Charles. 1947. "Biographical Memoir of Thomas Midgley, Jr., 1889–1944." National Academy of Sciences, Biographical Memoirs, vol. 24. Presented at the 1947 NAS Annual Meeting.

Litfin, Karen. 1994. *Ozone Discourses: Science and Politics in Global Environmental Cooperation*. New York: Columbia University Press.

The London Amendment. 1990. The Amendment to the Montreal Protocol Agreed by the Second Meeting of the Parties. London, June 7–29.

Lovelock, James, R. J. Maggs, and R. J. Wade. 1973. "Halogenated Hydrocarbons in and over the Atlantic." *Nature* 241 (January 19): 194–96.

Molina, Mario, and Sherwood Rowland. 1974. "Stratospheric Sink for Chlorofluoromethanes: Chlorine Atom-Catalyzed Destruction of Ozone." *Nature* 249 (June 28): 810–12.

Montzka, Stephen, Geoff Dutton, and James Butler. 2013. The NOAA Ozone Depleting Gas Index: Guiding Recovery of the Ozone Layer. NOAA Earth System Research Laboratory. Boulder, Colorado. http://www.esrl.noaa.gov/gmd/odgi/, accessed May 22, 2014.

National Aeronautics and Space Administration. 2002. Maximum Ozone Hole Area for 2000. Visualization by Greg Shirah (NASA/GSFC) and Paul Newman (NASA/GSFC), September 30. NASA/Goddard Space Flight Center, Scientific Visualization Studio. http://svs.gsfc.nasa.gov/cgi-bin/details.cgi?aid=2594, accessed October 12, 2014.

———. 2014. Ozone Hole Watch: Annual Records. Goddard Space Flight Center, National Aeronautics and Space Administration. http://ozonewatch.gsfc.nasa.gov/meteorology/annual_data.html, accessed May 22, 2014.

Russell, J. M., III, M. Luo, R. J. Cicerone, and L. E. Deaver. 1996. "Satellite Confirmation of the Dominance of Chloro-fluorocarbons in the Global Stratospheric Ozone Budget." *Nature* 379 (February 8): 526–29.

Schneider, Stephen. 2009. *Science as a Contact Sport: Inside the Battle to Save Earth's Climate*. Washington, DC: National Geographic Society.

Solomon, P. M., B. Connor, R. L. de Zafra, A. Parrish, J. Barrett, and M. Jaramillo. 1987. "High Concentrations of Chlorine Monoxide at Low Altitudes in the Antarctic Spring Stratosphere: Secular Variation." *Nature* 328 (July 30): 411–13.

Solomon, Susan, Rolando R. Garcia, F. Sherwood Rowland, and Donald J. Wuebbles. 1986. "On the Depletion of Antarctic Ozone." *Nature* 321 (June 19): 755–58.

United Nations Environment Programme. 2013. Information provided by parties in accordance with Article 7 of the Montreal Protocol on Substances that Deplete the Ozone Layer. UNEP/OzL.Pro/ImpCom/51/2. September 9.

US Census. 2012. Texas: 2010— Population and Housing Unit Counts, 2010 Census of Population and Housing. Report CPH-2-45. US Department of Commerce. Issued September.

US Congress. 1995. "Scientific Integrity and Public Trust: The Science behind Federal Policies and Mandates: Case Study 1—Stratospheric Ozone: Myths and Realities." A hearing before the Subcommittee on Energy and Environment, of the Committee on Science, US House of Representatives, 104th Congress, 1st Session. September 20. http://www.archive.org/stream/scientificintegr00unit/scientificintegr00unit_djvu.txt, accessed May 20, 2014.

US Environmental Protection Agency (EPA). 1993. Regulatory History of CFCs and Other Stratospheric Ozone Depleting Chemicals. EPA Press Release, April 23.

———. 2014a. Envirofacts: Toxic Release Inventory: EZ Search. http://www.epa.gov/enviro/facts/tri/ez.html, accessed May 22, 2014.

———. 2014b. Inventory of U.S. Greenhouse Gas Emissions and Sinks: 1990–2012. EPA 430-R-14-003. April.

World Meteorological Organization / United Nations Environment Programme. 2010. Scientific Assessment of Ozone Depletion. Scientific Assessment Panel of the Montreal Protocol on Substances that Deplete the Ozone Layer. http://www.unep.org/PDF/PressReleases/898_ExecutiveSummary_EMB.pdf, accessed June 6, 2014.

Tobacco and Secondhand Smoke

"Cigarette smoking particularly is associated with an increased chance of developing lung cancer."

—Surgeon General Leroy Burney, 1959, quoted in Bayne-Jones et al. 1964

"Involuntary smoking is a cause of disease, including lung cancer, in healthy nonsmokers."

—US Department of Health and Human Services, 1986

The idea of air pollution can bring up a vision of plumes of smoke billowing from tall chimneys and flares towering over large factories, refineries, and other facilities.

Secondhand tobacco smoke is both similar and different. It is certainly a pollutant, with a mix of more than ninety recognized toxins, including benzene, arsenic, cyanide, carbon monoxide, formaldehyde, and ammonia (US Food and Drug Administration 2012). But there is no industrial facility involved and no smokestack implicated. There is just a friend, family member, or coworker, with a small cigarette or cigar, at a familiar home or office, bar or restaurant.

Nevertheless, secondhand smoke is a serious health risk, tied to lung cancer, heart disease, and respiratory ailments that cost the United States nearly $6 billion in health expenses and lost productivity annually (Adhikari et al. 2008; Uccello 2006). At least twenty million Americans

died prematurely from 1964 through 2014 due to secondhand smoke (US Department of Health and Human Services 2014). In recent years, secondhand smoke is estimated to annually kill 4,300 nonsmoking Texans (Conde 2008).

The risk is all the more severe due to Americans' modern lifestyle, since Americans spend about 90 percent of the time indoors where concentrations of smoke and other pollutants can be two to five times higher than outside (US EPA 1987; 1989). Finally, secondhand tobacco smoke raises a troubling equity issue, since 25

percent of American nonsmokers (fifty-eight million people) and 40 percent of US kids (ages three to eleven) are exposed to secondhand smoke and the accompanying health risks without their choice and consent (Centers for Disease Control and Prevention 2015b, 2).

Despite the health hazards of tobacco, it has taken decades to develop the medical research, political support, and legislative rules to protect users and those nearby. However, over the past generation, indeed the last decade alone, remarkable strides have been made.

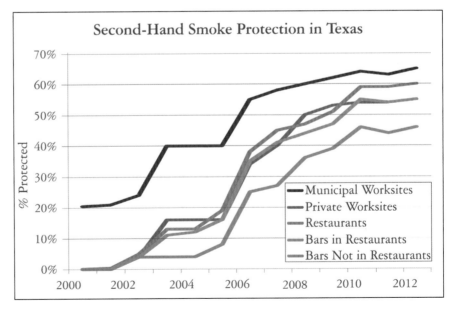

This chart tracks the rise in the number of Texans who are protected by municipal smoking ordinances. The ordinances represented here have a varied reach, affecting workplaces, restaurants, and bars (University of Houston Law Center 2015; Boerm 2013; Gingiss 2013; Gray, Gingiss, and Boerm 2013).

Federal Studies and Warnings

The federal government took critical early steps to control tobacco exposure by requiring health warnings on cigarette packs (1965) and by banning cigarette ads (1969) (Cigarette Labeling and Advertising Act of 1965, 15 U.S.C. 1331, P.L. 89-92; Public Health Cigarette Smoking Act of 1969, 15 U.S.C. 1331, P.L. 98-474). The United States has also been strong in supporting research and public information about tobacco's health risks. The surgeon general issued an initial report on smoking and health in 1964, stating that smoking caused lung cancer, chronic bronchitis, emphysema, and coronary disease (Bayne-Jones et al. 1964). The surgeon general and CDC followed up in subsequent work on secondhand smoke, including early discussions in 1972, and a full-blown indictment of its risks in 1986 (US Department of Health, Education, and Welfare 1972; US Department of Health and Human Services 1986). The EPA has also been involved in tobacco study, including its publication of a 1990 report finding that passive smoking causes 3,800 lung cancer deaths per year, and its classification of tobacco smoke as a Group A carcinogen (US EPA 1992).

Aircraft Flights

The first major federal effort to actually ban tobacco use due to secondhand smoke risks came in the regulation of commercial aircraft flights. The process began in the late 1960s as flight attendants began advocating for control of smoking on board flights. There was some success at first, when in 1972 the Civil Aeronautics Board (CAB) accepted a Public Citizen bid for requiring separate sections for smokers and nonsmokers. However, later progress was slow and haphazard. In 1973, the Federal Aviation Administration rejected a pilots' petition to ban smoking in cockpits, and in 1978, the CAB amended its rules to allow cigar and pipe smoking on board (Holm and Davis 2004). With time, though, the regulatory effort gained momentum. Key help came from a National Research Council report, "The Airliner Cabin Environment: Air

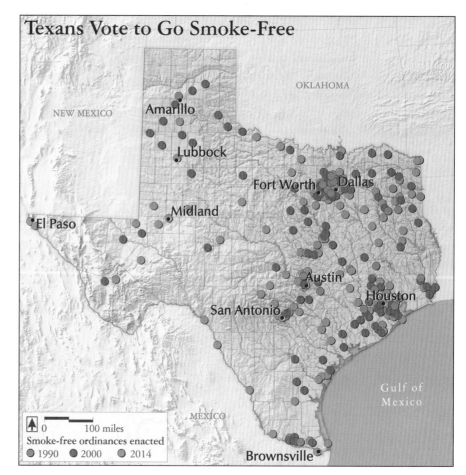

This map shows the growth of smoke-free ordinances in Texas, as they have been enacted through 1990, 2000, and 2015. As of May 2015, roughly 275 communities in Texas had some sort of protective antismoking ordinance, while thirty-six cities in Texas had comprehensive local ordinances. These ordinances affect over 16.3 million Texans, or 60 percent of the state's residents (American Lung Association 2013; University of Houston Law Center 2015).

Quality and Safety," that came out in 1986, and through congressional testimony by flight attendants in the same year (Committee on Airliner Cabin Air Quality 1986). In the spring of 1987, Congress responded by prohibiting smoking on flights of less than two hours, followed by a ban in 1990 that covered all domestic flights (Federal Aviation Act, 49 U.S.C. 1374(d)(1); Public Law 100-202; Public Law 101-164; 49 U.S.C. 40102 et seq.; 14 C.F.R. Part 252). Other federal restrictions on travel and public accommodations came soon after: the Interstate Commerce Commission banned smoking on interstate buses and trains in 1990, and President Clinton barred smoking in federal buildings in 1997 (Clinton 1997).

As a side note, advocacy from flight attendants and their union continued to affect the understanding and regulation of secondhand smoke far outside airliner cabins (Young 1989). In 1991, nonsmoking stewardesses Patty Young and Norma Broin filed a class-action lawsuit against the tobacco industry, joined later by 60,000 flight attendants. In 1997, the suit was settled out of court and resulted in a $300 million payment, which created the Flight Attendant Medical Research Institute. The institute has become an important source of funding for understanding and explaining secondhand smoke hazards (*Broin v. Philip Morris*, 641 So. 2nd 888 (Florida 3rd District Court of Appeal 1994); Pan et al. 2005; Young 1983–97).

Texas Law

While federal policy has led in the effort to protect against passive smoke, the state of Texas has had a more mixed record. The state traditionally has faced a general public allergy toward regulation of personal behavior. Also, despite support for smoking controls from the medical establishment, American Lung Association, American Cancer Society, Americans for Nonsmokers' Rights, and other nonprofits, restrictions faced well-organized opposition in the restaurant, bar, beverage, and tobacco industries (Jacobson and Wasserman 1997). Attempts to enact statewide bans failed in five legislative sessions from 2007 through 2015, while site-specific controls have been patchy (House Bill 9, 2007; House Bill 5, 2009; Senate Bill 544, 2009; Senate Bill 86 and House Bill 40, 2013; House Bill 1811, 2011; Senate Bill 87, 2015). The state does bar smoking at prisons, on school campuses, and in child-care centers (37 Texas Administrative Code 151.25(d), Texas Education Code 38.006; 40 Texas Administrative Code 746.3703(d)). Texas also limits smoking to designated areas within theaters, libraries, museums, hospitals, and buses. On the other hand, the Lone Star State still provides no restriction at all on smoking in government worksites, private workplaces, restaurants, casinos and gaming facilities, bars, or retail stores.

Nor does Texas have legislation protecting against smoking-related discrimination or retaliation (Texas Education Code § 38.006; Texas Penal Code Ann. § 48.01; Texas Education Code § 21.927; and Texas Administrative Code tit. 40, Part 19, Subchapter S, Div. 1 §§ 746.3703(d) & 747.3503(d)).

Texas Money

The story of tobacco-control funding in Texas has been uneven as well. Texas was one of four states in which the attorney general's office reached an early, trailblazing agreement with the tobacco industry for covering health costs, setting charges of conspiracy, racketeering, and consumer protection law. In 1997, tobacco firms agreed to pay the state of Texas $15 billion, payable over twenty-five years, in addition to $2.3 billion in initial payments due by 2003. The income was used to fund health and education-related endowments for the state (Texas Department of State Health Services 2003). In more recent years, though, the state has been reluctant to invest the level of funding for smoking control that is recommended by the Centers for Disease Control and Prevention (CDCP). Texas provides only 2.3 percent of the level advocated by the CDCP (American Lung Association 2013; Centers for Disease Control and Prevention 2015a, 187; Institute of Medicine 2007).

Local Texas Work

As smoking control advocacy struggled at the state level, antismoking efforts switched to local venues, with marked success (Jacobson and Wasserman 1997). State law had not preempted these local efforts, and so over 280 cities and counties within Texas have moved to take up the challenge of controlling secondhand smoke. The steps have been gradual and piecemeal, but now affect the lives of some sixteen million Texans. Early efforts, such as the 1978 ordinance in Tomball, Texas, focused on creating designated smoking areas, simply separating smokers and nonsmokers. Yet increasing evidence showed that ventilation systems could not filter out many of the harmful constituents of secondhand smoke, and so ordinances turned to building-wide prohibitions (Samet et al. 2010; University of Houston Law Center 2015).

Some municipalities and counties (such as the town of Weslaco, in 1987) moved first to regulate only their own properties (police stations, firehouses, court buildings, libraries, and such), leaving private property owners to develop their own approaches. However, policy makers soon learned that this focus on public spaces alone had shortcomings. For instance, in 1991, Llano passed an ordinance requiring that all workplaces, public or private, be smoke free. The city recognized that employees had little choice about showing up for work, smoky or not, and in fact faced the risk of retaliation in some cases (University of Houston Law Center 2015).

Smoking bans long exempted restaurants, bars, clubs, and casinos, which were seen as refuges for smokers. There was concern that cutting back on smoking in those establishments might curtail sales of food and liquor, undermining the viability of those businesses. However, critics pointed out that while patrons might choose to smoke there, the waiters, busboys, cooks, bartenders, and other workers in those venues were subjected to high and recurring secondhand smoke exposures. Also, there

Smoke-Free Rules' Varying Coverage

This figure shows the extent of protection provided by Texas smoke-free ordinances, as of 2015 (larger symbols indicate stronger protections). Ordinances are scored on a 1 to 5 scale in five categories—bans affecting municipal worksites, private worksites, restaurants, bars in restaurants, and freestanding bars. The highest grade of 5 is assigned in each category if no smoking is allowed in that setting. Lower grades of 4 are given if smoking in designated areas is allowed, but separately ventilated, of 3 if the ordinance's scope is limited by exceptions, ambiguities, or legal issues, of 2 if the ordinance allows or requires designated smoking areas, or of 1 if the ordinance places no restrictions on smoking. The map presents the sum of these five scores for each Texas community that has a smoke-free ordinance (University of Houston Law Center 2015).

was evidence that smoking bans did not hurt restaurant and bar revenues (Centers for Disease Control and Prevention 2002). West Lake Hills was the first Texas community to ban smoking in restaurants in 1993. Eight years later, Alvin banned smoking in bars that were located within restaurants, and the next year, 2002, El Paso was the first to ban smoking in stand-alone bars (University of Houston Law Center 2015).

Private Rules

While not required by statute or necessarily by ordinance, some private businesses have limited smoking on their properties. Private hospitals, both individual facilities and entire networks, have understandably taken the lead. A recent count indicated that 146 private hospitals in Texas, including large chains such as St. Anthony, Baylor, Chambers, Methodist, Presbyterian, Seton, and St. David's, prohibit all smoking. In addition, the fifteen Lackland and Randolph Air Force medical facilities are smoke free (Williams et al. 2009). Some Texas hospitals, such as the University Medical Center in El Paso and the Baylor Health Care System, have gone a step further, in simply declining to hire smokers in the first place (Sulzberger 2011).

Homes

Smoking areas are getting more and more limited, with restrictions even cropping up within homes. Some of the rules are voluntary and private. In fact, in Texas, the percentage of homes with no-smoking customs has risen from 65 percent in 1999 to over 81 percent in 2007 (Centers for Disease Control and Prevention 2015a, 186). Mandated smoking rules in public housing have proven more controversial. Proposed rules raise civil liberty concerns and worries over forcing the poor to face limited housing options elsewhere (Seelye 2011). Nevertheless, housing agencies realized that no-smoking rules reduced health hazards, fire risks, and even apartment cleaning costs (Henriquez and Gant 2012). Countrywide counts of smoke-free housing authorities have grown from two in 2000, to thirty-two in 2005, to 285 at the end of 2011, representing some 9 percent of the country's network of housing agencies (Smoke-Free Environments Law Project 2011; Watkins 2013). The national trend has reached Texas, where the Austin, Corpus Christi, Decatur, Freeport, Haltom City, Houston and San Antonio Housing Authorities have each banned smoking in their units since 2009 (George 2014; Housing Authority of the City of Austin 2014; King 2011).

The Great Outdoors

The most recent frontier for smoking legislation is in neither a house, nor a bar or restaurant, nor an office or public building, but actually outdoors.

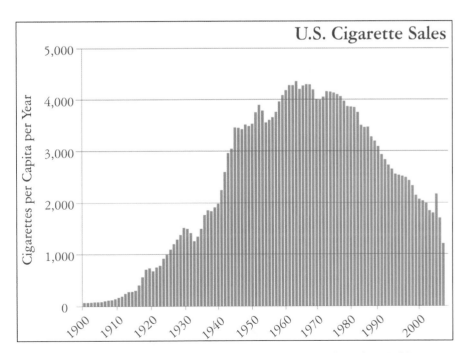

The 1900 to 2007 period has seen major declines in per-capita cigarette sales in the United States (American Lung Association 2011).

With urging from a nonprofit group, Smoke-Free Austin, data from the Austin Health and Human Services Department, and the idea of lowering fire risks during an ongoing drought, the city of Austin banned smoking in its public parks in December 2011 (City of Austin Code of Ordinances 10-6-2(A)). Currently, the city is discussing extending smoke-free areas to include patios, decks, balconies, and other outdoor spaces at local bars, restaurants, and live music venues (Coppola 2013). In January 2013, Travis County moved to ban smoking in all county property, including vehicles, garages, parking lots, lawns, and other areas (Olivieri 2013).

While it is encouraging to see the steady progress in limiting the hazards of secondhand smoke, it is important to remember that the real victory will be when all those who wish to stop smoking, or to never start, can. And there is good news there: per-capita cigarette sales in the United States and Texas are down over 70 percent from their 1963 and 1982 peaks, respectively (American Lung Association 2011; Orzechowski and Walker 2012). Fewer cigarettes are smoked by fewer smokers: smoking among adult Americans has fallen from a peak of 42.4 percent in 1965 to 18.9 percent in 2011, while teen smoking has declined from 36.4 percent (1997) to 18.1 percent most recently (Centers for Disease Control and Prevention 2013). Happily, these changes in smoking habits translate to enormous health benefits. A recent Rice University /

M. D. Anderson study found that US tobacco-control programs had prevented more than 795,000 lung cancer deaths between 1975 and 2000 (Moolgavkar et al. 2012).

Sources

Adhikari, B., J. Kahende, A. Malarcher, T. Pechacek, and V. Tong. 2008. "Smoking-Attributable Mortality, Years of Potential Life Losses—United States, 2000–2004." *Morbidity and Mortality Weekly Report* 57 (45): 1226–28. http://www.cdc.gov/mmwr/preview/mmwrhtml/mm5745a3.htm, accessed April 10, 2013.

American Lung Association. 2011. Trends in Tobacco Use. American Lung Association, Research and Program Services, Epidemiology and Statistics Unit, July.

——. 2013. State of Tobacco Control. http://www.stateoftobaccocontrol.org/sotc-2013-report.pdf, accessed April 9, 2013.

Bayne-Jones, Stanhope, Walter Burdette, William Cochran, Emmanuel Farber, Louis Fieser, Jacob Furth, John Hickam, Charles LeMaistre, Leonard Schuman, and Maurice Seevers. 1964. "Smoking and Health: Report of the Advisory Committee to the Surgeon General of the United States." U-23 Department of Health, Education, and Welfare. Public Health Service Publication No. 1103.

Boerm, Melynda. 2013. University of Houston, Department of Health and Human Performance, Health Network for Evaluation and Training Systems. Personal communication, April.

Broin v. Philip Morris. 641 So. 2nd 888 (Florida 3rd District Court of Appeals 1994).

Centers for Disease Control and Prevention. 2002. "Impact of a Smoking Ban on Restaurant and Bar Revenues—El Paso, Texas." *Morbidity and Mortality Weekly Report* 2004. Vol. 53, no. 7, pp. 150–52. http://www.cdc.gov/mmwr/preview/mmwrhtml/mm5307a2.htm, accessed April 11, 2013.

——. 2013. "Smoking and Tobacco Use: Trends in Current Cigarette Smoking among High School Students and Adults, United States, 1965–2011." http://www.cdc.gov/tobacco/data_statistics/tables/trends/cig_smoking/index.htm, accessed April 10, 2013.

——. 2015a. "Smoking and Tobacco Use: State Highlights, Texas." http://www.cdc.gov/tobacco/data_statistics/state_data/state_highlights/2010/pdfs/states/texas.pdf, accessed June 6, 2015.

——. 2015b. "Vital Signs Issues: Secondhand Smoke: An Unequal Danger." February. http://www.cdc.gov/vitalsigns/pdf/2015-02-vitalsigns.pdf, accessed June 5, 2015.

Cigarette Labeling and Advertising Act of 1965, 115 U.S.C. Chapter 36.

Clinton, William. 1997. "Executive Order 13058—Protecting Federal Employees and the Public from Exposure to Tobacco Smoke in the Federal Workplace." August 9. http://www.presidency.ucsb.edu/ws/?pid=54521, accessed April 10, 2013.

Committee on Airliner Cabin Air Quality. 1986. "The Airliner Cabin Environment: Air Quality and Safety." Board on Environmental Studies and Toxicology, Commission on Life Sciences, National Research Council. Washington, DC: National Academies

Press. http://www.nap.edu/catalog/913.html, accessed April 10, 2013.

Conde, Crystal. 2008. "Texas Medicine: Public Health Feature." Texas Medical Association. May.

Coppola, Sarah. 2013. "Austin Might Ban Smoking on Bar and Restaurant Patios." *Austin American-Statesman*, January 16.

George, Cindy. 2014. "Smoking Banned at Houston Public Housing." *Houston Chronicle*, January 24.

Gingiss, Phyllis. 2013. University of Houston, Department of Health and Human Performance, Health Network for Evaluation and Training Systems. Personal communication, April.

Gray, Patricia, Phyllis Gingiss, and Melynda Boerm. 2013. "Changes in Texas Ordinances in 2012 and Comparisons of Coverage of the Texas Municipal Population by Smoke-Free Ordinances." University of Houston. Submitted to Texas Department of State Health Services, Texas Tobacco Prevention and Control Initiative. January.

Henriquez, Sandra, and Jon Gant. 2012. Smoke-Free Policies in Public Housing. US Department of Housing and Urban Development. May 29. http://portal.hud.gov/hudportal/documents/huddoc?id=12-25pihn.pdf, accessed April 10, 2013.

Holm, A. L., and R. M. Davis. 2004. "Clearing the Airways: Advocacy and Regulation for Smoke-Free Airlines." *Tobacco Control* 13: i30–i36.

Housing Authority of the City of Austin. 2014. Proposed Smoke-Free Housing Policy, Effective September 1, 2015. City of Austin. December 18.

Institute of Medicine. 2007. *Ending the Tobacco Problem: A Blueprint for the Nation*. Washington, DC: National Academies Press, table 5.1.

Jacobson, Peter, and Jeffrey Wasserman. 1997. *Tobacco Control Laws: Implementation and Enforcement*. Santa Monica, CA: RAND. http://www.rand.org/content/dam/rand/pubs/monograph_reports/2006/MR841.pdf, accessed April 10, 2013.

King, Karisa. 2011. "SAHA to Ban Smoking in Public Housing." *San Antonio Express-News*, July 27.

Moolgavkar, S. H., T. R. Holford, D. T. Levy, C. Y. Kong, M. Foy, L. Clarke, J. Jeon, W. D. Hazelton, R. Meza, W. McCarthy, R. Boer, O. Gorlova, G. S. Gazelle, M. Kimmel, P. M. McMahon, H. J. de Koning, and E. J. Feuer. 2012. "Impact of Reduced Tobacco Smoking on Lung Cancer Mortality in the United States during 1975–2000." *Journal of the National Cancer Institute* 104 (7): 541–48. http://www.ncbi.nlm.nih.gov/pubmed/22423009, accessed April 10, 2013.

Olivieri, Joe. 2013. "Commissioners Vote to Ban Smoking on County Property." *Community Impact News*, January 30.

Orzechowski and Walker. 2012. The Tax Burden on Tobacco: Historical Compilation, vol. 47. http://www.taxadmin.org/fta/tobacco/papers/tax_burden_2012.pdf, accessed June 6, 2015.

Pan, Jocelyn, Elizabeth Bareau, Charles Levnstein, and Edith Balbach. 2005. "Smoke-Free Airlines and the Role of Organized Labor: A Case Study." *American Journal of Public Health* 95 (3): 398–404.

Public Health Cigarette Smoking Act of 1969. 15 U.S.C. § 1331.

Samet, Jonathan, Hoy Bohanon, David Coultas, Thomas Houston, Andrew Persily, and Lawrence Schoen. 2010.

"ASHRAE Position Document on Environmental Tobacco Smoke." American Society of Heating, Refrigerating, and Air Conditioning Engineers.

Seelye, Katharine. 2011. "Increasingly, Smoking Indoors Is Forbidden at Public Housing." *New York Times*, December 17.

Smoke-Free Environments Law Project. 2011. Housing Authorities/Commissions which have Adopted Smoke-Free Policies. January 20. The Center for Social Gerontology. Ann Arbor, Michigan. www.tcsg.org/sfelp/SFHousingAuthorities.pdf, accessed April 10, 2013.

Sulzberger, A. G. 2011. "Hospitals Shift Smoking Bans to Smoker Ban." *New York Times*, February 10.

Texas Department of State Health Services. 2003. "Texans and Tobacco: A Report to the 78th Texas Legislature." January. http://www.dshs.state.tx.us/tobacco/pdf/legrep03.pdf, accessed April 10, 2013.

———. 2011. "Texans and Tobacco: A Report to the 82nd Texas Legislature." January. http://www.dshs.state.tx.us/WorkArea/linkit.aspx?LinkIdentifier=id&ItemID=8589952884, accessed April 10, 2013.

Uccello, Cori. 2006. Costs Associated with Secondhand Smoke. American Academy of Actuaries. October.

US Department of Health and Human Services. 1986. "The Health Consequences of Involuntary Smoking." A Report of the Surgeon General. US Public Health Service, Centers for Disease Control. Rockville, Maryland.

———. 2014. "The Health Consequences of Smoking—50 Years of Progress."

A Report of the Surgeon General. US Public Health Service, US Department of Health and Human Services. Rockville, Maryland.

US Department of Health, Education, and Welfare. 1972. "The Health Consequences of Smoking." A Report of the Surgeon General: 1972. US Department of Health, Education, and Welfare, Public Health Service, Health Services and Mental Health Administration. DHEW Publication No. (HSM) 72-7516. Washington, DC.

US Environmental Protection Agency (EPA). 1987. "The Total Exposure Assessment Methodology (TEAM) Study: Summary and Analysis." EPA/600/6-87/002a. Washington, DC.

———. 1989. "Report to Congress on Indoor Air Quality: Volume 2."

EPA/400/1-89/001C. Washington, DC.

———. 1992. "Respiratory Health Effects of Passive Smoking: Lung Cancer and Other Disorders." EPA 600/6-90/006F. December.

US Food and Drug Administration. 2012. "Harmful and Potentially Harmful Constituents in Tobacco Products and Tobacco Smoke; Established List." Docket No. FDA-2012-N-0143. Federal Register, Vol. 77, No. 64. April 3.

University of Houston Law Center. 2015. Texas Smoke-free Ordinance Database. shsordinances.uh.edu, accessed November 30, 2015.

Watkins, Morgan. 2013. "Housing Authority Battles Bedbugs, May Ban Smoking." *Gainesville Sun*, April 3.

Williams, Scott, Joanne Hafner, David Morton, Amanda Holm, Sharon

Milberger, Richard Koss, and Jerod Loeb. 2009. "The Adoption of Smoke-Free Hospital Campuses in the United States." *Tobacco Control* 18 (6): 451–58.

Young, Patty. 1983–97. Patty Young Papers, 1983–1997. Dolph Briscoe Center for American History, the University of Texas at Austin. http://www.lib.utexas.edu/taro/utcah/01647/cah-01647.html, accessed April 9, 2013.

———. 1989. PM Exhibit, JD 023562, Hearing, "To Ban Smoking on Airline Aircraft," before the Subcommittee on Aviation of the Committee on Public Works and Transportation, House of Representatives, June 22. http://legacy.library.ucsf.edu/tid/het08h00, accessed April 9, 2013.

Upsets

A good deal of American environmental protection hinges on an idea called, "command and control," where agencies cap pollution with rules and permits. These licenses specify the kind and amount of pollution allowed and require monitoring, record keeping, and reporting.

For instance, much of modern US air pollution control revolves around limits and mandates for major industrial sources, such as refineries, chemical plants, power plants, and many other industrial facilities that are regulated under the federal Clean Air Act (42 U.S.C. § 7401).

However, not everything can be controlled and managed in this careful, rational way. Accidents happen. Things go wrong in unpredictable, chaotic ways. Many industrial processes operate with caustic chemicals running at high temperatures and pressures. Power drops out, motors

High flames and billowing dark smoke come from an upset at the Texas Petrochemicals plant in southeast Houston (Espinosa 2013).

fail, seals deteriorate, welds split, corroded and fatigued metal bursts, and gases escape, sometimes with a barely audible hiss, sometimes with a huge explosion.

This kind of pollution is generally known in the regulatory arena as an "upset," an "unplanned and unavoidable emission," an "episodic release," or somewhat mysteriously, as an "emission event." They are the burps, belches, flares, and leaks that escape from industrial plants during accidents and other mishaps. This chapter is about how agencies, companies, and nonprofits have struggled with this messy and untidy, and sometimes toxic and dangerous, problem (Carman 2013; Haragan 2013; Levin 2013).

The Dilemma

Upsets are viewed in a variety of ways. On the one hand, the law in Texas and many other states gives a pass to emissions that are technically considered "sudden or unavoidable," "beyond control," "unforeseen," "unscheduled," or "unplanned" (30 Texas Administrative Code §101.222). In a sense, these waivers are a pragmatic nod to the unpredictability of the real world.

On the other hand, historically, state and federal regulators have often exempted a very broad category of so-called upset emissions that are at least, to some degree, foreseeable. For example, agencies give some level of immunity to releases that occur as a result of routine and planned startups, shutdowns, and maintenance activities. These kinds of emissions are not bound by the facility's permitted pollution limits for their normal operations (Environmental Integrity Project 2004).

Critics ask whether all these releases are truly unexpected and unpreventable. Are the upsets just an instance of bad luck, or can they be foreseen and guarded against? Are

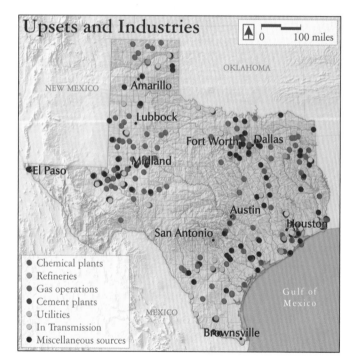
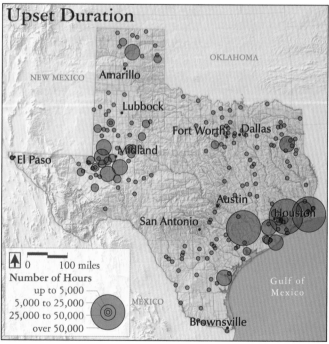

The Upsets and Industries map shows the upsets during 2012 at Texas chemical plants (purple), refineries (orange), gas operations (red), cement plants (gray), utilities (turquoise), in transmission (yellow), and from miscellaneous sources (brown). The markers in the Upset Duration map represent one or more facilities found in that community. The size of these markers indicates the cumulative number of hours that individual chemical upsets reported for that location during 2012 (TCEQ 2013a; Lyons 2013).

there patterns that can be found, root causes that can be identified? Are there ways that facilities can be reinforced, better maintained, or operated more safely to reduce these upsets?

Big, Diverse, and Widespread

Upsets involve big numbers. From 2007 to 2011, more than 2,400 facilities in Texas released close to 180 million pounds of upset emissions. These episodic releases were in addition to the 14.8 billion pounds of routine air emissions during that same period (Lombardi and Fuller 2013). For some individual facilities, their reported upsets overwhelmed their routine emissions. In 2011, the Enterprise Products plant in Mont Belvieu released 1.48 million pounds of volatile organic compounds (VOCs) in upsets, versus 1.08 million pounds during its normal permitted operations. In the same year, Flint Hills Resources' chemical plant in Longview emitted 1.43 million pounds of VOCs, while its routine emissions were permitted for just 209,680 pounds of VOCs (TCEQ 2013).

Upsets occur across the state and involve a variety of industries. Many along the coast come from chemical plants and refineries. Meanwhile, a large cluster of emissions are associated with oil and gas operations and pipelines in the Midland-Odessa area, the Panhandle, and Northeast Texas. Other upsets happen at electric power stations, cement plants, and brick kilns

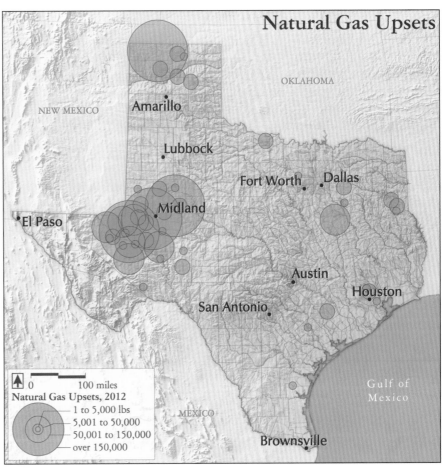

This map plots the cluster of natural gas releases (in terms of pounds) from upsets at wells, batteries, compressor stations, pipelines, and gas plants during 2012. If not completely burned, natural gas has potent greenhouse effects (TCEQ 2013a; Lyons 2013).

scattered throughout the state (TCEQ 2013).

In addition to their large size and wide variety, these upsets can be frequent and long lasting. Over 18,000 "emission events" were reported in Texas during 2012. Twenty-four of these upsets lasted a week or more, and one release lasted for over twenty-seven days (TCEQ 2013).

Natural Gas, Methane, and Climate

Natural gas holds great promise as a relatively clean-burning fuel that can help reduce climate change risks. However, before it is burned, natural gas (principally methane, but also including ethane, propane, and butane) is a potent greenhouse gas.

Unfortunately, the vast network of equipment that collects, compresses, transports, and distributes gas to the end consumer is prone to leaks. Upsets in wells, batteries, booster and compressor stations, pipelines, and gas plants release sizable amounts of natural gas, over 3.2 million pounds in Texas during 2012 (TCEQ 2013). There is research suggesting that methane emissions from the natural gas system may contribute as much as 17 percent to the US greenhouse gas inventory (Howarth et al. 2012).

VOCs, Smog, and Health

Upsets release chemicals that have serious health impacts. Some of the chemicals include volatile organic compounds that raise ozone levels, worsen smog conditions, and cause respiratory problems. VOCs released in upsets during 2010 accounted for nearly 10 percent of the total VOC emissions from all industrial sources in Texas (Environmental Integrity Project 2012). Nineteen counties, including the majority of the Houston-Galveston, Dallas–Fort Worth, and El Paso regions, currently violate federal ozone standards, and several other areas are near nonattainment for ozone. In those areas, air pollution from upset VOCs aggravates an already bad situation (US EPA 2012).

Some of the chemicals released in upsets are highly toxic, with carcinogenic, neurological, and respiratory impacts. During 2012, Texas facilities reported upsets that released significant amounts of chemicals identified under the Clean Air Act as hazardous air pollutants. These "air toxics" included 1,2-dichloroethane, 1,3-butadiene, acetonitrile, acrolein, acrylonitrile, benzene, dimethyl formamide, ethyl benzene, ethylene oxide, hexane, hydrogen chloride, hydrogen cyanide, hydrogen fluoride, methanol, styrene, toluene, 2,2,4-trimethylpentane, vinyl acetate, vinyl chloride, and xylene (42 U.S.C. § 7412(b); TCEQ 2013). Their toxicity can be magnified by the release's scale and intensity. Upset emissions can be very large, concentrated over a brief period, and even rival levels permitted for routine operations (Craft 2010).

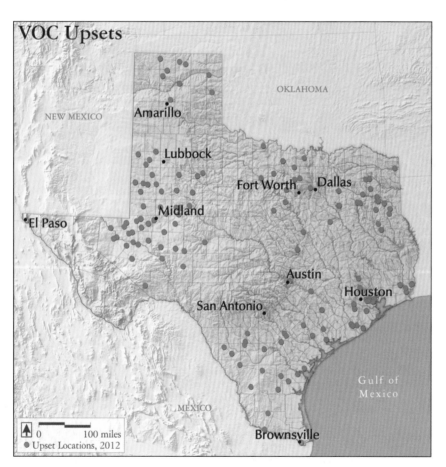

This map shows over 2,100 upset releases of VOCs that came from more than 460 facilities in Texas during 2012. VOC emissions from these upsets totaled more than 16 million pounds (TCEQ 2013a; Lyons 2013).

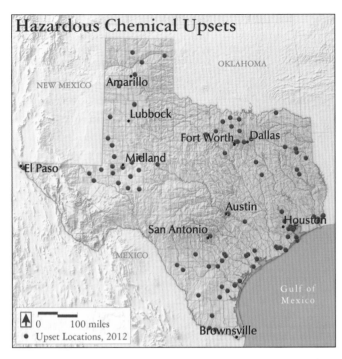

Over one thousand upsets involving hazardous chemicals occurred at Texas chemical plants, refineries, gas operations, transmission lines, and other industrial facilities during 2012. Only 199 facilities were involved; many of these upsets occurred repeatedly at the same operation (TCEQ 2013a; Lyons 2013).

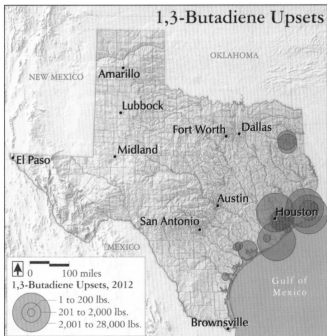

Unfortunately, upsets often involve carcinogens. The 1,3-Butadiene map shows that upset-related releases of this known carcinogen during 2012 were heavily clustered in the "Golden Triangle," among the industrial complexes in Houston and Beaumont/Port Arthur (TCEQ 2013a; Lyons 2013). The Benzene Upsets map plots upset-related emissions of this carcinogen during 2012 in Texas. Health effects have been linked to some of the upsets, such as a forty-day release of about 17,000 pounds of benzene in 2010 from the Texas City BP facility (Lyons 2013; D'Andrea and Reddy 2013; TCEQ 2013a).

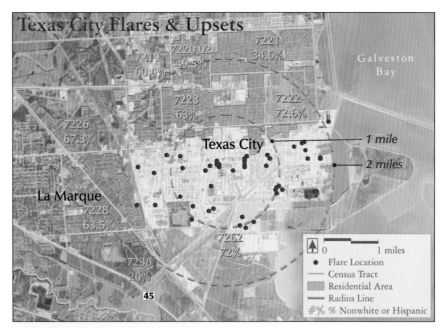

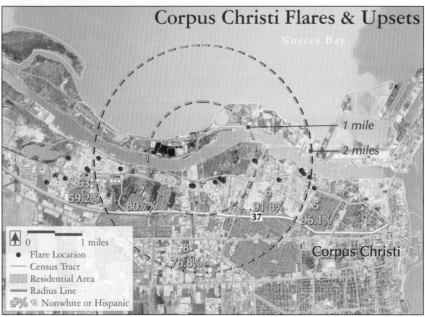

Upsets are sometimes flared off near residential neighborhoods. Some firms have attempted to buy out homeowners and create buffer zones, yet the problem persists. For example, the Texas City map shows that numerous flares (marked with red dots) in this industrial area of Galveston County are still located close to residential neighborhoods (portrayed here as purple polygons). The Corpus Christi map depicts Refinery Row, an example of how industrial neighborhoods can have much higher minority populations relative to the state as a whole, which is just 45 percent nonwhite or Hispanic. For scale, two orange concentric circles, with one- and two-mile radii, are shown in each map (Dickey 2013; US Census Bureau 2013).

Inequity

It is important to think about where these releases happen. Some upsets happen at compressor stations and other natural gas facilities that are in remote, unsettled areas. However, many upset emissions can be clustered in large industrial complexes that abut residential areas and that already face high continuous emissions. The combination of both these upset and permitted plumes brings up concerns about the unfairness of heavy and repeated impacts on fenceline communities.

Monitoring

Monitoring upset releases can be difficult and inaccurate. For many upsets, the released pollution surges out in a rapid spike and is not easily measured. And these inaccuracies can be very significant. Over the course of hours or days, the episodic releases can dwarf the accompanying routine emissions. For instance, a partial Texas inventory in 2000 found that the ratio of upsets to routine releases ranged from five to more than three thousand to one (measured in pounds, for chemicals such as butadiene, ethylene, and propylene) (Allen and Durrenberger 2003, 47).

Estimates of leaks from product storage tanks and wastewater treatment systems are another source of error. Many of these leak estimates are based on formulas that possibly understate the actual releases (Cuclis 2012). For instance, careful reviews of actual leaks at the Shell Deer Park refinery indicate that VOC emission factors may be off by a factor of thirty-one to as high as 132. This problem is likely not unique to a single plant. A study at the BP refinery in Texas City echoes these same doubts about the use of standard emission factors (Environmental Integrity Project 2012).

Also, upset gases are often burned at flares, 13,000 of which are found throughout the state (Dickey 2013). Regulators and industry typically work on the assumption that the flares bring 98–99 percent destruction of upset gases. However, these destruction estimates are based on studies that are decades old (McDaniel 1983; US EPA 1995). And there is evidence that combustion efficiency might be as low as 70 percent. For instance, flares may not be as effective as hoped if waste gases fail to burn easily, if conditions are windy, or if operators add steam to reduce smoking. With the lower combustion rates, flares can release much more pollution than is being reported (Environmental Integrity Project 2012).

The sketchy emission data lead to trouble in predicting and guarding against possible health effects. For example, the fuzziness of the upset monitoring data can make it hard to accurately model ambient air quality, due to the proverbial "garbage-in, garbage-out" problem. Next, if the airshed simulations are inaccurate, then it is hard to determine the level of permitted, normal-operation emissions that should be allowed.

With all these concerns, the city of Houston petitioned the EPA in 2008 to review and correct any old emission factors for petroleum refineries and chemical manufacturing plants that were shown to be inaccurate (White 2008; Data Quality Act). In 2009, the EPA promised to review the emission factors used to calculate releases at tanks, flares, cooling towers, and other sources in the petrochemical industry (Craig 2009). However, the federal response was seen as inadequate, and so in 2013 a group of nonprofits led by the Environmental Integrity Project successfully filed suit against the EPA to review correct emission factors for VOCs, NO_x, and carbon monoxide (90 Federal Register 26925 (May 11, 2015); *Air Alliance Houston et al. v. McCarthy*, No. 1: 13-cv-00621-KBJ (D.D.C.); US EPA 1995).

Reporting

Texans are fortunate to have an online reporting system for upsets, making the issue more transparent and accessible to the public. This rule came out of the 1999–2001 Sunset Review of the Texas Commission on Environmental Quality (then known as the Texas Natural Resources Conservation Commission) (Sunset Advisory Commission 2001, 178). Public interest advocates, including the Environmental Defense Fund, National Wildlife Federation, Public Citizen, Sierra Club, and others, participated in the review under the banner "Alliance for a Clean Texas."

They urged substantive limits and fines for upset emissions under House Bill 3584, but were unable to get these changes through the legislature. However, Representative Scott Hochberg (D-Houston) did manage to pass a law requiring a public, electronic database to follow these upsets (Texas Health and Safety Code § 382.0215(e)).

The database tracks the source, reason, chemical makeup, amount, date, duration, and location of upset emissions (TCEQ 2013). The data help regulators grasp the scope of the upset problem and help industry see patterns and possible origins for the releases. In a competitive business market where goodwill and public trust are very valuable, these data help press industries to work harder to clean up their operations and reduce emissions. And, for the public, the online information gives neighbors and nonprofits a clearer view and more complete tally of what is being released into the air (in fact, many of the maps in this chapter are based on those data).

Nevertheless, the data are far from perfect. As described above, many of the reported upset amounts are based on calculations (not actual monitoring) using EPA's old and sometimes inaccurate emission factors. Also, companies are not required to report all unpermitted emissions. If an uncontrolled release appears to be under the reporting threshold, as high as 5,000 pounds for some chemicals, plant operators do not need to file an incident report (Lombardi and Fuller 2013; 40 Code of Federal Regulations 302.4; 30 Texas Administrative Code 101). These "nonreportable" emissions can be frequent. Disclosure in a case against the ExxonMobil plant in Baytown revealed 2,158 "nonevents," dwarfing the 333 reportable upsets by more than six to one (Lombardi and Fuller 2013).

Violations

Upsets are considered to be violations under Texas and federal law. Technically, they are seen as unauthorized emissions (*Sierra Club v. Environmental Protection Agency*, No. 02-1135 (D.C. Cir. 2008); Texas Health and Safety Code, 382.0215(a)(1)). However, for many years, industry could avoid penalties if the company succeeded in proving one of a list of "affirmative defenses" (US EPA 2013). For example, a polluter could argue that the release was sudden and unavoidable, beyond its control, and could not have been saved by good design, operation, and maintenance practices (30 Texas Administrative Code 101.222(b)). These defenses date back to at least 1983 and have been widely used (Bennett 1983). During 2014, the TCEQ reported 3,878 "emission events," investigated 1,399, found eight to be excessive, and required just five corrective actions (TCEQ 2015a, 5-3, 5-13, 5-17). The days of using these affirmative defenses may be waning; recently, the courts

have supported EPA's move to greatly restrict their use, though the agency may start relying more on enforcement discretion (79 Fed. Reg. 55920 (September 17, 2014); *Luminant Generation Co. LLC, et al., v. US EPA*, 714 F.3d 841 (5th Cir. 2013); Mehta and Samuels 2015; *Natural Resources Defense Council v. US EPA*, 749 F.3d 1055 (D.C. Cir. 2014)).

Progress

Under Texas rules, upsets can eventually become "excessive" and subject to prosecution. The state rules define "excessive" based on how frequent, long lasting, and damaging the upsets have been, and whether they are tied to truly necessary startups, shutdowns, or maintenance work (30 TAC § 101.222(a)). For example, the state of Texas did secure a large, $50 million judgment in 2011 against BP for illegal emissions during a disastrous explosion (*State of Texas v. BP Products North America, Inc.*, Agreed Final Judgment, No. D-1-GV-09-000921, Travis County District Court, 201st Judicial District). The BP judgment resulted from a 2005 blast that killed fifteen workers and injured 180 others at its Texas City plant. This state suit is a reminder that upsets can be extremely dangerous accidents where plant workers and neighbors are very vulnerable.

While the state has pursued upset cases, there has also been legal pres-

sure from EPA's oversight of State Implementation Plans, and its federal claims against individual firms (75 Federal Register 62567 (October 12, 2010); *Luminant Generation Co. v. EPA*, 714 F.3d 841 (5th Cir. 2013); *U.S. v. BP Products North America*, 610 F.Supp.2d 655 (S.D. Tex. 2009); US EPA 2013). Citizen filings have also been a big factor in reducing upsets. The Clean Air Act of 1970, bolstered by its 1990 amendments, authorized such "private attorneys general" to provide a fail-safe measure to goad government into protecting clean air (42 U.S.C 7411, 7604; Greenbaum and Peterson 2011). Nonprofit groups such as the Environmental Integrity Project, Environment Texas, and the Sierra Club have taken advantage of these provisions. They have initiated enforcement cases against Chevron Phillips, ExxonMobil, Marathon, and Shell to reduce upsets and tighten releases (77 Federal Register 21808 (April 11, 2012); *Environment Texas Citizen Lobby and Sierra Club v. Chevron Phillips*, No. 4:09-cv-02662 (S.D. Tex. 2010); *Environment Texas Citizen Lobby, Inc. and Sierra Club v. ExxonMobil Corporation, et al.*, No. 4:10-cv-4969 (S.D. Tex. 2010); *U.S. v. Marathon Petroleum Company, LP and Catlettsburg Refining*, No. 2:12-cv-11544-DML-MJH (E.D. Mich. 2012); *U.S. v. Shell Oil Company, Deer Park Refining LP and Shell Chemical L.P.*, No. 4:13-cv-2009 (S.D. Tex. 2013)).

The good news is that these suits have brought impressive results. Several facilities, such as the Shell refinery in Deer Park and Chevron Phillips' Cedar Park plant, have made remarkable progress on reducing the scale and impact of upsets following the preventative work required under their settlements (Tresaugue 2013). Comparing the two years before and after the settlement with Shell, upset emissions declined dramatically, with sulfur dioxide discharges falling by 72 percent, and benzene by 89 percent (TCEQ 2013). Similarly, Chevron Phillips saw its upset emissions decline rapidly following its mitigation work, with upset-related NO_x emissions dropping by 46 percent, and upset VOC releases falling by 90 percent. These improvements undercut the claim that upsets are random and unavoidable, and encourage efforts to reduce upsets with foresight and hard work.

To err is human, but . . .

Texas companies and regulators are managing to ratchet down on many types of industrial air pollution. VOC emissions from Texas chemical plants, refineries, utilities, and other large industrial facilities fell by 6 percent from 2010 through 2013, by 10 percent for NO_x, and by 20 percent for SO_2 (TCEQ 2015b). However, overall advances in controlling emissions are undercut by the continuing challenges of reducing upsets. Emission events

increased 10 percent in number from fiscal year 2013 to 2014. And during fiscal year 2014, Texas emission events released over 34.8 million pounds of sulfur dioxide and more than 1.9 million pounds of volatile organic compounds (TCEQ 2015a, 5-2, 5-8). Upsets rightly remain a significant challenge for agencies, firms, workers, nonprofits, and fence-line communities.

In a larger sense, the persistence of these upsets is a sobering reminder of how hard it is to tightly manage technology. New devices and methods in industry have indeed led to better pollution control equipment. Yet at the same time, new technologies have brought their own complexities and risks. Upset air emissions, as well as accidents in other industries, such as the Deepwater Horizon oil spill and Fukushima radioactive release, underscore the difficulty of complete command and control of modern-day equipment. We are still frustrated by human error and machine breakdowns over a century and a half past the dawn of the Industrial Revolution. Each accident offers a reminder of our fallibility, and a cue for humility and caution. Humble pie still needs to be on the menu.

Sources

Air Alliance Houston, Community In-Power and Development Association, Louisiana Bucket Brigade and Texas Environmental Justice Advocacy Services v. McCarthy, EPA

Administrator, No. 1:13-cv-00621-KBJ (D.D.C. 2013). 2013.

Allen, David, and Cyril Durrenberger. 2003. "Accelerated Science Evaluation of Ozone Formation in the Houston-Galveston Area: Emission Inventories." University of Texas and the Texas Natural Resources Conservation Commission. February 5. http://www.utexas.edu/research/ceer/texaqsarchive/pdfs/Emission%20Inventoryv3.pdf, accessed July 15, 2013.

Bennett, Kathleen. 1983. "Policy on Excess Emissions during Startup, Shutdown, Maintenance, and Malfunctions." Memorandum from Assistant Administrator for Air, Noise and Radiation, sent to the Regional EPA Administrators, Regions I–X. Issued February 15.

Carman, Neil. 2013. Clear Air Director, Lone Star Chapter, Sierra Club. Personal communication, July.

Craft, Elena. 2010. "Upset about Upset Emissions." Texas Clean Air Matters Blog, Environmental Defense. http://blogs.edf.org/texascleanairmatters/2010/12/16/upset-about-upset-emissions-2/, accessed July 23, 2013.

Craig, Elizabeth. 2009. Letter from EPA Office of Air and Radiation, to Bill White, Mayor of Houston, April 7. http://www.epa.gov/QUALITY/informationguidelines/documents/08003-response.pdf, accessed July 17, 2013.

Cuclis, Alex. 2012. "Why Emission Factors Don't Work at Refineries and What to Do about It." Emissions Inventory Conference, Tampa, Florida. Environmental Protection Agency. August 13–16. http://www.epa.gov/ttnchie1/conference/ei20/session7/acuclis.pdf, accessed July 23, 2013.

D'Andrea, Mark, and G. Kesava Reddy. 2013. University Cancer Centers, Houston, Texas. http://www.prnews wire.com/news-releases/new-research-conducted-by-university-cancer-centers-links-bp-refinery-incident-to-increase-occurrence-of-cancer-in-texas-city-191390881.html, accessed July 30, 2013.

Dickey, Jill. 2013. Point Source Emissions Inventory Specialist, Texas Commission on Environmental Quality. Personal communication, July.

Environmental Integrity Project. 2004. Gaming the System: How Off-the-Books Industrial Upset Emissions Cheat the Public out of Clean Air. Environmental Integrity Project, August. http://www.environmental integrity.org/pdf/publications/Report_ Gaming_the_System_EIP.pdf, accessed July 4, 2013.

———. 2012. Accident Prone: Malfunctions and "Abnormal" Emissions Events at Refineries, Chemical Plants, and Natural Gas Facilities in Texas, 2009–2011. Environmental Integrity Project. http:// www.environmentalintegrity.org/news_ reports/documents/20120718Accident ProneFinal.pdf, accessed July 4, 2013.

Environment Texas Citizen Lobby, Inc. and Sierra Club v. Exxon Mobil Corporation, et al. 2010. US District Court, Southern District of Texas, Houston Division. Civil Action 4:10-cv-4969, filed December 13.

Environment Texas Citizen Lobby, Inc. and Sierra Club v. Chevron Phillips Chemical Company, LP. Consent Decree and Order. 2011. Civil Action No. 4:09-cv-02662, filed January 10.

Espinosa, Blas. 2013. Upset at Texas Petrochemicals facility, Houston, September 23, 2012. Photograph. Digital image. Texas Environmental Justice Advocacy Services.

Greenbaum, Roger, and Anne Peterson. 2011. "The Clean Air Act Amendments of 1990: Citizen Suits and How They Work." *Fordham Environmental Law Review* 2 (2): article 5.

Haragan, Kelly. 2013. Director, Environmental Law Clinic, University of Texas School of Law. Personal communication, July.

Howarth, Robert, Drew Shindell, Renee Santoro, Anthony Ingraffea, Nathan Phillips, and Amy Townsend-Small. 2012. "Methane Emissions from Natural Gas Systems: Background Paper Prepared for the National Climate Assessment, February 25." http://www.eeb.cornell.edu/howarth/ publications/Howarth_et_al_2012_ National_Climate_Assessment.pdf, accessed July 30, 2013.

Levin, Ilan. 2013. Associate Director, Environmental Integrity Project. Personal communication, July.

Lombardi, Kristen, and Andrea Fuller. 2013. "Upset" Emissions: Flares in the Air, Worry on the Ground. Center for Public Integrity. http://www.public integrity.org/2013/05/21/12654/upset-emissions-flares-air-worry-ground, accessed July 5, 2013.

Lyons, Thomas. 2013. Upset Emissions Inventory, based on Texas Commission on Environmental Quality data. Environmental Integrity Project.

McDaniel, Marc. 1983. EPA-600/2-83/052, Flare Efficiency Study.

Engineering Science, Inc., July. http:// www.epa.gov/ttn/chief/ap42/ch13/ related/ref_01c13s05_ jan1995.pdf, accessed July 15, 2013.

State of Texas v. BP Products North America, Case No. D-1-GV-09-000921. 201st Judicial District Court, Travis County. https:// www.oag.state.tx.us/newspubs/ releases/2011/110311bp_afj.pdf, accessed July 16, 2013.

Sunset Advisory Commission. 2001. Report to the 77th Legislature.

Texas Commission on Environmental Quality (TCEQ). 2013. Air Emission Event Report Database. http://www11 .tceq.texas.gov/oce/eer/index.cfm, accessed July 16, 2013.

———. 2015a. "Annual Enforcement Report, Fiscal Year 2014, Part One: Report and Tables." Texas Commission on Environmental Quality, Office of Compliance and Enforcement, Enforcement Division. November. https://www.tceq.texas.gov/assets/ public/compliance/enforcement/enf _reports/AER/FY14/enfrptfy14 .pdf, accessed June 6, 2015.

———. 2015b. Point Source Emissions Inventory Trends. http://www.tceq .texas.gov/airquality/point-source-ei/ psei.html, accessed June 7, 2015.

Tresaugue, Matthew. 2013. "Citizens' Lawsuits Lead to Less Air Pollution." *Houston Chronicle*. November 28.

US Census Bureau. 2013. American Fact Finder. US Department of Commerce. http://factfinder2.census.gov/faces/nav/ jsf/pages/index.xhtml, accessed July 22, 2013.

US Environmental Protection Agency (EPA). 1995. Compilation of Air

Pollutant Emission Factors Volume I: Stationary Point and Area Sources 1. AP-42. Office of Air Quality Planning and Standards, Office of Air and Radiation, US Environmental Protection Agency. www.epa.gov/ttn/chief/ap42/index.html, accessed July 16, 2013.

———. 2012. Currently Designated Nonattainment Areas, as of December 14, 2012. http://www.epa.gov/oaqps001/greenbk/ancl.html, accessed July 14, 2013.

———. 2013. Memorandum to Docket EPA-HQ-OAR-2012-0322, Statutory, Regulatory, and Policy Context for this Rulemaking, regarding State Implementation Plans: Response to Petition for Rulemaking; Findings of Substantial Inadequacy; and SIP Calls to Amend Provisions Applying to Excess Emissions during Periods of Startup, Shutdown, and Malfunction, February 4.

White, Bill. 2008. Request for Correction of Information under the Data Quality Act and Information Quality Guidelines. Office of the Mayor, City of Houston, Texas. July 9. http://www.bdlaw.com/assets/attachments/2008_City_of_Houston.pdf, accessed July 16, 2013.

Monarch Butterflies

Butterflies and Citizens

The massive 3,000-mile migration of millions of monarch butterflies (*Danaus plexippus*) through Mexico, the United States, and as far north as Canada, is one of the world's great natural events. Yet the story of the protection of this amazing spectacle, of this extraordinary species, is found in many small identification tags, larval monitoring reports, and little side-yard milkweed gardens contributed by thousands of citizens spread across North America. If ever there was a big conservation effort that showed the value of caring citizens, this is it. And much of the migration funnels through Texas, where many of the butterflies' human friends live and help out.

Fame and Mystery

The monarch's existence and its journeys have been known for centuries. In fact, Christopher Columbus is reputed to have seen its migrations in east-

A monarch butterfly (Danaus plexippus), *the state insect of Texas, is shown here feeding on milkweed at the Botanical Gardens in Grapevine, Texas (House Concurrent Resolution No. 94, 74th Legislature, Regular Session, 1995; Slade 2008).*

ern Mexico in the late fifteenth century (Commission for Environmental Cooperation 2008, 19). Over the years, its migration routes and timing came to be quite well understood. There are two populations, one on either side of the Rocky Mountains. The western group flutters north and south, from Southern California in the winter, to the Pacific Northwest in the spring for breeding. The eastern population breeds in the north central and northeastern band of the United States, as well as in the southeastern reaches of Canada. In the fall, this eastern group flies to Mexico to overwinter, coming to Texas and the southern United States to lay eggs the next spring. The Mexican returnees die within weeks of arriving. Their offspring, into the second, third, and fourth generations, continue the migration north again, until the cycle is repeated.

However, the full story of their migration, especially the location of their overwintering site, was not uncovered until 1975. This discovery was only made possible with the help of a legion of volunteer naturalists (Shoumatoff 1999).

Search

In 1937, Fred Urquhart, a zoology professor at the University of Toronto, decided to figure out the hidden story of the monarch migration. Over the years, and through many rounds of

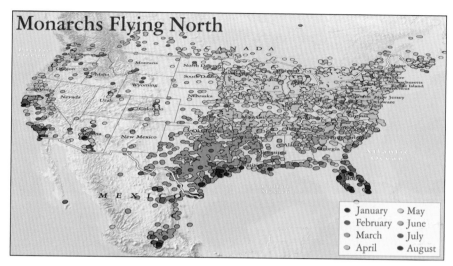

This map shows the multistage northward flow of monarch butterflies, from January through August, for the years 2000 through 2013. Colors for the smaller dots are assigned by two-week periods, with the darkest green corresponding with the first sightings of monarchs in early January, and the red marking the first arrival of the butterfly in mid-August. It is important to remember that no individual butterfly makes the entire northward trip. It is more of a multigenerational relay, with the first stage ending in Texas and other southern states, and the next steps succeeding from there (Howard 2014; Journey North 2014a and 2014b).

As shown here for 2002 through 2013, the northward butterfly migration coincides with the spring's first appearance of various kinds of milkweed, a key food and defense (a source of a cardiac glycoside toxin) for the monarch. The map marks are divided by month, with the dark green tones signifying the emergence of milkweed in January, and the orange showing the first sights of milkweed in June (Howard 2014; Journey North 2014a and 2014b).

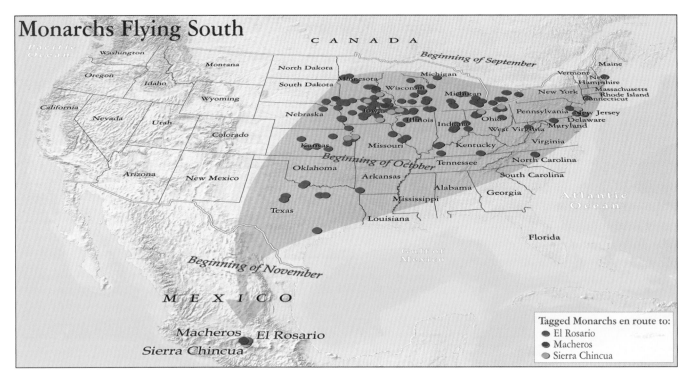

This map tracks the southward journey of a sample of individual monarchs, using tag data. The tags were applied from 2001 through 2011 in Canada and the United States. They were later collected on February 23, 2013, by citizen monitors in the monarchs' overwintering area in the highlands of central Mexico. The lines of text, "Beginning of September", Beginning of October", and "Beginning of November", are midpoint dates estimated for the southward progress of the decade's migrations. The dates can vary a great deal, depending on tail- or headwinds (MonarchWatch 2014a and 2014b).

trial and error, he and his wife, Norah, developed decals of special paper and adhesive that could accompany and identify individual butterflies in their travels. Marked with the plea, "Send to Zoology University Toronto Canada," the returned tags managed to trace the butterfly's flights throughout the United States and Canada.

The network of volunteers spread quickly after 1952, when Norah Urquhart penned a magazine article, "Marked Monarchs." Urquhart's story included an invitation to the public to join a tagging program and help solve the mystery of the monarch. Out of

this appeal grew the Insect Migration Association. By 1971, the association was marshaling the widespread efforts of over six hundred volunteer butterfly enthusiasts (Urquhart 1976).

Discovery

However, despite the association's work, the insect's trail seemed to disappear in Texas. Its overwintering habitat remained a secret. Then, in 1972, Mrs. Urquhart sent an advertisement to Mexican newspapers, asking for help in locating the monarch's winter hideaway. An American inven-

tor, Ken Brugger, and his wife, Cathy, responded to an ad in the *Mexico City News* and began a search. In January 1975, they finally managed to follow Mexican loggers' directions and track ragged butterfly remains to the monarch's winter roost (Urquhart 1976). To their amazement, they found thousands of monarchs clinging to the trunks and every branch and twig of over a thousand oyamel firs. Some colonies were so big and heavy that the limbs broke off under the insects' weight! Later on in the 1970s, others, including Lincoln Brower and Texan Bill Calvert, followed up on Brugger's work to identify yet more monarch sites in those same mountain forests of Michoacán and the Federal District (Brower 1995; Calvert 2014).

Study

The Urquharts' first outreach to the public helped build the core of a vast team of citizen scientists. Throughout the next three-quarters of a century, much of the research, appreciation, and support for the monarch butterfly has rested on volunteer work by amateur naturalists. From 1940 through 2014, 17 percent of monarch-related publications relied on citizen data. In recent years, the dependence on public naturalists has grown still more: since 2000, citizen science information has been used in fully two-thirds of the monarch field studies (outside of the Monarch Butterfly Biosphere Reserve in Mexico, where access is limited). Due to the monarch's wide range, a dispersed army of researchers has become a huge help. This broad network of volunteers has worked on many kinds of tasks, including tagging and recovering butterflies, recording monarch sightings, surveying habitat, breeding and rearing, and planting and tending milkweed plots for feeding. All these efforts add up. In 2011 alone, citizen scientists volunteered over 72,000 hours collecting records for monarchs and serving in general butterfly projects (Oberhauser 2014b; Ries 2014; Ries and Oberhauser 2015).

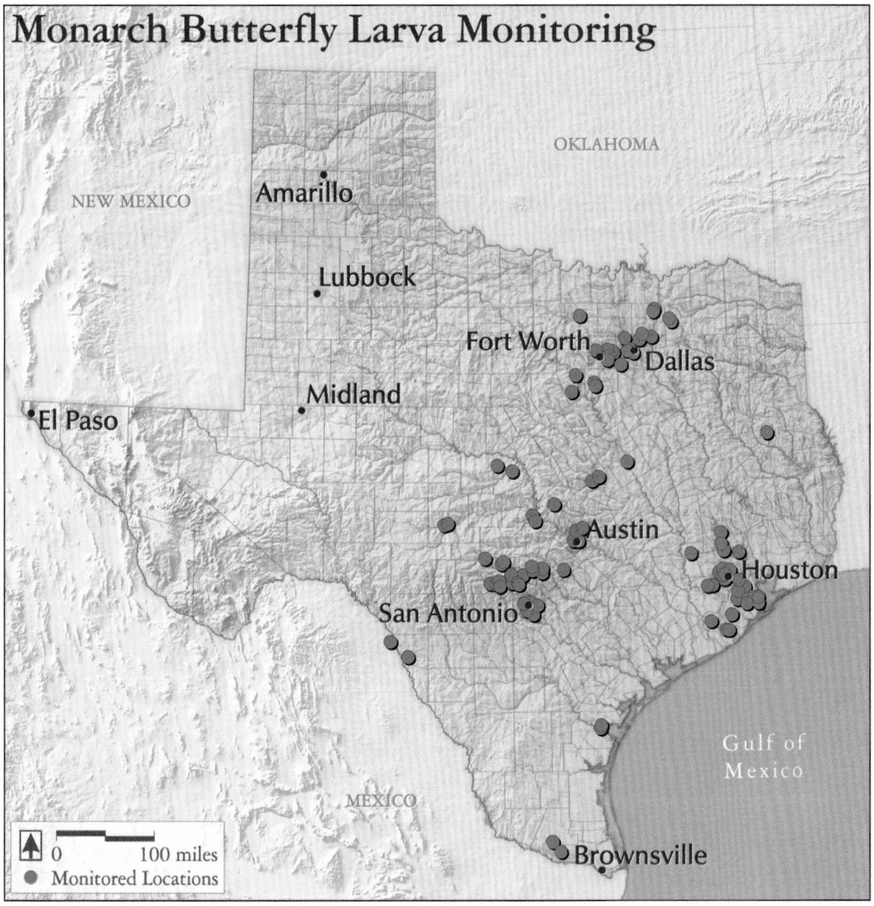

Connections

For many citizen scientists, participating in the larval surveys and or other field research gives them a valuable chance for hands-on, outdoor education. At the same time, the study provides communities a sense of their local habitat's importance, and its connection with the global ecosystem. As Carol Cullar, a teacher in the small border town of Eagle Pass, put it:

> We have monarch butterflies scattered all over the United States all the way from the Great Lakes region up into New England, North Carolina, all the eastern coast, down through central Kansas, Nebraska, North, South Dakota. They begin to migrate

Monarch Butterfly Larva Monitoring

Karen Oberhauser, a professor and ecologist at the University of Minnesota, coordinates an international monarch larva monitoring program. The larvae are found on milkweed, where they feed and gain a self-defense toxin, and in return pollinate the plant. From 1997 through 2014, Texas volunteer partners have checked for butterfly larvae on a variety of milkweed plants (including Asclepias asperula, Asclepias curassavica, Asclepias oenotheroides, Asclepias tuberosa, *and* Asclepias viridis*) at the more than one hundred markers shown here (Oberhauser 2014a and 2014b).*

south. Well, as they do so, they funnel down into a narrower and narrower path. The ones from the central, even New England and Nebraska, all that region between, they funnel down into what's called the central flyway.

By the time it gets here, the central flyway (which has been as wide as half the United States) [is] . . . only about a hundred miles wide. Well, Maverick County is thirty-two miles long and if you picture a bell curve of distribution—very few monarchs west of Del Rio, almost no monarchs south of Laredo—then you have a hundred-mile path and Maverick County sits right at the peak of the bell curve. Eighty percent of the entire migration passes through this part of the country! Well if it's a two hundred million butterfly migration, eighty percent of that is a lot of butterflies. So, starting about the ninth of October until near about the ninth [of] November, there will be hundreds of thousands of butterflies covering the trees in every spot you could imagine all over this county.

It's a perfect, perfect metaphor and opportunity for the kids here to realize that we are an important region. That we could in reality be very important to an entire species, and it connects us then with people in Canada and people in Mexico. So we're not just a little nothing place on a map or an empty place on a map. I want the kids here to see us as tied to the rest of the earth, that the ecology here and the environment here is

important nationally or internationally. (Cullar 2006)

Threats

Professional and amateur researchers are discovering many fascinating aspects of the monarch butterfly's life, but sadly their research has also revealed signs that the insect is declining very rapidly. As recently as the 1996/97 winter, the eastern population of monarchs numbered roughly one billion, yet by 2014, their count had fallen to just thirty-five million. Concern grew to alarm. A coalition of nonprofits and researchers filed a petition with the Fish and Wildlife Service to list the creature as threatened (Center for Biological Diversity et al. 2014, 13; US Fish and Wildlife

Service 2015). Some of the butterfly's decline has apparently been due to natural causes, especially extreme winter weather. However, humans are evidently responsible for other threats facing the monarch, including timber harvest in central Mexico, corn and soybean production in the northern United States, and habitat change throughout the monarch's route, including Texas (Pollinator Health Task Force 2015).

"Logging trucks starting to come around on rickety, terrible roads, shifting loads, dangerous. But they were starting to clear out the lumber."

—Hal Flanders, 2001, remembering a trip to the Monarch's winter habitat

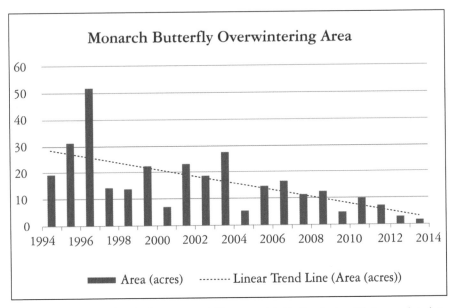

This chart shows the decline in the area occupied by monarch butterfly colonies at their overwintering sites in central Mexico. The colony area's shrinkage reflects both the drop in the insects' overall population and the logging of the oyamel fir forest where they spend their winters (MonarchWatch 2014b).

Mexican Oyamels

The monarch overwinters in a very limited and vulnerable area. Their winter range in the highlands of central Mexico includes only thirteen known sites, each less than 5 acres in size. Fortunately, a generation ago, the Mexican government recognized their great value and acted. In August 1986, Mexican leaders declared the monarch's home in these montane forests as the 33,500-acre Monarch Butterfly Biosphere Reserve. Five of the thirteen colony sites were granted total protection (UNESCO 2014). However, the legal protections have not been enough. By 2012, loggers had clear-cut the oyamel fir forest at one of these five presumed sanctuaries, and had done partial clearing in many other core and buffer areas (Brower et al. 2002; Carde and Resh 2012, 325, 326). While efforts are afoot to restore these forests, the acreage of the butterflies' winter roosts has plummeted by over 90 percent during the past twenty years (Forests for Monarchs 2015; MonarchWatch 2014b).

US Corn, Soybeans, and Milkweed

Corn and soybean farming also affects monarchs. There have been several steps to finding the connection. Using isotopic analysis of monarch wings, Keith Hobson and Leonard Wassenaar discovered that many of the butterflies breed in a 400-mile band that stretches from Kansas to Ohio,

overlapping with the Midwest farm belt (Wassenaar and Hobson 1998). Corn and soybean fields there are often sprayed with herbicides that kill competing plants, including milkweed, that turn out to form a key part of the monarch's diet. Herbicide use grew rapidly with the introduction of

glyphosate-tolerant soybeans and corn in 1996 and 1998, respectively. Then, from 1999 to 2010, records showed that milkweed declined by 58 percent in the Midwest, while at the same time, researchers saw an 81 percent decline in monarch egg production (Pleasants and Oberhauser 2013).

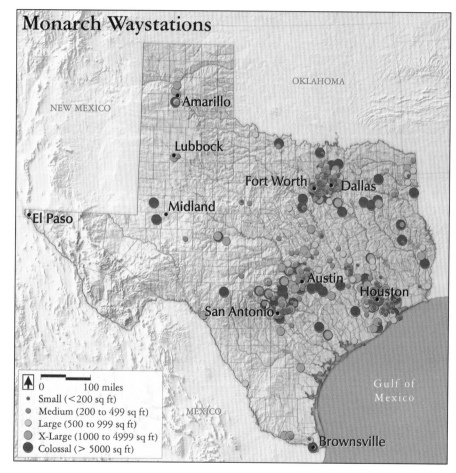

The nonprofit group Monarch Watch has organized a far-flung network of over 9,800 butterfly gardens nationwide where monarchs can find milkweed and other nectar-providing plants in their travels. Over 780 of the participating gardens are found in Texas, where they play a critical role since roughly two-thirds of the first generation of butterflies flying north out of Mexico arrive in the state, feed, reproduce, and die here. Without plentiful food sources in the Lone Star State, the entire chain of migration is undermined. Red markers refer to gardens over 5,000 square feet, orange, 1,000–4,999 square feet, yellow, 500–999 square feet, green, 200–499 square feet, and blue, less than 200 square feet (Howard 2014; Journey North 2014a and 2014b; MonarchWatch 2015).

Glyphosate use in American farm fields has not been the only problem for the monarch. In addition, John Losey and a team of researchers have found that genetically modified corn produces a pollen with an insecticide called Bt to protect the corn against European corn borers. Unfortunately, the Bt-laden pollen can blow and drift and land on milkweed leaves. In turn, many of the monarchs die after eating the contaminated milkweed (Losey, Rayor, and Carter 1999).

Ramarreros and More

Modern crop production and herbicide use certainly pose a risk for monarchs, but habitat conversion throughout the United States also presents a threat. Changes in habitat in Texas can have a particularly big and multiplying impact, since such a large percentage of monarchs funneling back from Mexico stop and reproduce here. An ethnobotanist in Rio Grande City, Benito Treviño explained the importance of native habitat along the Texas-Mexico border. He treasured the few remaining ramarreros, a thorny brush ecosystem of sugar hackberry, anaqua, ash, and cedar elms:

> We did have a ramarrero and . . . it is prime habitat . . . for the monarch butterflies and a lot of the migrating butterflies. For example, when the monarchs are moving south, when they come across the ramarreros, they use them as freeways, and if the ramarrero didn't exist, the butterflies would probably not be able to continue their journey because this particular ecosystem has flowering plants, it has moisture, it has minerals that the monarchs require. In the upland habitat the rest of the ranch doesn't have it . . . It's amazing to walk, . . . 100 acres and see four or five butterflies, and then go into the ramarrero and . . . stand in any one spot and you might spot thirty, forty different kinds of butterflies right there. Because this is a real precious belt of land that eventually connects with other little parcels and makes it all the way to where they're going. (Treviño 2000)

Nurturing

Fortunately, many citizens are working to create habitat that can offset losses from lumbering, agriculture, and urban development, and that can help sustain the monarch in its long travels. One of the leading groups involved is Monarch Watch (a descendant of the Urquharts' Insect Migration Association). Monarch Watch provides instructions, registry forms, and planting kits (including native seed for butterfly weed, common milkweed, swamp milkweed, Indian blanket, purple coneflower, and others) for participating gardeners. Diverse groups support over 9,900 of these monarch "way stations," including homeowners, schools, senior centers, churches, businesses, nature centers, zoos, and others (MonarchWatch 2015). These ideas of restoring habitat for the monarch, as well as other key pollinators, have taken wing with recent support from the Obama administration for enhancing highway rights-of-way, national forests, grasslands, and parks, as well as improving property owned by farmers, ranchers, and utilities (Pollinator Health Task Force 2015, 12).

A Reward

There is a magic to monarchs and their amazing migrations that touches and delights many. In fact, some have called these butterflies the "personification of happiness" (Lane 1993, 341). Sue Bailey, an Audubon warden from Bridge City, in southeast Texas, would probably agree. She summed up her own lifelong fondness for butterflies. "I loved the butterflies better than about anything. I still do for that matter. And I'm rewarded by having a migration of Monarchs come right here and spend the night!" (Bailey 1999). In a sense, just as many gardeners plant milkweed to nurture the traveling butterflies, so does the monarchs' simple existence and extraordinary life nurture those who study and love the butterflies. Perhaps that is the reward for the scientists, in academia and among the public, who work with monarchs and other wildlife.

Sources

Bailey, Sue. 1999. Oral history interview conducted on October 13, in Bridge City, Texas. Texas Legacy Project, Conservation History Association of Texas.

Brower, Lincoln. 1995. "Understanding and Misunderstanding the Migration of the Monarch Butterfly (Nymphalidae) in North America: 1857–1995." *Journal of the Lepidopterous Society* 49: 304–85.

Brower, Lincoln, Guillermo Castilleja, Armando Peralta, Jose Lopez-Garcia, Luis Bojorquez-Tapia, Salomon Diaz, Daniela Melgarejo, and Monica Missrie. 2002. "Quantitative Changes in Forest Quality in a Principal Overwintering Area of the Monarch Butterfly in Mexico, 1971–1999." *Conservation Biology* 16 (2): 346–59.

Calvert, Bill. 2014. Entomologist. Personal communication, June.

Carde, Ring, and Vincent Resh, eds. 2012. *A World of Insects*. Harvard University Press Reader. Cambridge, MA: Harvard University Press.

Center for Biological Diversity, Center for Food Safety, Xerces Society, Lincoln Brower. 2014. Before the Secretary of the Interior: Petition to Protect the Monarch Butterfly (*Danaus plexippus plexippus*) under the Endangered Species Act. Submitted August 26.

Commission for Environmental Cooperation. 2008. North American Monarch Conservation Plan. Communications Department, Secretariat of the Commission for Environmental Cooperation. Montreal, Quebec, Canada.

Cullar, Carol. 2006. Oral history interview conducted on February 22, in Eagle Pass, Texas. Texas Legacy Project, Conservation History Association of Texas.

Flanders, Hal. 2001. Oral history interview conducted on April 4, in Alpine, Texas. Texas Legacy Project, Conservation History Association of Texas.

Forests for Monarchs. 2015. Monarch Area. http://www.forestsformonarchs.org/projects/monarch-area/, accessed June 7, 2015.

Howard, Elizabeth. 2014. Founder and Director, Journey North. Personal communications, June and July.

Journey North. 2014a. "Critical Habitat: Percentage of Monarch Sightings from Each State, as of April 23, 2013." http://www.learner.org/jnorth/monarch/spring2013/c042513_habitat.html, accessed July 11, 2014.

——. 2014b. "Monarch and Milkwood Sightings: 2000–2014." http://www.learner.org/jnorth/monarch/DataReported.html, accessed June 10, 2014.

Lane, J. 1993. "Overwintering Monarch Butterflies in California: Past and Present." In *Biology and Conservation of the Monarch Butterfly*, edited by S. B. Malcolm and M. P. Zalucki. Los Angeles: Natural History Museum of Los Angeles County.

Losey, John, Linda Rayor, and Maureen Carter. 1999. "Transgenic Pollen Harms Monarch Larvae." *Nature* 399 (May 20): 214.

MonarchWatch. 2014a. Peak Migration Dates. http://monarchwatch.org/tagmig/peak.html, accessed July 9, 2014.

——. 2014b. Total Area Occupied by Monarch Colonies at Overwintering Sites in Mexico, Monarch Population Status, as of January 29, 2014. http://monarchwatch.org/blog/2014/01/monarch-population-status-20/, accessed July 9, 2014.

——. 2014c. 2012 Season Tag Recoveries in Mexico. http://monarchwatch.org/tagmig/2012-season-recoveries.html, accessed June 15, 2014.

——. 2015. Monarch Waystation Program Registry. http://www.monarchwatch.org/waystations/registry/, accessed March 27, 2015.

Oberhauser, Karen. 2014a. Monarch Larva Monitoring Project. http://www.mlmp.org/Results/ResultsState.aspx?state=TX, accessed July 10, 2014.

——. 2014b. Professor, Department of Fisheries, Wildlife and Conservation Biology. University of Minnesota. Personal communication, June.

Pleasants, J. M., and K. S. Oberhauser. 2013. "Milkweed Loss in Agricultural Fields Because of Herbicide Use: Effect on the Monarch Butterfly Population." *Insect Conservation and Diversity* 6: 135–44.

Pollinator Health Task Force. 2015. National Strategy to Promote the Health of Honey Bees and Other Pollinators. The White House. May 19.

Ries, Leslie. 2014. Ecologist, National Socio-Environmental Synthesis Center, University of Maryland. Personal communication, June.

Ries, Leslie, and Karen Oberhauser. 2015. "A Citizen Army for Science: Quantifying the Contributions of

Citizen Scientists to our Understanding of Monarch Butterfly Biology." *BioScience* 65 (4): 419–30.

Shoumatoff, Alex. 1999. "Flight of the Monarchs." *Vanity Fair*, November.

Slade, Ken. 2008. Monarch Butterfly Feeding on Red Tropical Milkweed, at Grapevine Botanical Garden, Grapevine, Texas, October 19. Digital image. Flickr. Creative Commons. https://flic.kr/p/afGug8, accessed July 7, 2014.

Treviño, Benito. 2000. Oral history interview conducted on March 1, in Rio Grande City, Texas. Texas Legacy Project, Conservation History Association of Texas.

United Nations Educational, Scientific, and Cultural Organization (UNESCO). 2014. Monarch Butterfly Biosphere Reserve. World Heritage Convention, UNESCO. http://whc.unesco.org/en/list/1290/, accessed June 10, 2014.

Urquhart, Fred. 1976. "Found at Last: The Monarch's Winter Home." *National Geographic*, August.

Urquhart, Norah. 1952. "Marked Monarchs." *Natural History*: 226–29.

US Fish and Wildlife Service. 2015. Endangered and Threatened Wildlife and Plants: 90-Day Findings on Two Petitions: Monarch Butterfly Petition. Proposed Rule. ID FWS-R3-ES-2014-0056-0001. Comment period closed, March 2.

Wassenaar, Leonard, and Keith Hobson. 1998. "Natal Origins of Migratory Monarch Butterflies at Wintering Colonies in Mexico: New Isotopic Evidence." *Proceedings of the National Academy of Sciences* 95 (December): 15436–39.

Energy

In recent years, Texas has seen a boom in wind energy and natural gas production (Texas leads the nation in both sectors). The resulting shift in utility boilers away from coal has helped lower the carbon intensity of the Texas economy by a full quarter during the first decade of this century (US Energy Information Administration 2014a, 2014b, 2014c).

Here we investigate how development of fossil fuels has affected the Texas landscape; we do this by tracking the oil and gas wells and the coal and lignite mines that dot the state. Also, we look at how renewable resources, particularly wind turbines and their state-spanning network of transmission lines, are changing the Texas countryside.

Sources

Agricultural Research Service. 2015. Plant Hardiness Zone Map, Previous Editions of the Map: 1990 US Map. https://planthardiness.ars.usda.gov/PHZMWeb/Images/USZoneMap.jpg, accessed May 7, 2015.

Arbor Day Foundation. 2015. Hardiness Zones, High Resolution Maps. https://www.arborday.org/media/highresolution.cfm, accessed May 7, 2015.

Daly, Christopher, Mark Widrlechner, Michael Halbleib, Joseph Smith, and Wayne Gibson. 2012. "Development of a New USDA Plant Hardiness Zone Map for the United States." *Journal of Applied Meteorology and Climatology* 51 (February): 242–64.

Friesen, Tammy. 2015. Member Services, Arbor Day Foundation. Personal communication, May.

Jacobson, Rebecca, and PBS NewsHour. 2012. "Plant Movement from Climate Change Revealed in Interactive Map." *Scientific American*, March 7.

US Energy Information Administration. 2014a. Electricity: Detailed State Data: Net Generation by State by Type of Producer by Energy Source. http://www.eia.gov/electricity/data/state/generation_monthly.xlsx, accessed August 3, 2014.

———. 2014b. Environment: State-Level Energy-Related Carbon Dioxide Emissions, 2000–2010: Carbon Intensity of the Economy, by State (2000–2010). Tables 1 and 8. http://www.eia.gov/environment/emissions/state/analysis/, accessed August 3, 2014.

———. 2014c. Natural Gas Gross Withdrawals and Production. http://www.eia.gov/dnav/ng/ng_prod_sum_a_EPG0_VGM_mmcf_a.htm, accessed August 3, 2014.

US Environmental Protection Agency (EPA). 2013. Greenhouse Gas Reporting Program: 2011 Data Sets. http://www.epa.gov/ghgreporting/ghgdata/2011data.html, accessed February 25, 2013.

———. 2015. 2013 Greenhouse Gas Data, Summary GHG Data 2013 (as of August 18, 2014). http://www.epa.gov/ghgreporting/documents/xls/ghgp_data_2013-FINAL-8-18-14.xlsx, accessed March 27, 2015.

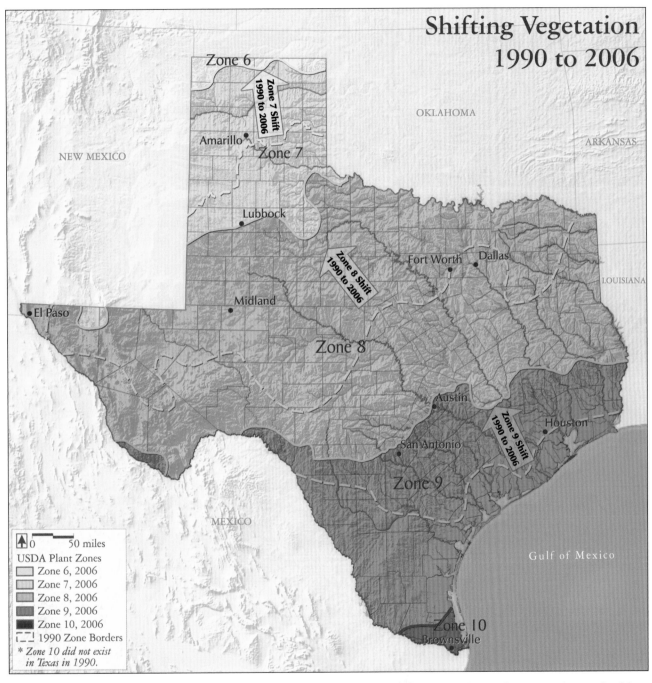

Shifting Vegetation 1990 to 2006

Zone 6

Zone 7 Shift 1990 to 2006

OKLAHOMA

NEW MEXICO

ARKANSAS

Amarillo • Zone 7

Lubbock •

Zone 8 Shift 1990 to 2006

Fort Worth • Dallas •

LOUISIANA

Midland •

• El Paso

Zone 8

Austin •

Zone 9 Shift 1990 to 2006

Houston •

San Antonio •

Zone 9

MEXICO

Gulf of Mexico

0   50 miles
USDA Plant Zones
☐ Zone 6, 2006
☐ Zone 7, 2006
☐ Zone 8, 2006
☐ Zone 9, 2006
■ Zone 10, 2006
☐ 1990 Zone Borders
* Zone 10 did not exist
in Texas in 1990.

Zone 10
Brownsville

With its large and mobile population, heavy industrial base, and high cooling demands, Texas is an energy-hungry place. Its appetites are often fed by burning various forms of carbon, including coal, lignite, natural gas, and oil (US EPA 2013). Unfortunately, our taste for carbon is changing the climate, heating our atmosphere and making it more unstable. The state is already growing warmer, as suggested by this map of northward shifts in plant hardiness zones from 1990 to 2006, echoed by similar shifts between 1960 and 2006, and from 1990 to 2012 (Agricultural Research Service 2015; Arbor Day Foundation 2015; Daly et al. 2012; Jacobson et al. 2012). Concerns over climate change are contributing to rapid declines in coal use, worries over the well technology used to extract transitional fuels such as oil and gas, and enthusiasm for renewable sources of energy, such as wind turbines (US Energy Information Administration 2015a, 2014b, 2014c).

Coal

Coal has long been a part of human life, culture, and industry. Coal has provided heat since 3000 BC for smelting metals, heating lime and ceramics, cooking meals, warming hearths, fueling engines and iron blast furnaces, and even firing altar braziers and funeral pyres. And for over one hundred years, cheap and plentiful coal has provided the vast bulk of the fuel for electricity generation.

However, the use of coal and its kin, lignite and coke, has recently started declining in Texas and throughout the United States. Utilities have retired scores of existing coal plants early and canceled many others before they were ever built. The decline in coal's use is accelerating in the United States: 2012 saw the greatest annual drop in coal-derived electricity on record, a loss of 12.5 percent (US Energy Information Administration 2013a). As of this writing, 139 existing coal, lignite, and coke plants in the United States, and an estimated seventeen older plants in Texas, are slated for early retirement

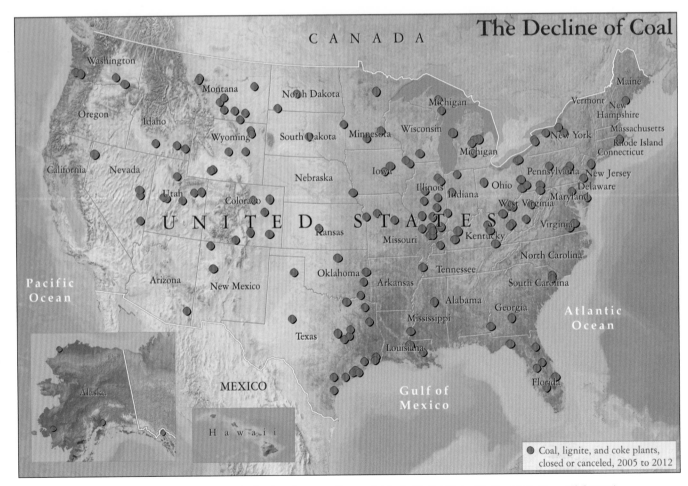

The map shows the coal, lignite, or coke plants or units that have been recently canceled in the United States (Mojica 2013; Sierra Club 2013).

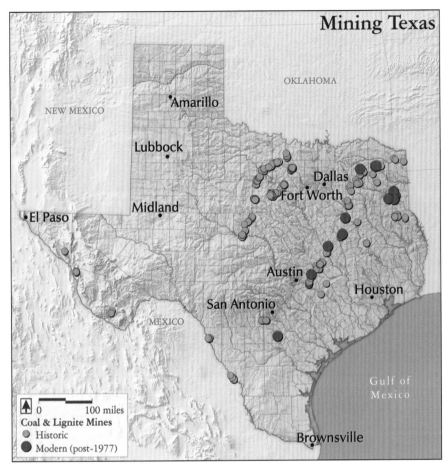

Mining Texas

Locations of 325 registered historic and modern coal and lignite mines in Texas are shown here. Note that many of the state's older coal mines were closed well before passage of the federal Surface Mining Control and Reclamation Act of 1977, and hence have been exempt from its recovery rules. Subsidence and sinkholes near some old shaft mines have appeared in the years since abandonment (Railroad Commission of Texas 2013a and 2013b; Brandt 2013).

Rauch 2009). While none alone has been overwhelming for the coal industry, together these drawbacks have had a big cumulative impact. This chapter looks into some of these causes of coal's retreat, and its repercussions in Texas and throughout the United States.

Mining

The effects of burning coal in Texas stretch far beyond the state's boundaries, and start long before coal reaches the power station. Massive shovels and extensive blasting operations have strip-mined wide stretches of Wyoming's Powder River basin, removed mountaintops and filled valleys in the coal-rich areas of Appalachia, and left many miners with debilitating cases of black lung.

Texas has also been marked by coal and lignite mining. Underground and surface mines have been identified at 325 sites within the state (Brandt 2013; Railroad Commission of Texas 2013a). The first coal mine was dug in Texas as early as 1819, at a seam near the Sabine River. Texas coal mining came into its own in the mid-1880s with the discovery of bituminous deposits near the booming town of Thurber, Texas. In its heyday, Thurber boasted an opera house, hotel, ice plant, and the world's longest horseshoe-shaped bar, manned by twenty-five bartenders! However, the town declined in the 1910s and 1920s as oil started replacing coal as a fuel source for train engines and

(Carman 2013). And according to some estimates, 177 coal, lignite, and coke power plants proposed for US sites, including nineteen for locations in Texas, have been aborted (Mojica 2013; Sierra Club 2013).

This stunning change in the American energy sector has powerful consequences for many businesses, including utilities, coal-mining con-

cerns, railroad companies, and renewable and natural gas rivals. Coal's decline could also have significant impacts on water use, air quality, climate, and public health. The reasons behind the fall-off of coal in the United States are many and diverse, and include environmental concerns, age and obsolescence, and market pressures (Lockwood, Welker-Hood, and

other uses, and its mines closed in 1921 (Ramos 1991). Texas miners turned to lignite in the 1920s, typically operating open pit mines tied to on-site power plants, such as that at Big Brown (Railroad Commission of Texas 2013b).

Later, mining in Texas began to draw its share of controversy. During the 1970s and 1980s, several central Texas nonprofit groups, including the Fayette County Resource Watch and Central Texas Lignite Watch, organized and spoke out against the proposed 10,000-acre Cummins Creek mine (Prager 2003). Pat Johnson, a volunteer who helped fight the mine, was concerned that many of the original mining leases had taken advantage of uneducated, elderly farmers in an isolated rural area. She also discovered that the planned mine would have cut through Native American sites, exposed uranium ore, severed a network of oil and gas pipelines, and pulled valuable land off the county tax rolls (Johnson 2003). As the mine plans were further developed, costs for transporting and drying the lignite began to rise, and dramatic charges of parties, junkets, and prostitution among senior contractors and agency officials were disclosed. Efficiency concerns arose as well: John Prager, a local activist and former coal miner, pointed out that the Cummins mine would have dug up lignite that burned less well than chicken manure! (Prager 2003). With a new executive director, David Freeman, and support from board members such as John Scanlan,

the Lower Colorado River Authority board was finally persuaded to scuttle the project in 1989 (Freeman 2007; Patoski 2008; Scanlan 2003).

Water

Coal-fired utilities require water, lots of it, to cool and liquefy steam as it leaves the turbines, and before returning it to the boilers. This is no different from other steam-cycle power plants, whether they be driven by nuclear fission, natural gas, or oil, but coal uses more water than its rivals (roughly 3.3 times as much as combined-cycle natural gas, for instance) (Ross 2012). Water efficiency is critical for the many arid parts of Texas, especially those that have faced serious drought in recent years.

Water for cooling power plants can come at the expense of competing uses, and lead to hard feelings, dry diversions, and litigation. For example, in November 2012 the Texas Commission on Environmental Quality suspended junior water rights in the Brazos River to ensure supplies to a single senior industrial user (Covar 2012; Covar 2013). With this curtailment affecting over 840 junior rights holders, the commission promptly got embroiled in controversy, with the Texas Farm Bureau filing suit against the agency (Texas Commission on Environmental Quality 2012; Price 2012).

Sometimes there are simply not enough water rights available. Water shortages have been a major factor in

crippling at least one proposed coal plant. The 1,320-megawatt White Stallion coal power plant in Matagorda County applied to the Lower Colorado River Authority for eight billion gallons of water per year, at a price of $55 million, for cooling use. However, after extensive negotiations, the authority rejected the water application in August 2011 (Lower Colorado River Authority 2011). In February 2013, the plant was canceled outright. Additional reasons were involved, but securing a water contract was evidently a key condition for the plant's financing (Galbraith 2011).

Sulfur

Sulfur dioxide (SO_2) emissions from coal power plants have been a long-running problem, due to their impacts on acid rain and respiratory illness. SO_2 discharges were first addressed in the 1963 Clean Air Act, again in the cap-and-trade programs of the 1990 Clean Air Act Amendments, and in the 2005 Clean Air Interstate Rule (42 U.S.C. 7401, P.L. 159, July 14, 1955, 69 Stat. 322, July 14, 1955; P.L. 101-549, 104 Stat. 2399, November 15, 1990; 40 CFR Parts 51 and 96, Federal Register, Vol. 70, No. 249, pp. 77101–77113, December 29, 2005). These programs drove shifts to low sulfur Western coal mines, emissions trades, and smokestack scrubbers. This all had a big effect: national SO_2 emissions fell by 79 percent from 1990 to 2012 (US EPA 2013c). However, there are still many plants throughout the United States, including Texas, that do not yet have scrubbers to remove sulfur dioxide from their stacks (US Energy Information Administration 2011). As of February 2011, 44 percent of Texas coal capacity, by megawatt, did not have scrubbers to cut emissions of sulfur and other contaminants (Gilbert and Catillaz 2011).

The Fayette Power Project, a three-unit coal plant east of La Grange, Texas, has been accused of damaging pecan orchards due to sulfur dioxide emissions (Price 2010). It has been difficult to confirm, but a botanist and a plant pathologist have seen a connection between sulfur discharges and vegetation damage. Further, similar impacts have been found in orchards in the airshed of the Coleto Creek power plant near Franklin, some 100 miles north of the Fayette Power Project. This same damage has appeared at pecan orchards near coal plants in Georgia and New Mexico (Associated Press 2010).

NO_x and Ozone

The majority of Texans live in areas where the EPA considers the air unsafe to breathe (US Census 2010; US EPA 2015). A critical air pollution problem in the state involves smog, also known as ground-level ozone. Ozone is typically associated with nitrogen oxide (NO_x) emissions, often coming from coal-fired plants. The Clean Economy Coalition and medical societies in Nueces, San Patricio, Refugio, and Aransas Counties all came out against the proposed $3 billion Las Brisas power plant, which would have been fired by petroleum coke (a coal-like material derived from oil residues). They feared that the NO_x emissions would bump Corpus Christi into "nonattainment" for ozone, causing asthma and other respiratory diseases (Clean Economy Coalition 2009). When the Texas Commission on Environmental Quality issued an air permit to the Las Brisas plant in January 2011, the Clean Economy Coalition, Environmental Defense Fund, and the Sierra Club filed suit against the TCEQ (*Environmental Defense Fund, Inc. et al. v. Texas Commission on*

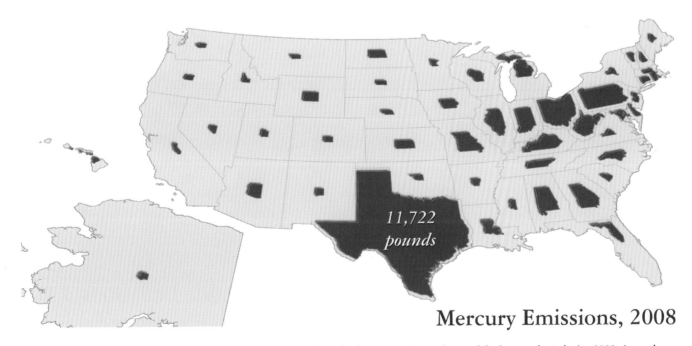

11,722
pounds

Mercury Emissions, 2008

The relative size of the state markers in this cartogram help contrast the scale of mercury emissions from coal-fired power plants during 2008. As seen here, Texas dominates the various states' emissions by a large margin (Environmental Integrity Project 2010, 8).

Environmental Quality, Cause No. D-1-GN-11-001364 (District Court, Travis County)). In July 2012, a state court overturned the permit, and by January 2013, the developer of the Las Brisas plant had announced that the plant was indefinitely suspended (Spruill 2013; *Texas Commission on Environmental Quality and Las Brisas Energy Center, LLC v. Environmental Defense Fund*, No. 03-12-0052-CV (Texas Court of Appeals, Third District, at Austin)).

Mercury

Coal-fired power plants generate about 46 percent of the emissions of US mercury, a potent neurotoxin especially damaging to children (Environmental Health and Engineering 2011, 11). As a result, coal-derived mercury releases have been at the center of a great deal of concern in recent years. Martin Lake Steam Station, near Tatum, Texas, has been one target. Martin Lake is the leading source of airborne mercury in the nation, contributing over 1,500 pounds of mercury in 2011 to the atmosphere (US EPA 2013b).

The effort to limit these coal-related mercury emissions has found its way into industry-wide rule making. In December 2011, the EPA issued new Mercury and Air Toxics standards, which apply to power plants across the country and touch on mercury emissions as well as discharges of arsenic, chromium, nickel, and acid gases (77 Fed. Reg. 9304; 246 DER AA-1, 12/22/11). Industry challenged these rules with the claim that the reduced emissions levels for mercury were not "achievable and measurable." In July 2012, the EPA agreed to reconsider the rules, and in March 2013 issued final rules focused on emissions from future power plants (US EPA 2013d).

Particulate Matter

Soot, or particulate matter, known as PM for short, is another problem that coal plants have faced. PM contributes to asthma, heart attacks, and climate disruption. Some Texas plants have violated their PM discharge

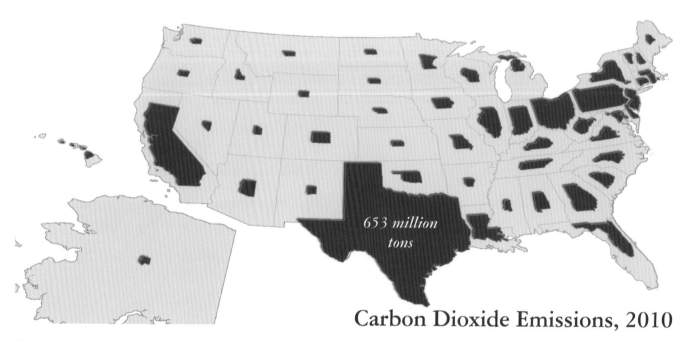

Carbon Dioxide Emissions, 2010

This cartogram shows the relative size of energy-related Texas CO_2 emissions. According to 2010 data, Texas CO_2 emissions were first among all American states, exceeding the second-ranking state, California, by 76 percent, and totaling more than both the second and third state (Pennsylvania). In fact, if Texas were an independent nation, its energy-related CO_2 emissions would rank seventh worldwide, just behind Germany (US Energy Information Administration 2013b and 2013c).

permits and have been brought to court. For instance, in May 2012, the Sierra Club and the Environmental Integrity Project brought a citizens' suit against the Big Brown power plant under the Clean Air Act for violations of the PM standards and opacity limits (*Sierra Club v. Energy Future Holdings Corporation and Luminant Generation Company, LLC*, Civil Action No. 6:12-cv-108; Texas Administrative Code 111.153(b)). Going forward, tightening of national PM standards may put further hurdles in front of yet-to-be-built coal plants (77 Fed. Reg. 38889, June 29, 2012).

Visibility

Coal emissions have also been tied to visibility problems, even in locations far removed from the plant and stack. The Carbon I and II coal-fired plants in Mexico, near Eagle Pass, Texas, provide an example. Although the pair of plants is some 135 miles away, the prevailing southeast–northwest winds cause the plants' plume to degrade Big Bend National Park's famously open skies. Visibility has been known to exceed 200 miles on some clear days in the park, but visibility has dropped as low as nine miles since start-up of the plants (Patoski 1996). EPA tracer and modeling studies concluded that sulfur emissions from the Carbon I and II plants were indeed largely responsible (Pitchford et al. 2004). Despite the fact that national parks get the strongest federal air quality protection, the Carbon stacks' location south

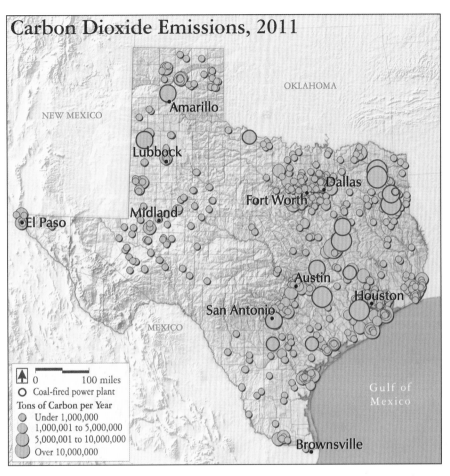

Carbon Dioxide Emissions, 2011

During 2011, carbon emissions totaling over 400 million metric tons of CO₂ equivalent, came from 770 major stationary nonbiogenic sources in Texas, including refineries, petrochemical complexes, cogeneration facilities, cement kilns, steel mills, natural-gas power stations, and coal-fired utilities (US EPA 2013b).

of the border have kept them out of reach of American scrubber requirements (Esty 1994, 187–88; Kiy and Wirth 1998, 194–203).

Carbon

Extensive scientific studies have discovered alarming trends in climate change (Intergovernmental Panel on Climate Change 2014, 6, 10, 21–25).

There are unfortunately many factors destabilizing the climate. Some of the smaller causes include emissions of methane (14 percent), nitrous oxide (8 percent), fluorinated gases, black carbon, and other materials. However, carbon dioxide, both from fossil fuel burning (57 percent) and land use (17 percent), plays the dominant role (Metz et al. 2007). And the greatest portion (26 percent) of that combustion-related

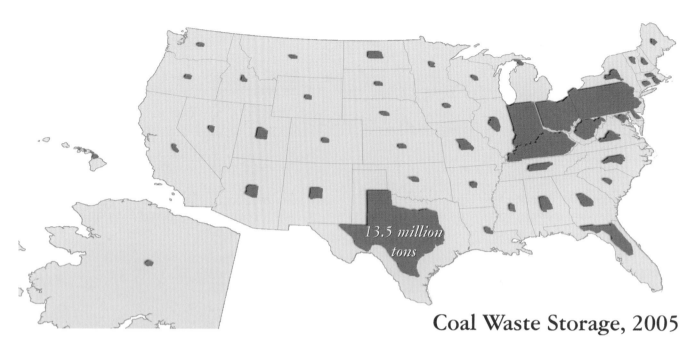

Coal Waste Storage, 2005

This cartogram portrays the relative amounts of coal waste stored among the various states. As of 2005, Texas had more coal waste stored within its borders than any other state (Natural Resources Defense Council 2013).

carbon dioxide comes from power plants, chiefly coal-fired units (US EPA 2013a). Texas power plants are significant here, with six power plants listed among the top fifty CO_2 emitters in the country, more than any other state (Environmental Integrity Project 2010).

Due to these concerns, the EPA has issued tighter standards for greenhouse gas emissions from new power plants (79 Fed. Reg. 1429–1519, January 8, 2014). These new limits will likely lower the number of new coal plants, although there have been efforts to find ways of controlling CO_2 emissions from coal. Most of the ideas have focused on costly and complex strategies that would capture the carbon dioxide from the stack and then rein-

ject it underground, perhaps to help with oil and gas recovery, or to use as a feedstock for urea fertilizer. Proposals for two large carbon capture and storage (CCS) power plants in Texas provide examples. One near Sweetwater was canceled by its developer in June 2013 due to a "challenging market climate." A second near Odessa is still proceeding with $450 million in federal assistance, but faces private costs for the plant that exceed $1.2 billion (Massachusetts Institute of Technology 2014). Since a natural gas power plant of equivalent size, with carbon capture, would cost only 40–45 percent as much, coal's carbon capture efforts do not seem competitive (Spegele and Smith 2012; US Energy Information Administration 2013b).

Operators and agencies will explore CCS and other generating options as states, including Texas, strive to meet the EPA's recently announced Clean Power Plan (Carbon Pollution Emission Guidelines for Existing Stationary Sources: Electric Utility Generating Units; Proposed Rule, 79 Federal Register 34829, June 18, 2014; 40 CFR Part 60). The plan proposes guidelines for fossil-fuel-powered utilities to drive them toward reducing greenhouse gas emissions.

On the Ground

While much of the concern over coal has focused on air emissions, there are also impacts at ground level. Burning coal creates enormous amounts of ash and other solid waste. Recent ash spills at Tennessee and Alabama coal plants brought this issue to the forefront for the more than 440 coal waste storage sites located throughout the United States (Dewan 2008; Dewan 2009). Four of the top ten storage and toxic metal sites are located in Texas, including Martin Lake, Limestone, Monticello, and Pirkey. As of 2005, Texas had more coal waste stored within its borders than any other state (Natural Resources Defense Council 2013).

Natural Gas

Tighter regulations and litigation pressures over environmental and public health concerns have cut back on coal's use. However, coal's decline is also due to market forces in the utility industry, especially from natural gas. Hydraulic fracturing ("fracking") in many tight shale deposits (including the Barnett and Eagle Ford shales in Texas, as well as the Bakken and Marcellus formations in North Dakota and Pennsylvania, respectively) has flooded the natural gas market and dramatically lowered its price. Together with the environmental and public health impacts associated with coal, the fall in gas prices, from over $13/mBtu as recently as 2008, to under $3 currently, has sped the conversion of many existing and planned coal plants to natural gas (US Energy Information Administration 2015). At the new lower prices, many natural gas plants can produce electricity at merely half

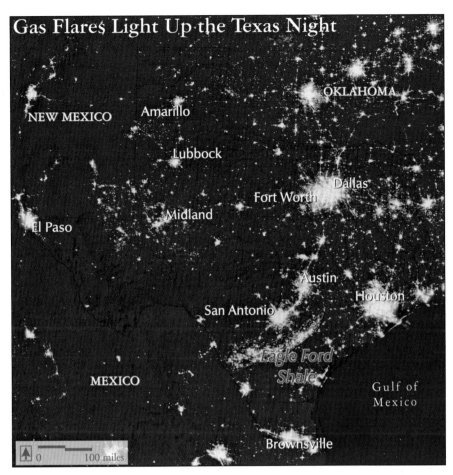

Gas Flares Light Up the Texas Night

This nighttime view of Texas shows the arc of light associated with development of the immense Eagle Ford shale play to the south and southeast of San Antonio. The lights in the Eagle Ford field are evidently tied to flaring of gas and lighting on drill rigs (NASA 2012).

the price of conventional coal, which puts a great deal of pressure on coal utilities in a deregulated market like that in Texas. This is even the case with the mine-mouth lignite power plant at Monticello, Texas, where its protection from coal delivery charges long kept it a low-cost producer of electricity. In fact, low gas prices recently caused two of the three units at Monticello to be idled for winter and spring (Galbraith 2012; Smith 2012).

As a result, we are now seeing a dramatic slide in the role of coal in the US utility industry, especially relative to natural gas. For example, in 2004, coal generated over 50 percent of American electricity, with only 20 percent coming from gas (Freme 2004, 7). Yet ten years later, coal has dropped to a 39 percent share as a supplier of US electricity, and natural gas had climbed to 27 percent (US Energy Information Administration 2014a). The numbers were even more lopsided in Texas, where coal provides 37 percent and natural gas supplies 45 percent of the state's electricity (Electricity Reliability Council of Texas 2014). These numbers represent truly major and rapid shifts in the huge and traditionally slow-changing utility industry.

Many welcome the substitution of natural gas for coal, since its use triggers far lower emissions of sulfur, nitrogen oxide, particulate matter, mercury, and carbon dioxide than does coal, all at a lower cost. In fact, many credit the rising use of natural gas as responsible for the 13 percent drop in American CO_2 emissions since 2007 (Porter 2013). Still, there are trade-offs. For instance, many critics are concerned that hydraulic fracturing uses excessive amounts of water and threatens aquifers with contamination from fracking chemicals. Natural gas production can also lead to releases of methane at the wellhead and compression stations that have serious greenhouse impacts on the climate. Also, there are repercussions from the lower price and greater availability of natural gas, outside of the utility industry. For example, booming shale gas supplies have triggered a number of Texas proposals to build ethylene, polyethylene, methanol and other petrochemical plants that use natural gas as a feedstock and/or fuel, and these plants have their own impacts on air and water quality (Kaskey 2013; Houston Business Journal Staff 2012).

Debt

Aside from the legal, political, health, environmental, and general market pressures on coal and lignite, big financial forces are also in play for individual companies in Texas. For instance, in 2007, the private equity firms Kohlberg Kravis Roberts and TPG bought TXU for a record $45 billion. Going into the leveraged buyout, TXU was the largest power generator and retailer in Texas and had recognized $2.6 billion in profits during 2006. To finance the purchase, the buyers took on $24.5 billion in debt. Saddled with that debt, TXU, later known as Energy Future Holdings, soon saw its fortunes sink. Competing against plants fired by cheap natural gas, operating in the tough post-2008 economy, and facing strong retail competition, Energy Future Holdings saw its debt load rise to $35 billion, its 2011 revenues fall to $7 billion, and its past profits turn to a single-year loss of $1.9 billion. While the Environmental Defense Fund had succeeded in 2007 in persuading Energy Future Holdings to shed plans for eight new costly coal plants planned for Texas, Energy Future Holdings' remaining assets went deeper into the red, valued at just 10 cents on the dollar (Lattman 2012). By April 2014, Energy Future Holdings had entered bankruptcy (Spector, Glazer, and Smith 2014).

Trade

Despite recent declines, Texas remains the largest importer of coal among the fifty states—a costly proposition for utilities and customers in the Lone Star State (US Energy Information Administration 2014b). The price of transporting that fuel to Texas (about two-thirds to three-fourths the cost of the delivered coal) has been a long-standing concern, given track outages, diesel fuel costs, and the control that a handful of railroads have on moving the coal (Texas Comptroller 2008). Also, the export of Texas dollars ($1.9 billion, annually, as of 2008) and jobs to Wyoming and Montana mines has left coal vulnerable economically and politically (Union of Concerned Scientists 2010).

Markets

Traditionally, the debates over coal use involved utility executives and investors, government agencies, and nonprofit organizations. Recently, though, electricity users have been given a vote as well in what had long been a monopoly industry. In 1999, the state legislature opened the wholesale generation end of the Texas utility industry to competition, and in 2002, unlocked the retail part of the business as well (Texas Electric Restructuring Act of 1999, Texas SB 7, June 18, 1999). As a result, electricity customers could now choose their provider. Some are now using that freedom to boycott investor-owned providers (such as TXU/Luminant) that use coal, and switch to those who don't, such as Green Mountain (Galbraith 2013). This pocketbook power has also been seen at the municipally owned utility Austin Energy, where ratepayers have been able to sign on for nonfossil electricity since 2000, leading to what is now the country's largest renewable market (National Renewable Energy Laboratory 2011).

Choices

Coal and its sister fuels lignite and coke have been criticized, regulated, and sued for many years, in many locations, by both government agencies and nonprofits. The industry has been challenged for its mining practices; its water use; its sulfur, nitrogen, mercury, and particulate emissions; its visibility impacts; and its climate change effects. However, these political and legal efforts to reduce coal use struggled to leave a lasting, industry-wide mark, until there were real options that were cheap, plentiful, and available in the market. The technology of hydraulic fracturing in the nation's shale formations, the release of huge and inexpensive supplies of natural gas to the country's utilities, and the openness of retail electric markets have recently provided that viable, and rapidly growing, alternative to coal.

. . . A Caveat

It is important to remember that environmental, public health, and economic pressures on coal may indeed limit its use in the United States, but those domestic trends may only increase the appeal of foreign markets for coal mining firms. Worldwide, coal remains a popular fuel, especially in fast-growing, energy-hungry developing nations. As evidence of this trend, we can look at recent proposals for coal exports through the Ports of Corpus Christi, Galveston, Houston, and Pasadena (Lobett 2012; Parker and Doan 2014; Wooten 2011). Some of these exports will go to China, Japan, Korea, India, and Germany (US Energy Information Administration 2014b, 11). Others do not go far at all; a mine planned for Maverick County on the Rio Grande is proposed to send coal to the Carbon I and II power plants in the Mexican state of Coahuila, just across the border (Campoy 2013).

Sources

Associated Press. 2010. "Fayette Power Project, Coal Plant, Blamed for 'Environmental Catastrophe.'" AP / *Huffington Post*, December 28. http:// www.huffingtonpost.com/2010/12/28/ farmers-pecan-growerssay_n_801945 .html#s2 16082&title=Vegetative_ Wasteland, accessed March 8, 2013.

Brandt, Jon. 2013. Geoscientist—Soils, Abandoned Mine Land Section, Texas Railroad Commission. Personal communication, March.

Campoy, Ana. 2013. "Texas Approves Border-Area Coal Mine." *Wall Street Journal*, January 29.

Carman, Neil. 2013. Sierra Club, Lone Star Chapter. Personal communication, February.

Clean Economy Coalition. 2009. "Clean Energy Coalition Ready to Fight Las Brisas Permit." Press Release. February 16. Clean Economy Coalition. www .cleaneconomycoalition.org/downloads/ pr_021609.pdf, accessed June 7, 2015.

Covar, Zak. 2012. Order Suspending Water Rights on the Brazos River Basin. Texas Commission on Environmental Quality. November 19.

———. 2013. Modification of Restrictions on Junior Water Right Holders in the Brazos River Basin. Texas Commission on Environmental Quality. January 8.

Dewan, Shaila. 2008. "Coal Ash Spill Revives Issue of its Hazards." *New York Times*, December 28.

———. 2009. "Waste Spills at Another T.V.A. Power Plant." *New York Times*, January 9.

Electricity Reliability Council of Texas. 2014. Energy by Fuel Type 2014, 2014 Demand and Energy Report. http:// www.ercot.com/content/news/ presentations/2014/ERCOT2014D& E.xls, accessed August 30, 2014.

Environmental Health and Engineering, Inc. 2011. Emissions of Hazardous Air Pollutants from Coal-Fired Power Plants. EH&E Report 17505, March 7. Prepared for American Lung Association. Washington, DC.

Environmental Integrity Project. 2010. "Dirty Kilowatts: America's Top Fifth Power Plant Mercury Polluters." March. http://www. environmental integrity.org/ news_reports/docu ments/EIP_Top50USPowerPlant

MercuryEmitters2010.FINAL042910 .pdf, accessed March 4, 2013.

———. 2012. Forty-Nine Coal-Fired Plants Acknowledge Groundwater Contamination in Response to EPA Data Collection. April. http://www .environmentalintegrity.org/news_ reports/documents/20120426_Final_ ICRDataReport.pdf, accessed March 17, 2013.

Esty, Daniel. 1994. *Greening the GATT: Trade, Environment, and the Future.* Washington, DC: Institute for International Economics.

Freeman, David. 2007. Oral history interview conducted on July 23, in Los Angeles, California. Texas Legacy Project, Conservation History Association of Texas.

Freme, Fred. 2004. US Coal Supply and Demand: 2004 Review. US Energy Information Administration. Washington, DC.

Galbraith, Kate. 2011. "Water Deal for Texas Coal Plant Postponed." *Texas Tribune*, June 15.

———. 2012. "Texas Coal Plant Scales Back Operations." *Texas Tribune*, August 31.

———. 2013. "Sierra Club Taking Aim at East Texas Coal Plants." *New York Times*, February 9.

Gilbert, Jesse, and John Catillaz. 2011. Retire or Retrofit? A Look at US Regional Scrubbed Coal Capacity. American Public Power Association. http://www.publicpower.org/files/ Retire%20°r%20retrofit%20-%20 %20A%20100k%20at%20US%20 regional%20scrubbed%20coal%20 capacity.pdf, accessed March 14, 2013.

Houston Business Journal Staff. 2012. "Billions of Dollars of Chemical Plants Planned in the Houston Area." *Houston Business Journal*, July 27.

Intergovernmental Panel on Climate Change. 2014. Summary for Policymakers. In "Climate Change 2014: Impacts, Adaptation, and Vulnerability. Part A: Global and Sectoral Aspects." Contribution of Working Group II to the 5th Assessment Report of the Intergovernmental Panel on Climate Change. C. B. Field, V. R. Barros, D. J. Dokken, K. J. Mach, M. D. Mastrandrea, T. E. Bilir, M. Chatterjee, K. L. Ebi, Y. O. Estrada, R. C. Genova, B. Girma, E. S. Kissel, A. N. Levy, S. MacCracken, P. R. Mastrandrea, and L. L. White, eds. New York: Cambridge University Press.

Johnson, Pat. 2008. Oral history interview conducted on February 24, in Fayetteville, Texas. Texas Legacy Project, Conservation History Association of Texas.

Kaskey, Jack. 2013. "Occidental Petroleum Seeks to Build Texas Ethylene Plant." *Bloomberg*, February 5. http://www .bloomberg.com/news/2013-02-05/ occidental-petroleum-seeks-to-build-texas-ethylene-plant.html, accessed March 6, 2013.

Kiy, Richard, and John Wirth, eds. 1998. *Environmental Management on North America's Borders.* The North American Institute.

Lattman, Peter. 2012. "A Record Buyout Turns Sour for Investors." *New York Times*, February 28.

Lobett, Ingrid. 2012. "Gulf Coast Joins Export Coal Rush." *Houston Chronicle*, October 20.

Lockwood, Alan H., Kristen Welker-Hood, and Molly Rauch. 2009. "Coal's Assault on Human Health." Physicians for Social Responsibility. http://www .psr.org/assets/pdfs/psr-coal-fullreport .pdf, accessed February 23, 2013.

Lower Colorado River Authority. 2011. August 10 LCRA Board Meeting Cancelled after White Stallion Water Contract Pulled from Agenda. August 3. http://lcra.org/newsstory/2011/ boardmeetingcanceledWStallion.html, accessed March 8, 2013.

Massachusetts Institute of Technology. 2014. Texas Clean Energy Project Fact Sheet. Carbon Capture and Sequestration Technologies. http:// sequestration.mit.edu/tools/projects/ tcep.html, accessed August 30.

Metz, B., O. R. Davidson, P. R. Bosch, R. Dave, and L. A. Meyer, eds. 2007. Contributions of Working Group III to the Fourth Assessment Report of the Intergovernmental Panel on Climate Change. New York: Cambridge University Press.

Mojica, Ruben. 2013. Conservation Department, Environmental Law Program, Sierra Club. Personal communication, March 19.

National Renewable Energy Laboratory. 2011. NREL Highlights 2010 Utility Green Power Leaders. Golden, Colorado. May 9. http://www.nrel.gov/ news/press/2011/1367.html, accessed April 18, 2013.

Natural Resources Defense Council. 2013. Contaminated Coal Waste: Coal Waste by State, Existing Plants. http://www. nrdc.org/energy/coalwaste/existing plants.asp, accessed April 18, 2013.

NASA. 2012. Earth at Night 2012. Images collected by *Suomi NPP* satellite in April and October. Data provided by NASA Earth Observatory / NOAA NGDC. http://eoimages.gsfc.nasa.gov/ images/imagerecords/79000/79800/

dnb_united_states_lrg.tif, accessed October 12, 2014.

Parker, Mario, and Lynn Doan. 2014. "Gulf Coast Embraces U.S. Coal Shippers Rejected by West." *Bloomberg Business*, November 20.

Patoski, Joe. 1996. "Big Bend, R.I.P." *Texas Monthly*, March.

———. 2008. "Full Stream Ahead." *Texas Observer*, February 8.

Pitchford, Marc, Ivar Tombach, Michael Barna, Kristi Gebhart, Mark Green, Eladio Knipping, Naresh Kumar, William Malm, Betty Pun, Bret Pun, Bret Schichtel, and Christian Seigneur. 2004. "Big Bend Regional Aerosol and Visibility Observational Final Report." US Environmental Protection Agency and National Park Service. http://vista .cira.colostate.edu/improve/studies/ BRAVO/reports/FinalReport/bravofinal report.htm, accessed March 8, 2013.

Porter, Eduardo. 2013. "A Model for Reducing Emissions." *New York Times*, March 19.

Prager, John. 2003. Oral history interview conducted on October 17, in Rosanky, Texas. Texas Legacy Project, Conservation History Association of Texas.

Price, Asher. 2010. "Is Power Plant to Blame for Poor Pecan Crop?" *Austin American-Statesman*, December 6.

———. 2012. "Farmers Battle State Environmental Agency in Brazos River Basin Dispute." *Austin American-Statesman*, December 26.

Railroad Commission of Texas. 2013a. Coal and Lignite Mines of Texas. http://www.rrc.state.tx.us/forms/maps/ historical/CoalMiningAreasShapefile .zip, accessed March 6, 2013.

———. 2013b. Historical Coal Mining in Texas. http://www.rrc.state.tx.us/

forms/maps/historical/historicalcoal .php, accessed March 6, 2013.

Ramos, Mary. 1991. Thurber, Texas Coal Town. Texas Almanac, 1990–91. http://www.texasalmanac.com/topics/ history/thurber-texas-coal-town, accessed March 8, 2013.

Ross, Lauren D. 2012. "Water for Coal-Fired Power Generation in Texas: Current and Future Demands." February 22. Prepared for the Lone Star Chapter of the Sierra Club. http://texas.sierraclub.org/press/ WaterForCoal20120229.pdf, accessed March 15, 2013.

Scanlan, John. 2003. Oral history interview recorded in Austin, Texas, on October 14. Texas Legacy Project, Conservation History Association of Texas.

Sierra Club. 2013. Stopping the Coal Rush. http://www.sierraclub.org/ envi ronmentallaw/coal/map/default.aspx, accessed March 13, 2013.

Smith, Rebecca. 2012. "Coal-Fired Plants Mothballed by Gas Glut." *Wall Street Journal*, September 11.

Spector, Mike, Emily Glazer, and Rebecca Smith. 2014. "Energy Future Holdings Files for Bankruptcy." *Wall Street Journal*, April 29.

Spegele, Brian, and Rebecca Smith. 2012. "China's Sinopec Pursues Big Energy Deal in Texas." *Wall Street Journal*, August 14.

Spruill, Rick. 2013. "Las Brisas Project Halted: Company Financing the Project Is Going out of Business." *Corpus Christi Caller-Times*, January 23.

Surface Mining and Reclamation Act of 1977. 30 U.S.C. Sections 1234–1324.

Texas Commission on Environmental Quality. 2012. "TCEQ Restricts

Junior Water Right in Upper Brazos." November 21. http://www.tceq.texas . gov/ news/releases/112112Brazos CallDrought, accessed March 17, 2013.

Texas Comptroller of Public Accounts. 2008. "The Energy Report: Coal." Publication 96–1266. http:// www .window.state.tx.us/specialrpt/energy/ nonrenewable/coal.php, accessed March 14, 2013.

Union of Concerned Scientists. 2010. "Burning Coal, Burning Cash: Ranking the States That Import the Most Coal." http://www.ucsusa.org/clean_energy/ smart-energy-solutions/decrease-coal/ burning-coal-burning-cash.html, accessed March 14, 2013.

US Census. 2010. 2010 Census, Demographic Profile 1, County Subdivisions. Shapefile. http://www2 .census.gov/geo/tiger/TIGER2010DP1/ CouSub_2010Census_DP1.zip, accessed June 7, 2015.

US Energy Information Administration. 2011. Coal Plants without Scrubbers Account for a Majority of U.S. SO_2 Emissions. http://www.eia.gov/today inenergy/detail. cfm?id =4410#, accessed March 14, 2013.

———. 2013a. Electric Power Monthly, Data for November 2012. US Department of Energy. http://www .eia.gov/electricity/monthly/index.cfm, accessed February 23, 2013.

———. 2013b. State CO_2 Emissions, 2010. http://www.eia.gov/environment/ emissions/state/state_emissions.cfm, accessed April 18, 2013.

———. 2013c. Total Carbon Dioxide Emissions from the Consumption of Energy, All Countries by Region, International Energy Statistics. http://www.eia.gov/

cfapps/ipdbproject/IEDIndex3. cfm?tid=90&pid=44&aid=8, accessed April 18, 2013.

———. 2013d. US Department of Energy. http://www.eia.gov/oiaf/beck_plant costs/excel/table1.xls, accessed March 11, 2013.

———. 2014a. Electric Power Monthly, Table 1.1. Net Generation by Energy Source: Total (All Sectors), 2004– June 2014. US Department of Energy. http://www.eia.gov/electricity/monthly/ epm_table_grapher.cfm?t=epmt_1_1, accessed August 30, 2014.

———. 2014b. Quarterly Coal Distribution Report, January–March 2014. June. US Department of Energy. http://www. eia.gov/coal/distribution/quarterly/pdf/ q1_coal_distribution14.pdf, accessed August 30, 2014.

———. 2015. Henry Hub, Spot Price, Natural Gas Spot and Futures Prices (NYMEX). Spreadsheet. US Department of Energy. http://www .eia.gov/dnav/ng/xls/NG_PRI_FUT_ S1_D.xls, accessed June 7, 2015.

US Environmental Protection Agency (EPA). 2013a. Global Emissions. http://www.epa.gov/climatechange/ ghgemissions/global.html, accessed March 4, 2013.

———. 2013b. 2011 Greenhouse Gas Emissions from Large Facilities. http://www.epa.gov/ghgreporting/ ghgdata/2011data.html, accessed April 18, 2013.

———. 2013c. Reconsideration of Certain New Source Issues. 40 CFR Parts 60 and 63. Dockets ID No. EPA-HQ- OAR-2009–0234 (MATS NESHAP) and No. EPA-HQ-OAR-2011-0044 (NSPS action). http://www.epa.gov/ mats/pdfs/20130328notic.pdf, accessed April 18, 2013.

———. 2013d. Table of National Aggregated Emissions, Emission Rates, Heat Input: 1990, 2000, 2005, 2010, and 2012. http://www.epa.gov/air markets/quarterlytracking.html, accessed March 14, 2013.

———. 2013e. Toxic Release Inventory. http://oaspub.epa.gov/enviro/ tris_control_v2.tris_print?tris_ id=75691MRTNL8850F, accessed March 8, 2013.

Wooten, Casey. 2011. "Kinder to Export Coal from Port of Houston." *Houston Business Journal*, April 25.

Oil and Gas, Water and Wastewater

Sins of the Father

The Abrahamic tradition is full of verses and parables regarding how the faithful should deal with "the sins of the father" (Numbers 14:18; Exodus 20:1–26; Ezekiel 18:19–20). Are future generations liable for the mistakes and shortcomings of their predecessors? Do the sins die with our forebears, or live on for us to atone for?

In environmental situations, we often have to confront our inheritance, both good and bad. Past blunders and errors, old spills and leaks, can long survive the original culprits and then cause all sorts of mischief far into the future. In each era, we must try to repair earlier damage and protect coming generations. Environmental conservation work in the Texas oil fields, both on its old production wells and its newer waste injection wells, gives one example.

This view of a forest of oil rigs south of Beaumont, circa 1901, suggests the vast number of oil and gas wells that have punctured Texas lands over the past century and more. In this scene, five hundred wells were reported to have been drilled on just 144 acres; derrick legs on some adjoining prospects touched one another. While the oil industry brought Texas great wealth, many wells in the state were unfortunately abandoned and left unplugged, remaining as an environmental liability for years to come (Trost 1901).

Oil and Gas Wells

The earliest oil well in Texas is reputed to date back to 1866, when Lyne Barret drilled a well in Oil Springs, near Nacogdoches (Barret 1966). In the intervening century and a half, over 1.5 million oil and gas wells have been drilled across the state (Texas Center for Policy Studies 1995, chap. 7, p. 2). Currently, the Railroad Commission has records of over 410,000 known wells in the state, more than 301,000 of which are considered active (Railroad Commission of Texas 2013, 2). There are more producing wells in Texas than in any other state in the Union (US Energy Information Administration 2011).

Oil, Waste, and Water

However, most of the wells in Texas are not producing. Many were dry holes from the outset or were pumped out over time. After the disappointed operators recovered their pump jacks and compressors, the remaining bore-holes presented their own problems. As nearby wells were drilled and pressurized, concerns arose many years ago about the chance that oil and gas and other chemicals might seep through open well bores. Leaked gas might ignite at the surface, or fluids might contaminate drinking water supplies in local aquifers (National Petroleum Council 2011, 16). These dicey connections between aquifers and oil reserves were grasped from the earliest days of the petroleum indus-

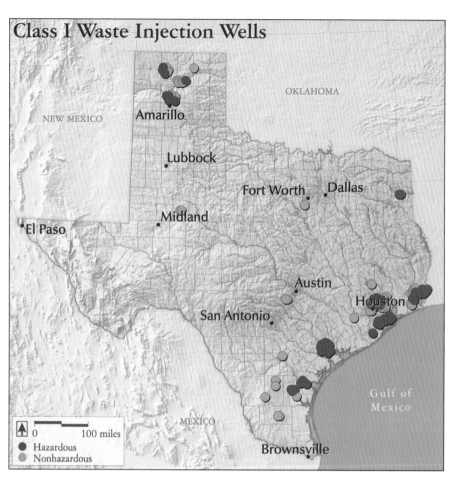

Class I Waste Injection Wells

This map shows 108 active Class I wells that inject materials underground in Texas, as of June 2014. Sixty-one of these Texas wells (marked in red) are permitted to handle hazardous waste, roughly half of all those reported for the United States. The waste is injected from 1,100 feet to 9,100 feet below grade. Of course, this is far beneath most wells tapping freshwater aquifers. However, concern has remained about the integrity of the thousands of feet of injection shaft that lie between the surface and the injection zone (Council 2014; Davis 2014; US EPA 2001, 3).

try; in fact, the first major oil discovery in the state, made in Corsicana in 1894, occurred while drilling for water (King 1970).

In more recent times, the possible interactions among water, oil, gas, and wastewater have grown more serious and complex. Complications flow from the hazardous wastes and brines that have been reinjected down-bore under great pressure. Risks also rise from production zones that have been hydraulically fractured with caustic chemicals and high pressures, especially when these new wells have been drilled into historic fields that are pockmarked with old shafts. There is a natural concern that the fluids may fol-

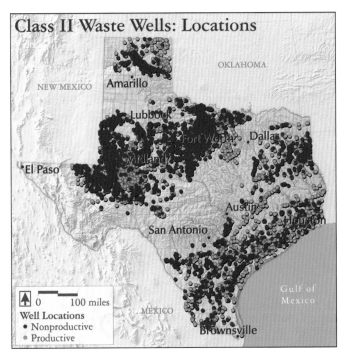

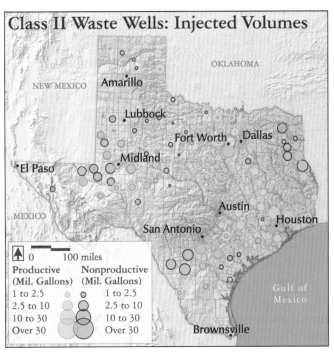

The "Locations" map marks over 7,700 active "Class II" injection wells registered by the Texas Railroad Commission. Its companion figure "Injected Volumes" shows the quantities of oil-field wastewater (summed by county for 2013) that are pumped underground by these same wells. The wastewater is mostly brine, but is also mixed with smaller amounts of drilling mud, fracture fluids, anticorrosion compounds, hydrocarbons, and radioactive materials. Over 4,100 Class II wells inject into formations that are "productive" of oil and gas, while the remaining Class II wells operate in formations that are "nonproductive." An additional 25,000 active injection wells (not shown here) are tracked by the commission and used for other purposes, largely storage or secondary recovery of oil and gas (injecting the fluids helps to maintain pressure in a formation and to "sweep" more hydrocarbons to the well) (Krueger 2014; Railroad Commission of Texas 2014a).

low the old abandoned boreholes and possibly contaminate aquifers.

Several kinds of these wells pump materials down into the substrata. The Texas Commission on Environmental Quality regulates one type known as "Class I" wells. They inject a variety of hazardous and nonhazardous wastes into the subsurface, mostly by-products of the refining, smelting, chemical, and pharmaceutical industries.

The Texas Railroad Commission monitors another kind of injection well, described as a "Class II" well. These wells pump fluids associated with oil and gas production, hydrocarbon storage, and wastewater. Impressive amounts of wastewater are injected underground through these Class II wells—as much as 31 billion gallons in 2013 alone (Railroad Commission of Texas 2014b). These figures exclude the large volumes that are injected to enhance oil and gas recovery, or to store products underground.

Caring for Wells

Modern injection wells have certainly complicated the dangers of mixing oil, chemicals, and water. However, the effort to cope with these risks goes back to the earliest days of production wells. Perhaps the state's years of managing oil and gas well risks will also help us look after the Class I and II wastewater wells going into the future. The Texas legislature began its environmental work with production wells in 1899, when it passed the original bill regarding the plugging of oil and gas wells. With the modern administrative, regulatory state still in its infancy, the legislature gave no agency the responsibility for carrying out that charge (House Bill 542, 26th Texas Legislature, regular session). However, in 1919, the legislature finally assigned that authority to the Railroad Commission, the first regulatory agency in the state (Senate Bill 350). Later that same year, the commission issued rules to protect underground water supplies, requiring operators to seal off productive layers and protect intervening aquifers (SB 350; Statewide Rules 10(b), 13, 20, and 23, Oil and Gas Circular No. 7, June 18, 1919). The legislature backed up these plugging rules with a 1923 law making water pollution from crude petroleum, oil, or similar materials a crime (1923 Tex. Gen. Laws, Ch. 85, repealed, 1969 Tex. Gen. Laws, Ch. 154).

"Plugging" is a tricky term, and it has taken years, and a good deal of rule making in Austin and evolution in the field, to refine its meaning by law and its practice underground. Over time, most abandoned oil and gas wells have been plugged with concrete, often together with drilling mud or bentonite (Arthur 2011, 10). However, especially many years ago, some wells were just plugged with rocks, buckets, tree stumps, cloth sacks, or even a glass jug (National Petroleum Council 2011; Suro 1992). The results were, in a word, inconsistent. So, in 1934, the commission issued express instruc-

tions on how to properly plug a well, a process that has improved greatly over the years (but that is still not foolproof, as the country saw in the case of the Deepwater Horizon spill) (Varela 2000, 6; Statewide Rule 13).

The seven-year drought of the 1950s seems to have brought special attention to the great value of freshwater, both on the surface and underground, and the danger that unplugged

or poorly cased wells could pose. In 1953, the legislature authorized plugging oil wells that were jeopardizing the water supply for the city of Callahan by leaking saltwater into the Frio River (1951 Texas Gen. Laws, Ch. 227; 1953 Texas Gen. Laws, Ch. 141). A few years later, in 1957, the commission promulgated rules specifically protecting freshwater sands (Railroad Commission of Texas 1957; Varela

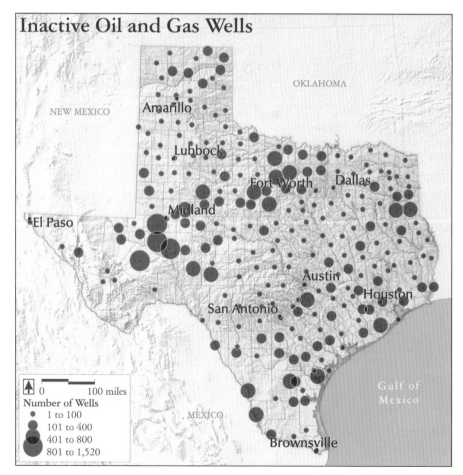

The Railroad Commission is tracking these 41,000 inactive, noncompliant oil and gas wells in the state that lack bonding, a subset of the larger universe of over 100,000 idled wells. Here they are shown summed by county, current as of 2014 (Railroad Commission of Texas 2013, 2; Railroad Commission of Texas 2014c).

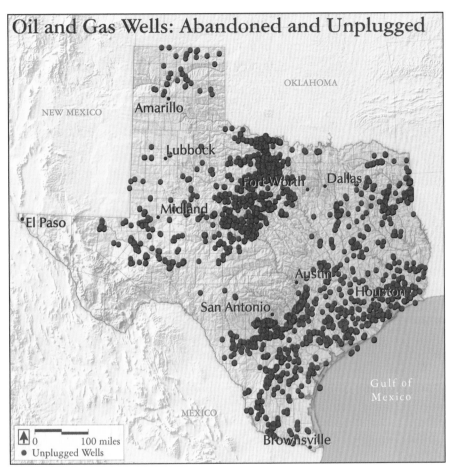

Oil and Gas Wells: Abandoned and Unplugged

The Railroad Commission has records of over 5,600 unplugged, abandoned oil and gas wells in Texas, distributed widely across the state (Krueger 2014).

However, given the enormous number of these idled wells (over 108,000 wells today in Texas), the Railroad Commission enacted new rules in 1992 requiring improved monitoring and testing of older, inactive wells (Statewide Rule 14; Railroad Commission of Texas 2013, 2). In 1993, to help bring more of these wells back into production, and avoid the risk of them being abandoned, the state of Texas began offering severance tax exemptions under its Inactive Wellbore Initiative (Texas Administrative Code Section 3.83; Tax Code Sections 201.053, 202.052, 202.056). Not only did this rule give operators an incentive to keep the wells intact and safe, but it also spun off taxes, jobs, and revenue.

Orphan Wells

In some cases, wells have gone beyond inactive, idle status and have become abandoned and finally delinquent in the eyes of the commission. At the end, they are officially considered "orphans." Orphan wells arrive with their own special plugging issues, since there is no ready source of private cash for sealing the wells. So Texas began a state program in 1965 to plug these orphans using general revenue (Texas Natural Resources Code Section 89.043). However, in 1983, after the collapse of oil prices and a decline in severance tax income, the legislature had to go a step further, creating a more secure, dedicated Well Plugging Fund. The fund drew

2000, 6). The regulatory sweep of the Railroad Commission grew yet more in 1982, with its receipt of delegated federal powers under the Safe Drinking Water Act's Underground Injection Control program (41 Federal Register 36730, August 31, 1976; 40 CFR 146; 47 Federal Register 618, January 6, 1982 and 47 Federal Register 17488, April 23, 1982).

Inactive Wells

Surprisingly, the owners of many of the wells in need of plugging have not permanently abandoned them. A national study found that 22 percent of unplugged wells were just idle or temporarily inactive, not abandoned. Often, the wells were just waiting for a more profitable time to pump (Interstate Oil and Gas Compact Commission 1996, 2).

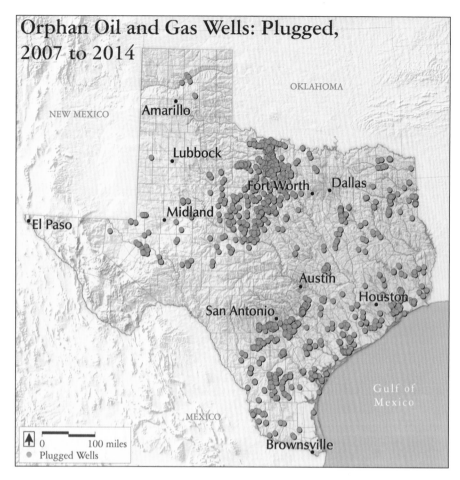

Orphan Oil and Gas Wells: Plugged, 2007 to 2014

As an effort to protect drinking water supplies in the state, the state of Texas has plugged close to 2,900 oil and gas wells from 2007 through 2014, as shown here, and over ten times as many in the 1984–2006 period (Krueger 2014).

2013, the state raised the fund's cap to $30 million (Texas Natural Resource Code Section 89.083; HB 3444, 1999; HB 3309, 2013). Court rulings have made a difference too, empowering the commission to recover plugging costs from well owners and operators who have sought bankruptcy protection (*Texas v. Lowe*, 151 F.3d 434, 439 (5th Cir. 1998)).

Despite these state efforts to plug orphan wells in Texas, over 8,600 still exist in the state. Nevertheless, the regulatory work has definitely had a good impact: the total number of these wells is down 48 percent over the past decade (Railroad Commission of Texas 2013, 2; Railroad Commission of Texas 2003, 2).

Costs

Despite the helpful state and industry funding, and the gradual progress in corking these wells over the years, the well-plugging challenge has been huge, long lasting, and very costly. From 1984 through 2014 (as of April 30, 2014), the state has plugged 34,158 wells at an expense of over $230 million (Fernandez 2014). Most of the plugging work has been on land, but offshore wells have proved particularly expensive to plug, even in relatively shallow bay waters. For example, a dozen wells lying off the Texas coast cost $170,000 each to plug in 2012 (Galbraith 2013). The state estimates that another 120 of these expensive orphan wells lie in Texas waters, yet to be plugged (Railroad Commission

on locked-in revenues from drilling permits, well-plugging reimbursements, and penalties collected by the Railroad Commission and attorney general (Texas Natural Resources Code, Section 85.2021). In 1991, the state upped the ante yet again, creating the Oil Field Cleanup Fund, a bigger and stronger version of the Well Plugging Fund (SB 1103, 72nd Legislature, 1991). The Cleanup

Fund required up-front bonds from operators and allowed money to be put toward capping wells as well as remediating spills and other problems (Texas Natural Resource Code Section 91.105).

In later years, the legislature enabled the Cleanup Fund to pull new income from sales of salvaged oil-field equipment (1993) and from fees on injection well permits (1999). By

of Texas 2013, 2). Nor is this Texas' problem alone. As many as two thousand idle wells are believed to sit in the Gulf of Mexico, some left behind in the 1940s, all eventually needing to be sealed (Saucier 2013).

Tikkun Olam

To come back to the ethical or religious theme where this legalistic and bureaucratic discussion began, the story of tending to this array of aging, corroding oil, gas, and wastewater wells might remind some of us of an age-old Jewish tenet, "tikkun olam" (Troster 2008). Tikkun olam roughly translates as humanity's shared duty to repair the world. The idea likely has many roots but could be traced back to the command to Adam and Eve to take care of the Garden of Eden (Genesis 2:15). Or, more simply, this call might be just a version of the kindergarten message to leave things neat and tidy, and better than you found them. In any case, the principle might give us some heart and courage, or even feelings of restoration and redemption, in caring for thousands of degrading wastewater and production wells.

Sources

Arthur, Daniel. 2011. "Plugging and Abandonment of Oil and Gas Wells." Paper No. 2-25. Technology Subgroup, Operations and Environment Task Group. National Petroleum Council North American Resource Development Study.

Barret, Lyne Taliaferro. 1966. Barret Papers, 1836–1966. East Texas Research Center. Stephen F. Austin State Library. Nacogdoches, Texas.

Council, Lorrie. 2014. Manager, Underground Injection Control Section. Texas Commission on Environmental Quality. Personal communication, June.

Davis, Jeff. 2014. Underground Injection Control Permits Section. Radioactive Materials Division. Texas Commission on Environmental Quality. Personal communication, June.

Fernandez, Ramon. 2014. "Monthly Report of State-Funded Well Plugging Activities, April." Field Operations Section, Railroad Commission of Texas. May 16. http://www.rrc.state.tx.us/media/19845/sfp-apr-14.pdf, accessed June 12, 2014.

Galbraith, Kate. 2013. "Abandoned Oil Wells Raise Fears of Pollution." *Texas Tribune*, June 8.

Interstate Oil and Gas Compact Commission. 1996. "Produce or Plug: The Dilemma over the Nation's Idle Oil and Gas Wells." Ad Hoc Idle Well Committee, Interstate Oil and Gas Compact Commission. December.

King, John. 1970. *Joseph Stephen Cullinan: A Study of Leadership in the Texas Petroleum Industry*. Nashville: Published for the Texas Gulf Coast Historical Association by Vanderbilt University Press.

Krueger, Trey. 2014. Systems Analyst, Information Technology Services, Railroad Commission of Texas. Personal communication, May and June 2014.

National Petroleum Council. 2011. "Plugging and Abandonment of Oil and Gas Wells." Paper #2-25.

Technology Subgroup, Operations and Environment Task Group. National Petroleum Council North American Resource Development Study.

Railroad Commission of Texas. 1957. Memorandum to District Supervisors, May 30, 1957 (Codified as Rule 15, effective June 1, 1964).

———. 2003. "Oil Field Cleanup Program, Annual Report—Fiscal Year 2003." Oil and Gas Division, Railroad Commission of Texas. February 24, 2004. http://www.rrc.state.tx.us/media/1562/ofcu2003.pdf, accessed July 8, 2014.

———. 2013. "Oil and Gas Regulation and Cleanup Program, Annual Report—Fiscal Year 2013." Oil and Gas Division, Railroad Commission of Texas. November 12, 2013. http://www.rrc.state.tx.us/media/18795/ofcu2013.pdf, accessed July 8, 2014.

———. 2014a. H10 Filing System: Injection Volumes. http://webapps.rrc.state.tx.us/H10/h10PublicMain.do, accessed July 2, 2014.

———. 2014b. "Inactive Well Aging Report, as of May 3, 2014." http://www.old.rrc.state.tx.us/iwar/iwarmay2014.xls, accessed June 8, 2014.

———. 2014c. "Oil Well Counts by County, as of February 2014." http://www.rrc.state.tx.us/media/2105/oilwellct_022014.pdf, accessed July 2, 2014.

Saucier, Michael. 2013. Decommissioning and Abandonment Summit. Bureau of Safety and Environmental Enforcement, US Department of the Interior.

Suro, Roberto. 1992. "Abandoned Oil Wells Polluting the Water." *New York Times*, May 3.

Texas Center for Policy Studies. 1995. *Texas Environmental Almanac.* Austin: University of Texas Press.

Trost, Francis John. 1901. Oil Rigs in Beaumont, Texas. Photograph, 1901. Digital image. Portal to Texas History. University of North Texas Library, crediting University of Texas at Arlington Library, *Fort Worth Star-Telegram* Photo Collection, Item Number AR406-5-20-8. Arlington, Texas. http://texashistory.unt.edu/ark:/67531/metapth41397/, accessed July 3, 2014.

Troster, Lawrence. 2008. "Tikkun Olam and Environmental Restoration: A Jewish Eco-Theology of Redemption." *Eco-Judaism.* Jewish Education News. Coalition for the Advancement of Jewish Education.

US Energy Information Administration. 2011. Distribution and Production of Oil and Gas Wells by State. January 1, 2011. http://www.eia.gov/pub/oil_gas/petrosystem/all-years-states.xls, accessed June 12, 2014.

US Environmental Protection Agency (EPA). 2001. "Class I Underground Injection Control Program: Study of the Risks Associated with Class I Underground Injection Wells." Report 816-R-01-007, March. Office of Water. US EPA. Washington, DC.

Varela, Richard. 2000. "Well Plugging Primer." Railroad Commission of Texas. http://www.rrc.state.tx.us/media/6358/plugprimer1.pdf, accessed July 2, 2014.

Brown Pelican

On December 17, 2009, the US secretary of the interior removed the brown pelican (*Pelecanus occidentalis*) from the endangered species list for Texas, Louisiana, and Mississippi (74 Fed. Reg. 59,443–59,444 (Nov. 17, 2009), codified at 50 C.F.R. part 17). Twenty-four years earlier, the Department of the Interior had delisted the bird for Alabama, Georgia, Florida, and the states along the eastern seaboard (50 Federal Register 4938–4945 (February 4, 1985)).

These moves completed the bird's arduous century-long tour through decline, protection, and recovery. Along the way, the brown pelican benefited from important chapters in the conservation movement, including the fight against the millinery and fishery trades, the development of the National Wildlife Refuge and Audubon Coastal Sanctuary networks, the regulation of pesticides, and the protections of the Lacey Act of 1900, the Migratory Bird Treaty Act of 1918, and the Endangered Species Act of 1970. It is a story that involves Texas in many steps along the way. The tale also ties in chapters from a small mangrove refuge in the Indian River Lagoon of Florida, a feather-trading exchange in London, a chemical factory in Memphis, a rookery in Louisiana, an oil rig in the Gulf, a dredge-spoil island in Matagorda Bay, and farms across America.

National Wildlife Refuges

The history of the brown pelican's fall and recovery began in Sebastian, Florida, where a German immigrant, Paul Kroegel, had settled in the 1880s. Kroegel took an interest in Pelican Island, five acres of mangroves in the Indian River Lagoon. The small island

A brown pelican adult and several fledglings are seen here on Chester Island, in Matagorda Bay (Spears 2013).

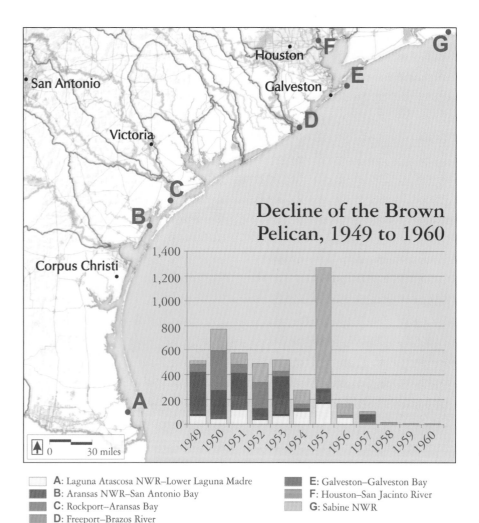

Decline of the Brown Pelican, 1949 to 1960

A: Laguna Atascosa NWR–Lower Laguna Madre
B: Aransas NWR–San Antonio Bay
C: Rockport–Aransas Bay
D: Freeport–Brazos River
E: Galveston–Galveston Bay
F: Houston–San Jacinto River
G: Sabine NWR

The chart and map track the decline of the brown pelican on the Texas and Louisiana coast during the 1949–60 period. Populations crashed in the late 1950s and early 1960s, with no brown pelicans seen at these major colonies in the immediate years after 1961 (King, Flickinger, and Hildebrand 1977).

dent, Theodore Roosevelt, with a plea to protect Pelican Island. Roosevelt responded on March 14, 1903, and signed an executive order establishing Pelican Island as a "reserve." Roosevelt chartered another fifty-one refuges during his first term, but this was a novel and untested strategy, using only implied presidential powers. As Roosevelt later wrote, "I acted on the theory that the President could at any time in his discretion withdraw from entry any of the public lands of the United States and reserve the same for . . . public purposes" (Roosevelt 1913). Despite the vagueness of the theory, the tactic worked. Pelican Island evolved into a National Wildlife Refuge, the first of over 540 in the country, covering more than 96 million acres.

"Mama, there's a woman with a dead body on her hat who wants to see you."
—Price 2004

Feathers and Hats

Refuges gave plumed birds some respite, but the widespread hunting and international trade in feathers persisted. The American Ornithologists' Union, the Audubon Society, and various antiplumage leagues worked to teach and shame those who might wear the feathers and skins on their heads. At the same time, legislatures were attempting to outlaw the plume trade (Doughty 1975). The Texas Plume-Bird Act of 1891 was an early step in this legislative effort. The Texas law

was home to thousands of brown pelicans and other birds. Many of the birds were under assault by the millinery trade that sought their feathers to decorate hats. Kroegel often sailed to the isle and stood guard over the rookeries. He also served as a guide and host to naturalists who stayed at the nearby inn, Oak Lodge, and toured the rookeries.

One of his visitors was Frank Chapman, curator of the American Museum of Natural History and a member of the American Ornithologists' Union. Chapman realized that this small island was the last surviving East Coast rookery for the brown pelican. So, together with another birder, William Dutcher, he approached the newly elected presi-

made it a misdemeanor to kill a pelican, seagull, tern, shearwater, egret, or heron, punishable with a fine of $5 to $25 (Rev. Stat., 1895, Penal Code, Art. 519, p. 100). Laws in other states, including Connecticut, Rhode Island, New Jersey, Florida, and Virginia, helped to gradually slow the trade in plumes (Palmer 1902).

However, the feathers were worth a great deal on the international market, more than the price of gold, and certainly more than the new penalties. Intervention all along the plume-trading route was required to make a dint in this global industry of hats, fascinators, and headpieces. Congress took action in 1900 with the Lacey Act, making it a federal crime to poach wildlife in one state with the goal of selling the proceeds in another. This law was squarely targeted at the killing of brown pelicans for the millinery trade (16 U.S.C. Sections 3371–3378). Then, in 1921, the English Parliament passed the Plumage Act, closing down London's feather market, the center of much international trade (Doughty 1975, 135).

"Kill the pelican or the
Kaiser will get you!"

—Pearson 1919

Fish, Fishermen, and Pelicans

While threats from the millinery trade subsided with time (and the turn to bobbed hair styles!), there were other threats to the survival of the brown pelican. Hunters and market fisher-

men charged that the pelicans were competing with their livelihood, even undermining the effort to feed the troops and the home front during World War I. In the 1910s, officials in Texas claimed that brown pelicans "consume more food fish than the people of Texas get in a year," while allegations in Florida were made that pelicans ate $950,000 of food fish every day. These were not just academic debates. In a furor, someone clubbed over four hundred pelican chicks in their nests on Pelican Island in 1918 (Pearson 1919, 509, 510).

Audubon biologists and activists sought to prove that pelican populations were much smaller than advertised and had less impact on fishing. They pointed out that the brown pelicans actually ate just the small bait fish, such as menhaden, mullet, pigfish, and minnows, and so did not truly compete with commercial and sport fishermen (Pearson 1919, 511).

Nevertheless, fishery conflicts continued, and brown pelican numbers dropped by more than 80 percent from 1918 to 1934 in Texas (Allen 1935). In fact, the attacks against brown pelicans as fish stealers persist even to the present day. As recently as 2011, a Texas fish farmer was convicted of shooting and killing ninety brown pelicans and was later fined $50,000 for the crime (US Attorney's Office, Southern District of Texas 2011). Some of the conflicts between brown pelicans and fishermen have been less intentional, but perhaps more pervasive; brown pelicans can

get tangled in monofilament fishing line, hurt on shrimp nets, or snagged by fishing tackle (Daerr 2002).

Laws to protect the pelican and other seabirds from fishermen and others who might harass them gradually took form over much of the twentieth century. The Migratory Bird Treaty Act of 1918 was an early and major piece of legislation protecting brown pelicans and other seabirds, including the individuals themselves and their nests and eggs (16 U.S.C. Section 703(a)). The Endangered Species Conservation Act of 1969 increased the penalties under the Lacey Act and extended prohibitions to reach all those who bought or sold rare species (Pub. L. No. 91-135, 83 Stat. 275 (repealed 1973)). In 1970, the brown pelican was one of the first creatures to be added to the 1969 act's list of endangered species. The bird was also later included in those protected by the Endangered Species Act of 1973 (Pub. L. No. 93-205, 87 Stat. 884; 35 Fed. Reg. 84960, June 2, 1970; 35 Fed. Reg. 16047, October 13, 1970).

Audubon Sanctuaries and Wardens

"Paper laws," though, have never been enough. The refuges have had to be guarded. Over one hundred years ago, the Florida Audubon Society realized that they needed "boots on the ground" and hired Kroegel as Pelican Island's warden. He became the first among a national network of Audubon

Chester "Chuck" Smith is at the helm here, on a Chester Island workday in October 2008. Mr. Smith, an oil industry retiree, served as Audubon Society warden on the island near Port O'Connor, Texas, from 1985 through 2010 (Spears 2008).

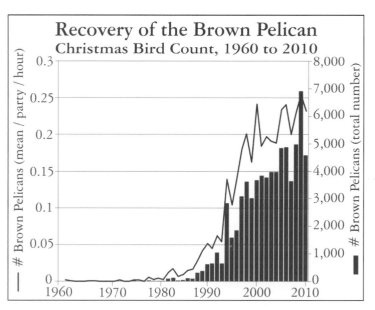

This chart traces the rebound of brown pelican sightings in Texas from fall 1960 through fall 2010. The vertical red bars show the total number of brown pelicans seen. The pink line reflects an adjustment for observation effort, by describing the mean number of pelicans seen per party, per hour of observation (National Audubon Society 2013; Ortego 2013).

wardens protecting public and private rookeries (Anderson 2000). Wardens soon came to defend the 13,000-acre network of coastal bird sanctuaries in Texas as well, beginning in 1923 (Graham 1991). The sanctuaries were staffed with gifts in the early years from James Carroll, a Piney Woods lumber baron and amateur naturalist. With help from Carroll and other Audubon supporters, wardens such as R. D. Camp, John Larson, Louis Rawalt, and others took on the lonely, tough, all-weather task of looking after the Texas rookery islands (Graham 1991).

Their commitment and creativity were carried on into modern days by such dedicated wardens as Chester Smith. Smith served for twenty-five years as caretaker of pelican rookeries at Sundown Island (now dubbed "Chester Island"). This 60-acre dredge-spoil isle lies offshore near Port O'Connor, one of the thirty-three islands that the Audubon Society now oversees on the Texas coast. With his infectious enthusiasm, Smith organized a volunteer team to guard the island against boaters and vandals, fishermen and hunters. The volunteers also protected the birds against coyotes, raccoons, and fire ants, and girded the island with bulwarks, shrubs, and trees (Hetsel 1987). With patience, their investment paid off. Chester Island has taken on a key role in restoring brown pelicans to the Texas landscape. By the time of Mr.

Smith's death in 2011, the island was hosting over 2,090 pairs of brown pelicans, more than two hundred times the number found when Mr. Smith first came to Sundown Island in 1986 (Barcott 2010). Mr. Smith's many contributions to the island are celebrated with a statue of a brown pelican erected there (Wilkinson 2013).

A Riddle

The protections against plumassiers, hunters, and fishermen, and the creation of refuges like Pelican and Chester Islands, definitely helped the brown pelican. However, another threat, a mysterious one at first, arose for the pelican during the post–World

War II era. During that time, birders recognized that flock numbers were falling fast to critically low numbers. In Texas, for instance, the brown pelican population had declined from five thousand in 1920 to only one hundred in 1963, with just twelve breeding pairs to be found in the entire state. And the birds were not reproducing: no brown pelicans at all were known to nest in Texas in 1964 or 1966, and only two nests were found in Texas in 1968. Moreover, the problem was not isolated to Texas. Researchers in neighboring colonies in Louisiana found similar drop-offs. While Louisiana hosted a population as high as 50,000 to 85,000 in 1920, the last nesting of brown pelicans in

the Pelican State had occurred in 1961 (King, Flickinger, and Hildebrand 1977; Nesbitt and Williams 1978).

"Elixirs of death."

—Carson 1962

Pesticides, Round I

The strange and rapid die-offs among brown pelicans in Texas and Louisiana were first ascribed to freezes, hurricanes, and disease (King, Flickinger, and Hildebrand 1977). However, Rachel Carson's book *Silent Spring* laid suspicion on the class of organochlorine pesticides, including DDT, that had come into use in the early 1940s. In her book, Carson

had reported on the 1960 discovery of hundreds of dead and dying pelicans, grebes, herons, and gulls in Tule Lake in southern California. The birds were soon found to have high levels of insecticide residues in their bodies (Carson 1962, 45).

Evidence confirming Carson's concerns came in from both coasts. On the Texas Gulf shores, Kirke King and other researchers found that high DDT levels were associated with the thinning of brown pelican shells (King, Flickinger, and Hildebrand 1978). Meanwhile, in Florida, Ralph Schreiber, an ornithologist at the University of Tampa, confirmed this same claim. Schreiber showed that DDT, and its metabolite, DDE, were

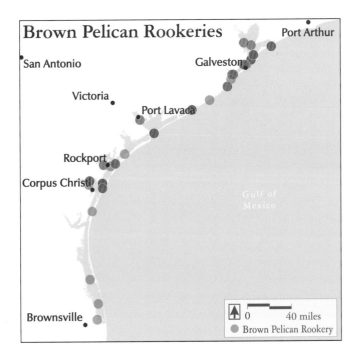

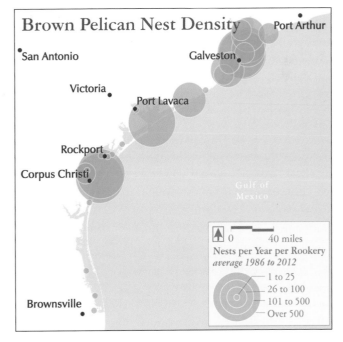

The Rookeries map plots the twenty-eight small and large nest sites where brown pelicans have been observed in Texas from 1986 to 2012, based on the Texas Colonial Waterbird Survey. The Nest Density map represents the number of nests seen during that same time, suggesting the degree to which the Texas brown pelican population is clustered, year after year, in a handful of rookeries on just a few small coastal islands (Johnson 2013).

indeed leaving pelican eggs so thin that they were crushed when the mother birds incubated them in their nests (Schreiber 1982). Their research hit a chord. In 1970, DDT was banned in Florida, and in 1972, with pressure from the Environmental Defense Fund, the EPA extended the ban to the entire nation (Fed. Reg. Vol. 37, No. 131, July 7, 1972). While DDT persisted in birds and fish for many years, the chemical gradually degraded as its use was eliminated in the United States (Gamble, Blankinship, and Jackson 1987; King et al. 1985).

Rookeries, Islands, and Habitat

Government refuges and Audubon sanctuaries, together with broader statutory protections, greatly helped restore the brown pelican in Texas and nationwide. However, the bird's hardwired habitat needs continued to put the pelican at risk in the modern world. The brown pelicans' tight clustering on a limited number of roost sites had become a major problem (Elliot 2006). For example, the Texas Colonial Waterbird Society counted 7,741 breeding pairs that had used sixty nesting sites along the Texas coast during the 1973–2012 period. In the aggregate, the number of birds and distinct rookeries was impressive. Yet over 80 percent of those birds were found on just three small, low-slung islets—North Deer Island, Shamrock Island, and Chester Island. These three islands totaled just 275 acres in size, and those few low-lying acres had

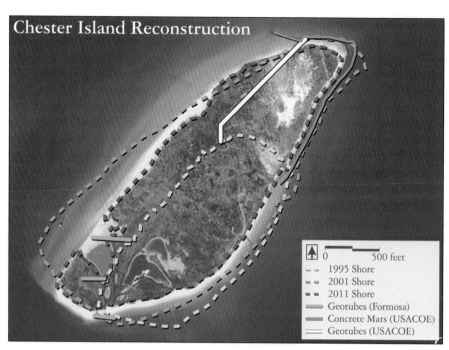

Chester Island Reconstruction

0   500 feet
- - -   1995 Shore
- - -   2001 Shore
- - -   2011 Shore
———   Geotubes (Formosa)
———   Concrete Mats (USACOE)
———   Geotubes (USACOE)

This map tracks the growth and stabilization of Chester Island (formerly known as Sundown Island) from 1995 to 2011. In 1962, the US Army Corps of Engineers created the island near Port O'Connor, Texas, as a site for spoil dumped from navigation dredging. In subsequent years, however, erosion from wind, tidal currents, and boat wakes had removed nearly half of the island. Major storms, such as 2003's Hurricane Claudette, chipped away at Chester Island's rookeries as well. However, repeated spreading of spoil, and deployment of sand-filled Geotubes, concrete mats, and other bulwarks have reinforced the island. Plantings of hardy casuarina, salt cedar, and eucalyptus (nurtured with irrigation from a windmill on the island!) have helped hold the soil against wind and water erosion, and also have provided roosting sites for birds (Wilkinson 2013).

to insure the futures of brown pelicans and many other species, including such rare birds as the reddish egret (Johnson 2013).

There have been efforts to spread the brown pelicans among more rookeries. For instance, the birds have been successfully reintroduced from Florida to Queen Bess-Camp and North Islands in Louisiana. Yet it is generally difficult to transplant birds and create new rookeries (Wilkinson, Nesbitt, and Parnell 1994). So protecting existing islands and rookeries

has become very important (Lowery 1974; Walter et al. 2013). As small as these islands are already, they constantly suffer from erosion that can whittle them down gradually, or scoop away at them in catastrophically rapid ways. The Texas rookery islands are very low, averaging only one to two feet in elevation. Consequently, any erosion from tug and barge traffic, dredging, wind-blown waves, and sea-level rise can have a dramatic impact.

Further, since many of the islands have been made from dredge spoil,

they consist of a combination of substrates that are hard to deal with. The
islands tend to be made partly of
hard-baked clays that are no friend to
grasses, shrubs, and other plants that
might hold the soil. The keys are also
built up out of light, loose, recently
dredged sands that can be very mobile
and easily swept away (Grantham
2013). As a result, the Texas rookery
islands tend to be dynamic and ephemeral at the best of times. However, from
time to time, major coastal storms,
such as Hurricane Carla of 1961, can
bring very high winds and waves, and
truly alarming wash-over and erosion
(Cornelius 1999).

Pesticides and Other Chemicals, Round II

Brown pelicans are known for their
spectacular dives from as high as 65
feet, twisting and plunging into coastal
waters to scoop up small schooling
fish. They are fishing acrobats of great
skill, but their diet has made them particularly vulnerable to chemicals such
as DDT that bio-accumulate in the
food chain. While the bird's risk from
DDT was greatly reduced after its banning in US markets, other types of toxins have remained a threat.

The insecticide endrin has been a
recurring danger to brown pelicans; it
is directly toxic to the birds and is also
lethal to the fish that pelicans feed on.
From the late 1950s through 1965,
endrin discharges from a Memphis
manufacturer were traced to over thirty
large fish kills in the lower Mississippi

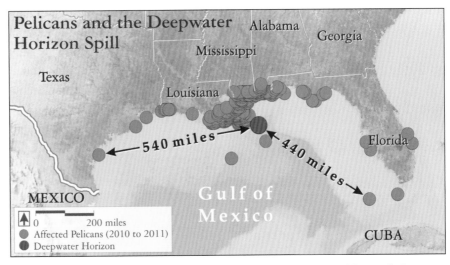

This map charts the location of brown pelicans retrieved through May 21, 2011, following the Deepwater Horizon blowout, explosion, fire, and spill that occurred from April 20 through September 19, 2010. Given the immense size of the leak, the largest spill in US history, it was fortunate that the immediate effects seem to have been confined largely to the coasts of Louisiana, Mississippi, and Alabama. However, it is remarkable how far away some impacts were felt (540 miles to a pelican retrieved in Corpus Christi, and over 440 miles to one found in Dry Tortugas). And it is still unclear how long the damage may last. In both respects, the Deepwater Horizon disaster is a reminder of the tight interconnections, and great vulnerability, of the Gulf, its industry, and its wildlife (US Fish and Wildlife Service 2011).

and Atchafalaya Rivers. The endrin
releases possibly caused local die-offs
in brown pelicans during that same era
(Lowery 1974; Souder 2012). Years
later, in early 1975, a major decline of
35–40 percent of the brown pelicans in
Louisiana was tied back to endrin used
by farmers to control the boll weevil,
bollworm, and sugarcane borer in the
Mississippi River and delta (Nesbitt
and Williams 1978; Schreiber 1982).
Finally, due to concerns about its toxicity to birds and other nontarget species, endrin was pulled off the market
in 1991 (US EPA 1998).

However, brown pelicans continue
to be threatened by other pollutants as
residential settlement and industrial
development of coastal areas proceed.

For example, National Wildlife Health
Laboratory staff found that untreated
sewage releases on the east coast
were associated with 47 percent of
212 brown pelican deaths during the
1976–83 period (US Fish and Wildlife
Service 2007). Petroleum and its many
by-products, either from tanker spills
or leaks and explosions on offshore
oil and gas platforms, have posed
another hazard (Blus 2007). The
Ixtoc I oil platform blow-out in 1979
drew great alarm, but oil booms kept
most of the slick from slipping into the
major pelican feeding areas in Corpus
Christi and Aransas Bays. However,
an oil pipeline rupture later that same
year did evidently kill a brown pelican
(King et al. 1979).

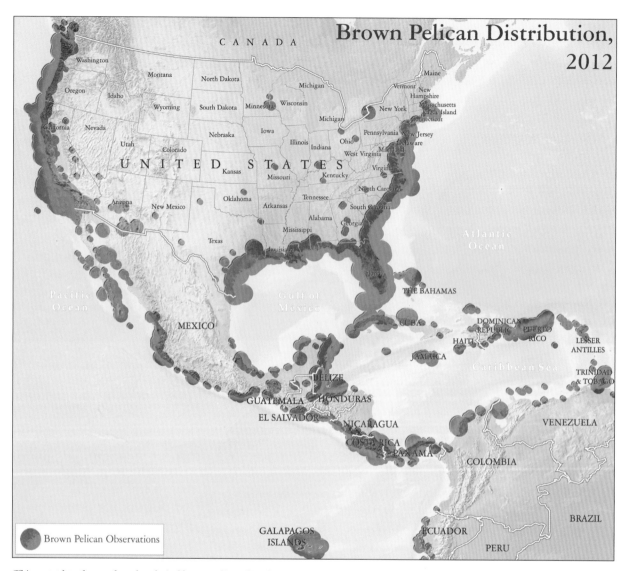

Brown Pelican Distribution, 2012

This map plots the very broad and vital brown pelican distribution in North America in 2012, after the strong recovery that began in the 1970s. The figure is based on over 56,000 observations reported to eBird, the citizen science site coordinated by the Cornell Lab of Ornithology and the National Audubon Society. Larger circles in the map indicate that more birds were observed in that area (eBird 2013; Johnson 2013).

After a long period of quiet restoration, the brown pelican was de-listed in 2009. The US Fish and Wildlife Service felt the bird had recovered sufficiently to no longer need Endangered Species Act protection. One of the de-listing factors was what scientists saw as a minimal 4–8 percent risk of major oil spills in the Gulf of Mexico (Fed. Reg., Vol. 74, No. 220, p. 59467, November 17, 2009). But then, just six months later, the Deepwater Horizon platform exploded and spilled over 4.9 million barrels of petroleum off the Louisiana shore (US Geological Survey 2010; Rudolf and Kaufman 2010). Following the spill, a 2011 survey along the Gulf Coast found 339 brown pelicans that had been covered with oil, 192 of whom died (US Department of the Interior 2011).

Back from the Brink

With over 12,000 pelicans now found along the Gulf Coast, 30,000 in the United States and 90,000 or more in Mexico, Panama, and South America, we can rightly celebrate the brown pelican's recovery from its many threats (Holtcamp 2010; NatureServe 2013; US Fish and Wildlife Service 2009). For a bird whose forebears date back forty million years, it has faced a tough and long century of plume hunting, nest destruction, DDT contamination, endrin poisoning, sewage leaks, oil spills, rookery erosion, and other problems. It is encouraging to see the resilience of an animal that could recover and coexist with a crowded world of people and industry, if given a fighting chance.

And the bird did have help from many decent and committed people. The brown pelican's recovery was aided by scientists who explored and explained the fate of pesticides, by legislators and advocates who enacted major wildlife laws, by stewards and wardens who worked to protect coastal islands from erosion and predation, and by volunteers who cared for oiled and injured pelicans. For the future, for both people and wildlife, perhaps the brown pelican has become yet another proverbial canary in the coal mine. Its story helps us all to appreciate the toxicity of chemicals, the fragility of our coastal ecosystems, and the intertwined connections among so many factors: islands in Florida, chemical plants in Memphis, oil wells in the deep Gulf, and rookeries in Texas.

Sources

Allen, R. P. 1935. "Notes on Some Bird Colonies on the Gulf Coast." *The Auk* 52 (2): 198–200.

Anderson, John "Frosty." 2000. *Wildlife Sanctuaries and the Audubon Society: Places to Hide and Seek.* Austin: University of Texas Press.

Barcott, Bruce. 2010. "Coast Guard." *Audubon* (August).

Blus, Lawrence. 2007. "Contaminants and Wildlife—The Rachel Carson Legacy Lives On." http://www.pwrc.usgs.gov/whatsnew/events/carson/Pres_Web/blus_pelicantalk051107.pdf, accessed May 18, 2013.

Burkett, Winnie. 1999. Oral history interview conducted on October 14, in Smith Point, Texas. Texas Legacy Project, Conservation History Association of Texas.

Carson, Rachel. 1962. *Silent Spring.* New York: Houghton Mifflin.

Cornelius, Bessie. 1999. Oral history interview, conducted on October 13, in Beaumont, Texas. Texas Legacy Project, Conservation History Association of Texas.

Daerr, Elizabeth. 2002. "A Pelican's Progress." *National Parks* (April–May).

Doughty, Robin. 1975. *Feather Fashions and Bird Preservation: A Study in Nature Protection.* Berkeley: University of California Press.

eBird. 2013. eBird: An online database of bird distribution and abundance. Ithaca, New York. eBird, Cornell Lab of Ornithology. http://www.ebird.org, accessed May 13, 2013.

Elliot, Lee. 2006. "The Texas Breeding Bird Atlas: Brown Pelican." Texas A&M Agrilife Extension. http://txtbba.tamu.edu/species-accounts/brown-pelican/, accessed May 16, 2013.

Gamble, Lawrence, David Blankinship, and Gerry Jackson. 1987. "Contaminants in Brown Pelican Eggs Collected from Texas and Mexico, 1986." Study Identification No. R2-87-01. US Fish and Wildlife Service, Corpus Christi, Texas.

Graham, Frank. 1991. *The Audubon Ark.* New York: Alfred A. Knopf.

Grantham, Jesse. 2003. Oral history interview, conducted in Rockport, Texas, on October 25. Texas Legacy Project, Conservation History Association of Texas.

———. 2013. Wildlife Biologist, US Fish and Wildlife Service. Personal communication, May.

Hetsel, Linda. 1987. "State Director Blames Vandals for Destroying Pelicans' Nests." *Victoria Advocate*, July 21.

Holtcamp, Wendee. 2010. "Brown Pelican Resurrection." *Texas Parks and Wildlife* (April).

Johnson, Erik. 2013. Texas Colonial Waterbird Society Data Manager, and Director of Bird Conservation, Audubon Louisiana. Personal communication, May.

King, Kirke, David Blankinship, Emilie Payne, Alexander Krynitsky, and Gary Hensler. 1985. "Brown Pelican Populations and Pollutants in Texas, 1975–1981." *Wilson Bulletin* 97 (2): 201–14.

King, Kirke, Edward Flickinger, and Henry Hildebrand. 1977. "The Decline of Brown Pelicans on the Louisiana and Texas Gulf Coasts." *Southwest Naturalist* 21 (4): 417–31.

———. 1978. "Shell Thinning and Pesticide Residues in Texas Aquatic Birds, 1970." *Pesticides Monitoring Journal* 12 (1): 16–21.

King, Kirke, Stephen Macko, Patrick Parker, and Emilie Payne. 1979.

"Resuspension of Oil: Probable Cause of Brown Pelican Fatality." *Bulletin of Environmental Contamination and Toxicology* 23 (1): 800–805.

Lowery, George. 1974. "Pelecanus occidentalis." *Louisiana Birds*. http://www.losbird.org/labirds/brpe.htm, accessed May 20, 2013.

National Audubon Society. 2013. "Brown Pelican Sightings, 1960–2010, in Texas. Christmas Bird Count Historical Results." http://birds.audubon.org/christmas-bird-count, accessed May 13, 2013.

NatureServe. 2013. NatureServe Explorer: An online encyclopedia of life (web application). Version 7.1. NatureServe, Arlington, Virginia. http://www.natureserve.org/explorer, accessed May 20, 2013.

Nesbitt, S. A., and L. E. Williams Jr. 1978. "Brown Pelican Restocking Efforts in Louisiana." *Wilson Bulletin* 90 (3): 443–45. http://research.myfwc.com/publications/publication_info.asp?id=57134, accessed May 13, 2013.

Ortego, Brent. 2013. Wildlife Biologist, Texas Parks and Wildlife. Personal communication, May.

Palmer, T. S. 1902. "Legislation for the Protection of Birds, Other Than Game Birds." Division of Biological Survey, Bulletin No. 12, US Department of Agriculture, Washington, DC.

Pearson, T. Gilbert. 1919. "The Case of the Brown Pelican." In *American Review of Reviews*, edited by Albert Shaw, vol. 59, January–June, 509–11.

Price, Jennifer. 2004. "Hats Off to Audubon." *Audubon* (December).

Roosevelt, Theodore. 1913. *An Autobiography*. New York: Macmillan.

Rudolf, John, and Leslie Kaufman.

2010. "Pelicans, Back from Brink of Extinction, Face Oil Threat." *New York Times*, June 4.

Schreiber, Ralph. 1982. "A Brown Study of the Brown Pelican." *Natural History* 91 (1).

Souder, William. 2012. *On a Farther Shore: The Life and Legacy of Rachel Carson*. New York: Random House, 348.

Spears, Marcy Crowe. 2008. Chester Smith, Chester Island, Texas. Photograph. Digital image. http://chesterisland.smugmug.com/Workdays/Devon-Energy-Workday-October/6525631_4P6BBV#!i=415560778&k=4gd3ZMn&lb=1&s=A, accessed May 20, 2013.

———. 2013. Brown pelican adult and fledglings, Chester Island, Texas. Photograph. Digital image. http://chesterisland.smugmug.com/BirdsofChesterIsland/PHOTOS-BY-SPECIES/Brown-Pelican-Photos/29452094 qBrk24#!I=25241236&k=vvHwfs7&lb=1&s=O, accessed May 19, 2013.

US Attorney's Office. 2011. "Seaside Aquaculture and Owner Must Pay for Killing Protected Species." http://www.justice.gov/usao/txs/1News/Releases/2011%20November/111108%20Seaside.htm, accessed May 21, 2013.

US Department of the Interior. 2011. Deepwater Horizon Bird Impact Data. DOI-ERDC NRDA Database, May 12, 2011. www.fws.gov/home/dhoilspill/pdfs/Bird%20Data%20Species%20Spreadsheet%2005122011.pdf, accessed May 20, 2013.

US Environmental Protection Agency (EPA). 1998. "Status of Pesticides in Registration, Reregistration, and

Special Review (a.k.a. Rainbow Report)." Special Review and Reregistration Division, Office of Pesticide Programs, US Environmental Protection Agency 401 M. Street SW, Washington, DC. Spring 1998.

US Fish and Wildlife Service. 2007. Five-Year Review of the Listed Distinct Population Segment of the Brown Pelican.

———. 2009. "Draft Post-Delisting Monitoring Plan for the Brown Pelican." US Fish and Wildlife Service, Ventura Fish and Wildlife Office, Ventura, California.

———. 2011. "Data by Individual Bird, Week of May 11, 2011." Bird Impact Data and Consolidated Wildlife Reports, FWS Deepwater Horizon Oil Spill Response. http://www.fws.gov/home/dhoilspill/collectionreports.html, accessed May 22, 2013.

US Geological Survey. 2010. Deepwater Horizon MC252 Gulf Incident Oil Budget. http://www.usgs.gov/foia/budget/08-02-2010.Deepwater%20Horizon%200il%20Budget.pdf, accessed May 19, 2013.

Walter, Scott, Michael Carloss, Thomas Hess, Giri Athrey, and Paul Leberg. 2013. "Brown Pelican (*Pelecanus occidentalis*) Colony Initiation Attempts: Translocations and Decoys." *Waterbird* 36 (1): 53–62.

Wilkinson, Philip, Stephen Nesbitt, and James Parnell. 1994. "Recent History and Status of the Eastern Brown Pelican." *Wildlife Society Bulletin* 22: 420–30.

Wilkinson, Tim. 2013. Warden, Chester Island Sanctuary, Audubon Texas. Personal communication, May.

Wind Energy

In many parts of Texas, the wind blows and blows and blows, steady and strong.

Early Days

Texans have taken advantage of wind as a source of power for many years. Railroads were some of the first businesses to build windmills in the state, using them to pump water for their steam engines as early as 1860 near Houston, and, by the 1880s, erecting huge Eclipse mills every 30 miles along their tracks in West Texas (Baker 1984; Galbraith and Price 2013). Windmills were also a crucial tool used for watering cattle in dry areas of the state, including ranches in the Trans-Pecos (Christopher Doty, 1882), Panhandle (Magnolia Cattle and Land Company, 1884, and the XIT Ranch, 1887), and South Texas (the Coleman-Fulton Pasture Company, 1885) (Welborn 2013). From the 1920s through the 1950s, some ranchers and farmers even installed Jacobs wind generators that charged automobile batteries, ran radios, and lit homes (Jones and Bouamane 2011).

Windmills' use only began to taper off in the 1930s, when electric lines reached many isolated homesteads and towns, following federal loans from the Rural Electrification Agency, leveraged by over sixty local electric cooperatives in the state. Even so, the old Aermotor, Baker, and Dempster windmills were seen less and less. While an estimated 80,000 windmills continued to spin and pump water in the state, most of the old windmills had been retired and removed (Texas State Energy Conservation Office 2007).

Fossil Fuel Crises

Then, in the 1970s, the United States saw a first surge of renewed interest in wind energy, triggered by events half a world away. In the fall of 1973, Egypt and Syria launched a surprise attack on Israel. As Israel fought back, President Nixon authorized Operation Nickel Grass to resupply Israel with arms. In retaliation, the Organization of Arab Petroleum Exporting Countries imposed an oil embargo on the United States. Oil prices quickly spiked, gas stations ran short of fuel, and the country realized that its energy habits were vulnerable to the vagaries of international geopolitics. At the same time, there was an American recognition that fossil fuels were, by their very nature, limited; US petroleum production had peaked in 1970, and was already starting a slow decline.

The uncertainties of the global fossil fuel industry made scholars, inventors, and policy makers turn to the possibilities of homegrown renewable energy, including hydroelectric, solar, geothermal, biomass, and wind power.

Pioneers

The federal government tried to spur interest in renewable energy. In 1973, the United States began providing money for wind research and development, beginning with $300,000 in 1973, growing to $67 million by 1980 (Nelson 2014). In 1978, Washington also sought to pry open the traditional utility market to renewables by passing PURPA, the federal Public Utility Regulatory Policies Act (Public Law 95-617). PURPA required utilities to buy electricity from small independent producers at reasonable prices, giving all sorts of young, alternative electric providers access to the huge American grid. Through the Energy Tax Act of 1978 and the Crude Oil Windfall Profits Act of 1980, the federal government also poured in tax credits to encourage early adopters to buy these newfangled devices (Public Law 95-618; Public Law 96-223).

At the same time, the state of Texas also took interest in energy alternatives. Pressed by severe market shortages of natural gas during the cold winter of 1972/73, and alarmed by the peaking of gas production in the state, governor Dolph Briscoe created the Governor's Energy Advisory Council (Executive Order No. D.B.-2, August 29, 1973). The council produced a report with the exciting promise that "the region of great-

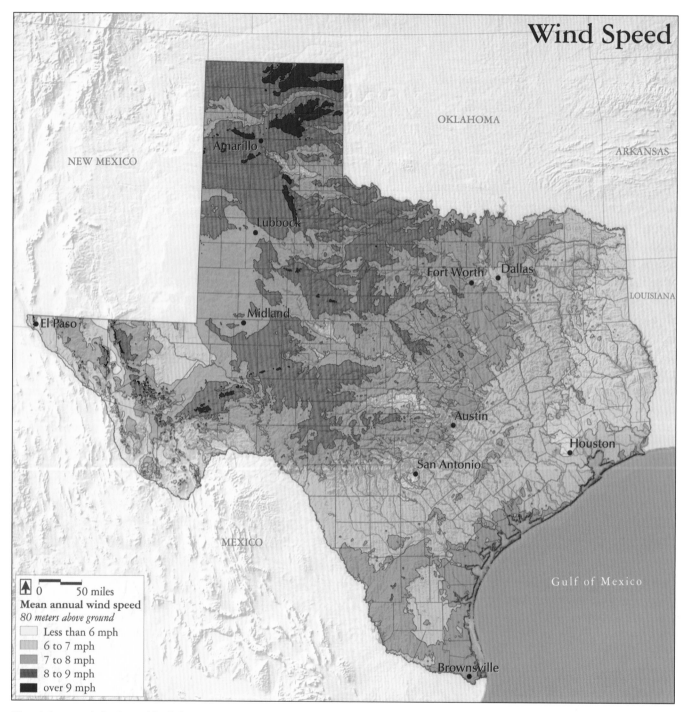

Wind Speed

Mean annual wind speed
80 meters above ground

0   50 miles

Less than 6 mph
6 to 7 mph
7 to 8 mph
8 to 9 mph
over 9 mph

Texas is fortunate in having a rich wind resource available throughout much of the state. This map shows the pattern of prevailing breezes in Texas at an elevation of 80 meters above the ground, close to the height of many modern wind towers (AWS Truepower 2013; Phelps 2013).

est wind energy potential in the United States is located mainly in the Panhandle of Texas," adding that Texas wind could supply 8 percent of the nation's electrical power by 1980 (Nelson and Gilmore 1974).

Enthusiasm about the potential for wind development spread to inventors and researchers as well. In 1977, Vaughn Nelson, Earl Gilmore, and Robert Barieu founded the Alternative Energy Institute at West Texas State University in Canyon to test windmill designs and collect data on wind patterns. By the late 1970s, the US Department of Agriculture research station in Bushland, Texas, had grown interested in alternative ways to drive the pumps for irrigating cotton and other crops, since natural gas supplies had become unreliable and costly. Soon, Nolan Clarke and his team at the Bushland facility had geared up with West Texas State to help test wind turbines.

These early wind turbines were developed by an array of inventors scattered around Texas. Lubbock-based Coy Harris worked with a local church to erect a wind turbine in the late 1970s, by which time Carlos Gottfried was building innovative "Hummingbird" direct-drive machines in Sweetwater. The Carter family in Burkburnett experimented with turbine designs, selling early models in 1978. Michael Osborne planted five of these Carter machines on a ranch near Pampa in 1981; these are believed to be the first wind turbines to feed the grid in Texas (Galbraith and Price 2013, 62–67).

Growing Pains

However, it took a long time for these early machines to scale up, multiply, and spread across the state. There were philosophical debates about whether big machines went against a "small is beautiful" ethic (Smith 2002). And there were technical problems with the early designs, especially in extreme weather. Blades came apart, transmissions failed, welds cracked, inverters dropped out, and controllers died (Galbraith and Price 2013, 67–70). An early, and notorious, accident occurred at the first large Texas wind farm, a 112-turbine complex in the Delaware Mountains. Built by Kenetech for the Lower Colorado River Authority and Austin Energy, the facility was damaged badly by 160-mph winds in January 1996, just a few months after construction was complete (Asmus 2001; Madrigal 2011, 248–49).

Wind developers faced financial challenges as well. High fuel costs drove powerful conservation efforts, energy demand fell, an oil glut grew, and petroleum prices slid from $38/barrel in 1981 to just over $11 in 1986 (Federal Reserve 2013). As oil and gas prices sagged, the appeal of wind power and other renewable energy sources declined as well. Utilities were reluctant to buy wind power, seeing it as too costly. In California, Pacific Gas and Electric and Southern California Edison were successful in blocking state pressure to purchase power from Kenetech, handing the leading wind company a staggering loss of over

$900 million and contributing to its bankruptcy in 1996.

Nevertheless, policy makers were concerned about the trends in the energy state; by the early 1990s, Texas had become a net importer of energy. With a state budget long buoyed by oil patch taxes and employment, this was a problem. And powerful political backers in Texas spoke out on behalf of wind, including Sam Wyly of Green Mountain Energy, a renewable energy vendor, and Ken Lay, head of Enron, a leading wind farm builder at the time (Galbraith and Price 2013, 113–21). A new trade group, the Texas Renewable Energy Industries Association, lobbied for wind energy support (Smith 2002). At the same time, concerns were growing in the environmental community about the impact of fossil fuels on climate change, as expressed in the IPCC reports of 1990 and 1995, and pressed by organizations such as the Environmental Defense Fund's Texas office (Intergovernmental Panel on Climate Change 1995; Tegart, Sheldon, and Griffith 1990).

The Boom

In 1999, the stars aligned. Led by state senator David Sibley and representative Steve Wolens, the Texas legislature passed Senate Bill 7, and governor George Bush signed the bill into law. SB 7 deregulated the utility industry, allowing big industrial customers to shop for cheaper electricity supplies, and also permitting power plants to seek large consumers outside their tra-

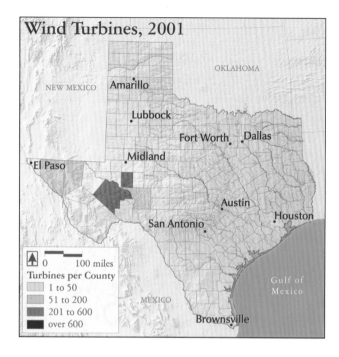

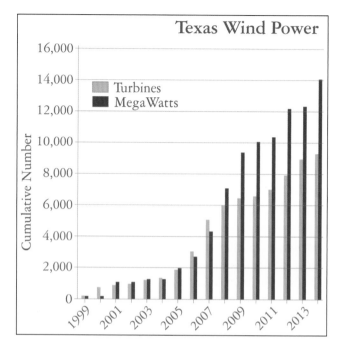

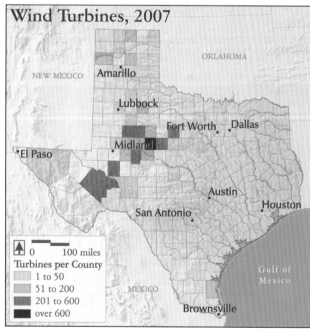

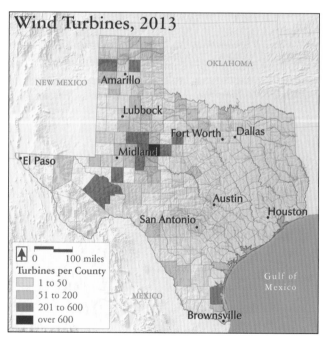

These wind turbine maps track the spread of grid-connected windmills, as they were built, showing the relative number of the machines per county in 2001, 2007, and 2013. Wind development in Texas has traditionally been centered in Far West Texas, and the Trans-Pecos, the Panhandle. Most recently, wind farms have come to the South Texas coast, where breezes blow more reliably during the heat of the day and the peak of electricity demand. Installation dates and locations are based on the FAA's efforts to monitor tall structures that might interfere with air travel. The chart shows the exponential growth in the total power and number of commercial wind turbines in Texas, over the last twenty years (Federal Aviation Administration 2015; US Department of Energy 2015).

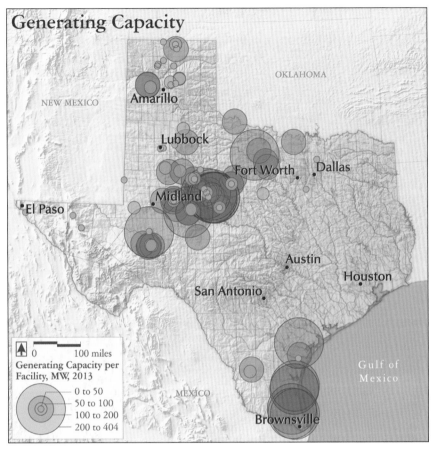

Generating Capacity

OKLAHOMA

NEW MEXICO

Amarillo

Lubbock

Fort Worth . Dallas

El Paso

Midland

Austin

San Antonio

Houston

Gulf of Mexico

MEXICO

Brownsville

0   100 miles
Generating Capacity per Facility, MW, 2013
— 0 to 50
— 50 to 100
— 100 to 200
— 200 to 404

This map shows the power of Texas wind farms that were built and in service as of May 2015 (Federal Aviation Administration 2015; Open Energy Information 2015; Posner 2013).

Big traditional utilities and manufacturers, including American Electric Power, General Electric, and TXU, signed up to finance and build the new wind farms. By the close of 2012, Texas had 12,214 megawatts of installed wind capacity, exceeding the state's ambitions for the year 2025 by over 20 percent. In fact, the Electric Reliability Council of Texas reported that Texas' main grid drew 9 percent of its 2012 electricity from wind farms. The Texas Public Utility Commission figured that fully 28 percent of the net new energy capacity added in Texas since 1995 had come from the new fleet of wind turbines (Public Utility Commission 2013b). And, at this writing, wind power generated in Texas exceeds that made in any other state (American Wind Energy Association 2013b).

Questions and Cautions

While wind energy has great value in diversifying the state's power supply and lowering its carbon footprint, winds are notoriously fickle. At times, they can fade and fail to blow at all. On a typical day, the Electric Reliability Council of Texas might see actual wind electricity production running at only 20 percent of installed capacity (ERCOT 2013). Also, breezes can blow out of sync with electricity demand and thus create storage and transmission problems. This is particularly true of wind turbines in West and North Texas, where the strongest winds tend to blow in the evening, well past afternoon peak loads.

ditional territories. And the new law made huge changes in the wind arena. SB 7 required utilities to develop 2,000 megawatts of new sources of renewable energy by 2009, enough to power 650,000 homes (24 Tex. Reg. 9142, October 22, 1999; Public Utility Regulatory Act, Section 39.904; Senate Bill 7, Act of May 21, 1999, 76th Legislature, Regular Session). This was a huge number, and a big gamble, at the time. The entire United States had less than 1,800 megawatts of

wind capacity, and Texas had only 800 megawatts of renewable energy of any kind (with over 80 percent of it coming from fifty-year-old hydroelectric turbines) (Galbraith and Price 2013).

Yet as turbine technologies and materials improved, federal subsidies flowed, and prices fell, SB 7's ten-year goal was reached quickly, by 2005 (Energy Policy Act of 1992, Ticket to Work and Work Incentives Improvement Act of 1999, Job Creation and Worker Assistance Act of 2002).

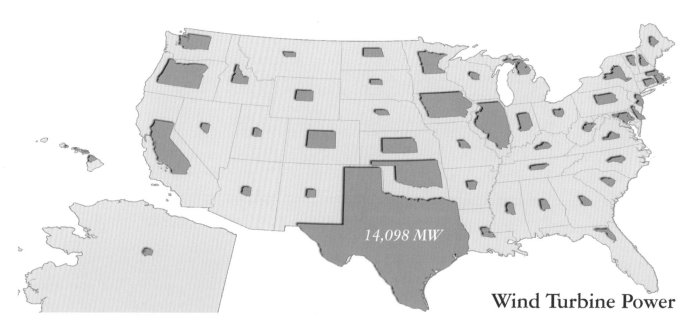

Wind Turbine Power

This map compares the installed wind turbine capacity in each state, 2014. Through a combination of politics, meteorology, pluck, and ingenuity, Texas' array of wind turbines makes up over 20 percent of the installed US capacity, with over twice the power of the second-ranking state, California (American Wind Energy Association 2013a; US Department of Energy 2015).

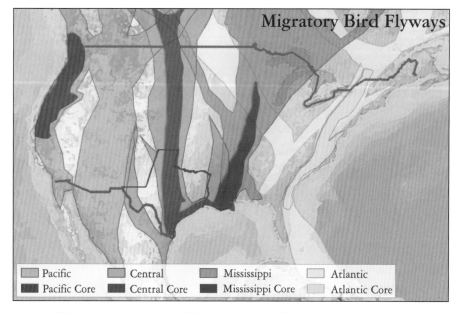

Migratory Bird Flyways

Pacific	Central	Mississippi	Atlantic
Pacific Core	Central Core	Mississippi Core	Atlantic Core

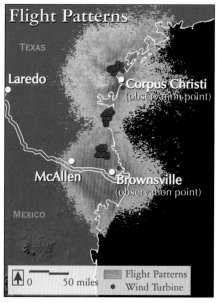

Flight Patterns

TEXAS

Laredo · Corpus Christi (observation point)

McAllen · Brownsville (observation point)

MEXICO

0 — 50 miles — Flight Patterns · Wind Turbine

Some wind farms are located in areas with heavy bird activity. This has been an issue in Texas, home to the great central flyway, as seen in the Migration map. Turbine/bird collisions can be severe in select areas, under certain weather conditions. The Flight Patterns map shows a network of wind farms in South Texas, matched with the bird (and bat) echoes identified by NextRad Doppler radar stations in Corpus Christi and Brownsville on a cold spring day, April 23, 2013. Wind turbines are marked in dark red, while bird and bat echoes are noted in yellow, orange, and red, with the highest density in red (Federal Aviation Administration 2015; Posner 2013; United States Avian Hazard Advisory System 2013; US Fish and Wildlife Service 2013; White 2013).

Birds, Bats, and Turbines

Wind energy can also present serious environmental problems. In certain places and times, birds and bats may collide with turbines. Early concerns arose in California, where over one hundred raptors, including thirty-four eagles, were estimated to have died in collisions or by electrocution at wind farms during the 1985–88 period (Anderson and Estep 1988). A more recent national study estimated that over 570,000 birds are killed annually by wind farms, and the concerns have even led to endangered species litigation (Glitzenstein 2014; Smallwood 2013). The exact scope of the problem is unknown, but some wags have called wind turbines "bird Cuisinarts." Unfortunately, since the Texas wind farms are largely privately owned and located on private lands, data for these collisions are proprietary, and recovering injured or dead birds before a hungry predator arrives is difficult (Newstead 2013).

It is suspected that South Texas wind farms, in the crossroads of the great central flyway, present a real challenge. Bird traffic there can be six to ten times that seen for any other migratory pathway, and during "fallouts" or foggy nights, tired or lost birds can fly lower than they typically would, and run head-long into a turbine tip spinning at 180 mph (Newstead 2013). Unfortunately, collaborative efforts among conservation and industry groups to develop siting guidelines were scuttled (Newstead

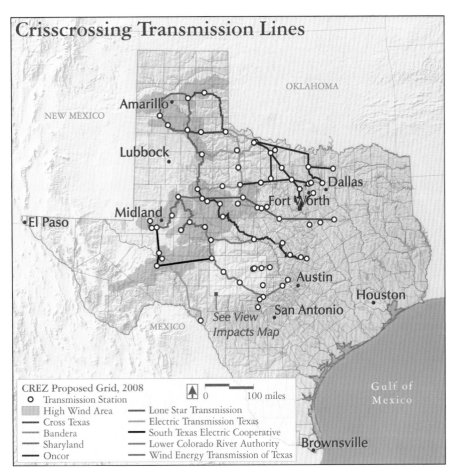

Power companies have built 3,595 miles of new Competitive Renewable Energy Zone (CREZ) transmission lines to move wind and other renewable energy from remote parts of West Texas and the Panhandle to major metropolitan demand areas. This $6.8 billion project to extend new lines has raised concerns about the sheer cost, in addition to the harm to bird migrations and the blot on rural landscapes (Farmer 2013; Public Utility Commission 2013a).

2013). The Coastal Habitat Alliance filed suit against Texas' General Land Office and Public Utility Commission for the state's failure to review siting of wind turbines under the Coastal Zone Management Act, but the case was dismissed (Blackburn 2008; Blackburn 2013).

There has been some optimism that on-site radar might alert turbine operators to incoming flocks and give the engineers enough notice to slow or stop the turbines. Yet contracted power delivery commitments, and grid compatibility concerns, may make wind farm managers reluctant to put the brakes on. And despite federal wind subsidies and Coastal Zone Management Act agreements, there is still very slight government over-

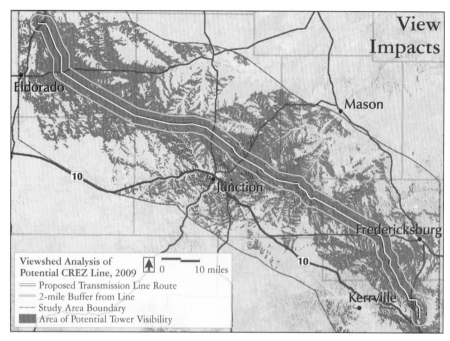

This map demonstrates how landowner groups such as Save Our Scenic Hill Country Environment and Clear View Alliance illustrated the visual effects of the proposed routes to decision makers, in trying to shift the new power lines or find capacity in existing routes (Ogren 2013).

ize many small communities (Smith 2013). On the other hand, building the enormous turbines, erecting the power poles, and stringing the high-voltage lines have ignited concerns about harm to migrating birds and foraging bats and raised hackles among property owners for disruptions to their peace, quiet, and rural landscape.

Wind power in Texas is perhaps another example of a new technology with exciting promise, and excited promoters, that manages to race ahead of complete transparency, full understanding, and careful safeguards. The irony is that many of the friends of wind power come from the environmental community, reminding us all of how difficult it can be to "do the right thing." Good intentions are not always good enough.

sight on turbine siting, beyond limited wetland construction restrictions (Blackburn 2013; Clean Water Act, § 404; Newstead 2013; Riley 2013).

Views, Towers, and Power Lines

There have also been concerns about new high-voltage transmission lines and the construction and maintenance roads that serve these new wind farms (Texas Utilities Code Section 39.904; Public Utility Commission Order 33672). The 110- to 200-foot-tall monopole and lattice towers, linking over 3,500 miles of new 345-kV power lines, have put a significant mark on remote Texas landscapes, and

a dent in utility budgets (the estimated cost has come in 37 percent over the projection). Public hearings and condemnation proceedings on the route of the lines have upset landowners and pitted neighbors against one another (Galbraith 2010; Neiman 2009; RS&H 2013; Steffy 2014).

Last Thoughts

Winds shift and spin, gust and ebb. In much the same way, debates in Texas over wind energy have swung wildly. On the one hand, Texas winds give wonderful opportunities for clean, sustainable electricity to fire a growing population and economy, and revital-

Sources

American Wind Energy Association. 2013a. Installed Wind Capacity: 2012 Year End Wind Power Capacity (MW). http://www.windpowering america .gov/wind_installed_capacity.asp, accessed September 26, 2013.

———. 2013b. State Wind Energy Statistics: Texas, June 3, 2013. http:// www.awea.org/Resources/state .aspx?ItemNumber=5183, accessed September 24, 2013.

Anderson, R. L., and J. A. Estep. 1988. "Wind Energy Development in California: Impacts, Mitigation, Monitoring, and Planning." California Energy Commission, Sacramento.

Asmus, Peter. 2001. *Reaping the Wind: How Mechanical Wizards, Visionaries, and Profiteers Helped Shape our Energy Future*. Washington, DC: Island Press.

AWS Truepower. 2013. Mean Annual Wind Speed Map for Texas, Estimated for an Elevation of 80 Meters above Grade. GeoTIFF digital file.

Baker, T. Lindsay. 1984. *A Field Guide to American Windmills*. Norman: University of Oklahoma Press.

Blackburn, Jim. 2008. "Coastal Update—Special Edition: The Kenedy Wind Farms, March 31, 2008." http://www .blackburncarter.com/downloads/ Blackburn_Coastal_Update%20 2008%20Special%20Edit.pdf, accessed October 2, 2013.

———. 2013. Environmental Attorney, Blackburn and Carter. Personal communication, September.

Electric Reliability Council of Texas (ERCOT). 2013. Forecasted and Actual Wind Power Production, Current System Conditions. http:// www.ercot.com/content/cdr/html/ CURRENT_ DAYCOP_HSL.html, accessed September 30, 2013.

Farmer, Steve. 2013. Consultant, Program Controls, RS&H. Personal communication, September.

Federal Aviation Administration. 2015. Digital Obstacle File, reflecting changes to March 20, 2015. Obstacle Data Team, Federal Aviation Administration. https://nfdc.faa.gov/tod/public/DOFS/ DOF_150329.zip, accessed April 1, 2015.

Galbraith, Kate. 2010. "Fighting the Power Lines to Protect Hill Country Vistas." *Texas Tribune*, September 9.

Galbraith, Kate, and Asher Price. 2013. *The Great Texas Wind Rush: How George Bush, Ann Richards, and a Bunch of Tinkerers Helped the Oil and Gas State Win the Race to Wind Power*.

Austin: University of Texas Press.

Glitzenstein, Eric. 2014. Notice of Intent to Sue for Violations of the National Environmental Policy Act, the Endangered Species Act, and the Bald and Golden Eagle Protection Act in Connection with the Fish and Wildlife Service's Final Rule Authorizing the Issuance of Eagle "Take" Permits for Thirty Years. Filed with the US Fish and Wildlife Service on behalf of the American Bird Conservancy. April 30.

Intergovernmental Panel on Climate Change. 1995. "IPCC Second Assessment: Climate Change, 1995." United Nations.

Jones, Geoffrey and Loubua Bouamane. 2011. "Historical Trajectories and Corporate Competencies in Wind Energy," Working Paper 11-112, Harvard Business School.

Madrigal, Alexis. 2011. *Powering the Dream: The History and Promise of Green Technology*. Cambridge, MA: Da Capo Press.

Neiman, Bill. 2009. "Scarred Forever: No Turning Back Once Transmission Lines are Built." *Mason County News*, September 23.

Nelson, Vaughn. 2014. *Wind Energy: Renewable Energy and the Environment*. 2nd ed. Boca Raton, FL: CRC Press.

Nelson, Vaughn, and Earl Gilmore. 1974. "Potential for Wind Generated Power in Texas." Governor's Energy Advisory Council.

Newstead, David. 2013. Environmental Scientist, Coastal Bend Bays and Estuaries Program. Personal communication, September.

Ogren, Jonathan. 2013. Cartographer, Siglo Group. Personal communication, September.

Open Energy Information. 2015. Map of Wind Farms / Data. CSV File. http:// en.openei.org/wiki/Map_of_Wind_ Farms/Data, accessed May 19, 2015.

Phelps, Byron. 2013. Product Manager, AWS Truepower. Personal communication, October 9.

Posner, Steve. 2013. Terrain and Obstacles Data Team, Aeronautical Information Management, Federal Aviation Administration. Personal communication, September.

Public Utility Commission of Texas. 2013a. CREZ Transmission Program Information Center. http://www. texascrezprojects.com/overview.aspx, accessed September 26, 2013.

———. 2013b. Summary of Changes to Generation Capacity (MW) in Texas, By Status and Resource Type, Updated January 23, 2013. http://www.puc .texas.gov/industry/maps/elecmaps/ gen_tables.xls, accessed October 2, 2013.

Riley, Cecilia. 2013. Executive Director, Coastal Bird Observatory. Personal communication, September.

RS&H. 2013. CREZ Progress Report No. 12. Prepared for the Public Utility Commission of Texas. July.

Smallwood, K. Shawn. 2013. "Comparing Bird and Bat Fatality-Rate Estimates among North American Wind-Energy Projects." *Wildlife Society Bulletin* 37 (1): 19–33.

Smith, Russel. 2002. Cofounder and Executive Director, Texas Renewable Energy Industries Association. Oral history interview conducted April 9, in Austin, Texas. Texas Legacy Project, Conservation History Association of Texas.

Smith, Smitty. 2003. Oral history interview conducted October 4, in Austin, Texas.

Texas Legacy Project, Conservation History Association of Texas.

Steffy, Loren. 2014. "Is Texas Souring on Wind Power?" *Forbes*, July 11.

Tegart, W. J. McG., G. Sheldon, and D. C. Griffith, eds. 1990. "Climate Change: The IPCC Impacts Assessment (1990)." Australian Government Publishing Service, Canberra.

Texas State Energy Conservation Office. 2007. "Roping the Texas Breezes." Fact Sheet No. 8. Texas Comptroller's Office. http://www.seco.cpa.state .tx.us/schools/infinitepower/docs/ factsheet08.pdf, accessed September 26, 2013.

US Avian Hazard Advisory System. 2013. AHAS Risk for Corpus Christi International Airport and for Brownsville South Padre Island International Airport, November 18, 2013, 4 pm. http://www.usahas.com/, accessed November 13, 2013.

US Department of Energy. 2015. Installed Wind Capacity, 12/31/2014. WINDExchange. National Renewable Energy Laboratory, US Department of Energy. http://apps2.eere.energy.gov/ wind/windexchange/docs/installed _wind_capacity_by_state.xls, accessed April 24, 2015.

US Fish and Wildlife Service. 2013. Biological Flyways. http://www .flyways.us/flyways/info, accessed December 12, 2013.

Welborn, Daniel. 2013. "Windmills." Handbook of Texas Online. Published by the Texas State Historical Association, http://www.tshaonline .org/handbook/online/articles/aow01, accessed December 12, 2013.

White, Ron. 2013. Aviation Hazard Advisory System Project Manager, Detect, Inc. Personal communication, December.

The Built World

Texas is the second most populous state in the Union, home to over twenty-six million people.
And for all the frontier lore, it is now an urban state. Texas has three cities among the ten largest
in America (Houston, San Antonio, and Dallas), and has more than 80 percent of its residents
living in metropolitan areas (US Census 2010).

To support all these citizens, and to power its economy, the second largest in the United
States, the state has an extensive pattern of cities and towns, stores and landfills, all tied together
by a network of roads and rails, pipelines, power lines, and other infrastructure (Bureau of
Economic Analysis 2014). These maps tell a story about how we have fitted out the state to sell
us what we might like and dispose of what we no longer want, to house our families and protect us from those whom we do not welcome, and to carry us from home to work to school and
beyond.

Sources

Bureau of Economic Analysis. 2014. Advance 2013 and Revised 1997–2012 Statistics of GDP by State,
    Embargoed for Release, June 11, 2014. US Department of Commerce. http://www.bea.gov/newsreleases/
    regional/gdp_state/2014/xls/gsp0614.xls, accessed June 8, 2015.
Federal Highway Administration. 2014. Functional System Lane-Length—2013, October 21, Table HM-60,
    Highway Statistics 2013, Highway Statistics Series. Office of Highway Policy Information. Federal Highway
    Administration, US Department of Transportation. http://www.fhwa.dot.gov/policyinformation/statistics/
    2013/hm60.cfm, accessed May 19, 2015.
Texas Natural Resources Information System. 2013. Strategic Mapping Program. http://tg-twdbgemss
    .s3.amazonaws.com/d/transportation/stratmap_trans_v2_fgdb.zip, accessed January 1, 2012.
US Census. 2010. Census Tracts, Demographic Profile, 2010 Census, TIGER/Line with Selected Demographic
    and Economic Data. US Census, US Department of Commerce. http://www2.census.gov/geo/tiger/
    TIGER2010DP1/Tract_2010Census_DP1.zip, accessed June 8, 2015.

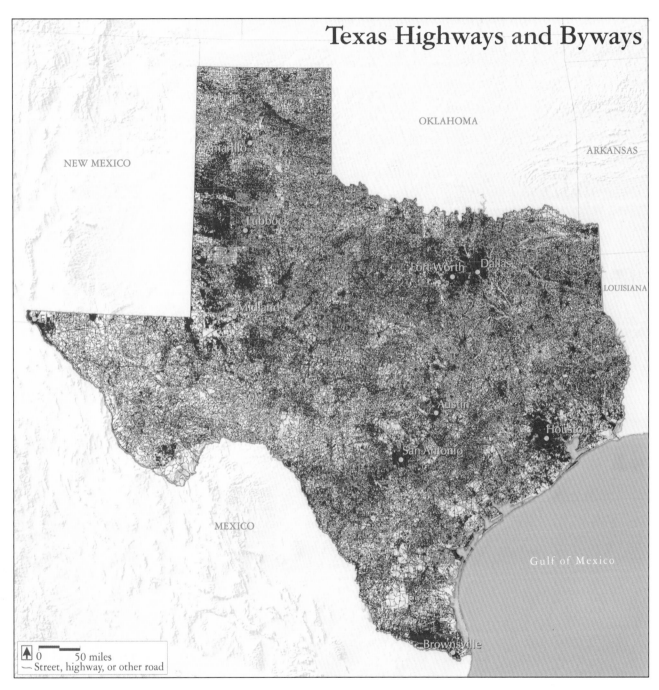

Texas Highways and Byways

NEW MEXICO

OKLAHOMA

ARKANSAS

Amarillo

Lubbock

Fort Worth · Dallas

LOUISIANA

El Paso

Midland

Austin

Houston

San Antonio

MEXICO

Gulf of Mexico

Brownsville

0   50 miles
— Street, highway, or other road

This built world of wood, steel, and concrete is overlaid on a natural world of soil, plants, water, and living creatures, and vitally depends on those natural resources. Unfortunately, that natural realm is not always constant and dependable—it moves between flood and drought, calm and storm, heat and cold—and our built world must flex with those changes. The maps in this chapter describe that interplay between our structures and the natural and durable, but shifting and evolving, foundations that they are based on.

This map shows some 675,000 lane-miles of highways, roads, and streets in Texas, which are just a small part of the vast infrastructure that ties Texas together (Federal Highway Administration 2014; Texas Natural Resources Information System 2013).

Population Growth and Shift

Tejas

Texas has long welcomed new residents. Its very name is translated from "tejas," the Spanish spelling of a native Caddo word, "taysha," meaning friend (Newcomb 1961). With a huge land area, plentiful timber and water, and rich soils, the state was a magnet for immigrants from its earliest days. While this population growth has built our state and filled our coffers, the surge has also had powerful and troubling impacts on the environment.

"The most important thing we need, of course, is population control. Without pulling our numbers back, we're sinking the planet. And so, when you're talking about saving open space and critters, it's very desperately needed."

—Terry Hershey, 2002

The United States Grows and Moves, 1790 to 2010

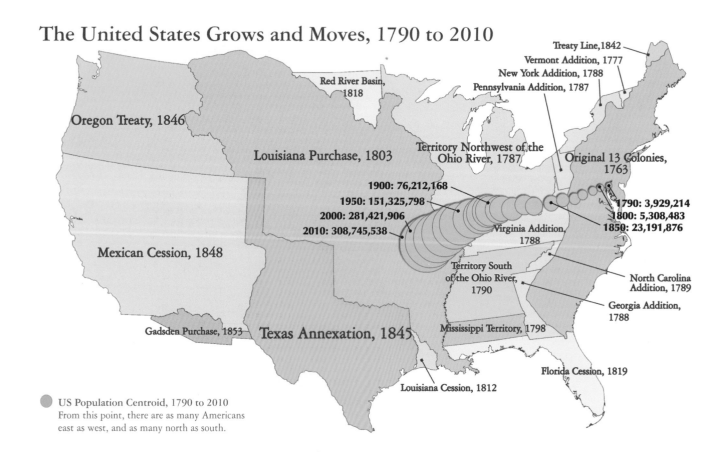

Oregon Treaty, 1846

Treaty Line, 1842

Vermont Addition, 1777

New York Addition, 1788

Pennsylvania Addition, 1787

Red River Basin, 1818

Louisiana Purchase, 1803

Territory Northwest of the Ohio River, 1787

Original 13 Colonies, 1763

Mexican Cession, 1848

1900: 76,212,168
1950: 151,325,798
2000: 281,421,906
2010: 308,745,538

1790: 3,929,214
1800: 5,308,483
1850: 23,191,876

Virginia Addition, 1788

Territory South of the Ohio River, 1790

North Carolina Addition, 1789

Georgia Addition, 1788

Gadsden Purchase, 1853

Texas Annexation, 1845

Mississippi Territory, 1798

Florida Cession, 1819

Louisiana Cession, 1812

● US Population Centroid, 1790 to 2010
From this point, there are as many Americans east as west, and as many north as south.

Westward ho! This map of the US population center shows the eightyfold growth (from 3.9 to 309 million) and movement of the American people, amid the addition of millions of acres in new territories to the United States. The blue dots' locations mark how the centroid of the American population moved from 1790 through 2010. The dot's size refers to the number of Americans (excluding many Native Americans, slaves, and undocumented aliens) counted during each of the decennial censuses (Gauthier 2002; Mackun and Wilson 2011; US Census Bureau 2013, 2014b).

Moving into and out of Texas, 1993-2010

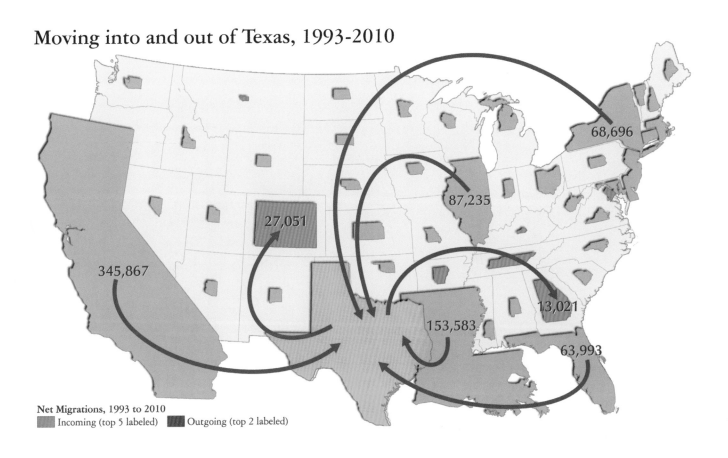

Net Migrations, 1993 to 2010
Incoming (top 5 labeled) Outgoing (top 2 labeled)

Where do new Texans come from? This figure shows the net migration between Texas and its sister states. Blue-colored states send more residents to Texas than they receive. Red-marked states receive more residents from Texas than they send. The size of the states describes the relative number of people involved. These estimates are based on the addresses of income tax returns filed for 1993 through 2010 (Tax Foundation 2014).

National Shifts

It may be helpful to first place Texas' big and rising numbers in a larger context. The move to Texas has been part of a more general western migration of the American people seeking new lands and opportunities. In fact, the mean center of the US population moved over 870 miles from Maryland to Missouri during the 1790 to 2010 period (US Census 2014b).

Texas' Growth

Texas' growth has been steady. In one of the first population estimates of Texas, made in 1744, the area had only 1,500 westerners, mostly clustered around San Antonio (Yoakum 1856, 87). However, it grew quickly from that early small start; upon its first American census in 1850, 213,000 citizens were reported. Fifty years later, the US Census Bureau found three million citizens within the

state's borders (Texas State Library and Archives Commission 2013). Recent growth has been no less rapid. By the year 2013, Texas claimed 26.5 million residents, close to nine times its 1900 count (Texas Department of State Health Services 2014b).

Interstate Moves

Much of the Texas growth has come from people packing up their things, leaving their homes, and moving into

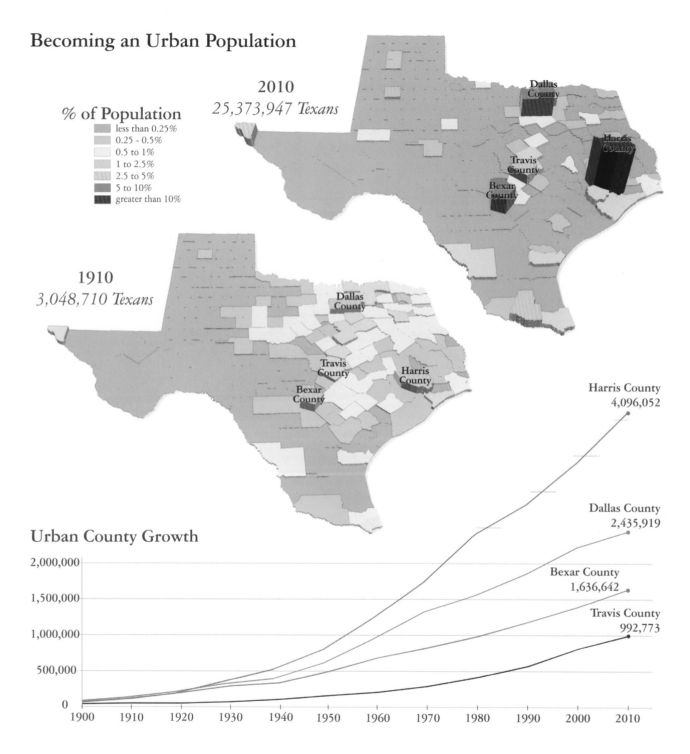

Becoming an Urban Population

% of Population
- less than 0.25%
- 0.25 - 0.5%
- 0.5 to 1%
- 1 to 2.5%
- 2.5 to 5%
- 5 to 10%
- greater than 10%

2010
25,373,947 Texans

Dallas County
Harris County
Travis County
Bexar County

1910
3,048,710 Texans

Dallas County
Travis County
Harris County
Bexar County

Urban County Growth

Harris County
4,096,052

Dallas County
2,435,919

Bexar County
1,636,642

Travis County
992,773

This pair of maps and the accompanying chart show how the population of Texas' major metropolitan areas has vastly outpaced the growth in the rest of the state over the past century (Texas Almanac 2013; Texas State Library and Archives Commission 2013).

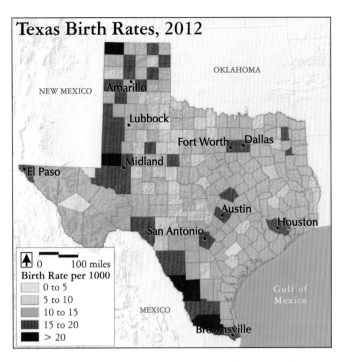

During 2012, Texas counties saw their birth counts range from under 2,100 to over 38,700. The crude birth rate for Texas counties during 2012 (the annual number of births per thousand citizens) ranged from under five to over twenty. The 2012 estimate of the number of citizens used here is based on the zero-migration scenario (Texas Department of State Health Services 2014a; Texas State Data Center 2014; Valencia, Flores, and Hoque 2012).

the state. U-Haul now reports that many Texas towns are found near the top of its list of US one-way truck rental destinations, including Houston (#1), San Antonio (#5), Austin (#6), and Dallas (#12) (U-Haul 2014). And it is not just the major cities that are seeing newcomers—it is a statewide influx. Since the early 1990s, forty-one of the fifty states have sent more residents to Texas than they have received back, according to an analysis of income tax returns. California, Louisiana, Illinois, New York, and Florida were the top five states supplying new Texans. While there have been some net losses to other states (principally Colorado, Georgia, and Arizona), over fourteen times more people immigrated to Texas than left for other states (Tax Foundation 2014; see US Census 2014a for moves mapped by county).

It is hard to pin down all the reasons why people are lured to Texas, and the reasons for their moves likely vary from year to year. Undoubtedly, though, many people come to Texas for financial reasons. They have pulled up stakes to work in the oil fields, health clinics and labs, technology fields, and military bases, and to enjoy a lower cost of living and reduced tax rate (Texas is one of just nine states without an income tax) (Batheja 2013). And perhaps the advent of air conditioning after the mid-1930s has made the move a bit more comfortable (Miller 2013).

Swings within Texas

Within the state, the population has gradually merged and bunched together. In 1900, the urban population of Texas was just 17 percent of the whole. Yet by 2000, the share of city residents in Texas had grown to 83 percent (State Data Center of Iowa 2014). This agrarian, small-town state became an industrial, commercial, big-city state in just one hundred years! And these cities were themselves grouping together. The population of the state has gradually been clustering in a nineteen-million-person megaregion known as the Texas Triangle, stretching from San Antonio to Dallas–Fort Worth to Houston (Neuman and Bright 2008; US Census 2014a).

Birth Rates

As we have seen, immigration to Texas is certainly a big part of Texas' population growth. However, more of the state's population rise (currently, about 54 percent) actually comes from births among residents already here. The state's major cities top the list of locations for the absolute number of children born. On the other hand, other regions, such as the Lower Rio Grande Valley and West Texas, lead in birth rates for the number of babies born per thousand people (Texas Department of State Health Services 2014a and 2014c).

While there are variations from county to county, it is interesting to see that the birth rate for the state as a whole has fallen remarkably over the last two generations. In 1952, the birth rate was 27.5 per thousand residents; seventy years later, it had dropped by almost half to 14.7 (Texas Department of State Health Services 2015). Although this general change does not reflect the shifts in the number of women in their child-bearing years, it does raise a question about what reasons there might be for the decline.

Family Planning

Some of the changes in fertility can be attributed to the widening availability of birth control, abortion services, and family planning education and advocacy as the twentieth century has carried on (Bailey 2012). There is a long history of family planning efforts in Texas. The origins of the birth control movement in Texas go back at least as far as 1935, when Katie Ripley helped found and support a Dallas clinic, affiliating it with Margaret Sanger's Birth Control Clinical Research Bureau (Smith 2011).

Change in birth control law, attitudes, and availability accelerated during the late 1930s, in Texas and nationwide. In December 1936, the New York federal appeals court authorized contraceptive distribution, and seven months later, the American Medical Association endorsed birth control education and devices (*United States v. One Package of Japanese Pessaries*, 86 F.2d 737 (1936)). In 1936, Agnese Carter Nelms ("the Margaret Sanger of Texas"), daughter of a Houston lumber magnate, helped organize the Birth Control League of Texas and proceeded to help organize the first clinics in Houston (1936), Austin (1937), Fort Worth (1938), San Antonio (1939), and Waco (1939) (Smith 2011).

Twenty years later, a second wave of clinic expansion hit, with family planning facilities founded in Corpus Christi (1958), Lubbock (1963), McAllen (1963), Odessa (1965),

Midland (1966), and Amarillo (1968). The clinics' impact was strengthened by new drugs, including G. D. Searle's new oral contraceptive, first approved by the FDA in 1960 (Marks 2001, 79). Subsidies for family planning grew during this time as well. With the belief that smaller families would struggle less with poverty, public funding for family planning began with wide bipartisan support in 1964 (Economic Opportunity Act of 1964, P.L. 88-452, 78 Stat. 508; Family Planning Services and Population Research Act of 1970, P.L. 91-572, 84 Stat. 1504; Smith 2011).

While recent years have witnessed harsh words and bitter politics over abortion and subsidies for family planning, it appears that birth control has managed to survive as a part of American custom and law, and as a means to limit our numbers and our mark on the environment.

Meaning

Disputes over birth control and abortion have reminded us all that population is a hot-button political issue. Still, the growth in Texas residents has brought many indisputable environmental impacts that deserve attention. Each of us has our own footprint, and there are more and more of us! The dramatic increase in Texas' total population has meant more land development, agricultural cultivation, water and energy use, pollution, and wildlife dislocations. Some worry that this growth must eventually bump up against the finite capacities of farm fields, rivers, aquifers, and other resources (Quinn 2003).

"Look at the population of Texas . . . at the beginning of the century it was three million. . . . It's going to be 36 million in thirty years. OK? But look at where those people are. They're not spread evenly across the geography of Texas. Seventy to eighty percent of those people are along I-35 or in the east of the state. Thirty years from now you're talking about a density of people on the upper Texas coast that's greater than the density of people in China. Think about that. . . . That's going to put a huge pressure on water and . . . the question is, are we going to have the vigilance to preserve any of our water for the ecological integrity of the state? And that's going to require the will of the people to want to do that."

—David Schmidly, 2002

As David Schmidly points out, the impact sometimes comes not so much from how many of us there are, but from where we are. For example, the movement of many Texans to the relatively arid IH-35 corridor and lower Rio Grande Valley has raised critical questions about supplying adequate water in a cost-effective, equitable way to the state's growing communities, while still protecting the ecological health of the watersheds supplying that water.

Opportunities

Although continued population growth in Texas puts more pressure on natural resources, it could be that there are still some positive signs. For one, our population's overall growth rate, on a percentage basis, is now actually below the torrid pace seen in the 1950s and 1970s (Texas State Library and Archives Commission 2013). As well, Texas' total fertility rate hit 2.075 in 2012, dropping below the replacement level of 2.1 (Centers for Disease Control and Prevention 2013, table 12, p. 38).

Also, the geography of our population increase is shifting, and possibly bringing benefits. Texas' current growth is concentrated in the metropolitan areas. While Texans' generational move to the big cities has removed many residents from an intimate, work-a-day contact with nature, it has raised the power of hunting, fishing, nature photography, and other forms of ecotourism as a conservation strategy (Eubanks 2002). Plus, packing more people into denser cities can increase both the efficiency and the creativity with which we confront environmental problems.

Finally, we need to remember that we are a clever and resourceful species. So perhaps these baby carriages and U-Haul trailers will bring new ideas for how Texas can cope with its environmental challenges.

Sources

Bailey, Martha. 2012. "Reexamining the Impact of Family Planning Programs on U.S. Fertility: Evidence from the War on Poverty and the Early Years of Title X." *American Economic Journal: Applied Economics* 4 (2): 62–97.

Batheja, Aman. 2013. "The Joys of No Income Tax, the Agonies of Other Kinds." *New York Times*, May 24.

Centers for Disease Control and Prevention. 2012. National Vital Statistics Reports, Vol. 61, No. 1. Births: Final Data for 2010. National Vital Statistics System, National Center for Health Statistics, US Department of Health and Human Services. December 30.

Eubanks, Ted. 2002. Oral history interview conducted on April 15, in Austin, Texas. Texas Legacy Project, Conservation History Association of Texas.

Gauthier, Jason. 2002. Measuring America: "The Decennial Censuses from 1790 to 2000. Appendix A: United States' Population and Census Cost." US Census Bureau. http://www.census.gov/prod/2002pubs/p0102-ma.pdf, accessed July 21, 2014.

Hershey, Terry. 2002. Oral history interview conducted on April 13, in Stonewall, Texas. Texas Legacy Project, Conservation History Association of Texas.

Mackun, Paul, and Steven Wilson. 2011. "Population Distribution and Change: 2000 to 2010." 2010 Census Briefs. US Census Bureau. March.

Marks, Lara. 2001. *Sexual Chemistry: A History of the Oral Contraceptive Pill.* New Haven, CT: Yale University Press.

Miller, Jeremy. 2013. "The Centroid." *Orion Magazine*, March–April.

Neuman, Michael, and Elise Bright. 2008. "Texas Urban Triangle: Framework for Future Growth." Research Report SWUTC/08/167166-1, Southwest Region University Transportation Center, Texas Transportation Institute, Texas A&M University System. http://swutc.tamu.edu/publications/technicalreports/167166-1a.pdf, accessed June 8, 2015.

Newcomb, William. 1961. *The Indians of Texas.* Austin: University of Texas Press.

Quinn, Daniel. 2003. Oral history interview conducted October 20, in Houston, Texas. Texas Legacy Project, Conservation History Association of Texas.

Schmidly, David. 2002. Oral history interview conducted October 11, in Lubbock, Texas. Texas Legacy Project. Conservation History Association of Texas.

Smith, Harold. 2011. "All Good Things Start with the Women: The Origin of the Texas Birth Control Movement, 1933–45." *Southwestern Historical Quarterly* 118 (1).

State Data Center of Iowa. 2014. "Urban and Rural Population for the U.S. and All States: 1900–2000." http://data.iowadatacenter.org/datatables/UnitedStates/urusstpop19002000.pdf, accessed July 24, 2014.

Tax Foundation. 2014. State to State Migration Data: Data Tools. http://interactive.taxfoundation.org/migration/, accessed July 17, 2014.

Texas Almanac. 2013. Texas Almanac: Population History of Counties from 1850 to 2010. http://www.texasalmanac.com/sites/default/files/images/topics/ctypophistweb2010.pdf, accessed April 28, 2013.

Texas Department of State Health Services. 2014a. Texas Health Data: Births to Texas Residents. http://soupfin.tdh.state.tx.us/birth05.htm, accessed July 19, 2014.

———. 2014b. Texas Population, 2013 (Projections). Center for Health Statistics. https://www.dshs.state.tx.us/chs/popdat/ST2013.shtm, accessed July 24, 2014.

———. 2014c. Vital Statistics Annual Reports, 2001 and 2012. http://www.dshs.state.tx.us/chs/vstat/annrpts.shtm, accessed July 24, 2014.

———. 2015. Births and Birth Rates, Texas Residents, 1946–2012. http://www.dshs.state.tx.us/chs/vstat/vs12/fig-4data.shtm, accessed June 8, 2015.

Texas State Data Center. 2014. Texas Population Projections Program: Data Downloads. Population Projections for the State of Texas and Counties. http://txsdc.utsa.edu/Resources/TPEPP/Projections/2012/2012allcntymigtot.zip, accessed July 19, 2014.

Texas State Library and Archives Commission. 2013. "United States and Texas Populations, 1850–2012." https://www.tsl.state.tx.us/ref/abouttx/census.html, accessed April 28, 2013.

U-Haul. 2014. "U-Haul Names Houston as the Number One Top 2013 U.S. Destination City." http://www.uhaul.com/Articles/About/2018/U-Haul-Names-Houston-as-the-Number-One-Top-2013-US-Destination-City, accessed July 25, 2014.

US Census. 2013. Center of Population and Territorial Expansion, 1790–2010. https://www.census.gov/dataviz/visualizations/050/, accessed December 10, 2015.

US Census. 2014a. Census Flows Mapper. http://flowsmapper.geo.census.gov/map.html, accessed December 10, 2015.

———. 2014b. National Centers of Population, 1790–2010. http://www.census.gov/geo/reference/centersofpop/natcentersofpop.html, accessed July 20, 2014.

Valencia, Lila, Miguel Flores, and Nazrul Hoque. 2012. "An Analysis of Texas Migration Patterns and Economic Implications." Applied Demography Conference, January 2012. https://idserportal.utsa.edu/Resources/Presentations/IDSER/2012/ADC/ADC2012_AnalysisofTexas_Valencia.pptx, accessed July 19, 2014.

Yoakum, Henderson. 1856. *History of Texas from Its First Settlement in 1685 to Its Annexation to the United States in 1846.* New York: Redfield.

Sprawl

Gone to Texas

Over the past several generations, Texas' built world has faced extraordinary growth, much of it channeled into the kind of sprawl that Mr. Draper, a Tennessee Valley Authority planner, first warned us about close to eighty years ago: diffuse, low-density construction running along strips and ribbons, leapfrogging among scattered tracts into the suburbs.

For Texas, sprawl has been fueled by the state's rapid population growth, an eightfold surge from 3.1 million in 1900 to over 26.1 million now (Texas State Library and Archives Commission 2014; US Census 2013; US Census 2014c). Today's Texans have increasingly tended to shun the smaller, more compact towns. It is estimated that as many as 88 percent of the state's residents have now settled in large metropolitan areas, including Houston, Dallas–Fort Worth, San Antonio, and Austin (Texas Department of State Health Services 2014). And within these metro regions, many Texans have found their way to the suburbs and exurbs. In fact, of the

fifteen fastest-growing American towns with a population over 50,000, fully six were satellite communities in the orbit of a Texas city. San Marcos, Texas, led the pack with a growth rate of 7.9 percent in the July 1, 2013, to July 1, 2014, period, followed by Georgetown (7.6 percent), Frisco (5.8 percent), Conroe (5.2 percent), McKinney (5.1 percent), and New Braunfels (4.8 percent) (US Census 2015).

Today, numerous cities in Texas, and for that matter, many towns throughout America, are known for or are even famous for their low-density character.

The Patterns of Sprawl

To get a sense of what these figures mean in Texas history and landscape, perhaps the following figures will help. As the global map below shows, Texas' urban sprawl is creating cities, such as San Antonio, with some of the lowest densities in the world. The next five maps show that San Antonio's growth pattern is shared by Austin, Houston, and Dallas–Fort Worth, as well as much of the exurban countryside.

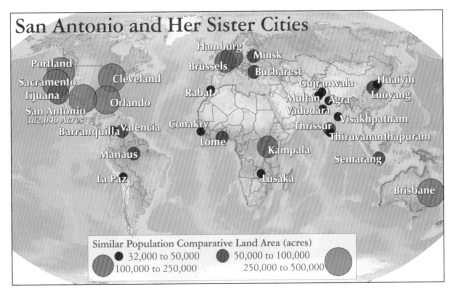

This map shows a set of thirty cities around the globe that might be considered San Antonio's peers, in that they have 2013-era populations within ± 5 percent of the 1.86 million people who call San Antonio home. However, despite their similar population counts, the average person in these sister cities uses only one-third the space of their fellow citizen in San Antonio. In fact, in some cases, he or she might occupy only one-twelfth the area of their compatriot in San Antonio (Demographia 2014).

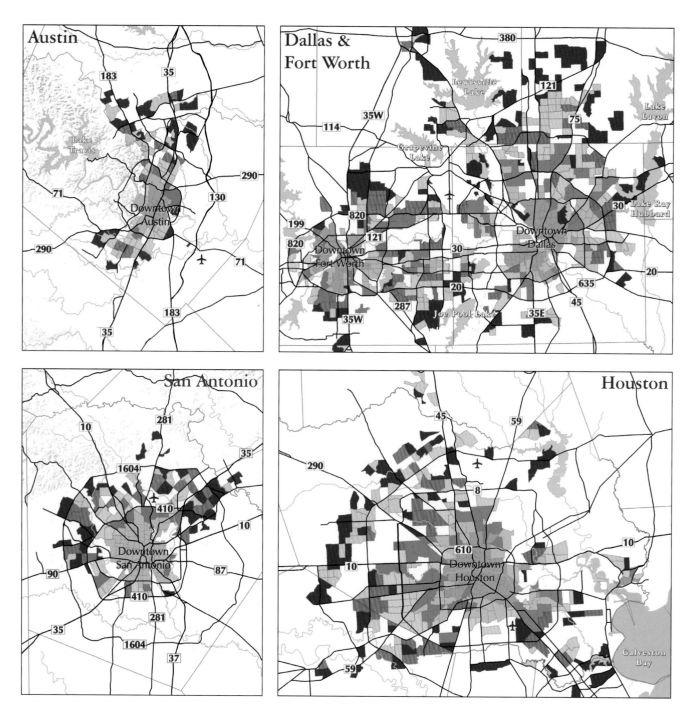

These maps show a short history of sprawl in Austin, Dallas–Fort Worth, Houston, and San Antonio. The polygons mark those areas that had developed to a density of five people per acre, or more, by 1960 (yellow), 1970 (light green), 1980 (pink), 1990 (orange), 2000 (violet), and 2010 (purple) (Minnesota Population Center 2014; Richmond 2014; US Census Bureau 2014a).

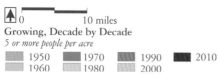

0   10 miles

Growing, Decade by Decade
5 or more people per acre

1950	1970	1990	2010
1960	1980	2000	

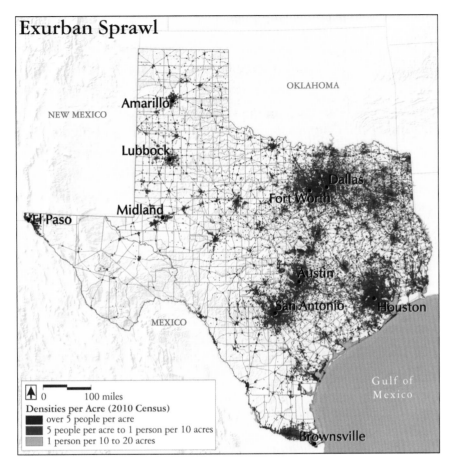

Exurban Sprawl

The effects of sprawl are not limited to the state's major cities and towns. Low-level development has leaked out into rural areas as well, particularly in the eastern third of the state. This map depicts 2010 census blocks that reported densities over five people per acre, between five people per acre and one person for every ten acres, and one person per ten to twenty acres (US Census Bureau 2014b).

Whys and Wherefores of Suburbs

As Earle Draper and current figures and maps tell us, this kind of growth has been with us for a long time and is certainly a widespread part of today's Texas landscape. Yet why does sprawl happen? There are many possible reasons.

Hardheaded, practical reasons, such as lower housing costs and better schooling, are often cited as motives to head for the suburbs, but perhaps those things are not always so important. Our look at Zillow.com data for the per-square-foot cost of housing found that suburban communities can often actually be more, not less, expensive than closer-in neighborhoods (Zillow 2014). Our review of Texas Education Agency records suggested that highly ranked public schools can be found in the inner city, as well as in the suburbs (Texas Education Agency 2014a and 2014b). Perhaps the true reasons for sprawl lie elsewhere.

Some argue that the move to the countryside was originally driven by xenophobia—immigrant communities had sprung up in the inner city during the early part of the last century (Jackson 1985, 70, 107). Other kinds of fear may have later been involved, including dread of a Cold War nuclear attack on US cities (Tobin 2002). Others believe that post–World War II federal programs supporting urban renewal and public housing in the city core triggered white flight to the suburbs (*Pruitt-Igoe Myth* 2012). Or, some say that more general, long-nurtured housing policies in the United States had a role; perhaps the thirty-year, federally insured, low-down-payment, tax-deductible mortgage helped build the Great American Dream house and yard in the suburbs (Revenue Act of 1913, Pub. L. No. 63-16; National Housing Act of 1934, Pub. L. No. 73-479, Servicemen's Readjustment Act of 1944, Pub. L. No. 78-346).

Others suggest that the move was more about lifestyle than politics. Perhaps sprawl grew from ambitions to adopt the expansive lawns found in European pleasure gardens or that later were used in the leisure-class sports of croquet, golf, archery, tennis, and lawn bowling (Jenkins 1994; Jenkins 1999, 117). Or maybe it was not so much a love of the sporting life, but more our fondness for drive-through fast food and big-box stores that has driven sprawl (Schlosser 2012, 293). Another thought: the expansion into the suburbs may have been part of the expansion of the American home itself, which picked up new amenities (some boasted a wine cellar, dance studio, sauna, juice bar, or theater) and grew in size by 44 percent from 1973 through 2010 (Cammel 2013; US Census 2012). Or, it could be that the move to the edge of town was fed by an almost tribal desire to be close to "people like us," with attitudes, faiths, and political leanings that made us feel comfortable (Bishop 2008). Finally, in one of those lovely perverse ironies, perhaps sprawl has been due to, of all things, environmental reasons, driven by people's desire to get closer to the nature that rings American cities.

It is tough to find simple, one-size-fits-all answers to the question of why people move to the suburbs. Each family weighs its options and chooses where to live, work, shop, and play for its own diverse reasons. But there is no question that there is a pervasive, powerful urge to move to (formerly) greener pastures.

Virtues and Sins of Suburbs

Motives for sprawl can be difficult to pin down; it is also hard to tell whether sprawl ends up being good or bad for people. Some believe that the growth and spread of cities is a good sign of vigor and prosperity. Some see sprawl's low-density development as allowing for a welcome array of lower-cost housing available to more people. The cul-de-sacs and quiet lanes of suburban bedroom communities may also provide a slower-paced, more private, and less crime-ridden lifestyle (Kahn 2006). On the flip side, some observers may recognize sprawl as a problem but believe that efforts to slow sprawl are gentrifying long-settled minority neighborhoods in the city core (Herrera 2003).

Other commenters are wholly unenthusiastic about sprawl. These critics use analogies of cancerous, out-of-control growth, lamenting a Levittown-style homogeneity in the suburbs, and even seeing a bigotry there traced back to red-lined neighborhoods of the 1950s. Detractors go on to say that suburban residents may see less crime but may also have to cope with higher traffic casualties (Ewing, Schieber, and Zegeer 2003). At the same time, suburbia's reputed slower pace may be outweighed by more road time and obesity (Smart Growth America 2014).

Some sprawl skeptics also condemn the costs that this kind of development imposes on the general public. Savings on private home prices in the suburbs may be exceeded by higher public infrastructure expenses (Blais 2010). For example, studies in Hays and Bandera Counties found that EMS, fire, police, schooling, and other government services for developed residential land in these suburban counties cost 10 to 26 percent more than the residents paid in through their taxes. Meanwhile, ranch and open lands in those two counties required only 26–33 cents in services for every dollar of tax paid (American Farmland Trust 2000 and 2001).

The debate about the good and bad sides of sprawl is hard to resolve when only considering its impact on humans. On the other hand, its effect on the natural world is clear. The bulk conversion of acres of habitat, rural watersheds, and farmland for human homes and offices and shops and roads damages wildlife, water, and food. Sprawl's impact is not just a quantitative one of sheer area, but can also involve a madly complicated set of interwoven factors, as new human neighbors introduce sterile St. Augustine lawns, invasive privet bushes, and prowling cats that upset the original native ecosystems.

Regardless of how one views our sprawling suburban world, its reasons and virtues, it is very much with us and makes it worth understanding more about where and how sprawl happens, and what its impacts might be. Please read on.

Pending Sprawl

Sprawl begins well before bulldozers, backhoes, and construction crews arrive; it begins with the quiet white-collar work of planning new roads and utilities, platting new subdivisions, and retitling new residential and commercial lots. This work can start a road map for future development before any spade hits the ground.

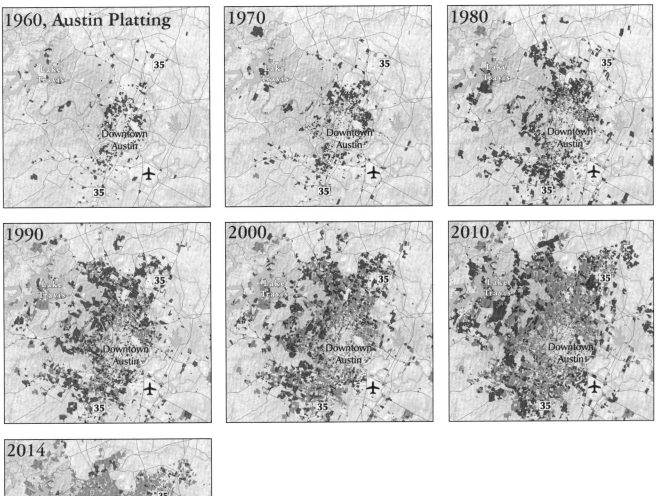

These maps of replatting in Austin show the process of splitting up land for development, prior to actual construction. The series of maps shows the city with plats having recording dates prior to 1960, 1970, 1980, 1990, 2000, 2010, and 2014 (City of Austin 2015).

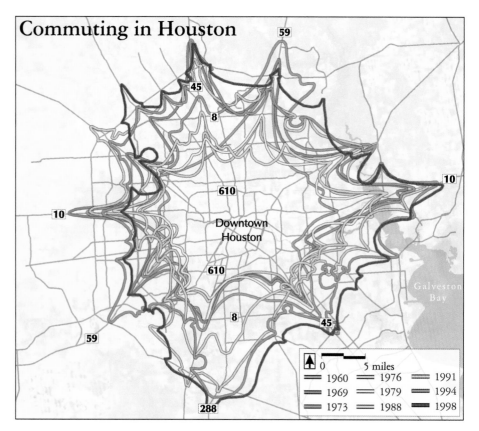

Commuting in Houston

This map shows the amount of time and distance taken by commuting in Houston, from 1960 through 1998. Each contour represents the distance covered in half an hour by a vehicle moving from downtown outward, during peak afternoon traffic. Contours marking this pulse of a low-density city are shown for 1960, 1969, 1973, 1976, 1979, 1988, 1991, 1994, and 1998 (Benz 2014; Harris County 1960, 1969, 1973, 1976, 1979, 1988, 1991, 1994, 1998).

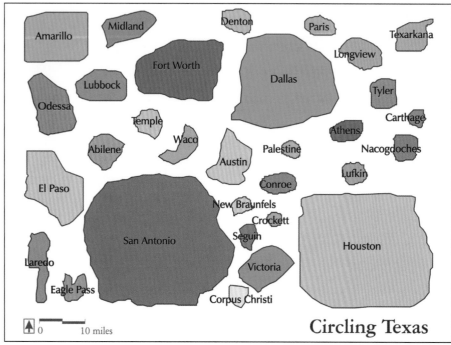

Circling Texas

This figure is an abstraction of the many ring roads in Texas, coalescing all of the major loops into one kind of paved Pangaea. Perhaps the figure helps show that these ring roads do have a cumulative effect, although sponsors have tended to look at them segment by segment (Sierra Club v. U.S. Army Corps of Engineers et al., Case number 4:11-cv-03063, US District Court, Southern District of Texas).

"The transportation infrastructure caused everything else to happen. All the lifestyles, the way people live, where they lived, how they moved around, all that was due to the plan for the transportation infrastructure."

—David Crossley—founder, Blueprint Houston, February 27, 2008, Houston

"There's a problem of this urban sprawl that's doing us all damage. I mean in the Houston-Galveston area, the eight counties, we're spending about 10 to 12 percent of our productivity in transport—going around, getting from A to B. And that's a terrible waste."

—David Marrack—physician and pathologist, October 23, 2003, Bellaire

Driving Sprawl

Low-density development living can require a lot of ricocheting among homes, schools, workplaces, and stores, and can consume a great deal of space and time (Shrank, Eisele, and Lomax 2012; Department of Transportation 2014). In fact, it is likely that the twentieth century's construction of a massive US fleet of cars, and a far-reaching US road system (and before it, the tram and interurban rail networks), have "driven" sprawl in American, and Texan, cities. Some of these patterns were set up long ago, when the Federal Highway Act of 1916 based its funding formulas on the area to span rather than the population to serve, and when the Hayden-Cartwright Act of 1934 dedicated gasoline taxes to highways (Gutfreund 2004).

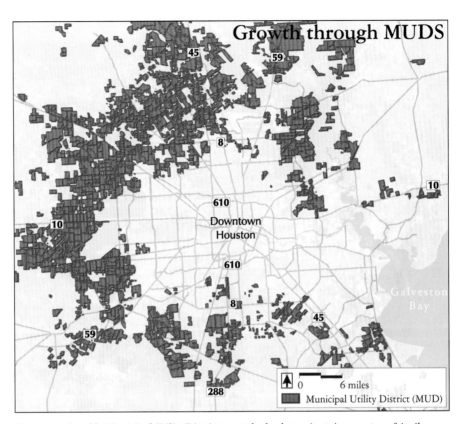

Houston is ringed by Municipal Utility Districts set up by developers (map is current as of April 2014). These districts can tap low-interest, tax-exempt bonds to finance private construction (Barber 2014; Patel 2014; TCEQ 2014b). Texas law also gives the districts powerful eminent domain rights of condemnation to access underground utilities (Texas Legislative Council 2012).

"Look at what's happened in Helotes where they put in their wall-to-wall housings.... The developers had bought dairy farms years ahead.... Their method of development is get good roads.... Then they'll push utilities, get the electric lines out here. And they'll push sewage. Then they'll get the school to build very expensive schools."

—Ed Scharf—retired armed forces, February 18, 2006, Grey Forest, Texas

"Houston's problems ... have to do with its incredible growth and sprawl. You're talking of a city of, what, 637 square miles. You're talking about a population in the region of about 4 million spread over a very large area—very low density. This creates a real problem for service delivery. Solid waste disposal works well under conditions of high density ... same with water supply.... So Houston's growth, which was considered its ally for a number of years, is probably its enemy."

—Marty Melosi—historian and professor, February 28, 2008, Houston, Texas

Financing Sprawl

Development is very costly. Builders must bring in new roads, sewers, water lines, and other utilities, and then put up new homes, shops, schools, and other buildings. Some of these costs may be offset by the lower prices of rural land and the sums paid by the first buyers and renters. However, much of suburban construction has often been underwritten by investor-owned, public-market firms, or leveraged with help from the public sector. Since their start in 1960, Real Estate Investment Trusts have provided one way to raise large sums of construction capital and disperse development's risk among many investors. In more recent decades, these REITs have been key vehicles for building regional malls and other green-field developments (Blackmar 2005; Cigar Excise Tax Extension of 1960). Municipal Utility Districts are another crucial financial tool for suburban builders. First authorized in 1971, MUDs have given suburban developers in Texas access to tax-exempt funds to help finance large new construction projects on the urban periphery (Galvan 2007; Texas Water Code Section 54).

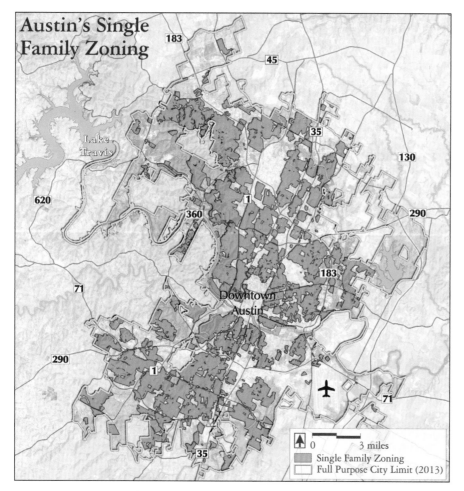

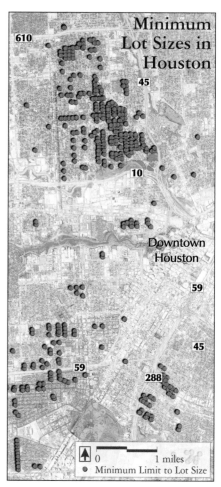

Near-town construction limits can squeeze new development out into the suburbs. The map of Austin shows those areas that have been designated for single-family dwellings (SF-1, SF-2, SF-3, SF-4, SF-5, and SF-6). The Houston map shows near-town locations where its city council, famously allergic to zoning, imposed minimum lot sizes (City of Austin 2014; City of Houston 2014).

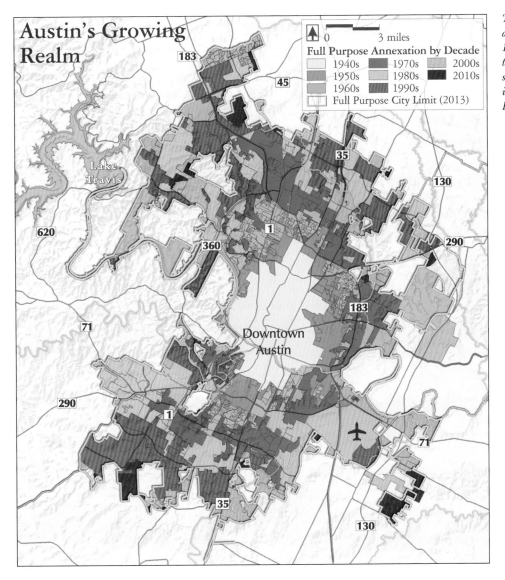

Austin's Growing Realm

Full Purpose Annexation by Decade
- 1940s
- 1950s
- 1960s
- 1970s
- 1980s
- 1990s
- 2000s
- 2010s
- Full Purpose City Limit (2013)

0 — 3 miles

This map depicts the stages of annexation in Austin's history over the 1946–2013 period. Core areas date to the 1940s, while successive rings and satellite neighborhoods were annexed in later decades (City of Austin 2014; Herrington 2014).

Zoning for Sprawl

Following the perplexing law of unintended consequences, some of the flight to the suburbs may be an odd side effect of efforts to protect current land uses and neighborhoods closer to town. For instance, zoning for single-family dwellings or ordinances mandating minimum lot sizes may have been drafted for worthy causes like encouraging homeownership, maintaining school enrollment, and stabilizing neighborhoods. However, these laws may also have ended up excluding high-density developments in the urban core and pushing more residents outward, into the suburbs.

Don't Leave!

After people move to the suburbs, the core city often seeks to annex these bedroom communities to keep its tax base from fleeing and to provide those suburbs with long-term infrastructure and services (Texas Local Government Code, Chapter 43). For cities' fiscal

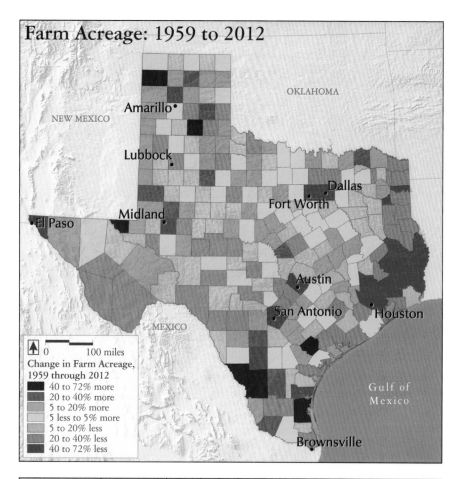

Farm Acreage: 1959 to 2012

0   100 miles

Change in Farm Acreage,
1959 through 2012
40 to 72% more
20 to 40% more
5 to 20% more
5 less to 5% more
5 to 20% less
20 to 40% less
40 to 72% less

The state map compares county-by-county farm acreage reported for 1959, and over fifty years later, in 2012. Green areas had gains in farmland, yellow showed little change, and orange to red areas saw significant losses. The state's metropolitan districts typically showed the highest declines in farmland (Borchers 2014; US Census Bureau 2014b: US Department of Agriculture 2014a, 2014b, and 2014c).

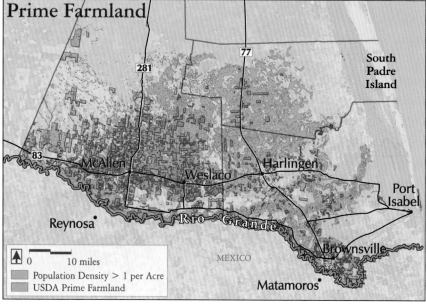

Prime Farmland

0   10 miles
Population Density > 1 per Acre
USDA Prime Farmland

Compared with the statewide view, the map of the Lower Rio Grande Valley gives a more detailed and current view of how agricultural land is slipping away as sprawl advances. In the Valley, communities (shown here as the neighborhoods with a population density over one per acre, inked in red) have built out across some of the most productive, prime farmland in the nation (marked with green) (Borchers 2014; US Census Bureau 2014c; US Department of Agriculture 2014d).

health, the stakes can be high; if San Antonio had kept its boundaries of 1945, it would reportedly have had more poverty and unemployment than Newark, New Jersey. However, the suburbs may not come back to the fold easily; neighborhoods near Houston, Wichita Falls, and New Braunfels protested that these annexations inflicted "taxation without representation" (Houston 2012, 5, 8, 9).

Sprawl and Food

The spread of Texas cities into the countryside has rewarded families with homes, shops, workplaces, and playfields. But there have been offsetting losses, such as the paving over of fertile agricultural lands that preceded those new streets, houses, stores, and offices. From 1982 to 2010, over 3.5 million acres of Texas land were developed, leading all states by a wide margin (USDA 2013, 34). From 1997 to 2012, 54 percent of those losses were concentrated in the twenty-five high-growth metropolitan counties that cover just 10 percent of Texas (Anderson et al. 2014, 6). In this way, urban sprawl can eat into nearby farm and ranch land, complicating the ability of cities to locally source their food. Fortunately, nonprofits such as the Texas Agricultural Land Trust, Austin's Sustainable Food Center, and Houston's Urban Harvest work to preserve working lands with easements, farmers' markets, and community gardens.

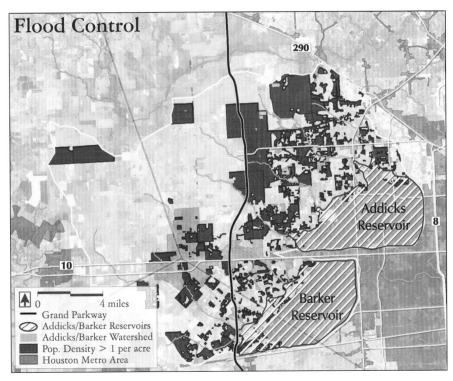

The Addicks and Barker reservoirs were built to control runoff after a catastrophic flood hit Houston in 1936, when seven people died, twenty-five blocks of downtown were inundated, and the Port of Houston was closed for months. This map shows the collision of roads (the Grand Parkway is marked in purple), development (tracts with a 2010 population density over one per acre are colored red) and flood control (the blue hatched areas). Rapid and extensive construction upstream from the Addicks and Barker reservoirs limits the levees' ability to hold back runoff and reduce downstream flooding (Melosi and Pratt 2007, 119; Texas Water Development Board 2014; US Census Bureau 2014c; US Department of Agriculture 2014d).

Sprawl and Runoff

Suburban growth can cut into agricultural lands, and the historic spread of cities has also limited other natural services that come from open space. Flood control is a good example. When construction and paving extend into the suburbs, impervious cover rises and flood runoff increases. The concern has grown acute in the Houston area, where the Sierra Club sued the Army Corps of Engineers, arguing that development and road construction upstream from the Addicks and Barker reservoirs had undermined the dams' ability to hold back storm water and protect the city downstream from flooding (*Sierra Club v. U.S. Army Corps of Engineers et al.*, Case number 4:11-cv-03063, U.S. District Court, Southern District of Texas).

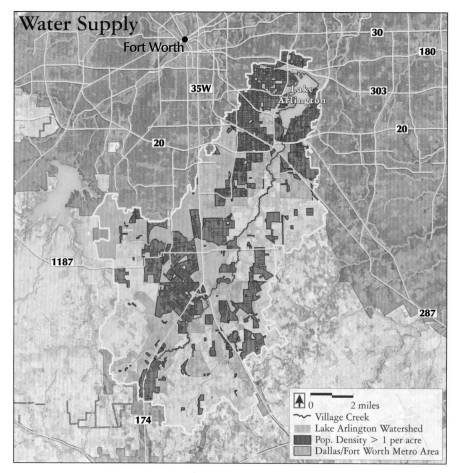

This map shows the spread of population upstream from Lake Arlington, raising the risk that runoff from the new roads, houses, cars, and other baggage of modern development will pollute drinking water that flows to over 500,000 residents of the city of Fort Worth. Areas marked in red had a population density over one per acre in 2010 (TCEQ 2013 and 2014a; Texas Water Development Board 2014; US Census Bureau 2014c; US Department of Agriculture 2014d).

"I suspect urban sprawl is more significant than any grazing or other misuse of land. We just keep expanding and expanding and once you build up a city, why that's the end of the natural vegetation. When I was teaching at A&M and I needed plants to study, I didn't have to go a half a mile to get plenty of different plants for us to study. And now you'd have to go 50 miles."

—Chester Rowell—botanist and professor, March 31, 2001, Marfa, Texas

"We have so much sprawl . . . A lot of the big ranches are being sold, and are now small subdivisions and ranchettes. These large tracts are so very important to wildlife, because wildlife move. . . . We're forcing animals into people's habitat."

—Bonnie McKinney—wildlife biologist, April 5, 2001, Marathon, Texas

"The word *ranchette* just turns my stomach."

—Tim Hixon—philanthropist and near-town builder, February 15, 2006, San Antonio, Texas

Sprawl and Habitat

Sprawl can end up swapping wildlife's dens, nests, and habitats for people's homes. Some animals, such as white-tailed deer, raccoons, coyotes, grackles, doves, and famously resourceful black rats, can be successful in sharing built-up lands with their two-legged relatives. However, other species are not so adaptable. This is especially true of many endangered species that fill very specific niches.

Sprawl and Drinking Water

Development into cities' outskirts has raised other complications for Texans. For instance, in Fort Worth, construction has spread throughout much of the watershed of Lake Arlington, a major source of drinking water for the city. Runoff from these upstream communities has brought unwelcome bacterial loads to the lake (TCEQ 2013). Lake Arlington's water quality woes are not an isolated problem. In Austin, the nonprofit Save Our Springs Coalition persuaded the city to limit impervious cover in sensitive watersheds to protect receiving waters (Save Our Springs Ordinance, City of Austin Ordinance 990225-70 and Ordinance 031211-11, 1992).

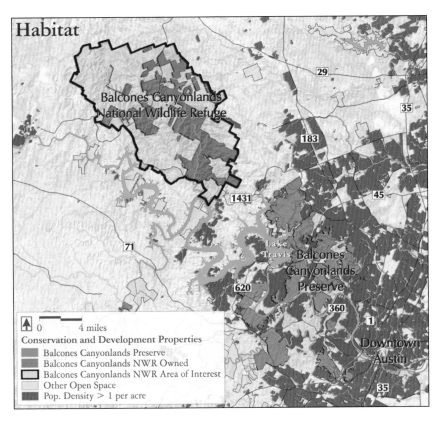

Habitat

Conservation and Development Properties
- Balcones Canyonlands Preserve
- Balcones Canyonlands NWR Owned
- Balcones Canyonlands NWR Area of Interest
- Other Open Space
- Pop. Density > 1 per acre

The Balcones Canyonlands National Wildlife Refuge (the authorized area is shown in light green, while the acquired lands are shown in dark green) and the Balcones Habitat Conservation Plan lands (olive green) have helped protect the endangered golden-cheeked warbler, black-capped vireo, and six types of karst invertebrates. Austin area development (shown here, in red, at a density of one person per acre) is growing closer to the sanctuaries (Umbehaun 2014; US Fish and Wildlife Service 2014).

Surface Parking   Structured Parking

Parking in Houston

Parking in Dallas

Sprawl can spread people far from the central core of Texas cities, too far to walk or ride a bike into downtown. As a result, large parts of downtown areas are used as parking lots. Houston and Dallas are both dominated by surface (red) and structured (pink) parking facilities (City of Dallas 2011; Downtown Houston Marketing Initiative 2014; Google 2014).

For example, sprawl in the Austin area has approached and threatened the traditional homes of two rare birds, the golden-cheeked warbler and the black-capped vireo. A pair of preserves, the Balcones Canyonlands National Wildlife Refuge and the Balcones Habitat Conservation Plan lands, has been set aside for the warbler, vireo, and other rare creatures, but sprawl has raised the price and limited the availability of lands for these refuges (Swearingen 2010, 193–96).

If we could imagine an abstract map that compared protected and developed lands in Texas, it might look something like this. This helps show how nonprofit groups, plus federal, state, and municipal governments (in addition to other agencies that include counties, river authorities, schools, and utility and water districts) have managed to protect significant parts of the state. Still, the amount protected is less than a third of that affected by development (Minnesota Population Center 2014; Ogren 2014; Texas Land Trust Council 2014; Texas Parks and Wildlife 2012; US Census Bureau 2014c).

Sprawl, Inside-Out

Sprawl unravels the fringe of cities. However, it can have a significant effect on the city's core as well. For example, sprawl, and its reliance on private automobiles for ferrying workers from the suburbs to central business districts and back again, have contributed to the recasting of downtowns as de facto parking zones. Some of these patterns may well be traced back into the deep intricacies of the tax code. Prior to 1984, the IRS treated free employee parking as a nontaxable fringe benefit (though transit commuting had no similar subsidy) (Deficit Reduction Act of 1984, Pub. L. No. 98-369).

Sprawl and Conservation

So what can we take away from this short and spotty history of sprawl? The concerns about suburban development's impacts on farmland loss, habitat fragmentation, storm water runoff, pollutant loads, highway traffic, and garage-rich downtowns suggest that sprawl is something worth reining in. Fortunately, there are many promising zoning, transit, educational, and marketing measures on the horizon that make compact cities more exciting and alluring for urban pioneers, and, at the same time, easier and more accommodating for families. Those kinds of long-term shifts in where people choose to live can have a huge impact. However, the speed with which popular modern cities can boom and grow and spread suggests that more imme-diate fixes are needed too. Fortunately, there have been lots of hard-working Texas nonprofits, agencies, and private individuals working to protect open space in the orbit of our cities, before it is developed or its price simply becomes prohibitive.

Sources

American Farmland Trust. 2000. "Cost of Community Services: The Value of Farm and Ranch Land in Hays County, Texas." American Farmland Trust. San Marcos, Texas. http://www.farmland.org/programs/states/documents/

AFT_COCS_HaysCounty_Texas.pdf, accessed April 22, 2014.

———. 2001. "Finding the Balance: Ranching and Rapid Growth in Bandera County, Texas—A Cost of Community Services Study." American Farmland Trust. San Marcos, Texas. http://www.farmland.org/programs/ states/documents/AFT_Bandera County_COCS.pdf, accessed April 22, 2014.

Anderson, Ross, Addie Engeling, Amy Grones, Roel Lopez, Brian Pierce, Kevin Skow, and Todd Snelgrove. 2014. Texas Land Trends, 2014: Status Update and Trends of Texas Rural Working Lands. Texas A&M Institute of Renewable Natural Resources. http:// txlandtrends.org/files/lt-2014-report .pdf, accessed June 9, 2015.

Barber, Elayne. 2014. Office of Water, Texas Commission on Environmental Quality. Personal communication, January.

Benz, Robert. 2014. Research Engineer, Texas A&M Transportation Institute. Personal communication, February.

Bishop, Bill. 2008. *The Big Sort: Why the Clustering of Like-Minded America Is Tearing Us Apart.* Boston: Houghton Mifflin.

Blackmar, Elizabeth. 2005. "Of REITS and Rights: Absentee Ownership in the Periphery." In *City, Country, Empire: Landscape in Environmental History,* edited by Jeffry Diefendorf and Kurk Dorsey. Pittsburgh: University of Pittsburgh Press.

Blais, Pamela. 2010. *Perverse Cities: Hidden Subsidies, Wonky Policy, and Urban Sprawl.* Vancouver: University of British Columbia Press.

Borchers, Allison. 2014. Economic Research Service, US Department of Agriculture. Personal communication, February.

Cammel, Erin. 2013. "The 'Growing' American Dream: An Analysis of Historic Trends in Housing." *Undergraduate Research Journal for the Human Sciences* 12.

City of Austin. 2014. City of Austin GIS Datasets: Zoning. ftp://ftp.ci.austin .tx.us/GISData/Regional/zoning/zoning .zip, accessed February 21, 2014.

———. 2015. Subdivision Boundaries, Base Map, GIS/Map Downloads. Shapefile. https://data.austintexas .gov/Geodata/Subdivisions/rqj4-hcbq, accessed May 20, 2015.

City of Dallas. 2011. Downtown Dallas Parking Strategic Plan, June 10, 2011.

City of Houston. 2014. Minimum Lot Size. https://www.houstontx.gov/plan ning/Neighborhood/docs_pdfs/2014 _MLS_MBL_MLSA_Applications .xlsx, accessed February 12.

Crossley, David. 2008. Oral history interview conducted on February 27, in Houston, Texas. Texas Legacy Project, Conservation History Association of Texas.

Demographia. 2014. World Urban Areas (500,000+): Population, Density. http://demographia. com/db-worldua .pdf, accessed February 9, 2014.

Downtown Houston Marketing Initiative. 2014. Visitor Parking Map. http:// downtownhouston.org /site_media/ uploads/attachments/2010-04-19/ Visitor_Parking_Map_ 2008-03.pdf, accessed February 20, 2014.

Ewing, Reid, Richard Schieber, and Charles Zegeer. 2003. "Urban Sprawl as a Risk Factor in Motor Vehicle Occupant and Pedestrian Fatalities." *American Journal of Public Health* 93 (9): 1541–45.

Galvan, Sara. 2007. "Wrestling with MUDs to Pin Down the Truth about Special Districts." *Fordham Law Review* 75 (6): 3041–80.

Google Inc. 2014. Google Earth, Version 7.1.2.2041. Software. Available from http://www.google.com/earth/.

Gutfreund, Owen. 2004. *Twentieth-Century Sprawl: Highways and the Reshaping of the American Landscape.* New York: Oxford University Press.

Harris County. 1960–98. Houston-Galveston Regional Transportation Study: Travel Time and Speed, 1960, 1969, 1973, 1976, 1979, 1988, 1991, 1994, 1998.

Herrera, Sylvia. 2003. Oral history interview conducted on October 16, in Austin, Texas. Texas Legacy Project, Conservation History Association of Texas.

Herrington, Chris. 2014. Watershed Protection Department, City of Austin. Personal communication, January.

Hixon, Tim. 2006. Oral history interview conducted on February 15, in San Antonio, Texas. Texas Legacy Project, Conservation History Association of Texas.

Houston, Scott. 2012. Municipal Annexation in Texas. Texas Municipal League, Austin.

Jackson, Kenneth. 1985. *Crabgrass Frontier: The Suburbanization of the United States.* New York: Oxford University Press.

Jenkins, Virginia. 1994. *The Lawn: A History of an American Obsession.* Washington, DC: Smithsonian Institution Press.

———. 1999. "'Fairway Living': Lawncare and Lifestyle from Croquet to the Golf Course." In *The American Lawn,* edited by Georges Teyssot. New York: Princeton Architectural Press.

Kahn, Matthew. 2006. The Quality of Life in Sprawled versus Compact Cities. http://greeneconomics.blogspot .com/2006/03/benefits-of-sprawl.html, accessed May 1, 2014.

Marrack, David. 2003. Oral history interview conducted on October 23, in Bellaire, Texas. Texas Legacy Project, Conservation History Association of Texas.

McKinney, Bonnie. 2001. Oral history interview conducted on April 5, in Marathon, Texas. Texas Legacy Project, Conservation History Association of Texas.

Melosi, Martin. 2008. Oral history interview conducted on February 28, in Houston, Texas. Texas Legacy Project, Conservation History Association of Texas.

Melosi, Martin, and Joseph Pratt, eds. 2007. *Energy Metropolis: An Environmental History of Houston and the Gulf Coast*. Pittsburgh: University of Pittsburgh Press.

Minnesota Population Center. 2014. National Historical Geographic Information System: Version 2.0. Minneapolis: University of Minnesota. https://www.nhgis.org/.

Ogren, Jonathan. 2014. Protected Lands in Texas. Personal communication, March.

Patel, Komal. 2014. Utility and District Section, Water Supply Division, Texas Commission on Environmental Quality. Personal communication, January.

The Pruitt-Igoe Myth. 2012. Documentary film. Chad Freidrichs, director.

Richmond, Lyndsey. 2014. Geographer, Geographic Areas Branch, Geography Division, US Census Bureau. Personal communication, January.

Rowell, Chester. 2001. Oral history interview conducted on March 31, in Marfa, Texas. Texas Legacy Project, Conservation History Association of Texas.

Scharf, Ed. 2006. Oral history interview conducted on February 18, in Grey Forest, Texas. Texas Legacy Project, Conservation History Association of Texas.

Schlosser, Eric. 2012. *Fast Food Nation: The Dark Side of the All-American Meal*. Boston: Houghton Mifflin.

Shrank, David, Bill Eisele, and Tim Lomax. 2012. "2012 Urban Mobility Report: Congestion Data for Your City." Texas A&M Transportation Institute. Texas A&M University. http://tti.tamu.edu/documents/ums/ congestion-data/complete-data.xls, accessed March 4, 2014.

Smart Growth America. 2014. Measuring Sprawl 2014. http://www.smart growthamerica.org/documents/ measuring-sprawl-2014.pdf, accessed May 1, 2014.

Sterba, Jim. 2012. *Nature Wars: The Incredible Story of How Wildlife Comebacks Turned Backyards into Battlefields*. New York: Random House.

Swearingen, W. Scott. 2010. *Environmental City: People, Places, Politics, and the Meaning of Modern Austin*. Austin: University of Texas Press.

Texas Commission on Environmental Quality (TCEQ). 2013. Watershed Protection Plans, May 2013. http:// www.tceq.state.tx.us/assets/public/ compliance/monops/nps/watersheds/ WPP_MapBook_web06_05_13.pdf, accessed May 1, 2014.

———. 2014a. TCEQ Segments. http:// www.tceq.state.tx.us/assets/public/gis/ exports/tceq_segments_2012_shp.zip, accessed May 1, 2014.

———. 2014b. Water Utility Database. http://tceq4apmgwebp1.tceq.texas .gov:8080/iWudSpatial/fmeDownload WaterDistrict.jsp, accessed April 24, 2014.

Texas Department of State Health Services. 2014. Projected Texas Population by Area, 2013. Center for Health Statistics. http://www.dshs .state.tx.us/chs/popdat/ST2013.shtm, accessed February 8, 2014.

Texas Education Agency. 2014a. 2013 Accountability Rating System. http:// ritter.tea.state.tx.us/perfreport/ account/2013/srch.html?srch=C, accessed April 22, 2014.

———. 2014b. School and District File with Site Address. http://mansfield.tea .state.tx.us/TEA.AskTED.Web/ Forms/DownloadSite.aspx, accessed April 21, 2014.

Texas Land Trust Council. 2014. Protected Lands Inventory, January 1.

Texas Legislative Council. 2012. Eminent Domain Authority in Texas.

Texas Parks and Wildlife. 2012. Land and Water Resources Conservation and Recreation Plan Statewide Inventory.

Texas State Library and Archives Commission. 2014. United States and Texas Populations, 1850–2012. https:// www.tsl.texas.gov/ref/abouttx/census .html, accessed January 29, 2014.

Texas Water Development Board. 2014. GIS Data: Natural Features: Existing Reservoirs: Shapefile. https://www

.twdb.state.tx.us/mapping/gisdata/
shapefiles/reservoirs_2001/existing
_reservoirs.zip, accessed March 4,
2014.

Tobin, Kathleen. 2002. "The Reduction
of Urban Vulnerability: Revisiting
1950s American Suburbanization as
Civil Defence." *Cold War History* 2 (2).

Umbehaun, Nancy. 2014. Senior Realty
Specialist, US Fish and Wildlife
Service. Personal communication,
February.

US Census. 2012. Mean and Average
Square Feet of Floor Area in New
Single-Family Houses Completed
by Location. http://www.census.gov/
const/C25Ann/sftotalmedavgsqft.pdf,
accessed May 2, 2014.

———. 2013. Population Estimates—State
Totals: Vintage 2013. http://www
.census.gov/popest/data/state/
totals/2013/tables/NST-EST2013–01
.xls, accessed February 8, 2014.

———. 2015. Table 1: The 15 Fastest-
Growing Large Cities from July 1,
2013 to July 1, 2014. US Department
of Commerce. http://www.census
.gov/content/dam/Census/newsroom/
releases/2015/cb15-89_table1.xlsx,
accessed June 9, 2015.

———. 2014a. Cartographic Boundary
Files—Places (Incorporated Places).
http://www.census.gov/geo/maps-data/

data/cbf/cbf_place.html, accessed
January 23, 2014.

———. 2014b. 2010 Census Population
and Housing Unit Counts—Blocks.
http://www.census.gov/geo/maps-data/
data/tiger-data.html, accessed March
4, 2014.

———. 2014c. Population Estimates:
State Population Estimates and
Demographic Components of Change:
1900 to 1990 Total Population
Estimates. http://www.census.gov/
popest/data/state/asrh/1980s/80s
_st_totals.html, accessed February 8,
2014.

US Department of Agriculture. 2013.
Summary Report: 2010 National
Resources Inventory. Natural
Resources Conservation Service,
Washington, DC, and the Center for
Survey Statistics and Methodology,
Iowa State University, Ames, Iowa.
http://nrcs.usda.gov/Internet/FSE
_DOCUMENTS/stelprdb1167354
.pdf, accessed June 9, 2015.

———. 2014a. Census of Agriculture:
Historical Census Publications.
National Agricultural Statistics Service.
http://www.agcensus.usda.gov/
Publications/Historical_Publications/
index.php, accessed February 3, 2014.

———. 2014b. 12 Digit Watershed
Boundary Dataset in HUC8,

NRCS Version. Natural Resources
Conservation Service. http://datagate
way.nrcs.usda.gov/, accessed March 5,
2014.

———. 2014c. Quick Stats. National
Agricultural Statistics Service. http://
quickstats.nass.usda.gov/, accessed
February 3, 2014 and June 24, 2014.

———. 2014d. Web Soil Survey. Natural
Resources Conservation Service.
http://websoilsurvey.sc.egov.usda.gov/
App/WebSoilSurvey.aspx, accessed
March 4, 2014.

US Department of Transportation. 2014.
Policy Information: Highway Statistics
Series: Annual Vehicle-Miles of Travel.
http://www.fhwa.dot.gov/policyinfor
mation/quickfinddata/qftravel.cfm,
accessed January 29, 2014.

US Fish and Wildlife Service. 2014.
USFWS National Cadastral Data and
Metadata: Balcones Canyonlands.
http://www.fws.gov/gis/data/
CadastralDB/index.htm, accessed
February15, 2014.

Zillow. 2014. Data: Zillow Home Value
Index (ZHVI): Median ZHVI per sq.
ft. ($): By Zip Code: January 2014.
http://files.zillowstatic.com/research/
public/Zip/Zip_Median ValuePerSqft
_AllHomes.csv, accessed March 4,
2014.

Fire Ants!

Red imported fire ants (RIFA), also known as *Solenopsis invicta Buren*, have a nasty, annoying sting, and the species is a certified member of the world of unwelcome pests. However, they are also a wonderful example of unintended consequences, global interconnectedness, and the difficulty of responding to invasive species.

The Arrival

The RIFA was likely introduced by accident into the United States from Brazil. The ant probably came as a stowaway in ballast aboard a freighter that docked in Mobile, Alabama, sometime during the 1930s (Ascunce et al. 2011; Callcott and Collins 1996). E. O. Wilson, the noted Harvard entomologist, was one of the first witnesses

This scanning electron microscope image gives an intimate close-up of the head of a red imported fire ant, or Solenopsis invicta Buren *(Nijhout 2013).*

to its arrival on American shores. In 1942, at the age of thirteen, Wilson reported discovering the RIFA in a vacant lot in Mobile (Wilson 2013).

The Reception

At first, RIFA's arrival raised little alarm. It was a very small creature, less than one-sixth of an inch long. And the ant did not seem remarkably unusual. It was just one of more than 280 species in its *Solenopsis* genus. In fact, it was just one of as many as twenty different kinds of New World fire ants, several native to the United States (including *S. xyloni*, the southern fire ant, *S. geminate*, the tropical fire ant, and two species found in desert habitats, *S. aurea Wheeler* and *S. amblyschila Wheeler*). When it first appeared in the United States, RIFA must have seemed insignificant, and was largely ignored. To the extent that there was concern about invasive ants, there was more attention paid to an earlier interloper, the Argentine ant, *Linepithema humile Mayr* (Williams, Collins, and Oi 2001).

The Advance

However, RIFA turned out to be a bold pioneer, colonizing the United States and beyond with amazing speed. After its arrival in Alabama in the 1930s, the RIFA spread north to Tennessee and west to California. The first Texas reports of the RIFA came from the eastern edge of the state (Gregg, Harris, Jefferson, Orange, and Smith Counties)

in 1953 (Culpepper 1953). By the first decade of the twenty-first century, its territory in the United States alone had spread to over 320 million acres (Williams et al. 2007). And over time, the ant even managed to find its way to Taiwan, mainland China, and Australia (Invasive Species Specialist Group 2013).

Natural Spread

The increase in the RIFA's range was extraordinary, but still natural. Much of its progress came through flights by mating queens (a mile or more with favorable winds), or in floating colonies carried by floods (Drees et al. 2000). Its spread was also due

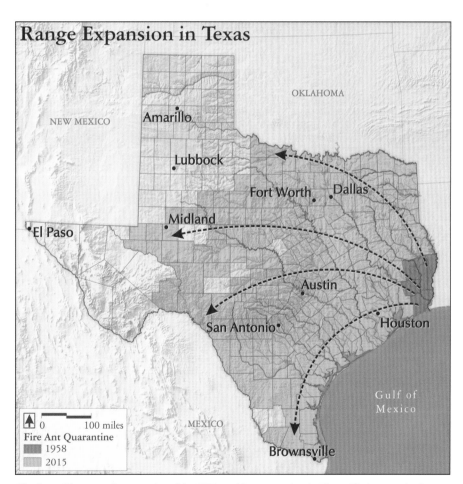

The figure illustrates the expansion of the RIFA, and its quarantine, in Texas. The increase in the ant's range is astonishing: its quarantined area grew from six counties and about 3.2 million acres in 1958, to 187 counties and over 112 million acres by 2015. Over the intervening fifty-seven years, the quarantined area shifted over 525 miles westward, quite an advance for a creature less than a sixth of an inch long (Callcott and Collins 1996; Code of Federal Regulations 2015; Texas Department of Agriculture 2015; US Department of Agriculture 2015).

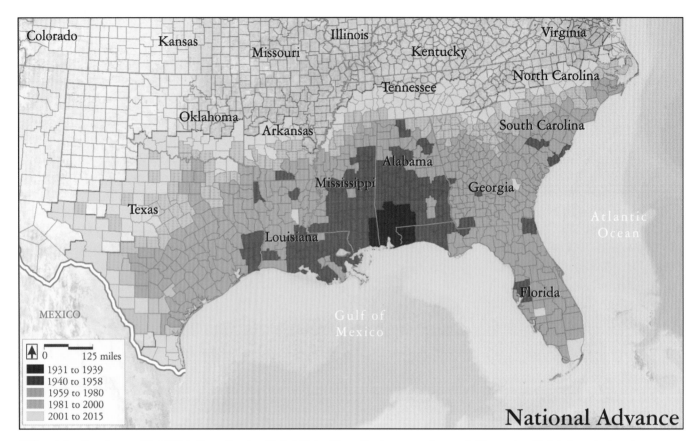

National Advance

This map logs the advance of the RIFA in the southeastern United States. The ant's advance was documented by a series of infestation reports and quarantine zones filed from 1931 through 2015. Please note that quarantine boundaries may lag the actual progress of the RIFA, since quarantines are usually not applied until RIFA colonies are positively identified. Also, limited funding and staffing for ant monitoring efforts may have missed some RIFA that had wandered farther than their documented territory (Brown 2013; Callcott and Collins 1996; Code of Federal Regulations 2015; Schechter 2013; Williams et al. 2001; US Department of Agriculture 2015; US Department of Agriculture 2009).

to its aggressive displacement of the southern fire ant (*S. xyloni*), tropical fire ant (*S. geminate*), big-headed ant (*Pheidole dentata*), Florida harvester ant (*Pogonomyrmex badius*), and other species of ants (Holldobler and Wilson 1990, 400, 429; Tschinkel 2006, 589).

At the same time, RIFA's rapid expansion drew from its diplomacy with members of other RIFA colonies. RIFA had originally formed discrete and well-defended colonies in its homelands of Brazil, Argentina, and Paraguay. However, in its new home in the United States, the ant created more of a federated suburban supercolony. This allowed the RIFA to move freely without challenge by their fellow RIFA neighbors (Flannery 2010).

The RIFA's success in North America was also founded on its farming skills, in how it milked nourishing fecal matter, more appetizingly known as "honeydew," from aphids. The honeydew gave the RIFA an energetic edge to out-forage competing ants and helped fuel its travel to many new territories (Zhou et al. 2013).

Hitchhiking

However, many of the long-range jumps in its range occurred with human help—usually unwitting, but effective nonetheless. RIFAs often

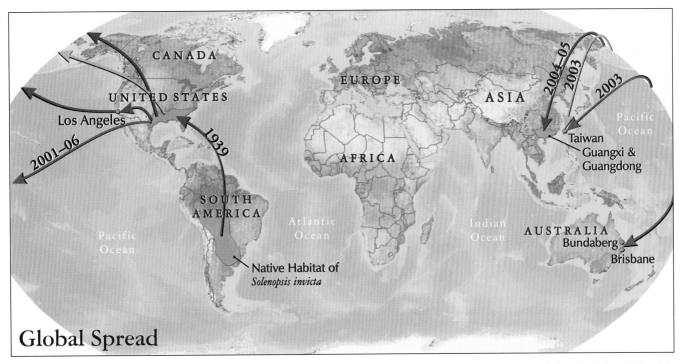

Global Spread

*The RIFA's range has expanded globally. The suspected routes and estimated dates of its travels are based on genetic analysis of selected colonies. While origi-
nally native to South America, the ant has spread throughout the United States and moved on to Australia, Taiwan, the Chinese provinces of Guangdong,
Guangxi, and Fujian, and elsewhere (Ascunce et al. 2011).*

found a convenient berth in garden
soil, mulch, potted plants, hay bales,
construction machinery, and other
cargo shipped around the world.
Sometimes the RIFA even found an
acceptable seat in insulation or foam
filters in automobiles, surviving on
dead insects in the radiator (Collins,
Lockley, and Adams 1993).

Part of its spread was certainly due
to this opportunistic hitchhiking. Yet
much of its ability to catch free rides
was due to its unusual multiple-queen
structure. The RIFA's polygyne organization allowed for small colonies of
queen, brood, and workers to easily

disperse, infest, and travel with multiple shipments of soil and nursery
stock (Taber 2000, 112).

Dominance

With its spread, RIFA came to out-
fight, out-forage, and simply out-
number native ants. A sense of the
RIFA's dominance is suggested by
their impressive counts and density.
Each mound might hold 250,000
ants. Single-queen colonies might
contain seven million ants per acre,
settled among twenty to 150 mounds
per acre. That alone presents a large

population. However, multiple-queen
colonies were even larger, occupying
100 to 1,000 mounds per acre, with a
total population of forty million ants
per acre. Overwhelmed by this competition, native ant abundance fell by 90
percent, and species richness dropped
by 70 percent after RIFA became
established (Stuble, Kirkman, and
Carroll 2009).

Ecological Damage

RIFA's scientific name, *Solenopsis
invicta Buren*, was well chosen.
"*Invicta*" translates as "invincible,"

and indeed, the RIFA was aggressive and its sting toxic to many of its fellow creatures. In fact, its sting was not only harmful to many of its rival ants, but was also dangerous to a wide variety of pollinators (ground-nesting bees), invertebrates, lizards, turtles, snakes, and ground-dwelling birds. Even young large mammals, including white-tailed deer and cattle, were vulnerable (Willcox and Giuliano 2006). Impacts on popular game birds, such as bobwhite quail, and on endangered amphibians (the Houston toad) and birds (the Attwater's prairie chicken) also drew concern (Allen, Demarais, and Lutz 1994; Allen et al. 2000; Giuliano, Allen, et al. 1996; Jones 2013; Lannoo 2005; Morrow et al. 2013).

Economic Effects

The ecological effects have been powerful, but economic damage by the RIFA has been impressive as well. Imported fire ants disrupt electrical circuits, and their mounds harm farm fields, golf courses, and cultivating and mowing equipment. RIFA can also cause health problems if multiple stings or allergic patients are involved. All together, this small ant costs the United States up to $6 billion annually on medical treatment, damage, and control (Lard et al. 2006).

The Embargo

To stem the RIFA tide, the federal government organized a quarantine in the 1950s to limit plant materials coming out of RIFA-affected counties of the United States, since it appeared that shipments of infested nursery stock were the main cause of the ant's expansion (Culpepper 1953). While the quarantine may have had an effect in slowing RIFA spread, many ants managed to elude the blockade. In fact, genetic research has confirmed that fire ants have been introduced no fewer than nine times from the southeastern United States to California, Asia, and Australia (Ascunce et al. 2011). At this point, it appears that the RIFA quarantine has largely failed, and that imported fire ants have occupied all parts of the United States that are warm and wet enough to support them (Plowes 2013 and 2015).

Chemical Warfare

In addition to the quarantine, agencies and individuals have made great efforts to stop RIFAs at the source: to kill RIFAs where they already exist. The first organized control efforts began in February 1937, with the use of calcium cyanide dust on 2,000 acres in Baldwin County, Alabama. In 1948, Mississippi, Alabama, and Louisiana began treatment of colonies with chlordane dust. By 1957, the effort had risen to the federal level. In that year, Congress appropriated $2.4 million for aerial and ground applications of heptachlor and dieldrin. Other chemicals were tried as well. From 1962 through 1978, 46.6 million acres were treated with mirex (Williams, Collins, and Oi 2001).

Defense!

Chemicals were found to have a variety of shortcomings. RIFAs had multiple lines of defense. They sometimes foraged underground or were inactive, so the ants might not always take a poison applied on the ground. Even if worker ants took the poison, the queen was protected, since she was only fed food eaten first by worker ants and larvae. Many poisons, especially fast-acting ones, never reached the queen. And even if a queen were killed, many mounds had multiple queens. Any surviving queen could decamp with just a half dozen workers and create a new colony elsewhere (Drees et al. 2000).

Collateral Damage

Chemical RIFA controls were all too effective elsewhere. Heptachlor residues were discovered in public meat and milk supplies, causing the federal insecticide program to be canceled. Mirex was found to wipe out many native ant colonies, while harming some birds, such as the loggerhead shrike. In 1971, the EPA issued a notice of cancellation for the chemical. By 1977, when mirex was reported to be a potential carcinogen, the agency went yet further, canceling its registration for all uses. Due to their toxicity to nontarget wildlife and humans, or just their lack of effect on RIFAs, chemical insecticides turned out to have limited value. The failure of insecticides was not for lack of trying. From 1958 through 1998, the USDA considered over 7,200 insecticides for use against the RIFA, yet only nine were approved (Williams, Collins, and Oi 2001).

Folk Remedies

Frustrated property owners have unleashed their own homemade creativity in dealing with RIFA. People have experimented with dousing and sprinkling mounds with club soda, coffee grounds, cinnamon, oak ash, cayenne pepper, diatomaceous earth, mixtures of orange oil and liquid compost, solutions of dish soap and water, or perhaps the most dramatic, the combination of gasoline and a

match (Blakely 2010; Williams 2012). Results have varied and appear difficult to verify and repeat.

Biological Controls

Consequently, in more recent years, efforts to manage *Solenopsis invicta* have turned to biological controls. Part of RIFA's extraordinary spread and success in the United States has been due to the lack of the typical predators, parasites, and pathogens that limit it in its home territories in South America. Without native predators, there are five times more RIFA per acre in the United States than in its former homelands in South America (Drees et al.

2000; Willcox and Giuliano 2006).

So entomologists have sought to find and introduce some of these natural enemies in the United States. These old foes of the RIFA include an infectious microsporidium (*Kneallhazia solenopsae*), a fungus (*Beauveria bassiana*), a parasitic ant (*Solenopsis daguerri*), a virus (SINV-3), a parasitic insect (*Caenocholax fenyesi*), a wasp (*Orasema*), nematodes (*Steinernema carpocapsae* and *Heterohabditis* species), and the straw itch mite (*Pymotes tritici*) (Oi and Valles 2012; Schowalter 2009; Thorvilson and San Francisco 2002; Valles and Hashimoto 2009). There are good prospects for these biological

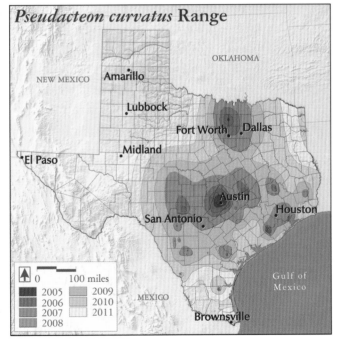

Following its introduction in Texas to control red imported fire ants, the Pseudacteon curvatus *has continuously expanded its range (Plowes 2013).*

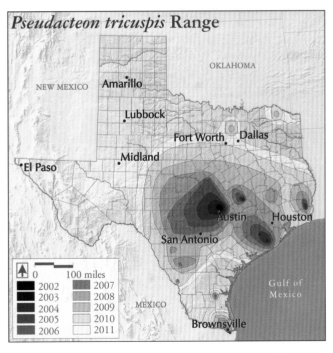

This map shows the consistent yearly expansion of the range of the Pseudacteon tricuspis *after it was brought to Texas for controlling RIFA (Plowes 2013).*

controls, but also limits. Researchers must weigh their danger to RIFA individuals and colonies. Entomologists need to study the logistics of raising, improving, distributing, and establishing the RIFA enemies. Scientists also have to review the risks that these introduced creatures might stray from their target, and affect other, possibly native, prey (Drees and Knutson 2002; Plowes 2013 and 2015).

Numerous species of phorid flies have shown particular promise as biological controls for RIFA. Phorid flies' attack begins as they inject their larva in the ant's thorax. Then, as the egg develops and moves into the ant's head, the ant is decapitated and dies, and the fly larva matures in the safety of the hard chitin shell of the ant's (former) head. Phorids are a menace to RIFA in other ways as well. The flies harass and disrupt the ants as they hover and search for a victim, distracting the ants from collecting food and defending their home. Also, the flies may damage colonies by carrying diseases from one colony to another.

With high expectations, two phorid species, the *Pseudacteon curvatus* and *Pseudacteon tricuspis*, were introduced from South America to control RIFA. They were successful in several ways. They rapidly became established in Texas, were indeed lethal to individual ants, and remained safely specific to the RIFA host. However, *Pseudacteon curvatus* and *tricuspis* have still failed in being a meaningful control on RIFA.

The work on using these two phorids has shown how very com-

plex and challenging biological measures can be with a resourceful social insect like the RIFA. For instance, the two dozen or more phorid fly species in the RIFA's home range in South America turn out to have very specific tasks: *Pseudacteon curvatus* and *tricuspis* attack worker ants only at the colony itself. This helps to some degree, but only 0.5 to 3 percent of the colony's ant population is exposed on the top of the mound at any given time. So even lethal phorid fly attacks on individual RIFAs that are roaming on the surface inflict very little harm to the colony as a whole. More recent research suggests that introducing phorid flies that specialize in attacks on foraging ants would be more effective against the RIFA. This strategy would cut the food supply to the entire mound's colony (Plowes 2013 and 2015).

The Silver Lining

The RIFA has certainly caused a great deal of damage. Yet it is important to recall that some of the harm has perhaps been balanced, to some extent, by benefits from the RIFA. RIFA actually have some redeeming qualities. They are an effective predator on a number of pests, including aphids, boll weevils, cotton leaf worms, horn flies, rice stink bugs, lone star ticks, soybean loopers, mosquito larvae, and sugarcane borers (Bhatkar 2013; Fleetwood, Teel, and Thompson 1984). And some of the RIFA impacts on wildlife have been anecdotal and

difficult to isolate and prove (Allen, Demarais, and Lutz 1994).

"Imported fire ants still are with us and will be with us in the foreseeable future."

—Williams, Collins, and Oi 2001

The White Flag

In recent years, experts have conceded that RIFA infestations may be managed and controlled to some extent, but eradication is very unlikely. What, then, is the next step?

First, a bit of perspective (or rationalizing) about RIFA/human conflicts may help. The spread of RIFA happened at the same time as massive growth in human populations within the Sun Belt. So who exactly is the invader? Who is the victim? Have they been unwitting allies? *Invicta*'s spread may have even been accelerated by human eradication efforts, especially the use of broad-spectrum insecticides that decimated rival ants (Gilbert 2015). Some of the damage blamed on the RIFA may have actually been due to prior human disturbance of habitat (King and Tschinkel 2006).

And second, perhaps patience may help. The RIFA may have enemies more formidable than its human opponents. Entomologists recommend that we tolerate and even encourage native ant species as a defense against imported fire ants (Drees et al. 1999). RIFA may have met its own bête noire anyway: a newer, and yet more imposing, invasive species called the crazy ant (*Nylanderia fulva*) (LeBrun, Abbott, and Gilbert 2013).

In the end, maybe a kind of détente will arise as the most realistic attitude. Given the rapid, global movement of people, cargo, and stowaway wildlife, eventually we may have to settle for a peace with ants and find a way to somehow coexist with both native and imported fire ants.

Sources

Allen, C. R., R. D. Willey, P. E. Myers, P. M. Horton, and J. Buffa. 2000. "Impact of Red Imported Fire Ant Infestations on Northern Bobwhite Quail Abundance Trends in Southeastern United States." *Journal of Agricultural Urban Entomology* 17: 43–51.

Allen, Craig R., Stephen Demarais, and R. Scott Lutz. 1994. "Red Imported Fire Ant Impact on Wildlife: An Overview." Nebraska Cooperative Fish and Wildlife Research Unit—Staff Publications. Paper 51. http://digital commons.unl.edu/ncfwrustaff/51, accessed June 6, 2013.

Ascunce, Marina, Chin-Cheng Yang, Jane Oakey, Luis Calcaterra, Wen-Jer Wu, Cheng-Jen Shih, Jerome Goudet, Kenneth Ross, and DeWayne Shoemaker. 2011. "Global Invasion History of the Fire Ant *Solenopsis invicta*." *Science* 331 (February 25): 1066–68.

Bhatkar, Awinash. 2013. Entomologist, Texas Department of Agriculture. Personal communication, June.

Blakely, Claude. 2010. "Fire Ant Control?" Issue 38, July 14. Laurens County Master Gardeners Association. Waterloo, South Carolina.

Brown, Charlie. 2013. National Program Manager, Animal and Plant Health Inspection Service, US Department of Agriculture. Personal communication, May.

Callcott, Anne-Marie A., and Homer L. Collins. 1996. "Invasion and Range Expansion of Imported Fire Ants (Hymenoptera: Formicidae) in North America from 1918–1995." *Florida Entomologist* 79 (2): 240–51.

Code of Federal Regulations. 2015. Title 7: Agriculture, Part 301: Domestic Quarantine Notices, Subpart 301.81-3: Imported Fire Ant. http://www.ecfr .gov/cgi-bin/text-idx?SID=33e143e84 cf068443896b77fc94e4c07&mc=true &node=se7.5.301_181_63&rgn=div8, accessed April 4, 2015.

Collins, Homer, Timothy Lockley and Dudley Adams. 1993. "Red Imported Fire Ant (Hymenoptera: Formicidae) Infestation of Motorized Vehicles." *Florida Entomologist* 76 (3).

Culpepper, G. H. 1953. "Status of the Imported Fire Ant in the Southern States in July 1953." USDA Bureau of Entomology Plant Quarterly Report E-867.

Drees, Bastian, Charles Barr, Donna Shanklin, Dale Pollet, Kathy Flanders, Beverly Sparks, and Karen Vail. 1999. "Managing Red Imported Fire Ants in Agriculture." Document B-6076, August. Texas Agricultural Extension Service, Texas A&M University System.

Drees, Bastian, Charles Barr, Bradleigh Vinson, Roger Gold, Michael Merchant, Nathan Riggs, Lisa Lennon, Scott Russell, and Paul Nester. 2000. "Managing Imported Fire Ants in Urban Areas." Document B-6043, June. Texas Agricultural Extension Service, Texas A&M University System.

Drees, Bastian, and Allen Knutson. 2002. "Potential Biological Control Agents for the Red Imported Fire Ant." Fire Ant Plan Fact Sheet #0009. https:// insects.tamu.edu/fireant/materials/ factsheets_pubs/pdf/fapfs009.2002 rev.pdf, accessed June 7, 2013.

Flannery, Tim. 2010. *Here on Earth: A Natural History of the Planet.* New York: Grove Press, 118–19.

Fleetwood, S. C., P. D. Teel, and G. Thompson. 1984. "Impact of Imported Fire Ant on Lone Star Tick Mortality in Open and Canopied Pasture Habitats of East Central Texas." *Southwestern Entomologist* 9 (2).

Gilbert, Larry. 2015. Director, Brackenridge Field Laboratory, University of Texas at Austin. Personal communication, January.

Giuliano, William, Craig Allen, R. Scott Lutz, and Stephen Demarais. 1996. "Effects of Red Imported Fire Ants on Northern Bobwhite Chicks." *Journal of Wildlife Management* 60: 309–13.

Holldobler, Bert, and Edward Wilson. 1990. *The Ants.* Cambridge, MA: Harvard University Press.

Invasive Species Specialist Group. 2013. *Solenopsis invicta* (insect). Global Invasive Species Database. http://www .issg.org/database/species/distribution .asp?si=77&fr=1&sts=&lang=EN, accessed June 1, 2013.

Jones, Ron. 2013. Board chair, Friends of Attwater Prairie Chicken Refuge. Personal communication, May.

King, Joshua, and Walter Tschinkel. 2006. "Experimental Evidence That the Introduced Fire Ant, *Solenopsis invicta*, Does Not Competitively

Suppress Co-Occurring Ants in a Disturbed Habitat." *Journal of Animal Ecology* 75 (6): 1370–78.

Lannoo, Michael. 2005. *Amphibian Declines: The Conservation Status of United States Species*. Berkeley: University of California Press, 416–17.

Lard, C. F., et al. 2006. "An Economic Impact of Imported Fire Ants in the United States of America." Texas A&M University, College Station.

LeBrun, Edward, John Abbott, and Lawrence Gilbert. 2013. "Imported Crazy Ant Displaces Imported Fire Ant, Reduces and Homogenizes Grassland Ant and Arthropod Assemblages." *Biological Invasions*. Netherlands: Springer.

Morrow, Michael, Rebecca Chester, Bastian Drees, and John Toepfer. 2013. "Brood Survival of Attwater's Prairie-Chicken (TX)." Final Report, National Fish and Wildlife Foundation, Grant Number 2010-0008-0000.

Nijhout, Fred. 2013. Fire ant (*Solenopsis invicta*) head: Electron scanning microscope image. Produced for Biology 222L, Duke University. http://biology.duke.edu/dukeinsects/sem gallery.php, accessed July 3, 2013.

Oi, David H., and Steven M. Valles. 2012. "Host Specificity Testing of the Solenopsis Fire Ant Pathogen, Kneallhazia Solenopsae, in Florida." *Florida Entomologist* 95 (2): 509–12.

Plowes, Robert. 2013 and 2015. Operations, Research and Teaching Coordinator, Brackenridge Field Laboratory, University of Texas at Austin. Personal communications, July 2013 and April 2015.

Schechter, Susan. 2013. User Services, National Agricultural Pest Information System, Purdue University. Personal communication, May.

Schowalter, Timothy. 2009. *Insect Ecology: An Ecosystem Approach*. Burlington, MA: Academic Press.

Stuble, Katharine, Katherine Kirkman, and Ronald Carroll. 2009. "Patterns of Abundance of Fire Ants and Native Ants in a Native Ecosystem." *Ecological Entomology* 34: 520–26.

Taber, Stephen. 2000. *Fire Ants*. College Station: Texas A&M University Press.

Texas Department of Agriculture. 2015. Red Imported Fire Ant Quarantined Area. https://www.texasagriculture.gov/RegulatoryPrograms/Plant Quality/PestandDiseaseAlerts/ RedImportedFireAntQuarantined Area.aspx, accessed April 4, 2015.

Thorvilson, Harlan, and Michael San Francisco. 2002. "Beauveria bassiana as a Biocontrol Agent against the Red Imported Fire Ant." Texas Imported Fire Ant Research and Management Project, Progress Report, June.

Tschinkel, Walter. 2006. *The Fire Ants*. Cambridge, MA: Belknap Press of Harvard University Press.

US Department of Agriculture. 2009. "Areas in Virginia Added to the Imported Fire Ant (IFA) Quarantine and Expansion of Existing IFA Quarantine Areas in Arkansas, Tennessee, and Texas for IFA." DA-2009-54, October 28, 2009. http://www.aphis.usda.gov/plant_health/ plant_pest_info/fireants/downloads/ da-2009-54.pdf, accessed April 5, 2015.

———. 2015. Imported Fire Ant Quarantine, last modified December 2011. Animal and Plant Health Inspection Service, US Department of Agriculture. http://www.aphis.usda.gov/plant_health/plant_pest_info/ fireants/downloads/fireant-2.pdf, accessed April 5, 2015.

Valles, S. M., and Y. Hashimoto. 2009. "Isolation and Characterization of *Solenopsis invicta* Virus 3, a New Positive-Strand RNA Virus Infecting the Red Imported Fire Ant, *Solenopsis invicta*." *Virology* 388: 354–61.

Willcox, Emma, and William M. Giuliano. 2006. "Red Imported Fire Ants and Their Impact on Wildlife." WEC 207, University of Florida IFAS Extension. http://edis.ifas.ufl.edu/pdffiles/UW/ UW24200.pdf, accessed June 5, 2013.

Williams, David, Homer Collins, and David Oi. 2001. "The Red Imported Fire Ant (Hymenoptera: Formicidae): An Historical Perspective of Treatment Programs and the Development of Chemical Baits for Control." *American Entomologist* 47 (3).

Williams, David, Timothy Davis, David Oi, Roberto Pereira, Herbert Bolton, Paul Horton, and H. Williams. 2007. "Biological Control of Red Imported Fire Ants." Extension publications, Agricultural Research Service, US Department of Agriculture.

Williams, Rob. 2012. "Entomologist Testing Puts Bite on Many 'Home' Fire Ant Treatments." Texas Imported Fire Ant Research and Management Project. Texas A&M University.

Wilson, Edward. 2013. *Letters to a Young Scientist*. New York: W. W. Norton.

Zhou, Aiming, Yongyue Lu, Ling Zeng, Yijuan Xu, and Guangwen Liang. 2013. "*Solenopsis invicta* Defend *Phenacoccus solenopsis* against Its Natural Enemies." *Environmental Entomology* 42 (2): 247–52.

Houston Lights

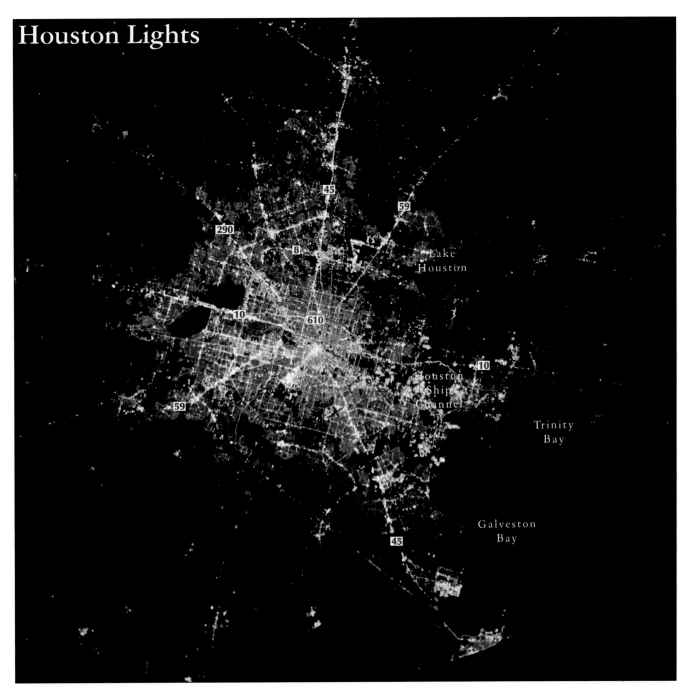

This is a February 28, 2010, view of Houston, shot by the International Space Station's Expedition 22 crew from an altitude of over 200 miles. The scale of the photo is immense: measuring roughly sixty miles across, east to west. The highways can be seen as a tracery of bright white lines radiating out from downtown. Intense yellow pools of light to the east of downtown mark the industries along the Houston Ship Channel. Reddish-brown and olive-green lights are the signature of residential areas with less intense lighting and more tree cover (NASA 2010).

Lights in the Night

Over the centuries, people have welcomed the discoveries of fire, oil lamps, candles, kerosene lanterns, gas jets, and incandescent light bulbs. These discoveries have brought light, comfort, and safety to our homes, workplaces, and communities (Bogard 2013; Schivelbusch 1988). From space, our towns and cities now sparkle and gleam like constellations on the ground.

Now flip your perspective. Viewed from the ground, these artificial lights have grown to rival the natural wonders of the night sky, to compete with the brilliance of the moon, the warmth of Mars, the glow of the Milky Way, the trails of meteor showers, and the twinkle of distant stars. The hundreds of millions of lights in homes and offices, above streets and parking lots, on signs and towers, create a kind of lit dome over our heads. These man-made lights overwhelm the blue-black field and the bright pinpricks of the night sky. For most observers, stars and planets have become a rare species, seldom seen and little known.

City

The change has come gradually over the past 120 years. Houston, San Antonio, El Paso, Dallas, Fort Worth, and Austin had started to install electric lighting in the 1890s, but since then, their arrays of lights have grown far wider and brighter. Austin may provide an example. Since 1894, when Austin purchased its famous 165-foot-tall carbon-arc moon towers, its utility has grown to feed over 420,000 customers and more than 70,000 streetlights (Bogard 2013). Since 88 percent of Texans now live in our major cities, these big metropolises have become the chief source of human light in the state (US Census Bureau 2013).

Country

For many years, Texas cities at night were just small lit patches in a vast dark landscape. Many rural areas of Texas did not get electrical connections until the 1930s or even into the mid-1950s. As late as 1935, over 97 percent of Texas farms were not connected to the grid. Commercial utilities could not make financial sense of extending service to so few users at the cost of so many miles of line (Davis 2013). This started to change in the mid-1930s, when the Rural Electrification Administration began to disburse federal loans to bootstrap consumer-owned cooperatives (Rural Electrification Act, 7 U.S.C. 901; Executive Order 7037). In 1935, Bartlett Electric Cooperative (BEC) was the first Texas group to get on its feet. BEC was followed in later years by the creation of over sixty-five co-ops serving 241 of Texas' 254 counties. These new utilities helped bring electric wells, refrigerators, ovens, washing machines, and other important conveniences, including lights, to millions of grateful Texans (Texas Electric Cooperatives 2013).

Skyglow

The lights from our cities, towns, and small rural homesteads now create a halo, or "skyglow," that can be estimated with an approach called Walker's Law (Walker 1977). Its creator was an astronomer named Merle Walker who helped plan the siting of a new dark-sky observing station for Lick Observatory. The new facility was proposed for Junipero Serra Peak near San Francisco, but even by the mid-1970s, skyglow had become a serious concern there. To calculate the impact of skyglow for the proposed observatory, Walker used photometers to measure the luminosity (the limiting magnitude) of the sky at various distances from nearby cities. He then did a regression of these readings and came up with a relationship. His formula is $I = 0.01Pd^{-2.5}$ where I is sky brightness, P is the population of the city, and d is the distance from that city. Basically, he found that skyglow in industrial nations varies with the number of people living nearby. People equaled light.

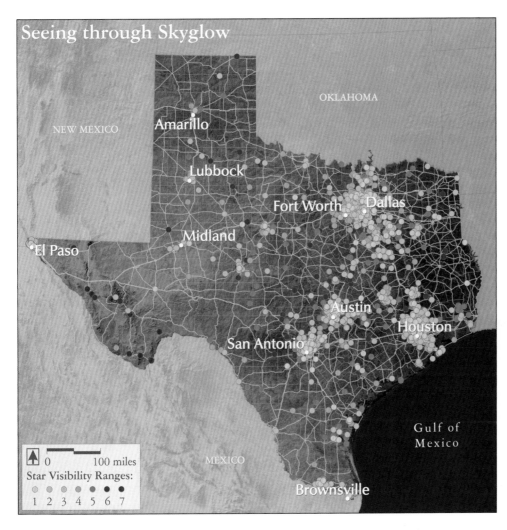

The map shows patterns of light pollution, or "skyglow," based on some seven thousand citizen reports from 2006 through 2014. The public submits estimates of darkness using Sky Quality light meter readings, or by comparing views of the constellation Orion with benchmark charts. The accompanying graph shows roughly how many stars are visible at different orders of magnitude (DIVA-GIS 2015; Globe at Night Citizen Science Campaign 2013; International Comet Quarterly undated; National Optical Astronomy Observatory 2015; Sinnott and Perryman 1997; Walker 2013).

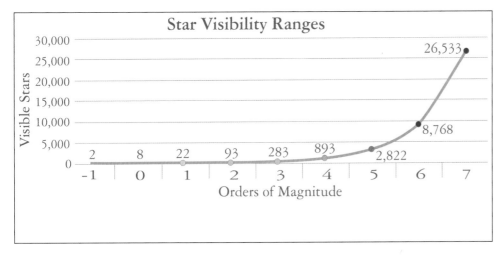

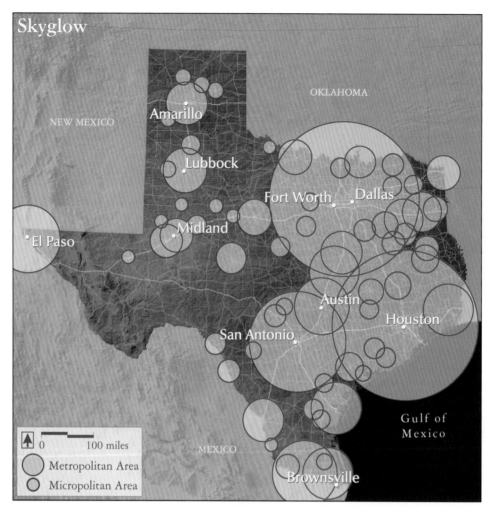

Skyglow

NEW MEXICO

OKLAHOMA

Amarillo

Lubbock

Midland

Fort Worth • Dallas

El Paso

Austin

San Antonio

Houston

Gulf of
Mexico

MEXICO

Brownsville

0   100 miles

Metropolitan Area
Micropolitan Area

Walker's Law helps calculate the expected amount of skyglow at various distances from cities of a given population. This map shows how far a skyglow of 10 percent can likely be seen (this is a conservative estimate, since people can usually sense skyglow as low as 6 percent). For some of the larger metropolitan areas (in red), skyglow can reach a long way: over 120 miles in both the case of the Houston/Woodlands/Sugar Land and Dallas/Arlington/Fort Worth areas, based on 2010 populations. The larger number and wider scatter of smaller, micropolitan areas (in blue) also contribute to skyglow in the state (US Census Bureau 2013; Walker 1977).

The Missing Milky Way

It is now estimated that two-thirds of Americans can no longer see the Milky Way, our home galaxy (Brox 2010). In fact, many were born too late to have ever seen the Milky Way in their hometown. Our "urban stars" have blotted out the real stars. In moderately light-polluted skies, our naked eye may still be able to see some 510 objects with a brightness greater than a third magnitude. However, at that level of man-made light, we will have lost sight of more than eight thousand fourth-, fifth-, and sixth-order stars (International Comet Quarterly undated; Sinnott and Perryman 1997).

It is a loss that many of us are still sorting through. Maybe we miss the stars because of nostalgia for what once was, but that is now quite rare. Or maybe we dismiss the washout of the night sky as just an aesthetic issue, a passing cocktail party topic, or one of those unanswerable questions like what is beautiful and what is ugly.

However, increasing research suggests that the spread of artificial light into the wee hours, and into rural and undeveloped areas, is a serious problem. There is evidence that light pollution affects human health, upsets nature's patterns, unhooks us from our past, and wastes large amounts of energy.

Human Health

Lighting at night can subtly, but significantly, hurt our health. Excessive artificial light after sundown essentially resets the length of day and night that we perceive. This disrupts our normal circadian rhythms and can worsen depression, obesity, insomnia, and stress from lack of sleep (Bower 2000). The shifts in our light/dark schedules can also upset our hormonal cycles, such as those involved in melatonin production, and perhaps affect breast cancer rates (American Medical Association House of Delegates 2012; Pauley 2004; Spivey 2010).

Wildlife

Artificial lights affect wildlife too. Consider that 30 percent of vertebrates and 60 percent of invertebrates are nocturnal. They have evolved over eons to operate in an uninterrupted darkness that may be scarcer and shorter-lived in current times. A few examples might give an idea of the surprising impact of our ordinary streetlights, security lights, and car lights. For instance, the lowly dung beetle is known to navigate by orienting itself to the Milky Way, keeping it from rolling its precious ball of fecal matter in endless looping circles (Dacke et al. 2013). Endangered loggerhead, leatherback, and green turtles nest on southern US beaches, and their hatchlings are drawn to the lights in seaside resorts. Unfortunately, the young turtles' attraction to the coastal lights sometimes delays their entry into the sea and exposes them to predators (Witherington and Martin 1996). Migrating birds are known to steer by using constellations, but they often veer off, like moths to a flame, to artificial lights on buildings, lighthouses, and communication towers. They sometimes become disoriented and exhausted, even colliding with one another, and with windows, walls, or floodlights (Bower 2000).

News from Afar

The white noise of neon, fluorescent, mercury vapor, incandescent, and LED lights on the earth's surface is also garbling the information we might otherwise be getting from the wider realm. Our lights interfere with light that may have come millions of miles through our solar system, galaxy, and the cosmos beyond. Mercury vapor bulbs are particularly troublesome; they create a wide spectrum of radiation that is hard for astronomers to filter and block. As sprawl approaches formerly isolated observatories, the seeing can be seriously affected; the huge 200-inch telescope at Mount Palomar was already compromised in the 1960s (Brucato 1991).

Legacy

Modern-day observatories are equipped with an arsenal of telescopes and teams of trained astronomers, but it is important to remember that generations of people who used their naked eye to study and understand the night skies preceded them. These forebears developed elaborate religious beliefs, navigation systems, and seasonal and multiyear calendars based on what they saw. With light pollution, we are losing our connection to this part of our heritage.

Cost

Finally, from a bottom-line approach, light that escapes to illuminate the neighbors down the street or the skies far above is likely wasted light. It is light that has slipped by its target and exceeded its need. In that sense, light pollution wastes dollars and squanders energy resources. In fact, some estimates claim that $2 billion is lost annually in the United States by illuminating the bottom of airplanes and clouds (Guynup 2003).

Spread

At the same time that we are learning about the impacts of light pollution, its extent and severity are growing. There are eyes in the sky that are tracking the spread of artificial lights on the earth's surface. Since the early 1970s, the US Air Force has operated a satellite sensor called the Operational Linescan System. The sensor flies on the Defense Meteorological Satellite System, orbiting every 101 minutes about 500 miles above the earth. In 2011, NASA and NOAA began running the *Suomi National Polar-Orbiting Partnership* satellite,

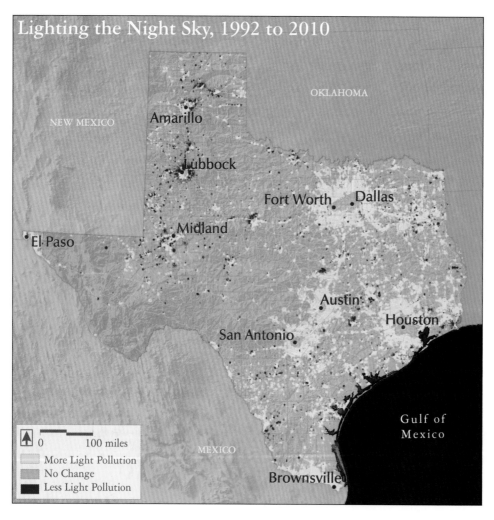

Lighting the Night Sky, 1992 to 2010

OKLAHOMA

NEW MEXICO

Amarillo

Lubbock

Fort Worth Dallas

Midland

El Paso

Austin

San Antonio Houston

Gulf of
Mexico

MEXICO

Brownsville

0   100 miles
More Light Pollution
No Change
Less Light Pollution

This map pairs nighttime satellite images shot in 1992 and 2010, showing the waxing (in yellow) and waning (in red) of artificial lights in the Texas landscape. It demonstrates how closely tied artificial lighting is to population growth and urban development. During that eighteen-year period, we can see that cities such as Houston have grown, that metropolitan areas such as Dallas, Arlington, and Fort Worth have joined, that smaller towns in the Valley have merged, and that development has stretched along the state's major highway corridors (National Oceanic and Atmospheric Administration 2013).

equipped with the Visible Infrared Imaging Radiometer Suite. Data from these sensors need to be culled and filtered, removing the moon-bleached images, deleting the cloudy and oblique views, erasing the flares from natural gas wells and the glare from brightly lit cities. However, once the images are sifted, compiled, and stitched together, we can now see how patterns of artificial light on the earth's surface have changed from 1992 through 2010 (Elvidge et al. 2013; National Oceanic and Atmospheric Administration 2013). The accompanying map shows how widely and quickly new light has spread across Texas' nighttime landscape.

Conservation

Fortunately, successful efforts have reduced light pollution in some situations. Several examples in Texas stand out and draw on the work of a wide variety of volunteers. They include green building professionals such as Andy Bergman, with Lights Out Houston, plus business and land-owners, such as those in the Hill Country Dark Sky Co-op. Educators, such as Bill Wren at the McDonald Observatory, and astronomers, such as Norman Markworth, with the Stephen F. Austin University Observatory, are also involved. Advocates, like Steve

Lights Out Houston

This figure demonstrates the impact that Lights Out Houston has had on reducing the energy use and skyglow from more than 155 million square feet of office and retail space in the city. The downtown buildings that take part in Lights Out Houston are shown in true color while nonparticipating buildings are shown in yellow. The program also includes structures in Houston's Greenway Plaza, Galleria, and major shopping centers, although they are not included in this view (Badoian-Kriticos 2015; Bergman 2013; Google Earth Pro 2014).

Bosbach and Julie Schaar with the Texas section of the International Dark-Sky Association, as well as federal park staff, such as Lisa Turecek, a building superintendent at Big Bend National Park, are also teaching about light pollution problems and solutions.

Volunteers

Lights Out Houston, a nonprofit, volunteer-run project, gives one answer to the light pollution challenge. Driven largely by energy conservation reasons, as well as just frugal common sense, Lights Out Houston has persuaded owners, tenants, and managers of over 155 million square feet of office space to voluntarily cut off their lights

after working hours. Millions of dollars and thousands of tons of carbon are at stake here. Roughly 25 percent of commercial energy use is dedicated to lighting (US Department of Energy 2008). From switching off all those lights in all those cubicles, corridors, and corner suites, these Houston firms reduce their operations' carbon footprint by over 52,000 metric tons of CO_2-equivalent and save over $7 million each year. Maybe that's why the program grew over fourfold in just its first five years (Badoian-Kriticos 2015; Bergman 2013).

Public efforts to dim the lights have not been confined to the big Texas cities like Houston. Some rural and small town proponents have invested

in the work as an energy conservation effort. Many times, support also comes from those who see it as a neighborly, considerate gesture to preserve a traditional part of the landscape. For instance, the Hill Country Dark Sky Co-op is seeking to "preserve the treasured natural wonder of the Hill Country's starry nighttime skies" (Hill Country Alliance 2013). The co-op has recruited and organized land owners (including the Bamberger, Double H, Hershey, Red Corral, and Reese Ranches), businesses, and residents in Bandera, Blanco, Comal, Gillespie, Kerr, Kimble, and Travis Counties to be careful with lighting fixtures, and to take other steps to control skyglow (Gandara 2013).

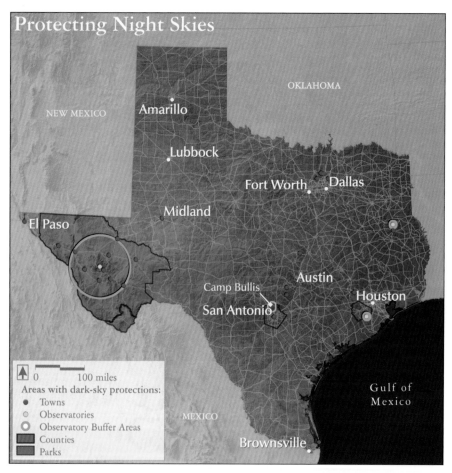

This map shows the Texas towns (red dots), counties (purple polygons), and parks (dark green areas) that have taken measures to protect dark skies. Observatories, which triggered a number of dark-sky protection efforts, are marked by a yellow dot, with a light green circle outlining the low-light buffer area. Camp Bullis is marked with a light orange boundary. The army had spurred light pollution control work in nearby San Antonio in order to protect nighttime field training at the camp (Bosbach 2013; City of Alpine 2000; City of Austin 2006; City of Boerne 2009; City of Dripping Springs 2000; City of El Paso 2005; City of Flower Mound 2002–4; City of Frisco 2011; City of Helotes 2009; City of La Grange 2011; City of Midland 2007; City of Nacogdoches 2005; City of Plano 2000; City of Port Aransas 2009; City of San Antonio 2008; Dark-Sky Association, Texas Section 2013; Schaar 2013; Town of Pecos City 2012; Village of Wimberley 2001; Wren 2010).

Early Legislation

Lights Out Houston and the Hill Country Dark Sky Co-op have recently taken a grassroots, voluntary approach, yet regulatory programs can be traced back quite far in the United States. Often the rules were developed to protect astronomical observatories, beginning with the 1958 passage of an ordinance against searchlights to help shield the Lowell Observatory in Flagstaff (City of Flagstaff, Ordinance No. 440, April 15, 1958). In 1970, David Crawford (later, a cofounder of the International Dark-Sky Association) led efforts to pass an outdoor lighting ordinance to protect Tucson's Kitt Peak Observatory (Owen 2007). Back in Texas, the legislature took its first steps in 1978 in resolving the problem of light pollution, authorizing counties within 57 air miles of McDonald Observatory to regulate their outdoor lights (Wren 2013). The legislature returned to the dark skies issue in 1995, when it enabled municipalities throughout the state to regulate outdoor lighting on public streets. Four years later, the state went further, requiring cutoff shielding on state-funded outdoor lights, including those on university grounds, prison properties, and highway rights-of-way (Texas Health and Safety Code, Title 5, Section 425; Texas Transportation Code, Title 6, Section 315.023).

Texas Counties and Cities

Since 1997, more than thirty Texas counties and towns have taken steps to regulate local outdoor lighting. Recognizing that skyglow and energy waste can be avoided just by better lighting design, these counties and cities have required fixtures to minimize excess glare and "trespass" of light beyond intended areas. And if precautions are not taken, a lot of light can escape. It is estimated that one-third to one-half of all outdoor lighting shines up, sideways, or otherwise misses its intended target (Ploetz 2003). The ordinances maintain good lighting for the work at hand, but keep light from making an easy getaway into the sky through clever use of automatic timers and controls, low-wattage bulbs, and light shields. In some cases, the commonsense solution is just to turn lights downward, away from the sky, and toward people's activities.

The State of Texas

Most of these regulatory efforts have been local. However, the state of Texas has gotten involved again recently, particularly where sensitive observatories and military bases are concerned. In 2007, the state authorized counties having large telescopes, with diameters over 69 inches, to regulate outdoor lighting (Texas Local Government Code, Title 7(B), Sections 240.032(b) and 240.033(b)). This statute applied to Fort Bend County (home of the George

Observatory), Nacogdoches County (site of the Student Observatory at Stephen F. Austin University), and Jeff Davis County (where the University of Texas' McDonald Observatory is located). In 2012, House Bill 2857 took effect, ratcheting up protection for McDonald Observatory by requiring counties and municipalities within 57 miles of the observatory to regulate outdoor lighting (Texas Local Government Code, Title 7(B), Sections 229.051–229.055 and 240.032–240.033). This affected a number of counties near the McDonald Observatory, including Brewster, Culberson, Hudspeth, Pecos, Presidio, and Reeves.

Military bases, where night-vision training often takes place, have also sought state help in dealing with light pollution. In 2007, the Texas legislature passed HB 1852, authorizing counties to adopt outdoor lighting ordinances within a five-mile radius of a military installation (Texas Local Government Code, Title 7(B), Sections 240.032(b-1) and 240.032(c)). Bexar County and San Antonio used this new law to protect Camp Bullis Army Training Facility from sprawl and related light trespass (Bexar County Commissioners Court Regulation No. 12.501.072208, July 22, 2008; City Code of San Antonio, Section 35-339.04).

A Dark Sky Park

Another effort to control light pollution has sought to protect and recognize areas that happily still have clear, natural skies. Big Bend National Park is one such place. The International

A photograph gives a semblance of how dazzling the night sky can be in Big Bend National Park (Nordgren 2008).

Dark-Sky Association declared it to be an International Dark Sky Park in 2012. In fact, Big Bend has the darkest skies in the lower forty-eight states, and is the largest park in the world that carries the dark-sky title. While some of its status is due to its remote location, the park's pitch-black skies can also be credited to an innovative partnership among an NGO, a business, and park staff. With gifts from the Friends of Big Bend National Park and equipment from the Musco Lighting Company, park staffer Lisa Turecek organized lighting renovations in the park that have limited light bleed, cut energy consumption by 98 percent, and helped open the night sky to thousands of park visitors (Wheeler 2010).

Familiar Stories

Although light pollution is a relatively new concern, it has the traits of many age-old environmental problems. For instance, it is a question that depends on one's perspective. If one has a billboard, service station, or stadium to illuminate, the bright lights may help earn extra eyeball views, gallons of gasoline pumped, or tickets sold. Any lost light is just an externality that is not one's concern (although for the neighbor, the invading light may not be so welcome). Second, artificial lights present a cumulative challenge, seldom worrisome for a few bedside lamps, but severe when thousands of outdoor spotlights, floodlights, and searchlights are involved. And last, light pollution is a creeper, a problem that can grow so gradually and subtly that we do not notice the change until it is quite serious.

Good Answers

Fortunately, unlike some tougher conservation challenges, there are good solutions at hand, many of which quickly pay for themselves. Light pollution is often costly wasted light, spilled and lost from where it is truly needed. As we have seen, voluntary efforts such as Lights Out Houston can both dim the lights and save huge amounts of money, electricity, and carbon. And many communities now have new ordinances moving us toward more task-focused lighting and less ambient and up-turned lighting, with more use of shields, timers, motion sensors, and other technical solutions. These ordinances can help us use less energy and fuel, while still enjoying a similar amount of useful illumination. Last, if we recognize, value, and set aside the places with exceptionally dark and beautiful skies, such as Big Bend National Park, we might start to realize what the fuss is all about and work toward having darker skies in our own backyards.

Sources

American Medical Association House of Delegates. 2012. "Adverse Health Effects of Nighttime Lighting." Council on Science and Public Health, Recommendations, Report 4-A-12.

Badoian-Kriticos, Marina. 2015. Senior Advisor, Office of Sustainability, City of Houston. Personal communication, April.

Bergman, Andy. 2013. Cofounder, Lights Out Houston. Personal communication, September.

Bogard, Paul. 2013. *The End of Light: Searching for Natural Darkness in an Age of Artificial Light.* New York: Little, Brown.

Bosbach, Stephen. 2013. International Dark-Sky Association, Texas Section. Personal communication, September.

Bower, Joe. 2000. "The Dark Side of Night." *Audubon* (March–April).

Brox, Jane. 2010. *Brilliant: The Evolution of Artificial Light.* Boston: Houghton Mifflin Harcourt.

Brucato, Robert. 1991 "Site Preservation at Palomar Observatory." In *Light Pollution, Radio Interference, and Space Debris*, edited by D. L. Crawford. ASP Conference Series, vol. 17, IAU Colloquium 112, pp. 20–24.

City of Alpine. 2000. An Ordinance to Improve Outdoor Lighting in the City of Alpine, Texas. Adopted May 23.

City of Austin. 2006. Article 2, Section 2.5. Site Design Standards: Exterior Lighting. Ordinance 20060831-068. Adopted August 31.

City of Boerne. 2009. Illumination Plan, Appendix A, Section 02, Parts 3.02.001 through 3.02.010, adopted as part of the Development Plat Regulations on July 28.

City of Bulverde. 2003. Article 3.09: Dark Sky Ordinance. Ordinance 128-03-07-08, Section 1.1. Adopted July 8.

City of Dripping Springs. 2000. An Ordinance Establishing Outdoor Lighting Regulation. Ordinance No. 1260.00. Adopted January 17.

City of El Paso. 2005. Outdoor Lighting Code, Adopted as Chapter 18.18 of the Building and Construction Code, as Ordinance No. 15996, on February 8.

City of Flower Mound. 2002–4. Code of Ordinances, Subpart B Land Development Regulations, Chapter 98—Zoning, Article IV—Supplementary District Regulations, Division 6—Outdoor Lighting. Ordinance Nos. 09-02, 14-03, 101-04, Adopted February 5, 2002, March 3, 2003, and December 20, 2004.

City of Frisco. 2011. Zoning Ordinance, Subsection 4.05—Lighting Standards. Adopted April 5.

City of Helotes. 2009. Outdoor Lighting. Article III, Sections 34–41 through 34–47. Ordinance No. 396, Section 1. Adopted February 26.

City of La Grange. 2011. Resolution to "promote outdoor lighting fixtures and practices that follow guidelines for efficient, non-intrusive lighting." Adopted December 12.

City of Marfa. 2000. An Ordinance Providing for the Regulation of Outdoor Lighting in the City of Marfa, Texas. Ordinance No. 00-01. Adopted July 11.

City of Midland. 2007. Article 3, Section 3.12: Lighting. Adopted 2007.

City of Nacogdoches. 2005. Code of Ordinances, Article VI, Outdoor Lighting, Section 34-181 through 34-188.

City of Plano. 2000. Part II—Code of Ordinances, Chapter 6—Buildings and Building Regulations, Article XI. Outdoor Lighting. Ordinance Nos. 85-5-27, 2000-4-16, 2001-6-7, 2001-6-7. Adopted May 13, 1985, April 24, 2000, June 11, 2001.

City of Port Aransas. 2009. Lighting. Code of Ordinances, Chapter 25, Division 2, Environmental Controls, Section 25–146. Adopted June 18.

City of San Antonio. 2008. Military Lighting Overlay Districts, in Chapter 35, Article II, Division 4 of the City Code of San Antonio, entitled Overlay Districts. Adopted December 11.

City of South Padre Island. 2011. Code of Ordinances, Regulation of Lighting, Sections 12–23 through 12–29. Adopted October 20.

County of Bexar. 2008. Order for Regulation of Outdoor Lighting in the Unincorporated Areas of Bexar County, Texas within 3 Miles of the Camp Bullis Boundaries, Commissioners Court Regulation, No. 12.501.072208. Adopted July 22.

County of Fort Bend. 2006. Orders for Regulation of Outdoor Lighting in the Unincorporated Areas of Fort Bend County, Texas.

County of Jeff Davis. 2007. Order of the Jeff Davis County Commissioners Court Governing Outdoor Lighting. Adopted October 9.

Dacke, Marle, Emily Baird, Marcus Byrne, Clarke Scholtz, and Eric Warrant. 2013. "Dung Beetles Use the Milky Way for Orientation." *Current Biology* 23 (4): 298–300.

Davis, Norris. 2013. "Rural Electrification." Handbook of Texas Online. Texas State Historical Association. http://www.tshaonline.org/handbook/online/articles/dpr01, accessed October 20, 2013.

DIVA-GIS. 2015. Spatial Data Download, Mexico, Administrative Areas. Shapefile. http://biogeo.ucdavis.edu/data/diva/adm/MEX_adm.zip, accessed April 7, 2015.

Elvidge, Christopher, Feng-Chi Hsu, Kimberly Baugh, and Tilottama Ghosh. 2013. "National Trends in Satellite Observed Lighting: 1992–2012." Earth Observation Group, NOAA National Geophysical Data Center. Cooperative Institute for Research in the Environmental Sciences, University of Colorado. Boulder, Colorado. Chapter 6 in *Global Urban Monitoring and Assessment through Earth Observation*, edited by Qihao Weng. Boca Raton, FL: CRC Press.

Gandara, Ricardo. 2013. "Hill Country Co-Op Lobbies to Save Dark, Starry Nights." *Austin American-Statesman*, July 6.

Globe at Night Citizen Science Campaign. 2013. Map the Data to Explore the Patterns of Light Pollution. National Optical Astronomy Observatory. http://www.globeatnight.org/analyze.html, accessed September 10, 2013.

Google Earth Pro, v. 7.1.2.2041. 2014. Houston, 29.753547N, -95.366733W, elevation 1,800 feet. Buildings data layer. Landsat imagery. Gray Buildings, copyright 2008, Sanborn. Provided by Google Earth. April 8.

Guynup, Sharon. 2003. "Light Pollution Taking a Toll on Wildlife, Eco-Groups Say." *National Geographic Today*, April 17.

Hill Country Alliance. 2013. Issue: Preserving the Night Skies. http://www.hillcountryalliance.org/uploads/HCA/NightSkyIPNew.pdf, accessed October 20, 2013.

International Comet Quarterly. Undated. The Astronomical Magnitude Scale. Cometary Science Center, Center Bureau for Astronomical Telegrams,

Minor Planet Center, Harvard University.

International Dark-Sky Association, Texas Section. 2013. Texas Municipalities with Specific Outdoor Lighting or Light Pollution Ordinances. http://www.texasida.org/LocalOrdinances.htm, accessed October 20, 2013.

National Aeronautics and Space Administration (NASA). 2010. International Space Station Imagery, Image ISS022-E-078463. http://spaceflight.nasa.gov/gallery/images/station/crew-22/html/iss022e078463.html, accessed October 18, 2013.

National Oceanic and Atmospheric Administration. 2013. Global DMSP-OLS Nighttime Lights Time Series 1992–2009 (Version 4) DMSP and VIIRS Data Download. Earth Observation Group, National Geophysical Data Center, NOAA. http://ngdc.noaa.gov/eog/download.html, accessed September 16, 2013.

National Optical Astronomy Observatory. 2015. Globe at Night, Maps and Data. http://www.globeatnight.org/maps.php, accessed April 7, 2015.

Nordgren, Tyler. 2015. 170° view of the rising Milky Way, as seen from south of Chisos Mountains, in Big Bend National Park, March 2008. Photograph. Department of Physics, University of Redlands. Personal communication, April.

Owen, David. 2007. "The Dark Side: Making War on Light Pollution." *The New Yorker*, August 20.

Pauley, Stephen. 2004. "Lighting for the Human Circadian Clock: Recent Research Indicates That Lighting Has Become a Public Health Issue." *Medical Hypotheses* 63 (4): 588–96.

Ploetz, Kristen. 2003. "Notes: Light Pollution in the United States: An Overview of the Inadequacies of the Common Law and State and Local Regulation." *New England Law Review* 36 (4): 985–1039.

Schaar, Julie. 2013. Founder, Texas chapter, International Dark-Sky Association. Personal communication, September.

———. 2015. Founder, Texas chapter, International Dark-Sky Association. Personal communication, April.

Schivelbusch, Wolfgang. 1988. *Disenchanted Light: The Industrialization of Light in the 19th Century*. Berkeley: University of California Press.

Sinnott, Roger, and Michael Perryman. 1997. Tycho Catalogue, Millenium Star Atlas. Sky Publishing Corporation and European Space Agency.

Spivey, Angela. 2010. "Light Pollution: Light at Night and Breast Cancer Risk Worldwide." *Environmental Health Perspectives* 118 (12): A525.

Texas Electric Cooperatives. 2013. History. http://www.texas-ec.org/about/history, accessed September 11, 2013.

Town of Pecos City. 2012. Ordinance 12-02-01. Adopted February 23.

US Census Bureau. 2013. CPH-T-5. Population Change for Metropolitan and Micropolitan Statistical Areas in the United States and Puerto Rico (February 2013 Delineations): 2000 to 2010. US Department of Commerce. http://www.census.gov/population/www/cen2010/cph-t/CPH-T-5.xls, accessed September 19, 2013.

US Department of Energy. 2008. Energy Efficiency Trends in Residential and Commercial Buildings. http://apps1.eere.energy.gov/buildings/publications/pdfs/corporate/bt_stateindustry.pdf, accessed September 15, 2013.

Village of Wimberley. 2001. Outdoor Lighting Ordinance. Ordinance No. 2001-24. Adopted October 4.

Walker, Connie. 2013. National Optical Astronomy Observatory and Globe at Night Program. Personal communication, September.

Walker, Merle. 1977. "The Effects of Urban Lighting on the Brightness of the Night Sky." *Lick Observatory Bulletin* 760: 405–9.

Wheeler, Camille. 2010. "Starstruck: The Quest to Save West Texas' Dark Night Skies." *Texas Co-Op Power*, December.

Witherington, B. E., and R. E. Martin. 1996. "Understanding, Assessing and Resolving Light-Pollution Problems on Sea Turtle Nesting Beaches." Florida Marine Research Institute Technical Report TR-2.

Wren, Bill. 2013. Public Affairs Specialist, McDonald Observatory, University of Texas. Personal communications, October and November.

Billboards

Billboards are a powerful part of the landscape in Texas, and indeed, throughout the United States. Based on state highway agency data, modern signs are tall (over 61 percent stand more than 40 feet in height), big (they average 430 square feet), and bright (78 percent are illuminated) (White 2015). And they exist here in the tens of thousands. One stakeholder, Scenic Texas, estimates that there are 35,000 off-premise signs in the state, with 550 new permits granted yearly (Scenic Texas 2013).

"Song of the Open Road"
I think that I shall never see
A billboard lovely as a tree
Indeed, unless the billboards fall
I'll never see a tree at all.

—Ogden Nash, 1941

Billboards have many critics. Mr. Nash is not alone. Scenic America, a nonprofit pledged to "preserving and enhancing the visual character of America" has called the signs, "sky trash," "litter on a stick," and "the junk mail of the American highway" (Chan 2014). Surveys have shown that much of the public also sees these signs as ugly, distracting, crassly commercial, and intrusive (Burnett 2007). For instance, a 1996 poll found that 81 percent of Houston residents favored banning new billboard construction, and 79 percent felt that there should

be no more billboards on Texas highways (Klineberg 1996).

On the other hand, billboards provide a cheap and effective way of distributing commercial information. Both sign supporters and critics acknowledge that outdoor ads are very difficult to ignore. One marketer wrote, "outdoor can't be beat. You can't zap it . . . you can't put it aside, turn the page, or toss it . . . you can't turn it off, turn it down, or tune it out" (Philip Morris Media and Leo Burnett 1993). As a result, these signs are the bread and butter for a large American industry, generating over $4.25 billion in revenue, seeing a twentyfold increase in billings since 1970, and currently enjoying double-digit income growth (Burnett 2007; Outdoor Advertising Association of America 2013). Moreover, the sign industry is national in scale, with heavily concentrated ownership (Outfront, Lamar, and Clear Channel Outdoor alone control 50 percent of the signs under TxDOT's purview, out of a pool of more than 990 regulated sign owners) (White 2015). With these ample resources, sign owners can and do undertake powerful lobbying and litigation efforts to support their industry.

Faced with a formidable foe, public resistance to billboards has not been simple, cheap, or quick. In the early days, the traditions and express

language of US law did not directly support sign regulation. Billboard critics could not challenge signs simply because they felt they were ugly. They had to contest them on public safety grounds, with arguments that the signs were likely to catch fire, fall on passersby, distract drivers, or hide criminals (Burnett 2007; Nowlin 2012). For many years, courts could not base their decisions on ideas of beauty that might be seen as hazy or subjective. As Lady Bird Johnson worried, beautification "sounds cosmetic and trivial and . . . prissy" (Bergeron 2008).

Nevertheless, sign critics were passionate about controlling the blight they saw in billboards. Thus much of the past century witnessed their effort to build a public movement and a legal structure to ban and pull down signs. Along the way, in fact literally along Texas and US roadsides, billboards have become the focus of a textbook conflict over a shared landscape. Sign control has become a classic clash between public opposition and private interest, between the power of public opinion and votes and the influence of special knowledge and money.

Early Efforts in Texas

The debate over billboards in Texas is not new. Texas and outdoor advertising have a long and mixed history. Numerous businesses have supported

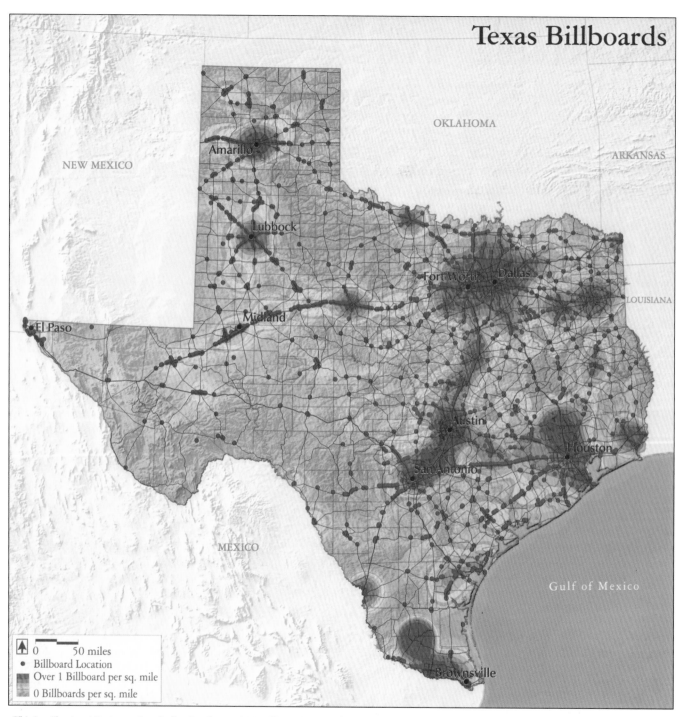

Texas Billboards

Legend:
- 0   50 miles
- • Billboard Location
- Over 1 Billboard per sq. mile
- 0 Billboards per sq. mile

This is a "heat map" representing the density of over 14,500 off-premise signs that are registered by the Texas Department of Transportation and located along federal and primary highways, as well as rural roads throughout the state. The map shows how the existence of these private signs depends heavily on the routes of public roads and the travel habits of motoring Texans. Please note that many signs fall outside of TxDOT's jurisdiction, so this is just a partial inventory of the billboards in the state, including perhaps a third of all off-premise signs (Texas Department of Transportation 2015; Trevino 2013; White 2015).

This image shows the downtown Houston skyline, accompanied by billboards, during the early 1960s (Eaton 2013).

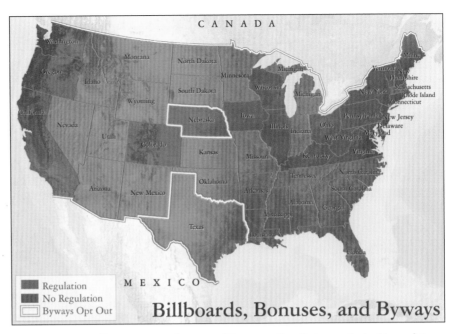

Billboards, Bonuses, and Byways

This map shows a split among states that were willing versus those that were reluctant to regulate off-premise signs. Red states refused the federal bonuses that were offered in the 1950s to police signage along interstate highways. In 1991, a group of four states opted out of the federal effort to create billboard-free "scenic byways." (Control of outdoor advertising, 23 U.S.C. §131(j, s); Federal-Aid Highway Act of 1958, a.k.a. "The Bonus Act," P. L. 85-381; Federal Highway Administration 2015; Intermodal Surface Transportation Efficiency Act of 1991, P. L. 102-240).

the use of billboards. Beginning in the 1890s, barn murals were painted for Bull Durham Tobacco and Lydia Pinkham's Compound, posters were made for Kodak film, and ads were tacked up for carnivals, shows, and circuses. And with the purchase of cars, the construction of roads, and the increasing habit of driving for fun and profit, there was a growing audience for these roadside signs. Also, in some communities, government welcomed and even supported the new signs. For example, during the 1910s and 1920s, an Austin sign painter and ad man named Godfrey Flury built mile markers for the county in exchange for using those mileposts as advertising platforms. He also sold "highly embellished" trash cans to the city that sported local ads (Meyers 1995).

However, as early as the 1920s, the opposition countered the sign builders and tried to protect the views along Texas roads. Growing from the nationwide City Beautiful movement, billboard limits were promoted locally by the Austin Art League, as well as by the Texas and Dallas branches of the General Federation of Women's Clubs (Meyers 1995). The growing effort to restrain signboards was not confined to nonprofits. During the 1920s, home-rule cities in Texas gained the right to regulate signs (Texas Local Government Code Annotated § 216.901(a)). There were efforts at the state level too: in 1933, the Texas Highway Department hired its first landscape architect, Jac Gubbels, who was charged with "beautification of highways." Gubbels declared that, with time, the public would insist on "safe and pleasant roadsides which in turn will develop pride, and will naturally eliminate unsightly dumps and ugly shacks as well as bootleg billboards" (Bergeron 2008). In more recent years, Texas has also led in other efforts at beautifying its waysides, including planting wildflowers, developing roadside parks, organizing adopt-a-highway programs, and promoting the famous "Don't Mess with Texas" ad campaign (Purcell 2013).

Bonus Act

Generally, though, there was reluctance in the United States, and in Texas specifically, to regulate outdoor signs even as they spread into the countryside during the post–World War II road-building boom. At a 1957 press conference, President Eisenhower mentioned that he was "against these billboards that mar our scenery" but was unsure how to legally proceed in regulating billboards that were built on land outside of the highway's public right-of-way (US Government Printing Office 1999).

Nevertheless, Congress did manage to pass the first federal outdoor sign legislation in 1958. The federal government provided a carrot, and hoped the states would wield a stick. Called the "Bonus Act," the law gave states a reward of an extra one-half percent of federal highway construction funding if those states agreed to limit billboards within 660 feet of interstate highways (Federal-Aid Highway Act of 1958, Pub. L. 85-381; 72 Stat. 95). Twenty-three states chose to regulate signs along interstates. Texas was not among them.

Although the Bonus Act of 1958 opened the door to federally encouraged sign regulation, the act's impact was limited. There was a big loophole: it allowed advertising signs that were within twelve air miles of the advertised activity. And, there was a major shortfall: funding for the program expired, leaving states with more than $10 million in unpaid bills. As a consequence, billboard regulations remained seriously lax in Texas and the other states.

Highway Beautification Act— Noble Beginnings

By the mid-1960s, the march of billboards across the landscape had once again drawn attention at the highest level. In 1965, President Johnson and Congress adopted the Highway Beautification Act (HBA) to control their spread (23 U.S.C. 131). The HBA was a high priority in Washington, seeing passage before the landmark Clean Air Act and Clean Water Act and some three hundred other environmental laws enacted during the Great Society initiative of the 1960s. The president was evidently pressed to promote the act because of his wife's deep passion for the issue. Billboard control, and beautification more generally, were near and dear to the heart of his wife, Lady Bird (Melosi 2012, 193–95; Wright 2007). She saw these issues in strong and broad terms, as more than isolated and prim aesthetic questions. As she put it,

> Getting on the subject of beautification is like picking up a tangled skein of wool. All the threads are interwoven—recreation and pollution and mental health, and the crime rate, and rapid transit, and highway beautification, and the war on poverty, and parks—national, state and local. It is hard to hitch the conversation into one straight line, because everything leads to something else. (Johnson 2007)

The general thrust of the act was to require the states to remove "noncon-forming" (legally built before passage) and "nonpermitted" signs (built after the act in a noncompliant way) that stood along federally supported roads. The act offered a reward (75 percent coverage of the cost of retiring the signs) and a penalty (states that did not follow suit would lose 10 percent of their federal road dollars). The act did not ban all billboards; it only controlled "off-premise signs" (exempting on-site signs that promoted businesses abutting the highway) that were not in "industrial and commercial zones."

However, during the course of congressional negotiations and with tremendous industry pressure, the law was whittled down. Loopholes were created that allowed the construction of many new signs and made their removal much more difficult and costly. The Government Accountability Office estimated that 587,000 signs were removed from federal highways in the United States from 1965 through 1983, at a cost of over $220 million. However, the Congressional Research Service found that somehow there were 150,000 more billboards on federally funded highways in 1991 than there were in 1965 (US Government Accountability Office 1985). Texas records echo the national struggle to remove signs. As of 2015, close to 6,500 Texas billboards had been removed, yet over 11,500 nonconforming signs and 4,200 nonpermitted signs remained in the state (White 2015). On account of its many loopholes, critics took to calling the Highway Beautification

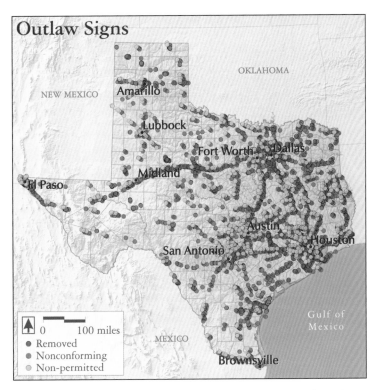

Outlaw Signs

0   100 miles

- Removed
- Nonconforming
- Non-permitted

This map marks over 6,500 off-premise signs that have been removed from Texas interstates, primary highways, and rural roads. The number of removed signs is greatly outstripped by the remaining nonconforming (11,500+) and nonpermitted (4,200+) billboards (Trevino 2013; White 2015).

Act the "Billboard Protection and Proliferation Act" (Vespe 1997).

The Location Loophole

One of the larger gaps in the 1965 act involved the permission it gave for billboards to be located in so-called industrial and commercial zones. The state of Texas is distinctive in having indirectly made many of these industrial and commercial zones that billboards now use to show their wares to passing motorists. The creation of this prime sign real estate began in the late 1940s, when Dewitt Greer served as the director of the Texas Department of Transportation. Under Greer, the agency designed and built frontage roads and extra ramps on major highways. As a policy stance, Greer felt that the interstates should not just support long-range, "through" traffic, but should also accommodate "interregional" traffic. Also, from a budget approach, Greer reasoned that giving road access to properties along the new interstates was cheaper than having to buy those access rights along with the right-of-way for the freeway itself (Beaumont et al. 2005; Purcell 2013).

These feeder roads and ramps affected the number and location of off-premise signs due to the way the federal Highway Beautification Act was structured, or at least the way its exemptions were designed. The act allowed signs in commercial or industrial areas along interstate highways (23 U.S.C. 131(d)). In many states, these sign-friendly business zones along interstates have been quite limited, because there is little access for local traffic and related stopping and shopping, especially in rural areas. However, in Texas, the extensive network of service roads, dating back to Greer's days, has allowed businesses to decamp to and flourish along interstate highways, and in turn, for signs to crop up along these newly minted "commercial" areas. Further, this business (and sign) development has been accelerated by the fact that exits and entrances from Texas interstates are closer together than those commonly found in other states (Purcell 2013).

Regulatory authority over Texas billboards has a limited scope. It is restricted to interstate highways, primary roads, tollways, incorporated cities, and cities' extraterritorial jurisdiction (Texas Transportation Code §§ 393.031, 395.001(a)(1)). This leaves a regulatory vacuum in rural parts of the state, where county commissioners do not generally have the statutory power to either prohibit billboards' construction or to mandate their removal. Also, because

Texas counties, and most of the state's towns, have no zoning regulations that declare an area "industrial" or "commercial," the HBA must look to whether there is a legitimate business within 800 feet of the sign. Unfortunately, this "industrial and commercial zone" criterion has often been manipulated and abused (Floyd 1982).

The Timing Bypass

Many of these sign laws came along late in the game. Numerous billboards along Texas interstates, especially in urban areas, were exempt from the Highway Beautification Act because the roads had been built before the act was passed. A number of Texas freeways had already begun construction in the late 1940s (such as the 1948 segments of Houston's Gulf Freeway) and were only later adopted into the Texas interstate system. Under the Cotton Amendment, portions of the interstate system built before July 1, 1956, received grandfathered protection for roadside signs (23 CFR § 750.01(a)(2)). Similarly, the Texas Rural Roads Act protects the off-premise signs among many state roads that were installed before September 1, 1985 (Texas Administrative Code, Title 43, Part 1, Rule § 21.407). Ironically, this grandfathering of old sign locations created a lucrative barrier to entry that enriches and entrenches existing sign operators.

The Valuation Detour

Appraisal of billboards can be an inscrutable fine art. Condemnation prices sometimes soar high above assessed values, making government buyouts very costly. For example, when a Houston highway was raised up and a nearby billboard was obscured, Clear Channel Outdoor filed suit claiming that Harris County owed it for curtailing the visibility of its sign. While the billboard was on the tax rolls for just $21,800, the county agreed to pay Clear Channel Outdoor $525,000 for the sign's "visibility easement" and also permitted Clear Channel to raise the billboard by ten feet to keep it in easy eyesight (Watson and McMahen 2008).

The Condemnation Roundabout

For decades, agencies had retired billboards through their police power, allowing the sign owners to recoup their investment over some period of years after notice, through a process known as amortization. In this way, government tried to avoid cash sign buyouts due to their well-known cost and delay (US Government Accounting Office 1978). However, in 1978 the Surface Transportation Act blocked this tactic (Public Law 95-599, 23 U.S.C. 131). The act required sign owners to be compensated, up front, in cash, for any bill-

boards that were taken down, not via amortization over the course of a number of years.

To add some frustration, earlier amendments to the Highway Beautification Act passed in 1968 indicated that these "nonconforming" signs did not have to be removed unless federal funds were available. Congress has generally failed to authorize these funds. While some dollars were available for billboard removal, the Intermodal Surface Transportation Efficiency Act of 1991 (ISTEA) put sign control costs in direct, zero-sum competition with popular and urgent highway construction projects (Public Law 102-240).

Attempts have been made to increase the cost of condemnation on nonfederal roads as well. In 1985, the Texas legislature passed House Bill 1330, allowing a handful of cities to amortize sign removal costs, but requiring the majority of cities to pay in cash (Texas Local Government Code §§ 216.003(b), 216.012(b)). Unfortunately, regulators have learned that removing a billboard can be a slow and tenuous process, often without enough agency staff available to carry out the project. Ironically, the removals have sometimes been known to merely finance a sign's move to a new site (Texas Local Government Code § 216.003(b)).

Scenic Routes

From the outset, the federal government tried to offer additional incentives to control billboards. However, from its early skittishness over the Bonus Act during the 1950s, the state of Texas continued to be wary of participating in national sign control efforts. For instance, in 1991 ISTEA created and funded the National Scenic Byways Program, providing over $500 million to promote and protect a "distinctive collection of American roads, their stories and treasured places" (23 U.S.C. § 162; Federal Register Vol. 60, No. 96, pp. 26759–26762, May 18, 1995; America's Byways 2013). Construction of new billboards along these scenic byways was banned. Most states chose to create at least some sign-free scenic byways within their borders. Texas and its sister states, Hawai'i, Nebraska, and Rhode Island, elected not to participate in the byway program, alone among all fifty states.

Although it sat out the American byways program, the state of Texas has declared some roads billboard free. These include a number of roads in national parks (Big Bend and Padre Island) and forests (Davy Crockett, Sabine, and Sam Houston) that are required to be unsigned by federal law. Others, though, were protected after public lobbying at the state legislature. They include picturesque rural roads in the Hill Country (Highways 16, 290, and 317), coastal prairie (Route 73), piney woods (Routes 105 and 2978), South Texas plain (Routes 281 and 77), and the rolling farmlands of the east central plains (Route 21). While it is important to give credit to the efforts to protect sign-free zones

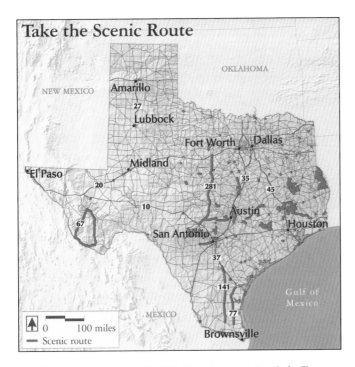

Scenic routes: under section 391.252 of the Transportation Code, Texas has banned off-premise signs along its designated "scenic" roads (Texas Department of Transportation 2015; Trevino 2013; White 2015).

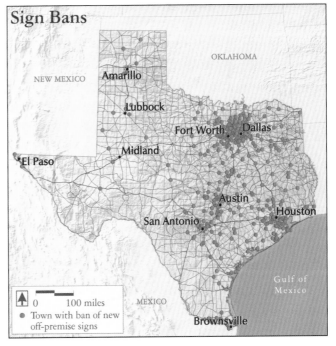

This map shows roughly 380 towns in Texas that have been identified by the nonprofit group Scenic Texas as having ordinances that bar construction of new off-premise signs. While effective against new billboards, these ordinances do not necessarily regulate or require the removal of existing signs (Culver 2013 and 2015; Eaton 2013; Franklin Legal Publishing 2015; Municode Library 2015).

along these roads, it remains true that the more valuable, heavily traveled interstates in Texas remain home to thousands of billboards.

Local Efforts

In addition to the efforts at the federal and state levels, a number of communities in Texas and other states have worked on regulating signs in their local areas. In fact, more than 260 Texas towns are estimated to have prohibited new billboards (Culver 2013; Eaton 2013). Many are small, master-planned suburban bedroom communities; however, some are very large metropolitan areas such as Houston, Dallas, Fort Worth, and Austin.

The Poster Child

In 1980, Houston was home to over 10,000 off-premise signs and was known as the Billboard Capitol of the World. Despite its reputation as an unzoned city comfortable with a diversity of land uses, a number of Houstonians were not happy with its billboard fame. So, in 1980, with leadership from council member Eleanor Tinsley, and support from a nonprofit group known as Billboards Limited (now dubbed "Scenic Houston"), the Houston City Council passed an ordinance banning construction of new billboards (Houston City Ordinance 80-351, March 26, 1980; Shaddock 2008).

As a result, the city has seen an impressive 85 percent decline in

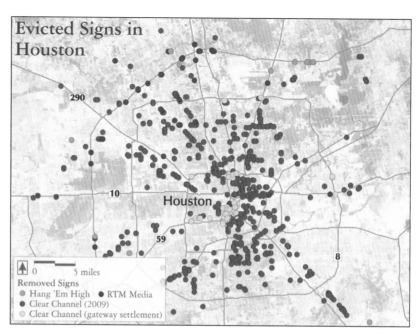

Here is an example of more than eight hundred signs that have been recently removed by the city of Houston through negotiation and litigation with three major firms. Clear Channel Communications took down six hundred signs in 2009. These were commercially insignificant signs that were relatively small (less than twelve feet in width). However, they were found scattered disproportionately among poor and inner-city residential neighborhoods. Clear Channel also tore down signs in a negotiated settlement to clear scenic and gateway routes in the city, including downtown, US 59, Beltway 8, the Hardy Toll Road, T. C. Jester, and Richmond/Weslayan. Other removed signs had been owned by Hang 'Em High and RTM Media. Both firms had erected the billboards in the regulatory no-man's land of the City's Extra-Territorial Jurisdiction (Eaton 2013).

billboards since 1980. The city has hewed to a strict municipal sign ordinance for over a generation and has made a large investment in enforcing the code, retiring old signs, and banning fresh signs from rising alongside 150 miles of new roads in the Houston area (including Texas 288, the Hardy Toll Road, and the Sam Houston Tollway) (Culver 2013). Many of the remaining signs are on interstate highways, and so are paradoxically protected by the federal Highway Beautification Act.

Constitutional Hurdles

While much of the debate over billboards has been in legislatures and city councils, some of the controversy has spilled over into courtrooms. Billboards are material things, just steel and wood and paper and vinyl, but they have been elevated to abstract and even constitutional levels.

Sign owners have regularly challenged regulators for violating the Fifth and Fourteenth Amendments, for taking without compensation and due process. Yet many courts have ruled that state and local governments are entitled, within their police powers, to limit signs for the sake of their citizens' health, safety, and welfare (*Lamar Corp v. City of Longview*, 270 S.W. 3d 609 (2008)). Sign companies have also protested that governments' efforts interfere with their customers' freedom of expression under the First Amendment. However, the Supreme Court settled this issue with its ruling that off-premise signs could be policed, so long as the regulation did not hinge on the sign's message (*Metromedia v. San Diego*, 453 U.S. 490 (1981)).

New Questions

With today's flood of competing distractions, sign owners have an increasingly challenging time getting and keeping the attention of enough "eyeballs." Static signs, even with their enormous size, bright colors, beautiful faces, and witty messages, may not be enough. As a consequence, the advertising industry is investing in new technology. Some advertisers have adopted new digitally lit signs. In 2007, the billboard industry succeeded in getting the Federal Highway Administration to let advertisers erect lighted LED signs, which flash a rotating variety of messages (Shepherd 2007). These signs can be very lucrative. They can host as many as 10,000 messages a day, shifting every eight seconds, lit around the clock. Sign owners argue that the LED signs can help the public by posting notices of impending storms, kidnapped children, or lost amnesiacs. Critics see them as distracting to neighbors, hazardous to drivers, destructive to dark-sky initiatives, and inconsistent with the letter and spirit of the Highway Beautification Act (Sharpe 2012). However, the courts have largely found that the digital signs are permitted under the act (*Scenic America, Inc. v. US Department of Transportation and Outdoor Advertising Association of America*, US District Court for the District of Columbia, Civil Action No. 13-93 (D.D.C., June 20, 2014)).

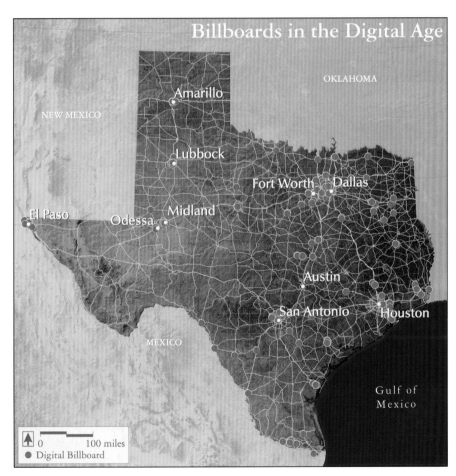

This is a map of over 282 new "digital billboards" in Texas that use light emitting diodes to show a revolving set of ads (Trevino 2013; White 2015).

The Conversation Continues

Over a century has passed since the first billboards appeared and the opposing hue and cry went up in Texas and beyond. Throughout, the same controversy has continued, with the same legislating and exempting, the same suing and condemning, and the same sign building and removing. Sign promoters see a media channel for commercials to reach consumers, generate ad dollars, and build sales revenues. Sign critics see a tacky mark on the sky, an ugly blot on a country view, and a messy flaw in a community's architecture. The same disputes over a shared landscape roll on. However, these debates are occurring in more and smaller communities, with more direct public involvement, affecting more and more new roads. And, increasingly, it does seem that people are agreeing that they indeed will never see a billboard as lovely as a tree.

Sources

America's Byways. 2013. America's Byways Fact Sheet. http://byways.org/press/fact_sheet.html, accessed August 1, 2013.

Beaumont, Penny, Rhonda Brinkmann, David Ellis, Chris Pourteau, and Brandon Webb. 2005. "Interstate Texas: Anywhere to Everywhere—The Development of the Interstate Highway System in Texas." Vol. 41, No. 4. Texas Transportation Institute, Texas A&M University System.

Bergeron, Kathleen. 2008. "The Environmental First Lady." *Public Roads* (March–April): 16–23.

Burnett, David. 2007. "Judging the Aesthetics of Billboards." *Journal of Law and Politics* 23 (Spring): 171.

Chan, Dawn. 2014. "All Across America, Artists Are Taking over Billboards." *New York Times*, August 18.

Culver, Anne. 2013 and 2015. Executive Director, Scenic Texas. Personal communications, August 2013 and April 2015.

Eaton, Holly. 2013. Project Manager, Scenic Texas. Personal communication, August.

Federal Highway Administration. 2015. America's Byways. Federal Highway Administration, US Department of Transportation. http://www.fhwa.dot.gov/byways/byways, accessed May 20, 2015.

Floyd, Charles. 1982. "Requiem for the Highway Beautification Act." *Journal of the American Planning Association* (Autumn).

Franklin Legal Publishing. 2015. Code of Ordinances. http://www.franklinlegal.net/codes.html, accessed April 7, 2015.

Johnson, Lady Bird. 2007. *A White House Diary*. Austin: University of Texas Press.

Klineberg, Stephen. 1996. Assessing Public Opinion Regarding Billboards in the Houston Area, conducted with Telesurveys Research Associates, for Scenic Houston. August.

Melosi, Martin. 2012. "Lady Bird." In *A Companion to Lyndon B. Johnson*, edited by Mitchell Lerner. New York: Wiley.

Meyers, Cynthia. 1995. "Godfrey Flury's Billboard Advertising Business: An Austin Ad Man in the 1910s and 1920s." *Southwestern Historical Quarterly* 158 (4): 568–83.

Municode Library. 2015. Code of Ordinances. https://www.municode.com/library/tx, accessed April 7, 2015.

Nash, Ogden. 1941. "Song of the Open Road." In *The Face Is Familiar: The Selected Verse of Ogden Nash*. Garden City, NY: Garden City Publishing, 21.

Nowlin, Caroline. 2012. "Hey! Look at Me: A Glance at Texas' Billboard Regulation and Why All Roads Lead to Compromise." *Texas Tech Law Review* 44: 429–61.

Outdoor Advertising Association of America. 2013. OOH Revenue by Format. http://www.oaaa.org/ResourceCenter/MarketingSales/Factsamp;Figures/Revenue/OOHRevenuebyFormat.aspx, accessed August 8, 2013.

Philip Morris Media and Leo Burnett. 1993. "Outdoor: It's Not a Medium, It's a Large." Adopt-A-Market. Houston. http://legacy.library.ucsf.edu/tid/mrp76e00/pdf, accessed October 14, 2013.

Purcell, Brian. 2013. Texas Highways Primer. http://www.texashighwayman.com/texhwys.shtml, accessed July 31, 2013.

Scenic Texas. 2013. Texas Counties: Billboard Facts. http://www.scenictexas.org/wpcontent/themes/uploads/County-Billboard-Facts.doc, accessed August 8, 2013.

Shaddock, Carroll. 2008. Cofounder, Billboards, Ltd. Oral history interview conducted on February 29, in Houston, Texas. Texas Legacy Project, Conservation History Association of Texas.

Sharpe, Susan. 2012. "'Between Beauty and Beer Signs': Why Digital Billboards Violate the Letter and Spirit of the Highway Beautification Act of 1965." *Rutgers Law Review* 64 (2).

Shepherd, Gloria. 2007. "Guidance on Off-Premise Changeable Message Signs." Federal Highway Administration, September 25. http://www.fhwa.dot.gov/real_estate/prac

titioners/oac/policy_and_guidance/ offprmsgsnguid.cfm, accessed August 15, 2013.

Texas Department of Transportation. 2015. Outdoor Advertising Signs, Off-Premise Signs Prohibited on Certain Highways: Transportation Code 391.252. https://ftp.dot.state.tx.us/ pub/txdot-info/row/scenic_prohibited .pdf, accessed April 10, 2015.

Trevino, Sam. 2013. Outdoor Advertising Compliance Agent, Texas Department of Transportation. Personal communication, August.

US Government Accountability Office. 1978. "Obstacles to Billboard Removal." CED-78-38, March 27.

http://www.gao.gov/products/ CED-78-38, accessed August 11, 2013.

———. 1985. "The Outdoor Advertising Control Program Needs to Be Reassessed." GAO/RCED-85-34, January 3. http://www.gao.gov/ assets/150/142372.pdf, accessed August 11, 2013.

US Government Printing Office. 1999. Unit Public Papers of the Presidents: Dwight Eisenhower, President's News Conference of April 17, 1957, p. 292. General Services Administration, National Archives and Records Service, Office of the Federal Register, Washington, DC.

Vespe, Frank. 1997. "High-Tech Billboards: The Same Old Litter on a Stick." *Journal of Public Policy and Marketing* (March 22).

Watson, Max, and Charles McMahen. 2008. "Letters: Why Subsidize Billboards?" *Houston Chronicle*, December 22.

White, Greg. 2015. Compliance Agent, Outdoor Advertising Regulatory Program, Right of Way, Texas Department of Transportation. Personal communication, April.

Wright, Lawrence. 2007. "Lady Bird's Lost Legacy." *New York Times*, July 20.

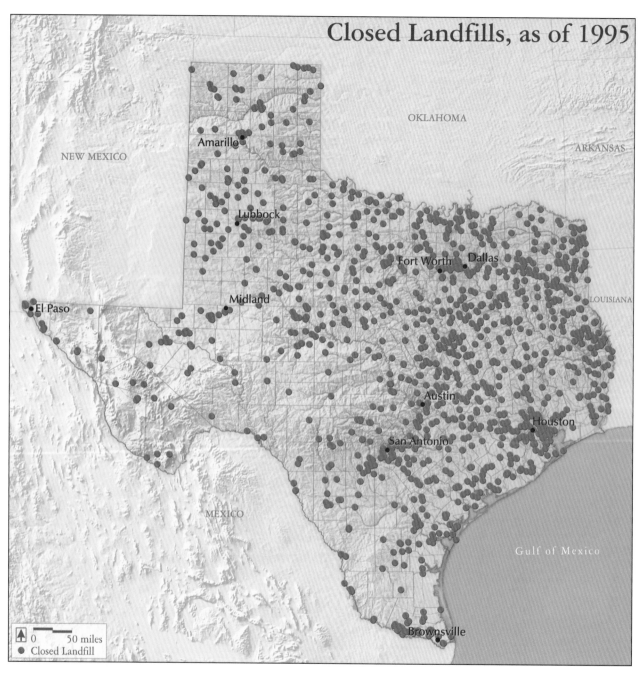

Closed Landfills, as of 1995

The map of closed landfills across Texas is the story of a (possibly belated) success. The map draws on the PERMAPP database and includes sites that had applied for or received a permit, as of 1995. Most had operated in the 1950s through the 1980s. Many of these landfills were originally located in places of convenience, such as ravines, brick pits, and sand and gravel mines. Many had serious problems with groundwater leakage, methane outgassing, litter, odors, and more. However, with passage of the Resource Conservation and Recovery Act in 1976 and development of ensuing regulations, over seven hundred of these older landfills closed, since they could not meet the new federal standards that required geotextile and clay liners, groundwater and off-gassing monitoring, and financial bonding (Rambaud 2012; Resource Conservation and Recovery Act, 42. U.S.C. § 6901 et seq.; TCEQ 2012; Schneider 2006; Untermeyer 2012).

Solid Waste

NIMBY, LULU, and NIABY

This is a small world; ecological benefits and harms are inevitably shared. Often, though, they are shared unequally, resulting in painful environmental injustice. The choice of solid waste sites is a good though troubling example. We sometimes read a shorthand, acronym-laced description of the problem. We learn that some places are protected by influential communities that cry out NIMBY! (Not In My Backyard!). We hear that other locales are surrendered repeatedly as "sacrifice zones" for LULUs (Locally Unwanted Land Uses). Neither approach is fair or sustainable, nor a complete view of the full story of environmental justice. Perhaps we can explore here how environmental justice has evolved in Texas and nationally, and how the debate is gradually, slowly shifting from discussions of NIMBY to NIABY (Not in Anyone's Backyard) (Brown 2004, 78).

Environmental Justice

Heartaches and debates over environmental inequity can be traced back at least as far as a tragic day in 1967, when an eight-year-old African American girl drowned at a garbage dump in the Sunnyside neighborhood of south Houston. Students at the nearby Texas Southern University campus protested, asking why a dump would be located in the middle of this community. The protest mixed with other racial tensions and riots broke out. Rocks, bottles, and gunshots were exchanged. A policeman was killed. Authorities arrested many of the student leaders and cleared nearly five hundred from the university dormitories. There was pain and anger on all sides (Bullard 2007, 218).

The Burdens of Bean

The issue arose again in 1979, not on the streets, but in a courtroom. The predominantly African American Northwood Manor neighborhood sued the state, challenging the health department's permit for the East Houston–Dyersdale Road municipal landfill (*Bean v. Southwestern Waste Management Corp.*, 482 F. Supp. 673, Southern District of Texas 1979, affirmed 782 F. 2d 1038 (5th Cir. 1986)). The *Bean* case, as it came to be known, was a trailblazer in the campaign for environmental justice. *Bean* is thought to be the first class action suit opposing a waste facility with the argument that its location had been chosen in a discriminatory way, as a violation of the neighbors' civil rights (Bullard and Johnson 2000, 556).

For the *Bean* case, research showed that all five city-owned garbage dumps in Houston, six of the eight local municipal garbage incinerators, and three of the four privately owned landfills were sited in African American neighborhoods (Bullard 1983). Yet at the time, African Americans made up only a quarter of Houston's population. The number of waste sites in African American neighborhoods seemed much higher than would be expected or considered fair. The *Bean* plaintiffs sought an injunction against the landfill's permit with the argument that the permit would be a violation of the Equal Protection clause of the US Constitution.

Yet ultimately, the claim failed due to two problems. First, there were difficulties in showing discriminatory intent: it was conceivable that the dump sites were chosen for their proximity to industrial facilities or for other nonracial factors. Also, there were perceived weaknesses in the statistical evidence: it was possible that the areas chosen for comparisons of racial makeup or distance to dump sites were not analogous (*Bean v. Southwestern Waste Management Corp.*, 482 F. Supp. 673, Southern District of Texas 1979, affirmed 782 F. 2d 1038 (5th Cir. 1986)). There was a high bar to show discrimination.

Warren County and Beyond

While the *Bean* claim was not successful in court, it did resonate among the public. Frustration with waste facility siting tied in with nonwhites' broader and longer-held anger over shortcomings in many governmental services to their neighborhoods. The waste facility siting problems seemed to be of a kind with police protection, schooling, and mass transit that were also seen as poor and unequal (Bullard 1983). The concerns over environmental racism raised in *Bean* were not unique to Houston, or other Texas communities. Similar controversy arose over the 1982 siting of a PCB landfill in Warren County, a rural area of North Carolina with a 75 percent African American population (Melosi 2001, 240). After a protest against the landfill ignited more than five hundred arrests, the US Government Accountability Office prepared a study on hazardous waste siting. The GAO report revealed that three-quarters of off-site commercial hazardous waste landfills in EPA's Region IV (which covers eight southern states) were located in predominantly African American communities, which made up only 20 percent of the region's total population (US GAO 1983, 1, 3).

A second and broader study, "Toxic Wastes and Race in the United States," was prepared by the United Church of Christ in 1987. It looked further, and found that this same pattern that had been found in Houston and in the eight southern states extended nationwide. Race was found to be the most powerful factor in predicting where waste sites, landfills, incinerators, and polluting industries might be located. Race was more influential for siting decisions than poverty, land values, or home ownership (Chavis and Lee 1987, xiii).

Texas Campaigns

The regional and national findings of bias were seen in local controversies across the country, including Texas. For example, in 1991, a grassroots group known as PODER became active in environmental justice work in Austin. PODER opposed and later removed a fuel storage tank complex in their predominantly Hispanic and African American, east Austin neighborhood. PODER later went on to confront a local waste-recycling facility, a metalwork and castings plant, a chip fabricator, and a power plant (Almanza 2003; Herrera 2003). Similar situations were playing out elsewhere, far beyond Austin. Beginning in 1992, an environmental law clinic at Texas Southern University took on environmental justice claims in cities across the state: College Station, Corpus Christi, Odessa, and Port Arthur (Hankins 1999).

Texas environmental justice concerns were appearing in smaller, rural communities as well. In 1992, Phyllis Glazer formed the nonprofit Mothers Organized to Stop Environmental Sins (MOSES). The MOSES group arose out of concern for the small, largely African American community of Winona that had been struggling with hazardous waste recycling, blending, and injection facilities for a number of years (Glazer 2000). Regional efforts, such as the Coalition for Justice in the Maquiladoras, took a hard look at the siting and behavior of plants in little towns and large cities along the Mexican border (Mika 2002). And a statewide effort grew up to connect some of these local campaigns, led by People against a Contaminated Environment, the Sierra Club, and other organizations (Malveaux 1999).

National Efforts

These Texas efforts did not happen in isolation. Similar campaigns were occurring across the country. In fact, a key national meeting was held in 1991, when the United Church of Christ convened over six hundred delegates for the first People of Color Environmental Leadership Summit (Melosi 2001, 240). African American, Asian American, Latino, and indigenous speakers at the meeting discussed the details and overarching patterns of environmental injustice. They voiced concerns about PCB facilities in North Carolina, chemical plants along the Mississippi, and maquiladora complexes in the Rio Grande Valley. The summit concluded by issuing the Principles of Environmental Justice, a list of essential rights to a clean environment that are shared by all peoples, regardless of color, culture, language, or belief (National People of Color

Environmental Leadership Summit 1991).

At the same time that public interest and neighborhood groups were speaking out against environmental injustice, governmental agencies were getting involved as well. In 1992, the EPA created the Office of Environmental Justice and, in 1993, established the National Environmental Justice Advisory Council (US EPA 1992a). In 1994, President Clinton issued an executive order mandating that federal agencies account and work for environmental justice in all their programs (Executive Order 12898, February 11, 1994).

Nevertheless, ten years later, a report found that efforts for improving environmental justice in the United States had stalled within the federal government, with inconsistent interpretations and weak implementations at the EPA (Carroll and Weber 2004, 7, 16). This critique of the agency's staffing and process turned out to be reflected in how hazardous facilities were actually being sited in the country, according to a 2007 report by the United Church of Christ. The church's analysis looked at industrial facility permits, together with data from the 2000 US Census, and found that many environmental justice challenges remained in the United States. For example, forty of the forty-four states with licensed and operating hazardous waste facilities continued to have racial disparities in the location of those sites (Bullard et al. 2007, 153).

Over 2,600 solid waste sites, including landfills, composters, recyclers, incinerators, transfer stations, processors, and other facilities were operating in Texas as of 2012 (Barnes 2012; TCEQ 2012).

Texas Sites

The church study noted that Texas also continued to suffer from these siting problems, in regard to both hazardous and municipal waste sites. Sixty-six percent of Texans in neighborhoods that hosted hazardous waste facilities were people of color, 19 percent higher than nonhost communities. In Houston, 79 percent of those living in host neighborhoods were people of color, 26 percent higher than those in nonhost neighborhoods (Bullard et al. 2007, 11, 61, 79). The siting of Texas solid waste facilities has also been skewed by ethnicity, as shown in the accompanying maps of Bexar, Harris, Tarrant, and Travis Counties. These maps indicate that whether intentional or not, fewer waste facilities are found in white neighborhoods, while predominantly nonwhite neighborhoods have more facilities

Siting Bias?

Nonwhite Population

- ☐ 0 to 10%
- ☐ 10 to 25%
- ☐ 25 to 50%
- ☐ 50 to 75%
- ■ over 75%
- ● Landfill

0 ——— 10 miles

Clustering

- ■ High-High
- ☐ High-Low
- ☐ Low-High
- ■ Low-Low
- ☐ Not Significant
- ● Landfill

0 ——— 10 miles

Significance Value

- ■ Very Significant (p = 0.01)
- ☐ Significant (p = 0.05)
- ☐ Not Significant
- ● Landfill

0 ——— 10 miles

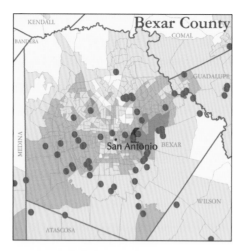

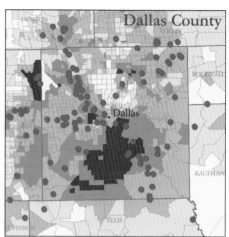

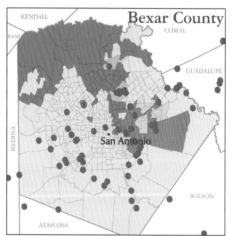

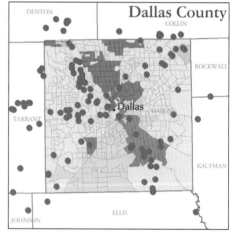

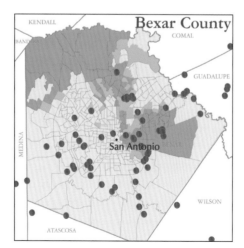

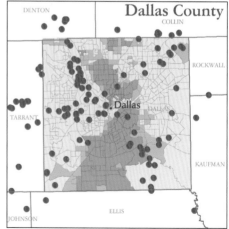

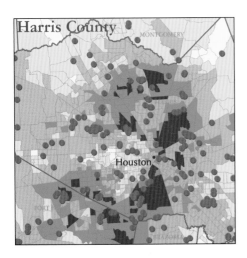

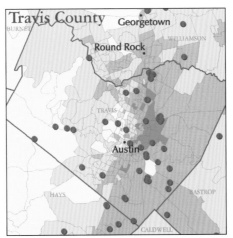

The maps in the top row of these two pages show the pattern of solid waste sites (as of 2012) and the ethnic makeup of census tracts (polled in 2010) in four major metropolitan areas of Texas: Bexar, Dallas, Harris, and Travis Counties. The US census data used here considers "nonwhite" to include those who identify themselves as African American, American Indian, Asian Indian, Chinese, Filipino, Japanese, Korean, Vietnamese, Guamanian or Chamorro, Samoan, "other Asian," "other Pacific Islander," or "other race."

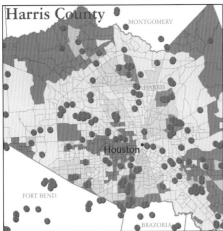

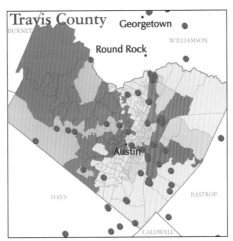

The maps in the middle row show the results of a Bivariate LISA cluster analysis. The BiLISA analysis looks at how the siting of solid waste facilities correlates with the location of nonwhite neighborhoods. Red ("high/high") indicates an area where there is a high number of sites and a high cluster of nonwhite neighbors; dark blue ("low/low") means that there is a low number of waste sites and a low number of nearby nonwhite residents.

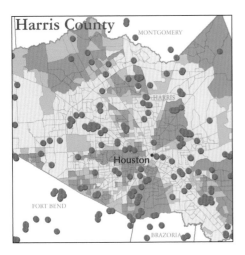

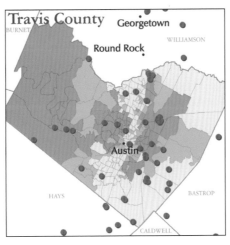

The maps in the bottom row show whether the spatial correlation of solid waste sites and nonwhite communities is significant, that is, nonrandom. The significant correlations are where high populations of waste sites coincide with high populations of nonwhite neighbors, or vice versa, where low counts of both exist. P-values of 0.01 (a lower probability that the correlation is random) are marked in dark green, while p-values of 0.05 (a higher, but still quite low, probability of a random correlation) are shown in light green. It is important to remember that a significant correlation between the location of waste sites and nonwhite areas does not necessarily show a causal relationship (Peter 2012; TCEQ 2012; US Census Bureau 2012).

nearby. This can probably be attributed, at least in part, to the fact that ethnic and environmental justice issues are not considered in state landfill regulations (Texas Administrative Code, Title 30, Part I; Worrall 2012).

Race and More

Race can often correlate with the location of solid waste sites. However, the burden of showing discriminatory intent and cause is very heavy. It is difficult to show that intentional racism is implicated since there are so many factors involved in siting. For instance, facilities may be built in areas where political opposition is weakest, because the nearby population is poor, scattered, or ill represented (Herndon 2006). Or, siting may track bottom-line costs, by going to locations where land is cheaper, particularly where parcels need to be large enough to allow an adequate buffer (Clark 2012). Similarly, siting may lean toward areas that have affordable infrastructure—the nearby roads and utilities that can support a facility. A waste site might also be chosen based on suitable geology, for instance, where low-permeability clay soils might protect against infiltration from a landfill (Worrall 2012). Finally, the location of a landfill or other industrial facility may just roll with the inertia of past decisions, of being sited in lands that are already dedicated to industrial purposes. Nevertheless, nonwhites are often poor, politically isolated, and found in the kind of industrial communities that

waste sites might settle in. It is much easier to see the results than to know the cause and aim. It is little comfort to know that these nonwhite neighbors could be victims of intent, or just casualties of a kind of heartless collateral damage.

Trash

This is a tough issue, and not one that will go away easily. Trash must always go somewhere. There is no escaping it entirely. Trash has been with us for time immemorial, as the many ancient shell middens that dot the Texas coast remind us. Moreover, the trash problem, apart from the siting issue, has grown. Garbage has mounded up as society has become more consumer oriented, as planned obsolescence has grown as a marketing strategy, and as disposable products have increasingly, and conveniently, arrived on store shelves. Hazardous waste aside, the growth of municipal waste alone has been impressive. Americans produce an amazing amount of garbage now, adding up to 7.1 pounds per day, per person, of trash, or some 102 tons over the course of a lifetime. This waste load amounts to twice the US rate of 1960, and close to three times the current rate in Japan (Humes 2012).

Landfills

The burgeoning amounts of garbage have led to larger and larger landfills. For instance, the Austin Community Landfill has a capacity of 39 million

cubic yards, over twenty-five times the volume of the Astrodome. Average landfill sizes in Texas have spread from 50 acres in 1986 to 190 acres in 2004, and their average height has jumped from just 13 feet to 69 feet in the same span of years (Schneider 2006). So in addition to the environmental justice problem of siting, society also needs to confront the question of how we can reduce the amount of garbage we generate. In the words of the mantra, can we effectively "reduce, reuse, and recycle"? Can we turn from arguments over "not in my backyard" to strategies for "not in anyone's backyard"?

Diversion

A number of larger Texas cities have tried to answer this "Don't Mess with Texas" charge. Many now have pay-as-you-throw trash pricing, curbside and single-stream recycling, and hazardous waste collection efforts. Some cities even take their sludge, lawn clippings, Christmas trees, and other organics and whip them up into a soil amendment (Dillo-Dirt in Austin and Hou-Actinite in Houston). In these ways, cities are reducing the amount of garbage they toss. In addition, some private companies, such as Dell, are promoting recycling of electronic waste laden with heavy metals and organic solvents (Schneider 2012). As a result, landfill diversion rates are climbing, albeit slowly, and with varied success among the state's leading cities. In 2011, Austin reported a landfill diversion rate of

This map shows the location of the 190-odd active landfills in Texas, as of 2011, illustrating the pattern, the scatter and density, of operating landfills throughout the state. The intent is that we also get a sense of the huge mark these landfills leave on the Texas landscape. The size and color of the map symbols indicates how the permitted volume of the given landfill compares with the Great Pyramid of Giza, the last survivor of the Seven Wonders of the Ancient World. Think of this: many of these landfills may well turn out to be the biggest and longest-lasting monuments of our age (Barnes 2012; TCEQ 2012).

The Great Pyramid of Giza was one of the Seven Wonders of the Ancient World, yet is small in comparison to many modern-day landfills (Hooper 1900).

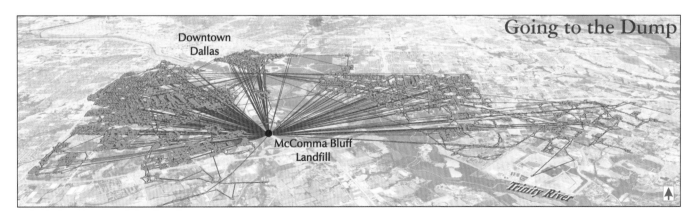

This map shows the movement of trash trucks out from their depot, through the community, and on to the McComma Bluff landfill. In a sense, this map illustrates the classic traveling salesman problem of finding how one can move most efficiently through one's route, whether selling encyclopedias, Fuller brushes, or in this case, moving solid waste. Perhaps the map also reminds us that black or white, Hispanic or Anglo or Asian, certain neighborhoods bear the brunt of solid waste disposal that benefits the entire city (Bonner 2012; City of Dallas 2012).

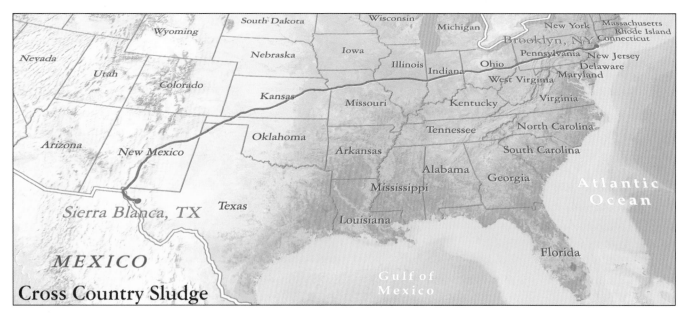

From 1992 to 2001, New York City sludge regularly made a 2,100-mile trip to Sierra Blanca, Texas. Its journey began with a barge from Brooklyn, led to a train from Jersey City, then a ride on the Union Pacific railroad to El Paso, and finally a shuttle by work train to Sierra Blanca. The route is approximate, as the path varied regularly, depending on the itinerary for other deliveries (Addington 2001; Lamarche 2012).

38 percent (City of Austin 2012). However, Houston recently reported a diversion rate of only 19 percent, and San Antonio had just an 18 percent diversion rate (City of Houston 2008; City of San Antonio 2011). Disparities occur within a single city too. Overall, Dallas diverted 7 percent from its landfills, but did much better, reaching 30 percent diversion, among single-family residents (City of Dallas 2012).

There is recognition that Texas residents can do better. Some Texas municipalities have high goals for the future. For example, the city of San Antonio has developed a plan to increase recycling from 18 percent to 60 percent by 2020 (City of San Antonio 2010). Meanwhile, the city of Dallas has set a goal of diverting 84 percent of trash headed to landfills by 2040, while the city of Austin has promised to reduce the amount of waste reaching landfills in 2040 by 90 percent (Swartswell 2012; City of Austin 2011). That would certainly be progress!

Poo-Poo Choo-Choo

Many siting controversies, like those mentioned above, are fought out as nasty, but relatively local, affairs within a single city or county. However, in at least one case, these questions of waste, place, and environmental justice were played out on a national stage. This story began in New York City. From 1924 through 1987, the city had been barging sludge from its sewage treatment plants and unloading it twelve miles offshore, in waters about ninety feet deep. The dumped sludge caused problems. Measurements turned up high bacterial levels and contaminated sediments at the disposal site. Agencies had to close polluted shellfish beds nearby. Reports began to come in about waste rolling up on New Jersey beaches. As a result, the ocean disposal site was moved in 1986 to a location farther offshore, to a site 115 miles east of New York, in waters about 7,500 feet deep. Two years later, Congress took the additional step of passing the Ocean Dumping Ban Act and signaling a nationwide end to offshore disposal (US EPA 1992b; Ocean Dumping Ban Act, P.L. 100-688, Title 1, 1988).

By 1992, New York had built dewatering plants and embarked on an effort to use land application to dispose of the sludge. The city hired Merco Joint Ventures for $168 million to find a spot to put the city's sludge. Merco in turn proposed disposal in Oklahoma and Arizona but was rebuffed by local opposition. However, the firm ultimately succeeded in finding a disposal site, and it turned out to be about ninety miles southeast of El Paso, near Sierra Blanca, Texas. There, Merco bought a failed resort and an 81,000-acre tract called Mile-High Ranch, gained a permit in record time (twenty-three days), and began spreading sludge in July of 1992. And it was a lot of sludge. Trains of fifty flatcars (affectionately known as the Poo-Poo Choo-Choo) arrived three times a week at the Merco site, bringing 250 tons of wet sludge per day at first, increasing to 400 tons per day by 1997 (Yardley 2001).

Some liked the jobs and payroll that the Merco operation brought to Sierra Blanca. Some people were excited that spreading the sludge was recycling "in its truest form," and was "enhancing the natural grass growth" (Grissom 2007; Yardley 2001). However, others felt that the disposal operation was abusive, threatening the air quality, groundwater, and public health of the region (Grissom 2007). Critics also believed that Merco, New York City, and the state of Texas were taking advantage of a small (553 residents), poor (46 percent below poverty levels), and minority (65 percent

Hispanic) community (US Census Bureau 2012).

In 1994 and 1999, Merco violated waste regulations and caught the attention of a prominent EPA whistleblower, Hugh Kaufman. Kaufman argued that the sludge was dangerous, declaring, "The fishes off of New York are being protected. The citizens and land of New York are being protected, and the people of Texas are being poisoned. Something is rotten in Texas" (Silverman 2007, 108–10). Local opposition from Sierra Blanca grocer and landowner Bill Addington and others grew (Addington 2001; Oliver 2001). In 1997, Sierra Blanca activists filed a civil rights complaint with the EPA against the permitting agency, the Texas Natural Resources Conservation Commission (Sze 2007, 63). Debates over the Merco operation in this remote town gained the notice of statewide media, including the *Texas Observer* and *Texas Monthly*, as well as the press back in New York City, the source of the gunk in the first place (Blakeslee 1997; Sharp 1992; Myerson 1995). Some of this unwelcome attention found its way to court: Michael Moore's lampooning TV show, *Sludge Train*, led to a defamation suit (*Merco Joint Venture v. Kaufman*, 923 F. Supp. 924 (W.D. Texas, 1996); *Scalamandre v. Kaufman*, 113 F. 3d 556 (5th Cir. 1997)). The controversy finally wound down in 2001, when New York City officials canceled the contract, claiming that the 2,065-mile disposal project was no longer cost effective. Shortly afterward, Merco

went bankrupt and then closed and sold the Sierra Blanca site (Royte 2005, 214, 215).

Questions after Sierra Blanca

Still, the question lingers, whether in Sierra Blanca or elsewhere, how do we fairly and sustainably deal with our solid waste? How do we keep situations like this one, shared by a small West Texas town and the Big Apple, from arising again? Perhaps the answer is in some combination of simply making less waste and caring more for our neighbors.

Rev. Roy Malveaux, pastor of the Shining Star Baptist Church, Beaumont, Texas, and director of People against a Contaminated Environment (PACE), explained the moral and religious foundation for environmental justice in this way: "Every man is my neighbor, because we're all tied together. We don't live an isolated life. We cannot live isolated from one another. And therefore, if I view you as my brother then I'm going to do all I can to keep from harming you" (Malveaux 1999).

Sources

Addington, Bill. 2001. Oral history interview conducted on March 28, in Sierra Blanca, Texas. Texas Legacy Project, Conservation History Association of Texas.

Almanza, Susana. 2003. Oral history interview conducted on October 16, in

Austin, Texas, Texas Legacy Project, Conservation History Association of Texas.

Barnes, Diane. 2012. Special Assistant, MSW Permits Section, Texas Commission on Environmental Quality. Personal communication, November.

Bean v. Southwestern Waste Management Corp., 482 F.Supp. 673 (1979).

Blakeslee, Nate. 1997. "The West Texas Waste Wars." *Texas Observer*, March 28.

Bonner, Vera. 2012. Sanitation Services, City of Dallas. Personal communications, October and November.

Brown, Phil. 2004. "Popular Epidemiology, Toxic Waste, and Social Movements." In *The Sociology of Health and Illness: A Reader*, edited by Michael Bury and Jonathan Gabe. New York: Routledge.

Bullard, Robert D. 1983. "Solid Waste Sites and the Black Houston Community." *Sociological Inquiry* 53 (2–3): 273–88.

———. 1993. "Environmental Justice for All." In *Environmental Justice and Communities of Color*, edited by Robert Bullard. San Francisco: Sierra Club Books.

———. 1994. *Dumping in Dixie: Race, Class, and Environmental Quality.* Boulder, CO: Westview Press.

———. 2007. "Dumping on Houston's Black Neighborhoods." In *Energy Metropolis: An Environmental History of Houston and the Gulf Coast*, edited by Martin Melosi and Joseph Pratt. Pittsburgh: University of Pittsburgh Press.

Bullard, Robert D., and Glenn S. Johnson. 2000. "Environmental Justice: Grassroots Activism and Its Impact on Public Policy Decision Making." *Journal of Social Issues* 56 (3): 555–78.

Bullard, Robert D., Paul Mohai, Robin Saha, and Beverly Wright. 2007. "Toxic Wastes and Race at Twenty, 1987–2007." Justice and Witness Ministries, United Church of Christ. Cleveland, Ohio.

Carroll, Daniel J., and Steven J. Weber. 2004. "EPA Needs to Consistently Implement the Intent of the Executive Order on Environmental Justice." Report No. 2004-P-00007, March 1. Office of the Inspector General, US Environmental Protection Agency. Washington, DC.

Chavis, Benjamin F., Jr., and Charles Lee. 1987. "Toxic Wastes and Race in the United States." Commission for Racial Justice, United Church of Christ, New York.

City of Austin. 2011. Austin Resource Recovery Master Plan, December 15. http://www.austintexas.gov/sites/default/files/files/Trash_and_Recycling/MasterPlan_Final_12.30.pdf, accessed November 7, 2012.

———. 2012. Austin Resource Recovery Annual Report: January–December 2011.

City of Dallas. 2012. Local Solid Waste Management Plan. City of Dallas, Transportation and Environment Committee, August 14. http://www.dallascityhall.com/committee_briefings/briefings0812/TEC_LocalSolidWasteMgmtPlan_081412.pdf, accessed November 5, 2012.

City of Houston. 2008. City Recycling Gets $1 Million Boost. Office of the Controller. http://www.houstontx.gov/controller/mail/Newt0808.htm, accessed November 5, 2012.

City of San Antonio. 2010. Ten-Year Recycling and Resource Recovery Plan for Residential and Commercial Services. City of San Antonio Solid Waste Management. June 24. http://www.sanantonio.gov/swmd/documents/2020Plan%20_6_1.pdf, accessed November 5, 2012.

Clark, H. C. 2012. Professor of Geophysics, retired, Rice University. Personal communication, October.

Executive Order 12898, Federal Register Vol. 59, No. 32 (February 16, 1994).

Glazer, Phyllis. 2000. Oral history interview conducted on October 21, in Winona, Texas. Texas Legacy Project, Conservation History Association of Texas.

Grissom, Brandi. 2007. "Sierra Blancans again Debate Possible Sludge Dump." *El Paso Times*, July 15.

Hankins, Grover. 1999. Oral history interview conducted on October 6, in Houston, Texas. Texas Legacy Project, Conservation History Association of Texas.

Herndon, Tootsie. 2006. Oral history interview conducted on February 21, in Spofford, Texas. Texas Legacy Project, Conservation History Association of Texas.

Herrera, Sylvia. 2003. Oral history interview conducted on October 16, in Austin, Texas. Texas Legacy Project, Conservation History Association of Texas.

Hooper, Franklin. Circa 1900. "Views, Objects: Egypt. Gizeh. View 03: Institute. Egypt." Brooklyn Museum Archives, Lantern Slide Collection. Item S10_08_Egypt_Gizeh03_SL1. http://www.brooklynmuseum.org/opencollection/archives/image/19314/image, accessed November 14, 2012.

Humes, Edward. 2012. *Garbology: Our Dirty Love Affair with Trash*. New York: Avery.

Lamarche, Alejandra. 2012. Department of Environmental Protection, City of New York. Personal communication, November.

Malveaux, Reverend Roy. 1999. Oral history interview conducted on October 8, in Beaumont, Texas. Texas Legacy Project, Conservation History Association of Texas.

Melosi, Martin. 2001. *Effluent America: Cities, Industry, Energy, and the Environment*. Pittsburgh: University of Pittsburgh Press.

Mika, Susan. 2002. Oral history interview conducted on April 17, in San Antonio, Texas. Texas Legacy Project, Conservation History Association of Texas.

Myerson, Allen. 1995. "Flood of Money Wins an Uneasy Home in Texas for New York City Waste." *New York Times*, July 17.

National People of Color Environmental Leadership Summit. 1991. Principles of Environmental Justice. Washington, DC. Adopted October 27.

Oliver, Gary. 2001. Oral history interview conducted on March 31, in Marfa, Texas. Texas Legacy Project, Conservation History Association of Texas.

Peter, Brad. 2012. Geographer. Statistical analysis and mapping. Personal communication, October.

Rambaud, Fabienne. 2012. Municipal Solid Waste Permits, Waste Permits Division, Texas Commission on Environmental Quality. Personal communication, October.

Royte, Elizabeth. 2005. *Garbage Land: On the Secret Trail of Trash*. New York: Little, Brown.

Schneider, Robin. 2006. "Texas Trash Rules Matter." Texas Campaign for the Environment and Public Research Works. Austin, Texas. January.

———. 2012. Executive Director, Texas Campaign for the Environment. Personal communication, October.

Sharp, Patricia. 1992. "Sludge Happens." *Texas Monthly*, December.

Silverman, David. 2007. *You Can't Air That: Four Cases of Controversy and Censorship in American Television Programming*. Syracuse, NY: Syracuse University Press.

Swartswell, Nick. 2012. "Dallas Looks at How to Produce Less Trash." *New York Times*, September 20.

Sze, Julie. 2007. *Noxious New York: The Racial Politics of Urban Health and Environmental Justice*. Cambridge, MA: MIT Press.

Texas Commission on Environmental Quality. 2012. Municipal Solid Waste Sites / Landfills. http://www.tceq.state.tx.us/assets/public/gis/exports/msw.zip, accessed August 22, 2014.

Untermeyer, Cheryl. 2012. Waste Permits Division, Texas Commission on Environmental Quality. Personal communication, November.

US Census Bureau. 2012. American Factfinder. http://factfinder2.census.gov/faces/nav/jsf/pages/index.xhtml, accessed November 9, 2012.

US Environmental Protection Agency (EPA). 1992a. "Environmental Equity: Reducing Risk for all Communities." EPA230-R-92-008A. Policy, Planning and Evaluation, US Environmental Protection Agency. June.

———. 1992b. "Reilly in New York to Mark End of Sewage Dumping." Press Release, June 30. http://www.epa.gov/history/topics/mprsa/03.html, accessed November 9, 2012.

US Government Accountability Office (GAO). 1983. "Siting of Hazardous Waste Landfills and Their Correlation with Racial and Economic Status of Surrounding Communities." Report GAO/RCED-83-168. June 1. Gaithersburg, Maryland.

Wahl, D., and R. L. Bancroft. 1975. "Solid Waste Management Today: Bringing about Municipal Change." *Nation's Cities* 13 (August): 18–32.

Worrall, John. 2012. Environmental services consultant. Personal communication, October.

Yardley, Jim. 2001. "New York's Sludge Was a Texas Town's Gold." *New York Times*, July 27.

Colonias

In Spanish, "colonia" means a community or neighborhood. Along the US-Mexico border, however, the word has taken on a different meaning. There, it is a settlement without potable water, sewage treatment, trash collection, paved roads, electricity, or safe and clean housing. In that sense, colonias also remind us of the importance of the environmental infrastructure and policies that we all need to keep our families, friends, and towns healthy.

While California, Arizona, and New Mexico host many colonias (roughly 33 in California, 123 in Arizona, and 129 in New Mexico), Texas is home to the largest number (HUD 2012). Approximately 500,000 Texans live in roughly 1,800 colonias in the state. Most are found in Hidalgo (44 percent) and El Paso (22 percent) Counties (Donelson and Esparza 2010, 3; Martinez 2010, 17; Federal

"A colonia is a shantytown that has sprung up, perhaps near an arroyo. . . . It has sprung up without any kind of sewage infrastructure, or water infrastructure. It is simply the will to have a place to live." —Meg Guerra, March 2, 2000, San Ygnacio, Texas (Guerra 2000; Weisman 2000)

A child plays in a colonia near Edinburg, Texas, on March 6, 1989 (Pogue 2012).

Reserve Bank of Dallas 2015, 2; Peña and Rosenthal 2010, 176; Texas Secretary of State 2012; USDA and US EPA 2014, 5). Studies suggest that Texas border colonias represent the largest concentration of people living without basic sanitation in the United States (Henneberger, Carlisle, and Paup 2010, 102).

Colonias grew out of Hispanic labor camps that provided contract ranch work and railroad construction in South Texas during the early 1900s (Wilson and Menzies 1997). Colonias spread in the 1960s as cotton farming and other agricultural uses of land along the border declined (Hill 2003, 146–47). Farmers and ranchers sold their excess or flood-prone lands to real estate developers who subdivided and resold small lots for low prices, perhaps $1,000 down, and $1,000 per year. Many were bought for residential use.

From the 1960s on, colonias grew rapidly. Increased immigration to the borderlands, fueled by the pressures of high unemployment and low wages in Latin America, was one factor driving their growth. American policy changes, starting as early as the Bracero farmworker program (1942), and continuing through the passage of the Immigration Reform Control Act (1986) and NAFTA (1994), also played a role in the greater numbers of migrants coming across the border (Immigration Reform Control Act, P. L. 99-603, November 6, 1986; Mexican Contract Labor Program Agreement, August 4, 1942; North American Free Trade Agreement, 32 I.L.M. 289 (1993); Ward 1999, 19, 70, 89). Primarily, though, colonias have not been so much a creature of immigration (only 15 percent of their residents are not US citizens) but more one of poverty and a shortage of affordable housing (Henneberger, Carlisle, and Paup 2010, 102).

Agua Dulce, Bougainvillea, Buena Vista, Country Aire Estates, Desert Meadows Estates, Enchanted Valley Ranch, Green Valley Acres, Homestead Meadows, Hueco Mountain Estates, Inspiration Heights, Plantation Oaks, Pleasant Valley Ranch, Rabbit Patch, Royal Palms Estates, Serene Acres, Southern Breeze, Spring Gardens and Stardust are examples of romantic but ironic colonia names in Texas. (USDA and US EPA 2014, 29–40)

Disease

In the late 1980s, concerns began to rise about colonias and the people who lived there. Disease outbreaks became a central worry. With a lack of safe drinking water, sewage treatment, and drainage improvements, colonias suffered from high rates of measles, hepatitis A, rubella, rabies, shigellosis, salmonella, tuberculosis, and dengue fever (May 2010, 164; Peña and Rosenthal 2010, 178; USDA and US EPA 2014, 14). The problems of poor community infrastructure and overcrowding

Colonias in the Borderlands

Here is a general overview of colonia locations known as of 2007, and found across the entire stretch of the US-Mexico border. Colonias exist in Texas, New Mexico, Arizona, and California, as well as the Mexican states of Baja California, Sonora, Chihuahua, Coahuila, Nuevo Leon, and Tamaulipas. The settlements often lack potable water, sanitary sewage treatment, adequate flood drainage, decent housing, and all-weather road access (Falk 2012; Kincy 2012; Parcher 2012; Parcher and Humberson 2007).

A birds-eye view reveals a colonia near Matamoros in the state of Tamaulipas, Mexico, as seen March 15, 1993 (Pogue 2012).

certainly raised health risks for residents of the colonias. However, their health troubles were also aggravated by the risks that many faced in their day-to-day work with chemicals and heavy equipment in crop fields and maquiladoras (Mika 2002).

Health Care

Moreover, medical care for many illnesses in the colonias was lacking, worsening the health problems that already existed. Health care in the colonias could be poor due to several reasons, mostly economic. Research has shown that colonia residents in Cameron, El Paso, Hidalgo, Maverick, Starr, and Webb Counties suffer from high unemployment (48 percent higher than non-colonia residents) and low pay (42 percent live in poverty) (Federal Reserve Bank of Dallas 2015, 2). Also, prior to recent Affordable Health Care Act initiatives, many residents carried no or minimal health insurance. Surveys suggest that roughly 42 percent of those living in the colonias of Starr and Hidalgo Counties had no coverage (Rogers 1993; Martinez 2010, 17; May 2010, 165; Ortiz, Arizmendi, and Llewellyn 2004).

Utilities

While working conditions and health care options have created serious problems in the colonias, many of the public health problems in the colonias trace back to land use issues. For instance, colonia infrastructure has often been lacking. In many cases, the original developers did not provide those improvements, in part to save costs, but also because the local governments did not require the infrastructure. For many years, the state of Texas did not grant counties the ordinance-making powers that would have required utilities in these rural areas (Donelson and Esparza 2010, 103). Later, the fault probably lay more with municipalities and counties. These local governments were unwilling to extend services to the distant and scattered areas where colonias were often found, sometimes due to the cost, but in some cases due to alleged bias among Anglo community leaders. In a Catch-22, connecting utilities to the makeshift homes in colonias has sometimes even been illegal, since the

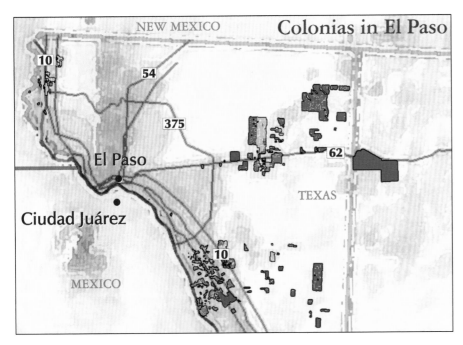

Colonias in El Paso

There are over 1,800 colonias in Texas, home to more than 400,000 people. These maps give a detailed view of the colonias located in the El Paso area and the Lower Rio Grande Valley, where the majority of the state's colonias are found. They are classified by color, current as of 2007. Red means that a given colonia lacks adequate wastewater disposal, does not have a potable water supply, or is not platted. Yellow signifies a colonia with potable water and adequate wastewater treatment, but with insufficient trash collection, unpaved roads, or inadequate drainage. Green colonias have platted records, potable water, adequate sewage treatment and trash collections, paved roads, and adequate drainage. A blue marking indicates that data are not available for the colonia (Falk 2012; Kincy 2012; Parcher 2012; Parcher and Humberson 2007; Texas Legislative Budget Board 2012).

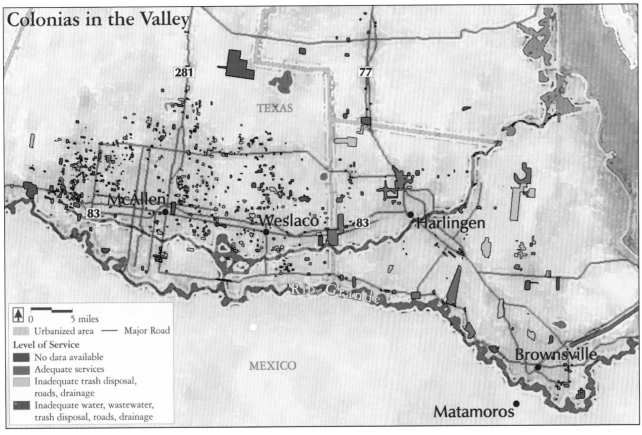

Colonias in the Valley

Level of Service

- No data available
- Adequate services
- Inadequate trash disposal, roads, drainage
- Inadequate water, wastewater, trash disposal, roads, drainage

buildings (tents, trailers, or structures of found materials, including cardboard or trash) may not have met code (Attorney General of Texas 2015).

Financing

Part of the concern about colonias has also been about abusive financial terms. For instance, many of the colonia tracts had been sold at high interest rates through "contracts for deeds," beginning as early as the 1950s (Ward, Way, and Wood 2012, 4: 1–2). Unlike standard mortgages, these contracts kept ownership of the land with the seller until the entire purchase price was paid. In this situation, if the buyer was late in his or her payments, the seller could repossess the property, including improvements. Often, the sales contracts allowed repossession to occur with only forty-five days' notice and without going through a typical foreclosure. In one Texas border county, these sales contracts failed 45 percent of the time, a much higher rate than the 6.4 percent level typical for institutional loans (Ward, Way, and Wood 2012, vii). Repossessing and flipping lots have destabilized colonias and undermined long-term investments in making the communities safe and healthy (Ward, Way, and Wood 2012, iv, 5: 39).

Help

Much of the challenge for colonias was likely due to their low visibility. Often sited in rural, isolated loca-

tions, colonias' difficulties were frequently little known, or at least easily ignored. However, reporters for the press and advocates with a variety of public interest groups (including the El Paso Interreligious Sponsoring Organization [EPISO], the Border Organization, and Valley Interfaith in the Rio Grande Valley) began to bring attention to the plight of the colonias in the early 1980s (Applebome 1989). Nonprofit and governmental efforts to improve conditions in the colonias followed at the local, state, and national levels.

Promotores

Some programs in the colonias have dealt with immediate health problems, often through paid and volunteer community health workers, also known as *promotores*. Early examples included Migrant Health Promotion, which was brought to the Rio Grande Valley in 1983 by the nonprofit Midwest Migrant Health Information Office. Somewhat later, in 1994, the Sisters of Charity established the Clínica Guadalupe on the outskirts of El Paso (Peña and Rosenthal 2010, 186–87).

Buildings

Work has also focused on repairing and improving individual buildings, often with sweat equity. For example, in the colonia of El Cenizo, in the Lower Rio Grande Valley, residents used funds in 1998 from lot payments, legal settlements, and Texas

Bootstrap Program loans to erect substantial brick homes and to install indoor plumbing (Henneberger, Carlisle, and Paup 2010, 112; Texas Legislative Budget Board 2012, 149; Texas Department of Housing and Community Affairs 2012). Self-help and state programs have been important here, but federal support has been helpful too. The US Department of Agriculture—Rural Development has distributed funds for bathrooms and plumbing, as well as water and wastewater systems, among the colonias (Federal Reserve 1997, 28).

Communities

Other efforts have targeted bringing water supplies, wastewater treatment, and other services to colonia communities as a whole. One early campaign began in 1967, with the Colonias del Valle's sweat-equity, hands-on work to bring drinking water lines to the Hidalgo County colonias (Wilson and Menzies 1997). Other efforts were more political. For instance, EPISO helped register more than 20,000 new El Paso area voters in 1987, pressuring the city council to extend water service to local colonias, using loans from the Texas Water Development Board (Cook 198; S.B. 2, Ch. 624, Regular Session, 71st Leg. and Texas Water Code, chaps. 15 and 16). In very recent years, market economics have played a role. The shale oil boom along the Texas-Mexico border has heightened interest among municipalities in annexing, collecting tax, and providing services to the now-valuable land under the colonias (Salinas 2015, 187).

Federal funding has had a hand in improving infrastructure too: the Cranston-Gonzalez Affordable Housing Act of 1990 directed major block grant funding to the colonias (Parcher and Humberson 2007, 3; Cranston-Gonzalez Affordable Housing Act, P. L. 101-625, November 28, 1990). As well, some of the support has come from the international arena. For example, the 1994 passage of NAFTA led to creation of the Border Environmental Cooperative Commission (19 U.S.C. § 3473). In turn, the commission helped coordinate and design environmental infrastructure, with financing from the North American Development Bank (22 U.S.C. Chapter 7, Subchapter XXVIII; Federal Reserve 1997, 28).

Developers

Perhaps some of the most crucial work has focused on breaking the cycle, by slowing unscrupulous developers' creation of yet more colonias. Some of the first state legislation was enacted in 1987, requiring subdivision plat filing and approval on the local level (S.B. 408, Ch. 1102, Regular Session, 70th Leg.; S.B. 896, Ch. 149, Regular Session, 70th Leg.). In 1989, the legislature went further, creating the Economically Distressed Areas Program, and enabling more direct state involvement. The program gave more affordable infrastructure funding, and critically, required developers to provide safe drinking water and sewer services (S.B. 2, Ch. 624, Regular Session, 71st Leg.). In 1995, the state passed the Colonia Fair Land Sales Act, which improved disclosure about purchases of colonia tracts and eased conversion of "contracts for deed" to better-protected, conventional mortgages (S.B. 336, Ch. 994, Regular Session, 74th Leg.). Finally, the Texas Office of the Attorney General has had an ongoing litigation program to control colonias by enforcing rules on subdividing, selling, and providing utilities to residential lots (Attorney General of Texas 2015).

Progress?

In these ways, over the past generation, long strides have been made in upgrading housing, water, wastewater, drainage, and health care in the colonias, through bootstrap efforts, grant funds, loan programs, and regulatory enforcement. However, along with poverty, colonias persist, popping up in a black market, as "pirate" settlements that both serve and prey on the poor.

Sources

Applebome, Peter. 1989. "At Texas Border, Hopes for Sewers and Water." *New York Times*, January 3.

Attorney General of Texas. 2015. Historical Sketch of Laws Related to Colonias Remediation and Prevention. Consumer Protection Division, Attorney General of Texas. https://www.texasattorneygeneral.gov/cpd/historical-laws-colonias, accessed June 10, 2015.

Cook, Alison. 1988. "Just Add Water." *Texas Monthly*, May.

Donelson, Angela, and Adrian Esparza, ed. 2010. *The Colonias Reader: Economy, Housing, and Public Health in U.S.-Mexico Border Colonias.* Tucson: University of Arizona Press.

Falk, David. 2012. Division Chief, Legal Technical Support Division, Office of the Attorney General, Texas. Personal communication, July.

Federal Reserve Bank of Dallas. 1997. "Texas Colonias: A Thumbnail Sketch of the Conditions, Issues, Challenges and Opportunities." http://www.dallasfed.org/assets/documents/cd/pubs/colonias.pdf, accessed June 6, 2012.

Federal Reserve Bank of Dallas. 2015. "Las Colonias in the 21st Century: Progress along the Texas-Mexico Border." Community Development, Federal Reserve Bank of Dallas. April. http://www.dallasfed.org/assets/documents/cd/pubs/lascolonias.pdf, accessed June 11, 2015.

Guerra, Maria "Meg." 2000. Oral history interview conducted March 2, in San Ygnacio, Texas. Texas Legacy Project, Conservation History Association of Texas.

Henneberger, John, Kristin Carlisle, and Karen Paup. 2010. "Housing in Texas Colonias." In Donelson and Esparza, *Colonias Reader*, 102–14.

Hill, Sarah. 2003. "Metaphoric Enrichment and Material Poverty: The Making of 'Colonias.'" In *Ethnography at the Border*, edited by Pablo Villa.

Minneapolis: University of Minnesota Press.

Kincy, Leon. 2012. GIS Analyst, Center for Health Statistics, Texas Department of State Health Services. Personal communication, June.

Martinez, O. J. 2010. "The U.S.-Mexico Border Economy." In Donelson and Esparza, *Colonias Reader*, 15–29.

May, Marlynn. 2010. "Living Betwixt and Between: Conditions of Health in Borderland Colonias." In Donelson and Esparza, *Colonias Reader*, 163–75.

Mika, Susan. 2002. Oral history interview conducted on April 17, in San Antonio, Texas. Texas Legacy Project, Conservation History Association of Texas.

Ortiz, Larry, Lydia Arizmendi, and Cornelius Llewellyn. 2004. "Access to Health Care among Latinos of Mexican Descent in Colonias in Two Texas Counties." *Journal of Rural Health* 20: 246–52.

Parcher, Jean. 2012. Senior International Relations Specialist, Land Remote Sensing, US Geological Survey. Personal communication, June.

Parcher, Jean, and Delbert Humberson. 2007. "CHIPS: A New Way to Monitor Colonias along the United States–Mexico Border." Open File Report 2007-1230. US Geological Survey.

Peña, Sergio, and Elizabeth Rosenthal. 2010. "Colonias Health Issues in Texas." In Donelson and Esparza, *Colonias Reader*, 176–89.

Pogue, Alan. 2012. Texas Center for Documentary Photography. Personal communication, June.

Rogers, George. 1993. "Cinco Colonia Areas: Baseline Conditions in the Lower Rio Grande Valley." Texas A&M University, Center for Housing and Urban Development.

Salinas, Alejandra. 2015. "Cleaning up the Colonias: Municipal Annexation and the Texas Fracking Boom." *Boston College Environmental Affairs Law Review* 42 (1): 163–94.

Texas Department of Housing and Community Affairs. 2012. Texas Bootstrap Loan Program. http://www.tdhca.state.tx.us/oci/bootstrap.jsp, accessed June 6, 2012.

Texas Legislative Budget Board. 2012. Fiscal Size-Up, 2012–13 Biennium, Submitted to the 82nd Texas Legislature, January. http://www.lbb.state.tx.us/Fiscal_SizeUp/Fiscal_SizeUp.pdf, accessed May 19, 2015.

Texas Secretary of State. 2012. Colonias FAQs. http://www.sos.state.tx.us/border/colonias/faqs.shtml, accessed June 5, 2012.

US Department of Agriculture (USDA) and US Environmental Protection Agency (EPA). 2014. U.S. Mexico Border Needs Assessment and Support Project: Phase I Scoping Assessment Report. April. http://www.rd.usda.gov/files/RD_RUS_Phase1ResearchRpt.pdf, accessed June 11, 2015.

US Department of Housing and Urban Development (HUD). 2012. Colonias, Houses, and Communities, U.S. Department of Housing and Urban Development. http://portal.hud.gov/hudportal/HUD?src=/program_offices/comm_planning/community development/programs/colonias, accessed June 7, 2012.

Ward, Peter. 1999. *Colonias and Public Policy in Texas and Mexico*. Austin: University of Texas Press.

Ward, Peter, Heather Way, and Lucille Wood. 2012. "Contract for Deed Prevalence Project." A Final Report to the Texas Department of Housing and Community Affairs. August.

Weisman, David. 2000. Maria "Meg" Guerra, March 2, San Ygnacio, Texas. Photograph. Digital image. Texas Legacy Project, Conservation History Association of Texas.

Wilson, Robert, and Peter Menzies. 1997. "The Colonias Water Bill: Communities Demanding Change." In *Public Policy and Community: Activism and Governance in Texas*, edited by R. Wilson, 229–74. Austin: University of Texas Press.

The Border and the Borderlands

The United States and Mexico share a vast 1,950-mile border that slices through landscape where wildlife and people have long lived, moved, and mixed. However, over the past twenty years, immigration, smuggling, cartel violence, and even terrorist fears have prompted efforts to close the border.

Immigration

There are political debates, but also undeniable facts, behind these concerns. Along the entire southwestern US boundary, the Border Patrol apprehended roughly 8.1 million people in the 2002–11 decade, and seized about

500 tons of smuggled drugs annually (US Department of Homeland Security 2012a; Powell 2008). Violence in Mexico has also increased concern along the border. Mexico has seen 50,000 die in organized crime disputes from 2006 to 2011, and 44 percent of those killed in 2011 died in

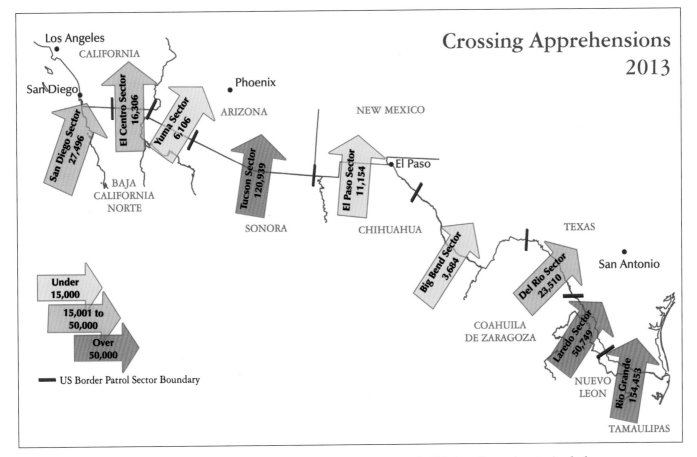

Apprehensions of illegal migrants crossing the US-Mexico border into Texas in 2013 fluctuated widely depending on the sector involved. Captures were highest in the Lower Rio Grande Valley and the Sonoran Desert (US Department of Homeland Security 2015a).

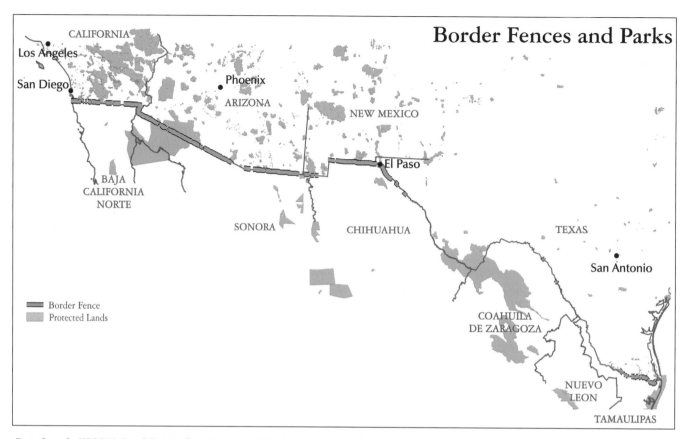

Border Fences and Parks

Data from the USGS National Gap Analysis Program and Mexican park system show that the border fence touches and affects a great deal of protected land on both sides of the border (Bezaury-Creel, Fco. Torres, and Ochoa-Ochoa 2007; Bezaury-Creel, Fco. Torres, Ochoa-Ochoa, Castro-Campos, and Moreno 2009; Corey 2014; Google Earth Pro 2015; Schwelling 2012; US Department of Homeland Security 2008; US Environmental Protection Agency 2013; US Geological Survey 2014).

the states bordering the United States (Molzahn, Rios, and Shirk 2012). The specter of international terrorism that arose after 9/11 also fueled fears about movement through the southwestern borderlands. During 2014, new worries rose from the sad sight of unaccompanied children coming to the border, in flight from gang violence in Latin America (Robles 2014).

Barriers

In response to these concerns, the federal government began trying to curtail illegal travel across the US-Mexico border. The effort began in 1990 when US Customs and Border Protection installed pedestrian barriers in the region south of San Diego, California (Abhat 2011; Clifford 2012). In 1994, President Clinton launched Operation Gatekeeper, rais-

ing Border Patrol presence along the California border (Nevins 2002). This program was followed by the 1996 passage of the Illegal Immigration Reform and Immigrant Responsibility Act (IIRIRA), which expanded the border-fencing program further and strengthened the kinds of barriers involved (Pub. L. 104-208, 110 Stat. 3009-3546, 104th Congress, September 30, 1996). IIRIRA required construction of 14 miles of triple-layered reinforced fencing near San Diego, with concrete and steel walls flanking a graded road tracking the border.

Waivers

However, there was resistance to the San Diego fence. In 2003, the California Coastal Commission signaled that completing the border wall within the Tijuana River National Estuarine Research Reserve would violate the federal Coastal Zone Management Act (16 U.S.C. §§ 1451–1464; California Coastal Commission 2003). Rebuking the commission, Congress passed the REAL ID Act in 2005 to allow the Secretary of Homeland Security to waive all "legal requirements such Secretary, in such Secretary's sole discretion, determines necessary to ensure expeditious construction of the barriers and roads under this section" (Pub. L. 109-13, 119 Stat. 302. 109th Congress, May 11, 2005). In 2006, the Secure Fence Act expanded the REAL ID Act's waiver powers beyond California, to extend them across the entirety of the US-Mexico border (Pub. L. 109-367, 120 Stat. 2638. 109th Congress. October 26, 2006).

Together, the REAL ID Act and Secure Fence Act greatly accelerated the construction of the border infrastructure throughout the southwestern United States. The two laws empowered the secretary of Homeland Security to waive all federal, state, and local laws to quickly build border fences and roads (Clark 2009). And, in fact, those powers did not lie idle for long. In 2007, Secretary Chertoff invoked the waiver rights beginning in the Barry Goldwater Range and the San Pedro Riparian National Conservation Area of Arizona (72 Fed. Reg. 2535–2536 (January 19, 2007); 72 Fed. Reg. 60870 (October 26, 2007)). In April 2008, with an unprecedented trumping of the nation's public health, safety, environmental, and cultural laws, the Department of Homeland Security (DHS) entered a wholesale waiver of thirty-five federal statutes across 500 miles of the US-Mexico border (73 Fed. Reg. 18293–18294 (April 3, 2008); Clark 2009). This was particularly alarming, considering that the border fence directly affected many protected lands and sensitive species.

The statutory waivers were followed by rapid condemnation of private property for the fence right-of-way. This was not so much of a factor in California, Arizona, and New Mexico, where the government owned many of the border properties. However, this was a significant and painful issue in Texas, where the fence route often passed through private land. Due process issues arose. In January 2008, DHS brought ex parte (that is, without the presence of the property owners) condemnation proceedings against six hundred Texas landowners who would not cooperate with agency surveys for wall construction (Von Drehle 2008;

This photograph of the border fence was taken near Brownsville, Texas, in February 2011 (Nottingham 2011).

Clark 2009). DHS actions also raised protests that the proposed fence routes avoided wealthy areas, and that seizures of some tracts were too quick and poorly compensated (Weber 2012). These concerns sparked a 2008 federal lawsuit by the Texas Border Coalition, a group of South Texas mayors and communities that sought, unsuccessfully, to block land acquisition and fence construction (Powell 2008).

The waiver of many of the typical regulations, and the streamlining of traditional processes affecting government projects, certainly sped construction of the border fence. Within just six years, over 670 miles of barriers were built along the border, at a cost of more than $2.4 billion (Stana 2009). This has become a huge structure, exceeding other famous fortifications such as Hadrian's Wall (73 miles) and the Korean DMZ (151 miles), and coming close in length to the 808-mile fence separating East and West Germany during the Cold War. Segments of the US-Mexico fence are now found in urban neighborhoods of San Diego, El Paso, and Brownsville, in the most remote areas of the Sonoran and Chihuahuan Deserts, in the heights of the mountains of the Sierra Madre, and in rich agricultural regions along the Colorado River and the Rio Grande.

The Texas Fence

One hundred and ten miles of wall exist in Texas currently, mostly in the Lower Rio Grande Valley, although some are in the El Paso area as well (McCorkle 2011). The fortified zone typically follows a sixty-foot-wide swath, with a barrier paralleled by cleared buffers and lit patrol roads (US Department of Homeland Security 2008). The original legislation required a more formidable pair of matching barriers, of which only 13.5 miles were built in Texas. In 2007, an amendment allowed the DHS flexibility to build a single line of fence, or take other measures (Senate Amendment 2480, Department of Homeland Security Appropriations Act, 2008, 110th Cong., 1st Session). The course of the barrier now swings between 100 feet from the border to as far as two miles away, depending on ownership, roads, canals, terrain, flooding issues, or other factors.

The fences themselves are substantial. They are typically fifteen to eighteen feet tall with three- to six-foot-deep foundations, and have been built with either no openings at all, or with gaps just one-half to 3 inches wide. In some cases, the barrier may be a wall, a fence, a levee (as in Hidalgo County), or a series of bollards (O'Brian 2011). As of January 2011, the majority of the fence is relatively porous and intended to just block vehicles, but tighter pedestrian fencing has stretched across 21 percent of the total

US-Mexico border. The more complete and impenetrable segments are located in the coastal ecoregions near the Pacific (62 percent of that segment) and Gulf of Mexico (48 percent) (Lasky, Jetz, and Keitt 2011).

Ties

The border fence was largely complete by 2010, but it had been inserted in an area that has long been a fluid place. For centuries, the US-Mexico border has seen frequent travel back and forth, bolstered by strong family, community, and economic ties joining the north and south sides of the boundary. This is especially true of the Lower Rio Grande Valley, where settlements have been established on both sides of the river since the mid-1700s, and many towns have kept close sister-city relationships across the border (Laredo and Nuevo Laredo, Reynosa and Hidalgo, or Brownsville and Matamoros). The fence has been particularly divisive for some families who live and farm close to the river. Almost two hundred US landowners in the Lower Rio Grande Valley have property trapped in the no-man's land between the American fence and the border with Mexico.

There are also strong ecological links between the north and south. Each side of the river originally shared a forest of Texas palmetto, sabal palm, and ebony-anaqua woodlands hosting more than 1,200 documented plant species. However, the integrity

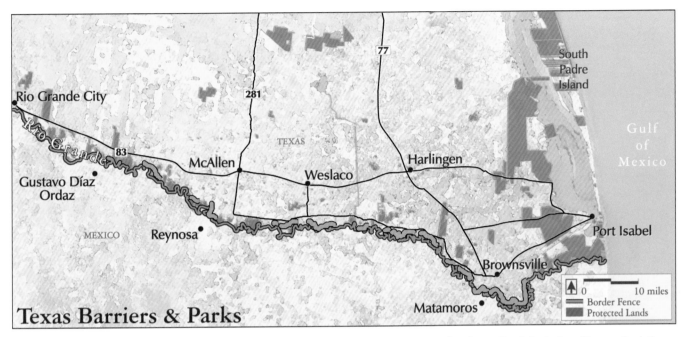

This detailed map shows the Texas border preserves in the Lower Rio Grande Valley, including those affected most directly by the fence (Bezaury-Creel, Fco. Torres, and Ochoa-Ochoa 2007; Bezaury-Creel et al. 2009; Corey 2014; Google Earth Pro 2015; Schwelling 2012; US Department of Homeland Security 2008; US EPA 2013; US Geological Survey 2014).

of this shared habitat has been fraying in recent years. Over the past century, both the American and Mexican sides of the fertile Lower Rio Grande Valley have been extensively developed as farmland, for cotton, citrus, and other crops. Now, less than 10 percent of the native riparian habitat remains (Reyes 2011). Public agencies and nonprofit conservation groups have recognized these trends, and have long worked to protect the valley's rich biota. Over the past thirty years, this public/private partnership has spent more than $150 million and worked toward restoring a 275-mile wildlife corridor of more than 180,000 acres, containing over 100 parcels, along the Lower Rio Grande (McCorkle 2011).

Walls and Parks

The rub has come in the last five years as the border fence and these Texas preserves have come into conflict. Over sixty of these parcels in the valley are now affected in some way by the border fence. The most directly affected preserves include private tracts owned by the National Audubon Society (Sabal Palm Grove), Gorgas Science Foundation (Rabb Plantation House), and the Nature Conservancy (Southmost Preserve). Impacts were also felt among many of the US Fish and Wildlife Service's sanctuaries, including numerous pieces of the Lower Rio Grande Valley National Wildlife Refuge. The preserves abut

the fence, levee, or other barrier; are severed by a segment of the wall; or are contained between the fence and the river. While the Fish and Wildlife Service prevailed on the Department of Homeland Security to insert about one hundred gaps in the fence in the Lower Rio Grande Valley, the openings are not large enough for many creatures. There is concern that the fence will fragment the habitat and disrupt the wildlife corridor that these preserves had been designed to maintain. In addition, critics worry that the wall will hinder the 2.3 million ecotourists who come each year to view wildlife in the valley, bringing some $300 million to the local economy (Woosnam et al. 2012).

Maps plainly show how the fence crosses or runs along or close to the preserves. It may be less clear how these barriers affect wildlife, but research suggests that the border fence intersects the range of numerous species, including thirty-eight types of amphibians, 152 reptiles, and 113 mammalian species. Many of the creatures affected by the border fence are rare. Fifty species that are globally threatened, or that are listed as threatened by the US or Mexican governments, occur within 30 miles of the border (Lasky, Jetz, and Keitt 2011).

This image provides a view of an endangered jaguarundi (Puma yagouaroundi) *(Muller 2013).*

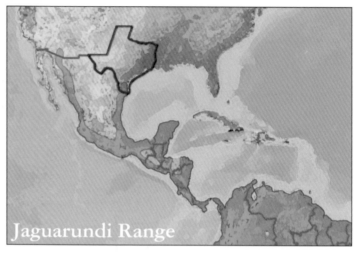

This map outlines the jaguarundi's range, including the small portions that extend into the United States, crossing through the fenced zone (Patterson et al. 2003).

Here is a picture of the rare ferruginous cactus pygmy-owl (Glaucidium brasilianum) *(Rae 2012).*

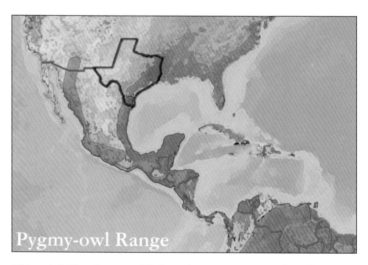

This map displays the range of the ferruginous cactus pygmy-owl, reaching from Latin America into the fenced borderlands of the United States (Ridgely et al. 2003).

Impacts

Two creatures, the jaguarundi (*Puma yagouaroundi*) and the ferruginous cactus pygmy-owl (*Glaucidium brasilianum*), can be seen as examples of the more general wildlife problem posed by the fence. Both species are quite rare in the United States. The jaguarundi was declared endangered in 1976 (41 Fed. Reg. 24062, June 14, 1976). The pygmy-owl was listed in 1997, but de-listed in 2006, and its status has been in litigation and political turmoil since (62 Fed. Reg. 10730, April 9, 1997; 71 Fed. Reg. 19452, April 14, 2006). Despite precautions, the fence presents a barrier to these two creatures. While the fence is not continuous, the lights and cleared roadway that parallel the fence create a formidable obstacle to the secretive, brush-loving jaguarundi. Also, while the fence is usually no more than 15–18 feet tall, only about one-quarter of the ground-hugging pygmy-owls' flights exceed that height. In these ways, the fence risks separating the US populations of both animals from water and suitable habitat and threatens to break the tie to relatives and a larger genetic pool to the south (Flesch et al. 2010). As a hindrance to south-to-north movements, the border fence may pose even more of a challenge as climate change and warming advances (Schlyer 2012).

Aside from the fence's effect on wildlife, there are both early answers and lingering questions about the wall's impact on the human world. It appears that the fence has indeed helped lower movement across the border, as its proponents sought. During fiscal year 2013, ending September 30 of that year, the Border Patrol apprehended over 414,000 illegal immigrants coming across the US-Mexico border (US Department of Homeland Security 2015a). These numbers are down dramatically since the peak of 2000, when 1.6 million illegal crossers were caught, and have returned to figures not seen since the administration of Richard Nixon in the early 1970s (Miroff and Booth 2011).

However, it is unclear if this downward trend is solely due to the fence. For the truly persistent, entry is still possible. Homeland Security has found numerous ladders, 149 tunnels, and as many as 4,000 holes cut through the fence (Clifford 2012). Some use carjacks to lift fence panels and create gaps to scurry through. Others scale the wall, leaving only scuffmarks and footprints behind. So could the decline in apprehensions be due instead to the chilling effect of heightened staffing in the Border Patrol and National Guard? Or is the fall in captures linked to the border's new virtual fence technology? Or perhaps immigrants are deterred because of arrests at US workplaces and the ensuing deportations (Preston 2012). The data are still inconclusive (Passel and Cohn 2012).

The doubts about the full effect of the border barriers on immigration, and the concerns about the barriers'

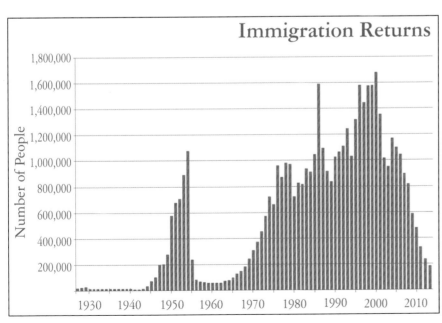

The chart shows long-term fluctuations in US returns from 1927 through 2011, most of which involve repatriating Mexicans to their home country (US Department of Homeland Security 2015b).

impact on wildlife movements, are joined by a third, and very troubling, issue: the deaths of migrants crossing the border. Many segments of the border fence were built in well-traveled, urban areas, slowing the traffic there but pushing desperate immigrants to find their way into the United States through harsh and remote parts of the Imperial Valley and the Sonoran Desert. As a consequence, up to 5,600 border crossers have died in the first decade of the twenty-first century, largely due to dehydration and exposure to the desert heat, particularly in the harsh country of southern Arizona (Jimenez 2009; Rose 2012; Humane Borders 2015; Christopherson et al. 2006).

Choices

We are left with a dilemma. In short, how can the country effectively protect its borders and national security, yet at a cost to humans and wildlife that we can all accept in good conscience? How can we maintain the boundary between the United States and Mexico and yet still protect the ties between the human and natural communities that straddle it?

The Future

With time, perhaps, there will be social, economic, political, and technological answers for the immigration question, and an eventual return to the more open frontier that existed prior to the 1990s. The speed and direction of human migrations can shift with changes in economic fortunes, population pressures, age structures, and political factors to the south and north of the border (Passel and Cohn 2012). Even if immigration pressures persist, technological improvements in radar, infrared sensors, drones, thermal imagers, and cameras may allow human immigration to be monitored while still allowing wildlife to pass unimpeded. And last, the existing fence policy may collapse under its own fiscal weight. The Government Accounting Office has estimated that maintaining the border fence will cost a hefty $6.5 billion over the next twenty years (Stana 2009).

Sources

Abhat, Divya. 2011. "Fenced Out: Wildlife Impacts of the U.S.-Mexico Border Fence." Wildlife Society. *Wildlife Professional* (Winter).

Bezanson, David. 2015. Land Protection and Easements Manager, Texas Chapter, The Nature Conservancy. Personal communication.

Bezaury-Creel J. E., J. Fco. Torres, and L. M. Ochoa-Ochoa. 2007. Base de Datos Geográfica de Áreas Naturales Protegidas Estatales, del Distrito Federal y Municipales de México— Versión 1.0, Agosto 31, 2007. Nature Conservancy / PRONATURA A.C. / Comisión Nacional para el Conocimiento y Uso de la Biodiversidad / Comisión Nacional de Áreas Naturales Protegidas.

Bezaury-Creel, J. E., J. Fco. Torres, L. M. Ochoa-Ochoa, Marco Castro-Campos, and N. Moreno. 2009. Base de Datos Geographica de Areas Naturales Protegidas Municipales de Mexico, 2009. http://www.conabio.gob.mx/informacion/gis/maps/geo/anpm09gw.zip, accessed May 1, 2015.

California Coastal Commission. 2003. Revised Staff Report and Recommendation on Consistency Determination, Coastal Zone Portion of 14-Mile Border Infrastructure System. No. CD-063-03. July 23.

Christopherson, Gary, Robin Hoover, John Chamblee, Daniel Deborde, and Mark Townley. 2006. Mapping Migrant Deaths in Southern Arizona: The Humane Borders GIS. ESRI Users Group Conference, September. http://proceedings.esri.com/library/userconf/proc06/papers/papers/pap_1464.pdf, accessed January 25, 2013.

Clark, Matt. 2009. "Protecting America's Borderlands." Defenders of Wildlife. http://www.defenders.org/sites/default/files/publications/protecting_americas_borderlands.pdf, accessed June 11, 2015.

Clifford, Frank. 2012. "The Border Effect." *American Prospect*, September 18.

Commission for Environmental Cooperation. 2015. Terrestrial Protected Areas, 2010. North American Environmental Atlas. http://www.cec.org/atlas/files/Terrestrial_Protected_areas_2010/TerrProtectedAreas_2010_Shapefile.zip, accessed May 1, 2015.

Corey, Michael. 2014. Open Street Map, Relation: U.S.-Mexico border fence (2266294). https://www.openstreetmap.org/relation/2266294, accessed April 8, 2015.

Flesch, A. D., C. W. Epps, J. W. Cain, M. Clark, P. R. Krausman, and J. R.

Morgart. 2010. "Potential Effects of the United States–Mexico Border Fence on Wildlife." *Conservation Biology* 24 (1): 171–81.

Google Earth Pro, version 7.1.2.2041. 2015. US/Mexico Border Zone. Elevation, 1,000 feet. http://www .google.com/earth/index.html, accessed April 8, 2015.

Humane Borders. 2015. 1999–2013 Recorded Migrant Deaths. http:// humaneborders.org/news/documents/ death_poster_2013_download.pdf, accessed June 11, 2015.

Jimenez, Maria. 2009. "Humanitarian Crisis: Migrant Deaths at the U.S.-Mexico Border." Mexico's National Commission of Human Rights and ACLU of San Diego and Imperial County. October 1. http://www.aclu .org/files/pdfs/immigrants/humanitari ancrisisreport.pdf, accessed February 5, 2013.

Lasky, Jesse, Walter Jetz, and Timothy Keitt. 2011. "Conservation Biogeography of the US-Mexico Border: A Transcontinental Risk Assessment of Barriers to Animal Dispersal." *Diversity and Distributions* 17: 673–87.

McCorkle, Rob. 2011. "Wildlife and the Wall: What Is the Impact of the Border Fence on Texas Animals?" *Texas Parks and Wildlife*. August.

Miroff, Nick, and William Booth. 2011. "Arrests of Illegal Migrants on U.S.-Mexico Border Plummet." *Washington Post*, December 3.

Molzahn, Cory, Viridiana Rios, and David Shirk. 2012. "Drug Violence in Mexico: Data and Analysis through 2011." Trans-Border Institute, University of San Diego. http://justi-ceinmexico.files.wordpress .com/2012/03/2012-tbi-drugviolence .pdf, accessed January 24, 2013.

Muller, Joachim. 2008. Jaguarundi. June 6, 2013. Creative Commons. https:// flic.kr/p/eQEUEo, accessed October 13, 2014.

National Park Service. 2015. Administrative Boundaries of National Park System Units, National Geospatial Data Asset. National Park Service, US Department of the Interior. http://gstore.unm.edu/apps/rgis/ datasets/7bbe8af5-029b-4adf-b06 c-134f0dd57226/nps_boundary .original.zip, accessed May 1, 2015.

Nevins, Joseph. 2002. *Operation Gatekeeper and Beyond: The War on "Illegals" and the Remaking of the U.S.-Mexico Boundary*. New York: Routledge.

Nottingham, Earl. 2011. Border Fence. Photograph. Digital image. Texas Parks and Wildlife. Austin, Texas.

O'Brian, Bill. 2011. Texas Border Refuge Cooperates with DHS. National Wildlife Refuge System, US Fish and Wildlife Service. http://www.fws.gov /refugesRefugeUpdateMarchApril _2011/texasborder.html, accessed December 20, 2012.

Olson, Lori. 2014. Executive Director, Texas Land Trust Council. Personal communication.

Passel, Jeffrey, and D'Vera Cohn. 2012. "Net Migration from Mexico Falls to Zero—and Perhaps Less." Pew Hispanic Center. Pew Research Center. April 23. http://www.pewhispanic.org/ files/2012/04/Mexican-migrants-report _final.pdf, accessed December 20, 2012.

Patterson, B. D., G. Ceballos, W. Sechrest, M. F. Tognelli, T. Brooks, L. Luna, P. Ortega, I. Salazar, and B. E. Young. 2003. Digital Distribution Maps of the Mammals of the Western Hemisphere, version 1.0. NatureServe, Arlington, Virginia.

Powell, Hugh. 2011. "Fencing the Border and Its Birds." Living Bird. Cornell Lab of Ornithology. http://www.all aboutbirds.org/Page.aspx?pid=1345, accessed December 20, 2012.

Powell, Stewart. 2008. "Texas Group Sues to Stop Construction of Border Fence." *Houston Chronicle*, May 16.

Preston, Julia. 2012. "Record Number of Foreigners Were Deported in 2011, Officials Say." *New York Times*, September 7.

Rae, Alastair. 2012. Ferruginous Cactus Pygmy Owl. Creative Commons. http://www.flickr.com/photos/ merula/8030252349/, accessed January 28, 2013.

Reyes, Ernesto. 2011. "Lower Rio Grande Valley Border Issues and Impacts to Wildlife." US Fish and Wildlife Service. February 20.

Ridgely, R. S., T. F. Allnutt, T. Brooks, D. K. McNicol, D. W. Mehlman, B. E. Young, and J. R. Zook. 2003. Digital Distribution Maps of the Birds of the Western Hemisphere, version 1.0. NatureServe. Arlington, Virginia.

Robles, Frances. 2014. "Fleeing Gangs, Children Head to U.S. Border." *New York Times*, July 9.

Rose, Ananda. 2012. "Death in the Desert." *New York Times*, June 21.

Schyler, Krista. 2012. *Continental Divide: Wildlife, People, and the Border Wall*. College Station: Texas A&M University Press.

Schwelling, Steve. 2012. GIS Analyst, Information Technology Division, Texas Parks and Wildlife GIS Staff. Personal communications, November and December.

Stana, Richard M. 2009. Secure Border Initiative: Technology Deployment Delays Persist and the Impact of Border Fencing Has Not Been Assessed. Testimony before the Subcommittee on Border, Maritime and Global Counterterrorism, Committee on Homeland Security, House of Representatives. GAO-09-1013T. http://www.gao.gov/new.items/d091013t.pdf, accessed February 5, 2013.

Steinbach, Mark. 2014. Executive Director, Texas Land Conservancy. Personal communication.

Texas Land Trust Council. 2015. Conservation Lands Inventory, Shapefile. http://www.texaslandtrust-council.org/index.php/what-we-do/cli, accessed March 2, 2015.

Texas Natural Resources Information System. 2015. StratMap Park Boundaries, Boundaries, Texas Statewide Datasets, Data Search and Download. Geographic Information Office, Texas Natural Resources Information System, Texas Water Development Board. https://tg-twdb-gemss.s3.amazonaws.com/d/stratmap_bnd/stratmap_park.zip, accessed May 1, 2015.

Texas Parks and Wildlife. 2012. Land and Water Resources Conservation and Recreation Plan Statewide Inventory 2012, Geodatabase. http://tpwd.texas.gov/gis/apps/lwrcrp/, accessed May 1, 2013.

———. 2015. State Park Boundaries, Shapefile. GIS Maps and Spatial Data. Texas Parks and Wildlife. http://tpwd.texas.gov/gis/data/baselayers/state-park-boundaries-zip, accessed May 1, 2015.

US Department of Homeland Security. 2008. Environmental Stewardship Plan for the Construction, Operation, and Maintenance of Tactical Infrastructure, US Border Patrol Rio Grande Valley Sector, Texas. US Department of Homeland Security, Washington, DC.

———. 2015a. Yearbook of Immigration Statistics: 2013 Enforcement Actions, Table 35, Aliens Apprehended by Program and Border Patrol Sector, Investigations Special Agent in Charge (SAC) Jurisdiction, and Area of Responsibility: Fiscal Years 2004 to 2013. Spreadsheet. http://www.dhs.gov/sites/default/files/publications/immigration-statistics/yearbook/2013/ENF/table35.xls, accessed April 8, 2015.

———. 2015b. Yearbook of Immigration Statistics: 2013 Enforcement Actions, Table 39, Aliens Removed or Returned: Fiscal Years 1892 to 2013. Spreadsheet. https://edit.dhs.gov/sites/default/files/publications/immigration-statistics/yearbook/2013/ENF/table39.xls, accessed April 8, 2015.

US Environmental Protection Agency (EPA). 2013. Public Lands. http://geodata.epa.gov/arcgis/rest/services/, accessed February 1, 2013.

US Fish and Wildlife Service. 2015. USFWS Interest Shapefile. Boundaries showing USFWS acquired lands (March 1). http://ecos.fws.gov/ServCatFiles/Reference/Holding/45000, accessed May 1, 2015.

US Forest Service. 2015. Administrative Forest Boundaries, Shapefile. FSGeoData Clearinghouse. US Forest Service, US Department of Agriculture. http://data.fs.usda.gov/geodata/edw/edw_resources/shp/S_USA.AdministrativeForest.zip, accessed May 1, 2015.

US Geological Survey. 2014. Protected Areas Database of the United States (PAD-US). http://gapanalysis.usgs.gov/padus/data/download/, accessed August 8, 2014.

Von Drehle, David. 2008. "The Border Fence: A Texas Turf War." *Time Magazine*, May 21.

Weber, Paul J. 2012. "Landowners on Border Say They Were Shortchanged." *The Big Story*, Associated Press, October 15.

Woosnam, K. M., R. M. Dudensing, D. Hanselka, and K. Aleshinloye. 2012. "Economic Impact of Nature Tourism on the Rio Grande Valley: Considering Peak and Off-Peak Visitation for 2011." Texas A&M University. http://rpts.tamu.edu/files/2012/05/STNMC-Final-report-4.16.12.pdf, accessed February 5, 2013.

Sparrows, Starlings, and Doves

Exotics and Natives

This is the story of the introduction of the house sparrow, European starling, and Eurasian collared dove to Texas and the New World. The chapter explains the logistics of how, when, and where the birds arrived, and then became established and later spread. Like the fire ants, nonnative fish, Old World grasses, and Chinese tallow previously discussed, these birds give an example of the ecological and economic risks posed by exotic species. They are just a few of 50,000 imported species in the United States, causing an estimated $134 billion in annual economic impacts and contributing to the decline of 42 percent of threatened and endangered natives (Pimentel 2002). In a more general way, though, these birds' history shows how human decisions, often made far away and long ago, can change and rebuild landscapes in Texas and beyond.

House Sparrow (*Passer domesticus*)

The history of house sparrows in the United States begins over 160 years ago. In the summer of 1850, caterpillars were devouring foliage on the trees along Flatbush Avenue in Brooklyn, New York. Nicholas Pike, the director of the Brooklyn Institute, had

learned that house sparrows were sworn enemies of such caterpillars, and so he brought eight pairs of house sparrows from England to a Brooklyn cemetery. He hoped the sparrows would control the caterpillars, in addition to other insects (Barrows 1889; Moulton et al. 2010).

At the time, insects of various kinds were indeed becoming a serious problem in many fast-growing American cities. The urban population of the United States was skyrocketing, on its way from 6.2 million in 1860 to 42 million just fifty years later. With the nation's growing needs for transport and industry, the US horse population tripled from 1850 to 1890, totaling 15.3 million, with each contributing some twenty pounds of dung daily, accompanied by a squadron of flies and other insects (McShane and Tarr 1997; Doughty 1978). Pigs, sheep, and cattle roamed through many American cities as well, adding their own waste and crews of flies and beetles. Meanwhile, the rise of cats and the decline of undisturbed habitat had killed or displaced many native birds that otherwise might have controlled those insects. Pike and others hoped that the house sparrow would help control the caterpillars and their insect kin.

Not all sparrow enthusiasts were so focused on horse dung and tree pests. A second sparrow introduc-

tion in the New York area occurred in 1872–74, when a pharmacist, Eugene Schieffelin, and his American Acclimatization Society brought numerous nonnative birds to the city. The society traced its ancestry (along with more than forty other similar groups around the world) to the esteemed Société zoologique d'acclimatation. The French biologist Isidore Geoffroy had established the Société in Paris in 1854 with the goal of enriching local flora and fauna, and providing more meat sources and better pest control through such foreign introductions (Bright 1998, 134–36). Schieffelin followed the Société's model with his New York sparrow releases and added the notion that the "enrichment" would be both ecological and cultural. Schieffelin endeavored to not only bring in the house sparrow but also all the birds mentioned in Shakespeare's works (Zimmerman 2013).

Whether for pragmatic insect control, or more literary goals, the last half of the nineteenth century saw over one hundred house sparrow releases in the United States. For example, sparrow releases were made in Boston (1858); Philadelphia (1869); San Francisco (1871–72); Portland, Maine (1854); and Salt Lake City (1873–74) (Lever 2005, 207–10). The enthusiasm for sparrows soon reached Texas. The first Texas introduction of sparrows appears to have been made in the late 1860s, in Galveston, by a local hardware store owner, James Brown (Doughty 1983).

Once released, the house sparrows' range expanded rapidly throughout the United States. In fact, a Texas bird list reported as early as 1912 that "this introduced species is now diffused over the entire state" (Strecker 1912). The bird's wide spread was due in part to human help. Repeated and widely scattered releases of the bird certainly helped the sparrow find new ecological niches and greater acreage to occupy. Also, the birds' human friends looked after them, shooting the hawks, owls, and shrikes that might otherwise prey on the sparrows (Doughty 1978). At the same time, Texas and other states passed laws giving house sparrows the same legal protection that many native songbirds enjoyed (Texas Revised Statutes, 1895, Penal Code, Title XII, chap. 5, p. 100, Art. 518).

In addition, house sparrows had some key biological advantages over other birds. Sparrows might produce two or three broods each season, rather than just one clutch raised by many native birds. And once laid, sparrow eggs hatched in just eleven days, and the fledglings became independent within just three weeks of their birth, about 30 percent faster than other birds of similar size. Also, sparrows were very flexible about their diet. Seed, waste grain, food leftovers, and insects were all fine with them. And they were amenable to all kinds of man-made and natural nesting options: siding, gutters, ledges, eaves, vents, pipes, ducts, and, critically, the nests of other birds, were all acceptable to house sparrows (Mann 2013). In fact, their broad-minded attitude about food and housing helped them quickly adapt to new habitat, and also sped them on their way to new lands. For instance, their palate often led them to rail yards where they ate up waste grain, while their fondness for built structures as nest sites introduced them to boxcars, flatcars, and cabooses that then carried them on to distant destinations (Doughty 1978).

By the 1870s, house sparrows grew to have many critics, who cursed them with names like "gamin," "tramp," and "hoodlum." Congressman John Lacey (future author of the Lacey Act, the main federal law against animal trafficking) considered the sparrow a "rat of the air, vermin of the atmosphere" (33 Congressional Record 4871–4872; 16 U.S.C. 3371–3378). Elliot Coues, director of the Biological Survey, called them "wretched interlopers" and "pestilent famine-breeders" (Comstock 1879, 152–53). Critics assailed sparrows for their role as carriers of disease, including Western encephalitis. They condemned them for their impact on native birds, such as the purple martin, tree swallow, and eastern bluebird.

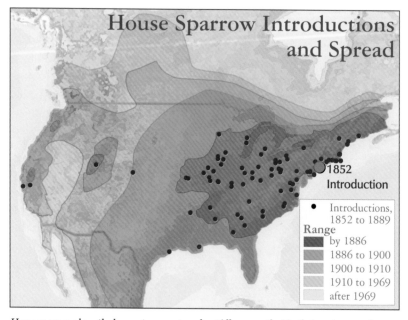

Here we can see how the house sparrow spread rapidly across the North American continent from 1886 to 1969. Markers and dates note the introduction sites (there have been in excess of one hundred release locations!). Interestingly, the 1886 boundary of the sparrow's range was based on a US Department of Agriculture compilation of 3,300 reports from the public. This may be one of the first examples of crowd-sourced citizen science (Barrows 1889; Robbins 1973).

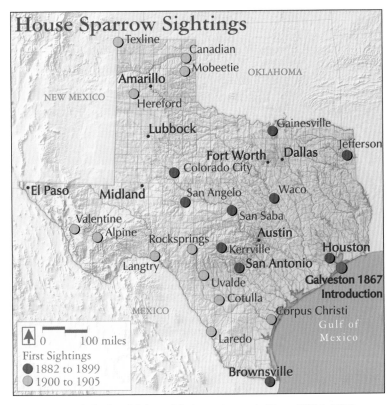

House Sparrow Sightings

Texline
Canadian
Mobeetie
OKLAHOMA
Amarillo
NEW MEXICO
Hereford
Lubbock
Gainesville
Fort Worth
Dallas
Jefferson
Colorado City
El Paso
Midland
San Angelo
Waco
Valentine
San Saba
Alpine
Austin
Rocksprings
Kerrville
Houston
Langtry
San Antonio
Galveston 1867
Introduction
Uvalde
Cotulla
Corpus Christi
Gulf of Mexico
MEXICO
Laredo
Brownsville

0   100 miles
First Sightings
● 1882 to 1899
○ 1900 to 1905

This map records the first sightings of the house sparrow in Texas, 1882 to 1905. The 1867 release of the sparrow in Galveston is noted in red (National Audubon Society 2013).

*The house sparrow is a common sight throughout Texas and much of the known world (*Passer domesticus*) (Fir0002 2006).*

And they counted the high cost of their big appetite for farmers' grains. Last of course, there was dismay at the birds' lack of interest in the insects that they had originally been imported to eat (Mitchell et al. 1973; Kalmbach 1940).

Nevertheless, the sparrow's introduction would not be the last. Other nonnative birds would soon be brought to American shores.

European Starlings (*Sturnus vulgaris*)

Despite the concerns over the house sparrow's wide and rapid spread, the late nineteenth century saw the release of another exotic bird in the United States. In April 1890, Mr. Schieffelin (the same one who was enamored of house sparrows) was involved in introducing eighty European starlings in New York City's Central Park. March 1891 brought the release of another eighty in New York (Cooke 1928). Sixteen pairs evidently survived to reproduce, and with time, the European starling grew to be one of the most common birds in the United States, with a flock of over 200 million, about one-third of the world's entire population. Only red-winged blackbirds are believed to exceed the US population of starlings (Linz et al. 2007). And the starling did not remain in the area where it was first released; it rapidly spread across the country. Specimens were seen as far south as Amelia Island, Florida, in 1918, as far north as Brockville, Ontario, in 1919, and indeed, as far to the west as Cove, Texas, in 1922. By 1950, they had even established themselves on the Pacific coast of the United States and Mexico (Lever 2005, 194–96).

The starling's rapid spread was in part due to its aggressive nesting and parasitism. Starlings have been known to displace eastern bluebirds, tree swallows, red-bellied woodpeckers, purple martins, great-crested flycatchers, wood ducks, kestrels, and other native cavity-dwelling birds. Starlings' ability to colonize new areas was also due to their diverse diet. They were known to forage and scavenge a great variety of food. In fact, their appetite led to concerns about the starling's agricultural cost. The bird enjoyed eating grain at feedlots and pecking away at potatoes, peaches, strawberries, figs, blueberries, and other fruit crops (Feare and Craig 2010).

Concerns about their ecological and economic impact broadened to worries over public health effects. Their great flocks left prodigious amounts of guano behind: eleven tons of starling dung once had to be shoveled off the dome of the Illinois state capitol (Cantwell 1974). And the concern was not just about the smell and muck: starlings could carry bacterial (salmonellosis, avian tuberculosis, streptococcosis, and vibriosis), viral (histoplasmosis, meningitis, and encephalitis), and fungal (aspergillosis) diseases. The bird has also been charged with disrupting air traffic when "murmurating" in large flocks.

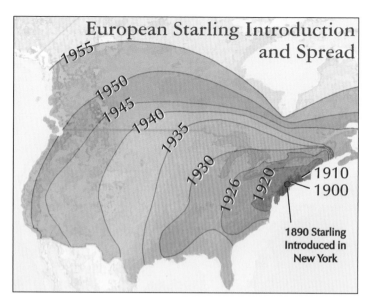

Here we can see the European starling's wave-like spread across North America from the end of the nineteenth century through 1955. The original American introduction is believed to have occurred in the New York area in 1890, with successful overwintering by 1895 (Cooke 1928; Cox and Moore 2010; Jung 1945).

In Boston, a flock of 10,000 starlings flew into a jet's engines in 1960, causing it to crash and kill sixty-two passengers. Accidents have seldom been so serious, but many minor collisions do occur. Starlings and blackbirds were involved in 852 aircraft strikes between 1990 and 2001 in forty-six states and the District of Columbia (Barras, Wright, and Seamans 2003).

Some of the charges against starlings admittedly may have been exaggerated. For instance, Christmas Count and Breeding Bird Survey data for Texas and the nation have not shown clear-cut declines in some of the cavity nesters of concern (for instance, the red-bellied woodpecker, tree swallow, purple martin, and eastern bluebird) (National Audubon Society 2013; Koenig 2003; Ortego 2013). And while starlings have been accused of crop damage, the charge may be only because of their tendency to flock with grackles, cowbirds, and red-winged blackbirds that do indeed have a fondness for corn and other grains. Except for the colder months, starlings appear to be more interested in insects. In fact, some of the starling diet includes agricultural pests such as weevils, grasshoppers, caterpillars, May beetles, June bugs, Japanese beetles, potato bugs, and corn borers (Jung 1945).

Nevertheless, numerous creative efforts have been undertaken to turn the tide on the invasion of sparrows and starlings. Control efforts have used itching powder, water sprays, electric wires, cobalt 60, pesticides (4-aminopyridine and fenthion), mechanical hawks, hawk kites, eyespot balloons, guns, fireworks, alarms, scarecrows, traps, glues, mist nets, antiroosting spikes, and even cats (Fitzwater 1994). Some cooks found it tasty (or romantic, given their reputed aphrodisiac properties) to add house sparrows to pies and other items on restaurant menus. None of these strategies, though, has had a lasting impact (Johnson and Glahn 1994). In their great and resilient numbers, starlings (and sparrows) have gradually become grudgingly accepted as part of the American landscape, and most folks have resigned themselves to just manage or control the most serious and local problems.

The rise of nonnative bird populations in the United States still does alarm naturalists and regulators. Over a century after its passage, the Lacey Act remains on the books as a bar to the introduction of foreign birds or animals (16 U.S.C. Sections 3371–3378; Anderson 1995). And government biologists and amateur birders are always on the lookout for introduced birds. Yet in this age of quick, common, and inexpensive international trade and travel, foreign birds continue to arrive in the United States. The story of the Eurasian collared-dove provides a modern-day cautionary example.

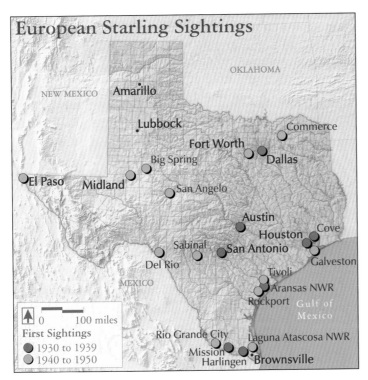

This map charts the first sightings of the European starling in Texas during the 1930–50 period. Please note that these reports may be late. They reflect what Christmas Bird Count observers might have been lucky to see under sometimes-harsh winter conditions on just a single day. Also, early arrivals could easily have been missed; bird counts were not established in many parts of Texas until well after starlings were established in large parts of the state (National Audubon Society 2013).

*The European starling (*Sturnus vulgaris*) sports an iridescent breast coat (Tanner 2009).*

*Here we see a pair of Eurasian collared-doves (*Streptopelia decaocto*).*

Eurasian Collared-Dove (*Streptopelia decaocto*)

The Eurasian collared-dove was originally native to India, Sri Lanka, and Myanmar, but gradually spread, on its own or with human help, to reach Turkey and the Balkans by the sixteenth century. From there, its range did not change markedly until the early 1900s, when, over the course of about fifty years, it colonized much of Europe and northwest Africa. In the mid-1970s, a Bahamian pet dealer was the first to bring the dove to the West. Then, in 1974, the bird escaped captivity in the Islands, and soon spread to the United States (Brown and Tomer 2002, 7; Smith 1987, 1371–79).

Like the sparrow and starling, the Eurasian collared-dove has attracted few friends. Bigger and more aggressive than the native mourning and white-winged dove, there is concern that they are supplanting them in Texas and elsewhere. Also, there is worry that the dove may be a carrier of West Nile virus and a disease-carrying parasite, *Trichormoas gallinae* (Rappole, Derrickson, and Hubalek 2000; Stimmelmayr et al. 2012). However, the collared-dove is popular in hunting circles and provides a subject for lively online debate about the right shot sizes to use:

> Beedubyacee: Due to their size I would recommend #6 shot to bring them down. Hit them with 8's and they keep right on flying!

> Hardy: I've had no problem killing them with 8's in my 20 ga. by the way. They fly nice and slow.

> Larryg: I don't have any problem knocking collared-doves down with my old 870 20 GA using 7 1/2 shot, (Texas Hunt Fish 2013)

There is also agreement on the joys of eating them:

> Cyphertex: I don't mind shooting [them] . . . bigger bird and I can't tell any difference in taste. They're all good wrapped in bacon! (Texas Hunting Forum 2013)

Just as sparrows, starlings, and doves are acclimating to their new American home, so are humans adapting to their new neighbors, or at least the targets and food they now provide. Perhaps some kind of welcome for these birds is only fair. In many places they are among the more common birds we see, and they do bring life, color, and song to our world.

Also, we need to accept our complicity in bringing these creatures to the Americas. We have carried them here, whether in a repeated, orchestrated way, like the house sparrow, or in a more isolated effort, like the European starling, or by careless accident, like the Eurasian collared-dove. And once here, we have made their spread easier and faster by controlling the raptors that might have picked off the sparrows, or by erecting martin houses that the starlings quickly usurped, or by filling feeders that the dove rapidly found and enjoyed.

Still, there is a certain amount of luck, bad luck, involved. While the sparrows, starlings, and doves have certainly done well, too well, introductions of many other foreign birds have failed. Mr. Schieffelin, who had

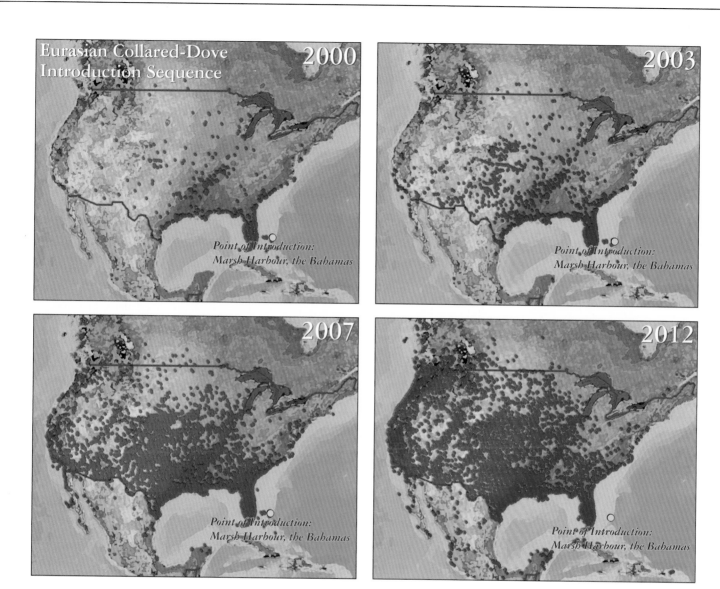

This series of continental maps shows the accelerating spread of the Eurasian collared-dove in North America, from 2000, to 2003, 2007, and 2012. Each dot represents a reported sighting of the bird (eBird 2013).

had such success with sparrows and starlings, made no headway with establishing US populations of the bullfinch, chaffinch, nightingale, and skylark. Even some modern transplants that were professionally managed have had little success, such as the aborted effort in the 1950s and '60s by the US Fish and Wildlife Service to establish the Erckel's francolin as a game bird on the mainland United States (Islam 1999).

And there, perhaps, is the most important lesson of all: experiments with nature are inherently unpredictable, the ultimate consequences are unknown, and the ramifications may be delayed, distant, and odd.

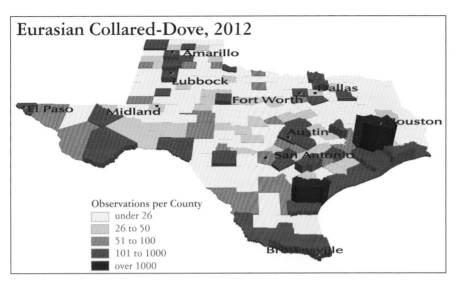

Eurasian Collared-Dove, 2012

Observations per County
- under 26
- 26 to 50
- 51 to 100
- 101 to 1000
- over 1000

This map shows the relative density of Eurasian collared-dove observations in the state, by county, during 2012 (eBird 2013).

Sources

Anderson, Robert. 1995. "The Lacey Act: America's Premier Weapon in the Fight against Unlawful Wildlife Trafficking." *Public Land and Resources Law Review* 16: 27–85.

Barras, S. C., S. E. Wright, and T. W. Seamans. 2003. "Blackbird and Starling Strikes to Civil Aircraft in the United States, 1990–2001." In *Proceedings of Symposium on Management of North American Blackbirds*, edited by G. M. Linz, 91–96. US Department of Agriculture, Animal and Plant Health Inspection Service, Wildlife Services, National Wildlife Research Center, Fort Collins, Colorado.

Barrows, W. B. 1889. "The English Sparrow (*Passer domesticus*) in North America, Especially in Its Relation to Agriculture." US Department of Agriculture, Division of Economic Ornithology and Mammalogy, Bulletin No. 1.

Bright, Chris. 1998. *Life Out of Bounds: Bioinvasion in a Borderless World*. New York: W. W. Norton.

Brown, Mary, and John Tomer. 2002. "The Status of the Eurasian Collared-Dove in Oklahoma." *Bulletin of the Oklahoma Ornithological Society* 35 (3): 5–8.

Cantwell, Robert. 1974. "A Plague of Starlings." *Sports Illustrated*, September 9.

Comstock, J. Henry. 1879. "Report upon Cotton Insects." US Department of Agriculture. Washington, DC: Government Printing Office.

Cooke, May Thacher. 1928. "The Spread of the European Starling in North America (to 1928)." US Department of Agriculture, Circular No. 40, November. Washington, DC.

Cox, Barry C., and Peter D. Moore. 2010. *Biogeography: An Ecological and Evolutionary Approach*, 8th ed., p. 73. Hoboken, NJ: John Wiley and Sons.

Doughty, Robin. 1978. "The English Sparrow in the American Landscape: A Paradox in Nineteenth-Century Wildlife Conservation." Research Paper 19. School of Geography, University of Oxford.

———. 1983. *Wildlife and Man in Texas: Environmental Change and Conservation*. College Station: Texas A&M University Press.

eBird. 2013. eBird: An online database of bird distribution and abundance. Ithaca, New York. http://www.ebird .org, accessed May 8, 2013.

Feare, Chris, and Adrian Craig. 2010. *Starlings and Mynas*. London: Christopher Helm.

Fir0002. 2006. House sparrow. Photograph. Digital image. Wikipedia. http://en.wikipedia.org/wiki/ File:House_sparrow04.jpg, accessed April 25, 2013.

Fitzwater, William. 1994. "House Sparrows, in Control of Nuisance Birds." Internet Center for Wildlife Damage Management. http://icwdm .org/handbook/birds/HouseSparrows/ HouseSparrows.pdf, accessed April 30, 2013.

Fujisaki, Ikuko, Elise V. Pearlstine, and Frank J. Mazzoti. 2010. "The Rapid Spread of Invasive Eurasian Collared-Doves (*Streptopelia decaocto*) in the Continental USA Follows Human-Altered Habitats." *Ibis, International Journal of Avian Science* 152: 622–32.

Islam, Kamal. 1999. "Black Francolin (*Francolinus francolinus*)." *The Birds of North America* Online, edited by A. Poole. Ithaca, NY: Cornell Lab of Ornithology; retrieved from the Birds

of North America Online, http://bna
.birds.cornell.edu/bna/species/395,
accessed May 9, 2013.

Johnson, R. J., and J. F. Glahn. 1992.
"Starling Management in Agriculture."
Coop. Ext. Publ. NCR 451, University
of Nebraska, Lincoln.

Jung, Clarence S. 1945. "A History of the
Starling in the U.S." In *The Passenger
Pigeon*, ed. N. R. Barger, vol. 7, no.
4, 111–16. Wisconsin Society for
Ornithology, October.

Kalmbach, E. R. 1940. "Economic Status
of the House Sparrow in the United
States." US Department of Agriculture
Technical Bulletin No. 711.

Koenig, W. D. 2003. "European Starlings
and Their Effect on Native Cavity-
Nesting Birds." *Conservation Biology*
17: 1134–40.

Lasley, Greg. 1997. Eurasian Collared-
Dove Status. Texas Bird Records
Committee. http://www.texasbirds.org/
tbrc/ecdo.htm, accessed May 8, 2013.

Lever, Christopher. 2005. *Naturalised
Birds of the World*. London: A & C
Black Publishers.

Linz, George, H. Jeffrey Homan, Shannon
Gaukler, Linda Penry, and William
Belier. 2007. *European Starlings: A
Review of an Invasive Species with
Far-Reaching Impacts*. Edited by
G. W. Witmer, W. C. Pitt, and K. A.
Fagerstone. Managing Vertebrate
Invasive Species: Proceedings of an
International Symposium. USDA/
APHIS/WS, National Wildlife Research
Center, Fort Collins, Colorado, 2.

MacKenzie, Alexandra. 2014. Eurasian
Collared-Dove, August 24. Photograph.
Digital image. Creative Commons collection, Flickr.com. https://flic.kr/p/
oWx8Ab, accessed October 13, 2014.

Mann, Charly. 2013. Oklahoma Birds
and Butterflies. http://oklahomabird
sandbutterflies.com/cat/3/35, accessed
April 29, 2013.

McShane, Clay, and Joel Tarr. 1997.
"The Centrality of the Horse to the
Nineteenth-Century American City."
In *Making of Urban America*, edited by
Raymond Mohl, 105–30. New York:
SR Publishers.

Mitchell, Carl, Richard Hayes, Preston
Holden, and Thomas Hughes. 1973.
"Nesting Activity of the House Sparrow
in Hale County, Texas, during 1968."
Ornithological Monographs, No. 14.
A Symposium on the House Sparrow
(*Passer domesticus*) and European
Tree Sparrow (*P. Montanus*) in North
America (1973), 49–59. Published
by University of California Press for
the American Ornithologists' Union.
http://www.jstor.org/stable/40168057,
accessed April 30, 2013.

Moulton, Michael, Wendell Cropper,
Michael Avery, and Linda Moulton.
2010. "The Earliest House Sparrow
Introductions to North America."
Biological Invasions 12: 2955–58.

National Audubon Society. 2013.
American Birds, the Annual Summary
of the Christmas Bird Count. http://
birds.audubon.org/american-birds-
annual-summary-christmas-bird-count,
accessed May 5, 2013.

Ortego, Brent. 2013. Wildlife Biologist,
Texas Parks and Wildlife. Personal
communication, May.

Pimentel, David, ed. 2002. *Biological
Invasions: Economic and
Environmental Costs of Alien Plant,
Animal, and Microbe Species*. Boca
Raton, FL: CRC Press.

Rappole, John, Scott Derrickson, and
Zdenek Hubalek. 2000. "Migratory
Birds and Spread of West Nile Virus in
the Western Hemisphere." *Emerging
Infectious Diseases* 6 (4).

Roberson, Jay. 2004. "New Dove in
Texas." *Texas Parks and Wildlife*
(April).

Smith, P. W. 1987. "The Eurasian
Collared-Dove Arrives in the Americas."
American Birds 41: 1371–79.

Stimmelmayr, R., L. M. Stefani, M. A.
Thrall, K. Landers, F. Revan, A. Miller,
R. Beckstead, and R. Gerhold. 2012.
"Trichomonosis in Free-Ranging
Eurasian Collared-Doves (*Streptopelia
decaocto*) and African Collared-Dove
Hybrids (*Streptopelia risoria*) in the
Caribbean and Description of ITS-1
Region Genotypes." *Avian Disease* 56
(2): 441–45.

Strecker, John K. 1912. "The Birds of
Texas: An Annotated Check-List."
Baylor University Bulletin 15 (1).
Waco, Texas.

Tanner, Linda. 2009. European Starling.
Photograph. Digital image. Creative
Commons collection, Flickr.com.
https://flic.kr/p/7qmNLL, accessed
October 13, 2014.

Texas Hunt Fish. 2013. The Doves of
Texas. http://www.texashuntfish.com/
app/wildlife-resources/23874/The-
Doves-of-Texas, accessed May 9, 2013.

Texas Hunting Forum. 2013. Eurasian
Collared-Dove. http://www.texas
huntingforum.com/forum/ubbthreads
.php/topics/3538239/Eurasian_
Collared_Dove, accessed May 9, 2013.

Zimmerman, E. A. 2013. "House Sparrow
History." Sialis. http://www.sialis.org/
hosphistory.htm, accessed April 25,
2013.

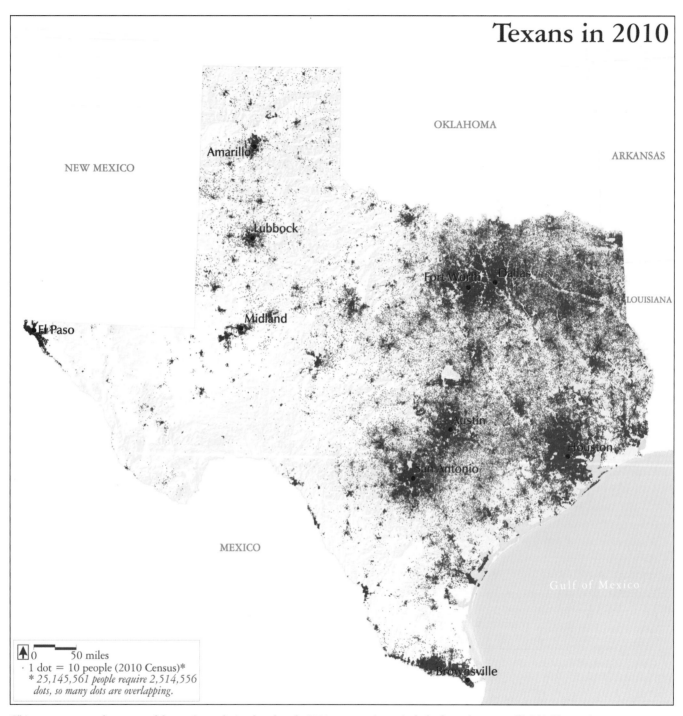

Texans in 2010

OKLAHOMA

NEW MEXICO

ARKANSAS

Amarillo

Lubbock

Fort Worth • Dallas

LOUISIANA

El Paso

Midland

Austin

Houston

San Antonio

MEXICO

Gulf of Mexico

0   50 miles
· 1 dot = 10 people (2010 Census)*
* 25,145,561 people require 2,514,556
  dots, so many dots are overlapping.

Brownsville

This map represents the pattern of the state's population, based on the 2010 census, using a single dot for each person tallied (Cable 2013).

Afterword

This book has chapters about water, land, wildlife, air, energy, and built structures. There are discussions about lakes and aquifers, prairies and forests, bison and pelicans, ozone and lead, wind and coal, billboards and landfills.

However, much of the book is really about us, seen through a kind of crazy funhouse mirror. These pieces of the Texas landscape are reflections of us, our tools, our needs, our wishes, and the things we would often rather not think about.

In other words, the water chapters can be seen as discussions of dams and boreholes, of irrigated fields and cooled power plants. The land articles can be viewed as explorations of both quiet parks and busy suburbs. The wildlife stories can describe our eclectic tastes for bison-hoof inkwells, ram horns, and pelican feathers. The section on the ozone layer can remind us of our affection for CFC-based hair spray, while the piece on lead reflects our appetites for smelted metals and no-knock cars. Similarly, the chapter on big coal plants can also tell us about our homes' energy-hungry gadgets and conveniences. Likewise, the billboards and landfills are of interest not only as large objects in the landscape but also as tangible signs of what we want and what we discard in our personal lives.

In these ways, for both good and bad, we are closely connected with the state's landscape. These marks are our footprints. We are tied to some scars in the state—the wastewater outfalls, dry springs, plant flares, border walls, outdoor signs, fire ant mounds, and sparrow nests. Equally, though, we are linked to the sites of recovery and redemption. We are hitched to the wind farms, pelican rookeries, artificial reefs, butterfly gardens, plugged wells, and public parks.

It has been said before, but there is great truth in Pogo's saying, "we have met the enemy and he is us" (Kelly 1972). And perhaps that is the nub of it—that we are both the confounding mark of many environmental problems and also the exciting sign of their solution.

Sources

Cable, Dustin. 2013. 2010 Racial Dot Map. Weldon Cooper Center for Public Service. University of Virginia. http://www.coopercenter.org/sites/default/files/node/13/US_RacialDotMap_HighResImage.zip, accessed August 29, 2014.

Kelly, Walt. 1972. *Pogo: We Have Met the Enemy and He Is Us*. New York: Simon and Schuster.

Acknowledgments

"John Glenn was the first to take his small camera and take a picture of an Earth glimpse . . . that shows very fuzzy layers of Earth's atmosphere . . . and the background of the curvature of the Earth. It was a discovery like Columbus."

—Kamlesh Lulla.
NASA Earth scientist,
October 5, 1999,
Clear Lake City, Texas

Kamlesh Lulla is a NASA earth scientist who trained many astronauts in photography and remote sensing. Dr. Lulla recalled that early Mercury and Gemini pilots lobbied to include a spacecraft window to peer through as they hurtled around Earth. Design engineers worried over safety risks in the harsh, unforgiving world of space, but ultimately relented. As a result, astronauts were able to use their curiosity about seeing and documenting the earth to build a treasure trove of hundreds of thousands of photographs of their home planet (Lulla 1999).

That same inquisitiveness is reflected in many other students' efforts to witness and understand the earth and all her ecosystems. We are extremely fortunate to have been able to base this work on the decades of data collection and research at countless schools, agencies, and nonprofits. We are very grateful for the information and advice that so many kind people have been willing to share.

Source

Lulla, Kamlesh. 1999. Oral history interview conducted on October 5, in Clear Lake City. Texas Legacy Project, Conservation History Association of Texas.

While we have attempted to fully credit our sources in the individual chapters, we would like to take the opportunity here, in one consolidated place, to again thank the organizations, researchers, and friends that our work has relied upon:

Acme Botanical Services: Bill Carr

Advanced Ecology: Matt Neuman

Alabama Department of Conservation and Natural Resources

American Rainwater Catchment Systems Association: Heather Kinkade

Applied Research Associates: Michelle Thompson, Beattie Williams

Audubon Texas: Marcy Crowe Spears, Tim Wilkinson

John Baker

Bandera County Appraisal District

Bexar County Appraisal District

Big Thicket Association: Pete Gunter, Mona Halvorsen, Maxine Johnston

Birdiview Photography Services: Stephen Ramirez

Jim Blackburn

Blucher Institute for Surveying & Science: Deidre Williams

Briscoe Center for American History: Amy Bowman, Aryn Glazier

Bureau of Economic Geology: Jeffrey Paine

California Department of Fish and Game: Derek Stein

Bill Calvert

Canadian Bison Association: Terry Kremeniuk

Center for Maximum Potential Building Systems: Pliny Fisk and Gail Vittori

Centers for Disease Control and Prevention: John Wood

City of Austin: John Abbott, Chris Herrington

City of Dallas: Greg Ajemian, Vera Bonner

City of Dripping Springs: Ginger Faught, Jon Thompson

City of Houston, Sign Administration: Marina Badoian-Kriticos, Myrna Franklin

City of New York: Alejandra Lamarche

City of Rollingwood: Michael Alexander

City of Round Rock: Jessica Woods

City of San Marcos: Jan Klein

City of Sunset Valley: Carolyn Meredith

Coastal Bird Observatory: Cecilia Riley

Conservation Fund: Margarita Carey, Andy Jones, Julie Shackelford

Cornell Lab of Ornithology eBird Project: Brian Sullivan

Donna Burdett Cotton

Dallas Historical Society: Samantha Dodd

Dallas Municipal Archives: John Slate

Defenders of Wildlife: Scott Nicol

Delaware Division of Fish and Wildlife, Fisheries Section: Jeff Tinsman

Department of Homeland Security: John Simanski

DESCO Environmental Consultants: Arthur Perkins, Justin Rowland

Detect, Inc.: Ron White

Ecological Recovery Foundation: Helen Besse

Energy Information Administration: John Powell

Environment Texas: Luke Metzger

Environmental Defense Fund: Ramon Alvarez, Scott Anderson, Pamela Baker, and Jim Marston

Environmental Integrity Project: Ilan Levin, Thomas Lyons

Fannin County Appraisal District: Mark Kinnaird

Far Flung Outdoor Center: Greg Henington

Federal Aviation Administration: Steve Posner

Federal Emergency Management Agency: John Bowman

Florida Fish and Wildlife Commission

Flower Gardens National Marine Sanctuary: Marissa Nuttall

Frederick, Perales, Allmon & Rockwell: Rick Lowerre

Georgia Department of Natural Resources, Coastal Resources Division: Jeff Mericle

Gladys Porter Zoo: Pat Burchfield, Jaime Peña

Dan Haas

Billy Hallmon

Hardin County Appraisal District: Theresa Crocker, Alex Stevens

Harris County Appraisal District: Thang Nguyen

Harris Galveston Subsidence District: Tom Michel

Help Endangered Animals— Ridley Turtles: Carole Allen

The History Center: Jonathan Gerland

History Colorado: Sarah Gilmor

Houston Chronicle: Joyce Lee

Houston-Galveston Area Council: Bill Bass

InterTribal Buffalo Council: Melissa Martin

International Boundary and Water Commission: Michael Tarabulski

International Crane Foundation: Elizabeth and David Smith

International Dark-Sky Association: Stephen Bosbach, Julie Schaar

Jefferson County Appraisal District

Journey North: Elizabeth Howard

KERA TV: Gila Espinoza

Kleberg County Appraisal District: Anita Garza

Landmark Wildlife Management: Keith Olenick

Lee College: David Rosen

David Lewis

Library of Congress, Historic American Building Survey

Lights Out Houston: Andy Bergman

Louisiana Department of Wildlife and Fisheries: Doug Peter

Lower Colorado River Basin Coalition: Kirby Brown

Madrono Ranch: Heather and Martin Kohout

Massachusetts Division of Marine Fisheries

McDonald Observatory: Bill Wren

Bonnie and Billy Pat McKinney

Mississippi Department of
Natural Resources

National Audubon Society,
Citizen Science: Kathy Dale

National Bison Association:
Jim Matheson

National Geophysical Data Center:
Barry Evans

National Oceanic and Atmospheric
Administration: Barry Eakins,
Charles Caillouet, and Jo Williams

National Optical Astronomy
Observatory: Connie Walker

National Park Service: Donna Shaver,
Scott Thompson-Buchanan, and
Jack Johnson

National Wildlife Federation:
Myron Hess and Norman Johns

Native Prairies Association of Texas:
Pat Merkord, Peter Quast

Natural Resources Conservation
Service: Shon Owens

Natural Resources Defense Council

Nature Conservancy: David Bezanson,
Jim Eidson, Charlotte Reemt

New Braunfels Utilities:
Mallory Doeckel

New Jersey Department of
Environmental Protection

North Carolina Department of
Environment and Natural Resources:
Jim Francesconi

Oklahoma State University:
Cody Edwards

Brad Peter

Plateau Land and Wildlife:
David Braun

Playa Lakes Joint Venture:
Ty Guthrie, Megan McLachlan

Asher Price

Public Citizen: Smitty Smith

Purdue University: Susan Schechter

Mike Quinn

Railroad Commission of Texas:
Jon Brandt, Trey Krueger,
Karen Sanchez

Rhode Island Department of
Environmental Management

Rice University: H. C. Clark

RS&H: Steve Farmer

San Marcos River Foundation:
Tom Hayes

Scenic Texas: Anne Culver,
Holly Eaton

Sierra Club, Lone Star Chapter:
Neil Carman

Siglo Group: Johanna Arendt,
Clare Crosby, Matt Fougerat

South Carolina Department of
Natural Resources: Bob Martore

Southern Methodist University,
DeGoyler Library: Katie Dziminski,
Cynthia Franco, Terre Heydari,
Anne Peterson

Sul Ross State University:
Thomas Janke

Tarrant County Appraisal District:
Mary McCoy

Texas A&M Transportation Institute:
Robert Benz

Texas A&M University, Department
of Geography: Daniel Goldberg

Texas A&M University, Gulf of Mexico
Coastal Ocean Observing System

Texas AgriLife Extension Service:
Billy Kniffen

Texas Campaign for the Environment:
Robin Schneider

Texas Center for Documentary
Photography: Alan Pogue

Texas Climate News: Bill Dawson

Texas Colonial Waterbird Society:
Erik Johnson

Texas Commission on Environmental
Quality: Kathy Alexander, Elayne
Barber, Diane Barnes, Prescott
Christian, Lorrie Council, Jeff Davis,
Morgan Dean, Jill Dickey, Alexander
Hinz, Michael Isley, Zach Lanfera,
Komal Patel, Fabienne Rambaud,
Andrew Sullivan, Michelle Tischler,
Cheryl Untermeyer, Walker Williamson

Texas Comptroller of Public
Accounts: Carmen Chavez,
Gwen Johnson

Texas Conservation Alliance:
Janice Bezanson, Gina and Richard
Donovan, Adrian van Dellen

Texas Cotton Gin Museum:
Jerry Moore

Texas Department of Agriculture:
Awirash Bhatkar

Texas Department of State Health
Services: Gary Heideman, Leon Kincy,
Michael Tennant

Texas Department of Transportation:
Greg White, Anthony Molina,
Julie Pollard, Sam Trevino

Texas Environmental Justice
Advocacy Services: Juan Parras,
Lucas Parras, Blas Espinosa

Texas Forest Service: Don
Hannemann, Jordan Smith

Texas General Land Office:
Craig Davis, Sterling Harris,
Michael Weeks

Texas Historical Commission:
Donald Firsching, Dan Julien,
Anne Shelton

Texas Land Conservancy:
Mark Steinbach

Texas Land Trust Council: Lori Olson

Texas Medical Association:
Betsy Tyson

Texas Natural Resources Information
System: Sam Norman, Erik O'Brian

Texas Office of the Attorney General:
David Falk, David Preister

Texas Parks and Wildlife Department:
Bob Baker, Heidi Bailey, Clay Brewer,
Cristy Burch, Linda Campbell,
James Edwards, Chase Fountain,
David Fowler, Blake Hendon, Gary

Homerstad, Ashton Hutchins, Doug
Jobes, Yanira Lacio, Mark Lange,
Chris Ledford, Meredith Longoria,
Earl Nottingham, Brent Ortego, Greg
Pleasant, Froylan Hernandez, Brooke
Shipley-Lozano, Jason Singhurst,
Vicki Sybert, Amie Treuer-Kuehn,
Joshua Turner, Matt Wagner, Ragan
White, Brendon Witt

Texas Renewable Energy Industry
Association: Russel Smith

Texas Rice Industry Coalition for
the Environment: Bill Stransky

Texas State Health and Human
Services: Whitney Michael

Texas State University, Department of
Geography: Lawrence Estaville

Texas State University, Meadows
Center for Water and the
Environment: Andy Sansom

Texas Tech University, Center for
Geospatial Technology: Lucia Barbato

Texas Water Development Board:
Rima Petrossian, Mark Wentzel

Travis County Appraisal District:
Amie Herrera, Richard Michalski

Rob Tranchin

US Army Corps of Engineers:
Stephen Sheedy

US Census Bureau:
Lyndsey Richmond

US Department of Agriculture:
Marcel Aillery, Allison Brochers,
Charlie Brown

US Department of Housing and
Urban Development: Jon Sperling

US Department of Transportation:
Dan Berman

US Fish and Wildlife Service:
Craig Farquhar, Jesse Grantham,
Tom Stehn, Nancy Umbehaun

US Geologic Survey: Matt Cannister,
Jeffery East, Pam Fuller, Natalie
Houston, Delbert Humberson, Mark
Kasmarek, Virginia McGuire, John
O'Malley, Jean Parcher, Janet Ruth

US Geological Survey, Woods Hole
Coastal and Marine Science Center:
John O'Malley

University of Houston: Melynda
Boerm, Phyllis Gingiss

University of Maryland: Leslie Ries

University of Minnesota:
Karen Oberhauser

University of Nebraska at Lincoln,
National Drought Mitigation Center

University of North Texas, Portal
to Texas History

University of Saskatchewan:
Geoffrey Cunfer

University of Texas at Arlington,
Special Collections: Ben Huseman

University of Texas at Austin,
Brackenridge Field Laboratory: Larry
Gilbert, Robert Plowes

University of Texas at Austin,
Department of Geography and the
Environment: Robin Doughty

University of Texas School of Law: Kelly Haragan

University of Texas at Austin, Texas Archeological Research Laboratory: Jonathan Jarvis, Laura Nightengale, Brian Roberts, Mary Beth Tomka

University of Texas at San Antonio Libraries, Special Collections

Upper Guadalupe River Authority: Tara Bushnoe

Virginia Marine Resources Commission: Mike Meier

David Weisman

Matt White

Wildlife Habitat Federation: Jim Willis

Wimberley Institute of Cultures: Clare Billingsley

John Worrall

Supporters

This project would not have been possible without the support of our big-hearted individual donors, and the backing of our foundation friends, including the Brown Foundation, Hershey Foundation, Houston Endowment, Knobloch Family Foundation, Price Foundation, Reese Foundation, Sasser Family Fund, Shield-Ayres Foundation, Still Water Foundation, Summerlee Foundation, Susan B. Vaughan Foundation, and the Trull Foundation. We are very grateful to them all.

We would also like to thank our board members—Janice Bezanson, Susan Petersen, Irene Pickhardt, and Ted Siff—for their great patience, wise advice, and heartening enthusiasm for the Project from its beginning to end. We have also been fortunate to have help from a skilled indexer and three editors, including Nancy Ball, Dawn Hall, Shelley Sperry, and Gina Wadas, respectively, who have improved the manuscript in many ways. The long and complicated process of bringing this work to print has been made much more fun and easy by our kind colleagues at Texas A&M University Press, including Donna Boswell, Christine Brown, Gayla Christiansen, Shannon Davies, Katie Duelm, Kevin Grossman, Mary Ann Jacob, Holli Koster, and Kristie Lee. And last, we should certainly thank Andy Sansom, a mentor and friend to us and many others in the Texas conservation world, for his generous foreword to this book.

Glossary

At its heart, nature is about water and air and animals and many familiar things that are easily described in a few short words. However, the world of environmental protection has grown into a thicket of acronyms, legalisms, scientific terms, and general jargon that can be almost impenetrable. With that in mind, we are providing this glossary to help get you through the more brambly parts of the woods. Toward the end of each definition, we mention the chapters where you might run across the term.

Acre-foot: An acre-foot is the amount of water that would cover one acre, a foot deep; it is equal to 325,851 gallons. [Dams in the Big Bend; The Neches Valley; Stream Flows and Water Rights]

Agricultural appraisal: An agricultural appraisal is keyed to a parcel's ability to produce livestock, crops, or recently, wildlife, rather than being based on its market value. [Cooperation; Wildlife, Land, and Taxes]

Allocation: Allocation is the process by which the state of Texas awards rights to surface water for a variety of beneficial uses. [Stream Flows and Water Rights]

Appropriated water right: Appropriated water rights are issued by the state, as opposed to the English common law tradition that held sway in Texas prior to 1889, by which all riparian landowners were entitled to make reasonable use of surface water. [Stream Flows and Water Rights; Water Planning and Interbasin Transfers]

Article 5 nations: Article 5 of the 1987 Montreal Protocol provided relatively loose ozone protection rules for 147 developing nations that were minor producers and consumers of ozone-depleting chemicals. [Ozone Hole]

Avulsive erosion: A 2010 Texas Supreme Court opinion held that private property rights were protected against "avulsive" (abrupt and storm-related) coastal erosion. Earlier, under the Open Beaches Act, the state had been entitled to claim lands that had dropped within the "wet beach" zone due to any type of erosion. [Storms and the Texas Coast]

Beneficial use: In Texas, water rights are issued for beneficial uses, which include municipal, domestic, agricultural, mining, hydroelectric, navigation, and recreational usage, but typically exclude support of wildlife or fisheries. "Beneficial use" also refers to the management of dredge spoil for wetland restoration, shoreline protection, and other alternatives to disposal. [Brown Pelican; Stream Flows and Water Rights]

Best Available/Conventional/ Practicable Control Technology: Air and water pollution permits are geared to various levels of technology and sophistication. Each level incorporates trade-offs among cost, complexity, energy consumption, and emission control. [Fishing, Swimming, and Polluting; Upsets]

Biocontrol: Biocontrol, or biological control, refers to strategies for using parasites, predators, or pathogens, rather than chemical pesticides, to attack plants and animals that have become a threat. [Exotic Fish in Texas; Fire Ants!]

Bottomland hardwood: Bottomland hardwoods are deciduous trees, including oaks, gums, and bald cypresses, that typically grow in floodplains and perform important tasks of filtering nutrients, reducing sediments, and providing mast and shelter for wildlife. [The Neches Valley; Reservoirs]

Bt: Bt, or *Bacillus thuringiensis*, is a gram-positive soil bacterium that has been genetically spliced into corn, canola, cotton, and other major crop plants to act as a pesticide. [Monarch Butterflies]

Buffalo jump: Native Americans hunted buffalo by herding the animals and driving them over cliffs, killing them instantly or injuring them to such a degree that they could be killed by spear or bow and arrow. [Fall and Rise of the American Bison; History and Prehistory of Lake Amistad]

Buyout: Buyouts are used to encourage private property owners to leave flood-prone areas, thus protecting against casualties and reducing the need for costly drainage and detention structures. Also, industrial facilities are known to buy out their neighbors in order to create a buffer around the facility and decrease local health risks and liability claims. [Houston Subsidence; Storms and the Texas Coast; Upsets]

Bycatch: When marine life of nontarget species, sex, or size is caught, those creatures are considered "bycatch." [Kemp's Ridley Sea Turtle]

Capture: "Capture" describes the situation in which agencies are swayed or even controlled by well-connected and economically powerful companies in a regulated industry. [Fishing, Swimming, and Polluting]

CDC: The Centers for Disease Control and Prevention originated in 1946 as the Communicable Disease Center, pledged to fight malaria. In the years since, the CDC has focused on combating infectious and chronic diseases, workplace risks, and environmental health threats, including the lead and tobacco exposures discussed here. [Lead, Smeltertown, and the Family Car; Tobacco and Secondhand Smoke]

CFC: Chlorofluorocarbons (CFCs) are a class of chemicals that deplete stratospheric ozone. [Ozone Hole]

Colonia: Substandard, often rural housing developments lacking potable water, wastewater treatment, flood control, paved roads, or other infrastructure are often known as colonias. [Colonias]

Command and control: Command and control, where pollutant discharge standards are set and enforced by statute, rule or permit, is a common environmental protection approach, distinct from more flexible, market-based incentives. [Upsets]

Conjunctive use: Conjunctive use describes strategies that couple surface and groundwater supplies in efficient ways. In Texas, these paired approaches are often complicated by the distinct statutory, agency, and private property rules that govern water found below and above ground. [Stream Flows and Water Rights]

Conservation easement: Conservation easements are legal agreements between a land owner and a private land trust or governmental agency to limit a parcel's development and protect the property's value as habitat or open space. [Barton Springs, Austin, and Nonpoint Source Pollution; Comal, San Antonio, and the Edwards; Land Protection; Sprawl]

Consumptive water use: Water that is diverted from a stream or lake, used for municipal needs, crop production, or industrial processes, and not later returned to the watercourse is considered a consumptive use. [Stream Flows and Water Rights]

Contributing zone: The contributing zone is that part of a watershed where rainfall is caught and runs off to a recharge zone that in turn feeds an aquifer. [Barton Springs, Austin, and Nonpoint Source Pollution; Comal, San Antonio, and the Edwards]

Co-op or Cooperative: A cooperative is a voluntary association of people who work for a shared goal and mutual benefit. In the environmental context, cooperatives have developed rural electric networks and wildlife management programs. [Cooperation; Lights in the Night; Wind Energy]

CREZ: In Senate Bill 20 (2005), Texas created Competitive Renewable Energy Zones (CREZ) where wind energy facilities could be built to supply electricity to major markets. [Wind Energy]

Critical resource: In 2005, the Texas legislature designated the proposed Fastrill reservoir site as a "critical resource," seeking to ensure that it could be developed as an artificial lake, pending full and formal permit applications, and in place of a National Wildlife Refuge planned for the same location. [The Neches Valley]

Desired future condition: The Texas legislature has mandated that groundwater conservation and subsidence districts develop and agree on "desired future conditions" (water volumes and levels, water quality, spring flows, and such) for an aquifer, before calculating the groundwater available for use from that aquifer. [Ogallala Aquifer]

DHS: The Department of Homeland Security (DHS) was created in 2002, combining the Customs Service, the Immigration and Naturalization Service, and a score of other federal agencies. DHS has drawn attention from the conservation community due to its responsibility for construction and operation of the US-Mexico border fence. [The Border and the Borderlands]

Diversion: A diversion entails taking water from a lake or stream for private use, usually requiring a state water right. A diversion can also refer to solid waste that is re-routed away from a landfill by recycling, composting, or some sort of reuse. [The Neches Valley; Solid Waste; Stream Flows and Water Rights; Water Planning and Interbasin Transfers]

Drought of Record: Texas' longest and most severe modern dry spell, running from 1947 through 1957 (sometimes referred to as just 1951–57) is considered the "Drought of Record." It was the spur to a major dam-building campaign in the state and became the worst-case benchmark for water planning. [Drought and Water Use; Reservoirs; Stream Flows and Water Rights; Water Planning and Interbasin Transfers]

Environmental justice: Environmental justice calls for the fair and equal protection of all citizens, regardless of race, color, national origin, or income, from environmental risks and natural hazards. [Colonias; Solid Waste; Upsets]

EPA: Created in 1970, the US Environmental Protection Agency (EPA) is the lead federal agency devoted to guarding human health and the environment. [Brown Pelican; Comal, San Antonio, and the Edwards; Desert Bighorn Sheep; Fishing, Swimming, and Polluting; High Plains Playas; Land Protection; Lead, Smeltertown, and the Family Car; Oil and Gas, Water and Wastewater; Ozone Hole; Reefs; Solid Waste; Stream Flows and Water Rights; Upsets]

ERCOT: The Electric Reliability Council of Texas (ERCOT) developed from the Texas Interconnected System, a World War II–era alliance created to supply energy to Gulf coast industries. It is now a nonprofit made up of generators, power marketers, electric cooperatives, and other members that schedules power on the electric grid and manages financial settlements for the energy market. [Wind Energy]

Ethanol: Ethanol, also known as ethyl alcohol, is made by fermenting sugars to create a solvent, antiseptic, or fuel. Its production has raised concerns about excessive corn cultivation and water use. [Ogallala Aquifer]

Exotic: Exotic species are those that have been intentionally or accidentally introduced to an ecosystem. If they become well established, these nonnative species can harm local biological diversity. [Exotic Fish in Texas; Fire Ants!; Sparrows, Starlings, and Doves; Water Planning and Interbasin Transfers]

Extraterritorial jurisdiction: The extraterritorial jurisdiction, or ETJ, of a municipality is the unincorporated area contiguous with the city's boundaries. In that area, the city can exercise annexation authority and limited regulatory powers over road access, lot size, and other development. [Billboards]

Fee simple: The term, fee simple, describes an unlimited or absolute ownership interest in land, as distinct from more restricted rights, such as a conservation easement. [Comal, San Antonio, and the Edwards; Land Protection]

FEMA: The Federal Emergency Management Agency (FEMA) supports planning and assistance to cope with hurricanes, tornadoes, floods, industrial accidents, and other disasters. [Houston Subsidence; Storms and the Texas Coast]

Fill: Excavated or dredged material, known as fill, can raise environmental concerns during its disposal in wetlands and open waters, but can also be used beneficially to build rookery islands. [Brown Pelican; Fishing, Swiming, and Polluting; High Plains Playas; Houston Subsidence; Land Protection]

Flint: "Flint," or hairless buffalo hides, became marketable after tanning innovations during the 1870s, greatly accelerating the bison's use and decline. Previously, only thick robes were easily sold; hides from the southern buffalo herd, or any hides taken during the nine warmer months of the year, had little value. [Fall and Rise of the American Bison]

Fossil aquifer: Fossil aquifers, such as the Ogallala, are large underground reserves of water that were created under past geologic or climatic conditions and that no longer receive significant recharge. With little natural inflow, they are vulnerable to overpumping. [Ogallala Aquifer]

Fracking: More formally known as hydraulic fracturing, fracking is a way of stimulating oil and gas wells in tight formations by injecting high-pressure fluids, often including water, sand, and chemical additives. Fracking has brought major new natural gas supplies online, undermining the coal industry, but simultaneously raising concerns over groundwater contamination and seismic activity. [Coal; Colonias; Oil and Gas, Water and Wastewater]

Gaia hypothesis: The Gaia hypothesis, first proposed by the chemist James Lovelock, theorizes that organisms interact with their inorganic surroundings to maintain a self-regulating, stable environment that is hospitable to life. [Ozone Hole]

Grandfathering: In the interest of keeping laws and regulations predictable and reliable, preexisting operations are often exempted, or "grandfathered," from rules issued later. Critics argue that this can hold back innovation in environmental protection and create a barrier to entry that protects vested interests from new rivals. [Barton Springs, Austin, and Nonpoint Source Pollution; Billboards; Comal, San Antonio, and the Edwards; High Plains Playas; Storms and the Texas Coast]

Greenfield development: Construction on previously open, unused land is considered greenfield development, as opposed to brownfield projects that involve building on previously used and/or contaminated sites. [Sprawl]

Home-rule city: Home-rule cities are chartered for extensive self-governance, with powers to pass ordinances (such as sign regulation) unless specifically barred by state law. [Billboards]

Hoof action: Heavy trampling from the hooves of bison, as well as cattle, sheep, and goats, can open hard-packed soil to water infiltration and new plant growth. [Fall and Rise of the American Bison; Prairies, Pastures, Cropfields, and Lawns]

Huevero: *Hueveros*, or eggmen, collected eggs from Kemp's ridley sea turtles that nested on eastern Mexican shores for sale as food and aphrodisiacs, greatly endangering the turtles' survival. [Kemp's Ridley Sea Turtle]

IBWC: The International Boundary and Water Commission (IBWC) inherited work from surveys associated with the 1848 Treaty of Guadalupe Hidalgo. The IBWC currently handles disputes and agreements over borderline demarcation, water supply, flood control, and sanitation along the US-Mexico border. [Dams in the Big Bend]

Infrastructure: "Infrastructure" is a catchall term that encompasses the roads, water lines, sewers, electrical grids, and telecommunication networks that support a modern industrial society. [Barton Springs, Austin, and Nonpoint Source Pollution; The Border and the Borderlands; Colonias; History and Prehistory of Lake Amistad; Reservoirs; Wildlife, Land, and Taxes, Storms and the Texas Coast; Trinity Barge Canal; Sprawl]

Junior water right: Under Texas' system of prior appropriation, the exercise of a junior water right to divert water from a stream or lake will be curtailed before a senior, older right during times of water shortage. [Coal; Water Planning and Interbasin Transfers]

Keystone species: A keystone plant or animal has a distinct, critical, and even essential role in ecosystem functions. [Fall and Rise of the American Bison; Prairies, Pastures, Cropfields, and Lawns]

Land application: Land application involves irrigating fields with wastewater, relying on anaerobic and aerobic bacteria to treat the waste. While land application can allow efficient reuse of water, the wastewater can contaminate crops, aquifers, and runoff to streams. [Barton Springs, Austin, and Nonpoint Source Pollution; Solid Waste]

Landfill: Landfills are disposal sites for solid waste. They are typically underlain by geotextiles or tight clay layers, covered with soil and compacted daily, and equipped with groundwater monitoring wells and methane recovery systems. They are the successors to the middens and dumps that were more common in the past. [Solid Waste]

LCRA: The Lower Colorado River Authority (LCRA) is a public utility created in 1934 that provides water supply, electricity, and park sites in the lower Colorado basin, reaching from Coleman to Bay City, and including Austin in its service area. [Coal; Comal, San Anatonio, and the Edwards; Reservoirs; Water Planning and Interbasin Transfers]

LULU: Locally Unwanted Land Uses include landfills, prisons, factories, power plants, and other facilities that are desired by the general public, but that are resisted by local host communities. [Solid Waste]

Midden: Middens are dump sites, often quite old, that can contain shells, animal bones, and other refuse, and that may mark a nearby human settlement and give clues to ancient diets and lifestyles. [History and Prehistory of Lake Amistad; Solid Waste]

Mitigation bank: A protected wetland, stream, or habitat restoration area can serve as a mitigation bank to consolidate and offset impacts to similar and nearby ecosystems from dredging, filling, paving, and other activities. [Land Protection; The Neches Valley]

MLD: The Texas Parks and Wildlife Department offers the Managed Lands Deer (MLD) program to provide incentives to white-tailed deer hunters, including more flexible and generous bag and season limits, in exchange for more active, large-scale habitat management. [Cooperation]

MUD: Municipal Utility Districts (MUDs) are political subdivisions of the state of Texas, typically organized by large-scale land developers to issue bonds, collect taxes, and provide water, sewage treatment, drainage, and other services. [Barton Springs, Austin, and Nonpoint Source Pollution; Sprawl]

NIABY: NIABY, short for the principle of "Not In Anyone's Backyard," holds that unpopular or unwise land uses should be limited generally, and not imposed on any neighborhood. [Solid Waste]

NIMBY: NIMBY, or "Not In My Backyard," is a pejorative term that implies that a neighborhood's rejection of an unwanted land use is selfish, narrow, or myopic. [Shared Sacrifice?]

NMFS: The National Marine Fisheries Service (NMFS) was founded in 1871 to protect food fish off the US coast. Its facility in Galveston has figured large in captive rearing, tagging, excluder device development and other work to restore the Kemp's ridley sea turtle. [Kemp's Ridley Sea Turtle]

NOAA: The National Oceanic and Atmospheric Administration (NOAA) is a federal agency focusing on climatic, weather, oceanic, and coastal issues, tracing its history back to the Coast and Geodetic Survey (1807), Weather Bureau (1890), and Bureau of Commercial Fisheries (1871). [Coal; Drought and Water Use; Kemp's Ridley Sea Turtle; Land Protection; Lights in the Night; The Ozone Hole; Reefs; Storms and the Texas Coast]

Nonattainment area: The Clean Air Act designates polluted regions that have failed to meet the National Ambient Air Quality Standards as "nonattainment areas," requiring an implemented plan to come into compliance or suffer loss of federal financial support. [Coal; Upsets]

Nonconforming signs: Nonconforming billboards were legally built before the passage of the Highway Beautification Act, but later failed to comply with the act's requirements for new signs. Removal of these signs has been a challenge for many communities. [Billboards]

NPS: NPS can refer to the National Park Service, the federal agency responsible for Texas preserves in the Big Bend, Big Thicket, Guadalupe Mountains, and Padre Island. The abbreviation can also describe "nonpoint source" pollution, in other words, diffuse waste that cannot be traced back to a single discharge from a pipe or channel. [Big Thicket; Comal, San Antonio, and the Edwards; Fishing, Swimming, and Polluting; History and Prehistory of Lake Amistad; Kemp's Ridley Sea Turtle; Land Protection; Storms and the Texas Coast]

NRCS: The Natural Resources Conservation Service (NRCS) grew out of the Soil Conservation Service, a federal agency chartered in 1935 in response to the Dust Bowl. Its modern successor focuses on limiting soil erosion, reducing flooding, restoring wildlife habitat, and improving water quality on private lands. [High Plains Playas; Ogallala Aquifer; Reservoirs; Sprawl]

NWR: The National Wildlife Refuge (NWR) system began in 1901 with the federal protection of Pelican Island and other areas frequented by colonial nesting birds, followed by the creation of preserves for bison, elk, migratory birds, and other creatures. [Brown Pelican; Land Protection; The Neches Valley; Prairies, Pastures, Cropfields, and Lawns; Storms and the Texas Coast]

Off-premise sign: Off-premise signs are a category of general-advertising billboards that are distinguished from on-site outdoor signage that promotes a nearby store, restaurant, hotel, or other facility. [Billboards]

Off-stem reservoir: Off-channel basins, or off-stem reservoirs, store water without direct impoundment of a stream and associated flooding of bottomlands. [Reservoirs]

Outfall: The discharge point for sewerage, cooling water, brine, or flood flows is known as an outfall. [Fishing, Swimming, and Polluting]

Oyamel fir: Oyamel fir (*Abies religiosa*) is an evergreen tree found in small parts of central Mexico at elevations of 7,800 to 11,800 feet that hosts monarch butterflies during their winter roosting. [Monarch Butterflies]

Ozone: Ozone is made up of three oxygen atoms and has several meanings in an environmental context. For example, ozone is used as an alternative to chlorine for water purification. In the air at ground level, ozone is created by the reaction of sunlight, hydrocarbons, and nitrogen oxide, and is considered a pollutant. Ozone also acts as a greenhouse gas, many times more potent than carbon dioxide on a per-molecule basis. In the stratosphere, ozone shields the earth from ultraviolet radiation, and is vulnerable to CFCs. [Air introduction; Coal; Ozone Hole; Upsets]

Pangaea: A supercontinent known as Pangaea existed from roughly 300 to 100 million years ago. It was created and later separated by continental drift, as shown by fossil, magnetic, and geologic evidence. Its clustering growth can be seen as a crude analogy for the connecting sprawl of nearby communities. [Sprawl]

PCB: PCB (Polychlorinated biphenyl) is a persistent, highly toxic, organic chemical once used as a coolant, plasticizer, stabilizer, and adhesive. [Fishing, Swimming, and Polluting; Reefs; Solid Waste]

Platform: Oil platforms are large off-shore structures with the ability to drill wells and then later pump, process, and temporarily store product. Platform oil spills have endangered aquatic life, but their underwater steel and concrete members often become substrates for coral reefs. [Brown Pelican; Kemp's Ridley Sea Turtle; Reefs]

Plugging: Plugging an abandoned oil, gas, or water well with concrete, clay, caliche, or other materials can protect aquifers and surface waters from leaks, spills, and contamination. [Oil and Gas, Water and Wastewater]

Prior appropriation: With the exception of the middle and lower Rio Grande below Amistad, Texas uses prior appropriation law as its system for allocating surface water rights, following the basic approach of "first in time, first in right." [Stream Flows and Water Rights]

Promotores: *Promotores de salud* are community health workers who have helped extend public health education and care to rural, marginalized, and lesser-served areas, such as colonias. [Colonias]

Recharge zone: Fractures, faults, fissures, and other openings in recharge zones collect and funnel water, and contaminants, to aquifers. [Barton Springs, Austin, and

Nonpoint Source Pollution; Comal, San Antonio, and the Edwards]

REIT: REITs, or Real Estate Investment Trusts, are securities that trade on major exchanges and that own or finance income-producing acreage and structures. [Big Thicket; Sprawl]

Replatting: Replatting refers to filing a land survey with a municipality or other local government. The survey map identifies a parcel's location, boundaries, easements, flood zones, roads, and access rights-of-way and is typically filed as part of a proposal to subdivide a property. [Sprawl]

Resaca: Abandoned channels of the lower Rio Grande are referred to as "resacas." These oxbows have been used as reservoirs and channels for irrigation since the start of the twentieth century. [Reservoirs]

RIFA: "RIFA" is short for red imported fire ant, the nonnative and very invasive insect formally known as *Solenopsis invicta Buren.* [Brown Pelican; Fire Ants!; Houston Subsidence; Wildlife, Land, and Taxes]

Riparian rights: Riparian rights to water are allocated among property owners who possess land along a stream. The rights are limited to their reasonable use, and subject to a duty to deliver water downstream undiminished in flow or quality. A system developed under English common law, it was later adopted and then largely abandoned in Texas. [Stream Flows and Water Rights]

Rotary drilling: Rotary drilling uses a spinning bit, driven by a rotating drill stem and cleared by circulating mud or other fluid. It is the common modern technology for augering oil, gas, and water wells. [Lost Springs and Old Trails; Ogallala Aquifer]

Rule of capture: The rule of capture is an English common law tradition adopted in Texas in which the first person to capture a resource (typically groundwater, oil, or gas) owns that resource. Texas laws for pooling, prorationing, and limiting nearby wells have limited its full use in oil and gas formations, but have had little impact on aquifer pumpage. [Houston Subsidence; Lost Springs and Old Trails; Ogallala Aquifer; Reservoirs; Stream Flows and Water Rights]

Saltwater barrier: Saltwater barriers, such as that at Wallisville, seek to block dense, bottom-hugging saline wedges from moving inland from the river mouth and contaminating fresh water supplies. [Trinity Barge Canal]

Saturated zone: An aquifer's saturated zone is the region where all the available spaces in a porous rock or unconsolidated sand or gravel stratum are filled with water. [Ogallala Aquifer]

Scalp: Some water resource managers, such as the Lower Colorado River Authority, have proposed "scalping" river flows by diverting floodwaters to storage reservoirs or aquifers. [The Neches Valley; Reservoirs]

SCS: The Soil Conservation Service (SCS), the predecessor of the NRCS described above, was founded in 1935 in the midst of the Dust Bowl to combat soil erosion with dams, contour plowing, cover crops, and other strategies. [Ogallala Aquifer; Prairies, Pastures, Cropfields, and Lawns; Reservoirs]

Section 1-d-1: Section 1-d-1 of the Texas Constitution allows lands used for agriculture and wild-life management to have reduced ad valorem tax appraisals, based on productive rather than market value. [Cooperation; Wildlife, Land, and Taxes]

Sisku: Sisku is an alternate term for a buffalo jump, in which bison were driven over cliffs to kill or immobilize them for Native Americans to harvest them. [Fall and Rise of the American Bison; History and Prehistory of Lake Amistad]

Skyglow: Skyglow is a term for light pollution, caused by spillover into the night sky from incandescent, fluorescent, mercury vapor, and other types of unshielded artificial lights. [Lights in the Night]

Slot: Slot limits are a game management strategy that limits harvest for fish, deer, or other animals to those that fall within a certain size range—neither juveniles that should be left to mature, nor trophy-sized animals that should be left to reproduce and improve the entire population. [Cooperation]

Sole source aquifer: Under the Safe Drinking Water Act of 1974, the

EPA defined a sole source aquifer as one that supplies at least half the drinking water consumed in the area overlying the aquifer. The Edwards Aquifer is considered a sole source aquifer for the city of San Antonio, and so qualifies for extra review of federally subsidized projects that might jeopardize the aquifer. [Comal, San Antonio, and the Edwards]

Storm surge: A storm surge is a coastal flood rising over and above the typical astronomical tide. It is caused by water being swept into shore by winds from a tropical storm or hurricane, and by water being raised by low atmospheric pressure within the cyclone. [Houston Subsidence; Storms and the Texas Coast]

Subsidence: The extraction of groundwater, oil, gas, sulfur, or coal, can collapse underground strata, and cause a gradual sinking or subsidence of the land surface. [Coal; Houston Subsidence; Water Planning and Interbasin Transfers]

Sunset review: In 1977, the legislature passed the Texas Sunset Act, providing for periodic review of state agency mission, operation, and performance, and allowing for agency improvement and even shutdown if shortcomings are identified. [Storms and the Texas Coast; Upsets]

Swampbuster: A program set up under the Farm Security Act of 1985, Swampbuster aimed to discourage private conversion of wetlands (including playas) to cropland use

by withdrawing various federal agricultural subsidies. [High Plains Playas]

Taking: A plaintiff alleges a "regulatory taking" by charging that the government is restricting his or her use of private property so fully, and without compensation, that the regulation is barred by the Fifth Amendment of the US Constitution. Billboard, historic landmark, zoning, wetland, and endangered species laws have encountered takings claims. [Billboards; Comal, San Antonio, and the Edwards; Drought and Water Use]

TCEQ: The Texas Commission on Environmental Quality, or TCEQ, has its origins in water rights administration by the Texas Board of Water Engineers (established 1913), but has since grown to be the chief state environmental agency in Texas, managing air, water, solid waste, and other programs. [Comal, San Antonio, and the Edwards; Coal; Drought and Water Use; Fishing, Swimming, and Polluting; Lost Springs and Old Trails; Ogallala Aquifer; Solid Waste; Sprawl; Stream Flows and Water Rights; Upsets]

TED: A TED, or "Turtle Excluder Device," is a grid of bars installed at the neck of a shrimp trawl to block turtles and other large bycatch, yet allow shrimp and other smaller creatures to pass into the net. [Kemp's Ridley Sea Turtle]

TIMO: TIMOs, or "Timber Investment Management Organizations," pro-

vide specialized technical advice to multipurpose institutional investors in finding, analyzing, acquiring, and managing forestlands. [Big Thicket]

Total fertility rate: The total fertility rate describes the average number of children born to a woman if she were to survive to the end of her reproductive life. This statistic is distinct from the crude fertility rate, which compares the number of births per thousand people in the entire population, male or female, of reproductive age or not. [Population Growth and Shift]

TPWD: The Texas Parks and Wildlife Department traces its history back to the state's Fish and Oyster Commission of 1895, and currently manages the state's parks and refuges, and its hunting, fishing, and nature tourism opportunities.

Tragedy of the commons: The biologist Garrett Hardin described "the tragedy of the commons" as a situation in which individuals following their own self-interest will typically degrade a commonly held resource. The theory can apply to overhunting a herd, overharvesting a fishery, overpumping an aquifer, or other similar scenarios. [Cooperation; Lost Springs and Old Trails]

TWDB: The TWDB, or "Texas Water Development Board," was founded in 1957, at the close of the great drought of the 1950s. It now has responsibility for studying, planning, and financially supporting development of water supplies in the state. [Colonias; Houston Subsidence; Lost Springs and Old Trails; The Neches Valley; Ogallala

Aquifer; Reservoirs; Sprawl; Stream Flows and Water Rights; Water Planning and Interbasin Transfers]

Unique reservoir site: Under section 16.051(g) of the Texas Water Code, the legislature may designate a "unique reservoir site" where state agencies and subdivisions may not acquire property interests that would significantly prevent construction of a reservoir at that location. [The Neches Valley]

Upset: An upset is an "unplanned and unavoidable" pollutant discharge from a facility, often associated with an accident, startup, or shutdown. Regulators typically treat upsets with greater leniency than they do ordinary permitted emissions. [Upsets]

USDA: The USDA, or United States Department of Agriculture, has had a large environmental role through its study and support of timber, farming, livestock, and other agricultural sectors. [Colonias; Drought and Water Use; Fire Ants!; High Plains Playas; Land Protection; Ogallala Aquifer; Prairies, Pastures, Cropfields, and Lawns; Sprawl]

Use and possession law: Early timber companies were known to amass large forest tracts in East Texas through developing roads and cutting forests and then citing those activities to assert ownership under the state's "use and possession" law. [Big Thicket]

USFWS: Programs of the United States Fish and Wildlife Service (USFWS) include biological study and refuge acquisition, and trace back to the US Fish Commission (founded in 1871) and the Division of Economic Ornithology and Mammalogy (established in 1885). [Barton Springs, Austin, and Nonpoint Source Pollution; The Border and Borderlands; Brown Pelican; Comal, San Antonio, and the Edwards; Cooperation; Dams in the Big Bend; Desert Bighorn Sheep; Exotic Fish in Texas; Kemp's Ridley Sea Turtle; High Plains Playas; Land Protection; Prairies, Pastures, Cropfields, and Lawns; The Neches Valley; Sparrows, Starlings, and Doves; Sprawl; Storms and the Texas Coast; Stream Flows and Water Rights; Wind Energy]

USGS: The United States Geological Survey (USGS) was chartered in 1879 largely for mineral surveys but has grown to collect and analyze environmental data, including information about wildlife populations, surface water flow and quality, aquifer characteristics, and other topics. [Barton Springs, Austin, and Nonpoint Source Pollution; The Border and the Borderlands; Brown Pelican; Colonias; Comal, San Antonio, and the Edwards; Dams in the Big Bend; Desert Bighorn Sheep; Fall and Rise of the American Bison; High Plains Playas; Houston Subsidence; Lost Springs and Old Trails; Ogallala Aquifer; Prairies, Pastures, Cropfields, and Lawns; Reefs; Stream Flows and Water Rights; Water Planning and Interbasin Transfers]

Water ranching: Water ranching involves the practice of property owners selling the right to pump groundwater that lies under their land for export to users elsewhere. [Ogallala Aquifer; Water Planning and Interbasin Transfers]

Wild and Scenic River: The National Wild and Scenic Rivers Act of 1968 authorized protection of the free-flowing, primitive, unpolluted, and scenic qualities of select river segments, with safeguards typically extending one-quarter mile on either side of the stream. [Dams of the Big Bend; The Neches Valley]

Wildlife management valuation: Section 1-d-1 of the Texas Constitution authorizes reduced property tax appraisals for land used for wildlife management, including providing food plots and water sources, controlling erosion and predation, surveying wildlife, and other practices. [Wildlife, Land, and Taxes]

WMA: Texas Wildlife Management Areas (WMAs) are state-protected lands that allow research, hunting, hiking, camping, and other activities. A WMA may also be an abbreviation for a Wildlife Management Association, a cooperative group of adjoining landowners and lessees that seeks to improve habitat, game, and other natural resources. [Cooperation; Desert Bighorn Sheep; Prairies, Pastures, Cropfields, and Lawns; The Neches Valley; Storms and the Texas Coast]

Index

Other titles in the Kathie and Ed Cox Jr. Books on Conservation Leadership, sponsored by The Meadows Center for Water and the Environment, Texas State University

Money for the Cause: A Complete Guide to Event Fundraising
Rudolph A. Rosen

On Politics and Parks: People, Places, Politics, Parks
George L. Bristol

Hillingdon Ranch: Four Seasons, Six Generations
David K. Langford and Lorie Woodward Cantu

Green in Gridlock: Common Goals, Common Ground, and Compromise
Paul Walden Hansen

Heads above Water: The Inside Story of the Edwards Aquifer Recovery Implementation Program
Robert L. Gulley

Fog at Hillingdon
David K. Langford

Border Sanctuary: The Conservation Legacy of the Santa Ana Land Grant
M.J. Morgan